W9-BAU-451

Andrew Johnson

THE AGE OF HATE
Andrew Johnson and the Radicals

923.73
m

THE AGE OF HATE

ANDREW JOHNSON AND THE RADICALS

by

GEORGE FORT MILTON

"The history of mankind is the history of its great men; to find out these, clean the dirt from them, and place them on their proper pedestal, is the true function of a historian."

CARLYLE

ARCHON BOOKS
HAMDEN, CONNECTICUT
1965

Wingate College Library

COPYRIGHT, 1930, BY
COWARD-McCANN, INC.

REPRINTED 1965 WITH PERMISSION
IN AN UNALTERED AND UNABRIDGED EDITION

LIBRARY OF CONGRESS CATALOG CARD NUMBER: 65-14191
PRINTED IN THE UNITED STATES OF AMERICA

THIS BOOK

I DEDICATE TO ONE WHO HAS
INSPIRED, GUIDED AND AIDED ITS
WRITING MORE THAN
ANY OTHER—

MY WIFE

27294

CONTENTS

ILLUSTRATIONS

ACKNOWLEDGMENT

THE author wishes to acknowledge his gratitude to the many who have contributed by suggestions, information, prudent criticism and scholarly advice to the work upon this book.

To Mr. T. R. Preston of Chattanooga I am indebted for the original suggestion as to the need for a careful study and reappraisement of the life of Andrew Johnson.

To Mr. Claude G. Bowers of New York; Dr. Archibald Henderson and Dr. J. G. de Roulhac Hamilton of the University of North Carolina; Dr. Benjamin B. Kendrick of Greensboro, N. C.; Dr. Edward McMahan of the University of Washington; Dr. William B. Hesseltine of the University of Chattanooga; Dr. Frank L. Owsley of Vanderbilt University; Mr. Denis Tilden Lynch of New York; Mr. David Rankin Barbee, of Washington, D. C.; Dr. Thomas P. Martin of the Library of Congress, Washington; Dr. Howard K. Beale of Bowdoin College; Hon. A. W. Chambliss of Chattanooga; Colonel Fay W. Brabson, United States Army, and Mr. Gilbert Govan of Chattanooga, the author is under great obligation for a careful reading of the manuscript or proof sheets, and for criticisms, corrections and suggestions thereon.

In the collation of hitherto unused source material, and the suggestion of other information of value in the writing of this volume, the author desires to acknowledge his gratitude to the following:

Mrs. Marguerita Hall Albjerg of Purdue University; Mr. Matthew Page Andrews of Baltimore; Mr. Garnett Andrews of Chattanooga; Senator Henry F. Ashurst of Arizona; Mrs. Fanny Perry Beattie of Sumter, S. C.; Mr. Perry Belmont of Washington, D. C.; Mr. Desha Breckinridge of Lexington, Ky.; Hon. Foster V. Brown of Chattanooga, Mr. Walter G. Brownlow of Knoxville; Dr. James E. Barnes of Washington, D. C.; Mr. Elwood Baker of Cleveland, Ohio; Mrs. H. H. Coffey of Knoxville; Mrs. Elizabeth S. Chandler of Los Angeles, Calif.; Mrs. Mary D. Clagett of Washington, D. C.; Miss Nora Crimmins of Chattanooga Public Library; Hon. Josephus Daniels of Raleigh, N. C.; Mr. James F. Duhamel of Washington, D. C.; Mr. James F. Finlay of Chattanooga; President C. O.

ix

Gray, of Tusculum College, Greeneville, Tenn.; Bishop Thomas
F. Gailor of Sewanee, Tenn.; Mr. Christian A. Herter of Bos-
ton; Mrs. Annie Bachman Hyde of Chattanooga; Mr. C. C.
Hemenway of the Hartford *Times*, Hartford; Mrs. John B.
Henderson of Washington, D. C.; Colonel A. M. Hughes of
Washington, D. C.; Mr. George Hensel, Jr. of Quarryville, Pa.;
Dr. E. K. Kline of the University of Chattanooga; Hon. Breck-
inridge Long of Washington, D. C.; Mrs. S. B. LaRue of
Greeneville, Tenn.; Colonel Simms M. Latta of Columbia, Tenn.;
Mr. R. W. McGrath of Fredonia, Kansas; Mr. Franklin J.
Meine of Chicago, Ill.; Mr. James S. Murray of Baltimore;
Judge George H. Moore of St. Louis; Mrs. John Trotwood
Moore of Nashville; Mr. Arthur V. Morton of Philadelphia;
the late Selden Nelson of Knoxville; Miss Helen Nicolay of
Washington, D. C.; Colonel W. M. Nixon of Chattanooga; Mrs.
W. H. O'Keefe of Greeneville, Tenn.; Mr. Adolph S. Ochs of
New York City; Mr. Richard T. Oulahan of Washington,
D. C.; Mr. J. L. Pemberton of Knoxville; Dr. J. G. Randall of
the University of Illinois; the late Colonel E. C. Reeves of
Johnson City, Tenn.; the late Winslow Russell of Hartford,
Conn.; Mr. Ernest Spofford, Secretary of the Pennsylvania
Historical Society, Philadelphia; Dr. St. George L. Sioussat
of the University of Pennsylvania; Mrs. Fowler Shankland
of Los Angeles; Mr. C. T. Steven of Hartford, Conn.; Mr.
Floyd C. Shumaker, Secretary of Missouri State Historical
Society of Columbia, Mo.; Judge George C. Taylor, of Knox-
ville; Mr. Lillard Thompson of Lebanon, Tenn.; Mr. W. H.
Vickers of Baltimore; Mr. Oswald Garrison Villard, editor of
the *Nation*, New York; Mr. Charles T. White of New York, and
Mrs. Sophia Banker White of Staten Island, New York.

Colonel Andrew Johnson Patterson of Greeneville, Tenn.,
has supplied me with every possible assistance as to family
data as to his grandfather. Judge Robert W. Winston of
Chapel Hill, N. C., made available to me his notes for his own
notable Johnson biography.

Dr. J. Franklin Jameson, Chief of the Manuscript Division
of the Library of Congress, and Dr. Thomas P. Martin, Assistant Chief of the Division, have been extremely helpful, particularly in causing to be undertaken the transcription of the
shorthand diary of Colonel William G. Moore, a secretary to
President Johnson. Dr. Martin furthermore has made me
many thoughtful suggestions of comparative source material.

Mr. Wilfred Goodwyn, of Washington, D. C., was of much help in securing material connected with Vinnie Reams' career. Miss Maude L. Kimberly, of the staff of the New York *Nation*, searched the files of that journal for references which proved most useful in the writing of this book. To them both I express my thanks.

Mr. Thomas Ewing, 3d of New York, and the late Mr. George Ewing of Columbus, Ohio, have proven of great assistance in making available to me the Hugh Ewing manuscript.

To Mr. Edward Young Chapin of Chattanooga, a faithful friend who carefully and thoughtfully scrutinized every line of the manuscript, I am most grateful. And finally, the author was fortunate in a secretary, Mrs. Ellen Douglas Pennington, whose faithful and untiring attention has been invaluable in the completion of the manuscript.

GEORGE FORT MILTON.

Chattanooga, Tennessee
Dec. 28, 1930.

I. WAR-TIME WASHINGTON

I N the late forenoon of December 2, 1863, a crowd had gathered on the Capitol lawn at Washington. Senators and Congressmen mingled with masons and artisans, while blue-clad sentries leaned idly on their bayoneted muskets. Thad Stevens' gaunt figure was conspicuous; he regarded the scene with a sardonic smile. Cannons boomed forth their salute as a long queue of workmen plied at a rope through block and tackle, carrying aloft the headpiece of the great Statue of Freedom to crown the Capitol dome, veritably a symbol of Liberty triumphant in the midst of Civil War. As the last section swung into place, applause burst from the assembled thousands. Above the statue, the flag of Union was unfolded to the breeze.

During the war, work had continued on the Federal Capitol, and its great dome, surmounted by the colossal Statue of Freedom, "secure in its bright bronzed armor and lifting its flashing helmet to the sunlight," had been "completed in the midst of the darkest hour of the nation's life." It did not escape acid-tongued Thad Stevens' notice that Freedom was standing "with her face toward the loyal States, and her back turned to the Rebellion."

Most of the throng of onlookers were happy at the symbolic spectacle; but to a reflective few, it was invested with a sense of ironic mockery. Thus Greeley, in his *Tribune*, thought the figure might prove either "a mentor, a censor, a scoffer, or a satirist," or perhaps "no more than a mocking memorial of fading traditions and of virtues which have grown antique," and wondered whether it would not have been best to have left aloft on the dome the unfinished and uncrowned torso. None the less the scene had drawn to war-girt Washington an unusual throng of visitors, and had hastened the tardy advent of the members of the nation's legislative arm, due that day to open the short December term.

When Thad Stevens left his home at Lancaster, Pa., on the early morning of the first of December, he might well have remarked upon the safety and dispatch of the trip to Washington. Some thirty years before, when he had first to make this journey, it took a full week, but in 1863, it could be done in less than two days' time, including all the changes and ferries one had to make!

The traveller coming to Washington from North, East or West had but a single way of reaching the city. Unless he elected to trudge afoot, to come on horseback with flapping saddlebags, or to jolt along in one of the few remaining stage-coaches over country roads of almost unfathomable mud, he must travel over the Washington branch of the Baltimore and Ohio Railroad. The last portion of the journey was made over a small line, beginning at the Relay House, nine miles west of Baltimore.[1]

The trip by railroad from Baltimore to Washington was one of the outstanding accomplishments of transportation in this fourth decade of the acclimatization of the Iron Horse to the Western World. Between Baltimore and Washington there were eight passenger trains a day each way, the slowest operating on a schedule of one hour and fifty minutes, while the most rapid needed only an hour and twenty minutes for its transit. The fare for the journey was the modest sum of $1.60, a pittance in comparison with the charges of the stages which the railroad had replaced.[2]

Probably the famous locomotive, "Ten Wheel Perkins," or a similar product of Engine Builder Thatcher Perkins' inventive genius, had drawn Thad Stevens from Baltimore. This engine was a voracious wood burner, and occasions were not infrequent upon which the train must halt at a convenient wood-pile to replenish the fuel supply. In 1864, passenger cars were widely variegated, some resembling nothing so much as a goods-box mounted on wheels, while others were of a design surprisingly similar to those of today. All had open platforms, with hand brakes, and, inside, immense cast-iron stoves, which during winter months were kept a cherry-red by the frequent feeding of lightwood and pine knots. The train crew were outfitted in double-breasted uniforms of light blue, with large brass buttons and military caps bearing a large metal plate legend of the employee's title on the front. At least once a minute, as an exasperated English correspondent recorded, the door at either end of the car would be opened and closed with a bang. This, he observed, was done by a periodical visitor, a "young gentleman with chain and rings," who bore a tray before him and solicited orders for "gum drops" and "lemon

[1] *Notes will be found, pages 685-754.*

drops." Tobacco, apples and cakes were also liberally consumed by the passengers, who were "crowded as close as they could pack."[3]

Both before and after the war, the stations between the Relay House and Washington were mere hamlets, presenting an infinitely desolate appearance. Shortly after the war, an observer made careful note of the region's "hard times" look. There were a few dirty, dingy farmhouses, most of them whitewashed rather than painted. The fields were full of stagnant pools, with geese, pigs and children swarming about "on a footing of perfect equality."[4]

In the winter of 1863-64, however, the traveller escaped this doubly dilapidated atmosphere, for practically the entire distance from Baltimore to Washington was alive with soldiers, camps, warehouses and artillery parks. After passing through this backwash of war, the train reached the Washington railroad yards and threaded its way cautiously through the maze of tracks, to the frame station, with its tower and clock, which stood at the corner of New Jersey Avenue and C Street. The railroad edifice was termed by some a dirty cheerless hall, but contemporary railway magnates considered it "a marvel of beauty and convenience."[5]

Emerging upon New Jersey Avenue, the visitor would be greeted by the wordy battle of the Jehus, a series of shouts and yells which would startle and bewilder him unless he were "a man of uncommon nerve." At train-time, a dense line of omnibuses and hacks would be drawn up before the station, all the porters and drivers crowding around the entrance and yelling at the top of their lungs the names and good points of their caravanseries.

"Willard's, whose a-goin' to Willard's? Every *gentleman* knows Willard's."—"Metropolitan 'otel, sir? Best 'ouse in the city, sir."—"The National, National! This way, sir. Only first class 'ouse in Washington." These cries, mingled with the no less vigorous shouts of pirate hackmen, gave the visitor to the war-time capital his first greeting.[6]

The traveller could not fail to be impressed with the great Capitol which would burst upon his view as he left the station. Under Major L'Enfant's plan, the Capitol was the center and starting point of the whole system of the city. Situated by George Washington's express selection on the western brow of a commanding hill, it overlooked Washington and the surrounding country. The early builders had determined its position with tedious astronomical exactitude.[7] It was finished during the presidency of James Monroe. Americans of that period considered it "a grand affair," but it soon proved inadequate for the needs of a growing Congress, which reflected the growing country, and in 1850 a great extension was voted.

The effect of this Capitol was "indescribably grand." The "pure white marble glitters and shines in the sunshine, and the huge structure towers above one like one of the foreign palaces of the past." Yet the visitor was more impressed with the magnificent dome, constructed entirely of iron and on close inspection shown to consist of an inner and an outer shell, joined and held together by an "infinity of bars and bolts." An iron stairway led up to the lantern; half way up to the dome, and much visited by tourists, was a gallery running around the exterior of the outer shell. Mounting still higher, the visitor entered the gallery just beneath the canopy, where he might look down nearly 200 feet to the floor below, to see persons moving about like "so many pygmies." The Library of Congress, containing Thomas Jefferson's private library and housed in the western wing of the Capitol, was conducted under strict rules, visitors being requested to remove their hats and prohibited from loud talking; no one under sixteen years of age was admitted under any circumstances.

The superintendent of the Capitol was proud of the heating and ventilating apparatus, the noise of which in the winter season added a constant monotone of clanging machinery and hissing steam to senatorial discussions. Capitol attendants took pride in the "members' baths," which were finished in black walnut, possessed shower baths as well as tubs, and had the floor laid with marble tiles. The Capitol restaurant was managed by "a gentleman of color," who had "decidedly the most elegant manners to be seen in the Capitol." His bill of fare listed every delicacy of the season, and his dishes "were served in a style which would not shame Delmonico himself."

The visitor would probably be driven around the northern flank of the Capitol grounds, which were enclosed by an iron railing mounted on a stone wall, with stone gateways. At the base of Capitol Hill, his carriage would swing into Pennsylvania Avenue, once paved with cobblestones from the Capitol to Georgetown. However, in less than six months after the war began, the "Avenue became so grooved and hammered by army wagons and the increased traffic that its surface suggested that of corrugated iron roofing."[8] In many places, more than ten inches of mud buried the pavement, and teams of army mules often stalled. The surface was churned into "fearful canals of almost unfathomable mud," which in dry weather was changed into clouds of dust. The brick sidewalks along the Avenue and elsewhere were in wretched condition.

During the war, mud and dust were the distinctive features of Washington. The weather had been bright for Lincoln's first inauguration, and tornadoes of dust swept through the streets; at his second, "the streets were covered with a thick coating of mud, carrying out the saying that Washington alternates from dust to mud, or vice versa."[9] Capital residents were fearful of maintaining private carriages, an English visitor noted, because "people are afraid of bringing good horses to be mired by the rut tracks."[10] The Secretary of the Interior lamented that the great width of the streets "quite discourages any attempt to completely pave them."

But for all its insufficiency of paving, Pennsylvania Avenue was generally full of life and motion. In winter, with Congress in session, the Avenue had its ebbs and flows, "like the main artery of Manhattan Island." With the wartime influx, it put on a metropolitan aspect.

One found venders on its corners, "with patent soaps warranted to remove grease spots most tenacious, in an amazingly short space of time." Close by was a man with artificial insects attached to elastic strings, jumping up and down in such a way as to cause passing children to tug at their escorts' sleeves, begging them to pause and purchase. Candy men by the dozens stood by their little stands, on which were displayed "huge rocks of the variegated article," from which they chipped with little hammers, according to demand. Italians roasting chestnuts, telescope men offering their spyglasses at "ten cents a look," and proprietors of "lung-testing machines" asking passers-by if they "want to take a blow to see wot kind of a chist you've got," vied with organ-grinders with their dancing monkeys. Newsboys and bootblacks were everywhere, the former exclusively white, the latter mostly "little inky fellows who would swarm at the crossings and make a dive at your foot as you passed." Mounted guards sat at every street corner, with swords drawn, waiting to pounce upon the unwary speeders of those days. The horsecars clanged along every two or three minutes over the double track from the Navy Yard to Georgetown.

Despite its fathomless mud, the Avenue was filled from early morning until late at night with wheeled conveyances—government wagons, ambulances, private carriages with liveried coachmen and lackeys, and in greatest number, hacks driven by darkies, many of whom were local characters. Verily, it was a museum without a Barnum. In one shop you could buy a satin slipper; next door, a load of hay, while at the next were exhibited coffins up on end, with a "transparency suggesting that you be embalmed." At the heels of a member of the President's Cabinet would tag a shriveled itinerant crying out "um-ber-ellas to mend." The sidewalks were edged with second-hand furniture; ice cream venders camped beneath the trees. In many places on the south side of the Avenue and in a few on the north, painted index fingers pointed out the whereabouts of the aspiring washwoman and the perspiring cook. On the north side, the buildings were higher and more pretentious than on the south, where they were irregular in height and insignificant in appearance. On one side was "sunshine and bustle and pretty shops, and on the other, shadow, dullness and dinginess." It was an Avenue "where almost at every step, Yesterday seems looking over the shoulder of Today, and Tomorrow peers smilingly between."[11]

But for all of the glamor of The Avenue, Washington was a disappointing capital. A Prussian traveller gave it as his opinion that there was "no State in the world which possesses proportionately so small, scantily populated and shabby a capital as the American Union."[12] In 1863-64, it had but one theater, no modern school buildings, and its statues and monuments were few and far between. North of K Street and west of Fourteenth Street, houses were infrequent until Georgetown was reached. East of the Capitol, dwellings were likewise well scattered. The White House, the Treasury Building, the Capitol and the Interior Building were the only imposing official edifices of the nation.[13] Secretary Seward's quarters as Secretary of State were in a tumbledown brick building attached to one end of the Treasury.

The battered and shattered war building to which Lincoln made so many anxious, weary trips had originally been of two stories built of brick, painted drab, with a wooden porch and heavy wooden columns. By 1864 a story had been added to it.[14] The city as a whole was a vast mass of straggling buildings "with little architectural display and few signs of permanent business activity and wealth. . . . " The great government structures of later days—the State, War and Navy Building, the Bureau of Engraving and Printing, the National Museum, the Agricultural Building, the Congressional Library, the Pension Bureau—had not been built. By the end of 1863 the Postoffice had been finished, and the Patent Office nearly so. The Center Market was a low row of sheds, open on both sides. The unfinished Washington Monument, which had climbed to only a third of its projected height, stood forth in bold relief against the distant green of the Virginia hills, a pathetic reminder of the nation's forgetfulness and neglect. At its base clustered ugly sheds and huge piles of rock and lumber.

The odorous B Street canal and Tiber Creek, a little muddy stream, which in summer was "hardly liquid enough for geese," made the city "one vast stench." The canal ran through the center of the city, cutting off what was known as "The Island."[15] There were many other open pools, swamps, ditches and sewers. A further vexation was the way in which horses, cows, goats and pigs roamed at will. Seven years later, George F. Edmunds of Vermont, in a senatorial debate, lamented "the infinitely abominable nuisance of cows, horses, sheep, and goats running through the city," and supported a bill the object of which he described as being to protect "the national representatives and national citizens . . . from being obliged to share the sidewalks and streets with animals that ought to be kept enclosed."[16]

In 1864 Washington was still "the city of magnificent distances," but under the pressure of war-time, the gaps between the White House and the Capitol had begun to fill. No longer was the city the "quiet retired place" of *ante bellum* days. With the coming of Lincoln and the war, Washington's social as well as physical metamorphosis began.

Even before the firing on Sumter, Southern statesmen, with their "long hair, gold-headed canes, and free and easy bearing," had disappeared, to be replaced by "the solid, heavy-stepping, sunburned, rough-handed yeomanry from the Northeast, the East, and the Middle States."[17] Lincoln's inauguration had brought a throng of this new type of visitors to the capital. Hardhanded, rugged men of the West came by the hundreds, to the astonishment and dismay of Society. Morals "were at a very low ebb." Honesty, both private and official, had been replaced by rascality, a visitor declared, and "female virtue was at a discount." The "real inhabitants" held aloof, protesting against the orgies of the newcomers—"barbarians," they dubbed them—by refusing to take part in them. An army of contractors and speculators, "men not sufficiently patriotic to enlist as soldiers, but greedy enough to make the largest possible profit out of the necessities of war," swelled the population. Many of these were as shoddy, both morally and socially, as the goods they sold to the government.

The social standards of the capital were "peculiar." Those "in trade" were looked down upon until they either amassed large fortunes or secured high political place. To work was a reproach. On inheriting a fortune, a Washingtonian remarked, "I never did a day's work, and I never will."[18] Women of social standing lost caste by soiling their hands with toil. Secluded poverty was held preferable to self-help. Education was considered "dangerous to the masses."

One of the sights of the war-time city was the Sunday promenade of "the ladies and gentlemen of color." On Sundays, the city appeared to belong almost entirely to the negroes, to judge from the way in which they, and especially their wives, paraded "in the most elegant costumes, the most blaring colors, the broadest crinolines, rustling in silks, and most closely imitating the white ladies and gentlemen." Even so, Washington was not too friendly to negro aspirations for equal rights. Despite Radical protests voiced by Sumner and backed by Chase, the street car system ran separate cars for white and colored almost throughout the war. "Why can not colored people ride on the cars?" Chase wrote to his friend Jay Cooke, chief owner of the lines; "their seclusion is a disgrace." But the Washington and Georgetown company would not cease its separation of white and black until Senator Sumner announced his purpose to move to forfeit its charter.[19] District residents were adamant against negro suffrage. No negro could testify in legal proceedings.

With the war, Washington became more than the capital of the nation; it became a great military post. Camps, sheds and trains crowded the plains around the city; soldiers and temporary clerks filled every available building and the cost of living rose to unprecedented heights. The householders of pre-war days charged "fabulous" prices, while others threw up hasty shacks for which they charged exorbitant rents.[20] In a few months, the population swelled from sixty-odd thousand to nearly a quarter of a million, and this remained Washington's average size throughout the war.

One of the familiar sights was the streams of ambulances carrying wounded soldiers through the streets to the many hospitals of the city. At the height of the war, the twenty-one hospitals scattered in various parts of the city cared for more than 14,000 wounded, and there was an "endless army of wounded, mangled, ragged, limping, bandaged, and smoke-blackened soldiers, that boats, trains, and ambulances hurried to the city."[21] The huge convalescent camp at Alexandria at one time held 10,000 patients, "some of whom in midwinter had to sleep on the ground."

At all hours of the day and the night, Washingtonians heard "the rumble of the artillery, the galloping of cavalry, the clank of sabres, and the rhythmic tread of marching infantry, the noisy screeching of carts and wagons overburdened with supplies for the commissary. Martial music and the bugle-call's shrill notes kept the population constantly reminded of the roar and thunder of distant battle." Armed sentries were everywhere. The profanity of mule-skinners, marshalling thousands of mules through the streets, added to the excitement of the war-time scene. Soldiers, mostly undisciplined, thronged the streets and increased the burden of police and provost guard.

The soldiers presented one of the greatest problems of war-time Washington. The provost guard was often helpless to restrain them, particularly after pay-days. One of General McClellan's first endeavors, on taking command late in 1861, had been to reduce the number and increase the discipline of the soldiers in Washington by directing that no officer or soldier should visit that city "except on public duty." The mayor coöperated by changing the closing hour for saloons from midnight to nine a. m., but as this did not affect the hours of hotel bars and restaurants, the relief was negligible.

Congress passed an act prohibiting the sale of liquor to soldiers, under penalty of fine or imprisonment; but in vain. Wherever soldiers were stationed, beer barrels and whiskey demijohns were in evidence. Provost Marshal Baker estimated that not less than thirty-seven hundred "fountains of ruin" were in active operation.[22] Two sides of a square were

occupied by the "lowest places of intoxication." The entire
stock of trade of many of these drink purveyors was a cask of
lager beer and "a gallon of unknown and villainous Bourbon
whiskey, dealt out in an old rusty tin cup at ten cents a drink."
On the eve of an important battle, an imperative call for a
train of a hundred wagons to carry supplies to the front found
not five government teamsters sufficiently sober to move forward.

Only second in corrupting influence to the bars and saloons
were the Canterburies, a species of concert hall where the per-
formances were "disgusting, oftentimes brutal."[23] There, "decency, law and humanity were nightly outraged"; men were
drugged, robbed, maltreated and sometimes murdered. The
flashy company was largely made up of thieves and street-
walkers, whose victims were unsophisticated "boys in blue."

Closely akin were Washington's numerous houses of ill-
fame, a few being "superbly furnished" and conducted "in the
most magnificent style." The inmates "were either young or
in the prime of life, and frequently beautiful and accomplished."[24] Few were native Washingtonians; most of them
came to the capital from New York, Boston, Philadelphia, and
Chicago, stayed while Congress was in session and departed
upon its adjournment. The patrons were men "of nominal re-
spectability," Governors, lawyers, doctors, Senators, Congressmen "and the very best class of the city population." They
came openly, would exchange greetings with each other in these
dens of infamy, and "then go away and talk eloquently about
morality and virtue. . . ."[25]

War-time Washington was a very paradise of gamblers.
In August, 1863, Provost Marshal Baker formally reported to
Secretary Stanton that "no less than 163 of these establishments were in full blast"; most of them were on or close to Pennsylvania Avenue and some of them were sumptuously furnished.
The heavily curtained windows, the general air of silence and
mystery and the brightly lighted halls were significant features.
A typical establishment, in which many of Thad Stevens'
lighter moments were spent, was fitted up in "a magnificence
which is princely."[26] "The floor was thickly carpeted, the
walls and ceilings exquisitely frescoed and adorned with choice
works of art." Chandeliers with scores of gas jets shining
through cut glass globes shed a brilliant glare on costly furniture. Negro attendants in splendid livery "attended your every

want with a grace and courtesy positively enchanting." The table groaned under a cold collation, and at stated hours a banquet was served. Food and wine were free to all without obligation to engage in the games of chance, although few accepted this hospitality without playing a little by way of payment. The proprietor was, "as gamblers understand the term," a gentleman of the bluest blood. "If you did not know his trade," a visitor remarked, "you would take him for one of the high officials of the republic, so courtly are his manners, and so lofty his bearing."

In such "first class" establishments, "square" games alone were played, the principal one being Faro. Money was seldom seen on the tables, for ivory counters were generally used. Thousands of dollars changed hands in a single night. The patrons were drawn "largely from members of Congress." The great men of the country could be seen at the principal Faro banks on the nights when no official reception was scheduled. The proprietors told great tales of the nation's statesmen; and in 1864, and for many years after, "the greatest men" frequented these parlors of chance. Nine in every ten of the defalcations by paymasters and others in the employment of the government "were occasioned by losses at the card table."[27] But these were by no means the only gambling houses. There were many "of a lower and viler character," some with "female dealers to lure the unwary to their fate." Decoys for these houses haunted the Capitol and the hotels. The unwitting visitor was made drunk, forced to play and swindled out of his last cent.

Cheek by jowl with these temples of chance on and off The Avenue were Washington's famous hotels, the Metropolitan, the National and Willard's. The National, the largest hotel in the city, at the corner of Pennsylvania Avenue and Sixth Street, had been the chief stopping place of the Southern gentry before the war. During Buchanan's days it had had the distinction of having a disease named for it, "the National Hotel disease," the outcome of too-elementary kitchen sanitation. From its proprietor, John Gadsby, a famous boniface, it was colloquially known as "Gadsby's." On the opposite corner was Jesse Brown's establishment, opened under the name of the Indian Queen, in the late 40's called Brown's Hotel, in Civil War days finally emerging in full titular glory as the Metropolitan. Further up the avenue, at the corner of Twelfth

Street, was Andrew Johnson's favorite Kirkwood House, an unpretentious but bountiful inn.

Two blocks further west stood Willard's, a rambling tribute to the genius of Caleb Willard, perhaps the most enterprising hotel keeper early Washington ever knew. It was "a quadrangular mass of rooms, six stories high and some hundred yards square." Obscure or unpretentious guests were usually assigned to a top floor room farthest removed, and had the painful task of climbing five flights of stairs. During the war, Willard's was packed to its capacity by the onrush of patriotic politicians, and was said to contain "more scheming, plotting, planning heads, more aching and joyful hearts, than any building of the same size ever held in the world."[28]

When he first stopped there, W. H. Russell, war correspondent of the London *Times,* was startled by the way in which, up and down the long passages, doors kept opening and shutting for men with papers bulging out of their pockets. Fully four-fifths of the people in the hotel seemed to be busily engaged in seeking Senators and Congressmen in the great lobby and, on finding them, in presenting heavily documented recommendations for federal jobs; the very floor shook with the tread of the candidature. Not less than 2,500 people a day dined in the Willard's public room, "a vast apartment without carpets or any furniture but plain chairs and tables, ranged in close rows." The business of dining was so serious that one could scarce hear his neighbor speak. To judge from one American's breakfast, the items of which the English correspondent carefully noted, eating must indeed have been more of a business than an art. It consisted of black tea and toast, scrambled eggs, fresh spring shad, wild pigeons, pig's feet, two robins on toast, oysters, Thomas' bread and an ample supply of waffles. The ladies at Willard's were accorded "a handsome drawing room, with pianos, sofas, and easy chairs all to themselves," while the men enjoyed a barber shop, in which shaving was carried on "to a high degree of publicity."[29]

Washington was a city of hotel dwellers; a scathing editorial critic complained that "too many people in that Federal Babylon live in hotels. . . . If the Government were to provide for every Senator and Representative a comfortable house to live in, surrounded by his family . . . public morals would be visibly improved and private manners visibly refined."[30]

To the visitor, there was uncommon pleasure in sauntering beyond Willard's, past the Treasury Building at the next corner, to the "President's House," around which were the most pleasing gardens of the capital. In this neighborhood, the city assumed an almost idyllic aspect. "The kine pasture in the streets," says one chronicler. "The bullfrogs croak and roar in the side-lanes, the birds of passage twitter in all the trees, and the humming-birds flash around every flower." Yet the White House was not considered a desirable residence because of the "ague and fever" that came with Spring and Autumn.

The grounds in front of the President's House were handsomely ornamented, while in the rear a park stretched to the Potomac's edge. The structure itself, modeled on the lines of the palace of the Duke of Leinster, had been partially destroyed in 1814 by Admiral Cockburn's raiders, only to be immediately rebuilt. Its material was freestone, painted white, from which fact, or perhaps from the Widow Custis' home in the Peninsula being so named, it was called the White House. It contained two lofty stories, and the roof was surrounded with a balustrade. Ionic pilasters ornamented the exterior walls. On the north front was a handsome portico with four Ionic columns. The main entrance led from this portico through a massive doorway opening into the main hall.[31]

Within the structure were thirty-one rooms "of considerable size." From the walls of the handsome hall, divided midway by a row of imitation marble pillars, the portraits of former presidents somberly stared down. To the left, occupying the entire eastern side of the house, was the East Room, a "beautiful apartment," handsomely furnished, where the formal levees and receptions and great state dinners were held. Its one fault was that, despite its four fireplaces, it was generally cold. The Green Room, Blue Room, and Red Room adjoining the East Room, each furnished in the colors named, formed "one of the handsomest vistas in the country." West of the Red Room was the large dining room used on the smaller state occasions, and adjoining it the smaller dining room, generally used by the President and his family.

On the north front of the second floor were six rooms used as bedrooms by the President and his family, and to the south were seven rooms—ante-chamber, audience room, Cabinet room, the President's private office, the ladies' parlor, and two others not assigned to any specific purpose. There were eleven

Wingate College Library

rooms in the basement, used as kitchens, pantries, butler's rooms, etc. On the left of the main entrance were the stairs to the upper story, where a doorkeeper was always stationed to prevent "improper characters" from mounting. The White House had an air of elegance and of comfort, its furniture giving an impression of costliness but not of taste.[32]

Throughout his tenancy of the President's House, Abraham Lincoln was easily accessible to visitors—too easily, Mrs. Lincoln thought—but would see no one before nine o'clock in the morning. At the door was Edward McManus, a shrewd little Irishman, who always had a pleasant smile and a cheery word. His duties as buffer for a succession of presidents had endowed him with remarkable insight into character; he could "tell from a look the business and hopes of almost all callers."[33] Lincoln's whole day was consumed with seeing office-seekers and officeholders, holding hastily called meetings of his Cabinet, and reading the Washington newspapers, to which he always gave the greatest care.[34]

Every summer after that of 1861, the President and his family had lived at the Soldiers' Home, some three miles north of the city. Lincoln would call for his carriage every morning at about the same hour, and by 8:30 Washingtonians would see him "coming in to business."[35] One summer morning Walt Whitman observed Lincoln and his cavalcade *en route* to the White House. The President was riding an easy-going gray horse. "Mr. Lincoln is dressed in plain black, somewhat rusty and dusty, wears a black stiff hat, and looks about as ordinary in attire, etc., as the commonest man. A lieutenant, with yellow stripes, rides at his left, and following behind, two by two, come the cavalrymen in their yellow-striped jackets. They are generally going at a slow trot, as that is the pace set them by the one they must wait upon. The sabres and accoutrements clank, and the entirely unornamental cortège, as it trots toward Lafayette Square, arouses no sensation; only some curious stranger stops and gazes."[36] Little Tad "with his cape flying in the wind" kept his pony trotting briskly at his father's side.

Such was the Nation's capital in the battle-drenched days of 1863-64. In Washington was played the greater part of the drama of Andrew Johnson, the Tennessee tailor so strangely destined to hold the national stage for the next five years—

fateful years of recklessness and passion, years in which a prostrate people is to be sacrificed to hate. The stage is set, the actors are ready. Raise the curtain for Ariel and Prospero and clubfooted Caliban.

O N the first of January, 1864, in accordance with the presidential custom, the Lincolns opened the White House for a great New Year's reception. The old year had gone out to the accompaniment of a severe northeasterly storm, but on Friday morning a bright sun ushered in the infant year. At noon the White House doors were thrown open and for two hours a continuous stream of humanity, rich and poor, great and humble, surged through.

Presidential receptions had been conducted in very much the same outward style since Monroe's days, and their etiquette had become so well regulated that even 1861's onrush from the West had not changed it.[1] Social observances were prescribed and followed with the utmost exactness.[2] The President stood in one of the smaller parlors, Mrs. Lincoln by his side, the Cabinet Members surrounding him. Visitors entered from the hall and were presented to the President by an usher, who first asked the name, residence and vocation of the guest. Lincoln shook each one cordially by the hand, presented him to Mrs. Lincoln, and the visitor then passed on into the East room.

These New Year's affairs were more interesting to the guests than to the presidential hosts, for by custom the President must shake hands with every visitor presented. At his Inaugural reception 1861, "the downright serious hard work of the evening" had been performed by Mr. Lincoln, who for more than two hours had shaken hands "in right good earnest" with all comers, at the rate of twenty-five per minute.[3] At the end of such an affair, more often than not the Chief Executive's right hand would be so swollen that for hours afterwards he could not use it.[4]

This New Year, Mrs. Lincoln was receiving by her husband's side. For the last two years, at his evening receptions, the President had almost invariably selected a lady from among the guests to join the promenade with him, leaving Mrs. Lincoln, to her displeasure, to choose another escort. Finally she issued an ultimatum. "Our guests," she said, "recognize the position of president as first of all. Consequently you take the lead in everything. Well, now, if they recognize your position, they should also recognize mine. I am your wife and should lead with you. And yet you offer your arm to any other lady in the room, making her first, and placing me second. The custom is an absurd one, and I mean to abolish it. The dignity I owe to my position as Mrs. President demands that I should not hesitate any longer to act."[5] Mary Todd Lincoln's sharp tongue won her fight. At the New Year's reception of 1864 she determinedly emphasized her primacy, while the rather scornful society of the capital snickered at her triumph.

After three years of daily association, Abraham Lincoln's Cabinet Members still marveled at his physique and physiognomy. The President seemed invariably to be dressed in an ill-fitting wrinkled suit of black, an impression the best tailor in Washington had vainly sought to change. His eyes and brow were his finest features, the eyes dark, full and deep-set, both penetrating and tender, the brow lofty, but covered by irregular strands of thick hair carelessly brushed across it.[6]

Mary Todd Lincoln, the Kentucky planter's daughter whose girlhood ambition to become a president's wife had been so unexpectedly fulfilled, was as short and plump as her husband was tall and gawky. Many of her pictures show her an almost comely woman, though contemporaries seldom so depicted her. To Russell, of the *Times*, describing her appearance at a state dinner he attended, she seemed of middle age and medium height; her face plain, her nose and mouth ordinary, her appearance "homely."[7] Yet, after all the things he had heard of her, Russell had never been more surprised in any person than in Mrs. Lincoln; "her manners," he said, "would adorn a court."[8] Rose Greenhow, who saw through a glass darkly and hated every Northerner, described her as having "a very broad flat face, with sallow, mottled complexion, light gray eyes with scant, light eyelashes, and exceedingly thin, pinched lips."[9]

None the less, "Mrs. President" was far from being the unattractive person pictured by the bitter ladies of Secessia. A French visitor found her "well dressed, according to my taste, in spite of what the simpletons say. . . ."[10] At this New Year's reception Mrs. Lincoln, dressed in purple silk trimmed with black velvet and lace, looked exceedingly well, "receiving and dismissing her guests with much apparent ease and grace."[11]

The Members of the Cabinet grouped about the Lincolns held little levees of their own as the crowd thronged past. Chief among them were Seward, Welles, Blair and Chase. Seward, the "Premier," was a slight man with a sedentary stoop. When he was seated, his large, well formed head, mounted on a long slender neck seemed to project over his chest "in an argumentative kind of way." His mouth was large and flexible, his nose prominent and aquiline, his penetrating eyes were "lively with humor." His broad brow was crowned with a fine head of silvery hair. A subtle, quick man he was, rejoicing in power, fond of a jest and full of oracular utterances. Blair had a "hard, Scotch, practical looking head." One man thought his small, deep-set eyes "rat-like." The Postmaster-General usually spoke with caution, as though weighing his words. "Father Gideon," as Secretary of the Navy Welles was called in a tone of commingled affection and derision, was a small man, with a great, outspreading, long gray beard.

Salmon P. Chase, Secretary of the Treasury, would have struck anyone as the most intelligent and distinguished looking Member of the Cabinet. Tall and of good presence, he had a well formed head and fine forehead. His face indicated energy and power, but a peculiar drooping motion of the lid of one eye detracted from the agreeableness of his countenance and gave it a touch of the sinister.[12] Chase seemed "somewhat perplexed" at the reception.[13]

Throughout the affair Lincoln was in excellent spirits, cordially shaking the hand of each caller, many times halting the procession while he told a quaint joke to some intimate friend in the line. Yet, for all his high spirits, he was looking unduly worn. The President had been ill that winter, but it was more than his physical condition which had brought those deep black circles under his sad and solemn eyes. He was worried, perplexed and embarrassed, for 1864 was the year of the presidential election, and Abraham Lincoln had determined to seek a second term.

In was the political rather than the military situation which so perplexed this master politician of the age. The prospect of the armies of the Union was better than it had been since General P. G. T. Beauregard had opened fire on Fort Sumter. But the political situation, as Lincoln perceived it, was discouraging. The people of the North were so weary with the three years' drain of war that they could not see the promise of peace with victory within the next few months. Yet this vision was not denied the profound observer. In the West, Sherman was at Ringgold, Georgia, facing Johnston, and developing the masterly strategic conception of the Atlanta campaign. Following Vicksburg's surrender, "the Father of Waters flowed unvexed to the seas." Missouri and Arkansas had been pacified, Tennessee largely cleared of Southern troops. The situation in the West was better than Lincoln had seen it since the Civil War began.

In the East, the military situation strategically was little different from that existing in the spring of 1863. But at last President Lincoln had succeeded in his most critical military problem: He had found a general who would fight and who would keep on fighting. Soon he was to place Grant in chief command of the armies; in March the victor of Shiloh, Vicksburg and Chattanooga was to be confirmed as lieutenant general and to come to the East to take personal charge on the Virginia battle front. On the seas the Federal situation was decidedly better. Wilmington, N. C., Charleston, S. C., and Brownsville, Texas, were the only ports remaining open to the swift gray side-wheel blockade runners with their precious freights. The *Alabama* still ranged the seven seas, but her career was shortly to be brought to an end off the coast of France.

In spite of all the improvement in military status of the Federal Government, the North was war-weary. There seemed no surcease from slaughter, and the economic exhaustion of the South was not manifest. The Southern States were on the verge of sudden collapse, but the Northern people did not know this—only their leaders saw it, and they mistrusted their own eyes.

The North's political battles lacked the drama of the military campaigns, but were little less influential upon the final result. Study of the various maneuvers on the Northern political stage reveals still another aspect of Abraham Lincoln, that of the master politician, as cautious and farseeing in appointing postmasters and federal marshals as in choosing generals for the Federal troops. "Father Abraham" had no choice in this—he had to be a politician. Had he confined himself to statesmanship, both Radical North and Conservative Border would quickly have repudiated him, and the Union would not have been maintained.

In 1861 Lincoln was far from having the support of a homogeneous and united North. The Abolitionists, the original secessionists and disunionists, were not pleased with him. Not only had William Lloyd Garrison carried at the masthead of the *Liberator* the stinging statement that the Constitution was "a covenant with death and an agreement with hell," but he had also called Lincoln "the slave hound from Illinois." The Radical Republicans, an immoderate, determined and bitterly influential group, were quite as opposed to Lincoln as were the Abolitionists themselves. The great moderate middle body of Republicans chiefly desired to maintain the Union, but hoped for emancipation of the slaves. The War Democrats and the Conservative Unionists of the Border States, many of them slave-owners, chiefly pinned their faith to "the Union as it was and the Constitution as it is." Then there were the Peace Democrats, many of them loyal, but others on the fringe of treason.

Lincoln's problem was to secure and maintain the support of the majority of each of these groups, and the life of the Union depended on his success. Without proper political support at home, he could neither keep his armies manned and supplied, nor maintain their morale. His first stroke of genius was in keeping the Border States in the Union. His mild and tolerant course toward them through 1861 greatly irritated the Abolitionists. "Mr. Lincoln would like to have God on his side, but he must have Kentucky,"[14] was a typical gibe.

The Northern Abolitionists considered him shamefully tardy. As late as August, 1862, a Radical diarist sourly noted that Lincoln, with the Sewards and Blairs, would "rather see every Northern man shot" than to interfere with slavery, "the palladium of the Rebels."[15] Horace Greeley's faultfinding letter to Lincoln and the latter's magnificent, evasive reply are well known. Committees of Northern ministers called on the President to present emancipation petitions little short of insolent. Congressional Radicals felt that the President was an enemy rather than a friend. The "great political shuffler," they charged, had never yet acted up to his letters.

By the late autumn of 1862, the Border States had been irrevocably committed to the Union cause; but now Lincoln began to fear that, as a result of his inaction on emancipation, he was losing the support of the anti-slavery people of the North. The preliminary Emancipation Proclamation, following Lee's repulse at Antietam, secured for the President little more than the grudging support of the Radical leaders; but it won the enthusiastic loyalty of the Republican rank and file. Even so, its immediate political effect was disastrous. The result of the October elections of 1862 was "utterly discouraging," and those of November were quite as bad.[16] Emancipation proved a boomerang in the five leading free States. Democrats won fourteen Ohio congressional districts. The Republicans lost eight Indiana seats in Congress. In Pennsylvania, which had given Lincoln 60,000 majority in 1860, the Democrats had a lead of 4,000. No state election could have been more harmful or distasteful to the Administration than that of New York, where Horatio Seymour, a peace Democrat—considered by contemporaries "almost a Copperhead"—defeated James S. Wadsworth, Radical Republican brigadier, by nearly 10,000. The overwhelming loss of Illinois filled Lincoln's cup of mortification to the brim. In nearly all of the free States, the administration majorities were sharply cut.

New England and the Border States gave the President a little solace. The former remained Republican, and the Border States vindicated Lincoln's "sagacity and wisdom."[17] Missouri went decisively Republican, and Administration strength was augmented in Kentucky, West Virginia, Maryland, and Delaware. But for the aid of these Border States, the Administration would have been overwhelmed in Congress. As it was, its majority was slender enough. The 1862 elections marked Lincoln's political ebb-tide.

The elections in the fall of 1863 were more encouraging. The military victories of the summer had given heart to the people. Pennsylvania veered around. New York rebuked Seymour's course by electing a Republican state ticket. A wave of popular indignation in Ohio led to the defeat of the Copperhead Vallandigham for Governor by over 100,000 votes.

None the less, Lincoln's Administration was far from having regained its prestige. It had to conduct its battle on Capitol Hill with an undependable, makeshift leadership. Appreciation of Lincoln as a statesman was heartbreakingly slow in growing.

Early in 1863, various Radical leaders started quiet campaigns to secure the nomination of another than Lincoln the next year. By July, Washburne of Illinois was "already making a business of committing men to Grant for the presidency." In September, a Pennsylvania friend of General Butler wrote him that he planned to announce his name for president the next month, and James Parton, a historian who seems also to have acted as Butler's press agent, arranged an interview between Horace Greeley and the General, at which they could discuss the coming political campaign. Two months later, Parton's book on Butler in New Orleans came from the press, a timely campaign document, and its author wrote its hero that "H. G. is sot."[18]

The Radicals termed the oration of Edward Everett, the "chief" speaker at the Gettysburg Memorial, in the fall of 1863, "a masterpiece, noble and warm," but they sneered that Lincoln "also spoke," with one eye on the future platform and on reelection.[19] Immediately after the delivery of the address, some of the President's best friends regretted that it had been a failure.[20]

By the beginning of the presidential year of 1864, the President indubitably desired both to be renominated and reelected. In this his purpose was not chiefly selfish—his zeal was for the Union and his anxiety was for the restoration of peace and friendship after the seceded States had been restored. He was convinced that a Democratic president would not preserve the Union; and he feared that a Radical Republican executive would tread the South under an iron heel.

Lincoln was by no means lacking in shrewd, faithful and effective friends. In and out of his Cabinet, he had a group of lieutenants who could undertake successfully the very type of political maneuver which his renomination and reëlection required. It was a group of politicians of exceptional shrewdness, sagacity and finesse, men much more competent in practical politics than any of the Radical leaders, unless Thad Stevens be excepted. In the Cabinet, Seward and Blair were no mean politicians; out of it Simon Cameron, Thurlow Weed, Henry J. Raymond, A. K. McClure, Ex-Governor Morgan and several others were even more competent. And they had already set to work.

Montgomery Blair, valuable in himself, was even more valuable in his father, the famous Francis Preston Blair, chief member of Jackson's "Kitchen Cabinet" and one of the General's staunchest and shrewdest friends. Although now in his seventies, the old gentleman was still an intimate and confidential counsellor and correspondent of hundreds of important people throughout the North.

Seward's chief political assets were his two friends, advisers and allies, Thurlow Weed and Henry J. Raymond. Seward and Weed were politically the same person; this Seward himself acknowledged in his oft-quoted epigram, "Weed's Seward, and Seward's Weed."[21] Of the two, Gideon Welles held the Albany editor-politician to be "of vastly more vigor of mind, reckless and direct, persistent and tortuous, avaricious of late, and always corrupt." Weed did not look the part of a politician. A tall man, slightly stooped, with an air of benevolence, he could easily have been mistaken for a college professor or clergyman. He usually walked alone, with a soft, catlike tread, his head inclined to one side. When he talked, it was in low tones, almost in whispers, as if he had trained himself to extreme caution in his utterances lest he be overheard. An unerring tactician, farsighted and eminently practical, he always looked for success, and generally it came his way.[22]

Raymond, who had begun as a reporter, had slowly worked his way up. After Raymond had managed to found the *Times*, Greeley, with whom he had served several years, always referred to him as "that little devil of the *Times*." Welles thought him a man of considerable talent, and regretted that "under Weed's teaching he is destroying himself."[23] Like Weed, he was an effective controversial writer, and unlike him, a popular and effective orator. Raymond, now in his middle forties, looked ten years younger. He was short and thickset, a handsome face making up somewhat for his unimpressive stature. Even in the thick of caucuses and conventions, he was very much of a swell, carrying a monocle and toying with a gold-headed cane.

The third of this trio, Simon Cameron, was one of the great politicians of the day. In his later career, he was to dominate Pennsylvania Republicanism as few have done before or since. A slight man with a thin calculating mouth, deep-set keen gray eyes and gray hair, he gave those who met him an impression of ability joined to unscrupulous adroitness.[24] He had been Lincoln's Secretary of War not quite a year when rumors of fraudulent war contracts began to be bruited about, and the

President "kicked him upstairs" as United States Minister to Russia.

Cameron was the shrewdest of the Pennsylvania politicians. Seldom did a clash between him and Stevens, Governor Curtin, or John W. Forney, result in the old intriguer's defeat. By the autumn of 1863 he was back in the country and had his ear to the ground. His almost unerring intuition informed him that, even if the Radical leaders looked upon Lincoln as a menace and a fraud, the rank and file of Northern Republicans believed in him. Thereupon Cameron forehandedly assumed the leadership of the Lincoln forces in Pennsylvania, doubtless as much to rehabilitate himself as to strengthen the President.

The Radicals were very loath to contemplate Lincoln's renomination.[25] They considered his first Administration a failure. They had neither confidence in nor respect for him. "The people," they felt, "does not support Lincoln's shiftless, heartless, incapable Administration." For more than a year, these self-styled "patriotic, devoted, courageous, self-sacrificing" Radicals had been laying plans to push Lincoln aside, and to put a "real patriot" in the presidential chair—intrigues which had backing in the Cabinet itself!

In mid-February, 1864, Attorney-General Bates found the President "fully apprehensive of the scheme of the Radical leaders." Lincoln told him that these men "were almost fiendish." The President was well aware that his enemies "would strike him at once, if they durst, but they feared that the blow would be ineffectual, and so they would fall under his power as beaten enemies." Thus, because of fear that they might fail as enemies, they still pretended to be Lincoln's friends.[26]

Radical backing for the nomination had been hawked around through most of 1863. Sumner approached Vice President Hamlin with a "tender" of the 1864 Republican presidential nomination, which Hamlin declined.[27] Another who appealed to the Radical mind was Wadsworth of New York. After his defeat by Seymour, Radical thought turned from him to the notorious Benjamin F. Butler, who, they felt, differed from Lincoln in being "no joker, no sham, but a most thorough pro-consular reality."

Butler had been a Massachusetts Democrat. As a delegate to the Charleston National Convention, he had cast his vote, through more than forty ballots, for Jefferson Davis for presidential nominee. Butler's war career was rather spotted. In 1862, as military governor of New Orleans, he had issued an order respecting the women of the city which soon brought him the title of "Beast" Butler. At New Orleans he gained the further sobriquet of "Silver Spoon"—or simply "Spoon"— Butler, because of his reputed appropriation of some Southern table silver. Later in the war, he was given a Department command in Virginia, and in the fall of 1863 and early in 1864 was being anxiously and vainly looked to by Radical leaders to make a great military success, so that he might be nominated for president in Lincoln's stead.

Resembling a cross between a pig and a peacock more than a man-eating tiger, in physical appearance Ben Butler was not a very formidable "beast." He was short and thickset, strongly built, "with gross limbs."[28] His head, completely bald, gave his forehead an appearance of elevation not properly its own. His manner, decided and abrupt, was marked by extreme pomposity—he strutted sitting down. He generally wore a magnificent major general's uniform and an enormous sword. Butler was given to making stump speeches, even in casual conversation. His eyes seemed to have a peculiar obliquity of vision, the eyelid hanging with a heavy droop over the eye. When the Hero of the Silver Spoon looked at one, he had to cock his head at an almost neck-breaking angle. Lincoln thought him "as full of poison gas as a dead dog."[29]

Gurowski[30] wrote in his diary on January 28, 1864: "Ben Butler would make an excellent president. He has all the capacities of a statesman. Butler can destroy and build, organize and administer. He is bold, with keen insight, and with prompt unerring decision. Could only Butler make some *coup d'éclat* before Richmond!" Two days later he wrote to remind the General that "in the last hour," "the people will go for the ablest man, provided that man accomplishes some brilliant action, and accomplishes it in the *nick of time*. . . . A lightning-like blow dealt from Fortress Monroe on Richmond, putting you in possession of the nest of the Rebellion, transforms you into an irresistible favorite, and a candidate for the presidency." "Of course Lincoln . . . will never put you in possession of sufficient means for such a *coup*," Gurowski added, advising sagacious duplicity in accumulating the troops needed for it. Then, "when the hour comes, strike the blow without letting out your secret. Report to the rulers—when half-way before Richmond. . . . A great action, a bold action, and Lincoln's chances vanish as a nightmare."[31]

Butler acted with promptness. On January 31 he telegraphed to a friendly general in Baltimore to send him a plan of Richmond, explaining that he sought it thus outside the usual channels because "my sending to buy one would cause remark."[32] For a week he collected and prepared troops for a raid. The War Department and Meade's Army seemed loath to cooperate, but Butler worried Sedgwick until the latter reluctantly agreed to make a demonstration.

The raid was an inglorious failure. The Army of the Potomac, in its demonstration, lost 200 killed and wounded, and Sedgwick wired the War Department that Butler had "spoiled the best chance we had for a successful attack on the Rapidan."[33] The politician-general characteristically sought to shift the blame for the failure. He reported to President Lincoln that the Confederates had been warned by a deserter, a New York soldier under sentence of death, who "would have been hung long ago but for the President's order suspending till further orders the execution of capital sentences." Butler's Radical friends were much annoyed at the failure of the raid.[34] "Everyone is disappointed," a Massachusetts friend wrote him; "the report continually made is, if that had succeeded, Butler would have been the next President, and nothing could have prevented."[35]

After Butler's failure, the Radicals reluctantly turned to Chase. In many ways this new Richmond approached greatness. He was a remarkably able executive, with extraordinary powers of analysis, of decision and of dispatching great masses of work in a competent and satisfactory way. Undoubtedly he was a great Secretary of the Treasury, but not nearly so great as a man. He was almost a zealot on the question of negro suffrage. Able, self-centered, completely lacking in humor, Chase during most of his Treasury incumbency felt contempt for Lincoln and considered the President inferior to himself. It is altogether possible that he really believed that Lincoln would surely lose the 1864 election and that he himself could surely win it. Nor was Chase alone in so comparing himself and Lincoln to the latter's detriment. A large group in and out of Congress felt this keenly, among whom were Sumner, Stevens, Howard of Michigan, Henry Winter Davis, Ashley of Ohio, "Bluff Ben" Wade and S. C. Pomeroy of Kansas. Greeley,

Beecher and Tilton preferred Chase. Joseph Medill didn't much care.

Gideon Welles had long suspected Chase of disloyalty to Lincoln. As early as June 26, 1863, he made note of a remark of Montgomery Blair: "The tendency of things . . . is to make McClellan and Chase candidates," in which event Blair expects "McC. will beat C. five to one."[36] In October Chase made a speech in Baltimore which Gurowski thought had "the flavor of a presidential candidate." Late in December, Senator Doolittle of Wisconsin called upon Welles to say that "there is an active, zealous and somewhat formidable movement for Chase, . . . Chase clubs are being organized in all the cities to control the nominating convention." For several months the Secretary of the Treasury had avoided attending Cabinet meetings, doubtless because of his embarrassment at sitting across the council table from the President whom he was secretly attempting to displace.

The New England Republicans gave all possible aid and comfort to the Chase movement. The day after Lincoln's New Year's reception, Senator Sumner of Massachusetts complained to Welles of Lincoln's cautious moves toward reëlection. The President "has spoken to several persons on the subject very explicitly," Sumner charged. Welles replied that Lincoln had "exchanged no word with me on the subject," but confessed that he had taken it for granted that Lincoln would be a candidate; "all presidents entertain dreams of that nature." The Secretary added that he thought a strong current was setting in Lincoln's favor, a remark received in sullen silence by Sumner, leaving his host to believe that "his thoughts are in another direction"—that of Chase.[37]

Early in January, soon after the Pennsylvania legislature convened, Simon Cameron bestirred himself to commit the Republican party of that State to Lincoln's renomination. After some maneuvering, he prepared a paper which was signed by every Republican senator and representative at Harrisburg. In doing so, he stole a march on Thad Stevens, who was strongly opposed to Lincoln's having a second term.[38]

About this time, the Blairs became active. On January 10 the venerable Francis Preston Blair brought Governor Dennison of Ohio to see Gideon Welles, and the three went thoroughly over the situation. Thurlow Weed quietly began to bestir himself. And more than all three, the voice of the people

back home began to be heard. Resolutions of other state legislatures indorsing Mr. Lincoln began to roll in. The Radicals
suspected that Weed, "that prince of dark deeds," was the
secret manager of these pro-Lincoln pronunciamentos. Some
of the Radicals slowly and reluctantly concluded that, strive as
they might, "the masses are taken in by Lincoln's apparent
simplicity and good naturedness, his awkwardness, his vulgar
jokes." They saw that "in the people's belief, the great shifter
is earnest and honest."[39]

The leaders of the anti-Lincoln movement at last perceived
that they must act, and act quickly, if the President's renomination were to be prevented. They decided that Chase was the
man, organized a secret committee for him, and in February
sent out a circular, pointing out the political and public dangers attendant upon Lincoln's renomination, and calling for
the choice of Salmon P. Chase. The circular, although a joint
product of Sumner, Stevens, Davis, Wade, Pomeroy and others,
bore Pomeroy's name alone. It was intended for private and
confidential distribution, but in some way got into the hands of a
Washington newspaper and was generally reprinted.

It referred to the endeavor "recently made throughout the
country to secure the renomination of President Lincoln" which,
it stated, necessitated counter-action on the part of "unconditional friends of the Union." The machinery of government,
it charged, was being devoted "to secure the perpetuation of
the present administration"; and therefore "those who conscientiously believe that the interests of the country and of
freedom demand a change" had no choice other than an appeal
to the people.

Even if Lincoln's reëlection were desirable, the circular held
that "it is practically impossible"; if he were to be reelected,
"the cause of human liberty and the dignity of the nation"
would suffer from the President's "manifest tendency toward
compromises." The authors of the circular found "united in
the Hon. Salmon P. Chase more of the qualities needed in a
president . . . than are combined in any other available candidate." Accordingly, "a central organization" had been established to promote his nomination, and the aid and assistance
of all true patriots were solicited.[40]

The publication of this amazing document greatly embarrassed its supposed beneficiary. On February 22 Chase wrote
Lincoln a curious and uncandid letter, in which he claimed to

have had "no knowledge of the existence of this letter," before he saw it in the *Constitutional Union.* A few weeks before, he related, several friends had called on him to urge that he allow his name to be submitted for consideration; he had replied that he feared "such use might impair my usefulness as head of the Treasury Department," and that he much preferred to continue his labors where he was. There were several further interviews, he wrote, at all of which the backers of his candidacy expressed their united judgment that "the use of my name as proposed would not affect my usefulness in my present position." Chase "accepted their judgment as decisive; but at the same time told them distinctly that I could render them no help, except what might come incidentally from the faithful discharge of public duties. . . ."

The Secretary of the Treasury added that he knew nothing further about the enterprise and had never wished that his name "should have a moment's thought in comparison with the common cause of enfranchisement and restoration, or to be continued before the public a moment after the indication of a preference, by the friends of that cause, for another." In conclusion, he wrote the President that for him he cherished "sincere respect and esteem, and, permit me to add, affection," and did not wish "to administer the Treasury Department one day without your entire confidence."[41]

Lincoln allowed Chase to remain on tenterhooks until February 29, when he wrote him that he had not yet read, "and I think I shall not," the Pomeroy circular, but, had "in spite of myself, known of its *existence* several days before." He was neither shocked nor surprised by its appearance, for he had knowledge of the Pomeroy committee "for several weeks." As to Chase's remaining at the head of the Treasury, that "is a question which I will not allow myself to consider from any standpoint other than my judgment of the public service; and, in that view, I do not perceive occasion for a change."

In truth, premature publication of the circular had played into Lincoln's hands, for the plans of the Radicals had not matured and could readily be frustrated. It did not take long to nip the Chase movement in the bud, and it was done with an ingenuity which suggests that Thurlow Weed was the engineer. Only three days after the issuance of the Pomeroy circular, the Ohio legislature, representing Secretary Chase's home state, passed a resolution calling upon the party to renominate President Lincoln as the man to win the war! Shortly after this pointed repudiation by the legislature of his own State, Chase published a letter declining to permit his name to be used.

Although Wendell Phillips made speeches terming Lincoln an "imbecile," an "honest incompetent," and urged Fremont or Butler, and although the General's friends informed him that Chase would "advise his friends at just the right time to give their influence" to Butler,[42] Lincoln's managers were never in doubt as to his renomination; but, as his prospects improved, Lincoln himself seemed to have grown more anxious, to have become apprehensive of a slip and to have set about to strengthen himself. About the time of the ill-fated Pomeroy circular, the President had made up his mind to get a new running mate for the 1864 campaign. He came to the conclusion that the existing situation demanded a War Democrat, and both he and Stanton determined to swallow their personal feelings and to draft Benjamin F. Butler.[43] They submitted their tentative plan to Simon Cameron, who heartily indorsed the scheme. Lincoln then asked the Pennsylvania politician to go down to Fortress Monroe and tell Butler what they had in mind. Cameron agreed, and in a few days left for Butler's headquarters, accompanied by William H. Armstrong, a Pennsylvania Republican politician.

Lincoln's envoy told Butler that "the President . . . intends to be a candidate for reelection, and as his friends indicate that Mr. Hamlin is no longer to be a candidate for vice president, and as he is from New England, the President thinks that his place should be filled by someone from that section." Cameron continued that, "aside from reasons of personal friendship which would make it pleasant [to Mr. Lincoln] to have you with him," the President believed that, as the first prominent Democrat who volunteered for the war, "your candidature would add strength to the ticket, especially with the War Democrats." Would not the General allow his friends "to cooperate with Lincoln to place him in that position?"[44]

To Cameron's astonishment, Butler refused. "There is nothing in the vice presidency," he sneered. "I prefer to stay in the army." Obviously the General had not yet given up hope for the timely *coup d'éclat* and the resultant first place on the ticket. "Please say to Mr. Lincoln," Butler told Cameron, "that while I appreciate in the fullest sensibility this act of

friendship and the compliment he pays me, yet I must decline."
He added, laughing, "Tell him with the prospects of the campaign, I would not quit the field to be vice president, even with
himself as President, unless he will give me bond with sureties,
in the full sum of his four years salary, that he will die or resign within three months after his inauguration."[45] But this
unexpected rebuff did not cause Lincoln to give up his plan to
have a War Democrat at the tail of the ticket. In April,
Lincoln decided to go to Fortress Monroe himself to see Butler,
and wrote him cautioning him not to make public the projected interview.[46]

Left without an outstanding candidate by Chase's sullen
withdrawal, the Radicals were now in a stew. Sumner was still
anxious for another nominee, as were Governor John A. Andrew of Massachusetts, "Bluff Ben" Wade and Thad Stevens.
They pursued their plans a little further, only to find their
hopes quite vain. The politically competent among them concluded that, however much they might dislike it, they would
have to accept Lincoln again. But it was different with the
Abolitionists and the Missouri Radical Republicans, who followed General John C. Fremont and hated the very shadow of
the Blairs.[47] Accordingly, between May 6 and May 14 several
calls for a Republican National Convention were issued. It
was to be held in Cleveland, on the last day of May.

Referring to "the imbecile and vacillating policy of the
present Administration in the conduct of the war," one call
demanded "the immediate extinction of slavery throughout the
whole United States," with "the absolute equality of all men
before the law, without regard to race or color." Another
urged that all patriots "unite to resist the swelling invasion of
an open, shameless, and unrestrained patronage." Among the
signers were Elizabeth Cady Stanton, B. Gratz Brown, Stephen
S. Foster, Emil Pretorius, Nathaniel P. Sawyer and many
others of lesser note. Wendell Phillips wrote a letter of enthusiastic approval.[48]

The Cleveland affair could term itself a Republican convention without any conflict with the Baltimore meeting which
had already been called to effect Lincoln's renomination. With
the utmost sagacity, the President had determined that not
the Republican, but a new party, the National Union party,
should offer him to the country for a second term. The Re-

publican National Committee, meeting in Washington on
Washington's birthday, had invited delegates chosen by "all
qualified voters who desire the unconditional maintenance of
the Union, the supremacy of the Constitution, and the complete suppression of the existing rebellion, and the cause thereof by vigorous war, and all apt and efficient means" to a
convention to meet in Baltimore on June 7, to present candidates for president and vice president.[49]

The use of the title "National Union" proved to be a master
stroke of political strategy. In 1860, the Republican party
had been frankly sectional, and in eight Southern States it had
not received a single vote. During the early part of the war,
the chief grievance against Lincoln's Administration had been
that it was based on a sectional party which did not represent
even the North in arms. But Lincoln received the support of
many Northern Democrats—War Democrats, they were called
—Stephen A. Douglas, as true a patriot and as magnanimous
as Lincoln himself, taking the lead. Their backing had been
of immense value in upholding Lincoln's hands. In his campaign for reelection, the President desired to appeal not alone
to Republicans, but equally to War Democrats, to old Whigs
and Native Americans, to Conservative Unionists of the Border
and Radical Abolitionists of the Northern fringe. Abraham
Lincoln had determined to make himself the presidential candidate of all men who loved the Union and wished it preserved.
He would nationalize the Republican party by embodying in
himself the Union cause. Thus Lincoln was not unwilling for
the ultra-Radical Abolitionist fringe, temporarily at least, to
assume the Republican name.

The Radicals duly met at Cleveland. The resolutions
adopted were distinctly immoderate. Wendell Phillips' letter
terming the Administration "a civil and military failure, and
its avowed policies ruinous to the North," evoked much applause. The delegates unanimously nominated General John
C. Fremont for president and General John B. Cochrane of
New York for vice president, adopted resolutions roundly denouncing the Lincoln Administration, and adjourned. There
had been a number of ridiculous occurrences during the convention. The four hundred delegates who attended were chiefly
known to the people as cranks, fanatics and men of extreme
bitterness and rancor.

Lincoln received the news of the Radicals' convention calmly. A friend giving him an account of it said that, instead of the many thousands who had been expected, there were present at no time more than four hundred men. The President, struck by the number mentioned, reached for the Bible which commonly lay on his desk, and after a moment's search read these words: "And everyone that was in distress and every one that was discontented gathered themselves unto him, and he became a captain over them; and there were with him about four hundred men."[50]

While the Radicals were preparing for their ebullitions of wrath, Lincoln's managers were planning their pacification. The election of delegates to the Baltimore convention quickly proved Lincoln's hold on the Union masses. The New York *Evening Post* had taken up his campaign cause in February, printing two columns of Lincoln anecdotes, one of which was the President's remark that "it is never best to swap horses in crossing a stream."[51] This homely figure appealed to the humor and common sense of the country, and greatly assisted the energetic endeavors of Lincoln's political managers. The legislatures of State after State indorsed Lincoln's reëlection. Successive conventions selected delegates, instructing them to vote as a unit for his renomination. Much of this was due to the shrewd management of his political lieutenants, but more was due to the common sense of the people themselves.

In April, Charles Sumner, Senator from Massachusetts, began a curious intrigue to oust Hannibal Hamlin from the vice presidential chair. Sumner was generally deemed the genius of the Radical Republicans, the American Charles James Fox. The currents and cross-currents of these troubled times cannot be understood without a study of this eerie, evil genius who sat in Daniel Webster's seat in the Senate, spinning tenuous spiderwebs of far-fetched theory about negro equality—theories to improve the legal status of the very negroes whose physical presence left him cold.[52] In his own opinion Charles Sumner was almost a demigod. He permitted none the right to question the logic of what he said, the language in which he said it, or the illustrations from four tongues with which he brocaded his carefully prepared remarks. To New England Abolitionists and to the Radicals throughout the country, Charles Sumner was the hope of the Western world. Yet few men so generally disliked by his associates as Sumner ever sat in a legislative hall.[53]

This unpopularity with his colleagues did not spring from Civil War differences. Sumner seemed possessed of a very genius for antagonisms. By the time he had been in the Senate two or three years, many of his fellow Senators would not even speak to him. "Bully" Brooks' attack on him in 1856 failed to arouse as much sympathy among his Republican senatorial colleagues as it did through the North, because of the general contempt in which Sumner was personally held by his associates.

Thad Stevens' view was characteristic. One day he remarked to a friend: "I go neck and neck with Sumner a long way, but we differ essentially in one particular. The god of my idolatry is my country. The god of his idolatry is Charles Sumner." A mention of Sumner in Grant's presence evoked an unusual flash of wit from the General. Someone said that Sumner did not believe in the Bible. "Why should he?" Grant asked. "He did not write it."[54] Even Bluff Ben Wade disapproved of the "suspicion of arrogance, the flavor of sham," in the splendid Sumner.

Handsome, able and learned, as he was quite aware, he spoke in deep sonorous tones, modulated his voice carefully and enunciated clearly, interspersing his delivery with appropriate but studied gestures. In the debate provoked by Sumner's "Crime Against Kansas" speech, Stephen A. Douglas charged that the Senator from Massachusetts "had his speech written, printed, committed to memory, practiced every night before a glass, with a negro boy to hold a candle and watch the gestures, and annoyed the boarders in the adjoining rooms until they were forced to quit the house."

Thoroughly versed in the classics, Sumner carefully interspersed his speeches with quotations from Greek and Latin poets, from Shakespeare, Milton, Voltaire and Rousseau. Some writers believe him "sincere, high-minded and morally courageous"—others quite the reverse. But it is undisputed that Sumner enraged his opponents and irritated those who should have been his friends. This unfortunate trait is illustrated in a story which Attorney-General Bates carefully confided to his diary on May 20, 1864.

Mrs. Julia Ward Howe of Boston had had occasion to go

to Washington. During her stay, she called upon the Senator, and in the course of their conversation, this colloquy occurred:

> Mrs. Howe: Ah, Mr. Sumner, have you heard Booth yet? He's a man of fine talents and noble hopes in his profession.
> Mr. Sumner: Why, no, madam, I long since ceased to take any interest in individuals.
> Mrs. Howe: You have made great progress, sir. God has not yet gone so far—at least, according to the last accounts.

This anecdote throws a revealing light upon Charles Sumner. Devoid of humility, he was equally lacking in consideration for the feelings of others. Anyone who had the hardihood to disagree with him, he immediately set down as either a knave or a fool, and probably both.

No one was more provoked by Sumner's calm assumption of being the sole repository of the best of American idealism than his New England colleague, William Pitt Fessenden of Maine, a man of substance and of courage, a real fighting man. Nor was the Maine Senator altogether lacking in a grim sense of humor, an ironic ability to take the wind out of soaring senatorial sails. He evolved a technique which gave him considerable amusement and the Senate real relief. At the apogees of the Massachusetts statesman's eerie flights it became Fessenden's custom to arise "for the purpose of a question." Then, with a brusque and annihilating phrase, he would pluck the feathers from the soaring eagle's wings, greatly to the amusement of the assembled Senators and infinitely to Charles Sumner's ire.[55]

Vice President Hannibal Hamlin also came from Maine. Until March, 1861, he had himself been a member of the Senate, taking great pleasure in its verbal brawls. Sumner believed that Hamlin was not happy, immured in the forced neutrality of the vice presidential chair. It imposed upon him the obligation of impassivity, no matter how hot the dispute. The Massachusetts statesman concluded from a few of Hamlin's chance remarks that the Vice President would be much happier were he once more to be a Senator from Maine.

Fessenden was to come up for reelection in 1865. Were Hannibal Hamlin free of the vice presidency, he would return to Maine and regain his seat in the Senate: and then Fessenden would trouble Sumner no more.   Thus ran the thoughts of Massachusetts' matchless theorist.   He would perform this true service for Hamlin, and would at the same time pluck out the offending Fessenden and return him to private life.   He seems not to have deemed it necessary to consult the Vice President. A supplement readily suggested itself.   Not only would Sumner drive Fessenden from the Senate by the repatriated Vice President, but he would have a hand in naming a new Vice President and would see that he came from New York.   Either John A. Dix or Daniel S. Dickinson would make a magnificent vice president.   With a staunch New York War Democrat on the ticket, William H. Seward, whom Sumner regarded as a national menace, would have to retire to private life!

III. THE NATIONAL UNION CONVENTION

L ATE in May, two Maine politicians set out on a leisurely journey to Baltimore. Josiah H. Drummond was a delegate from Maine's first district to the coming National Union Convention and Charles J. Talbot, although not a delegate, was an influential local figure. Both were friends of Vice President Hannibal Hamlin and neither expected any difficulty in his being again selected for Lincoln's running mate. Breaking their journey at Boston, they proceeded to visit friends and acquaintances. They had not been long on these casual calls before they learned of a secret caucus of the leaders of the Massachusetts delegation, then in progress.[1] The Maine visitors walked boldly in.

To their amazement, the caucus proved nothing more nor less than a meeting of a steering committee seeking Hamlin's defeat. The Massachusetts leaders frankly expressed their dissatisfaction with the Lincoln Administration, and their desire to have "a more Radical Republican" in Lincoln's stead. But the renomination of the President, they had regretfully concluded, was "a foregone conclusion, . . . it was no use to make any attempt to nominate anyone else. . . ." None the less these Radicals deemed it of the greatest importance that the influences about Lincoln be altered, so that the conduct of the Administration should be more in keeping with their views. They were especially determined to get rid of Seward.

Much to the discomfiture of Hamlin's two friends, the caucus agreed that the best way to oust Seward from the Cabinet was to nominate a vice president from New York. It was Sumner's formula. Manifestly it would be politically unthinkable for a single State, even New York, to be allowed to furnish both the Vice President and the Secretary of State. Drummond and Talbot vainly pleaded the cause of Hamlin, and continued on their journey to Baltimore, carrying the unwelcome intelligence that Charles Sumner had unsheathed his sword.

It was substantially the first information Hamlin's managers had of the stealthy fight against their chief, and they did not attach much importance to it, for Sumner was often a general without an army. But they did attempt to start a backfire in Massachusetts: perhaps the Bay State delegation could be brought back into line. After Governor John A. Andrew had seen that Lincoln's renomination was inevitable, he had asked his alternate to represent him at Baltimore and to vote for Lincoln if need be. Now the Hamlin men appealed for help, and the Governor hurried to the convention. Senator Henry Wilson, too, hastened to Baltimore to intercede.[2] Wilson went so far as to tell delegates that he had "full authority to represent the views of President Lincoln privately," and that it was Lincoln's earnest desire that Hamlin be renominated!

But Sumner did not intend to have his plan overturned at the last moment. He also took the train to the convention city. The delegates listened respectfully to Andrew and to Wilson, but Sumner won the day.

The nomination of a New Yorker in Hamlin's stead was an indispensable feature of the Massachusetts scheme—not merely a New Yorker, but a War Democrat, one who had supported Lincoln through thick and thin. The choice of such a man, it was urged, would be the best evidence that it was not a Republican, but a Union party, concerned with the preservation of the nation and the victorious conclusion of the war. Two such men were prominently named in the discussions: Daniel S. Dickinson and John A. Dix. One of these, it was believed, would be Lincoln's running mate.[3]

More than a politician, almost a statesman, Daniel Stevens Dickinson was an attractive figure. He was an effective stump speaker with a sharp wit, a rich fund of anecdote and sparkling humor. His singular facility in using Biblical illustrations had won him the nickname of "Scripture Dick." Long flowing silvery locks added to his impressiveness. Dickinson came from Binghamton and Seward's home was at Auburn, in the same Southern Tier. When men of opposing political faiths live in the same section, they generally develop a bitterness toward one another unknown to rival partisans who live further apart. Seward never learned to trust his Democratic foe, and the latter often complained bitterly of the attitude of Seward and his friends.[4] After supporting Stephen A. Douglas in 1860, Dickinson offered his warm support to Lincoln and maintained it throughout the war. With him, men had become of little moment; it was "the great cause of the Union" he was determined to promote.[5]   Even in the spring of 1864, with the Democrats girding their loins for a great campaign to recapture the White House, Dickinson came out bravely for the Emancipator.

The other New York War Democrat discussed for Vice President was John A. Dix, a major general in the Federal Army.   He had entered Buchanan's Cabinet as Secretary of the Treasury near the stormy close of that unfortunate administration.   As Secretary of the Treasury in 1861, Dix had electrified the North by his famous telegram to a subordinate at New Orleans: "If any man attempts to haul down the American flag, shoot him on the spot."   He was generally considered "a man of excellent ability, of wide experience in affairs, of spotless character, and a most zealous friend of the Union."[6] In 1864, he was commanding the Military Department of New York.

Dix was also in Secretary Seward's bad books, the chief unpleasantness between them dating back to less than three weeks before the Baltimore convention day.   On May 18, a spurious presidential proclamation calling for a fresh draft of men to bolster the failing Federal armies had appeared in the New York *World* and in the *Journal of Commerce*.   Joe Howard, a former *Tribune* man and a member of Henry Ward Beecher's church, had perpetrated the hoax and the editors of the two papers had printed the proclamation, only to bring down the wrath of Washington upon their heads.   As both were "Copperhead" anti-Administration papers, Seward chose to believe that the responsible editors were parties to the fraud— although in fact they were guilty at most of gross carelessness —and ordered their immediate suppression.

In view of the editors' proof that they had been guiltless of a part in the plot, General Dix disapproved of this order and so protested to Seward.   The latter countered with a stern direction that the order be obeyed.   Dix suppressed the papers, threatening at the same time to resign his command.[7]   There is good authority that Lincoln did not approve of Seward's procedure.[8]

The General's attitude in this episode rendered him quite as obnoxious to Seward as was Daniel S. Dickinson, and correspondingly as acceptable to Sumner and his friends.   But Dix quickly put an end to the possibility of his nomination, and reduced the Radicals' New York choice to Dickinson alone. On the day before the opening of the convention, he publicly announced that he was unwilling even to be a candidate for the vice presidency, and asked his friends not to embarrass him by putting forward his name.

As the meeting of the Baltimore Convention drew near, political leaders large and small showed an increasing anxiety to learn Lincoln's wishes. It was not the President's wont to take too many into his confidence, but it was then, as now, the habit of the American politician to wish to be "close to the throne." Though Lincoln was besieged by letters, telegrams and personal calls to make his desires known, he revealed them to only a very few. Aside from Cameron, Weed, Raymond, Seward and the Blairs, only one or two men ever learned of them. Even to his own faithful secretaries, John George Nicolay and John Hay, the President disclosed no faintest hint of his intentions, while to the casual politician of small caliber—or even to the more important Republican leaders in whose loyalty or sagacity the President had not full confidence —he remained enigmatically and anecdotally silent. Nicolay insists that to all such unofficial inquiries Lincoln "returned an energetic refusal to give any word of counsel, or to express any personal desires."[9]

The week before the convention, Washington was "overrun with politicians, contractors, and busybodies of all kinds and sizes," so that Radicals sneered that "the ravens made due obeisance at the White House."[10] Whether they really sought to learn something of the President's wishes or were merely anxious to impress their own faces and names on his anxious and expectant mind, the callers at the White House were all welcomed with genial and cordial courtesy, but almost invariably "received not the slightest intimation of what would be agreeable to him."

"The most powerful politicians from New York and Pennsylvania," Nicolay declared, "were listened to with no more confidential consideration than the shy and awkward representatives of the rebellious States who had elected themselves in Butler's tents. . . ." On the eve of his own departure for Baltimore to observe the convention for his chief, Nicolay himself sought a confidential word from Lincoln about the latter's desires as to his running mate, but received no satisfaction.[11]

There were a few, however, to whom Lincoln did not hesitate to disclose his desires and purposes. On the morning of June 6, S. Newton Pettis of Pennsylvania, a political figure of some note in his State, found Lincoln in his study in the White House, and told him that he had called "especially to ask him who he desired to put on the ticket with him as vice president." Lincoln leaned forward and replied, in a low but distinct tone of voice: "Governor Johnson of Tennessee."[12]

Three days before the convention was to meet in Baltimore, Lincoln telegraphed Colonel Alexander K. McClure, an intimate friend and political adviser, that he wanted to see him. McClure, at the time editor of a small paper in Chambersburg, Pa., and later to become editor of the Philadelphia *Times*, was one of the leaders of the Curtin faction and hence hated Cameron bitterly. He reached Washington on June 6 and immediately went to the White House, where he was startled by Lincoln's "stating that he desired me to support Andrew Johnson for vice president," for reasons which the President "earnestly explained":[13]

First: foreign recognition of the Confederacy was still a grave peril to the Union cause. The nomination and election of a vice president from a reconstructed State in the heart of the Confederacy, a distinctly representative man who had filled every office in the gift of the State, would add more strength to the friends of the Union in England and France, who were struggling against the recognition of the Confederacy, than could be gained in any other way save by the complete overthrow of the Confederate military power.

Second: there was strong political necessity for the nomination of a distinctive War Democrat not then connected with the Republican party. Such a nomination would bring to the support of the Administration many thousands of War Democrats who were followers of men like Johnson, Dickinson, Butler, Dix and Holt.

Finally, Johnson's nomination would "de-sectionalize" the Republican party. Johnson's choice on the ticket with Lincoln would demonstrate effectively the substantial progress being made in the restoration of the Union by the reconstruction of a State in "the very inner circle of rebellion."[14]

The Pennsylvania editor-politician "had no particular affection for Hamlin," but was not a friend of Johnson—whom, indeed, he later termed "a very able and dangerous demagogue." Yet McClure considered Lincoln's reasons so logical and conclusive that he said, "I would have voted for Johnson as a matter of duty to the party and to the country, regardless of my willingness to accede to the wishes of the President." He accepted the decision in good stead and hurried to Baltimore to do what he could with the Pennsylvania delegation.[15]

Lincoln was not the only Administration leader whose views were sought. Almost as many called upon Seward as upon the President, and the visits to the Secretary of State were more productive of definite suggestion to casual visitors than were those to Lincoln. Among the visitors to Washington were Chauncey M. Depew, a young man from New York on his way to his first national convention. He had attached himself to a Westchester County veteran, Judge W. H. Robertson, a shrewd and able politician and a lieutenant of Seward.

At dinner with the Secretary on a late Sunday afternoon, they found him fairly communicative. It was an open secret, he said, that the nominee for vice president should this time be a War Democrat, but the nomination of Mr. Dickinson would be a bad mistake, for he had been "one of the most pronounced, extreme and radical Democrats the State had had."[16] The man to nominate, Seward advised, was Andrew Johnson. Thereupon he eulogized the Tennessean, describing warmly the courage and patriotism with which Johnson, at the risk of his life, had advocated the cause of the Union and had kept his State practically loyal. "You can quote me to the delegates, and they will believe I express the opinion of the President," the Secretary instructed, "that while the President wishes to take no part in the nomination for vice president, yet he favors Mr. Johnson." Robertson and Depew did not linger to call at the White House. Their delegation was to caucus on Monday night, and they departed forthwith for the convention city.

Although Baltimore displayed great activity in preparing for the convention, somewhere along the line things struck a snag—Baltimore's one commodious convention hall had been secretly rented on the dates set for the convention! On May 13, when Governor Morgan, the party chairman, discovered the trick, he was greatly perturbed. He told Welles that the hall had been "hired by the malcontents through the treachery and connivance of H. Winter Davis," in whom he had confided. The chairman had the choice of taking the Front Street Theater in Baltimore, of building a temporary structure, or of changing the meeting place to Philadelphia. He finally rented the

Front Street Theater, and had it altered for the occasion.[17] Its scenery and stage effects were removed and the parquet was floored over.

It is all very well to look upon the Baltimore Convention as a gathering of patriots of purest gold, of statesmen assembled without thoughts of self to further the cause of Union and of Freedom. Yet for all its name of "National Union" it was nevertheless a political convention—a gathering mainly of Republican politicians, whose primary purpose was to reelect Abraham Lincoln because he was the fountainhead of Federal jobs. It was a motley crew which gathered in the Baltimore hotel lobbies, a "crowd of scar-faced greedy politicians," it seemed to a Radical onlooker, who pitied "the patriots, who, in this crowd, seemed isolated, like hills in a marshy, unhealthy, desolate plain." His catalogue of those on hand included "officeholders, postmasters, contractors, lobbyists, expectants, pap-editors," and the like, and the very atmosphere seemed filled with greedy and devouring eyes. Spoilsmen, as well as statesmen, were on hand at Baltimore.[18]

Seward himself stayed in Washington, but his friends, Thurlow Weed and Henry J. Raymond, were in the forefront. Weed was early established in a parlor of the Eutaw House, sending for delegation leaders and dropping subtle hints. Within the week, Raymond, Weed's pupil and Seward's friend, was to prove himself the "true master" of the convention itself, to exert an influence on party affairs which neither Weed nor Greeley possessed, and to place himself at the head of the Republican National Committee with the task of reelecting Mr. Lincoln in his hands.

Then there were Mr. Lincoln's trusted friends, chiefly delegates from the Middle Western States, men of Illinois, Iowa and Michigan. Burton C. Cooke, who headed the Illinois contingent, a man of standing but of little discernment, was very much impressed with his importance as chairman of the delegation from the President's home State. Leonard Swett, a former law partner of the Executive, was on hand, as were Henry Wilson of Massachusetts and Zachariah Chandler of Michigan. Nicolay was sending frequent telegrams and notes to Hay at Washington, but Cameron was Lincoln's political "manager" and right well did he fulfill his rôle.

Although in their White House talk on June 6, Lincoln had

discussed the vice presidential matter at length with McClure, characteristically he had not revealed to him that Simon Cameron had long before been enlisted in his vice presidential plan. However, Colonel McClure had not been long in his room in the Eutaw House when Cameron called on him. The former War Secretary first pulled the service bell, ordered a bottle of wine, and then informed the leader of the rival faction that he had come to discuss the question of the vice presidency. Cameron's first suggestion was for the Pennsylvania delegation to cast a complimentary vote for him for vice president. This did not go well with McClure. "We have a very important duty to perform," he replied, "and we will settle down at once, without playing marbles to see what Pennsylvania will do."

Thereupon Cameron presented his plan. He was friendly to Hamlin, he said, but the Vice President could not be renominated; to this McClure agreed. Cameron next said that he was inclined to favor Johnson of Tennessee; McClure again assented. Then Cameron said that he was "somewhat embarrassed" by the pleasant relations he had had with Hamlin when they were in the Senate together. Would it not be well if both he and McClure should line up their friends on the delegation to cast a unanimous vote for Hamlin when Pennsylvania was called; but at the end of the roll call, and before the vote was announced, to change Pennsylvania to a unanimous vote for Johnson? McClure again agreed. And thus, for the first time, Cameron knew that Lincoln had enlisted McClure and McClure knew that Cameron was carrying out Lincoln's plan.

They experienced little difficulty in executing their program. The only man on the delegation who objected was Thad Stevens. At the caucus, when McClure voted to have the delegation give a solid support first to Hamlin and then to Johnson, Stevens, who was seated by McClure's side, turned his cold gray eyes upon him and said, in a tone of profound contempt: "Can't you get a candidate for vice president without going down into a damned rebel province for one?"[19]

Poor Nicolay was not having an easy time of it. Many leaders were coming to him, insisting on his confiding the President's real desires, and they were dissatisfied and disgruntled with his necessarily equivocal replies. Burton Cooke would not let himself be put off with Nicolay's standard formula: "The President is taking no hand in the matter." He picked up the

In Chowan county, on the 31st ultimo, the Rev. Job Pettijohn, of the Baptist Church; and, on the 9th instant, Mrs. Sarah Newbern, consort of Mr. John Newbern.

At South Washington, on the 11th inst. Mr. James Usher, Jr. aged 21 years

Ten Dollars Reward.

RAN AWAY from the Subscriber, on the night of the 15th instant, two apprentice boys, legally bound, named WILLIAM and ANDREW JOHNSON The former is of a dark complexion, black hair, eyes, and habits. They are much of a height, about 5 feet 4 or 5 inches The latter is very fleshy freckled face, light hair, and fair complexion. They went off with two other apprentices, advertised by Messrs Wm. & Chas. Fowler When they went away, they were well clad—blue cloth coats, light colored homespun coats, and new hats, the maker's name in the crown of the hats, is Theodore Clark. I will pay the above Reward to any person who will deliver said apprentices to me in Raleigh, or I will give the above Reward for Andrew Johnson alone

All persons are cautioned against harboring or employing said apprentices, on pain of being prosecuted.

JAMES J. SELBY, Tailor.
Raleigh, N. C. June 24, 1824.   26 3t

Louisburg Female Academy.

THE second Session will commence on Mon-

REWARD FOR THE RUNAWAY

This Advertisement Appeared in the Raleigh, (N. C.) *Star*, on June 26, 1824. Interestingly Enough, Its Descriptions of the Two Johnson Brothers Are Reversed. Original in North Carolina State Historical Association, Raleigh, N. C.

idea that Leonard Swett was working at cross purposes with Lincoln, was disturbed at Swett's advice to put Joseph Holt of Kentucky in Hamlin's place on the ticket, and forced Nicolay to write to Washington "to find out Mr. Lincoln's real desire." Hence Nicolay's note to Hay:

"I told Cooke Lincoln would not even wish to indicate a preference . . . Cooke wants to know confidentially whether Swett is all right."

The answer came the very next day; Lincoln himself had scribbled on the back of Nicolay's letter:

"Swett is unquestionably all right. Mr. Holt is a good man but I had not heard of him for V. P. Wish not to interfere about V. P. Cannot interfere about platform. Convention must judge for itself."

Cooke was not satisfied with this declaration. Thinking that the President might be reluctant to commit to writing the secret wishes of his heart, he took the next train to Washington. The President's oral statement to Cooke confirmed the scribbled note to Nicolay. As was not unnatural with a man who had long found it a good political rule not to let his right hand know what his left hand was doing, Lincoln told the loquacious Illinois chairman that he was "particularly anxious" not to make known his preference. But Cooke concluded to his own entire satisfaction that "Hamlin was his favorite."[20] Austin Blair, Michigan's famous war Governor, went to Washington to satisfy himself that the hotel lobby rumor of Lincoln's preference for Johnson was true, but got no satisfaction from the interview.[21]

There were Radicals a-plenty on hand as delegates, but they were far from having a majority in the convention. In many cases, they came under instructions from their districts to support the Lincoln program despite their personal views.[22] But few states had instructed their delegations as to the tail of the ticket, and here was a needed safety valve for pent-up Radical wrath.[23]

A large group of Southern Union delegates were there— Union either by conviction or by force of arms. From Tennessee, Virginia, Louisiana, Arkansas and South Carolina they had come. There were all kinds and characters of these Southerners: "Rebel" turncoats, Old Line Whigs, holders of Federal jobs. Many of them, in Nicolay's phrase, had "elected themselves in the shadow of General Butler's tents." Lincoln had shown much sympathy toward these Southern attempts to resume normal political relations with the national political bodies. "What is that crowd of people in the hall?" he asked Nicolay one day shortly before the convention. "It is a delegation from South Carolina—they are a swindle," his secretary answered sneeringly. "Let them in," Lincoln said, "they will not swindle me."[24]

Perhaps the most sincerely devoted Union delegation from the South was that from Tennessee, with Horace Maynard at its head. Tall, angular, with a fiery gleam in his eye, Maynard was a commanding, almost a fear-inspiring figure. With him was William G. Brownlow, the famous Fighting Parson, a slave owning, soul stirring, pistol carrying Union preacher of East Tennessee. There was grave doubt whether any of these men, even the Tennesseans, would be seated as delegates, inasmuch as they came from States, large parts of which were even at the moment in armed rebellion against the Constitution and the Flag.

The New York delegation met early Monday evening and canvassed the subject of the vice presidency.[25] An "informal" ballot was soon taken "merely to ascertain the preferences of individual members," the result being: Hamlin twenty, Dickinson sixteen, Tremaine six, and Andrew Johnson eight.[26] The caucus then adjourned until Tuesday morning.[27] Dickinson's friends were much encouraged by their success in the informal caucus; and they began active solicitation among the delegations of the various States in their candidate's behalf. The Seward supporters were correspondingly despondent; none of them yet dared oppose Dickinson's selection on any other grounds than those of expediency.

Lyman Tremaine, Old Line Democrat and Dickinson's chief lieutenant, opened the adjourned caucus Tuesday morning with "a careful, eloquent and effective speech" of half an hour. He insisted that it would be unjust and unwise to disregard the sacrifices of political feelings and of party ties which the War Democrats had made. "I have never been a Republican," he said, "and I would feel that I have no place in this organization if both candidates were selected from the Republican party." Setting forth the noble manner in which Dickinson "had broken away from the Democratic party when it became disloyal," and listing his sacrifices for the good of the country, Tremaine urged on the New York delegates every consideration of state pride to induce them to give solid support to Dickinson. Then he moved that, when the roll of States was called, the New York delegation present a New York man as candidate for vice president.

While this speech was in progress, Weed, Raymond, and Preston King, one of their chief lieutenants, were busy making a hasty poll of the delegation. The result showed that while the Dickinson men were numerous, the Seward faction still controlled the delegation by a slender margin. The night before, most of the Seward men had indicated their liking for Hamlin. Accordingly, on Tuesday Raymond was about to move that New York indorse both candidates on the 1860 ticket.

At this moment, the Seward leaders received disquieting news from Massachusetts—they heard that the Bay State had refused Hamlin.[28] A messenger was sent in haste to find out the facts. In a few minutes he returned with the unequivocal reply: "Massachusetts will not support Hamlin under any circumstances." Quick to take advantage of this sudden break, Tremaine called for an informal ballot, which showed Dickinson ahead. New York's Civil War politicians, like the tribe in general, were utter realists. They saw that there must be a quick change and that even then it was doubtful if Seward could be saved.

Weed whispered, "Take Johnson." The quick-witted Raymond made a parliamentary point; there was a motion before the body, he said—Tremaine's motion that New York present a candidate herself, and he arose to speak to it.

He acquiesced in everything the Dickinson man had said as to the claims of War Democrats to the gratitude of the country and the favor of the convention. He concurred in all the tributes to Dickinson. But, he thought, "we shall do injustice to ourselves and to the War Democracy of the whole Union if we restrict our acknowledgments to our own State." And he added that, "much as Dickinson had suffered and done in the cause of the nation," there were other Democrats who had done and suffered more.

"I believe that the salvation of the country will be due," said Raymond, "primarily and mainly to those noble hearts in those Border States who have not only discarded every party tie, but who have thrown to the winds all the prejudices of the section in which they live, all the teachings of their childhood, all the pride of States' Rights, all their interests in slavery, everything which might be supposed to have most weight with men in their condition—and have suffered in their property, their families and their persons to a degree of which we in the Northern States can form but a faint conception." Andrew Johnson was the man to whom, "more than to any other one person not in the government or in the army, the country is indebted for aid for putting down the rebellion," and Raymond proposed that Andrew Johnson be the War Democrat honored by New York's vice presidential choice.

Preston King was on his feet as soon as Raymond yielded the floor, to emphasize the "impolicy" of taking a candidate from New York. Several Dickinson speakers warmly attacked this position, and George W. Curtis, secretary of the delegation, charged that it was very evident that "the main reason which leads so many delegates to oppose Mr. Dickinson's nomination is the certainty that it will render necessary Mr. Seward's withdrawal from the Cabinet, as two such posts cannot be given to one State, and I think it quite time that the real motive of the opposition to Mr. Dickinson shall be understood."

This was the opportunity for which the Seward men had been praying. Quick as a flash, Raymond replied that he could only regard this as a declaration that Dickinson must be nominated for the purpose of ejecting Seward from the Cabinet. "While I should very gladly assent to any change in the Cabinet which the good of the country may require," he stormed, "I protest against any such attempt to use Mr. Dickinson as an instrument for degrading Mr. Seward." The Dickinson men's disavowals of any such purpose fell on unheeding ears. Raymond demanded that Tremaine's motion be put, and it was lost by a narrow margin. New York had voted that it would not present a New York candidate for second place!

Thereupon Raymond himself moved that each member be allowed to name his own candidate, without any unit rule. This proposal was carried, and the ballot resulted: Johnson thirty, Dickinson twenty-eight, Hamlin seven, Holt one. Before it could be announced, two more votes were given to Johnson, making the result Johnson thirty-two, Dickinson twenty-eight, Hamlin six. On Raymond's further motion it was ordered that, on the convention roll call, this be announced as New York's first ballot vote. Thereupon the caucus adjourned.

The impending defeat was not perceived even then by Ham-

lin's leaders. As a whole, the evening's caucuses had turned
out to their satisfaction. The chief manager, Senator Lot M.
Morrill of Maine, received the reports of his aides at eleven on
Monday evening and concluded that the battle had been won.[29]
Simon Cameron had "delivered" Pennsylvania! New Jersey
sent word that she would be for Hamlin, with Maryland and
Delaware. Encouraging reports came from the very Mid-
Western States in which defections had been chiefly feared.
Michigan, Minnesota and Wisconsin had stood firm for Hamlin.
Informally, so as "not to commit Mr. Lincoln," Illinois had
expressed a desire for the renomination of both men on the
1864 ticket. Even Iowa, which had been expected to be solid
for Andrew Johnson, in its caucus gave Hamlin half the votes.

The guileless Morrill was especially pleased with Massachusetts—he had called in person at this point of danger, had
been informed that there had been a caucus, without formal
action, and that "Massachusetts would do Hamlin no harm"!
Only they wanted to wait a little before giving any formal
pledge! Yet for all these pleasant lies, the Sumner scheme had
not changed at all, and even then the Massachusetts delegates
were sowing disaffection to Hamlin among the delegates from
Rhode Island and Connecticut; and Pennsylvania's Hamlin
vote was to be shifted to Johnson before the result of the first
ballot could be announced. At midnight Senator Morrill went
to bed, sure of victory and proud of his fine day's work. And
while he lay in sultry slumber, Sumner's henchmen were working on the delegates from New Jersey, Maryland and other
Middle Seaboard States, and the New York caucus, in its final
poll, had given Hamlin a bare half-dozen votes.

The convention's first session was scheduled for noon on
Tuesday. The theater doors were thrown open at eleven. It
was a tight squeeze to get all the delegates into the pit. The
alternates and spectators had to be satisfied with the galleries.
A large part of the audience was made up of ladies, and Mr.
Yerkes' ice water brigade was kept active because of the heat
of the day.[30]

A little after noon, Governor Morgan, chairman of the executive committee, opened the meeting with a brief speech.[31]
His one significant sentence was that the party of which they
were the delegates and honored representatives would fall short
of accomplishing its great mission unless, among other results,

it should declare "for such amendment of the Constitution as would positively prohibit African slavery in the United States." He then turned the convention over to the temporary chairman, the Rev. Dr. Robert J. Breckinridge of Kentucky.

After having been Vice President of the United States and a candidate for president, John C. Breckinridge had become a Confederate General; but his cousin, Dr. Robert J. Breckinridge, bitterly reprehended secession and was active and effective in preventing Kentucky from joining her fortunes to those of the seceded States. He was a warm friend of President Lincoln and, according to a tradition in the Breckinridge family, Lincoln had suggested to the Kentucky minister that he could have the 1864 vice presidential nomination, only for the latter to decline it because he did not think it proper for a minister to accept a political post. But President Lincoln wanted to pay Dr. Breckinridge a conspicuous compliment for his stand for the Union and had him made temporary chairman at Baltimore.[32] Yet the selection of a Border cleric was more than a personal compliment by the President to a friend. It was part and parcel of Lincoln's adroit reelection strategy. It was, and was meant to be, further conspicuous evidence of the national character of Lincoln's campaign.

Dr. Breckinridge's introduction of the President's name early in his speech occasioned tumultuous cheers. It was no lengthy manufactured demonstration with cheer leaders regimented and standards sweeping by in organized review, like the convention devices of later years, but a spontaneous ovation, heartening to the Lincoln men. As soon as the shouts had died away, the chairman called attention to the fact that he, a minister of the Gospel, was there presiding over a political convention and announced, paradoxically enough, that he considered himself absolutely detached from politics—that is, from partisan and Abolition politics. "As a Union party," he said, "I will follow you to the ends of the earth and to the gates of Death. But as an Abolition party, as a Republican party, as a Whig party, as a Democratic party, as an American party, I will not follow you one foot."[33]

The temporary chairman's speech and the chaplain's convention prayer had no sooner been concluded than the question of the right of Southern delegates to seats in the convention forced its way to the floor. Thad Stevens objected to the inclusion in the roll of States of those which were "in secession."

Pennsylvania's Commoner said he had no doubt that "there are many very excellent men here from such States," but protested against any "recognition of the right of States which now belong to the Southern Confederacy to be represented here, and of course, to be represented in the electoral college."

In the ensuing debate, Horace Maynard seized his chance.[34] As he pleaded the cause of the Southern Unionists who had risked their all in the Federal cause, he presented an unforgettable appearance. Tall and spare, Horace Maynard was a natural "rabble-rouser." His harsh, high voice carried even to the edge of the largest outdoor crowd. His hair was long and of a deep black; his brow high, his nose prominent and straight. He had a particularly forceful gesture with the index finger of his right hand. Without a drop of Indian blood in his body, Maynard was nicknamed the "Narragansett Indian," looked like one and spoke with the passion and force of the famous orators of the native American race.

His theme at Baltimore was not so much the political rights of his delegation as it was the suffering, loyalty and patriotism of the hundreds of thousands of Unionists in the South. He appeared before the convention as the chairman of the Tennessee delegation, "sent here by the loyal Union portion of the population of that old State, extending as they do from the mountains to the banks of the Mississippi River." This particular convention purported to consist of delegates representing that part of the American people who, in the field and at home, seek to "sustain the honor and existence of the government." In any such assemblage, the "much enduring Union-suffering men who sent us here must not be passed by, or their existence forgotten or ignored."

"For you that drink in the cool breezes of the Northern air," he said, "it is easy to rally to the flag, . . . but we represent those who have stood in the very furnace of the rebellion, those who have met treason eye to eye, and face to face, and fought from the beginning for the support of the flag and the honor of our country." As he described the grim devotion to the cause of the Federal Union of these outnumbered, often outlawed patriots, his eyes grew wet with tears and many in the audience sobbed aloud. Maynard told of the depredations by the guerrillas, the insults continually heaped upon the loyalists, the burning of their homes, the confiscation of their property, the conscription of their sons into Confederate armies,

and the imprisonment, sometimes execution of their leaders!
It was a moving speech, a masterpiece, the story of a little bit
of Hell by one who had himself passed through the flames. At
his conclusion, there arose a wild outburst of applause. It
swept the pit and aroused the galleries. Horace Maynard
had won his case.[35]

After this preliminary bout, the committees on credentials,
organization and resolutions were named, and withdrew to
thresh out the matters before them. At three o'clock Tuesday
afternoon, the convention adjourned until 7:30 that evening.
By the night session, the Committee on Permanent Organization reported, proposing Governor William Dennison of Ohio
for permanent president, with a long list of vice presidents and
secretaries representing the various States. The report was
adopted by acclamation. After Dennison's drab speech, it was
noted that no rules committee had been appointed that morning, and one was accordingly named. The other committees sent
word that they could not hope to report before the next day.
Consequently, Thad Stevens moved adjournment until nine the
next morning, but withdrew his motion in order to give the
convention a chance to hear a speech from the fiery "Parson"
Brownlow of Tennessee.

The "Fighting Parson," although just out of a sick bed,
was in the mood for a rattling speech and quickly captured the
humor of the crowd. He warned the convention against recognizing secession by "so rash an act" as excluding the delegation from Tennessee. "We don't recognize it in Tennessee,"
he gibed, amidst applause. "We deny that we are out. We
deny that we have been out. We maintain that a minority first
voted us out, and then a majority whipped the minority out
of the State with bayonets. . . ."

Brownlow suggested, "as an inducement not to exclude our
delegation, that we may take it into our heads, before the thing
is over, to present a candidate from that State in rebellion for
the second office in the gift of the people." The gallery burst
into applause at this reference to the Johnsonian vice presidential boom, and the Parson continued: "We have a man down
there whom it has been my good luck and bad fortune to fight
untiringly and perseveringly for the last twenty-five years—
Andrew Johnson. [Applause.] For the first time in the Providence of God, three years ago we got together on the same

platform, and we are fighting the devil, Tom Walker, and Jeff Davis side by side."[36] The convention then adjourned until ten o'clock Wednesday morning.

The second day's session was opened by the Committee on the Order of Business, which reported various rules of procedure. One of these established that States should vote in geographical rather than alphabetical order. Another established the order of business: First, the credentials report, next the platform report, and then balloting for candidates for president and vice president.

The report of the credentials committee was presented by Preston King, its chairman, a huge bull-necked man with a *basso profundo* voice. The majority report seated the "Radical Union" delegation from Missouri, with votes, and seated the delegations from Virginia, Tennessee, Louisiana, Florida and Arkansas without the right to vote. Two minority reports were presented, and King himself, aided by Senator Jim Lane of Kansas, led the fight to amend the majority report.

Union men were present from Tennessee, Virginia, South Carolina, Florida, Louisiana and Arkansas. It was inevitable that their right to seats would be sharply challenged. First of all, their seating might have an important bearing on the vice presidential nomination. With the possible exception of those from Tennessee, these Southern Unionist delegations were Conservative rather than Radical. Geography would enlist them against Hannibal Hamlin, so Hamlin men as well as Radicals wished to refuse them seats.

The question involved collateral issues which went to the bottom of the whole restoration question. For over a year, the Radicals in Congress had shown petulance and anger over President Lincoln's views and consequent acts as to the legal status of the redeemed States. Three rival theories were rapidly developing. There was Sumner's gossamer-spun theory of "state suicide"; Thad Stevens insisted that secession had been accomplished, and that the former Southern States of the American Union therefore were now foreign territory, conquered by the sword and held as spoils of war. Lincoln's theory was that no State could secede, therefore none had seceded, and that they were still States of the Union. Men could be traitors —States could not. If Lincoln was right, loyal Union delegations from the Southern States were entitled to seats in a

National Union convention. If Sumner or Stevens spoke truly, these delegates were not Americans; however "loyal" they might be, they had no right to vote.

King's fight for the seating of the Blair delegates from Missouri along with the anti-Blair men was lost, although Dr. Breckinridge warned the convention that the delegation about to be seated came from a party in Missouri whose platform was to support Lincoln only "on the condition that the President of the United States will agree to be browbeaten by them." He lamented the judgment of the convention in seating such men in the place of a delegation "whose main business for the past two years has been to support and sustain the President of the United States." None the less, in accordance with Weed's crafty plan, the sullen Radicals were allowed every safety valve for the ebullition of dissatisfaction with the Administration, and the anti-Blair men were seated by 440 votes to four.

The next question was the admission of the Southern delegations without the right to vote. The question was finally divided, and an amendment was offered to admit Tennessee with a vote. This resulted in an individual roll call, which resulted in 310 delegates voting to seat the men who had come from "the furnace of treason," and 151 against. In this important test, the negative votes came chiefly from the New England States, Pennsylvania and Maryland, although strangely enough Kentucky's delegation voted against the seating of Tennessee. On the next roll call, Arkansas and Louisiana were likewise admitted with votes, while Virginia was admitted without a vote. South Carolina's men were not even permitted seats on the convention floor. The seating of Tennessee did much more than gain rights for the contested delegation. It gave powerful momentum to the Andrew Johnson boom.

Next in the order of business came the adoption of a platform. Here the Radicals hoped to admonish and perhaps to reprimand Lincoln for his unsatisfactory Cabinet.[37] But the President's friends were too adroit. Strong resolutions indorsed the war for the Union, indorsed Lincoln's practical wisdom, unselfish patriotism and unswerving fidelity, and advocated an amendment to the Constitution now and forever prohibiting slavery in the nation. One resolution administered the *coup de grâce* to a favorite Radical plan by vaguely reciting "as worthy of public confidence and official trust those only who cordially indorse" the principles above outlined.[38]

The words were those of Henry J. Raymond, distilled by Thurlow Weed. Their purpose was the same as that behind the admission of the Missouri fanatics: To assuage the dissatisfaction of the Radical rank and file. The words themselves, however, were susceptible of various interpretations. Although it was generally understood that under its terms Montgomery Blair, if no other, would be forced to leave the Cabinet, not all of the delegates who voted for the plank would have agreed upon any further details of Cabinet change.

The nomination of a candidate for president was next in the adopted order of business. An Ohio delegate made the customary motion to proceed to the nomination. At this point, there was once more evidence of Simon Cameron's fine Italian hand. He had accomplished another of the missions Lincoln had entrusted to his care—it was now certain that Johnson would be nominated as Lincoln's running mate. But the Pennsylvanian was also anxious that responsibility for Hamlin's defeat be laid neither at the President's door nor at his own. The almost too obvious disclaimer for both Lincoln and himself was for Cameron—Lincoln's manager—to propose an ineffective move in Hamlin's behalf.

Thus Cameron moved a substitute: That Lincoln and Hamlin be renominated by acclamation.[39] Almost as if by prearrangement, objection was immediately made to the proposal; its mover did not defend it and it was emphatically tabled by *viva voce* vote. Cameron then withdrew his proposition, only to submit a new one for Lincoln's nomination by acclamation. An excited debate ensued, to which Raymond gave the quietus; he pointed out that whatever opposition existed should have the fullest opportunity of expression and demanded that the roll of States be called; to this Cameron straightway agreed. On the roll call of States, Lincoln's name alone was designated, and he received the entire vote of the convention, except that of the Missouri Radicals, who stubbornly voted for Grant.[40]

The President's renomination was accomplished by 2:30 in the afternoon.[41] Immediately after the applause had died down, Governor Dennison read the convention a message just received from the Secretary of War. It told of a Federal victory in the Valley of Virginia the night before, in which General Hunter had routed the Confederates beyond Staunton. This welcome news was received with tumultuous applause by the delegates, who realized full well that the success of the Union ticket in November depended more on the victorious armies on the battlefield than it did on the resolutions adopted at Baltimore.[42]

The roll call of States for nominations for vice president was next in order. "I am instructed by the State of Pennsylvania," said Cameron, "to present the name of Hannibal Hamlin." Daniel S. Dickinson was proposed by his devoted friend Lyman Tremaine, "on behalf of a portion of the New York delegation." Andrew Johnson was proposed by C. M. Allen of Indiana, under instructions of its state convention. Horace Maynard seconded Johnson's nomination on behalf of Tennessee. "When Andrew Johnson sees your resolutions," he said, "he will adhere to those sentiments and the doctrines therein set forth as long as his reason remains unimpaired, and as long as breath is given him by his God." The balloting then began.

Maine, the first State to be called, responded with a solid vote for its native son. But New Hampshire defections showed that New England, the Vice President's home section, was not unanimous in his support. Its vote was announced: Hamlin four; Dickinson three; Butler two; Johnson one. At the vote for Andrew Johnson, a burst of enthusiasm in the rear of the theater and in the galleries made a distinct impression on the convention. The anti-Hamlin trend in Vermont, Massachusetts and Rhode Island further increased the confusion. Johnson had five votes in Vermont, Dickinson one, Butler two, and Hamlin two. Massachusetts gave Dickinson a big vote—seventeen, only three to Hamlin, and two to Butler. Rhode Island announced Hamlin three, Butler two, Burnside two, and Dickinson one. A renewal of the Johnson demonstration occurred when Connecticut gave Johnson a solid vote of twelve, for which the Hamlin men blamed "Father Gideon."[43]

The delegates awaited announcement of the vote of New York with mingled feelings of hope and apprehension. The chairman announced it with due solemnity: Johnson thirty-two; Dickinson twenty-eight; Hamlin six. With it came a roar from the galleries—Johnson was getting into his stride! New Jersey gave Dickinson twelve; Johnson two. As had been determined at the Pennsylvania caucus, in accordance with the Cameron-McClure understanding, Pennsylvania announced a solid vote for Hamlin, and as she did so, her chairman remained

on his feet awaiting a chance to obtain the recognition of the
president of the convention, so as to change the vote to Johnson. Delaware threw her six votes to Dickinson, and Maryland
gave the New Yorker eleven votes to Johnson's two, and Hamlin's one.

With the Southern and Western States, however, the Johnson totals began to soar. Louisiana split her delegation of
fourteen evenly between the New York and the Tennessee candidates; Arkansas' solid ten went to Johnson. The Missouri
Radicals characteristically rushed to Ben Butler, with
twenty votes to two for Johnson. Tennessee naturally was
solid for her Military Governor, with fifteen votes. Kentucky
threw her strength away on a compliment to General L. H.
Rousseau, a native son, with a single vote to David Tod, of
Ohio. But Tod's State went solidly for Johnson, as did Indiana.

Illinois cast a complimentary Hamlin vote, as did Michigan.
Wisconsin split: Hamlin four; Johnson two; Dickinson ten.
Iowa which followed, announced and recorded a solid Johnson
vote.[44] Minnesota cast Dickinson three; Hamlin five. Cali-
fornia split her ten votes evenly between Hamlin and Johnson.
Oregon complimented Schuyler Colfax with a solid vote, why,
no one could tell. Kansas' six votes were evenly divided among
Hamlin, Dickinson and Johnson. West Virginia cast a solid
Johnson vote. Nebraska scattered a vote each to Preston
King, Hamlin and Dickinson, and gave three to Johnson. Colorado cast all six votes for Dickinson, while Nevada wound up
the roll call with a solid Johnson vote of six.

Then began a stampede of delegations anxious to clamber
on the band-wagon. When the roll call had been completed,
its result was: Johnson 200; Dickinson 113; Hamlin 145.
Kentucky was the first to change to Johnson, followed in quick
succession by Oregon and Kansas. Simon Cameron then claimed
the floor to say: "I am directed by the Pennsylvania delegation
to change her vote, and give her fifty-two votes for Andrew
Johnson." At this there was an outburst of great applause.
New Jersey followed suit, and Senator Morrill of Maine, Hamlin's sanguine manager of the night before, changed the vote
of Hamlin's State to the Plebeian from Tennessee. State after
State followed suit "for the noblest Roman in the country."[45]
When these corrections had been made, and the convention
clerk was able to announce the result of the first and only ballot, Andrew Johnson had received 494 of the entire 521 votes

cast for the Union nominee for vice president. Hannibal Hamlin had only nine.[46]

Thus were nominated for president an Illinois rail-splitter, and for vice president a tailor from Tennessee. The latter selection was quickly made unanimous and became the occasion for great rejoicing among the delegates. Seward was happy, Sumner, half-happy,—and only Hamlin sore at heart.

Lincoln had spent the morning at the War Department, in constant telegraphic touch with Grant. At noon he strode to the White House, snatched a hasty snack and hurried back, without pausing at his private office. The first dispatch he saw told of Johnson's nomination. "This is strange," Lincoln said. "I thought it was usual to nominate the candidate for President first." The telegrapher was astonished. "Mr. President," he asked, "have you not heard of your own renomination? It was telegraphed to you at the White House two hours ago." He dug into his pile of flimsies and showed Lincoln a copy. He glanced at it. "Send it right over to the Madam," he commented. "She will be more interested than I am."[47]

The news did not reach Nashville until June 9. "What will the aristocrats do?" Andrew Johnson inquired, "with a rail-splitter for President, and a tailor for Vice President?"[48]

THERE was a curious irony in this nomination of two Southern men to lead the North in its endeavor to keep the South within the Union. The origin of the Tennessee tailor thus put on the National Union ticket as candidate for vice president had been as obscure and humble, his early struggle as unremitting and his career as picturesque as Abraham Lincoln's. While the spotlight has been turned upon every ascertainable fact or fiction concerning the birth of a son to Nancy Hanks, the circumstances surrounding the nativity of this boy born to Mary McDonough, the wife of Jacob Johnson, in Raleigh, N. C., on December 29, 1808, are even yet somewhat shrouded in obscurity and doubt.

In 1808, Raleigh had outgrown being a backwoods settlement; it had almost a thousand inhabitants, and to it, as the capital of the State, flocked the great and the near-great of North Carolina: politicians and lawmakers, lawyers and clients, and travellers commercial and uncommercial. Raleigh's courtrooms rang with the battle of giants, especially when John Marshall held circuit court there. Socially, Raleigh was a miniature Charleston or Richmond, with evening teas at the homes of the Haywoods, Boylans and Polks; during the season, fox and deer hunts amused the notables. The taverns likewise played their parts in the Capital's social life. They were the scenes of many a cotillion, ball and levee, their well-stocked bars lending zest to jollifications which sometimes ended on the duelling ground.[1]

Peter Casso's Tavern, on the main North and South road, and immediately to the southeast of the Capitol, was the leading inn of that day and generation, its bars being unexcelled for imported and domestic brands of liquor, its stable equal to any on the Continent and able to accommodate forty head of horses at a time. The inn-yard contained a modest two-story house, almost a cottage. In 1808 it was occupied by the family of Jacob Johnson, handy man of the tavern.

Jacob's origin and early life are not authentically recorded, but recently discovered evidence inclines one to the conclusion that he probably was a native of the North of England. Under this story, the date of his birth is uncertain, but he had been a house carpenter for several years when, in 1794 or 1795, he emigrated from Newcastle to Boston. The vessel in which he was voyaging was taken by a French privateer, but Jacob and two of his companions escaped and made their way to the American states. For a short time he kept up a correspondence with his brother Thomas, in the old country, but then contact between the two was lost. His son Andrew had little information of his father's origin or family until in 1868, when, in the midst of impeachment proceedings, he received a letter from a cousin in Northumberland giving the family tree. There is, additionally, a claim that Jacob was of an old Virginia family, one of the children of an Andrew Johnson living in what is now Pendleton County. There is no record of this Jacob Johnson having been the man of the same name who went to Raleigh early in the century, but the traditions of the Skidmore family, a collateral branch, so hold.[2]

In any event, about the turn of the century, Jacob made his way to Raleigh and established himself there, winning the confidence and respect of the best people of the little capital. In the year with which this chapter opens, Jacob had very definitely found his niche in life. More than a porter and less than a clerk, he was anything but an aristocrat. He recognized that he belonged to the "mudsills," and shed no tears about it. But he was a brave and likable fellow, and at various times was city constable, sexton, porter of Colonel William Polk's state bank[3] and a captain of the State Militia.[4]

Andrew's mother, whose maiden name was Mary McDonough, was an humble woman of ancestry difficult to trace for more than a generation, although we know that it was definitely Scotch-Irish. For many years "Polly" Johnson, or "Aunt Polly," as she was called, supplemented her husband's income by her work as laundress and seamstress, caring for the linen of the members of the North Carolina Supreme Court in particular.

In the spring of 1811, Jacob Johnson had joined a large fishing party on Walnut Creek. Colonel Thomas Henderson, editor of the Raleigh *Star*, and two companions ventured forth in a skiff; all had too much to drink; for sport, Editor Henderson started rocking the boat. When it upset, one of the men went to the bottom, dragging the editor with him. Jacob Johnson leaped into the water, dived for the two men and finally succeeded in bringing them up. But these efforts so exhausted the rescuer that his health broke down.[5] Although he lived nearly a year afterward, he collapsed from exhaustion one day while tolling the statehouse bell for a funeral, was carried home and died a few days later.

In his Raleigh *Star*, on January 12, 1812, Editor Henderson said that Jacob, who had occupied "a humble but useful station in society," was visited in his last illness by the élite of Raleigh, "by all of whom he was esteemed for his honesty, industry, and humane and friendly disposition." "None lament him more . . . than the publisher of this paper," the notice concluded, "for he owes his life to Johnson's boldness and humanity." He was buried in the Citizens' Cemetery. Many years later, after the close of the Civil War, the citizens of Raleigh erected a tablet bearing these words: "In memory of Jacob Johnson, an honest man, loved and respected by all who knew him."

His death caused a crisis in the humble family. "Aunt Polly" worked harder than ever as seamstress and washwoman. William, the oldest boy, was now nine, and in a short while became of some assistance to his mother. But Andrew, five years younger, although a good son, was too small to be of any help. So he spent many hours at games with the boys of the neighborhood, his favorite being "Cat and Bass Ball and Bandy," the last the "choyst" game of all.[6] But this happy-go-lucky life did not quite satisfy the fatherless lad. He wanted an education. There were no free public schools at Raleigh in that day and generation; as for a pay school, Andy's mother could scarce keep clothes on the backs of her children, let alone pay tuition.

Thus Andy fell into the habit of visiting a local tailor shop every day, to listen to the reading aloud to the workers, a custom of that trade at the time. The journeymen and apprentices would sit cross-legged, sewing and cutting industriously, while a paid reader, often on a raised dais, would read newspapers, novels, poems—even Congressional debates—to them for hours at a time. It was no mean substitute for the "blab-school" of the day.

Years later, Tom Lomsden, one of the journeymen of the establishment,—it was that of James J. Selby—at the time when Andrew began to frequent it, told how the lad began his education. "I was always a great reader," he related, "and although Andy didn't know one letter from another, he was always pestering me out of work hours to read to him. He was a pert sort of a boy, and I always told him he would be a great man some day. One fall, business was brisk, and the boss wanted a 'prentice. He took in Andy, and the boy was right glad to get something to do to help along his old mother. A 'prentice usually worked the first year for his keep and his clothes; but Andy couldn't leave his mother, and the boss agreed to give him what it would cost to feed and clothe him in money."[7]

The boy's mother—she had meanwhile married a worthless ne'er-do-well named Turner Doughtry, or Daugherty—gladly complied with the legal formalities necessary to enable her son to take advantage of this unexpected opportunity to become a "bound boy." A paper was drawn up:[8]

> This is to certify that it is my desire that my son, Andrew Johnson, is bound an apprentice to James J. Selby, to learn the tailoring trade and that he is to serve him faithfully until he is twenty-one years old.
> Andrew Johnson was born in 1808, December 29th.
>
> MARY DOUGHTRY.
By TURNER DOUGHTRY.

Accordingly it was ordered by the Court of Pleas and Quarterly Sessions at Raleigh, in February, 1822, "that A. Johnson, an orphan boy and son of Jacob Johnson, deceased, 14 years of age, be bound to Jas. J. Selby till he arrived at lawful age, to learn the trade of a tailor."[9]

Under the apprenticeship law then prevailing in the State, Selby was entitled to the boy's services without salary until he should become of age. In return, the master pledged to feed and clothe young Andy and to teach him his trade. Under the law, during the stipulated term a lad so apprenticed was virtually the bond-servant of his master. None could hire him but the master without the latter's formal consent. A "bound boy" who had run away, could be brought back by force and recommitted to his master's keeping, almost as if he were a runaway slave. The master likewise was legally entrusted with rigorous disciplinary powers, including that of flogging.[10]

The foreman of Selby's shop during Johnson's apprentice-

ship remembered Andy as a wild harum-scarum boy, who however had no "*un*honorable traits about him."[11]   The lad, he
recalled, had been of an exceedingly restless disposition, and
had constantly climbed picket fences, so that his clothes were
usually in a state of dilapidation.   The mistress was greatly
concerned over this unnatural wear and tear; and the old foreman related that once she made Andy "a coarse, heavy shirt
of homespun goods, and the young gentleman for a short time
was obliged to wear a whole undergarment."   But despite these
boyish scrapes, the fatherless apprentice learned the tailoring
trade: learned it so well that, when eventually he had need to
set up for himself, he was able to build and maintain a successful business of honest workmanship on honest goods.

In June, 1824, Andy's youthful exuberance led him into
trouble.   There lived in Raleigh at that time a lady by the
name of Wells, with two "right smart" daughters.   One Saturday night Andy and another apprentice "chunked" the old
lady's house.   Next day Mrs. Wells learned the names of the
boys who had thrown rocks at her windows, and sent word that
Monday morning she intended to "persecute" them.   Very much
frightened, the two culprits ran away that night,[12] along with
Andy's elder brother William, who at that time was likewise
articled to Selby.

The master tailor promptly "advertised" for the Johnson
boys, offering a reward of $10.00 for the delivery of William
and Andrew, "or I will give the above reward for Andrew
alone."[13]   Oddly enough, in his notice Selby reversed the descriptions of the two apprentices.   He had William "of a dark
complexion, black hair, and eyes," and Andrew, "very fleshy,
freckled-faced, light hair, and fair complexion."   When the
boys went away, the advertisement stated, both were well clad
in blue cloth coats, light-colored homespun coats, and new
hats.   "All persons are cautioned against harboring or employing said apprentices, on pain of being prosecuted," it concluded.

The runaways first stopped at Carthage, N. C., about
seventy-five miles south of Raleigh, where they opened a tailor
shop, and soon had an excellent trade.[14]   But Andrew did not
feel safe in North Carolina, and pushed across the South
Carolina border to the town of Laurens.   There he again

opened up a tailor shop and worked at his trade the better part of a year, making clothes to the complete satisfaction of the gentry of the district.

Johnson arrived in Laurens in the fall of 1824, but he stayed in the South Carolina town only about a year. An incipient love affair seems to have been responsible for his departure. He had fallen in love with a young girl named Sarah Word, and had asked for her hand in marriage. Tradition has it that she was beautiful, and that she reciprocated the tailor's love.

It was an idyllic romance, in the course of which young Andy gave his sweetheart a tailor's goose, and helped her draw designs of fruits and flowers on a quilt, and to make it. He asked to be allowed to embroider his initials on it, as a mark of his affection, but this Sarah's "maidenly modesty forbade," so only the initials "S. W." appeared. But while Sarah was charmed with her tailor swain, her mother was "indignant" at the idea of her daughter marrying a runaway apprentice. Andy was very much mortified, and abandoned his suit. The next day he closed up his tailor shop, and started back to Raleigh. Before 1825 had ended, Sarah had become the bride of one William Hance.[15]

There may have been other reasons besides love's difficulties that induced the young runaway to return to North Carolina. It seems that Selby had written that if Andy would come back and go to work, his sins would be forgotten. But when he talked the matter over with Selby, the two were unable to reach a working agreement. At any rate, the adventuresome young tailor determined to seek his fortune in Tennessee.

Tom Lomsden, as yet one of Selby's journeymen and still a great friend of Andy, recalled that the sixteen year old boy was always talking about the West, and that one day he had said to him, "Tom Lomsden, I am going to quit Raleigh and go to Tennessee." The older man replied, "All right, Andy, do what you think best; but you are bound to be a great man some day." Andy laughed.

The next night the young tailor left Raleigh. Lomsden well remembered the scene. "He was a gawky sort of a boy, and his clothes never did fit him," the old tailor recounted. "He had on a little cap, and a bundle of shirts and socks thrown over his shoulder. It was a bright moonlight night, and I walked out of town with him a matter of two miles. He was talking all the time about the great things he intended to do out West; and when we shook hands, and he bade me goodby, the tears just rolled down his cheeks."

"Cheer up, Andy," Lomsden told him. "Raleigh is no place for you. You'll succeed out there, and some day I hope to see you President, for you are bound to be a great man." This made the boy's spirits brighter, and he turned away and went whistling down the road.[16]

About this time a North Carolina gentleman named Brown was moving across the Smokies to Tennessee with his train of covered wagons, his slaves and his household goods. After he had crossed the mountains and reached Tennessee, his attention was attracted to a boy, poorly clothed, sitting on the side of the road, with his little pack beside him. It was Andrew Johnson. He asked Brown to let him ride along, which favor was granted.[17]

After reaching Knoxville, young Andy floated down the Tennessee River on a flatboat to Decatur, Alabama, landed there and walked the seventy miles overland to Columbia, Tennessee.[18] In this flourishing center of a rich farming country —incidentally, the home of James K. Polk, Johnson's fellow North Carolinian, and like him destined to become President of the United States—the lad had no difficulty in finding employment with James Shelton, Columbia's leading tailor.

Shelton took a great fancy to young Johnson, who lived with his employer's family during most of his six months' stay in Columbia. Years later, when Johnson had become famous, Mrs. Shelton took much pride in recounting to her friends that it was she who taught him his letters and how to read. On the occasion of a visit to Columbia, after his Presidency, Johnson was asked whether her boast was true or not. He answered kindly: "She did not, but she seemed to get so much pleasure out of saying that she did that I have not denied it. ‧ I am glad to give her all the pleasure that I can, for she was a mother to me when I lived with them and worked at my trade with her husband."[19]

Johnson stayed at Columbia, working for James Shelton, about six months. At the end of that time he received disquieting intelligence from Raleigh about his mother's condition. Her second marital venture had not improved her lot in life and she was living in direst penury. So Andrew left the

Sheltons, and trudged back to Raleigh to see what he could do to amend his family affairs.

When the young tailor returned to Raleigh in the summer of 1826, he found it impossible to secure employment at his trade. Legally, he was still bound by the articles of indenture of the Raleigh court, as he had not yet arrived at lawful age. His friend Litchford, who had set up shop for himself in the meantime, dared not employ the lad. Selby had moved away from Raleigh in the meantime and Johnson walked the twenty miles to his legal master's new home to try to secure either re-employment on terms, or a release of the indenture. But Selby was surly and stubborn. He would not take Andy back without sureties the boy could not furnish, and he would not release him.[20] Under these circumstances, no tailor in the State dared employ the runaway apprentice. He could not hope to escape this ban in North Carolina until four more years had elapsed. So he now determined to take the greater venture and move the entire family to Tennessee.

At the age of seventeen, Andrew had already become the accepted head of the family. His mother depended upon his judgment, and his stepfather was willing to do whatever he said. Brother William had already gone ahead across the mountains and settled on a fine farm in the rich valley of the Sequatchie River, in southeastern Tennessee. So, in the month of August, the Johnsons sold or gave away what possessions they could not load in a rude cart and set out on the long and dusty road. They were accompanied for the greater part of the journey by A. D. February, another adventurous Raleigh tailor.[21]

The family followed the same route which Andrew Jackson had taken when he rode over the mountains forty years before. But the outfit of the two adventurers was quite different. When he left the State of North Carolina, Andrew Jackson had already been admitted to the bar ; he set forth with a span of fine horses, duelling pistols in his holsters, well packed saddlebags flapping behind, and several hundred dollars of gold in his pocket.[22] But Andrew Johnson did not ride from Raleigh. He trudged on foot most of the way along the narrow rutted road.

There is an appealing legend about this journey of the Johnsons, an unlikely tale with no historical evidence to sustain it other than that it is part and parcel of the old folklore of upper East Tennessee.[23] As the Johnson expedition was toiling westward, the story goes, a party of horsemen came riding toward them. They rushed past the creaking cart, cursing at the unwieldy obstacle in their road. One of them splashed mud on the trudging Andy and swore at him for being in the way. This drew a rebuke from a grim and tight lipped warrior, who chided his obstreperous companions, reined in his own horse, and descended to comfort the bespattered lad. Legend has it that this courteous horseman assured young Andrew that Tennessee was truly a land of promise; there a man could make his mark. "I am General Jackson," he said, as he turned to mount.

It was not an easy journey, this westward path across the Smokies. There were many long hard days of travel through the mountains. Forty-two years later, February was to write Johnson how well he remembered the hard time they had on their journey. He also recalled some exciting incidents: "Do you remember the panther that came and knocked the skillet off the fire where we camped one night?" Then too there was an occasion "on the top of the Blue Ridge, where you snapped your shotgun so often at a bear."[24]

At last the humble party made its way across the mountains and reached the green clad valleys of upper East Tennessee. One Saturday afternoon in September, 1826, residents of the little village of Greeneville saw coming down the North Carolina road, a wrinkled, swarthy, little old woman who was driving a cart, followed by a man and a boy, leading a cow. It was the Johnsons. They were very weary, and while Greeneville was by no means their final destination, it afforded a needed resting place. The group passed across the hollow into the village of Greeneville.[25]

Andy spied a pretty young girl standing on the lawn in front of a rather pretentious house. The boy approached the gate and asked her if she knew where there was an empty house his family could rent for a few days. She told him of a cabin, described its location and walked along with him to point it out, as well as the store of the owner, one Armitage.[26]

Andy made terms for the rent of the cabin and installed his family. As they were getting settled, he remarked to his mother that he liked the young lady who was so friendly, and intended to marry her. Her name, he had learned, was Eliza McArdle, and she was the orphaned daughter of a Scotch shoemaker,[27] a girl as good as she was beautiful. She supported her widowed mother and herself by piecing crazy quilts and making cloth-topped sandals. Eliza, on her part, was not unimpressed with Andy, dirty and forlorn as he appeared. Upon her return home, some of her girl friends who had seen her walking up the street with this "tramp" began to tease her and to ask, "Eliza, who is your new sweetheart?" She tossed her head, and answered, "He's all right," and added, with a chuckle, "I might marry him some day."

The storekeeper drew out the lad's story, remarked that he had some cloth he wanted to get "made up" and offered Andy a temporary job. The Johnsons stayed on in Greeneville while Armitage's stock of cloth was being made up. At the end of six weeks the temporary tailoring job came to an end. Thereupon the family hitched up the blind pony to the rickety cart, and resumed the westward journey, probably with Columbia as their goal.

Andy must have left Greeneville with extreme reluctance. How could he forget the girl who had guided him to the Armitage cabin? When the family reached the little town of Rutledge, seventy-five miles to the southwest, it halted again. John Cocke, on his way to take his seat in the Federal House at Washington, turned over his little brick law office to Andy for his shop.[28] There for the next six months the young tailor made clothes and began to build up a fine trade. But presently he had word from Greeneville that the only tailor in the town had departed. Immediately Johnson, his mother, and his stepfather moved back to Greeneville.

Upon his return, Andy prospered in the tailoring business and even more so in his suit for the hand of Eliza McArdle. On May 17, 1827, they were married, the knot being tied by 'Squire Mordecai Lincoln, a distant cousin of the Kentucky Abraham. This love match proved a happy one. Andy was but nineteen at the time and his bride seventeen. Eliza brought to him "youth, beauty, culture, and a love which never failed him in his darkest hour." She was indeed a very attractive girl, with soft hazel eyes, nut-brown hair, generous mouth, fine Grecian nose, ample forehead and tall shapely form. Those who knew her later, when she had reached womanhood, termed her "a beautiful woman" and referred to "her soft features and graceful form, her wavy light brown hair, and her large hazel

Drawn by Harry Fenn, from a photograph

ANDREW JOHNSON'S TAILOR SHOP, GREENEVILLE, TENNESSEE

JOHNSON'S GREENEVILLE TAILOR SHOP

Drawing Made by Harry Fenn, from a Photograph, *Century Magazine,* 1883.

eyes, and withal, her intelligent expression and pleasing address."[29]

The legend persists that his child-wife taught Andrew Johnson to read and write. It is a pretty story, but half of it is not true. Andy learned to spell his letters and to read while an apprentice at Raleigh. There is unmistakable evidence that, during his runaway year in South Carolina, he was hungry for books. Old Litchford, Selby's foreman, believed that the boy knew his A B C's when he came to the shop. "But I think I taught him to read," he said. "He deserves unbounded credit, for some people say as how they had a grand start, and I reckon he started underground."[30] Dr. Hill, a man of leisure and wealth, made a practice of reading to the Raleigh working men at their noon hour extracts from the speeches of the great orators of the past. His lexicon was the famous "United States Speaker."[31] One day Andy heard him read from the "Speaker," was stimulated to read it himself, and went to Dr. Hill to borrow it. Hill offered to give Andy the book if he could prove that he could read. The boy took the book, read from it, and Dr. Hill presented it to him. This "United States Speaker" came across the mountains in the cart, and was the most treasured volume of Johnson's library.[32]

Nor is this the only evidence of Johnson's fondness of books. When he had his shop in Laurens, he boarded at the same house with a young man named Simmons, and many years later Simmons, who had become the proprietor of the Laurens Hotel, told Benjamin F. Perry that he remembered Johnson well during his Laurens experience, and that the future president "could then read, and always had a book before him."[33]

Yet there is no doubt that, at the time of his marriage, the ambitious young tailor could only write his name, if that. With a loving heart, his girl-wife undertook the task of teaching him to write and to cipher to the rule of three. She had an eager pupil, for Andrew Johnson was afire with the zeal for knowledge. He borrowed continually from the private libraries of Greeneville, few in number and restricted in quality, and made it a habit to seek out the heart of every person's knowledge by eager questioning and debate.

Greeneville was by no means a rude and uncultured community but boasted of two fledgling colleges, zealously conducted by the devoted educators of the day. In 1794, Dr. Hezekiah Balch had crossed the mountains from Mecklenburg

County, North Carolina, to Greeneville, to found Greeneville College, under a charter from William Blount, Governor of the Federal Territory South of the Ohio River. This college was the first institution of higher learning south of the Ohio and west of the Alleghanies.[34] The next year Samuel Doak, a dour Presbyterian Divine, likewise crossed the mountains, took out a charter in Washington County, established Washington College and became its first president. A Calvinist of the Jonathan Edwards school, he brought across the mountains a library, large for that time, of church history and theological disputation. In 1818 Dr. Doak severed his connection with Washington College, moved to Greene County and founded Tusculum Academy, four miles west of the county seat.

Thus, in 1828 and 1829, when young Andrew Johnson began to seek further training in self-expression, he found close at hand two young colleges with ambitious debating societies. He was quick to avail himself of these opportunities for self-improvement. He first affiliated himself with the debating society—"Polemic Society," they termed it—at Greeneville College, and was wont to walk the four miles to this pleasant campus several times a week. This school then had a library with something like 3,000 volumes, collected by its second president, Dr. Charles Coffin, from friends in New England. The books came chiefly from the private libraries of the Mathers, Jonathan Edwards and other New England theologians of the day; and while there were histories among them and some rare and valuable books[35] they were mainly volumes of sermons and theological discussions. Undoubtedly Johnson ransacked this library and borrowed from it, so as to get the volumes over which he pored until late in the night.

A Greeneville College student of that day later recalled Johnson's persistent endeavors to cultivate his mind and recounted how the young tailor belonged to the "Polemic Society," connected with the college, and how, to attend its meetings, "he walked the four miles out and back every week. I well remember his fascinating manners, his natural talent for oratory, his capacity to draw the students around him, and make all of them his warm friends."[36] Others, however, recalled him at this period as "a very timid speaker, afraid of his own voice." But probably the most valuable results of his walks to Greeneville College were the friendships which he formed. The most conspicuous of these was that with Sam Milligan, who was then teaching at the college.

The Greeneville College debating society suspended in the winter of 1828, whereupon Johnson transferred his attendance to Tusculum.[37] The Doak institution at that time had a very scanty library, probably containing little other than theological books, but it had a live and active literary and debating society, called the Philomathean Literary Society. It met every Friday evening and Johnson walked four miles from Greeneville to the college and back regularly, for more than a year, to take part in the debates. Tusculum has no records of the questions fought out by the society while Johnson was a member, but doubtless they were the great political issues of the day: The Federal Government's constitutional right to make internal improvements; the re-charter of the United States Bank; the Kentucky-Virginia Resolutions of 1798, and other spacious controversies.

These college arenas were not the only forum for Johnson's self-instruction in the art of debate. About the time he entered politics, he took part in the organization of a debating society formed by the young men of Greeneville. But he had one much closer at hand and in session nearly every night—the back room of his tailor shop.

At his marriage Andy had his shop in a two-room building on Main Street: his tailoring establishment in the front room, his kitchen and dining room, parlor and bed chamber in one in the rear. Here Andy and Eliza lived until 1831. In this rear room was born Charles, the first son, and Martha, the future mistress of the White House. By the end of four years, Johnson's rigid economy enabled him to think of buying a house. On February 24, 1831, he attended a court sale, and purchased a dwelling and smith shop on Water Street, paying about $1,000 for it.[38] Soon afterwards he heard of the sale of a Main Street building, bought it and rolled it a block and a half to the smith lot, where it was transformed into the famous tailor shop.

This fine new shop now replaced the front room as the debating society, and in it Johnson continued his quest for knowledge and truth. He was wont to employ a bright schoolboy,[39] at fifty cents a day, to read aloud to his assistants and himself, as they worked; not the novels of Jane Austen and Maria

Edgeworth, but Eliot's debates, Jefferson's messages, and over
and over again the Constitution of the United States.   And in
this room every Saturday evening there would be a throng of
students, come to debate again with the eloquent tailor the
matters discussed in the college debating society the night
before.[40]   The influence of the much worn copy of the "United
States Speaker," in forming Johnson's style of speaking must
not be overlooked.   It had been both a mentor and a mine of
information.   His mind was perfectly fresh and the style, language and sentiments impressed his youthful imagination.
"Through the power of Chatham, the solidity of Burke, the
popular acumen of Erskine, the vehemence of Fox, . . . this
volume molded into form and inspired into suitable action the
elements of his mental character, and thus laid the foundation
of his fame and fortune."[41]

It was during these years that he formed some of his fast
friendships, among them those with Blackstone McDannel,[42]
the devoted friend of his early years, and Sam Milligan, who
became his political mentor, legal adviser and lifelong guide.
This time of study, debate and self-education was likewise a
time of building up a successful tailor shop and the foundations
of a modest fortune.   Johnson was a good tailor; he hired
competent workmen and taught his apprentices well.   The shop
in which he plied his trade is still preserved in Greeneville, with
the early tailor's bench, and the simple, time-battered sign:
"A. Johnson, Tailor," which hung outside.   From 1827 to
1843, Andrew Johnson's interest was turning more and more to
public affairs; yet during these years, by the practice of rigid
economy and spurred on by the remembrances of early want,
he purchased "one of the best residences" in Greeneville,[43] secured and paid for his tailor shop, a brick store building, and
a farm of more than a hundred acres.   On the latter he settled
his mother and stepfather.

No story of the beginning of Andrew Johnson's political
career would be complete without some notice of the Greene
County Democracy, which came to regard him as the reincarnation of Old Hickory, and stuck by him to the day of his
death.   He often told the Greene County Democrats that to
them he owed all that he was.   For years he molded their political opinions—and Andrew Johnson knew how to build men
as well as how to clothe them.   He knew the people of Greene
County, men, women and children; and they would travel from

the fastnesses of the mountains to get a chance to hearken to his beloved voice. A political comradeship and understanding grew up between him and the Greene County Democracy, a sympathy which no sly attack could embarrass and no sledge-hammer blow could budge.

I N 1829, Andrew Johnson was elected alderman, his first step in a lifelong career in politics. This initial plunge was a result of the affection of the young men of the town who frequented his tailor shop debating society. For the little twelve by twelve log cabin had become the loafing place of the young men of Greeneville. Their conversations were accompanied by much boisterous merriment, but this did not disturb their tailor host at all.

"Andy, however, neither lost his temper nor suspended his twofold employment of reading and sewing," one of them relates.[1] "The moment the needle passed through the cloth, his eye would return to the book, and anon to the needle again; and so, enter when you would, it was ever the same determined read and sew, and sew and read. His sober industry and intelligence won the favor of the grave and sedate, and his genial tolerance of the jovial groups which frequented his shop secured him unbounded popularity with the young men of the place."

They were so impressed with the tailor that they determined to give him a substantial proof of their admiration by electing him to the town council. Accordingly, on the Saturday night preceding the Monday town election, a dozen of his admirers gathered to make up their slate at the counting room where Alexander Hawthorne, a ringleader in the plan, was employed. "The first name we put down for alderman," Hawthorne tells us, "was Andy Johnson, the rest were soon selected, and as there was no printing office in the place, we wrote out the ballots. We resolved to keep everything secret until Monday morning. Then we went to the polls and worked for our candidates. Our whole ticket was elected by a sweeping majority."

The tally sheet of this election, which has been preserved, shows that while Johnson was elected, his vote of eighteen was the smallest received by any of the seven successful candidates. Interestingly enough, not alone Andrew Johnson, a tailor, but also Blackstone McDannel, a plasterer, and Mordecai Lincoln, a tanner, were elected. The success of these three plebeians gives strength to the story that the artisans waged a campaign against the aristocrats of the little town.[2]

In any event, the "best people" of the town were astounded at the idea of a tailor's election to the council. But Andy filled his office to the people's satisfaction. He took pride in his humble origin and, whenever occasion arose, battled for the rights of the mechanics and artisans of the town. They responded loyally to his championship. In 1830 he was reelected to the council; the next year he was chosen mayor, holding that post for three successive terms. In 1832 the county court made him a trustee of the Rhea Academy, no small honor for a twenty-three year old tailor who had never gone to school a day in his life.

Johnson next turned his thoughts to the legislature. In those days modes of candidature were informal. It was in the decade when King Caucus was dying and King Convention was not yet crowned. The young tailor's nomination to represent Washington and Greene Counties in the legislature was achieved with ease and informality. The coming canvass had been thoroughly discussed in his tailor shop debating society, and Andy's ambition had been fired. One Saturday night in the spring of 1835, the usual crowd gathered in Jones' store, smoking, chewing and "swapping lies." They began discussing the men who had entered the race.[3] After listening to this talk a few minutes, Andy sprang from his seat to say: "I, too, am in the fight."[4]

At the time he was but twenty-seven years old; his friends feared he would be no match for his opponent, Major Matthew Stephenson, a wealthy citizen of character and social position.[5] But as soon as Andy "went after him," the aristocratic Major cut a sorry figure. An appeal to the common people against the aristocrats elected Johnson to the legislature. He "hacked and arraigned" Stephenson until the latter's friends pitied him, and Andy was elected by a small plurality.[6]

Johnson's service in the Tennessee House was not conspicuous. That body's Journal records that he opposed a motion to invite the ministers of the Gospel at the capital to open the daily sessions with prayer. He opposed the chartering of the Hiwassee Railroad Company on the ground that railroad charters were unconstitutional, being monopolies and perpetuities. As a strict constructionist, Johnson was against the State's undertaking a great scheme of building macadamized turnpikes, a program very popular in mountain-bound East Tennessee;[7] and his consequent defeat in the legislative race of 1837 by Brookins Campbell, who stood for internal improvement, is not surprising.

Two years later Johnson had another battle with Campbell and defeated him. In this canvass the Greeneville tailor was a very advanced State's Rights Democrat, almost a follower of Calhoun, but this phase was not lasting. From 1840 onward, "Old Hickory" was Andrew Johnson's political pilot, the model of his conduct and the idol of his heart.[8]

When Johnson first took the leap from village politics to those of State and nation, the Democracy of Greene County was in a plastic, almost a chaotic state.[9] Almost its only fixed principle was an immutable faith in Andrew Jackson. In the nation at large politics was almost as chaotic as in East Tennessee. The period from 1830 to 1850 in American politics was marked by party flux. The Whig party had been born with little to cement its membership save a common opposition to Andrew Jackson and Jacksonism. It attracted the rich and the aristocratic and had "no reason for existence other than its devotion to things that were passed."[10] The fact that the Whigs were bound together by their hatred of Jacksonism caused true Democrats everywhere to make the person and principles of "Old Hickory" their guiding star. The constancy with which Johnson preached Andrew Jackson to his Greene County neighbors was not empty demagogism, and his tactics proved him a master of political stagecraft.

A record of this process shows that in the winter or spring of 1840, Johnson called the Greene County Democracy in mass meeting at Greeneville. It proved so successful that it became the model for the Jackson-Johnson Democratic rally in Greeneville every year. Loyal partisans poured forth from the Democratic strongholds until there was scarcely an able-bodied man left at home. Afoot, on horseback, or in wagons, they came, without banners or music, but "in the strength and simple power of an irresistible outpouring."[11] A few empty boxes set up against the courthouse wall formed Andrew Johnson's rostrum. Between ten and eleven in the morning the speaker ascended the impromptu stand. Immediately George Foute, clerk of the Greene County court, a lieutenant of Johnson, came forward to read in a clear, sonorous voice, resolutions which Johnson himself had prepared.

These resolutions ran the gamut of American political history. They flayed Hamilton, the father of Federalism, and lauded Jefferson, the founder of Democracy. John Adams and his Alien and Sedition Laws were excoriated. Henry Clay and the "corrupt bargain" of the 1824 election were denounced, and Andrew Jackson, the second savior of the country, the conqueror of the octopus of the United States Bank, held final place.

After Foute, who always acted as chairman, had read these resolutions, Andrew Johnson spoke for two or three hours. It was not an oration, but a speech, all the more effective because he did not rant. Even in 1840, Andy was a compelling public speaker, and his power to move the minds of men grew steadily for the next twenty years. He would begin in a low soft tone, which grew stronger as he warmed up. It was no turgid outpouring, yet there was no hesitation, no groping after words. An excellent judge of the temper of a crowd, at the outset of his career Johnson interlarded his speech with wit and humor and anecdote; in the 'Sixties he did so much less often. He did not seek for oratorical effect, but his voice rang out and was heard for a great distance; contemporaries thought it particularly adapted to the open air. His tones were loud but not unmusical, his articulation was amazingly clear, his choice of words appropriate and simple. Temple was struck by "the exact language coming to his lips to express the idea in his mind."[12]

The Democracy of Greene County came to believe that Andrew Johnson was the reincarnation of Andrew Jackson, and that he too was destined to be President of the United States. On the firm foundation of the confidence of his home folks, the tailor-politician builded his political career. He never forgot or grew cold toward this Greene County Democracy. At least once every year, until the Civil War, this scene was repeated. The meeting would begin with the reading of these resolutions, which George Foute carefully preserved from year to year and read with great oratorical effect. On Andrew Johnson's great days, Richard M. Woods, for many years Greene County's high sheriff, would be present "to preserve order"—and more especially to give to the crowd a sign, by a smile or a nod, when to laugh and when to shout.

At the perorations on these occasions—when Johnson would inform his auditors that "eternal vigilance is the price of liberty," and that "power is always stealing from the many to give to the few"—the individuals in the crowd would furtively glance around them to see if anyone was trying to steal from them. Johnson had one rhetorical figure especially dear to the hearts of Greene County's Democracy. It was an impassioned appeal to the party to stand together, "hand in hand, shoulder to shoulder, foot to foot, and to make a long pull, a strong pull, and a pull together." This delicate reference to the time-honored custom among the wagoners of the day of helping one another out always set the old wagoners in the crowd wild with delight, and their war whoops could be heard for miles. After the speaking had ended, Greene County Democracy would take the homeward road. Often it would be late in the afternoon when Johnson finished, and some of the wilder of his partisans would visit Greeneville's grogshops and make their way home much later, ready to fight at the drop of the hat any man who doubted that Andrew Johnson was the greatest man in the United States.

Such was the testing block upon which the ambitious young politician tried out his rapidly forming theories of national affairs. It was not long before he had a chance to use them in a larger arena than that of the General Assembly of the State. In 1840, he was chosen one of the Democratic electors from the State-at-large. It was a distinct honor. In picking him, such men as James K. Polk, A. O. P. Nicholson, Aaron V. Brown and Felix Grundy were passed over. In 1841 Johnson was elected State Senator, and in 1843 he ran for Congress in a strong Whig district and carried his fight.[13] His opponent was Colonel John A. Aiken of Jonesboro, a lawyer of repute and a forceful orator.[14] The campaign centered about the United States Bank, with Johnson defending "Old Hickory's" views in opposing the bank.

In the 'Forties, congressional customs of punctilio were pronounced, and the new Solon must tread cautiously lest he commit some blunder which might mar his career. Andrew Johnson did tread with caution and was well regarded during his first term. While Congress was in session, Washington was alive with parties, receptions, routs, levees and balls, only to languish like a stricken city during the long recess. Johnson had little aptitude or heart for society. He constantly borrowed books from the Congressional Library and devoted himself to mastering the details of public affairs. He was attentive to his committee assignments and was always eager to respond to the wants and wishes of his friends back home. With his devoted friend, George W. Jones of Tennessee, Johnson impressed the country with the way in which he, "a sentinel at the doors of the Treasury," used his voice and recorded his vote against jobs and grabs of all description.[15]

Johnson was painfully scrupulous about taking pay from the Government. He had been named a member on a committee to investigate a contested election, the type of *per diem* assignment most congressmen were eager to get because of the extra pay. Not so Johnson. He caused to be entered in the account book of the Sergeant-at-Arms of the House of Representatives, "I have no doubt of the legality of the charge of $768.00, but I doubt my *moral* right to more than pay for the days actually engaged in the service, and accordingly decline to receive the balance."[16]

His maiden speech warmed the hearts of the Greene County Democracy. It was a defense of Andrew Jackson, made in connection with a resolution Johnson had offered to refund to the aged hero the fine imposed on him for having declared martial law in New Orleans in 1815.[17] In Johnson's first term, an increased tariff was urged; he placed himself squarely against such increases, terming the tariff "an oppressive and nefarious system of plundering the great masses of the people for the benefit of the few." The Texas question was soon injected by John C. Calhoun, and Johnson was a staunch annexationist.

In 1845, William G. Brownlow, a young Methodist preacher and spitfire Whig editor of Jonesboro, entered the lists against Andy. The Parson knew he was no match for Johnson on the stump, and did not attempt to meet him there; but he employed the columns of his paper, the Jonesboro *Whig*, to blast his opponent's reputation. Of these efforts the most amusing to a modern reader is Brownlow's scathing card, *"Ten Reasons For Believing Andrew Johnson To Be An Atheist."*[18] The Parson's *Whig* "extra" of June 25, 1845, took note of his opponent's denunciation of him in a speech at the courthouse as a "hyena," a "devil," a "coward," and "a man of no character," and replied: "Andrew Johnson is a VILE CALUMNIATOR, AN INFAMOUS DEMAGOGUE, A COMMON AND PUBLIC

LIAR, AN IMPIOUS INFIDEL, AND AN UNMITIGATED VILLAIN . . . Mr. Johnson knows where to find me, at all times."

A few issues later, the Whig Parson printed two columns of excited brevier charging Andrew Johnson with having hired a rapscallion brother of Brownlow's to assassinate him. Politics was politics, indeed, in those days in East Tennessee. Another charge was that Johnson was not the son of Jacob Johnson at all, but a "by-blow" of John Haywood, in 1808 Judge of a North Carolina Superior Court; "the very spit of the Judge's nephew." This aspersion raised Johnson's temper to the boiling point and he denounced it.

Johnson's indignation at the insinuation about his birth was slow to cool, and shortly before the election, after a trip to Raleigh to seek testimony on the matter, he issued an open letter to the public. "These vandals and hyenas," he wrote, "would dig up the grave of Jacob Johnson, my father, and charge my mother with bastardy." He then cited numerous affidavits to disprove the charge. "As for my religion," he added, "it is the doctrines of the Bible, as taught and practiced by Jesus Christ."[19] Brownlow's canards did not carry the election, for Johnson registered a triumph.

Johnson's second term coincided with the Presidency of James K. Polk, a fellow Tennessean and fellow Democrat. But Polk was an aristocrat, Andy a plebeian, and their relations soon became strained. The Congressman quarreled with Polk over patronage and his avoidance of the White House became conspicuous. After "a frank conversation" of an hour's length between the two, the President committed to his diary his belief that Johnson "wished to play the demagogue. . . . I would almost prefer to have two Whigs here. . . ."[20]

On the very next day, Johnson wrote a friend in Tennessee that Polk, "very deficient in moral courage," was not thought "competent to lead a great party," had acted "with great duplicity to the party" and was not "respected as a man." "Polk's appointments, all in all," he added, "are the most damnable set that was ever made by any President since the government was organized. . . . He has a set of interested *parasites* about him, who flatter him until he does not know himself. He seems to be acting upon the principle of hanging an old friend for the purpose of making two new ones. . . . There is one thing I will say . . . *I never betrayed a friend or [was] guilty of the black sin of ingratitude.* I fear Mr. Polk cannot say as much."[21]

Johnson was sorely depressed by the general disfavor with which his home folks viewed his feud with Polk. On January 10, 1847, he wrote to Blackstone McDannel, at Greeneville, addressing him as "My dear friend,—*if there is one left that I can call my friend.*" It was a letter of despair. "When I reflect upon my past life and that of my family," he wrote, "when I sum up the many taunts, the jeers, the gotten-up and intended slights to me and mine, . . . I wish from the bottom of my heart that we were all blotted out of existence, and even the remembrance of things that were." He had even come to doubt Sam Milligan's loyalty to him, and as for Greeneville, he was sick of the "backbiting, Sunday-praying scoundrels of the town. I never want to own another foot of dirt in the damned town while I live."

On February 2, 1847, Johnson made a speech destined to plague him in Tennessee for several years. "I wish to Almighty God," he said, "that the whole American people could be assembled in one vast amphitheater in Washington, so that the veil that now conceals from their view the many abuses could be drawn aside," to disclose to them "the secret springs of the entire proceedings of things in this government, of all the intriguings of officers in authority, from the highest to the lowest. . . ."[22] Toward the close of his term, Polk claimed to be unaware if he had ever given Johnson cause for offense, but lamented that the latter had been "politically, though not personally, hostile to me during my whole term. He is very vindictive and perverse in his temper and conduct. . . ."[23] However, the Congressman from East Tennessee had more to occupy him than quarrels with the White House over patronage. He warmly supported Polk's Mexican War policy; as to Oregon, at first he insisted upon the 54° 40″ line, tweaking the Lion's tail as he did so, and then supported Polk's compromise.

On March 27, 1846, Johnson first introduced his Homestead Bill, a measure particularly designed to aid the landless whites, the "mud-sills" whence Johnson himself had sprung.

His most noteworthy legislative service prior to secession was his unflagging advocacy of Homestead legislation. The problem of the disposition of government land was particularly important to the people of the trans-Appalachian states. Thomas H. Benton—the famous "Old Bullion"—had early advocated Homestead legislation.   Indeed the technical excuse for the historic debate between Hayne and Webster was a resolution of a Connecticut Senator concerning public lands. Southern Members of Congress had been actively antagonistic to Homestead legislation in the Thirties. But in the next decade, as nine new territories grew up and knocked at the portals seeking statehood, Southern politicians were aghast.   They feared that these new States in the West, settled by free men and offering free state constitutions, would unbalance the South's federal control.

Nor were the Southerners the only enemies of such a Homestead law as Johnson urged.   The "Know-Nothings" feared that Catholic immigrants would monopolize the free lands; railroad promoters wanted them for themselves as a governmental bonus for road building, and the advocates of a high tariff feared that large government revenues from land sales would eliminate the need for tariff revenue and thus cause a cut in tariff duties.[24]

The Tennessee Congressman's plan was simple.   His object was not to swell federal revenues but to put settlers on the land. He wanted the Government's western holdings to be divided into homesteads to be given without cost to real settlers.   Each head of a family, if an American citizen, should be given a quarter-section, if he would settle and cultivate it for a certain number of years.

The House was slow in warming up to this farsighted project.   Representatives of such alien interests as Thad Stevens and Jefferson Davis united in crushing it, but by 1850 Johnson was gaining more support.   On May 12, 1852, he succeeded in passing his bill in the House.   But the Senate stood out against it.

Johnson's advocacy of a Homestead bill attracted attention to him in the North.   He had many invitations to speak to labor and land reform organizations, and in a labor convention he even received votes for nomination as a labor candidate for President.   In his own Southland, Johnson was the target of sneers and abuse.   "It was an infamous and a nefarious scheme," said the Raleigh *Register*.   The Richmond *Whig* called him "the greatest of national humbugs."

During these years of the Homestead fight in the House, Johnson was in a delicate position.   Himself a representative of a slave State, an owner of slaves and a believer in slavery, he had to march in step with his Southern colleagues in the great slavery fights. But he undoubtedly recognized that the ultimate effect of the adoption of the Homestead plan would be to strike a body blow at the future of the entire slave system. To reconcile these two divergent forces was no easy task. While Johnson's attitude on slavery in the Forties and early Fifties was orthodox enough from the Southern point of view, it was mainly due to his recognition of the necessities of his political situation—"compulsory," Winston terms it. But as a "mudsill" himself, "free land for free labor," the underlying idea of the Homestead Bill, stirred him to the core. The results of Johnson's Homestead campaign in the House were only educational, but in 1857, when he entered the Senate, he resumed the battle for free land and for free labor.

Johnson's speech of February 2, 1847, against Polk, played a large part in his next contest. It had been the general expectation of the district that Landon C. Haynes, an eloquent and ambitious Democrat, would run against Johnson at the next election; had this occurred, the latter's speech would have won him general Whig support. But Haynes belatedly decided not to run and toward the end of the summer, Oliver P. Temple, a young Whig, entered the fight. Temple made much capital of such Johnsonian phrases as "the intriguings of officials in authority from the highest to the lowest"; and the Democrats, indignant at Andy, voted for Temple by the hundreds. On election night, when it seemed that Temple had won, Johnson "shed tears, and almost broke down with emotion."[25] The next day the last returns from two distant counties gave Johnson the election by 314 votes.

He made no more anti-Polk speeches.[26] Indeed, in 1848, he delivered a powerful address in defense of the presidential right of veto—a defense of Polk which has unusual significance in view of Johnson's later career. The veto was a "constructive" thing, one which "enables the people, through their tribunitian officer, the President, to arrest or suspend unconstitutional, hasty or improvident legislation, until the people . . . have time and opportunity to consider of its propriety. . . ." In 1849, Andy was reelected over Nathaniel G. Taylor, the Whig candidate, by a majority quite as great as those of his first two campaigns.

Finally, in 1851, Landon C. Haynes measured his strength against Johnson in a bitter personal campaign. Haynes and

Johnson bandied epithets and exchanged accusations "for six hours each day" throughout the long canvass. Haynes denounced Johnson's Homestead plan as bearing fraud and robbery upon its face and having its origin in the hotbed of Jacobinism in France. Johnson's newspaper supporters made much capital out of this, and it contributed to Haynes' defeat.[27] Although an eloquent speaker, the Democrat-aristocrat was "glittering rather than solid," and Johnson's superior ability, courage and tact triumphed. "In truth," wrote a reminiscent Whig, "eloquence never availed much against the irresistible logical facts always so dexterously used by this artful man. No rhetoric, no amount of word painting, could withstand the trenchant blows he struck."

It is little wonder that, in January, 1852, a Tennessee friend wrote Franklin Pierce, who was even then hoping for the Democratic presidential nomination, without expecting it, that "the great man of this district is the Hon. Andrew Johnson, our representative. His stronghold is with the people, and he can command more votes in the district than any man."[28]

Back in Washington, Johnson was disgusted at the Congress, "the poorest . . . I ever saw," he wrote Milligan, "it deserves the curse of every honest man." Already, Johnson saw "breakers ahead." In the debate over the Compromise of 1850, he gravely reprehended the slavery agitation in Congress and appealed "to the North and to the South, to the East and to the West—to Whigs and to Democrats—*to all*—to come forward and join in one fraternal band and make one solemn resolve that we will stand by the Constitution . . . as our only ark of safety."

The Whigs now took counsel as to how to bring the tailor's political career to a close. As they controlled the new Tennessee legislature, they redistricted the State, Gustavus A. Henry introducing the bill by which Greene County, Johnson's political bulwark, was cut off from the First District and attached to one overwhelmingly Whig.[29]

The tailor-statesman made up his mind "to bid adieu to political life," a decision which he made with less unwillingness in view of his forebodings over the prospect of Franklin Pierce's presidency. The latter's "transit has been too sudden," Johnson wrote Sam Milligan; Pierce lacked "that political preparation so necessary to prepare *ordinary* men" for presidential responsibilities. In addition, the Democratic Party now seemed bound together only by the "cohesivity of public plunder." Ill health increased Johnson's willingness to abandon a political career.

A little later, however, he seems to have improved in political and bodily health, for he began to write Tennessee friends that, "under a proper set of circumstances," he would run for governor.[30] In his swan song in the House, he said that the General Assembly "had parted my garments, and for my vesture are casting lots," adding warmly, "but there is much in the future."[31]

The outcome of the gerrymander was to prove discomfiting to these clever political engineers. William B. Campbell, Governor of the State, and Tennessee's outstanding Whig, refused to seek a third term, thus depriving his party of its strongest candidate. The Whigs fell back on Gustavus A. Henry, a politician familiarly known as "the Eagle Orator." The Democratic county conventions urged many local figures,[32] but Andrew Johnson, indorsed by more counties than all the rest combined, was hailed as "a man of the people, and the people's man."[33]

When the state convention met in Nashville in April, jealous leaders sought to prevent the favorite's choice. At a secret caucus on the night before the convention, three test votes were taken and each time Johnson had a majority. But the leaders neverthless determined to offer Andrew Ewing of Nashville as the choice of the caucus.

When this was announced the next day, turmoil ensued. Several speakers denounced the caucus, demanding that Johnson be voted on. Finally Ewing withdrew in Johnson's behalf. Then an opposition leader announced capitulation, saying, "It seems that Johnson is strong enough to run all the Democrats out of the convention, and can run Henry out of the State." The Greeneville man was unanimously nominated.

It was charged that Johnson, taking advantage of a casual promise Ewing made several months before, had craftily written to Ewing to commit him and that a keen sense of personal honor had caused Ewing to sacrifice a nomination practically his, to keep a faith which Johnson did not deserve. But the facts as to Ewing's pledge and Johnson's letter disclose no self-abnegation on Ewing's part.[34]

He attended the preconvention caucus, at which Johnson's

majority had been unmistakable; yet he shared in the plot to
have himself nominated by acclamation. Until it was obvious
that the convention would not nominate him, Ewing made no
move. His withdrawal arose from his fear "to have the roll
called when no names were before the convention except his own
and that of his 'friend' Johnson."[35]

Henry, the Eagle Orator, proved no match for Johnson on
the stump.[36] The two made a joint canvass of the state, from
the Mountains to the Mississippi. Johnson told the voters
that he had been not gerrymandered, but "Henry-mandered,"
out of Congress, and made great headway with this charge.
This spirited canvass occasioned an enormous vote and Johnson
was elected, with 63,413 votes to Henry's 61,163.

Johnson's inauguration as Governor took place on October
17, 1853. In the inaugural address, he struck some popular
notes, particularly in emphasizing the crying need for the
general education of the people and for better economic treatment of the laboring classes. The inaugural became known as
the "Jacob's Ladder" speech, because of the Governor's ingenuous declaration: "Democracy and religion are handmaidens
to each other. They are two converging lines extending from
earth to heaven, where they unite in theocracy." This remark was severely censured, not alone by the "conservative
statesmen of this country, but by the aristocratic press of
England and France," though the Western Democrats thought
it a magnificent philosophy.[37]

The new Governor devoted two months to a penetrating
study of state conditions before he sent in his first message, a
state paper of high rank. He analyzed the state's debt and
made recommendations for alleviating it. He proposed a road
building tax. He wanted the State to get out of the banking
business and gradually to liquidate the Bank of Tennessee. He
criticized the competition of products of prison labor with
those of free labor. He demanded a thoroughgoing reform of
the judiciary.

A striking feature was Johnson's insistence on aid for education. "The time has surely arrived," he said, "when the legislature and the people should lay hold of this important question with a strong and unfaltering hand. Tennessee ranks last,
except one. The difficulty is that there is not enough funds,
and there is no way except to levy and collect a tax from the
people of the whole State. . . ." Millions were being spent for

internal improvements. "Can there be nothing done to advance the great cause of education?"[38]

Although the House was Whig and the Senate Democratic, Johnson's first term was marked by progressive legislation. A Bureau of Agriculture was established. The Assembly heeded Johnson's urgent appeal for education and passed an act levying heavier taxes for schools than any theretofore. Its internal improvement bill increased state aid in railroad construction. The Iron Horse went galloping over Tennessee at state expense.

Johnson was Tennessee's first Governor to give nearly all his time to his public duties. During this term he rarely discussed national affairs. He paid no attention to the rise of the Know-Nothings and had little to say about the much discussed Kansas-Nebraska Act. When he had a task to do, he stuck to his last.[39]

He was one of the first of the Progressives, in the modern sense of the word. As a disciple of Jefferson and an apostle of Jackson, he thought democracy must be something more than an empty word. He believed the common man was the cornerstone of the republic and that the people, voting directly, should elect their officials. Thus, in his first message Johnson submitted several proposals for amendments to the Federal Constitution. One provided for the election of the President and the Vice President by the people of the States, rather than by the fictitious electoral college. A second made the tenure of judges of United States courts twelve years, instead of for life. A third sought to have the United States senators elected by direct vote of the people. The tailor-statesman never lost his enthusiasm for these reforms.

In the 'Fifties, passions were hot and bowie knife and pistol often supplemented verbal argument. A man could not be Governor of Tennessee without being physically as well as politically brave. Johnson well met this test. One morning a placard was posted in Nashville, announcing that the Governor was to be shot "on sight." His friends went to his house to serve as a bodyguard to escort him to the Capitol. "No, gentlemen," he replied, "if I am to be shot at, I want no man to be in the way of the bullet." And he walked alone and with his usual deliberation from his home to Capitol Hill![40]

Thoroughly alarmed by Johnson's achievements, the Whigs determined to put him down at all costs. Consequently they entered into an alliance with the Know-Nothings, that mushroom political growth then sweeping South and Nation. Bottomed on anti-Catholicism and similar proscriptions, it had already gained a hundred thousand members in Tennessee.[41] Soon after their party merger, the Whigs began advocating that both parties dispense with state conventions to select candidates for governor. Indeed there was no occasion for the Whigs to do so, for the secret conclaves of the Know-Nothings had already determined upon Meredith P. Gentry, "the best natural orator in Congress," as their candidate. And so, on February 12, Gentry issued a card to the papers of the State, referring to "the generous sentiments expressed for me" and adding, "I deem it my duty to respond by respectfully announcing that I am a candidate for the office of Governor of Tennessee, at the next election."

The Democrats, however, were unwilling thus informally to launch their campaign. Their papers insisted on a meeting so they could organize "and fight the fight on religious and political freedom." Governor Johnson was indorsed by nearly every Democratic county, and the delegates to the state convention met in Nashville on March 27 in a fighting mood. Not only was the Governor renominated by acclamation, but resolutions were adopted reprehending Know-Nothingism in the strongest terms.

The two candidates met, agreed on sixty joint meetings, beginning at Murfreesboro on May 1, and ending at Chattanooga on August 1.[42]

Temperance likewise was destined to play a part in the contest. Maine's abolition of the liquor traffic had aroused interest and support in the South as well as in the North. In February, 1855, a state-wide temperance convention appointed a committee to ask Johnson where he stood. The committee wrote him, bluntly: "Are you in favor of a law prohibiting the sale of intoxicating liquors as a beverage? Will you, if elected, recommend to the Legislature the passage of such a law . . . ?"[43]

He responded with equal bluntness. He believed "some of the leading provisions of that law are incompatible with the rights and privileges of freemen," and in conflict with the spirit, "if not the very letter of the Constitution of the State." If elected governor, he could not recommend such a law. He added: "I hope that I have succeeded in making myself understood."[44]

In the opening debate at Murfreesboro, Johnson carried the war into Africa. He arraigned the secret party for "its signs, grips and passwords, its oaths and secret conclaves, its midnight gatherings, its narrowness, littleness and proscriptiveness." In joining the order, he charged, its members "swore to tell a lie." There came a sudden stillness over the audience, full of Know-Nothings, as Johnson, weighing his words, exclaimed: "Show me a Know-Nothing, and I will show you a loathsome reptile, on whose neck every honest man should put his foot."

Under this terrible denunciation, the crowd became "pale with rage" and "still as death." Upon his declaration that the order was "no better than John A. Murrell's clan of outlaws," many voices burst out, "It's a lie, it's a lie!" The sound of cocking pistols was heard from many quarters, and men ceased to breathe. But Johnson looked on, grim, unmoved and undaunted. Pausing a moment, he resumed his speech. There was no outbreak. His next appointment to speak was in another Know-Nothing stronghold, and a committee of Democrats waited on him, urging him to omit the speech. "I'll make that speech tomorrow," he answered, "if it blows the Democratic Party to hell."[45]

The two candidates canvassed the State from Sullivan to Shelby in a campaign of great bitterness. Many threats were made against Johnson. Word was sent him that if he appeared in a certain Know-Nothing stronghold, he would not leave the hall alive. At the appointed hour, the Governor advanced to the desk, and laid his pistol upon it.

"It is proper," he began, "when free men assemble for the discussion of important public interests that everything should be done decently and in order. I have been informed that part of the business to be transacted on the present occasion is the assassination of the individual who now has the honor of addressing you. . . . Therefore, if any man has come here tonight for the purpose indicated, I do not say to him, let him speak, but, let him shoot."

Thereupon he placed his right hand on his pistol, with the other held open his coat, and looked blandly at the crowd. After a half minute's pause, he announced that it was apparent he had been misinformed, and proceeded with his speech.[46] The boldness of the attack on the Know-Nothings set the State on end. Gentry devoted his best platform oratory to a defense of the secret order, but his words were wasted. Johnson was reelected, thanks to the heavily increased majorities he received in rural Protestant counties, and thenceforth Know-Nothingism was impotent in the State.

The keynote of his Inaugural was his declaration that "the people have never deserted me; and, God being willing, I will never desert them." His second term was largely given over to continuation of the policies of the first. A new touch was his recommendation that the State sell its stocks and turnpikes, railroads and banks, and liquidate as much as possible of the state debt. He annnounced with pride that the State had purchased the Hermitage, home and tomb of Andrew Jackson.[47]

When the Democratic state convention met in Nashville on January 8, 1856, Johnson made a short talk, the keynote of which was his statement that, "slavery exists. It is black in the South, and white in the North, and it will continue to exist." Anxious to put Johnson forward as the State's favorite son, the convention resolved "that Andrew Johnson, as a statesman and patriot, has no superior; that he is our first preference, and we would delight to honor him with the highest office in the gift of the American people."

After the Cincinnati convention, Johnson loyally accepted the Buchanan nomination, and was soon drafted for a speaking campaign throughout Tennessee. He opened in Nashville on July 25 with three hours of closely reasoned argument, the speech evoking unbounded satisfaction from both friends and foes, so much so that the governor was forced to repeat it throughout the State. Although the "Black Republicans" had not put out an electoral ticket in Tennessee, Johnson contended that Millard Fillmore, the Know-Nothing candidate, was a greater Abolitionist than Fremont. After pillorying Fillmore as a compromiser, Johnson said: "My own opinion is that the South has been engaged in compromises, as they are termed, long enough. We have been engaged first in one compromise and then another, until our rights have been all compromised away. It is now time to stop. For me, I have nothing to conceal in reference to my political sentiments; and when I say I am no compromiser, I think there are many who agree with me."

Lest this be misunderstood as a veiled secession threat, he added these significant statements, containing a germ of his later stand in 1861: "I am no alarmist, but I speak what I think.

This Union shall be preserved. Our Southern institutions depend upon the continuance of the Union, and upon non-interference."[48]

The Tennessee Democrats registered a notable triumph at the polls, carrying the State for their presidential nominee for the first time since Andrew Jackson's day. Not only did the Buchanan electors receive a majority of 7,500 votes, but also the two Houses of the State legislature were safely Democratic, and thus Johnson's election to the United States Senate, should he desire that preferment, was assured.

Johnson did not aspire to a third term as governor. "If I make a move for the Senate," he wrote Milligan in December, 1856, "now is the time to do it while public opinion is setting in that direction."[49] His friends promptly set to work and early in 1856, the Tennessee legislature sent him there. He was chosen not by the leaders, but by the Democratic masses, whose wish was so manifest that the leaders did not dare say them nay. He always spoke with contempt of the aristocratic leaders and humiliated them whenever chance presented. "Old Andy" was the idol of the Democratic rank and file. He trusted them and they trusted and honored him. "In robust strength," says a contemporary, "Johnson stood alone in his party. His reign at this time was absolute."

From the time he entered the Senate, Johnson verged more and more away from the leaders of the Slave States. There was little sympathy between him and the Davis, Cobb, Toombs contingent. They generally considered him a plebeian upstart and he hated what they represented. He was likewise quite unimpressed with Buchanan. "I fear his administration will be a failure," Johnson wrote his son Robert on January 23, 1858. "It is too timid to venture upon anything new or risk much upon anything old." He predicted that there would be much "grannyism" in the conduct of affairs and, as to "Old Buck" himself, "to hear him talk, one would think that he was quite bold and decided, but in practice he is timid and hesitating."

The Tennessean's first address to the Senate, directed against an increase in the regular army, gave him "rank among the first debaters."[50] In 1858 he protested against the Federal Government's fixing the qualification of voters in Minnesota, then seeking statehood, and denied "that this government has

power to go inside a sovereign state and prescribe the qualifications of her voters at the ballot box."

In this same year, Johnson had an untimely altercation
with John Bell, his Whig senatorial colleague from Tennessee.
In 1854 Bell had been one of the few Southerners to vote
against the Kansas-Nebraska bill. In his speech he had expressed the view that a Senator whose opinions were "in direct
opposition to the settled sense of his constituents" should resign. The Tennessee legislature, which favored the Kansas-
Nebraska bill, promptly passed a resolution calling on Bell to
resign. When Bell sought to answer these resolutions in the
Senate, he excoriated some of Johnson's friends in the General
Assembly at home. The tailor-statesman felt called upon to
defend the legislature. In doing so, he incidentally referred to
Bell as "a competitor." Bell resented the reference and replied
that Johnson was neither big enough nor good enough to be so
classed.

The latter, now thoroughly angry, almost made a scene in
the Senate. He told Bell he had had competitors "worthy of
my steel, men who recognized me as such." He added that a
gentleman, "a well bred man will respect me; all others I will
make do it." He knew his rights and the right of the State he
represented, and would maintain these "at all hazards and to
the last extremity." It looked for a while as if the Tennesseans might meet on a duelling ground, but next day both
apologized, and though they never became friendly again,
formal relations were resumed.[51]

Johnson's main attention was now given to his Homestead
Bill. As soon as he reached the Senate, he reintroduced it, and
pressed it with all the force he had. With very few exceptions,
the Southern Senators opposed it with every parliamentary
device at their command. On May 20, 1858, when he had
finally managed to have his favorite project made the special
order of the day, Johnson made one of his greatest efforts,
taking up the cudgels for the free farmer.

Not long before, Senator Hammond of South Carolina had
told the Senate that the working classes were "the very mud-
sills of society," and had compared the "slaves" of North and
South. This provoked Johnson, who scorned the idea that the
free workers of the North were slaves because they had to earn
their daily bread with the sweat of their brows. Such a comparison as the South Carolinian had made would make a slave

of every man who was not a slaveholder. He concluded with a peroration in support of his Homestead plan.[52] Even so mild a rebuke as this did not suit the Senators of the Slave States. Mason of Virginia called Johnson "almost an Abolitionist." The Homestead Bill failed again.

Johnson brought in his bill again in the first session of the 36th Congress, and on April 11 made another powerful appeal for its passage, in the course of which he engaged in several sharp colloquies. When the measure came to final roll call, most of the Southern Senators who had interposed parliamentary obstacles to its passage did not dare to vote against it, and it was passed by forty-four to eight, the yeas including Chestnut and Hammond of South Carolina, Clay and Fitzpatrick of Alabama, Jefferson Davis of Mississippi, Hemphill of Texas, Sebastian of Arkansas, Slidell of Louisiana, and Yulee of Florida! The House quickly passed the measure with amendments, a compromise was agreed on in conference, and on June 20 it was presented to Buchanan for his signature. On June 23, despite what Johnson had deemed the President's commitment to the Homestead Bill, "Old Buck" returned it with an argumentative veto.

Johnson suspected that most of the Southern slavery phalanx which had voted for his measure had done so after a secret understanding with the President that he would veto it and they would then sustain his negative. When the ultra Southern Democrats, who were Buchanan's main bulwark of support, forced his hand, Johnson believed he quickly forgot his promise and returned the desired veto. And so it proved. A number of Southerners sufficient to keep the bill from repassing changed their vote, in spite of Johnson's despairing efforts.

Early in 1859, Senator Johnson said he did not believe "all the factionists of this government can pull it to pieces." In that December, when John Brown made his raid on Harper's Ferry, Johnson displayed a moderation and good temper in striking contrast to the bitterness and acrimony of the Senatorial extremists of South and North. He made an earnest defense of the Constitutional rights of the Slave States, without the usual threat of secession. "I am no disunionist," he announced. "Because we cannot get our constitutional rights, I do not intend to be one of those who will violate the Constitution. . . . I intend to place myself on the Constitution which I have sworn to support, and to stand there and battle for all its guarantees."[53]

Early in 1860, Johnson's Tennessee advisers thought they saw a real chance for him to become the beneficiary of the war between Douglas and Buchanan, and, by playing a shrewd game, to win the Democratic nomination. They were in doubt as to his wishes, however, and had to send many messages to Washington before gaining his consent. At that, it seems to have been the necessity of the local factional situation rather than any real nomination hopes which induced Johnson to countenance the enterprise. The Tennessee Convention met in Nashville on January 17. The Douglas men quickly discovered the impossibility of their securing the delegation, and perforce joined the Johnson party; the next day the convention formally instructed its delegation to the coming Charleston Convention to present Andrew Johnson's name. But he felt there was little or no hope of his securing the nomination,[54] and looked with anxiety upon the prospect. "The whole Senate," he wrote, were aspirants, and Jefferson Davis, "burning up with ambition, is nearer consumed by an internal heat than any man I ever saw. . . . What Jeff will do if he is not nominated, *God* only knows." The Tennessee Senator could see little ahead save the division and destruction of the party.[55]

Johnson understood the grim determination of the Western Democrats to nominate the Little Giant. "Sentiment is almost universal and determined in favor of Douglas," A. Ten Eyck wrote Johnson from Detroit in February. "The gentlemen of position and influence in the South should not shut their eyes to the fact that if Mr. Douglas is not the nominee of the Charleston convention, Mr. Seward is almost certain to be elected. With any other candidate than Mr. Douglas, we cannot hope to carry a single Northern State, except perhaps Illinois. . . . Accept at Charleston the Cincinnati platform intact, without note or comment, if you please. Give us Douglas for our candidate."[56] Thus, while Johnson wanted to pay the expenses of his son Robert and Sam Milligan at the coming convention, he seems to have entertained no serious hope of nomination. His anticipations were well founded.

Throughout the Charleston deadlock the Tennessee delegation stood loyally by the tailor-statesman, but without any real hopes of success. True, Milligan convinced himself that Douglas' friends were Johnson's friends, and believed that when

JOHNSON AT 33

From an old daguerreotype belonging to Colonel Andrew Johnson Patterson, of Greeneville. This picture was taken by a traveling daguerreotypist in 1842.

Douglas withdrew, his forces would turn to the Tennessean. But the convention tension became so great that the Douglas men were too angry to compromise or change.

During the platform debates, threats of a bolt by Gulf State delegations greatly disturbed the Tennesseans. On April 29, W. C. Whitthorne, the delegation's chairman, telegraphed from Charleston: "Have you declared for Douglas in the event of the adoption of the minority report? Six or more States will withdraw. What ought Tennessee to do?" Johnson answered promptly and firmly, "I recommend and acquiesce in the nomination, Nicholson, Wright and Avery concurring." Later that same day, he telegraphed again: "I would hold out; acquiesce in the nomination." These telegrams gave Milligan, Whitthorne and Andrew Ewing the added force they needed to restrain the delegation hot-heads, and to prevent Tennessee's joining the Gulf States bolt.

On May 2, after the bolt, Douglas reached a majority, Johnson was temporarily withdrawn, and a delegate telegraphed him: "We have withdrawn you. Douglas has majority. Ought we support him?" The Senator answered immediately: "The delegates present with all the facts before them are better prepared to determine what course to pursue than I am."[67]

But regardless of Johnson's views, the Tennessee delegation was unwilling to go to Douglas. They felt that a Douglas victory "by a purely sectional vote would of itself, more effectively than the secession of the Gulf States, denationalize the party." As soon as the Illinois man seemed to have a chance of nomination under a loose construction of the two-thirds rule, the Tennesseans joined Virginia, Maryland, North Carolina and Kentucky, in insisting upon such a strict construction that Douglas could not possibly win.

Despite the turmoil between the Charleston adjournment and the Baltimore opening, Sam Milligan continued to nurse hopes that Johnson still had a chance. "Your friends lie in the North and Northwest," he wrote the Senator, "and I do believe, by a little concert of action with Mr. Douglas and the conservative men of those States, your nomination at Baltimore is by no means improbable." But he felt, as did Whitthorne, that "the election is lost in any event, and the Extreme South is responsible for it." But the Senator had no delusions, and instructed Milligan not to let his name be presented. In an hour of serious apprehension for the future of the Government, Johnson felt it incumbent on all to secure harmony, that "the Union, with the blessings, guarantees and protection of its Constitution be perpetuated forever." He therefore wished the Tennessee delegation to be free to vote for others, and thus to help avert any more deadlocks or bolts.　But Milligan's hopes would not be downed; on June 22, he telegraphed Johnson, from Baltimore: "If the withdrawing delegates from the Moderate States North and South should recommend your name for the presidency, would you object?"　Johnson would, and the Tennesseans remained with the main convention, stubbornly voting for Andrew Johnson until the thirty-sixth ballot.[59]

After the Democratic split, Johnson supported the Southern Democratic ticket of Breckinridge and Lane.　He could not believe that there was any real danger of secession in the event of Lincoln's election, and thought the talk of the Rhetts and Yanceys and Toombses empty campaign bluff.　Following the election, when the Cotton South started its secession, Johnson was shocked and indignant.　He was himself a State Rights man and owned a few slaves.　But first of all, he was an Andrew Jackson Democrat.

A good epitome of Johnson the Senator was offered by Jefferson Davis in 1865, while a prisoner of state in Fortress Monroe, held for trial on the grave charge of high treason. One day Dr. Craven, the prison physician, fell into conversation with him about the ante bellum Senate and Senators.　The doctor asked the head of the late Confederate states for his opinion of President Johnson.　Davis replied that he knew only what the papers told him of President Johnson.　But of Mr. Johnson, when in the Senate, he could speak.　Johnson's position with his associates from the South had never been pleasant.　In the midst of associates, many of whom pretended to aristocracy, Johnson seemed to keep ever present with him his own plebeian origin as a bar to warm social relations. Davis charged him with having an "almost morbidly sensitive" pride —"the pride of having no pride."

The other senators, said Davis, respected Johnson's "ability, integrity, and great original forces of character. . . .　He was an immense worker and student, but always in the practicalities of life.　His habits were marked by temperance, industry, courage, and unswerving perseverance; also by inveterate prejudices or preconceptions on certain points, and these no arguments could change. His faith in the judgment of the people was unlimited, and to their decision he was always ready to submit. One of the people by birth, he remained so by conviction."

Johnson's honesty of character, justice, kindliness and generosity were notable. "He was eminently faithful to his word," said his imprisoned foeman, "and possessed a courage which took the form of angry resistance if urged to do or not to do anything which might clash with his convictions of duty. He was indifferent to money, and careless of praise or censure, when satisfied on the necessity of any line of action."[59]

VI. "IN THE FURNACE OF TREASON"

IN December, 1860, when the Senate reconvened, Andrew Johnson was in his seat to do battle for "the sacred cause of the Union." It was a time that tried men's souls. Immediately upon Lincoln's election, Georgia, Mississippi and Alabama had dispatched agents to the North to purchase arms "without regard to expense."[1] It was South Carolina's mission to sever "the accursed Union," Mr. Rhett told the Palmetto State's legislators. Jefferson Davis, addressing the people of Vicksburg, termed "submission to the rule of the arrogant and sectional North infamy and degradation" and urged an appeal to the God of Battles.

President Buchanan, in his message on December 4, took the position that, while South Carolina's grievances justified secession, yet she had no right to secede, and that the Federal Government had neither right nor power to coerce her. Four days later, Howell Cobb of Georgia resigned as Secretary of the Treasury, assigning as his reason his duty to his State. On the 14th, the venerable Lewis Cass gave up the Secretaryship of State; he could not remain in a Cabinet "that confesses that the General Government is subordinate to the State."

On this same day appeared an address to the People of the South, signed by Senators and Congressmen from that section. "All hope of relief in the Union is extinguished," declared such men as Davis and Brown of Mississippi, Benjamin and Slidell of Louisiana, Hemphill and Wigfall of Texas and Iverson of Georgia. "The honor, safety and independence of the Southern people require the organization of a Southern Confederacy." On December 17, South Carolina's Constitutional Convention assembled and speedily adopted its Secession Ordinance. On Christmas Eve, Governor Pickens proclaimed South Carolina a "Separate, Sovereign, Free, and Independent State."

During these fevered days the Senate was in continual debate. The Southerners were either delivering their Union swan songs or hurling maledictions at the Federal compact. In this last, they were aided by several doughfaces—"Northern men with Southern principles"—and by none more offensively than by Senator Joe Lane of Oregon—the same Lane whom Andrew Johnson had supported for vice president a few weeks before.

Andrew Johnson studied the situation, read copiously on loyalism in American history and prepared for his most notable senatorial address.[2] He began his speech late in the session of December 18, concluding it the next day. He commenced by suggesting again the three changes to the Constitution which he had urged for years. The first two dealt with the election of the president and of United States senators by direct popular vote. His third plan for limiting judicial tenure, was reshaped to fit the existing sectional situation. He urged altering the mode of appointment and tenure of office of the Supreme Court by dividing its membership into three classes, the term of the first to expire four years from the date of reclassification, the second eight, and the third twelve. As vacancies occurred, half should be filled with men from Slave States, and half with appointees from Free States. At each election, either the president or the vice president must come from a slaveholding State. He felt that the South would thus gain true security.

Johnson then arraigned disunionists of whatever section. In reviewing the fears and grievances of the Slave States, he admitted that there should be redress, but such redress must be sought within the Union itself: "If this doctrine of secession is to be carried out upon the mere whim of the State, this government is at an end." The Senator's dislike for a consolidated government was well known; but it must be "strong enough to preserve its own existence," and not "fall to pieces . . . whenever a little dissatisfaction takes place in one of its members." If the State had the right to secede at will, he warned, the government was no stronger than a rope of sand.

He next considered the spectre of "coercion." He did not think the Federal Government had the power to coerce a State, but it did have ample and complete right and power "to pass laws, and to enforce those laws upon individuals within the limits of each State." A State's secession would not call for coercion. The government had power to execute its constitutional duties; to carry the mails, to establish post offices and post roads, to establish courts, to levy and collect taxes, etc. It was no invasion of the State for the Union to execute its laws and the government undertaking to maintain its authority did not become an aggressor—"it is only acting within the scope of the constitution." But a State that resists it "becomes the aggressor, and places itself in the rebellious or nullifying attitude."

As to the effect of secession upon the South's peculiar institution, Johnson had a flash of insight. "The continuance of slavery," he said, "depends upon the preservation of this Union." With its dissolution, slavery would be overthrown. Speaking for Tennessee, Johnson said, "We do not intend that you shall drive us out of this house that was reared by the hands of our fathers. It is our house. . . . We have a right here."

At this point he delivered a striking apostrophe:

> I intend to stand by the Constitution as it is, insisting upon a compliance with all its guaranties. I intend to stand by it as the sheet-anchor of the Government; and I trust and hope, though it seems to be now in the very vortex of ruin, though it seems to be running between Charybdis and Scylla, the rock on the one hand and the whirlpool on the other, that it will be preserved, and will remain a beacon to guide, and an example to be imitated by all the nations of the earth. Yes, I intend to hold on to it as the chief ark of our safety, as the palladium of our civil and our religious liberty. I intend to cling to it as the shipwrecked mariner clings to the last plank, when the night and the tempest close around him. It is the last hope of human freedom.

What was South Carolina's grievance? Did she want to carry slavery into the territories? In the very last session, South Carolina's Senators had voted "it was not necessary to make a statute now for the protection of slavery in the territories." Was South Carolina going out "for a grievance . . . which your own Senators then said had not occurred?" No, the reason was the election of Lincoln—"It is because we have not got our man."

Johnson then riddled the logic of the South. True, Lincoln was a minority president, but elected according to the Constitution. Johnson intended to maintain his place in the Senate, to "put down Mr. Lincoln and drive back his advances upon the Southern institutions, if he designs to make any." In the Senate, the South could checkmate Lincoln completely. "Let South Carolina and her Senators come back, . . . and on the

4th of March we shall have a majority of six in this body against him. Lincoln cannot make his Cabinet . . . unless the Senate will permit him. He cannot send a foreign minister, or even a consul, abroad, if the Senate be unwilling. He cannot even appoint a first-class postmaster. . . ."

"I voted against him," Johnson exclaimed dramatically, "I spoke against him; I spent my money to defeat him: but still I love my country; I love the Constitution; I intend to insist upon its guaranties. There, and there alone I intend to plant myself." In conclusion, he again expressed his abiding faith, his unshaken confidence in man's capacity to govern himself. He would stand by the Republic, and he entreated "every man throughout the Nation who is a Patriot" to come forward "and rally around the altar of our common country, . . . that the Constitution shall be saved and the Union preserved."

Even as Johnson spoke, the fate of a nation of 35,000,000 people hung in the balance. The North was "petrified with amazement, if not with fear." This speech, "the first message of courage to the almost despairing North," flashed "as a powerful light on the darkness and gloom of the hour." This slaveholding Southern Senator had done what no other Union man in Congress, North or South, had dared to do. Johnson "at once became the most popular man in the North except the President-elect."[3] Alexander H. Stephens was later to pay tribute to the effectiveness of this speech by terming it "the most masterly effort ever delivered by man on earth"; Johnson's influence alone had gained a hundred thousand Southern men for the Union armies, and but for him, the Confederate leader said, the South would have gained her independence.[4] On the other hand, the speech startled and enraged the Southern Senators. That a Southern Democrat who had supported Breckinridge should hurl such thunderbolts at secession was unendurable; and with relentless malignity, Johnson was assailed by Wigfall, Benjamin, Toombs and Iverson, aided always by the vindictive Joe Lane. It was an attempted "reign of terror," the Tennessee Senator wrote a Nashville friend.[5]

When Johnson's speech was printed in Tennessee, it evoked irritation, indignation and protest among the Secessionists. In many places in Middle and West Tennessee he was burned in effigy, so that his son Robert wrote him from Greeneville on

New Year's Day: "I presume you have heard of the burning of your effigy. As John Tyler once said, they merely give you light for a man to walk by." On December 30, a Nashville lieutenant reported his disappointment over the ill success of a Union gathering of the day before. "It almost resulted in a secession meeting. The truth was," he continued, "that you have been in the way of a good many of our would-be great for a long time. At heart, many of us never wanted you to be Governor, only none of the rest of us could have been elected at the time. . . . Now we are afraid of the people and a little of you, but notwithstanding this, we must give vent to our feelings. . . . Now keep cool, wait, keep your powder dry. Don't write, but when you come home, call us together, and call things by the right name." Johnson was denounced throughout the State by Buchanan appointees to Federal jobs, as in Knoxville, where the United States Attorney, the Pension Agent and the Postmaster were his chief detractors. When it was too late, Buchanan ordered several to be removed from office.

But Johnson kept sending good advice to leaders in the State. There was no need for haste. He declaimed against "the follies of South Carolina." He wrote John Trimble, "If Tennessee will stand firm, in the end she can and will act a very important part in bringing back the seceding States into the Confederacy." He was "satisfied that if the Middle States will remain in the Union, they can obtain any reasonable guarantee they may demand from the Northern States which will protect and secure slave property in the Border States, which would be much better than being separated into the two hostile powers."[6] "The best government in the world," he concluded, "is in the most imminent peril," and neither editorials nor effigy burnings would prevent his battling for it.

The Senator's mail contained many insolent letters, mainly anonymous. One from Grand Junction, Mississippi, ran thus:

> I have a mulatto slave remarkable for his impudence. . . . As a means of humiliating my slave it has been recommended to me to send him to Washington City with a *cowhide* and instruct him to give your back and shoulders some *marks of his attention* . . . If he shall happen to wound you badly in the encounter, employ Senator *Sumner* to send daily bulletins of your condition to your friends about Grand Junction.

With his usual precision, Johnson filed away the letter, indorsing on its envelope, "Threatened assault from Mississippi. Attended to."

But assurances of warm support came from all parts of his State, from outstanding men, many heretofore his opponents. "You and I differed very widely during the last canvass," wrote W. R. Hurley, Editor of the Nashville *Democrat*, "but when I see you stand up boldly for your country, I say, 'Well done, thou good and faithful servant.' I am proud of a representative who has the manliness to discharge his duty." After reading Johnson's speech, John Trimble of Nashville wrote that "as a man and a citizen, I thank you for the true voice it utters." A Knoxville friend informed the Senator on December 27: "Your worst political enemies, *Brownlow* for instance, now speak of you in the highest terms. Brownlow said to me yesterday: 'Johnson is right. He is a true Jackson Democrat, and occupies the same position now that he did in 1833, and I will defend him to the last.' " . . . Sturdy words came from Sam Milligan: "If any law is violated or the security of any portion of the people imperiled, it is not the duty of the President to exercise any discretion about it, but he is bound to vindicate the law. . . . The law is one thing and the consequences another. The President should attend to the one, and God will look after the other. . . ."[7]

On February 5 and 6, Andrew Johnson defended himself against Lane. He stated that the vice presidential nominee during the campaign had been charged with being the embodiment of Secession; Johnson had repudiated the charge, seeking to convince his people that Breckinridge and Lane were loyal Union men. He next considered the case of Jefferson Davis and his covert sneers at the lowborn tailor. "When I consider his early associations," Johnson said of Davis, "when I remember that he was nurtured by this Government, that he fought for this Government, . . . I cannot understand how he can be willing to hail another banner. . . . It seems to me that, if I could not unsheathe my sword in vindication of the flag of my country, . . . I would return the sword to its scabbard; I would never sheathe it in the bosom of my mother; never, never!"

In the final scenes of the debate on March 2, Johnson uttered words which helped to sustain the Union cause in the North more than any single incident thus far. "Show me who has been engaged in these nightly and secret conclaves plotting the overthrow of the government," he exclaimed. "Show me who has fired upon our flag, has given instructions to take our forts, and our custom houses, our arsenals, and our dock yards, and I will show you a traitor!"

The excitement in the galleries could no longer be suppressed. A faint cheer in one gallery was taken up in the others and ended in a tremendous outburst of cheers. J. B. Grinnell of Iowa led in three cheers for the Union and three cheers for Andrew Johnson of Tennessee.[8] Southern Senators demanded that the galleries be cleared; threats of arrest came from the Chair; a spectator swung his hat and shouted: "Arrest and be damned!"

Johnson resumed: "Were I the President of the United States, I would do as Thomas Jefferson did in 1806 with Aaron Burr, who was charged with treason. I would have them arrested and tried for treason; and if convicted, by the Eternal God, I would see that they suffer the penalty of the law at the hands of the executioner."

About that time a friend in Springfield, Illinois, informed the Tennessean that many visitors to Lincoln were urging Johnson for the Cabinet, and he quoted the President-elect as having replied to one such solicitation: "Gentleman, I have no idea Mr. Johnson would accept such a position. His course is truly noble, but just as [is] to be expected from a man possessing such a heart as his." E. Littell of Boston, publisher of the *Living Age*, wrote to Johnson: "It is generally acknowledged that *you* have saved the Border States from joining the traitors. How the whole Northern people would have rejoiced if you had taken a seat in Mr. L's Cabinet!"

During these tense days and nights in Congress, there had been exciting scenes in most of the Southern States. Isham G. Harris, Governor of Tennessee, was a determined secessionist, but the people were not disposed to follow his lead. In January the legislature ordered an election as to whether a convention should be called to determine if Tennessee secede or not. On February 9, 1861, this question was submitted to the people at the polls. East Tennessee Unionists threw prudence to the winds and stumped the State in defense of the permanence of the nation. Tennesseans rejected the secession project by an unmistakable vote.

Not content with the result of the referendum, Governor Harris soon called another session of the legislature, which docilely summoned a constitutional convention, and provided for a popular vote to ratify or reject the expected secession ordinance. In April, after Sumter and Lincoln's call for troops, the impatient Harris, unwilling to await the people's verdict at the ballot box, entered into a "Military League" with the Confederate Government, called for 55,000 men for the Southern armies and levied heavy taxes to pay Tennessee's cost of war.[9] Southern troops on their way to Virginia streamed through the State. Expression of Union sentiment became dangerous. Men were whipped, shot and hanged.

Early in April, Johnson determined to return to Tennessee to take part in the new election. Virginia had seceded and Confederate pickets were at the south end of the Long Bridge. At Alexandria he found a great crowd wildly cheering Wigfall of Texas, who had boarded the same train and was being cheered at nearly every station. Johnson sat by a slender lad who later described him as a big, broad-shouldered, stumpy man, with short legs.[10] Some time after dark when the train reached Lynchburg, the largest crowd yet gathered was awaiting it, many men bearing torches. Here there were no cheers for Wigfall, but cries of "Hang the traitor!" "Here's the rope!" "Bring him out!" A maddened mob swirled about the car. Suddenly the door opened, a man rushed down the aisle and, leaning over the boy, said to his seat-mate, "Are you Andy Johnson?" Upon an affirmative reply, the stranger said, "Well, I want to pull your nose!" and made a reach for Johnson's face. Johnson jumped to his feet and repelled his assailant. A scuffle followed.

Then Wigfall entered and asked Johnson to go out to the platform with him. After the Texan secured silence and urged the mob to give Johnson a hearing, the latter began his speech by saying, "I am a Union man!" He held them spellbound until the train departed, and, as it pulled out, his last words were, "I am a Union man!" But the last words from the crowd were, "Hang him!"

At Bristol a similar incident occurred. Some of the Confederates who had learned that Johnson was about to pass through that city determined to lynch the Unionist Senator. A mob hurried to the station. When the train arrived, a young Confederate officer named Greenwood ordered the engineer to pull on to Jonesboro immediately, without making the usual stop at Bristol. It was not a moment too soon, for the mob had already surrounded Johnson's car and was preparing to carry out its plan. The officer stated that his instructions to save Johnson from the mob had come from Jefferson Davis, at Richmond.[11]

On reaching home, Johnson immediately took the stump. There was a loyal band of East Tennessee leaders—Johnson, T. A. R. Nelson, an eloquent Knoxville Whig; "Parson" Brownlow, with his equipment of sarcasm, invective and scorn; Horace Maynard, the Narragansett Indian, one of the most eloquent men who ever debated in Tennessee; Oliver P. Temple and others of less note. These men presented the cause of the Union throughout East Tennessee. In the middle and western grand divisions, Harris' troops made it dangerous to advocate the Union cause.

Johnson's and Nelson's joint speaking tour was notable. Nelson spoke to the Whigs and Johnson to the Democrats in nearly every county in East Tennessee. The crowds, numbering thousands, were powerfully swayed by their force and patriotism.[12] Threats of violence were plentiful. Before they came to Kingsport, "awful threats" were made against them.[13] They spoke in the church, where Johnson took out his pistol, placed it on the pulpit, covered it with his handkerchief and made his usual address. With Confederate bayonets at the polls in most of the state and Secession a *fait accompli*, the result of this election was not in doubt. But East Tennessee voted down Disunion by a majority of 19,141, only a little less than the number by which it had voted it down in February.

The Greene County results were illuminating. In 1860 the plurality of Breckinridge, whom Johnson had supported, had been 1,006 votes. In June, 1861, the Union majority was 1,947![14] In the supreme hour of the nation's peril, Johnson had pleaded for his country with a passionate earnestness that moved men's hearts as he had never moved them before. The loyalty of East Tennessee to the Union is but another evidence of Johnson's dominating power over the minds of his homefolks. "The transfer of allegiance of the Democrats from the party of their love . . . to a union with the Whigs whom they hated, and infinitely worse, to a union with Free-Soilers and Abolitionists, whom they both feared and abhorred, affords an example of devotion and confidence without parallel."

Johnson's stalwart Union stand led the Secession authorities at Nashville to determine, not to arrest him, but to have him summarily shot. W. G. Brownlow was similarly to be disposed of. A high-placed Nashville friend of Johnson came to Knoxville to apprise him of his danger, but found Brownlow, who, on June 3, wrote Blackstone McDannel, at Greeneville to turn Johnson "through Kentucky to Washington, at once. . . . There is no attempt at sensation, and there is no humbug in it. . . . He will be assassinated in less than ten days, if he does not get out of the way."

Thus warned, and at the earnest urging of his family and friends, Johnson determined to leave for the North. On June 14, in open daylight, accompanied by a few friends, he left home, traveling overland by the public road. A militia general issued a call to arrest Johnson as a traitor, but not a man responded. The Senator passed quietly on, and reached Cumberland Gap. In Kentucky he was safe.[15]

In Washington again, Johnson plunged at once into the work of the war. On July 26 he offered a resolution in the Senate as to the causes and purposes of the war. This, it recited, had been forced on the country by the disunionists; none the less, Congress, "banishing all feeling of passion or resentment," would remember only "its duty to the whole country." The war was not being prosecuted "in any spirit of oppression, nor for any purpose of conquest or subjugation," nor for the purpose of interfering with the rights of established institutions of the South. The nation was at war "to defend and maintain the supremacy of the Constitution" and "to preserve the Union, with all the dignity, equality and rights of the several States unimpaired. . . . As soon as these objects are accomplished, the war ought to cease." This was adopted by a vote of thirty to five. John J. Crittenden, now in the lower House, there offered an almost identical resolution. By these resolutions, the Union purposes in the war were formally and magnanimously declared. In the House, Thad Stevens refrained from voting; in the Senate, the magnificent Sumner also refused to vote.

Throughout the fall of 1861 and the spring of 1862, Senator Johnson, bereft of a State, kept pressing upon Lincoln, Cameron, McClellan and any important Union officer whose ear he could reach, the story of the hardships and privations of the tens of thousands of loyal citizens in East Tennessee. Lincoln made valiant efforts to move Buell and McClellan to protect them, but was openly disobeyed. East Tennessee remained largely in Southern hands until 1864.

In Middle Tennessee, Grant's capture of Forts Henry and Donelson in the winter forced the Confederacy to evacuate Nashville late in February, 1862. The Southern troops retreated almost to the line of the Cumberlands. Rejoicing at this first practical gain of the war, Lincoln began to think of the restoration of civil government. Soon afterwards, he asked Johnson to leave his seat in the Senate, return to Tennessee and attempt to reestablish loyal civil government there, with restoration of federal relations as speedily as possible. The latter consented, and on March 4, 1862, the President nominated and the Senate confirmed Andrew Johnson as Military Governor of Tennessee, with the rank of Brigadier General.

Stanton's letter of appointment conferred on him "authority to exercise and perform, within the limits of that State, all and singular, the powers, duties and functions pertaining to the office of Military Governor (including the power to establish all necessary officers and tribunals, and suspend the writ of *habeas corpus*) during the pleasure of the President, or until the loyal inhabitants of that State shall organize a civil government in conformity with the Constitution of the United States."

When it became known in Confederate Tennessee that Andrew Johnson was coming to Nashville to be Military Governor of the State, the fury of the State's secessionists descended upon his head. It seemed to them infamous that this "vile wretch, this traitor to the State," should thus become the instrument of dragooning them back into a Federal Union they despised. Johnson's mail teemed with letters of threats and insults. "Go it, Andy," read one such. "This is your day, But while you are going so high you must not For get that evry dog has his day And the day is not far advanse when you will have your Just day, and that day cannot come untill you are tared and fethered and burnt. . . ."

Guerrillas plotted to ambush his train and Bragg authorized an elaborate scheme to kidnap the new Military Governor on his way from Louisville to Nashville. When Johnson arrived at Louisville, he found a letter from General Buell.[16]

"You must not expect," it said, "to be received with enthusiasm, but rather the reverse, and I would suggest to you to enter without any display."

On March 12 Johnson reached Nashville and entered "the very furnace of treason."[16] Governor Harris reëstablished his government at Memphis, Bragg's army was no further away than Murfreesboro, forty miles southeast, and Nashville's population was Confederate to the core.

Johnson had not been long established at Nashville before the Confederates in East Tennessee adopted harsher measures toward his family. General E. Kirby Smith's provost marshal sent a note to Mrs. Johnson "to respectfully require that you and your family pass beyond the Confederate States' line (through Nashville if you please) in thirty-six hours from this date." She responded that she could not comply. A little later, Robert Johnson, who had gone to Cumberland Gap seeking news about his mother and sister, telegraphed his father: "Be on your guard about assassination. Three of Morgan's men left Knoxville on Tuesday for that purpose." Johnson wrote his dear Eliza that he felt like giving up in despair, "but we must hold out to the end."

On March 18 the Military Governor issued a proclamation. "The state government has disappeared," it recited; "the executive has abdicated, the legislature has dissolved, the judiciary is in abeyance. The great Ship of State . . . has been suddenly abandoned by its officers and mutinous crew." But the Federal Government, which had guaranteed a republican form of government to every State, was conscious of its obligation. As a preliminary, it had made him Military Governor. He would extend the protection of the government to all the people; "all their rights will be duly respected, and their wrongs redressed when made known." Loyal Unionists would be honored, while the erring and misguided would be welcomed on their return. "Intelligent and conscious treason in high places" would be punished, but to others, complete amnesty was offered, if only they would again yield themselves "peaceful citizens to the just supremacy of the laws."

Passions were still too excited, however, for this appeal to carry much weight. The Nashville municipal authorities were belligerently Southern. When the Military Governor ordered them to take an oath of allegiance to the United States, they "respectfully asked to be excused." Johnson promptly ousted them. This stirred Confederate indignation, but gained warm approval in the North.

Johnson found that Confederate sermons were being preached from nearly every pulpit in Nashville. The most obnoxious speakers were straightway arrested, and again the Military Governor was charged with tyranny. But he had a good defense. In two cases, "they were not arrested as ministers of the Gospel or chaplains, but as traitors inculcating treasonable doctrine." "The assumed ministers of Christ," he wrote, "have done more to poison and corrupt the female mind of this community than all others, in fact changing their entire character from that of women and ladies to fanatics and fiends. One of those very ministers, in leaving here for Louisville, told those who were collected to see him off: 'Don't forget your God, Jeff Davis and the Southern Confederacy.'"

After the Battle of Shiloh, Union sentiment grew and Johnson's reorganization proceeded apace. Rich secessionists began to take the amnesty oath, and Unionists to take fresh heart. Nashville became a garrison city. By April 30, Ex-Governor William B. Campbell, Colonel William H. Polk, brother of the former President, Bailie Peyton, William B. Stokes and others met with the Governor to plan Tennessee's restoration to the Union.[17]

The Governor first believed he possessed constitutional power to appoint two senators from Tennessee. Horace Maynard, who, without challenge, in Washington represented the Second Tennessee District in the House of Representatives, broached the subject to Lincoln, Stanton and others, and wrote Johnson that "the President was in favor of the power being exercised; that it existed he expressed no doubt. The Secretary of War, with his usual fanatical tone, not only asserted the power, but developed the means of its exercise." But Johnson determined not to exercise it.[18]

He soon turned his attention to reprisals for Confederate mistreatment of East Tennessee Unionists. On June 5 he telegraphed Lincoln that he had that day "taken steps to arrest seventy vile Secessionists in this vicinity and offer them in exchange" for seventy East Tennesseans then in prison at Mobile, many of whom he declared were being treated "with more cruelty than wild beasts of the forest." . . . He continued: "Our people must be redeemed and if they refuse to exchange, I will at once send them South at their own expense and leave them beyond our lines, on condition that, if they return, . . . they shall be treated as spies. It is no punishment now to send Secessionists North. In most instances, they would rather go to the Infernal regions than to be sent South."

Through Stanton, Lincoln approved this seizure of hostages. Maynard wrote the Military Governor that the President had expressed himself "gratified in the highest degree that you do not let them raise any 'nigger' issues to bother him. . . . Your administration so far has commanded the approval, I might add the admiration, of the whole country." In a letter asking Johnson to indorse him, as an aid in his Congressional campaign, Schuyler Colfax wrote that "the President has told me twice that, while he has had troublesome questions to settle from other military governors and officers, as in North Carolina, New Orleans and so forth, 'Andy Johnson has never embarrassed me in the slightest degree.' You enjoy his fullest confidence, as you so richly deserve."[19]

In May and June Johnson and the Union leaders stumped Middle Tennessee. On May 12 the delegates at a Nashville meeting "seemed electrified" by Johnson's presence. On May 24 he spoke at Murfreesboro to an audience that was a queer mixture of bluecoats and "butternuts." At first hostile, these former secessionists warmed up as Johnson proceeded, and applauded with cries of "Good for Andy!"

These meetings, which were profoundly affecting the sentiment of Middle Tennessee, had to be suspended in July, when Forrest's Cavalry, the advance guard of Bragg's army, swept into the middle of the State. By mid-August, Nashville was filled with refugees. On September 5 Bragg recaptured Murfreesboro, and the next day Buell announced that he would abandon Nashville.

Granville Moody, the famous Methodist evangelist and anti-slavery orator, entered Nashville the day that Buell had notified Johnson of his purpose. When the preacher called at the Capitol, he inquired, "How are matters going, Governor?"

"Going? Moody, we are sold. Buell has resolved to evacuate the city. He called on me this morning, requesting me to leave also."

Moody replied that he would stay there with Johnson. "I have faith in God that he will deliver us from falling into the hands of the enemy."

"I am glad to hear you talk of faith in God," Johnson rejoined. "Moody, can you pray?"

In a moment the Governor and the Evangelist were both on their knees, with their backs toward each other. Moody began to pray with great fervor, while Amens came with greater and greater rapidity from his fellow suppliant. Soon the Governor had crept on his knees across the room and, throwing his arms around the preacher, cried out vehemently, "Amen! Amen! God hear Moody's prayer."

Then both men arose. "Moody, I feel better," said the Governor. "I believe that God Almighty sent you here, and that Nashville will be saved. That prayer has been answered. I feel it. I know it. Buell can go. I stay right here."

In a calmer mood, he added: "Moody, I don't want you to think that I have become religious because I asked you to pray, but, Moody, there is one thing that I do believe: I believe in Almighty God; and I also believe the Bible; and I say, *I'll be damned if Nashville shall be surrendered!*"[20]

Nor was it surrendered. Failing to win Buell over, Johnson kept the wires hot to Lincoln at Washington and forced him to interpose. General Thomas was instructed to hold the city at all cost.

By late September the siege was under way. Bragg's main army had swept on into Kentucky, leaving a beleaguering force behind. For two months Nashville was cut off from the world. The garrison was in a frenzy of activity preparing against the assault. Rations were getting scarce. The Governor's "wise and energetic measures . . . inspired courage and confidence among Union men."[21]

During all the struggle, Johnson remained unimpressed with the pomp of war. In the days of bloodiest battle, his heart yearned for the return of peace. Late in October, when Rosecrans had been appointed to command, and reinforcement and relief were at hand, came a relaxation of strain. Thereupon Captain Morton, chief engineer of the Army of the Ohio, began to assign names to the hastily constructed fortifications in and around the city. The bastion on Capitol Hill he called "Fort Andrew Johnson," provoking from the Governor an illuminating private letter.[22]

While thankfully acknowledging the compliment, Johnson doubted the propriety of having his name so honored, and "as a citizen and public man" did not desire it. His adopted State had already accorded him "every honor that a State can confer upon one of her citizens, and in this the measure of my ambition has now been filled." He continued:

> I certainly am not entitled to it for any military service or prowess, and such compliments should be accorded only to those who are entitled to them. I had rather an inquiring public would ask why my name was *not* given, than to ask why it was. It is not safe at all times, and in all instances, to name children, cities, forts, after the living, for the bestowal is often regretted and repented. . . .
>
> It may be that in the shock of battle some devoted one, now unknown, may yet pour out his heart's blood upon the massive altar stones of our Capitol, as a libation to the sacred cause of Liberty and Union, and history will proclaim *that* man, officer or private, entitled to the honor which you have assigned me. . . .
>
> War is not the natural element of my mind. I have always endeavored to cultivate the arts of peace, and have therefore not pursued a military life. For my part, I would rather wear upon my garment the dust of the field and the dinge of the shop as badges of the pursuits of peace, than all the insignia of honorable and glorious war.
>
> My heart would swell with joy to see the sword and the bayonet laid aside, and the soldier restored to his peaceful associations. Heaven grant that ere long peace and good will may be restored to a misguided and divided people. . . . I feel more than flattered at the compliment conferred, but a consciousness of duty performed is my present remuneration, and the only reward I ask in the future is the lowly inscription of my name with those who loved and toiled for the people.

On November 14 Rosecrans finally arrived up the Cumberland with relief, and Nashville was safe. Johnson's courage and energy had won him the admiration of all who watched him. Glenn, the New York *Herald's* correspondent, who had observed it all, paid voluntary tribute. "From first to last," he said, "Governor Johnson was a model of abstinence. He never played cards for amusement or gain. He never indulged in drink on any single occasion to a greater extent than perhaps a clergyman would at a sacrament, and as for the smaller vices, he was free from them all."

With Buell's replacement by Rosecrans came a new policy in the treatment of the people of Tennessee. Hitherto Johnson and the military authorities had proceeded on the theory that the people of the reoccupied territory had not had their hearts in secession, but had been either misled or dragooned. After a six months' trial of a lenient policy based on this belief, Johnson reluctantly concluded he had been wrong, and Rosecrans felt the same way. Thenceforward, Johnson was determined to reconstruct Tennessee with only "unconditionally loyal Union men."

The war Governor was sorely tried by the army commanders and their staffs.[23] The conduct of civil government in the midst of military rule was one of immense difficulty. The generals were generally unmindful of political aspects, with which Johnson was particularly concerned, and he was not sufficiently mindful of strategic considerations. Constant friction ensued.[24]

The correspondence of the Military Governor was laden with complaints against one Colonel Truesdail, a "Rosecrans' pet," whose high-handed confiscations of property rendered him objectionable. "From all I know personally and what I have learned from others," Johnson wrote to an inquirer in Cincinnati, "I am well satisfied in my own mind that he is a base and unmitigated Jesuitical parasite. . . . I have refused and rejected the application for the release of fifty convicts, confined in the cells of our State prison, who are better and more worthy men than he is."

Johnson complained to Washington and received support, Halleck instructed Rosecrans that the position of Military Governor had been created specifically to mitigate the evils of a purely army control. "The army," wrote Halleck, "was not to interfere with the loyal officials of the state government, except in cases of urgent and pressing necessity."[25] To Johnson it seemed that the military was determined to undo everything he sought to do to restore civil rule and at a time when he had his hands full of delicate and difficult political problems.

In the spring of 1863 a rumor came to President Lincoln's ears that Johnson was contemplating raising negro troops.

This met with the warm approval of the harassed Chief Executive and on March 26, he sent Johnson a note of encouragement.[26]

"I am told," Lincoln wrote, "you have at least *thought* of raising a negro military force. In my opinion the country now needs no specific thing so much as some man of your ability and position, to go to this work. When I speak of your position, I mean that of an eminent citizen of a slave State, and himself a slave holder.

"The colored population is the great *available* and yet *unavailed-of*, force for restoring the Union," he continued. "The bare sight of fifty thousand armed and drilled black soldiers on the banks of the Mississippi, would end the rebellion at once. And who doubts that we can present that sight, if we but take hold in earnest? If you *have* been thinking of it, please do not dismiss the thought." However, despite Lincoln's approval, Johnson was able to do little to develop this plan.

One of his constant concerns was to build up Union sentiment by holding elections, and in this, too, he had the urgent support of President Lincoln. In October, 1862, the President had sent commissioners to Louisiana, Arkansas and Tennessee, to stimulate sentiment favoring the holding of congressional and state elections. The Military Governors of these States were instructed "in all available ways" to give the people "a chance to express their wishes at these elections." So far as convenient, the forms of law should be followed, but the main thing was "to get the expression of the largest number of people possible."[27] Johnson called for an election for December 29, but the effort proved abortive.

Tennessee Unionism numbered in its ranks tens of thousands of Old Line Whigs, and even as a war measure, the Emancipation Proclamation irritated and alienated a large part of this group, who thereupon became obstructionists to the Lincoln-Johnson policy in the State.

Furthermore, the political success of restoration depended on the military status. During the greater part of 1863, the Federal forces were pushing forward. In January, after the battle of Murfreesboro, Bragg retreated almost to the Cumberlands. During the summer, Rosecrans outflanked him and Bragg retreated to Chattanooga. As soon as he heard of Bragg's evacuating Chattanooga, Lincoln, overjoyed, telegraphed Johnson: "All Tennessee is now clear of armed insurrectionists. You need not be reminded that it is the nick of time for reinaugurating the loyal state government. Not a moment should be lost." But the President did not lose sight of the need to have loyal men do the inaugurating. The enemies of the Union must not be put in the saddle; this would make the whole struggle "profitless to both State and Union." Johnson must exclude all but men who "can be trusted for the Union."[28]

The fair promise came to naught. Bragg turned on Rosecrans on the field of Chickamauga, routed him and but for Thomas, would have demolished the Federal forces. The siege of Chattanooga, Longstreet's expedition into East Tennessee and the siege of Knoxville followed. Johnson's plans were again held up until the Battle of Chattanooga in November and Sherman's relief of Knoxville finally completed the Federal occupation of Tennessee. In 1864, Johnson was enabled to set to work in earnest to carry out Lincoln's dear desires.

His course politically in 1863 had caused great opposition from the Conservatives and his perseverance in it was due to the fact that he was carrying out President Lincoln's direct wish. In the spring of 1864, Johnson persisted, grim and relentless, in his determination to entrust the task only to faithful Union men. A Union League was organized that claimed to represent 60,000 votes, a broad enough base to sustain a successful election.[29] The Governor arranged for a large meeting at Nashville on January 21, and addressed it in a speech of great power and force.

Tennessee had never been out of the Union, said the War Governor, its federal functions had merely been paralyzed. The President now proposed to restore to the people the Republican form of government. There must be a beginning somewhere, and the people who should take part in it must be loyal. Those engaged in the Rebellion had by their own act, expatriated themselves and should not take part. This, however, was easy to say and hard to enforce. Some standard of inclusion and exclusion must be set up. There was a difference between the enjoyment of pardon for misdeeds by the president's amnesty and the right to take part in the reorganization of the State. Hence the oath he was about to prescribe was vital.

As to the negro, "the rebels commenced the destruction of the government for the preservation of slavery, and the government, . . . in the preservation of its own existence, has put slavery down justly and rightfully." In Tennessee, in fact, the negroes are emancipated. The only remaining question is to assign the negro "his new relation to society." He would be governed by the same laws and compelled to fall back upon his own resources as were all other human beings. "Political freedom means the liberty to work and at the same time enjoy the products of one's labor. If he [the negro] can rise by his own energies, in the name of God, let him rise!"

The meeting indorsed the Governor, and messages from throughout the State praised his plan.[30] On January 26, 1864, he issued a proclamation for an election on the first Saturday in March. The would-be voter must solemnly swear henceforth to support the Constitution and to defend it against assaults, and must take oath henceforth to be and conduct himself as "a true and faithful citizen of the United States."

In addition—this was the clause which chafed—he must swear "that I ardently desire the suppression of the present insurrections and rebellion against the government of the United States, and the success of its armies, and the defeat of all those who oppose them," and that the Constitution "be speedily and permanently established and enforced over all the the people," and that he would "hereafter aid and assist all loyal people in the accomplishment of all these results."[31]

It is not difficult to see why ex-rebels choked over these words. They could take the oath only by a complete change of heart or by black perjury. Many Conservative Unionists felt Johnson had gone too far. Some carried their wrath to Washington, but President Lincoln gave them cold comfort. To one inquirer he replied "You had better stand by Governor Johnson's plan; otherwise, you will have conflict and confusion."[32] A little later he wrote that he had "seen and examined Johnson's Proclamation," and was "entirely satisfied with his plan."[33] But the ex-secessionists and the Union Conservatives continued their opposition. On February 28, the Nashville *Press* openly advocated taking the oath without respecting it. Confederate leaders, too, advised this course. The cavalry leader Richardson exhorted, "Take any oath that Federals may prescribe, but . . . control the election at all hazards."

As a result the election on March 5 was almost "a serious farce." Although the total vote was between forty and fifty thousand, the numbers cited do not reflect the election conditions. In many counties, no election was held. Ultra-Unionists were indignant at having their loyalty questioned by being required to take the oath.[34] Johnson's prestige was weakened but his resolution was only strengthened by the storm which raged around his head. He concluded that so long as slavery was not constitutionally abolished in Tennessee, conditions would not improve, and he moved directly for a Constitutional Convention.

A few days after the Battle of Resaca, Benjamin C. Truman, a lieutenant of Johnson, returned to Nashville from the Georgia front and ran into an old newspaper friend whom he had not seen in several years. The latter disclosed to Truman that he was in Nashville as a volunteer aide to General Dan Sickles, whom the President had sent to Nashville "on an important mission."

"He is coming down here to look after Johnson," Truman's friend continued, "to see what he is doing. To look into his habits. The President wants Johnson on the ticket with him if his habits will permit; and the General has been sent here to investigate."

It was eleven at night, but Truman hurried to the Military Governor's house, awakened him and repeated his conversation. Johnson sat bolt upright in his bed. "I want you to leave for Washington tomorrow," he instructed Truman. "Go direct to Colonel Forney and repeat to him what you have said to me and ask him to look out for my interests." Truman left the next morning.[35]

None the less, Johnson did not divert his attention from the restoration of Tennessee to his vice presidential prospects.[36] In April, he reassembled the East Tennessee convention of 1861. But many of the leaders were Conservatives whose opinions had not grown with the war. After acrimonious debate, the convention yielded a majority only on the question of adjournment.

About this time a call went out for the election of Tennessee delegates to the coming Baltimore Convention. The proceedings were irregular, but little else could have been expected. At meetings throughout the state, resolutions were passed indorsing Johnson's course. At assemblies at Nashville, Knoxville and Chattanooga, the nomination of Lincoln for President and Johnson for Vice President, was demanded. The delegates thus selected, an able and thoroughly loyal group, departed forthwith by way of Kentucky and Ohio for the great gathering of patriots and postmasters in process of assembling at Baltimore.

THE night when the news reached Nashville that Andrew Johnson had been placed on the ticket with Lincoln, his enthusiastic friends turned out to accord him an old-fashioned, jubilating serenade. A huge throng gathered in front of the Capitol, with brass bands playing patriotic airs. The candidate for Vice President stepped out upon the portico, to be greeted with thunderous applause. Let us pause to note what manner of man this was, so loyally acclaimed.

"He says he is in every respect a *sound* man," an insurance examiner reported in April, 1865, thus indorsing Johnson's own belief.[1] The Tailor-Statesman was of medium height, his compactly shaped figure giving a hint of sinew, strength and power. Ben Truman, his secretary, thought Johnson "matchlesssly perfect in figure." He always held himself erect, his fine shoulders thrown back. His chest was broad and deep. A large but not unshapely neck sustained a massive, well formed head,[2] which so impressed Charles Dickens that he wrote to his son that Johnson's head was splendidly shaped, and that no judge of human nature could look upon Johnson and doubt that he was an extraordinary man. His skin was slightly swarthy, his hair dark and luxuriant; under the stress of the Presidency, it was to thin out to a silver gray.

The striking features of his countenance were his eyes, dark, deep-set, and piercing. Major Truman tells us that they were small, "black, sparkling, and absolutely beautiful." His forehead, a contemporary asserts, "was not exceptionally high, but very wide and perpendicular." Above his eyes were two "remarkable bumps or protuberances, swelling out from his brow."[3] He had a large nose, a large and mobile mouth and a firm chin. Colonel Crook, a White House attendant, says it was very square, jutted out at an obstinate angle and had a combative cleft in it.[4] His hands and feet were small.

He did not smile readily. "On his front," says George W. Jones, who loved him, "deliberation sat, and public care." But when he did smile—and it was chiefly with children—his face became marvelously attractive. One little boy who lunched at the White House with Johnson's grandson, remembered throughout a long life the President's dazzling, tender beautiful smile. A little girl attending a children's party at the White House remembered him as a very kindly man. "His face beamed," she said, "and his eyes smiled with the greatest affection."[5] While not stately, his appearance was easy and graceful. When he chose, Johnson could be delightful, and as he grew older, he became more and more so to his intimates.

Aside from politics, Johnson's only game was checkers, which he played "indifferently." In 1862 he told Truman he had never gone to the theater—he would rather study or work. He looked on all sorts of gambling as wrong. He liked circuses and minstrels but seldom attended such shows, for he "never had much time for frivolity."

And yet this was no backwoods bumpkin, no uncouth demagogue, but a man of distinction and of impressiveness. Probably at this very serenade, he wore his usual costume of black broadcloth frock coat and waistcoat, black doeskin trousers and high silk hat. He was scrupulously clean, almost dainty about his linen.

In demeanor he was not a blustering, Ben Butlerish sort of person, but was habitually calm and reserved. There was an uncanny magnetism about him—with a simple gesture he could sway the mind of the crowd. His voice was a magnificent physical organ—he could make himself heard in a whisper over great throngs. Indeed, he must have been an impressive figure as he stood on the Capitol portico, about to answer the thousands who loved him even in the heart of Secession Tennessee.

To this milling crowd, Johnson made what was virtually a speech of acceptance. "Slavery," he said, "is dead. It was not murdered by me. I told you long ago what the results would be if you endeavored to go out of the Union to save slavery. In trying to save slavery you killed it. . . ." He served notice that the man who gave his influence and his means to destroy the government should not participate in the reorganization of the State. The war continued "that treason might be put down and traitors punished." The traitor has forfeited his right to vote with loyal men, and should be subjected to a severe ordeal before restoration to citizenship.

Such was the general theme of this informal acceptance speech. In it, he took occasion to reaffirm his party allegiance. "I am a Democrat," he said, "in the strictest meaning of the term. I am for putting down the rebellion, because it is a war against democracy." He concluded with a ringing appeal in the best Johnsonian manner for all to pull together for the maintenance of the Union and the salvation of free government in the new world. "For myself," he ended, "I mean to stand by the government until the flag of the Union shall wave over every city, town, hilltop, and crossroads, in its full power and majesty."[6]

Although Johnson's mail was full of congratulations, the most scrupulous search has failed to disclose any record of messages of mutual congratulations on their nominations between Lincoln and Johnson. But we have evidence of Lincoln's cordial reception of the selection of his running mate. S. Newton Pettis, who wrote Johnson that he had been with the President ten minutes after the latter had learned of the choice of his running mate, proceeded to inform the latter of Lincoln's manifest satisfaction. Another correspondent, who had talked with Lincoln the evening after the convention, "was rejoiced to hear him speak as he did, of the perfect accord of feeling and sympathy upon public questions between yourself and himself, and his satisfaction at the nomination. . . ."

Seward told Judge Kellogg of Michigan: "Johnson is the best man we could have got on the ticket, for you and I may go back and un-say what we have said, but Johnson can't go back if he would. There is no way for the Union men of the Border States, but to go forward . . . !" A. P. Gorman, the Senate postmaster, quoted Governor Hicks of Maryland: "The country should be congratulated, instead of Johnson." Indeed, there were those who thought Johnson on the wrong end of the ticket. "God bless old Brownlow for his speech at Baltimore," wrote E. T. Carson of Cincinnati, "he did it. The only fault I have to find in the nominations is that they were not REVERSED. . . ." When George L. Stearns wrote from Boston: "If anything can reconcile me to the nomination of Abraham Lincoln, it is the association of your name on the same ticket," he but voiced Sumner's views.[7]

But the Baltimore outcome did not please many of the extreme elements. Both Ultra-Radicals and Ultra-Conservatives were chagrined. Attorney-General Bates, an outstanding member of the latter group, was greatly surprised and mortified. Though Lincoln had been nominated, it was "in a manner and with attending circumstances as if the object were to de-

feat their own nomination. They were all (nearly) instructed
to vote for Mr. Lincoln, but many of them hated to do it, and
only kept the word of promise to the ear, doing their best to
break it to the hope."[8]   Adam Gurowski, on the other fringe
of the political world, was equally savage in his expressions.
"Mr. Lincoln is nominated. But what a chill runs through the
best men! . . . Terrible is the dilemma of the true men and
patriots; the issues awful, and black despair at the end of
both of them. To swallow a Lincoln, dissolved in Seward and
Blair, to try to save the country with that not heavenly compound, or to facilitate the dark, humanity destroying victory
of the Democrats."[9]   On June 11 Ben Butler wrote a hurried
note to his wife: "Hurrah for Lincoln and Johnson! That's the
ticket! This country has more vitality than any other on
earth if it can stand this sort of administration for another
four years."[10]

In July Johnson began to be plagued with requests to go
North to speak. From Indiana came pressing demands. "This
State will be fiercely contested," A. J. Fletcher of Evansville,
wrote him on July 30. "The result, from present appearances,
is doubtful." Vallandigham was to canvass Indiana and
Fletcher held that it was "the aim of these Northern traitors
to make Indiana the South Carolina of the Northwest." Governor Johnson must speak at several points in Indiana, if that
State was to be saved.[11]

"I do believe," wrote John B. DeFrees, superintendent of
Public Printing at Washington, "you can do more good in
Indiana than any other dozen men." Schuyler Colfax urged
that the October elections would settle the presidential election
as they had done in '56 and '60, and that Indiana was far the
hardest of the three States to carry. "No one man living can
do us more good than you," he continued, offering to pay Johnson's expenses on the trip.[12]   J. W. Wright, the Indiana Union
Committee chairman, kept up a constant stream of telegraphic
appeals.

At first Johnson declined these invitations, writing letters
that might be published to aid the campaign. In response to
one of Wright's appeals, he observed shrewdly that "a separation of the South from the North will only be the entering
wedge to other divisions, resulting in an intermissable [sic]
Civil War." This argument was then used with great effect
throughout the Central West.[13]   But Wright would not be

satisfied with letters, and finally, in September, the Union candidate for Vice President made a swing around Indiana with great success.

The Illinois chairman wrote in late June asking for a few speeches in Southern and Central Illinois, with the warning that "the vote will be a very close one in our State." Robert G. Ingersoll wanted Johnson to speak at a large Union mass meeting at Peoria. "Your name would secure an additional attendance of at least 20,000," Ingersoll urged. "The name of Andrew Johnson has become a household word all over the great West." The Ohio State Central Executive Committee wanted him to speak in that State a week or two following the Democratic convention.

On September 11, 1864, Henry J. Raymond, chairman of the Union National Committee, asked if it would not be possible for Johnson to make a trip through the North and East. "I think that in Ohio, Pennsylvania, and New York, your presence would be especially useful," he wrote. "Your position, reputation, and ability continue to give great weight and influence to your words." Raymond added encouragingly that "everything just now looks well."[14]

Through most of these exciting political calls, Johnson stayed in Nashville and attended to his work. His correspondence of this period shows him to have been a man of indefatigable energy, of scrupulous attention to detail, of wide interests and, one learns with surprise, of great heart. While Johnson's letters show no evidence of any wirepulling with Lincoln on his own behalf, either before or after his nomination, he was in constant telegraphic communication with the President in matters of promotion for others, of the pacification of Tennessee, and in appeals for Lincoln's clemency to be extended to soldier boys sentenced to be shot.

It was not without reason that the Middle Western politicians had been beseeching Andrew Johnson to come into their States and speak, for the political firmament was becoming overcast. There were dissensions in the Cabinet and Lincoln had only the grudging support of a divided party. The military situation, too, which in June had seemed so promising, turned dark again in July. Chase had added to the President's perplexities by further pettiness. The Secretary of the Treasury stubbornly refused to help Lincoln out of a difficulty with patronage, and seemed to feel that this provided another occasion for registering a triumph over the President by resigning. To Chase's chagrin, Lincoln accepted the resignation and brought Chase's house of cards tumbling down upon his head. This resignation gave relief rather than disappointment to the country. Welles looked upon it as a blessing—Chase "had been a load of late," disappointed, dissatisfied, captious and uncertain, favoring the faultfinders and encouraging opposition to the President.[15]

Soon after the nominations, the controversy between Congress and the President over Reconstruction came to a head. On December 8, 1863, President Lincoln had offered a general pardon to all Confederates who would lay down their arms and return to their obedience to the laws. In this he embodied his initial plan for restoration: Whenever in any one of the subdued States, a number of persons equalling one-tenth of the voters in the 1860 presidential election, who were qualified voters under the 1860 laws should reëstablish a state government republican in form and not contravening the oath under the Amnesty Proclamation, it would be recognized as the state government.[16]

The President's message put the matter before Congress. On December 15, Thad Stevens reported a special resolution to refer as much of Lincoln's message as related to the treatment of "rebellious States" to a special committee. Henry Winter Davis offered a substitute which Stevens accepted, Davis being made chairman of the committee thus authorized. On February 15, the Maryland Radical introduced his bill; on March 22 it came up for final reading and debate, and on May 4 it passed the House by a vote of seventy-three to fifty-nine.

The measure authorized the President to name, for each State declared in rebellion, a provisional governor to conduct civil administration until a civil government existed therein and was recognized. When armed resistance had been suppressed, the governor should direct the Federal marshal to enroll all white male citizens of the United States. Whenever a majority of these took the oath, the governor should invite loyal people of the State to elect a convention to reëstablish state government.

These conventions must insert in their new state constitutions these provisions:

First: No person who had held or exercised any office, civil or military, except offices merely ministerial and military offices below colonel, State or Confederate, under the usurping power, shall vote for or be a member of the Legislature, or Governor.

Second: Involuntary servitude is forever prohibited, and the freedom of all persons is guaranteed in said State.

Third: No debt, State or Confederate, created by or under the sanction of the usurping power, shall be recognized or paid by the State.

In the Senate, Ben Wade promptly took this measure under his especial care, but it did not come up until July 1. Nearly all the Radicals supported it. As amended, it passed the Senate on July 1, twenty-six to three. The next day, the Senate receded in its amendments, agreed to the House bill, and the measure was then sent to the President.

On the morning of July 4, the date on which Congress was to adjourn, Lincoln had come to the Capitol and was in the President's room, signing bills as they were brought before him. When the Wade-Davis bill appeared, he glanced at it and laid it aside. Several intense Radicals hovered about it in a state of intense anxiety. At length Zach Chandler broke the silence and asked Lincoln if he intended to sign it. He replied that it had been placed before him just a few moments before Congress adjourned and was a matter of too much importance to be "swallowed" in that way.

Chandler persisted until Lincoln rebuked him, saying that he doubted the authority of Congress to act thus, and the Senator went out in high dudgeon. Lincoln declared to the Members of the Cabinet seated about him: "I do not see how any of us now can deny and contradict what we have always said, that Congress has no constitutional power over slavery in the States." He resolutely refused to sign the bill. In his carriage on the way back to the White House, he discussed the Radical threats. "I do not doubt that they can do harm," he said. "They have never been friendly to me. At all events, I must keep some consciousness of being somewhere near right."[17]

On July 8 the President issued a proclamation about the bill he had allowed to die. He was unprepared "by the formal approval of this bill," he said, "to be inflexibly committed to any single plan of restoration." He was also unprepared to declare that the free state constitutions and governments already adopted and installed in Arkansas and Louisiana should be set aside. He profoundly hoped and expected that a constitutional amendment abolishing slavery throughout the nation might be adopted. None the less, he felt that the Wade-Davis method was "one very proper plan for the loyal people of any State choosing to adopt it," and was prepared to aid any State which wished to employ it.

The Radicals were enraged at this proclamation. Wade and Davis hastened to issue a manifesto against the President, the bitterest attack made upon him during his presidential career. Published prominently in Greeley's *Tribune* on August 5, it charged that Lincoln had been moved by the lowest personal motives and termed his action a "studied outrage on the legislative authority of the people." It warned the President "that the authority of Congress is paramount and must be respected; . . . and if he wishes our support, . . . to obey and execute, not make the laws—to suppress by arms armed rebellion, and leave political reorganization to Congress."[18]

In July and August the country was further agitated by the ill-starred Niagara Falls Peace Conference. On July 7 Horace Greeley wrote the President that he had information that two ambassadors of "Davis & Company" were in Canada, ready to negotiate peace. The autocrat of the *Tribune* broadly hinted that the Administration was not anxious for peace, and insisted that "a frank offer by you to the insurgents of terms, which the impartial will say ought to be accepted, will, at the worst, prove an immense and sorely needed advantage to the national cause; it may save us from a Northern insurrection."[19]

Lincoln was embarrassed by this ingenuous injection, but with the sagacity of a master politician took steps to spike Greeley's guns. On July 9 he wrote to the cantankerous editor, appointing him his agent for the negotiation. Greeley objected strenuously, but the President wrote in reply: "I not only intend a sincere effort for peace, but I intend that you shall be a personal witness that it is made."[20] Greeley perforce went to Niagara Falls, fearful that he had been hoist by his own petard. Upon his arrival, it proved that the whole thing was a Confederate hoax.

Nevertheless, on July 18 Lincoln sent John Hay to Greeley with this letter:

> To Whom It May Concern: Any proposition
> which embraces the restoration of peace, the integrity
> of the whole Union, and the abandonment of slavery,
> and which comes by and with an authority that con-
> trols the armies now at war against the United
> States, will be received and considered by the execu-
> tive government of the United States, and will be met
> by liberal terms on other substantial and collateral
> points, and the bearer or bearers thereof shall have
> safe conduct both ways.

After this proposition, it became quickly apparent that the
Davis agents in Canada had no title of authority to open negotiations. Greeley was put completely in the wrong. He sought
to throw the blame on the President. Lincoln could have
cleared himself by publishing the correspondence, but he feared
that the news that the *Tribune* "was ready to sacrifice everything for peace," would prove "a disaster equal to the loss of a
great battle."[21]

Overshadowing even these political disturbances was disaster in the field. The North seemed about to lose its faith in
Grant. Cold Harbor and the Wilderness had been bloody
shambles. Hospitals back of the lines were choked with wounded.
The casualty lists first stunned the North and then evoked rage
and indignation. General Jubal Early made a spectacular
raid in force which brought Washington under the Confederate
guns. Welles hastily prepared a vessel to carry Lincoln down
the Potomac. Only the timely arrival of a corps from Grant's
army saved the capital. Greenbacks fell to forty cents on the
dollar. The North was overcast with gloom.

The inevitable political reaction ensued. On August 9
Greeley wrote that if the election were held the next day, New
York and Pennsylvania would go Democratic by 100,000 ma-
jority. About this time, Thurlow Weed told Lincoln that his
reelection was altogether impossible, and made overtures to the
New York Democrats, while old Francis Preston Blair made
the rounds of New York City pleading with Greeley, William
Cullen Bryant, James Gordon Bennett and even General Mc-
Clellan to support Lincoln, or, if that were impossible, not to
oppose him.[22]

The dissatisfied Radicals, both Republican and Democrat,
began to turn to Ben Butler, in spite of new evidence on the

part of that general of such incapacity in the field that a subordinate wrote piteously to Grant: "How you can place a man in command of two army corps who is as helpless as a child on the field of battle and as visionary as an opium eater in council?"[23]

Even after Butler's disastrous failure at Bermuda Hundreds in July, the Radicals agitated for both Fremont and Lincoln to withdraw in Butler's behalf. On July 4, Wade told a friend of Butler that "he believed you could be triumphantly elected president if you were nominated, and thinks there would be scarcely any trouble over that."[24] Congressman Ashley of Ohio wrote Butler that he had seen and talked confidentially with Thurlow Weed, Thomas Corwin, John W. Forney and others, and that all wished a national convention of War Democrats to nominate the General.[25] A New Yorker suggested the ticket: Benjamin F. Butler and Benjamin F. Wade, "two earnest men for country, humanity, God's truth and eternal justice."

Keenly apprehensive over the combined difficulties of battlefield, dissatisfied Radicals and militant Democrats, Lincoln was unwilling either to remove Butler from field command, although Grant requested it, or to reprimand the General for a highhanded suspension of civil law in Norfolk late in July, over which Governor Pierpoint of Virginia had protested vigorously. When Lincoln brought the matter before his Cabinet on July 19, the details caused Welles to exclaim that "while Butler has talents and capacity, the more I see of him, the greater is my distrust of his integrity."

None the less, Lincoln would not act. Following an ineffectual appeal to him, Bates wrote in his diary: "Alas, that I should live to see such abject fear, such stolid indifference to duty. . . . My heart is sick when I see the President shrinking from the correction of grave and heinous wrong because he is afraid 'General Butler will raise a hub-bub about it'! . . ." The next day Bates added: "The President knows what is right, as well as any man, and will be glad to *see it done*, but unhappily lacks the nerve to do it."[26]

In this dismal August Lincoln did a characteristic thing. He probably felt that he would be defeated in November. If his administration should lose at the polls, his duty was so clear to him that on August 23, he wrote down on a little slip of paper:

Executive Mansion.

Washington, August 23, 1864.

This morning, as for some days past, it seems
exceedingly probable that this administration will not
be reelected. Then it will be my duty to so coöperate with the president-elect as to save the Union between the election and the inauguration; as he will
have secured his election on such grounds that he
cannot possibly save it afterward.

A. Lincoln.

When the Cabinet met that day, Lincoln presented this
folded slip to the members, asking them to write their names
on its back. Lincoln had made a compact with his conscience
as to what he should do in case of defeat.[27]

The Democrats were having their own embarrassments.
The bulk of the party wished to preserve "the Union as it was,
and the Constitution as it is." The extreme peace Democrats
—the "Copperheads"—led by Clement C. Vallandigham of
Ohio and Fernando Wood of New York, wished to commit the
party to peace at any price, even though that meant a separate
South. The gloomy military aspect had given this group great
encouragement.

The other wing, led by August Belmont, American agent of
the Rothschilds and chairman of the Democratic National Committee, sought the nomination of a soldier, inclining to General
George Brinton McClellan, the Little Napoleon. In opening
the convention, though Belmont termed Lincoln's reelection a
calamity, he appealed for "the sacred cause of the Union, the
Constitution, and the laws."[28]

The real battle of Chicago took place in the Resolutions
Committee, where Vallandigham forced the fight. This Ohio
Copperhead was the hero of the convention. Crowds followed
him through the streets.[29] The Conservatives were overwhelmed.
The platform, while pledging "unswerving fidelity to the Union
under the Constitution," asserted "as the sense of the American people," that "justice, humanity, liberty, and the public
welfare demand that immediate efforts be made for a cessation
of hostilities," with a convention to establish peace "on the
basis of the Federal Union of the States." In other words, the
war was a failure. Upon the reading of this platform, the
crowd surrendered itself to the wildest enthusiasm.[30] Vallandigham had carried the day.

Flushed with this victory, he sought to prevent the choice of McClellan. One speaker said that if General McClellan accepted a nomination on the peace platform he would stultify himself and be unworthy of support. But McClellan was nominated on the first ballot.[31]

Meanwhile the Radicals had kept up the movement to displace Lincoln, the Massachusetts Republican leaders going so far as to publish a letter calling for the withdrawal of "both Republican nominees" in favor of a new man. At David Dudley Field's house in New York, on August 14, Horace Greeley, smarting over his peace fiasco, Parke Godwin of the *Evening Post*, Henry Winter Davis, Dr. Francis Lieber and about twenty more outstanding Republicans formed a committee to ask Lincoln to withdraw. Greeley thought that Lincoln was already beaten and that Grant, Sherman or Butler must be selected to save the cause from complete overthrow! In sympathetic correspondence with these leaders, Sumner referred freely to Lincoln's personal and political defects. He wrote to Richard Cobden that Lincoln was an American Louis XVI; the President "lacks practical talent for his important place." However, although he thought another candidate desirable, Sumner counselled the leaders that Lincoln's withdrawal must be "free and voluntary."[32]

In the light of these and other circumstances, the candidacy of Fremont and Cochrane assumed a new importance. No longer could Lincoln jestingly dismiss the Radical ticket with a jocular reference to an apposite Biblical text. Lincoln's advisers began to point out to him proven instances of the disastrous effect of third party movement. Accordingly, a series of conferences began in Washington early in September, with Zach Chandler as leading spirit in insisting that Lincoln make terms with Fremont. Chandler at last secured the consent of the President, went to New York and sought out Fremont's political adviser, David Dudley Field.

Lincoln's emissary easily convinced Field that Fremont should secure the best terms he could from Lincoln and withdraw. On behalf of the President, Chandler promised that Fremont should immediately be given active service in high command, and that "those who had long persecuted him" would be humbled. To Chandler, this last ambiguous promise referred only to the Blairs; but Field and Fremont considered that it also assured the immediate dismissal of Stanton and that Seward should not be reappointed Secretary of State.

Before making up his mind, Fremont consulted several of his close friends. Important among these was Nathanial P. Sawyer of Pittsburgh, who was also a close friend and great admirer of Andrew Johnson. In August Sawyer had sent Johnson his congratulations. "O, how I wish it had been for the presidency!" he wrote. "Then the Union party would have not been divided. Fremont would have supported you, and we could have taken you to the White House without any trouble. I am sorry, very sorry, that you have not been associated with a better man than Lincoln. But He that doeth all things well, have no doubt, will control this matter, and should Lincoln be successful, may, in His own good time, make Andrew Johnson President, and restore our Unf[ortunate] country once more to peace and happiness."

When Fremont laid the President's proposal before Sawyer, he thought it generous, and advised its immediate acceptance. On September 13 he wrote to the General: "If you have assurance of Mr. Blair's immediate removal and also Mr. Stanton's, and the assurance that Seward will not be reappointed, my advice is that you withdraw as soon as practicable in favor of Lincoln and Johnson.. Something tells me that Lincoln will not fill a second term. If I am right, Johnson will be the President, a man whom I have loved ever since '61. I have no doubt he will do you and your friends justice. There is no man living I would sooner see President. . . ."[33]

Within a week of Sawyer's advice Fremont retired, ungraciously. He said that he was not interested in the proposal made him. So late in the war, he did not want another high military command. His enemies had already done their worst. But as an act of pure patriotism and for the welfare of the Republican party, he would withdraw. Certainly he had not been moved by admiration of Lincoln. "I consider," he announced, "that his Administration has been politically, militarily, and financially a failure, and that its necessary continuance is a cause of regret for the country."[34] Though Fremont was unwilling to demand Montgomery Blair's decapitation, other bitter enemies of that worthy leaped at the chance. Stanton and Blair did not speak. Blair was barred from the Union League, Chase despised him and Radical rank and file hated him with a fiendish hate.

On September 22 Fremont published his withdrawal. The next morning Lincoln wrote a short note to the Postmaster-General asking for his resignation. Bates set down in his diary that Blair thought this action "a result of a compromise with the leaders of the Fremont party—the extreme Radicals—and circumstances seem to warrant the conclusion." He added: "It is announced that *Ben F. Wade and H. Winter Davis* (notwithstanding their fierce manifesto) are to take the stump for Lincoln. The result will probably be to insure Mr. Lincoln's election over McClellan; and the Radicals, no doubt, hope that they will constitute the controlling element in the new party thus formed, and as such will continue to govern the Nation. . . . But, perhaps, their success is a melancholy defeat for their country."[36]

During these recurring crises, Andrew Johnson had remained in Nashville, seeking to carry out his triple task. He must sustain and administer civil government in the State, prepare Tennessee for resumption of practical relations with the national government and, most important of all, he must carry Tennessee for the Union ticket in the autumn.

On July 2 the Union nominee for vice president addressed a letter to Governor Dennison, President of the Baltimore Convention, formally accepting the honor accorded him. In the main, Johnson's letter followed the lines of his Nashville serenade speech, but he added an appeal to the Democrats. "The hour has now come," he said, "when that great party can justly vindicate its devotion to true Democratic policy." If Secession wins, "free government North and South fails. . . . This is not the hour for strife and division among ourselves. Such differences of opinion only encourage the enemy, prolong the war, and waste the country."[36]

Careful maneuvering was essential to make sure that the Tennessee election could be held in such a way that the Administration would be sustained. Unless drastic tests for voters were established, victory at the polls could not be assured in any section of the State. Word from West Tennessee was particularly alarming; Confederate guerrillas cowed Middle Tennessee and the emancipation program had irritated the Conservative Unionists in the East.

In the political battles of Civil War days, war chests were quite as necessary as campaign plans and Tennessee was no exception. One of Johnson's zealous subordinates sent a circular to all officers and contractors in his division. "It is expected," read the blunt message, "that you who have received the liberal patronage of the government will willingly lend your means. I am authorized to say, gentlemen, to those who respond cheerfully to this call, that the patronage herefore extended to them will without doubt be continued." The size of the subscription, he added, was expected to "correspond with the patronage you have received." When objection was made to this forthright method, its author defended it by exhibiting the results achieved—"not less than $20,000 in Tennessee, and I hope for a good deal more."[37]

Thus sustained, Johnson and his lieutenants began a program to win the election, equally regardless of Forrest's Cavalry and of the Conservative Union men. On August 2 a group of "loyal citizens" met in Nashville and asked the state executive committee to call a convention of loyal men. Two days later the call appeared, listing three subjects for the meeting: The general condition of the country; ways of reorganizing civil government in the State; and the expediency of holding a presidential election in Tennessee. Later that same month, the Governor issued a proclamation inviting the people to return to their allegiance and to aid in protecting themselves against lawless bands, and warning them that "criminal opposition" against the laws and constitution and adherents thereto must cease, or the people could no longer expect the protection of the government.[38]

The convention which gathered on September 5 was a nondescript assemblage, liberally sprinkled with soldiers, and with the Radicals obviously in thorough control. Horace Maynard, J. B. Bingham of Memphis, Leonidas C. Houck of Knoxville and J. S. Fowler, all powerful and uncompromising Radicals, were among the leaders. The Conservatives put up a fight, but in vain. When T. B. Thomas of McMinn County, the Conservative leader, moved that the convention be governed by the Constitutions of the United States and Tennessee, a storm broke about his head. This was intensified the next day when he presented the Conservative ultimatum that all truly loyal men must have a chance to vote as they might see proper. Thomas' resolution was promptly laid on the table, to the accompaniment of such personal abuse that he and his followers left the convention. The now untrammeled Radicals proceeded on September 7 to put through their program, recommending the holding of an election in November by those "who are now and have been attached to the National Union." A complicated system of registration and qualification was set up, the most important phase of which was the oath which anyone seeking to vote must take:

> I solemnly swear that I will henceforth support the Constitution of the United States, and defend it against the assaults of all its enemies; that I am an active friend of the government of the United States; that I sincerely rejoice in the triumph of its armies and navies, and in the defeat and overthrow of the armies, navies and all armed combinations in the interest of the so-called Confederate States; that I will cordially oppose all armistices or negotiations for peace with rebels in arms, until the Constitution of the United States and all laws and proclamations made in pursuance thereof shall be established over all the people of every State and territory embraced within the National Union; and that I will heartily aid and assist the loyal people in whatever measures may be adopted for the attainment of these ends; and further, that I take this oath freely and voluntarily and without mental reservation. So help me God.

The convention indorsed the Lincoln-Johnson ticket, approved Johnson's course as governor, demanded the immediate abolition of slavery in Tennessee and asked the Military Governor to put into effect its plan of election "in such manner as he may think will best subserve the interests of the government."[39] This Johnson proceeded to do. On the same day, he issued a proclamation pledging the support of the military government. On September 30 he issued a second proclamation, expressing his desire to coöperate with the efforts of the convention, and ordering an election on November 8, to take part in which voters must take the exact oath the Nashville resolutions had prescribed.

Although apparently the Military Governor was merely carrying out the will of the assembled delegates, the truth was too transparent to deceive anyone. The oath was cunningly contrived to exclude not only Rebel sympathizers but also the Conservative Union men who preferred McClellan to "Honest

Abe." As its full force became apparent, a storm of indignation rose. The peace Democrats had at first placed an electoral ticket in the field in Tennessee. When they saw the impossibility of success under the oath, their wrath boiled over, and a deputation of McClellan electors traveled to Washington to protest to the President against the outrage done them.

Among the names signed to this able document were those of such outstanding Union men as T. A. R. Nelson, Ex-Governor William B. Campbell and Emerson Etheridge. When he learned of the protest, Nelson denied that he had been consulted, and had not authorized his signature, and repudiated the document. None the less, on October 15, a committee representing the indignant Democrats saw Lincoln. John Lellyett of Nashville read their protest.

"May I inquire," Lincoln asked, "how long it took you and the New York politicians to concoct that paper?" This brusque query took the delegation aback. Lellyett protested that none but Tennesseans had had a hand in it.

"I expect to let the friends of George B. McClellan manage their side of this contest in their own way," Lincoln retorted, "and I will manage my side of it in my way." He added that he might make some further answer in writing, abruptly closed the interview, and the fuming McClellan electors filed out.

On October 22 Lincoln replied in writing to the protest and made plain that "Governor Johnson, like any other loyal citizen of Tennessee, has the right to favor any political plan he chooses, and as Military Governor, it is his duty to keep peace among and for the loyal people of the state." "I cannot discern," he continued, "that by this plan he proposed any more. But you object to the plan. Leaving it alone will be your perfect security against it. It is not proposed to force you into it. Do as you please, on your own account, peaceably and loyally, and Governor Johnson will not molest you, but will protect you against violence as far as in his power." After this unsatisfactory reply, the McClellan electors saw the hopelessness of their attempt and withdrew from the race.

On October 24 Johnson wound up the Tennessee campaign with a speech to the colored population of Nashville. Cedar Street was packed so close that the negroes could not move. Torches and transparencies cast a ruddy glow over the sea of dusky faces.

A Johnson IIII IIII IIII III — 18   1
J W Harold IIII IIII IIII IIII IIII IIII I 31   2
M Lincoln IIII IIII IIII IIII IIII I 26   3
J Maloney IIII I 6
James Johnson II 2
W Stone IIII III 8
B McDaniel IIII IIII IIII IIII IIII I 26   4
A Brown IIII IIII IIII IIII 19   5
J Sister IIII IIII IIII IIII 19   6
D Alexander IIII IIII IIII IIII IIII 25   7
A Aiken IIII IIII IIII 14
M Payne IIII IIII III 13
V Sevier / 1
W Brannon IIII II 7
Thos. Lane III 3
Saml McGaughy III 3
R N Woods II 2
McDowell / 1
Bassett IIII 4
Bob t Rhea / 1
Lowry II 2
Baker / 1
B West II 2
Knowles / 1
Russell / 1
Isaac Brannon / 1
Morris / 1

A Johnson 18
J W Harold 31
M Lincoln 26
B McDaniel 26
A Brown 19
J Sister 19
D Alexander 25

ANDY'S FIRST TALLY SHEET

This Tally Sheet Was Used in Counting the Votes in Johnson's First Election Contest—That for Alderman, in 1829. Used by Courtesy of Mrs. S. B. LaRue, Greeneville, Tenn.

The hour had come, Johnson announced, when the last vestiges of slavery must be removed. Therefore, "without reference to the President or any other person," he had a proclamation to make: "Standing here upon the steps of the Capitol, with the past history of-the State to witness, the present condition to guide, and its future to encourage me, I, Andrew Johnson do hereby proclaim freedom, full, broad and unconditional, to every man in Tennessee." Upon these words, the correspondent of the Cincinnati *Gazette* recorded, a roar of delight burst from 3,000 throats; flags, banners, torches and transparencies were wildly waved or thrown aloft, and drums and trumpets added to the tumult.

The Military Governor proceeded to denounce slavery and harsh masters. "This damnable aristocracy," he said, "should be pulled down. No longer should the wives and daughters of the colored men of Tennessee be dragged into a concubinage compared to which polygamy was a virtue." "If the law shields those whom you hold dear from the unlawful grasp of lust," he asked, "will you endeavor to be true to yourself, and shun . . . the path of lewdness, crime and vice?" Shouts burst from the multitude: "We will! We will!"

Much moved as he watched the freedmen's happy faces, Johnson voiced the hope that, "as in the days of old," a Moses might arise "to lead them safely to their Promised Land of freedom and happiness."

"You are our Moses!" shouted many voices, and the assembled masses cheered wildly. "We want no Moses but you!"

In the emotion of the moment, the Governor caught the phrase and responded: "Humble and unworthy as I am, if no better shall be found, I will indeed be your Moses, and lead you through the Red Sea of war and bondage to a fairer future of liberty and peace."[40]

This wound up the Tennessee campaign. Under the oath prescribed, the result was a foregone conclusion. After their unsuccessful interview with Lincoln, the Tennessee McClellan electors had withdrawn in disgust. Although the advance of Hood's army and the wide scourgings of Forrest's Cavalry prevented the opening of the polls throughout much of Middle and West Tennessee, the election was held and Lincoln and Johnson carried the State. The return was duly certified to Congress, but when the electoral voters came to be canvassed by the two

Houses, those for Tennessee were excluded, in deference to the
Radical protest against presidential reconstruction in the
South.

The results of the early elections were vastly encouraging
to the Union cause. Fremont's withdrawal, Blair's departure,
Johnson's speeches, Sheridan in the Shenandoah, Farragut at
Mobile and Sherman's capture of Atlanta had turned the tide.
The effect of military victory was just as Lincoln had foreseen.
"With reverses in the field," he had said, "the case is doubtful
at the polls. With victory in the field, the election will take
care of itself."[41] In September, Vermont and Maine elected
Republican state tickets by significant majorities, and in October Pennsylvania, Ohio and Indiana, three decisive States,
foretold the presidential verdict in November. During the last
month of the campaign, the swing to the Union ticket went on
unabated; the Republican politicians were confident, the Democrats depressed.

By the vote of the electoral college, the presidential election was an overwhelming triumph for the Administration. Of
the twenty-two States whose votes Congress counted, McClellan
carried only three. Of the eighteen free States, he carried New
Jersey alone. In the popular vote, the election was not quite
so one-sided. In New Hampshire, Lincoln received less than
4,000 majority out of 69,000 votes; in Connecticut, only a
little more than 2,000; in New York less than 7,000 out of
700,000 votes cast; in Pennsylvania, a change of 10,100 votes
out of a total of 572,000 would have lost Lincoln the State.
The total vote was 4,115,902, and the Lincoln-Johnson ticket
had a lead of about 300,000.

Strengthened by the indorsement of the people at the polls,
Lincoln determined to press his restoration plans with all the
power he had. Indeed, with the opening of the second session
of the thirty-eighth Congress, in December, 1864, it seemed as
if at last he had a chance to get Congress to agree to presidential reconstruction. Many of the Radicals were now more
willing for the President to have his way.

The test came in the case of Louisiana, which had been reorganized under Lincoln's plan. General Banks had made a
success of it. Louisianians took the Lincoln oath by tens of
thousands; a new state constitution in line with the presidential
wishes was adopted, a state election was held, and a loyal gov-

ernment installed. The new Louisiana legislature elected
Charles Smith and R. King Cutler United States Senators, and
the various districts had elected congressmen. On the reopen-
ing of Congress, a complete body of national representatives
from Louisiana appeared in Washington, claiming the right to
seats.

The Radical protest was of less intensity than theretofore.
Some senators took the position that Smith and Cutler could
not be seated so long as the presidential proclamation declaring
Louisiana in insurrection remained unrecalled. In the Senate,
the matter was referred to the Judiciary Committee, and on
February 17, 1865, Senator Lyman Trumbull of Illinois made
his report. As a preliminary, he offered a joint resolution
"that the United States do hereby recognize the government
of the State of Louisiana as the legitimate government of the
said state, and entitled to the guaranties and all other rights
of a state government under the Constitution of the United
States."

This resolution seems to have received general assent. John
W. Forney, Secretary of the Senate, made a private poll, concluded that the only person opposed to the admission was
Charles Sumner, "who possibly might be followed by Wade,
Wilkinson, and Chandler," and wrote to Johnson that Tennessee's members would quickly enter, upon the Louisiana precedent.[42]

But Sumner was adamant. The crucial point with him was
whether the negro should be allowed to vote. He realized he
would secure but meager support in a frank fight for negro
suffrage, so he resorted to every device of parliamentary tactics at his command to harass and delay Trumbull's resolution.
Finally he resorted to filibuster. Ben Wade and Howard of
Michigan later entered the debate in behalf of Sumner, but the
great majority of the Senate wanted to adopt Trumbull's resolution, which had Lincoln's backing, so that something practical would be done.

As days passed in fruitless debate, and March 4, the legal
end of the session, crept upon them, the Senators became irritated and alarmed. Sumner made so manifest his determined
and unyielding purpose to speak against time so that this resolution should fail, that the Administration forces began to
weaken.[43] The calendar contained a great mass of important
legislation. The army and navy appropriation bills had not

been passed. Trumbull did not like to yield the question, but as Sumner's obduracy continued and the army and navy appropriations bills remained unconsidered, he finally capitulated. The Senate dropped the recognition resolution and proceeded to other things.

They may not have known it at the time, but this decision marked a great crisis in reconstruction. Congress definitely rejected Abraham Lincoln's policy of peace and mercy to his defeated fellow countrymen. It foreshadowed bayonet rule of the conquered provinces. It was the unhallowed triumph of Charles Sumner.

VIII. ANDY MAKES A BAD SLIP

Now that he had been elected, Andrew Johnson was far from anxious to assume his new duties as Vice President of the United States on March 4. He well knew that there was no particular urgency in assuming his duties as constitutional presiding officer of the Senate, inasmuch as Congress would not regularly meet until December. His work in Tennessee was as yet uncompleted, and he felt that there was a certain ignominy in leaving Nashville before the State had been restored to practical Federal relations, a consummation upon which he had set his heart.

There were many loose ends in Johnson's restoration program, and one or two major matters demanded his closest attention. He had issued a call for a constitutional convention to meet in December, to strike slavery from Tennessee's basic law. But so much of the State was in the hands of Hood's army—as yet not come to grips with Thomas at Franklin and Nashville—that the meeting was postponed to early January. Then "Parson" Brownlow had to be installed as governor in Johnson's stead and then there was much accounting and reporting to be done, to say nothing of the new burdens of correspondence, for the Tailor-Statesman had been deluged with congratulations and sage advice.

His part in the election had not been overlooked by his well-wishers. Lewis D. Campbell, a sturdy friend and sagacious Ohio politician, wrote that "Mr. Lincoln was not *per se* so popular in Ohio. . . . Nothing but the fact that your name was on the ticket prevented a general stampede." Campbell had just returned from Washington, where he had seen "Father Abraham," and reported that "he looks careworn and dilapidated."[1]

A letter full of flattery and guile came from Secretary of the Senate Forney, who wished his new chief to believe that for twenty-five years the latter had been his *"beau ideal* of a representative and Radical Democrat." Whatever his relations with the Executive might be, the Vice President must be on his guard. "I regard it as your duty," Forney insisted, "to see that the Union Democrats represented by Dix, Dickinson, Holt,

Sickles, Dougherty, Logan, Wright of Indiana, and others of that class, shall be considered and recognized in every possible way by Mr. Lincoln. . . . If it is not done, in less than a year we may find ourselves a divided party. *No man in the Union is more concerned in this than Andrew Johnson, and you know what I mean when I say this.*"[2]

Interspersed among the many letters of this type, were one or two of poignant pathos. Early in December, the widow of ex-President James K. Polk asked Johnson to transmit to Lincoln an appeal she had written begging for the exception of "this little lot of cotton (only sixteen bales) from the restrictions of the cotton trade. . . . You know my pecuniary circumstances. I have been deprived of all income since the war commenced. My husband was faithful to the country, and I claim protection and think it due me; I am now sixty years of age." One is glad to find this letter indorsed "Attended To."[6]

While Johnson no doubt appreciated the praise of his friends and the advice of the politicians, he was not to be diverted from completing his Tennessee task. The delegates to the postponed constitutional convention met in Nashville early in January and, under the Military Governor's guidance, proceeded to adopt an amendment to the State Constitution declaring slavery forever abolished in the Volunteer state. On January 13, the Vice President-elect telegraphed the good news to the White House. The next day Lincoln wired back: "Thanks to the convention and you," adding "When do you expect to be here?"

While Johnson was bending all his energies to these tasks, typhoid fever, the scourge of the armies during the Civil War, laid its heavy grip upon him.[4] He was forced to stay in bed several weeks with a high fever. Not only did the disease weaken him physically, but it delayed the completion of his self-allotted task.[5]

Johnson now grew very anxious not to be required to leave Nashville until he could regain his strength and conscientiously feel that his work in Tennessee had been done. He sought to discover if there were not some legal precedent which would enable him to remain in Nashville, there take the oath of office as Vice President, and come to the National Capital at a later date. He wrote Lincoln of his hopes, and also asked the Secretary of the Senate to have precedents checked up.

President Lincoln was so anxious about this new complication that he took up the question with his Cabinet and on January 24 telegraphed Johnson that, "While we fully appreciate your wish to remain in Tennessee until that state government shall be inaugurated, it is our unanimous conclusion that it is unsafe for you not to be here on the 4th of March. Be sure to reach here by that time."[6]

Forney's first consideration of the question submitted caused him to telegraph Johnson that there was no obstacle in the way of his remaining in Nashville. But the next day, he wrote at length, enclosing a memorandum prepared by the Chief Clerk of the Senate, "from which you will ascertain that there are sufficient precedents to allow your absence on the day of the inauguration," but protesting against any such step. "All our friends," Forney wrote, "will be greatly disappointed if you are not in Washington at a very early date. Not alone your own interests, but the interests of the country, demand your presence. You are in fact the representative of the Democratic element, without which neither Abraham Lincoln nor yourself could have been chosen. The present partisans of Mr. Lincoln will be on the ground, and I think you should be here, if only for a few days, to see the people who look to you to assist in shaping generous, magnanimous and national policies. If this is not done, my dear sir, the great Union party will be a failure."[7]

These considerations among others induced Johnson to abandon his first plan to take the oath of office in Nashville. He began to get ready for the inauguration. A Washington tailor wrote him to be sure not to get a new suit, as he was "having one built here." Forney asked the "diagram or dimensions" of his head, so that a Philadelphia hat maker could present an evidence of his art. Many others sought to compliment and to honor the Tennessee tailor. Captain Clinton sent him, with his compliments, "1 box sparkling Catawba." Many of the cities on his line of progress to Washington invited Johnson to stop and speak. The Pennsylvania legislature, then in session, clamored for an address; a committee in Pittsburgh said he must stop there; and the American Union Commission in New York asked for an address on Southern Reconstruction. Because of his weakness he was able to do none of these things.

On February 22, R. L. Stanford wrote from Louisville, "You would do well to be cautious in traveling over the railway between this city and Nashville on your way to Washington. The road will be closely watched by guerrillas . . . to catch you. There are some of the *worst* men in Kentucky that are to be found upon earth; they hate you, and would make any *sacrifice* to get you."[8] But there is no record of Johnson's having taken any especial precautions on his journey to Washington. Leaving Nashville on the morning of February 25, accompanied by General Gillem, Joseph Fowler, his comptroller, and four others,[9] he arrived in Washington on March 1, and established himself at his favorite stopping place, the Kirkwood House.[10] On the very next day Senator Lyman Trumbull, chairman of the Congressional Committee to notify him of his election as vice president, wrote to arrange the place and hour to give him personal notice of his election. There was a heavy demand for Johnson's pictures and M. B. Brady, Washington's favorite photographer, wrote requesting a sitting at once.

The day before the inauguration, Johnson sent his formal resignation as Brigadier General and Military Governor to Secretary of War Stanton. With it went a note to Stanton "to express my high regard for you personally, and also to thank you sincerely for the uniform kindness which you have been pleased to extend to me personally and officially during my service. . . ."

Stanton responded by tendering Johnson "the thanks of this department for your patriotic and able service during the eventful period through which you have exercised the high trust committed to your charge." He paid lavish tribute to the Tennessean. "In one of the darkest hours of the great struggle," he wrote, "the government called you from the Senate and from the comparatively safe and easy duties of civil life, to place you in the front of the enemy, and in a position of personal toil and danger perhaps more hazardous than was encountered by any other civil or military officer of the United States. With patriotic promptness you assumed the post, and maintained it under circumstances of unparalleled trials, until recent events have brought safety and deliverance to your State and to the integrity of that constitutional Union for which you so long and so gallantly periled all that is dear to man on earth." The Secretary concluded by expressing "the sincere wish of one who in every official and personal relation has found you worthy of the confidence of the government and the honor

and esteem of your fellow citizens," that "you may be spared
to enjoy new honors. . . ."[11]

On the eve of Inauguration Day, Colonel Forney and several
other admirers of Johnson celebrated the Tennessean's career
and accomplishments with a party at which the wine flowed as
freely as the oratory. It was an unfortunate night for the
Vice President-elect. He awoke the next morning chagrined at
his unsteady condition.[12]

The day had dawned far from pleasantly. A drizzling rain
was falling, transforming the streets of the capital into channels of churned-up mud.[13] Senator Doolittle of Wisconsin, the
member of the committee on arrangements designated to accompany the Vice President-elect to the Senate chamber, called
at Johnson's hotel at half past ten.[14]

Hannibal Hamlin also called at the Kirkwood House that
morning, and Doolittle, Hamlin and Johnson rode down Pennsylvania Avenue to the Capitol, according to program. During this ride Johnson was perfectly sober. When the party
had entered the Vice President's Room, he remarked to Hamlin:
"I am not fit to be here, and ought not to have left my home,
as I was slow recovering from an attack of typhoid fever. But
Mr. Lincoln telegraphed me, as did other friends, that I must
be here, and I came. I am now very weak and enervated, and
require all the strength I can get. Can you give me some good
whiskey?"[15]

"No," the virtuous Hamlin responded. "When I became
vice president, I gave an order prohibiting the sale of liquor in
the Senate restaurant, but if you desire I will send across the
street for some."

Accordingly, Hamlin sent out for a bottle of whiskey and
Johnson "drank a good potation." The two remained seated
for some minutes, until it was announced that it was time for
them to go into the Senate chamber for the ceremony. Johnson said again "I will take some more of the whiskey, as I need
all the strength for the occasion I can have."

In his "weak and feeble condition of health," the liquor
played havoc with the Vice President-elect.[16] The heating arrangements of the Capitol were that day working far too well.
The heat of the Senate chamber and the whiskey proved too
much for the enfeebled Johnson, who made "a rambling and
strange harangue, which was listened to with pain and mortifi-

cation by his friends." Through it ran a strain of plebeian
pride, crudely expressed and ill-fitted to the occasion.

The Vice President wanted it to be understood that he had
presented himself there, not "presumptuously to thrust myself
in a position so exalted," but to discharge a constitutional duty.
He gloried in being "one who claims no high descent, one who
comes from the ranks of the people." He then proceeded to
tell each group there that "the people" stood above them.

"You, Senators," he said, "and you who constitute the
bench of the Supreme Court of the United States, are but the
creatures of the American people; your exaltation is from
them." He next singled out Seward and Stanton for similar
admonition; and legend has it that then, turning his eyes to the
Diplomatic gallery, he thus addressed the assembled plenipo-
tentiaries: "And you, gentlemen of the Diplomatic Corps, with
all your fine feathers and gewgaws."[17]

This same strain of the power of the people and the insignificance of their rulers ran through the whole maudlin speech.
"Humble as I am, plebeian as I may be deemed," great are the
people. As a plebeian, one not learned in parliamentary law,
one who had "only studied how I may best advance the interests
of my State and of my country, and not the technical rules of
order," he implored the kindness and indulgence of the Senate.
Once more, "I, though a plebeian boy, am authorized by the
principles of the government under which I live to feel proudly
conscious that I am a man, and grave dignitaries are but men."

In conclusion, he proclaimed that Tennessee was free. "She
has bent the tyrant's rod, she has broken the yoke of slavery,
and today she stands redeemed. . . . She is now as loyal, Mr.
Attorney-General, as is the State from which you come. . . .
It is the doctrine of the Federal Constitution that no state can
go out of this Union; and moreover, Congress cannot reject a
State from this Union. . . . She is still in the Union, and I am
her representative. . . ." Thereupon the speaker declared
himself prepared to take the oath, which he did, while Senators
were struck with consternation, and diplomats with difficulty
restrained their laughter.

Soon after Johnson began, several Senators on the Republican side began to hide their heads.[18] The righteous Sumner "covered his face with his hands, and bowed his head down
on the desk."[19]

Up in the press gallery, some reporters were too ashamed to write the news. "The second official of the Nation—drunk—*drunk*—when about the take his oath of office, bellowing and ranting and shaking his fists at Judges, Cabinet and Diplomats, and making a fool of himself to such a degree that indignation is almost compelled to pity," Charles Dudley Warner's Washington correspondent privately wrote him, adding that he felt such a revulsion at the spectacle that he could not write it.[20]

Lincoln and the assembled Cabinet members were astounded at the turn things had taken. Speed, the new Attorney-General, who sat at Gideon Welles' left during the ceremony, whispered to him: "All this is in wretched bad taste." As it went on, he leaned over again to say: "The man is certainly deranged." Welles whispered to Stanton at his right, "Johnson is either drunk or crazy," and Stanton replied, "There is evidently something wrong." Seward tried to put a good face on the matter by saying that it was the emotion of returning and revisiting the Senate. "I can appreciate Johnson's feelings. I myself am very much overcome." Welles hoped Seward was right, but didn't concur with him. There was, he whispered, "something wrong—I hope it is sickness." He first wrote in his diary: "My impression is that he was drunk," then struck out the short stark word and substituted "under the influence of stimulants," adding in exculpation "he has been sick and is feeble—perhaps he may have taken medicine, or stimulants, or his brain from sickness may have been over-active in this new responsibility. Whatever the case, it was all in bad taste."[21]

Hamlin, too, was mortified and chagrined, and at the time sought to assume the blame for the incident. "Perhaps I am responsible for this matter," the departing Vice President said in an interview a few weeks later. "Andrew Johnson is not an intemperate man. He is sober and in his right mind, and is the right man in the right place, and may God keep him and preserve him."[22]

During this painful scene, Senator John B. Henderson of Missouri, who had escorted Lincoln to the Capitol, sat by the President's side. Henderson noticed Lincoln's head drooping in the deepest humiliation, and as the Senator offered him his arm for the procession to the steps of the Capitol where he was to deliver his own Inaugural, the President turned to the Marshal and said: "Do not let Johnson speak outside." When Lincoln himself kissed the Bible, his lips are said to have been pressed to the passage in Isaiah: "Woe unto them that rise up early in the morning that they may follow strong drink."

This amazing inaugural was the talk of Washington—and indeed of the country. "Very disreputable," Orville H. Browning noted in his diary, adding that the Vice President had "disgusted all decent people who heard him." Johnson's enemies were elated, his friends depressed. Many Senators claimed to be deeply shocked. The scene was so humiliating that a few days afterward a Senatorial caucus "seriously considered the propriety of asking him to resign as their presiding officer."[23] While this was not done, the Senate in a moment of consternation and repentance suddenly voted to exclude liquor from the Senate wing of the Capitol, causing the *Independent* ironically to comment that if the Senate could prevent its officers and its members from drinking to excess by passing a resolution, the country might well rejoice. The Senate went further. It voted to drop McDougall of California and Saulsbury of Delaware from all its standing committees, "because of their habitual inebriety and incapacity for business."[24]

According to the usual accounts of the matter, Johnson betook himself to bed in illness and mortification after this disgraceful inaugural.[25] A week later a Washington newspaper asserted that several physicians had been called in by the Vice President "for consultation, with the view of making out a case of temporary insanity."[26] Very sensibly Johnson made no attempt to preside over the Senate. The Blairs took him out to Silver Spring, the patriarchal estate of the sire of the family, to give him a chance to rest and recuperate, and there he stayed about a fortnight, slowly recovering his strength and letting the general furore die down. During his stay he completely captivated the Blairs.

Old Francis Preston Blair insisted that Johnson was "all right," that he hadn't said anything "that was bad sense, only bad taste," and that it would not have been "nearly so much of a thing if Sumner hadn't been so exquisite about it."[27]

At the Cabinet meeting on Tuesday, March 7, Johnson's infirmity was the chief topic, and Welles noted that "Seward's tone and opinion were much changed since Saturday. He seems to have given Johnson up now, but no one appears to have been aware of his failing." Welles also had experienced a change and was now inclined to believe Johnson's drunkenness on March

4 a temporary ailment, which might be overcome if rightly treated.[28]

McCulloch, too, was gravely concerned. He had not known the Tennessean before and was highly alarmed at the prospect of what would happen to the country if President Lincoln should suddenly be removed. A day or two after the inauguration, the Secretary of the Treasury took occasion to say as much to Lincoln. After a moment's hesitation, the President answered, with unusual seriousness: "I have known Andy for many years; he made a bad slip the other day, but you need not be scared. Andy ain't a drunkard."[29]

Whatever may have been Lincoln's feelings on the matter, the country as a whole was horrified. Solemn editorials hectored the erring Vice President. Democratic organs seized with avidity upon this opportunity to denounce the dereliction of the supposedly Radical Vice President. The New York *World* termed Johnson "an insolent drunken brute, in comparison with whom Caligula's horse was respectable."[30] On March 11 the Washington *Times* accused Weed and Seward of having been responsible for Johnson's nomination. The *Independent* fulminated against the "humiliating spectacle," about which it refused to keep silent.[31]

"I would gladly pass over the scene in silence," wrote its correspondent, "but Washington is in a ferment over it, the Senate feels disgraced, and it is better to invoke the judgment of intelligent and sober people upon such conduct, that Mr. Johnson may hereafter hold a tight rein upon his appetite for liquor, and save the Senate from further shame on his account."

The Vice President-elect, it charged, "presented himself to take his solemn oath of office in a state of intoxication. . . . It is the plain duty of Mr. Johnson either to apologize for his conduct, or to resign his office." And the Radical organ, "in the name of an insulted people," felt itself "compelled to demand that so great an affront to the dignity of the Republic, shall be made to bear a fit penalty, atonement and warning."

In its next week's number, the *Independent's* Washington correspondent noted that newspaper criticisms were having a salutary effect on Johnson's conduct, and on that of others as well. It seemed he had been under the care of a physician for a week, and "he asserts that he is in a shattered condition, resulting from a severe illness and severe labor. He would never have committed the terrible blunder on Inauguration Day if he had been well, and it is asserted that he is determined never again to give offense to the Senate and the country by use of intoxicating liquors. But if he is to keep this noble resolution, he must part company with some of the Senate officials, or they must throw their whiskey demijohns out of the windows of their official apartments."

At Grover's Theater on E Street, the matter got into doggerel:

> *At Washington the other day,*
> *There was a brilliant display,*
> *For some were drunk*
> *And some were gay*
> *At the Inauguration.*
>
> *O, was it not a glorious sight,*
> *To see the crowd of black and white,*
> *As well as Andy Johnson tight*
> *At the Inauguration.*
>
> *There is a place well known to all;*
> *To senators both great and small,—*
> *A grog shop called*
> *"A hole in the wall,"*
> *At the Capital of the nation.*
>
> *And there Great Andy Johnson got*
> *And took a brandy-toddy hot,*
> *Which made him drunk as any sot,*
> *At the Inauguration.*
>
> *And now to wipe out the disgrace,*
> *The President has closed the place*
> *Where Andy Johnson fell from grace,—*
> *At the Inauguration!*

On March 9 the Vice President himself had written from Silver Spring to Mr. Sutton, chief reporter of the Senate: "I am not very well, having been confined to my room for some days and unable to call and see you. I see from the *Congressional Globe* that the proceedings of Saturday the 4th inst. have not as yet been published, and as I understand there has been some criticism upon the address delivered by me in the

Senate chamber, will you do me the favor to preserve the original notes and retain them in your possession, and furthermore, at your earliest convenience bring me an accurate copy of your report of what I said on that occasion?"[32]

Some of Johnson's loyal friends at Nashville took up cudgels in his defense. James A. Bishop, one of his quartermasters, prepared a lengthy article for the Nashville *Times*, which listed Johnson's many services to the cause of Union and asked if "for the one lapse, is it right now to gibbet Andrew Johnson in eternal infamy?"[33]

The Vice President returned from Silver Spring much improved in health. Congress not being in session, he thought to take an opportunity to return to Greeneville for his first visit to his beloved home since he had fled from it four years before. On March 25, A. P. Gorman, the Senate postmaster, telegraphed Colonel Robert Johnson, at Greeneville, that the latter's father would leave Washington the next Tuesday for home.

But the rapid rush of war developments checked the Vice President's trip. Throughout January, February and March Federal armies on many fronts had been hemming in the Southern forces, and late in March it was apparent that the war was almost won. Johnson stayed on in Washington to be close at hand when Richmond fell.

Throughly apprised of the situation, Lincoln was anxiously awaiting news from Grant. The President had not been well. Throngs of politicians had haunted the White House importuning him for positions. Friends said that he was sick of office-seekers. After a two weeks' siege by job-hunters, he went to City Point, Grant's headquarters, almost within rifle shot of Richmond, perhaps as much to escape the greedy politicians as to observe the army in the field.

Grant quickly relieved the President of any apprehensions he might have had as to the military situation, but Lincoln remained at army headquarters for a number of days. While he was at City Point the last week in March, Sherman's army reached Goldsboro, N. C., General Sherman decided that his forces needed a few days to refit, and that he needed to get in touch with Grant, so he hastened to the Lieutenant General's headquarters. There he found the President. On March 27, Grant and Sherman had a long talk with Lincoln, whom they found "in an exceedingly pleasant mood." The next day the two generals paid a second call, Admiral Porter accompanying them. The three spent an hour and a half with the President, in which they went thoroughly into the entire situation and envisaged the steps to be taken to secure an early peace.

Sherman asked Lincoln if he was all ready for the end of the war. What was to be done with the Confederate armies? What about the political leaders, Jeff Davis, and others? Did Lincoln wish Davis to be allowed to escape? The President answered he was prepared. All he wanted of the generals was to defeat the armies against them and to get the Confederates back at work on their farms. As to Davis, he answered with an anecdote: One day a man who had taken a total abstinence pledge visited a friend, and was invited to take a drink. He declined because of his pledge, but he did accept the offer of lemonade. The friend pointed to the brandy bottle and said the lemonade would be more palatable with a little brandy. The guest answered, "If you can do so unbeknown to me, I will not object." From this story, Sherman inferred that Lincoln wanted Davis to escape "unbeknown" to him.

On the topic of Restoration, Lincoln "was full and frank." He assured Sherman that he was all ready for the civil reorganization of the South, and authorized him to inform Governor Vance of North Carolina that, as soon as the army surrendered, "they would at once be guaranteed all their rights as citizens of a common country; and that to avoid anarchy the State governments then in existence, with their civil functionaries would be recognized by him as the government *de facto* until Congress could provide others."[34]

Sherman was struck by Lincoln's haggard, careworn look, his deep sympathy for the people's afflictions and his earnest desire to bring the war immediately to an end. Both generals thought there would first have to be a great battle: That Lee would make a sudden breakaway, join forces with Johnston and try to overwhelm Sherman, in which event Grant would come in hot pursuit, and the Confederates would be annihilated after a decisive battle. This prospect grieved Lincoln very much. "Enough blood has been shed," he ejaculated. "Can't another battle be avoided?"

Admiral Porter was so impressed with the conversation that he took notes of it. Sherman told Lincoln again and again that he could make Johnston accept any terms necessary to be imposed and that Johnston would have to yield. "But the

President was very decided about the matter," Porter relates, "and insisted that the surrender of Johnston's army must be obtained on any terms. General Grant was evidently of the same way of thinking. . . ." Lincoln "wanted peace on almost any terms," the Admiral continued. "His heart was tenderness throughout, and, as long as the Rebels laid down their arms, he did not care how it was done."[35]

Following these conferences, the President returned to Washington to await the final episodes of the war. On April 1, after Sheridan had won a triumph at Five Forks, Lee saw that he could no longer hold the Richmond-Petersburg line and sent Davis a hasty note which the latter received while attending church the next morning, to this effect. Lee's orderly found Davis in the African Church, at Richmond, attending services. He handed the Confederate President the dispatch, and added verbally, "Petersburg is to be evacuated." The congregation heard the words, and rose in unison. As Davis left, there was an impromptu prayer. At two that afternoon Richmond was abandoned. Early Monday morning, Wisconsin troops under the command of General Weitzel occupied the Confederate capital.

The fall of Richmond occasioned an outburst of rejoicing throughout the North, "a bedlam of good cheer."[37] But it was far from evoking any feeling of brotherly love. Theodore Tilton's *Independent* exulted "at the fall of Babylon, the great mother of harlots and abominations of the earth," and voiced a demand for the punishment of "Southern traitors." The administration, it insisted, "owes to God and man a duty that can only be discharged by meting out exact and even justice. The welfare of society and all the interests of humanity demand that Davis, Lee & Company, shall be tried, found guilty, and hanged by the neck until they are dead." The North in large part remained in the grip of an ugly war psychosis.

Immediately upon the news of the fall of Richmond, Abraham Lincoln determined to inspect the condition of the captured Confederate capital. The story of his progress up a James River filled with mines and torpedoes, his entry into the heart of Richmond and the almost unbelievable enthusiasm with which the negroes greeted him, to the accompaniment of the sullen scowls of the late Confederates, forms an exciting page in the last chapter of the great President's life.

On April 5, Vice President Johnson joined the President in

Richmond. He came at the request of Lincoln himself.[38] The Vice President, accompanied by Preston King, Colonel William B. Browning and several servants travelled on the *Dictator*, a Government dispatch boat. Among the few other passengers was young Henry C. Warmoth, soon to depart for New Orleans for a stormy political career. To him, the Vice President expressed himself in vigorous, almost angry language that "treason must be made odious." The Johnson party put up at the Spottswoode House, where the Vice President found occasion to pour into the ear of Charles A. Dana, Assistant Secretary of War, a vigorous homily on the sins of the Rebels.[39]

During his stay in Richmond, President Lincoln matured plans for the reassembly of the Virginia legislature, so as to take the Old Dominion out of the Confederacy and to recall its troops from Lee's army. The President here met J. A. Campbell, a friend of happier days before the war, and held a long conference with the despondent Southern leader, suggesting to him a means by which Virginia could end her national apostasy.[40]

On April 5, following a conversation of considerable length with Campbell, Lincoln sat down in General Weitzel's office and carefully wrote out a paper, which he handed to the Confederate. Perhaps from haste, perhaps from caution, he did not sign it, but certainly it represented Lincoln's state of mind at the time.

"As to peace," the paper recited, "I have said before, and now repeat, that three things are indispensable. 1. The restoration of the national authority, throughout all the States. 2. No receding by the Executive of the United States on the slavery question from the position assumed thereon in the late annual message to Congress, and in preceding documents. 3. No cessation of hostilities short of an end of the war and the disbanding of all force hostile to the government. That all propositions coming from those now in hostility to the government, and not inconsistent with the foregoing, will be respectfully considered, and passed upon in a spirit of sincere liberality."

It was useless, the President continued, for him to be more specific with those who would not say they were ready for these indispensable terms, even on conditions named by themselves. But "if there be any who are ready for those indispensable terms, on any conditions whatever, let them say so, and state their conditions, so that such conditions can be distinctly known, and considered." As the remission of confiscations was within his power as President, Lincoln promised that such confiscations—except as referred to supposed property in slaves—would be remitted "to the people of any State which shall now promptly, and in good faith, withdraw its troops and other support from further resistance to the government."[41]

When he reached City Point again on April 6, Lincoln wrote General Weitzel that he might allow "the gentlemen who have acted as the legislature of Virginia . . . to assemble at Richmond, and take measures to withdraw the Virginia troops and other support from resistance to the general government."[42] In pursuance of this liberal offer and an additional verbal suggestion by Lincoln, Campbell matured plans and issued a call for the members of the 1861 Virginia Legislature to reassemble, to undo the secession ordinance and to remove the State from rebellion. Such was the status of affairs on April 7, when Lincoln left the captured Confederate capital.

On Sunday April 9, the very day that Lee's capitulation to Grant was signed, the President returned to Washington. Monday morning a salute of several guns was fired in Washington. As the tidings spread over the country, the North was delirious with joy. "Guns are firing, bells ringing, flags flying, men laughing, children cheering . . .; all, all, are jubilant," it seemed to Gideon Welles. The Army of General Joseph E. Johnston had not yet laid down its arms, but Sherman's forces were so overwhelming that it was generally felt Johnston could not much longer resist.

On Tuesday, April 11, a rejoicing throng visited the White House; to it Lincoln made what was destined to be his final speech. He had prepared it carefully, and read from his notes by the flickering light of a candle.[43] The President began by alluding to the prospects of a righteous and speedy peace, therefore giving thanks to Him from whom all blessings flow. By the military successes, he pointed out, reconstruction was pressed more closely on their attention. It was fraught with great difficulty. Disorganized and discordant elements must be molded into States. There was a substantial added embarrassment in the differences among the loyal people as to mode, manner and means of reconstruction.

He examined the case of Louisiana with great care. "As a general rule," he said, "I abstain from reading the reports of attacks upon myself, wishing not to be provoked by that to which I cannot properly offer an answer. In spite of this precaution, however, it comes to my knowledge that I am much censured for some supposed agency in setting up and seeking to sustain the new state government of Louisiana. In this I have done just so much as, and no more than, the public knows." He pointed out the position he had taken in his annual message of December, 1863, and the reconstruction plan therein contained. He recited that he had then said it was not the only plan which might possibly be acceptable, and emphasized that "this plan was, in advance, submitted to the then Cabinet, and distinctly approved by every member."

The new Louisiana constitution was the result of loyal men of Louisiana seeking to work out a plan in accordance with the President's proclamation. As to sustaining the new government, his promise was out; "but as bad promises are better broken than kept, I shall treat this as a bad promise, and break it whenever I shall be convinced that keeping it is adverse to the public interest. But I have not yet been so convinced."

A letter had been shown him, Lincoln continued, supposedly an able letter, in which the writer regretted that the President had not definitely made up his mind as to whether the seceded States were in or out of the Union. The truth was, "I have *purposely* foreborne any public expression upon it. As appears to me, that question has not been, nor yet is, a practically material one." It is "a merely pernicious abstraction."

"We all agree," he went on, "that the seceded States, so-called, are out of their proper practical relation with the Union, and that the sole object of the government, civil and military, in regard to those States, is to again get them into that proper practical relation. I believe it is not only possible, but in fact easier to do this without deciding, or even considering, whether these States have ever been out of the Union, than with it. Finding themselves safely at home, it would be utterly immaterial whether they had ever been abroad. Let us all join in doing the acts necessary to restoring the proper practical relations between these States and the Union, and each forever after innocently indulge his own opinion whether, in doing the acts, he brought the States from without the Union, or only gave them proper assistance, they never having been out of it."

Following this gentle raillery aimed rebukingly at Sumner's theory of state suicide, and Stevens' theory of the South as a conquered province, Lincoln resumed his analysis of the Louisiana plan. Its outstanding aspect, it seemed to him, was that it was a feasible and immediate way to restore Louisiana to practical relations with the Federal Government. As to the negro and his desire to vote, would he not attain the franchise sooner "by saving the already advanced steps toward it than by running backward over them?"

Here the President indulged in another of his homely similes. "Concede," he said, "that the new government of Louisiana is only to what it should be as the egg is to the fowl; we shall sooner have the fowl by hatching the egg than by smashing it. . . . What has been said of Louisiana will apply generally to other States." Lincoln told his hearers that he felt "it may be my duty to make some new announcement to the people of the South." Who can doubt that this announcement would have been one of forgiveness and peace?[44] To give a touch of mingled waggery and pathos, Lincoln concluded by announcing he was about to call on the band to play a piece of Confederate music. It was one "we captured yesterday, and the Attorney-General gave me his legal opinion that it is now our property. So I ask the band to play 'Dixie.'"[45]

"The President's speech," Sumner wrote a friend, "and other things, augur confusion and uncertainty in the future, with hot controversy. Alas! Alas!"[46] Alas, indeed.

Two days later, Lincoln discussed his Virginia plan with Welles. He told the Secretary that Stanton and others had shown marked displeasure at his act in having General Weitzel assemble the legislature. Welles himself expressed doubts, for he feared that the secessionist lawmakers, with their hostile feelings, might conspire against the government. "I have no fear of that," Lincoln responded. "They are too badly beaten, too much exhausted." His idea was that the members of the legislature, the prominent and influential men of the various counties of the State, had better come together and undo their own work. Civil government must be reëstablished as soon as possible; there must be courts and law and order, or anarchy would ensue. But he reluctantly withdrew his permission for the assemblage.

The next day—April 14—there was a Cabinet meeting. General Grant had been especially invited to be present, and remained throughout the session. Almost the sole topic was

what should be done about the Southern States. The first
necessity was the reestablishment of commerce and trade relations. Stanton proposed that resumption should be effected
by his issuing an order. Welles felt that the President should
issue the proclamation.

Taking as an excuse Lincoln's admitted overzealousness in
his Weitzel letter, Stanton asked the Cabinet to hear the "rough
draft" of a proposed ordinance he had prepared for "reconstruction in the Rebel States." It seemed to Welles "a plan
of subjugation, tending and I think designed to increase alienation and hatred between the different sections of the Union."

For several months Lincoln had expressed his solicitude as
to what would happen in the South after the Southern armies
had disbanded. Emancipation was sure to break up social
and domestic relations, the Southern governments would be
nullities, and "civil governments must be introduced at once to
prevent anarchy and punish crime." Although Stanton's proposal was cunningly contrived to seem to satisfy the President's
desires, it really furthered Radical plans at variance with
Lincoln's will. The War Secretary's rough draft placed Virginia and North Carolina in a single military department under
the supervision of the War Department, without recognizing
their separate statehood.

Welles took exception to this failure to preserve state in-
dividuality. "Your point is well taken," the President commented, "the same difficulty has occurred to me." He therefore
directed Stanton to take the document and separate it, adapt-
ing one plan to Virginia and her loyal government, and another
to North Carolina, destitute as she was of legal state authority.[47]

Inquiry was next made as to the news from Sherman. Grant
had heard nothing, but was expecting news any hour. Lincoln
remarked: "I have no doubt such news will come, and come
soon, and come favorable." "Last night," he continued, "I
had the usual dream which I have experienced preceding nearly
every great and important event of the war. Generally the
news which succeeded this dream has been favorable, and the
dream itself is always the same."

Welles inquired what this remarkable dream could be. "It
relates to your element, the water," Lincoln answered. "I
seem to be in some singular, indescribable vessel, and I am
moving with great rapidity towards an indefinite shore. I had

this dream preceding Sumter, Bull Run, Antietam, Gettysburg, Stone River, Vicksburg, and Wilmington." General Grant remarked, "Stone River was certainly no victory, and I know of no great results which followed from it." Lincoln answered that however that might be, his dream had preceded that fight. "I had this strange dream again last night," the President concluded, "and we shall, judging from the past, have great news very soon. I think it might be from Sherman. My thoughts are in that direction, as are most of yours."[48] There was great news that night, true enough. But it was not from Sherman.

ON the night of April 14, Andrew Johnson was occupying his usual quarters on the second floor of the Kirkwood House. He had not yet fully recovered from the depressing effects of his typhoid fever siege back in Nashville. Friday had been an exhausting day at the Capitol, and that evening he early retired to bed.

That evening it happened that L. I. Farwell, a former governor of Wisconsin, went to Ford's Theater, not so much to see Laura Keane in her benefit performance of "Our American Cousins," as to gain an opportunity between acts to take up a matter with President Lincoln, who was occupying a box that night in especial compliment to Miss Keane.

The moment the quick-witted Wisconsin politician heard a shot ring out, followed by a wild cry from Mrs. Lincoln and a histrionic voice shouting *"Sic Semper Tyrannis,"* Farwell realized that the Great Emancipator had been the victim of an assassin. His alert imagination fed his fears of a widespread plot for the assassination of the other leading officers of the government —Johnson, Seward, Stanton and Grant. Perhaps the offer of a reward for such a wholesale assassination in a Selma, Alabama, paper, a few months before aroused Farwell's apprehensions. At any rate, he rushed from the theater and ran at top speed down F Street to the Kirkwood House. He was obsessed with fear that the Vice President too had been killed. Noticing one of the hotel clerks, named Spencer, standing outside the hotel door, Farwell shouted: "Place a guard at the door. President Lincoln is murdered!" Inside he found another clerk at the office desk and shouted to him: "Guard the stairway and Governor Johnson's room. Mr. Lincoln is assassinated."

Without stopping, he knocked on the door of No. 68, the Vice President's room, and hearing no response, he knocked again and called out in the loudest tones he could command: "Governor Johnson, if you are in the room, I must see you." He heard Johnson spring from his bed and exclaim: "Farwell, is that you?" "Yes," he answered, "let me in." The door opened, Farwell entered, turned and locked the door, and told the startled Vice President the fearful news.

Both were overwhelmed and, grasping hands, fell upon each other as if for mutual support. This sense of overpowering surprise, shock and grief lasted but a moment. Then Johnson, without expressing any apprehensions as to his own safety, began planning the proper course for them to pursue in the emergency. The guards whom Farwell had demanded as he rushed into the Kirkwood House were soon placed at the stairway downstairs and in front of Johnson's door. In a few minutes, these volunteer defenders were relieved by soldiers sent by Stanton for the task.[1]

In a few minutes the hotel lobby downstairs and the corridors upstairs were thronged by anxious personal friends of Johnson who had come to satisfy themselves as to his safety. The Vice President inquired several times about Lincoln's condition and about that of Secretary Seward, who, he had just heard, had likewise been a victim of the fiendish plot. He asked Farwell to go in person and see the President, and not to be satisfied with any second- or third-hand information as to his condition. A few minutes later, the Vice President resolved to go himself to Lincoln's bedside.

His friends tried to persuade Johnson that he must not leave the house when there was so much danger, but he was determined. When Major James O. O'Beirne, commander of the provost guard, insisted on sending a detachment of troops with the Vice President, he would not have it, but buttoned up his coat, pulled his hat well over his face and told Farwell to lead the way and O'Beirne to accompany him. "And thus," says Farwell, "we went through the multitude that crowded the streets and filled the passageway, 'till we joined the sad circle of friends who were grouped around the bedside of the dying President."

There are many records of the exact time of this visit. It was about two o'clock in the morning; Lincoln was unconscious and could not communicate any word to his successor destined in five hours' time to take his place as President of the United States.[2] After about half an hour, Johnson left and returned to the Kirkwood House.

It was a night of horror. The President had been shot at the theater. The Secretary of State had been assaulted in his bedroom. Rumors were current of plans to assassinate the Vice President, the Secretary of War and General Grant. The streets of Washington were filled with excited, grief-stricken people. A feeling of uncertainty and depression pervaded the atmosphere and everyone was wondering what would happen next. There was a general sentiment that, in such a critical emergency, the government must not be without a head for a single day; no one could tell what might happen, in the state of the country, if there were, even for a day, no president of the United States.[3]

The sorrowful group which had held that sad and solemn vigil about the bedside of Abraham Lincoln had yet to witness the death struggle, which occurred a little after seven o'clock on Saturday morning, April 15. A little before seven, Gideon Welles entered the room and joined the mourners gathered about the bedside. Mrs. Lincoln made a last, tearful visit. Robert Todd Lincoln stood at the head of the bed, struggling to maintain his self-control, once or twice breaking into uncontrollable sobs and leaning on Charles Sumner's shoulder. At twenty-two minutes past seven, the patient's stertorous breathing ceased. Stanton whispered: "He now belongs to the ages."

After a short and simple prayer led by Dr. Gurley, the members of the Cabinet—all were present except the stricken Seward—filed out of the room of death into the back parlor, to take counsel on what they should do next.

When Lincoln's heart had ceased to beat, Sumner left his place at the head of the bed and went down into the gray drizzling rain. He found General Halleck getting into his carriage and went with him, asking to be set down at Seward's. Halleck replied that first he must stop at Mr. Johnson's hotel. The carriage drove to the Kirkwood House, and Halleck went in to tell the new President that he "must not go out without a guard." By this word Andrew Johnson knew that he had become President of the United States.

As soon as they had closed the door, McCulloch grasped Stanton's coat lapel, and asked: "How will this affect us?" Stanton answered: "We will all have to resign, and if the President accepts our resignation, we must go. If not, why, we must remain." Somewhat alarmed, McCulloch exclaimed: "We don't doubt him. I am prepared for it. I have made all my arrangements to stay here, and I can not resign."[4]

The Cabinet members quickly determined on their course. Attorney-General Speed prepared a letter to Johnson informing him that, by the death of Abraham Lincoln, he had become President, and that it was the common desire of the heads of departments that he take the presidential oath at the earliest possible moment. When all the members had signed this document, the question arose as to who should deliver it.

Stanton proposed that Attorney-General Speed, with some other member of the Cabinet, should carry the notification. Dennison, who presided at the conference, named Gideon Welles, and the Secretary of the Navy noted in his diary that when Dennison did so and all assented, it obviously disconcerted Stanton, "who had expected and intended to be the man." Welles refused the honor and named McCulloch, the Secretary of the Treasury, next in rank after the stricken Seward, as the man to go with Speed.[5]

That Saturday morning Chief Justice Chase was up with the light; a heavy rain was falling, and the sky was black. He first walked to Seward's to inquire about his condition, and then to the house in which Lincoln was lying; there he was told that the President was already dead.[6] Chase went immediately to the Kirkwood House to see Johnson, and found him "apparently calm, but very grave." In a few minutes McCulloch and Speed came into the room and informed the Chief Justice that they were on the way to his house to ask him to administer the oath to the new President. It was agreed that a simple ceremony should take place in Johnson's quarters at ten o'clock that morning. Chase then went with Speed to look into the precedents as to such successions in the cases of Tyler and Fillmore, and to examine the Constitution and the laws.[7]

After an adequate examination of the authorities, the Chief Justice and the Attorney-General returned to the Kirkwood House. At the entrance Chase encountered his erstwhile enemy, Montgomery Blair, and Blair's fine old father. In the emotion of the moment, old bitternesses were forgotten, resentments were buried and a friendly and affectionate greeting was interchanged between the three. They entered the hotel parlor and found assembled there twelve or fourteen gentlemen, among them McCulloch, Senators Foote and Ramsey, former Senator Hale and a number of others.

All were deeply impressed with the sad solemnity of the occasion. Every countenance was overcast. Andrew Johnson, grief-stricken like the rest, and oppressed by the suddenness of the call made upon him and its occasion, was none the less calm and self-possessed.[8] The Chief Justice administered the oath by repeating it word by word, while the Vice President repeated it after him "very distinctly and impressively." At its close Johnson kissed the Bible. Chase noted that the new President's lips had pressed the 21st verse of the 11th chapter of Ezekiel: "But as for them whose heart walketh after the heart of every detestable thing and their abominations, I will recompense their weight upon their own hands, saith the Lord God."

When the Chief Justice received the Bible back in his hands, he said very earnestly: "You are President. May God support, guide and bless you in your arduous duties." Then Chase left the room.[9] The others present congratulated the new Chief Executive, but seemed to feel the usual phrases cold and unsuited to the occasion. After a few moments they found others of a warmer, more spontaneous nature, and presently the new President responded to them:

> Gentlemen: I must be permitted to say that I have been almost overwhelmed by the announcement of the sad event which has so recently occurred; I feel incompetent to perform the duties so important and responsible as those which have so unexpectedly been thrown upon me. As to an indication of any policy which may be pursued by me in the administration of the Government, I have to say that that must be left for development as the Administration progresses. The message or declaration must be made by the acts as they transpire. The only assurance that I can now give of the future is reference to the past. The course which I have taken in connection with this rebellion must be regarded as a guarantee for the future. My past public life, which has been long and laborious, has been founded, as I in good conscience believe, upon a great principle of right, which lies at the basis of all things.
>
> The best energies of my life have been spent in endeavoring to establish and perpetuate the principles of free government; and I believe that the Government, in passing through its present perils, will settle down upon principles consonant with popular rights, more permanent and enduring than heretofore. I must be permitted to say, if I understand the feelings of my own heart, I have long labored to ameliorate and elevate the condition of the great mass of the

American people. Toil and an honest advocacy of
the great principles of free government have been my
lot. The duties have been mine—the consequences
God's.[10] This has been the foundation of my political
creed. I feel that in the end the Government will
triumph, and that these great principles will be
permanently established.

In conclusion, gentlemen, let me say that I want
your encouragement and countenance. I shall ask
and rely upon you and others in carrying the Government through its present perils.

I feel, in making this request, that it will be
heartily responded to by you and all other patriots
and lovers of the rights and interests of a free
people.[11]

After the Chief Justice and other spectators had retired,
the new President expressed to McCulloch and Speed, who had,
at his request, remained in the room, his desire that the present
Cabinet should stand by him in his difficult and responsible
position. McCulloch reported that this wish had been expressed in the language of entreaty and that Johnson appeared
relieved when he was assured that, while the secretaries felt it
their duty to place their resignations in his hands, he should
have the benefit of their services until he saw fit to dispense
with them.[12]

The Cabinet met at noon in McCulloch's office to make
plans for any necessary steps to preserve the public peace.
Attorney-General Speed reported that Johnson had taken the
oath; there was some discussion as to the propriety of his then
issuing an inaugural address to the people. Welles took the
position that this would be in bad taste, and the proposal was
dropped. Johnson himself said that his acts would best disclose his policy; an inaugural he thought unnecessary. In all
essentials this policy would be the same as that of the last president. He desired all members of the Cabinet to go forward
with their duties without any change. Pending Seward's recovery or death, the Chief Clerk of the State Department was
deputed to act as Secretary of State.

The members of the Cabinet were much gratified at the way
the new President conducted himself. Welles noted that Johnson had deported himself admirably.[13] McCulloch was struck
with Johnson's proper conduct. "When we left him," he said,

"the unfavorable impression which had been made upon us by the reports of his unfortunate speech . . . had undergone a considerable change. We all felt as we left him, not entirely relieved of apprehensions, but at least hopeful that he would prove to be a popular and judicious president."[14]

The suggestion was made that Johnson open an office in the White House, but he refused. He did not wish to disturb the family of the murdered President, and preferred temporary offices in some Department. Welles suggested the State Department, but Stanton objected that Seward's papers would be disturbed. Welles acridly suspected that Stanton feared certain documents would thus fall under Johnson's eye which Stanton did not wish him to see. McCulloch offered the room adjoining his own in the Treasury building, and there the new President established himself for several weeks to come.

For a temporary home, he accepted the offer of Representative Samuel Hooper, of his house on Massachusetts Avenue. The first morning he found that there was no food in the larder, and he had to send to market before he could have any breakfast. He asked the servants if there was any wine. "Yes, a few bottles," was the reply. "Well, you had better take good care of them," he replied ironically. During his stay, Johnson had to pay the wages of the Hooper servants, and even to buy feed for the horses.[15]

The stories as to Andrew Johnson's drinking and drunkenness while president would seem to be disproved by McCulloch's testimony. During these first weeks, his office was next door to that of Secretary McCulloch and the latter was intimately associated with him in work, hour by hour and day by day. For six weeks after he became President, McCulloch relates, Johnson "occupied the room adjoining mine. . . . He was there every morning before nine o'clock and he rarely left before five. There was no liquor in his room. It was open to everybody. His luncheon, when he had one, was like mine,—a cup of tea and a cracker."

"It was in that room," the account continues, "that he received the delegations that waited upon him, and the personal and political friends who called to pay their respects. It was there that he made the speeches which startled the country by the bitterness of their tone. . . . So intemperate were some of these speeches that I should have attributed them to the use of stimulants if I had not known them to be the speeches of a sober man, who could not overcome the habit of denunciatory declamation which he had formed in his bitter contests in Tennessee. . . . But none of them could be charged to the account of strong drink. For nearly four years I had daily intercourse with him, frequently at night, and I never saw him when under the influence of liquor. I have not hesitated in saying that whatever may have been his faults, intemperance was not among them."[16]

On the evening of Johnson's first day as President, Sumner called to see him, found him in the "common room" of the Kirkwood House and had a long interview. The Senator's theme was the vital necessity of giving the negroes the right to vote.

On Sunday morning there was another Cabinet meeting, in which the general policy of the treatment of the South was discussed at length. Stanton had divided his "rough draft" and submitted two plans, one for Virginia and a second for North Carolina. Johnson listened to the discussion but did not indicate his decision as to either State.

That evening, in response to a request from Stanton, Welles called at the War Department to discuss a matter of business. After the two secretaries had disposed of the points in question, Welles remained a while, talking of the recent catastrophe.[17] Soon Senator Sumner, Representatives Gooch and Dawes of Massachusetts, Schuyler Colfax, John Covode of Pennsylvania and several other Members of Congress and one or two generals of the army came into the room. Welles was startled, but said nothing.

In a few minutes, Stanton took from his desk the draft of his proposed order for setting up government in the South, and to Welles' astonishment and embarrassment, proceeded to read this secret Cabinet paper, point by point. He was suddenly interrupted by Senator Sumner who demanded: "What provision is made for enfranchising the black man?" Stanton replied he thought it would be impolitic to press *that* question there, since there were differences of opinion on the point "among our friends"; it would be better to go forward with the great essentials wherein all agreed.

"I will not move a step, not an inch," Sumner responded, "if the right of the colored man to vote is not secured."

Welles, embarrassed and outraged at this secret discussion of the proposed proclamation in the making of which none of these men except Stanton was concerned, abruptly said good-night and left. Sumner later disclosed to him something of what had occurred after he had left. Stanton's desire had been to insert nothing which would cause the new President and his friends to suspect the Radicals' intentions. Thus, in discussing what qualification should be prescribed for North Carolina voters, they determined to propose that "loyal citizens are to vote."

This wording was adopted and agreed on that Sunday evening, but Sumner complained to Welles the following December that "the Administration would not accept it." He also gave Welles to understand that by "loyal citizens," they meant blacks as well as whites. Welles deemed this "a cunning contrivance" and said that it was the Radicals who had deserted the Lincoln principles, and not Johnson.

This incident gives a revealing glimpse of the almost fevered activities of the Radicals. It is usual today to depict the death of Lincoln as having occasioned an universal outburst of grief throughout the North and particularly among the leaders of the Republican party, by whom "the Great Emancipator" has since been made a party god. When a searcher for the truth examines the private records of the time, he can scarce repress a feeling of surprise, for the fact is that the Radical leadership of the Republican party, while not pleased with the sacrifice of Lincoln, the individual, almost rejoiced that Lincoln, the merciful executive, had been removed from the helm of state.

Sumner and Fremont, Davis and Chase, Butler and Wade had sought desperately to prevent Lincoln's renomination, or to force his withdrawal in favor of "a better man." George W. Julian, an Indiana Radical Congressman of the day, said that the renomination "was not only very distasteful to the large majority of Congress, but to many of the most prominent men of the party throughout the country." Of the Republicans in both Houses "probably not one in ten really favored it."[18] The pocket veto of the Wade-Davis bill greatly increased their wrath, and presidential pressure behind the Trumbull Louisiana resolution raised their feelings to the boiling point.

So upon Lincoln's assassination, among the Radicals there was "a nearly universal feeling that the advent of Andrew Johnson to the presidency would prove a godsend to the country." Lincoln's restoration views, Julian related, "were as distasteful as possible to Radical Republicans." They had been given a particular obnoxiousness by Lincoln's reiteration three days before his death of his policy of peace and reconciliation to the Southern States.[19]

Almost in the hour when Johnson took the Presidential oath, Radical politicians flocked about him, pressing him to abandon Lincoln's plan. On the afternoon of that very day, the Radicals held a political caucus to discuss "the necessity for a new Cabinet and a line of policy less conciliatory than that of Mr. Lincoln."[20] It was a protracted session, extending far into the night. Among those present, in addition to the Indiana Radical, were "Bluff Ben" Wade, Zach Chandler, Wilkeson, the Washington correspondent for Greeley's *Tribune* and others of that kidney.

At this gathering of Republican leaders, "the hostility for Lincoln's policy of conciliation and contempt for his weakness" were "undisguised." It was "the universal sentiment" that the President's "death is a Godsend to our cause." The caucus thought the time opportune "to get rid of the last vestige of Lincolnism." As a beginning, Ben Butler should become Secretary of State! Interestingly enough, the Blairs had plans of their own for this position, urging the new president to name Montgomery Blair in Seward's stead. Frank Blair they urged for Secretary of War. "The Blairs are a peculiar family," Johnson later told his secretary.[21]

The day after the caucus, Wade carried his Committee on the Conduct of the War to the President's office in the Treasury Department and revealed his secret hopes thus: "Johnson, we have faith in *you*. By the gods, there will be no trouble now in running the government!" Johnson received them cordially and briefly reiterated his views on treason. "We were all cheered and encouraged," Julian relates. The Radicals were sure that the new President "would act upon the advice of General Butler by inaugurating a policy of his own."

"In fine spirits," Ben Butler hastened to Washington to offer advice to the President. He "must not administer on the estate of Lincoln," the General informed the caucus, and set to work to prevent it, calling on Johnson frequently.[22] A few days later, he sat down in his room in Willard's Hotel and addressed a twenty page letter to the President, giving his views on some questions Johnson had voiced as to the legal status of the prisoners of war under the Appomattox Convention. Butler insisted that a parole of the prisoner "in no way lessens his liability to be tried and punished for any crime theretofore committed. . . . A parole confers no *rights* on the prisoner." General Lee was properly liable to be tried for treason, and Butler thought he should be so tried.

Lee heard of this, and appealed, through Reverdy Johnson, to General Grant. The latter, determined to maintain the rights of his paroles, suggested that Lee make a formal pardon application. The latter did so, and also forwarded a statement of his proposed indictment. Grant took the two papers to the President to plead—successfully—that neither Lee nor his men could honorably be tried unless they violated their paroles.[23]

While the Radicals thought that they had Johnson in leading strings, they were very anxious for him not to call Congress in extra session. Elihu B. Washburne, an Illinois Radical, telegraphed that he trusted the President would forego an extra session: "It would lead only to evil." Congressman Ashley of Ohio wrote to the President "indorsing with pleasure your short and emphatic speech," suggesting Daniel S. Dickinson for Seward's place, and adding and underscoring, "I hope no extra session of Congress will be called."

The general tone of the flood of messages which poured in upon Johnson was one of affection and esteem. On April 16 the citizens of Boston, in meeting, sent a message to the new President expressing their determination to give him their "undivided and unfaltering support." The next day 15,000 Indiana patriots assembled in a great meeting at Indianapolis and adopted resolutions, written by Governor Oliver P. Morton, confiding fully in the ability, patriotism and integrity of Andrew Johnson: "The loyal men of this city will rally round him and give his administration the same cordial and generous support which was accorded to that of his lamented predecessor. . . ."

Hiram Walbridge, an important New York financier, reported that great meetings had been held both on the Produce Exchange and in Wall Street and that in both, resolutions were passed, "with the greatest enthusiasm," pledging vigorous determined support. "The whole people will sustain you. Give us a firm Jacksonian administration. . . ."

On behalf of the Union men of New Jersey, Charles P. Smith, chairman of the Union State Committee, tendered

Johnson their confidence and coöperation, and assured him of their "unfaltering faith that God . . . has made you His instrument for restoring peace and prosperity to our distracted land. . . ." Such messages by the hundreds showered in on the new President.[24]

But in public, all was lamentation. Monday and Tuesday were taken up with arrangements for the funeral solemnities at the Capitol, and on Wednesday the funeral itself was held. Business was suspended everywhere and the people crowded the streets. After a solemn procession to the Capitol, Lincoln's remains were placed in the rotunda for the sorrowing throngs to gaze upon. Men and women and little children thronged the streets. The poor colored people "exhibited their woe, bewailing the loss of him whom they regarded as a benefactor and father."[25] Distress was depicted on nearly every countenance. Even the Radicals gave the impression of grief. Lincoln's body lay in state in the Capitol Wednesday afternoon and all day Thursday. Shortly after six o'clock Friday morning, the casket was removed, taken to the station and placed upon the funeral train.

That very day a new turmoil arose in Washington. Word was received from Raleigh of an armistice between General Sherman and the Confederate General Johnston, on terms very disturbing to Stanton, Johnson and Grant. But Sherman was not altogether without authority for his terms. Both President Lincoln and the Secretary of War had given definite expressions to their desire for immediate and merciful peace. In January, when the General had reached Savannah, Stanton had rushed down on a revenue cutter "to pay court to Sherman."[26] The Secretary was much depressed over the length and the cost of the war, and talked freely to the General "of the financial problems that threatened the very existence of the government itself," hinting that there was danger of national bankruptcy "and appealing to Sherman as a soldier and a patriot to hurry matters up so as to bring the war to a close."[27]

Later Sherman had been so impressed with the merciful nature of the President's terms as expressed in their talks at City Point that he repeated them several times to fix them firmly in his memory. They were in his mind when, on April 13, he received a message from General Johnston asking an armistice, "to permit the civil authorities to enter into the needful arrangements to terminate the existing war." The Union General responded by undertaking to abide by the terms Grant had made to Lee. "I really desire," he continued, "to save the people of North Carolina the damage they would sustain by the march of this army." He immediately forwarded this news to Grant, who received it on the 18th, and was immensely pleased, telling Browning that "the great masses of the people South must be received as citizens. We could not get along in the work of reconstruction if we excluded more than half the people of the South from participation."[28]

At eight o'clock on the morning of April 17, as Sherman was about to board the train, the telegraph operator ran down to tell him that an important cipher dispatch was even then being received. It was from Stanton, saying that Lincoln had been assassinated! Stunned by the news and fearful of its effect upon the soldiers, the General pledged the operator to secrecy pending his return. As soon as he was alone with General Johnston, Sherman told him the news. The Confederate general was appalled. Perspiration broke out on his forehead and he denounced the act as "a disgrace to the age."

General Johnston agreed that "any further fighting would be murder," and thought that he could arrange for the surrender of all the Confederate armies rather than for that of his own alone. When Sherman inquired if he had the necessary authority, Johnston answered that he could get it from Davis, and they adjourned to enable Johnston to obtain authority for a general surrender. The next morning the Confederate general assured Sherman that he had authority over all the Confederate armies so that any would obey his orders to surrender, but argued that the Confederates should be given some assurance of their political rights after surrender. Sherman explained Lincoln's amnesty proclamation, but Johnston remained obdurate. Confederate Secretary of War Breckinridge likewise stressed Southern uneasiness about political rights. After considerable further debate, Sherman wrote out, as the very best terms to which he would agree, those which Lincoln had outlined in the conference at City Point late in March.[29] Sherman then read his paper and the Confederates "readily assented."

Under the terms of the agreement, the Confederate armies were to disband and be conducted to their several state capitals to deposit their arms and public property, each officer and man agreeing to cease all acts of war and to abide the action of the authorities. The President was to recognize the Southern State governments, "on their officers and legislators taking the oath prescribed by the Constitution of the United States." Where there were rival state governments, the United States Supreme Court should determine which was legitimate. Another section called for the reestablishment of Federal courts in the South.

A further provision would have guaranteed to the people of all the Southern States, so far as the Executive could do so, "their political rights." Sherman undertook that the executive authority should not disturb the Southern people as long as they lived in peace and quiet, abstained from armed hostility and obeyed their local laws. The final clause provided for "the war to cease," pledging the President to a general amnesty conditional on the disbandment of the Confederate armies and the soldiers' resumption of their pursuits of peace. Its last sentence stated that, "Not being fully empowered by our respective principals to fulfil these terms," the two generals submitted them to their respective civil authorities.[30]

When the paper had been copied and signed, there was general rejoicing among both staffs that the war was over. The next morning, April 19, Sherman gave the documents to an aide, Major Henry Hitchcock, to rush them to Washington for submission to the new President. In his letter to Grant, the General took pride that the agreement would "produce peace from the Potomac to the Rio Grande." Hitchcock reached Washington on the afternoon of April 21, the day on which the Lincoln funeral train had left for Springfield, and delivered his message immediately. On reading it Grant was exceedingly perturbed, and ordered the messenger to wait in his office and discuss the matter with no one until Grant should instruct him what to do.[31]

It is probable that Sherman's terms to Johnston would have seemed altogether satisfactory to Lincoln. Sherman always contended, with a good deal of reason, that in his pact with the Confederate General he was merely carrying out instructions Lincoln had given him in their conference at City Point. But the armistice was more than an armistice; it was virtually a treaty of peace. Viewed from the distance of the third decade of the Twentieth Century, its terms seem very sound. But Lincoln had been assassinated. The feelings of the North had changed with the shot of John Wilkes Booth. From a general desire for peace, reconciliation and early readjustment, there had arisen an ugly, glowering demand for the stern punishment of the South.

As soon as Grant gave the letters to Stanton, the latter called upon Johnson for a Cabinet meeting. The members gathered at eight that evening, General Grant and Preston King also being present. Stanton read the paper and as soon as he had concluded, there was general and emphatic disapproval.

Stanton was particularly vehement in his denunciation, and Speed not far behind. Stanton feared that Sherman might be marching on to Washington at the head of his victorious legions, and wanted to put Sherman under arrest. Speed believed that the General deemed himself the American Napoleon. They pictured Sherman as almost a traitor, and credited him with making plans for a *coup d'état*.[32]

President Johnson decided to inform Sherman immediately that the armistice was disapproved and that he must resume hostilities at once, and Grant was sent posthaste to Raleigh to take personal command. Stanton wrote a terse dispatch to Sherman reprimanding the great strategist. At ten o'clock Hitchcock was summoned to Grant's office, and at midnight the General of the Army started with him to Raleigh. Sherman's loyal subordinate did not know what was in the wind, but he expected the worst. When they reached Raleigh, officers crowded around the Aide, asking: "Well, Major, do you bring back peace or war?" He answered: "I brought back General Grant."

The whole matter became public on Sunday, when Stanton gave the Associated Press a dispatch incorporating a copy of his order, and accompanied it with a statement of nine reasons "among others," why the Sherman-Johnston armistice had been disapproved. But the President had not known of Stanton's pontifical bull.[33]

At the Cabinet meeting, the dispatch recited, General Sherman's action "was disapproved by the President, Secretary of War, by General Grant, and by every member." Sherman had been ordered to resume hostilities immediately and a copy of the instructions Lincoln gave Grant in regard to peace proposals from Lee had been sent him.[34] It added that Sherman's

ANDREW JOHNSON IN THE FIFTIES

At the Time of this Picture, Andrew Johnson Had Just Taken His
Seat in the United States Senate in 1857.

orders to Stoneman would "probably open the way for Davis to escape . . . with his plunder!"[35]

The reasons given in Stanton's unsigned statement for disapproving Sherman's action were that he had no authority to make such a peace; that it was a practical acknowledgment of the Confederate government; and that "it undertook to reestablish the rebel state governments." Stanton also made the point that, under this pact, the South would be enabled to reestablish slavery, and he contended that the armistice agreement might obligate the government to pay the Confederate debt. His eighth "reason" delivered a stinging rebuke to Sherman. The armistice, Stanton said, "gave terms that had been deliberately, repeatedly, and solemnly rejected by President Lincoln, and better terms than the Rebels had ever asked in their most prosperous condition." [36] After this diatribe, little wonder that Sherman's wrath was great!

Sherman took the President's orders and Grant's visit, in good stead, denounced the armistice and soon received Johnston's surrender on Appomattox terms. He did not know of Stanton's bulletin until he received a copy of a New York paper at Raleigh. He termed it "an outrage on me . . . a personal and official insult"—as indeed it was.

There was an almost universal chorus of Radical disapproval of the Sherman pact. On April 27 the General's brother, Senator John Sherman, wrote that he was "distressed beyond measure at the terms. . . . There should now be literally no terms granted. We should not only brand the leading Rebels with infamy, but the whole Rebellion should wear the badge of the penitentiary. . . ."[37] Fessenden called it a "stupendous blunder." Perhaps no popular "idol," Stanton's panegyrist declares, "was ever before so discredited."[38]

Within less than a week, the Conservative Republicans recovered their balance. On April 23, Welles commented that the manner of Stanton's announcement was "not particularly commendable, judicious or correct." The Navy Secretary had already concluded that Sherman had been "hasty" rather than "wicked or ambitious" in his scheme.

When, on April 25, in Cabinet meeting, Speed charged that Sherman had been seduced by Breckinridge into making himself dictator, Welles termed this a strange phantom and admitted that the Cabinet had suffered itself "to be hurried in the unjust and ungenerous suspicions by the erroneous statements of the Secretary of War."[39]

Mention has been made of the haste with which Sumner had called upon Johnson on the first evening of his presidency. The overtures made by Julian, Wade and other Radicals to the new executive were other instances of the almost frantic Radical effort in April and May to capture the new president. Several usually authoritative historians contend that Johnson did submit unreservedy to the Radical program, and then became a Judas to their cause.[40] On what evidence does this charge depend? Was Johnson dazzled by the Massachusetts sun god? Was this inexperienced Tennessee tailor hypnotized by Bluff Ben Wade? Was Lincoln's successor more intrigued by Chase's hobby than Lincoln himself had been?

Sumner from the beginning deliberately cultivated Johnson. Following his first visit at the Kirkwood House, when he used a minor detail of public business in his hands as chairman of the Foreign Relations committee of the Senate as pretext to make a Radical plea,[41] he saw Johnson "repeatedly." Sumner thought the President's manner "excellent, and even sympathetic, without any uncomfortable reticence." At times he called on Johnson alone, at others he took Chief Justice Chase with him. Again, Bluff Ben Wade was the chosen chorus to the Senatorial doctrinaire.

On Saturday, April 22, Sumner and Chase made an evening visit on the President, "especially with the view of conversing on negro suffrage." They "urged earnestly" all the "rights and necessities of the case," and were "light-hearted" when they left. Sumner wrote a friend a day or so later, "I am confident that our ideas will prevail."[42]

At this time, like the rest of the Radicals, Sumner was anxious that there be no extra session of Congress. "I should not be surprised," he wrote, "if we had this great question settled before the next meeting of Congress." On the suggestion of an extra session, he said, "I hope not." With Johnson committed, why have a Congress to interfere?

Radicals were urging Sumner to exert pressure on the new President. A Boston friend asked if Johnson would surround himself with wise advisers and insisted "that *you* should establish . . . intimate relations with him, and save him from the Blairs."[43] George Loring of Salem wrote that Lincoln's death "has opened the way . . . I pray you to keep President Johnson true. . . . Urge him to adopt a policy based on federal authority." Another letter declared that Lincoln's "goodness, benevolence, and magnanimity" were much out of place, while a third anticipated with delight "an entirely new order of things under Mr. Johnson." Many hinted to Sumner that he should take Seward's place as Secretary of State, and George L. Stearns wrote "how grandly Andrew Johnson looms up. . . . Let us thank God that with Abraham Lincoln Whiggery died." Stearns too was not greatly grieved over Lincoln's death. "What he refused us while living," this Boston Radical wrote his Senator, "his death has given to the country." In one week it had "doubled the antislavery strength of the North, and made justice to the black loyalists a necessity."[44]

On the second Sunday night succeeding his visit with Chase, Sumner called on the President again and had a long talk with him. "Of course," the Senator wrote John Bright the next day, "my theme is justice to the colored race." Sumner insisted that the President "accepted this idea completely, and indeed went so far as to say, 'There is no difference between us.'" The Senator expressed his joy that there would be no breach within the party and quoted Johnson as answering, "I mean to keep you all together." One of the Senator's biographers states that "as he walked away that evening, Sumner felt that the battle of his own life was ended."[45]

This letter of Sumner, who wrote similar exultant epistles to other Radical friends, is the chief basis for the contention that, after letting himself be taken in by the Radicals and pledging himself to their policies, Johnson later broke his faith. But a careful examination of Sumner's letter to Bright reveals that Johnson was far from committing himself unreservedly. For Sumner wrote further of the President's views at this interview: "He deprecates haste; is unwilling that States should be precipitated back; thinks there must be a period of probation, but that meanwhile all loyal people, without distinction of color, must be treated as citizens and must take part in any proceedings for reorganization. He doubts at present the expediency of announcing this from Washington. . . ."

Thus we know that Sumner had not been able to persuade Johnson to take any immediate steps. The President had merely said that he was not opposed to negro suffrage. Nor was he—if a State itself should confer it. Johnson's position from beginning to end was that suffrage was the function of the State alone. Sumner himself admitted that his confidence was "founded in part upon the essential justice of our aims and the necessity of the case."

That same day Sumner wrote to a foreign diplomat, comparing Lincoln and Johnson "on the important question" to the advantage of the latter. The next day he informed Francis Lieber that he was "charmed" by Johnson's sympathy, "entirely different from his predecessor's," and that Johnson had reiterated "that colored persons are to have the right of suffrage." But once more he sets down that "the President desires that the movement should appear to proceed from the people."

There was another interview which should have shown Sumner the light. The Massachusetts Senator had been disturbed because Brownlow's Tennessee government had not provided for votes for negroes and he had besought Johnson to interfere; but this the President refused to do. If he were at Nashville, Johnson said, he would do so, but it was beyond his proper sphere as President.[46] When the Virginia proclamation was announced, some of Sumner's Radical friends became alarmed at the prospect. Thad Stevens wrote to him from Philadelphia: "I see the President is precipitating things. Virginia is magnified. I fear before Congress meets he will have so bedeviled matters as to render them immovable. It would be well if he would call an extra session of Congress. But I almost despair of resisting executive influence."[47]

But Sumner's hopes still sustained him. On May 12 a caucus of Radicals was held in the National Hotel, in Washington, with the purpose of exerting Radical influence on the President. Sumner and Wade both addressed the meeting and both declared that President Johnson was thoroughly Radical and favored negro suffrage as much as anyone there.[48] But they did not so much as hint that the President favored negro suffrage only if accorded by the States.

Before Sumner left Washington about the middle of May, he had another interview with the President and once more repeated his views. Johnson listened pleasantly and said with a smile, "Have I not always listened to you?" Sumner interpreted this enigmatic expression of courtesy as positive presidential assurance that Johnson was completely committed to his views.

Wade also saw Johnson, and always urged stern Radical views. There is a record of one such interview. The President had asked the Ohio Senator: "What would you do, were you in my place?" The Radical quickly answered "I would either force into exile, or hang ten or twelve of the worst of those fellows—perhaps, for full measure, I should make it thirteen, just a baker's dozen." Johnson asked how to select such a small number. Wade quickly named Davis, Toombs, Benjamin, Slidell, Mason, and Howell Cobb and added: "If we did no more than drive these half dozen out of the country, we should accomplish a good deal."[49] But of negro suffrage, no word of Johnson promise is preserved by Wade's biographer.

In April, shortly after the interview of Sumner and Chase with President Johnson, Chase determined to make a speaking tour through the South, his addresses to be "reserved for the masses of freed negroes, not for the sullen whites." Sumner declared that Chase had been authorized to represent Johnson's policies, "and to do everything he can to promote organization without distinction of color."

But Chase gave another impression. He submitted the rough draft of a reorganization plan in which he had "incorporated a distinct recognition of the loyal colored men as citizens entitled to the right of suffrage." After he had read it and re-read it to the President, the latter told him: "I agree to all you say, but I don't see how I can issue such a document now. I am new and untried, and cannot venture on all I please." On April 18, Chase wrote Johnson in great anxiety about hints of a North Carolina restoration. "Is this expedient?" he inquired. "Would it not be far better to make Florida and Louisiana really free States with universal suffrage . . .? Everything now, under God, must depend on you." When the Chief Justice left on his Southern tour, he was far from claiming that he had Johnson's pledge. All he would say was that he "almost hoped that the President's reluctance was conquered."[50]

The evidences of Johnson's "apostasy" do not, then, seem striking. Sumner seems to have misinterpreted Johnson's careful courtesy for agreement, and to have taken the Tennessean's bitterness toward "the conscientious and intelligent leaders" of Secession as meaning that he was willing to override State Rights and impose negro suffrage on the South at the bayonet point. It was quite like Johnson not to dispel such a misunderstanding, for it was a habit of the President, Gideon Welles disapprovingly recounts, to listen to anyone's opinions; "but unless he squarely and emphatically disapproves, [he] is disinclined to controvert. This trait has led many to misunderstand and to misrepresent him. They make statements themselves which he does not deny and dispute, and he is consequently represented as entertaining the views of his auditor or adviser."[51]

This Radical beguiling was not the only types of advice tendered to the new President. Preston King, Senator Doolittle of Wisconsin and Thurlow Weed were with him much during these days when he was living in Representative Hooper's comfortable home, waiting for the Lincolns to leave the White House. It was at this period that Doolittle wrote his wife: "God is still with us. O, if we are only true to the country all will yet be safe. . . . Mr. Johnson, King and myself are a trio whose hearts and heads sympathize more closely and more deeply than any other trio in America just now." "I know that his first solicitude was to ascertain and carry out the policy of Mr. Lincoln," Weed later recounted. "I know he went to the White House with that determination." This testimony of Seward's *alter ego* as to Johnson's unyielding attachment to the policy of his martyred predecessor is unnecessary, for the new President considered Lincoln "the greatest American that has ever lived."[52]

Francis Preston Blair, who had so recently befriended Johnson in a time of need, was also on terms of intimacy with him now as President; and conservative Union leaders throughout the country depended upon the prop of Andrew Jackson to prove a prop to Andrew Johnson too. On April 17, George W. Childs, owner of the Philadelphia *Ledger*, wrote Blair asking him to tell the new President that the independent press of the country would stand by him, "and we hope he will carry out the wise policies of Mr. Lincoln." The Conservatives were all looking to Blair, Childs added, to keep Johnson out of the hands of the Radicals, for if they should control him, there would be trouble ahead. The columns of the *Ledger* were at the service of the new President. Edward Bates wrote from St. Louis that "at such a time as this, the nation needs, humanity needs, a Chief Magistrate brave, firm, moderate, law-abiding, a man that reverences the Constitution of his country. . . ."

But the dominant Republican sentiment throughout the North was otherwise. In offering the President his cordial support, Lyman Trumbull insisted that the control of state organizations in the South must be given to new men having no sympathy with the slaveholding aristocracy. A Michigan Attorney-General named Williams believed that Booth should suffer, but asked "Why should Davis, Lee, and others," whose pupil Booth was, "and who are infamous beyond the power of description, be allowed to escape with impunity? Hang the very worst of them, expatriate many more, and disfranchise the still larger class than the second, thereby teaching them treason is a crime."

The servants of the Gospel of the Man of Galilee were not silent. The Rev. G. L. Griffitt, pastor of the Central Baptist Church of Trenton, N. J., informed the President that "Copperheads alone gnash their teeth at the prospect that treason is to get its due. Go on and God prosper you." B. Gratz Brown, Radical politician, wrote: "I yet believe that God in His Providence has called you to complete the work of rebuilding this nation that it might be stamped with a creed of Radical Democracy in all its parts." John Cockburn wrote from Indianapolis urging Johnson to offer a reward for the capture of Jefferson Davis. "The country is prepared," he said, "to see these men properly dealt with as outlaws and criminals. The arrest and punishment of Jeff Davis alone would do more for our future peace than the most destructive battle of the war."

The new President's speeches and actions had brought him general commendation in the North during these first few weeks. On April 22 Greeley's *Tribune* said that Johnson was gaining "steadily in public confidence and esteem." Its Washington correspondent termed him "not only one of the nation's foremost patriots and statesmen," but also "a fitting type of a modest, yet self-reliant and accomplished gentleman." The Philadelphia *Press*, equally lavish in its praise, called Johnson "the most popular man in America."

For a short period the President had the approval and support of elements which in their nature were irreconcilable. Remembering his insistence that treason must be made odious, the Radicals relied upon him to be their Moses. The Conservatives prayed that Johnson would consider himself the trustee of Lincoln's policies, and the Southern Unionists believed in him because he was one of them. But the leaders of the Secession

and the Civil War feared harsh measures at his hand. When
Jefferson Davis was captured in Georgia, he told General Wilson that he feared the new President would display a "vindictive
and unforgivable temper" toward himself and the South. Nor
did the rank and file respect him. "I think to hold an office
under Andy Johnson, even for the good of the country, would
be a disgrace," the daughter of a distinguished Georgia Unionist declared. She thought her father "too honorable a man" to
have relations with "that vulgar renegade."[53]

Johnson's speeches in the first few days of presidential
service contained expressions which might have justified
Southern apprehensions. When, on April 18, an Illinois delegation headed by Governor Oglesby called upon the President
in his Treasury office in reply to their expressions of support,
he repeated his bitter phrases about treachery and treason.

Immediately after Lee's and Johnston's surrenders, some of
the Confederate Governors had summoned their legislatures to
restore relations with the Union. But Stanton found these
advances unwelcome and ordered the military commanders affected to disperse the legislatures by force and to drive the
governors out of office.[54]

On April 21, Governor Oliver P. Morton, spokesman of an
Indiana delegation, was unqualified in his pledge of support.
The Radical Julian joined the delegation which, he believed,
"had a decidedly political significance." Morton, who was then
supreme in Indiana, "the idol of his party and of returning
soldiers," spoke at length on reconstruction. A State, he insisted could "neither secede nor by any possible means be
taken out of the Union." If the States which had been brought
back by force should be dealt with as conquered provinces,
Morton believed that the nation itself would be obliged to pay
any debts contracted by them before the war.[55]

Johnson's impromptu response was a homily on treason
which, he said, was none the less treason whether in a free or a
slave State.[56] There might be some excuse for a traitor who
had slaves, "but a traitor in a free State has no excuse but
simply to be a traitor." The President did not mean that any
man should be exonerated from the penalties and punishment
of treason. "The time has arrived," he said, "when the American people should understand what crime is, and that it should
be punished, and its penalties enforced and inflicted. . . . If
you take the life of one individual for the murder of another,

and believe that his property should be confiscated, what should be done with one who is trying to assassinate this nation?"

"Treason," he said, "must be made odious, . . . traitors must be punished and impoverished, . . . their social power must be destroyed." But then he struck another note: "I say, as to the leaders, punishment. I also say leniency, conciliation and amnesty to the thousands whom they have misled and deceived."

He ended with a reference of appreciation of Morton's remarks as to the status of the Southern States. Here Johnson stood firmly on Lincolnian ground. "Yes, if rebellion had . . . set aside the machinery of the State for a time, there stands a great law to remove the paralysis and revitalize it, and put it on its feet again." His views on the theory of state suicide were well known. The States' "life breath has been only suspended, and it is a high constitutional obligation with them to secure each of those States in the possession and enjoyment of a republican form of government. . . . I care not how small the number of Union men, if enough to man the ship of state, I hold it, I say, a high duty to protect and secure to them a republican form of government."[57]

A few days later Johnson substantially repeated his homily on treason, this time in a talk to a delegation of Southern refugees with whom he discussed the problem of amnesty and showed clearly the division in his mind between the leaders of Secession and its rank and file. "I say justice toward the leaders, the conscious leaders," he declared. "But I also say amnesty, conciliation, clemency, and mercy to the thousands of our countrymen whom you and I know have been deceived or driven into this infernal rebellion."[58]

Some of Johnson's Tennessee friends became alarmed at these savage speeches and a committee went to Washington to seek to ameliorate his attitude. They found him in the bathroom shaving; and he had them ushered in and talked with them while he completed his morning toilet. "Boys," he said, "I know exactly why you have come here. Give yourselves no uneasiness. I am not going to hang anybody."[59]

These interviews and successive delegation speeches proved wearing on the President. In May, to Welles' delight, the pressure somewhat lessened. Father Gideon felt that, while they might have been useful to some extent "in giving the President an opportunity to enunciate his opinions in the

absence of any inaugural," none the less they had been annoy-
ing, irksome and obstructive to business. But through them all
Johnson had "borne himself well," and had won "the good
wishes of the country."[60]

These speeches, while time consuming, formed a minor part
of the presidential burden. It was the multifarious problems of
ending war and establishing enduring peace that chiefly oppressed Johnson. The problems were diverse, numerous, important and bitterly contested. How should justice be administered to the Lincoln conspirators? Should the blockade
of Southern ports immediately cease? Should Jefferson Davis
be tried for treason, and if so, by a civil or military court?
Was it wise to confiscate the property of the Confederates?
Had the Southern States legally seceded, or were they still
States of the Federal Union, with merely suspended functions?
How should the currents of trade be reestablished, so as to
reanimate the prostrate South? How would the millions of
freedmen be protected? What would be the attitude of the
ex-masters toward their former slaves? Who were citizens and
by whom should government be reorganized? These and myriad
similar thorny questions were pressing for immediate consideration and action.

The President and his Cabinet members were working under tremendous pressure. For the first three months of his
presidency, Johnson took no recreation at all. On July 9,
Welles persuaded him to take a "short excursion" down the
river, and noted that a month had passed since Johnson had
moved to the White House, "and he has never yet gone outside
the doors."[61]

During these first few weeks, the Cabinet held not only the
regular Tuesday and Friday meetings but had many called
sessions on other days of the week, Sunday being no exception.
The questions mentioned above came up for discussion not once
but many times. The problems most frequently recurring in
these Cabinet meetings in April and May, were those of Amnesty and Restoration. Whenever more immediate matters had
been disposed of, the Cabinet would turn to them.

At the second meeting of the Cabinet in May, the Virginia
branch of Stanton's April proclamation came up again for
discussion. After severe amendment on Welles' suggestion, it
was adopted and was issued on May 9. By its terms, the task

of restoration was committed to the existing State government
—the hypothetical government which Pierpoint had trumped
up at Alexandria. Inasmuch as this Virginia government was
"loyal," the Virginia proclamation had little in it to cause any
particular stir. Attorney-General Speed also presented his
draft of an Amnesty Proclamation, which in the main followed
the lines of the various Lincoln amnesties, its general tone
being one of reserve toward the Secession leaders and of great
indulgence toward the rank and file.

At this same meeting, the North Carolina issue came to a
head. When Stanton read his draft of the plan for the restoration of that state, his phrase as to "loyal citizens" was critically
examined. Did it mean negroes as well as whites? Trapped,
Stanton admitted that it did, and asked his colleagues to vote
thereon.[62] He was anxious that they "not discuss the question,
but each express his opinion without preliminary debate." The
Cabinet was found to be evenly divided. Welles, Usher and
McCulloch opposed inserting the negro suffrage provision;
Stanton, Dennison and Speed approved of it.

Welles was painfully struck with the "fanaticism" on the
subject of negro suffrage. Such persons persuaded themselves
"that the cause of liberty and the Union is with the negro and
not with the white man. White men, and especially Southern
white men, are tyrants," he continued. "Sumner is riding this
one idea at top speed. There are others, less sincere than
Sumner, who are pressing the question for party purposes," he
noted on May 9.[63] "No one can claim that the blacks, in the
slave States especially, can exercise the elective franchise intelligently," he continued. "In most of the free States, they are
not permitted to vote. . . . If the negro is to vote and exercise the duties of a citizen, let him be educated to it."

Stanton had executed an about face on the subject of negro
suffrage; a short time before he had objected to such plans,
"but aspiring politicians will generally take that road."[64] On
May 19, Seward was able to return to the State Department
and resume his duties. When he arrived he ranged himself
with the Conservatives in the Cabinet, but Johnson, as a
staunch States' Rights Democrat, did not need the weight of
Seward's judgment to determine him.

On May 22, the President, by proclamation, opened all
Southern ports to world commerce except a few in Texas.[65]
On that same day, all Washington was thrilled by a great cere-

monial, the magnificent spectacle of the review of the armies of the North. On the first day the Army of the Potomac marched by the reviewing stand, regiment after regiment, brigade after brigade, and divisions without end; on Tuesday Sherman's Armies of the West marched by.

During the second day's review, a significant incident occurred. The President, his Cabinet and General Grant were standing on the reviewing stand. When Sherman reached it, he left the line of march and joined the group on the platform. The Cabinet crowded about him to shake hands and offer congratulations. Sherman shook the President cordially by the hand. Stanton approached him with his hand held out for greeting, but Sherman gave him a withering glance and put his hand behind him. "I do not shake hands with clerks," he said, and turned upon his heel.[66]

This great review was the closing act of the Civil War. As the thousands trod the dusty streets, their rhythmic march omened the coming of peace to a reunited Union.

About the middle of May, Johnson had made up his mind as to the form of the North Carolina proclamation and the details of the Amnesty. There yet remained the question of whom Johnson would select as Provisional Governor of North Carolina to carry out the plan the President had in mind?

Early in May, he summoned a number of the Unionist and Conservative leaders of North Carolina to Washington for consultation. Chief among them was W. W. Holden, the Raleigh politician and editor, whose efforts in 1864 to be elected Governor on a peace platform had been watched with rapt attention through the North. Before Holden reached the capital, several other North Carolina Conservative and Unionist leaders conferred with the President, among them D. L. Swain, president of the University of North Carolina, B. F. Moore, William Eaton and John H. Wheeler.

Johnson showed them his proclamation. Moore vehemently objected on the ground that it was unconstitutional. The legislature should be allowed to meet to call a constitutional convention. The President said that the legislature had no legal status and asked what he could do if, after he had recognized a Secession legislature, it should refuse to do the things which had to be done. Moore answered that there was "no one of that body who might not be led back into the Union by a silken thread." But the President remained courteously insistent on his plan.[67]

Upon Holden's arrival, there was another conference. This time Johnson did not submit his plan for criticism, but made it obvious that the consultation was to aid him in naming the proper man as Provisional Governor. During the discussion. Swain called Holden aside and appealed to him not to accept the appointment. Holden thought Swain feared he was an enemy of the University and assured him such was not the case. When they returned to the White House, they were greeted with the information that Holden had been appointed to the post.[68]

The Provisional Governor remained in Washington seven or eight days and had several talks with the President concerning the problems of reorganizing the State, in which he said he had urged a policy "as generous as possible." Johnson called attention to the exceptions in his Amnesty Proclamation, and said that whenever applied to by any person falling within one of these fourteen classes, he would "give immediate attention, and pardon where he could."[69] As a means of financing the provisional government during its initial stages, he promised to turn over to Holden all the war property that had been collected by Governor Vance and seized by the Federal authorities.[70]

Radical though he later became, Holden's testimony puts a quietus to the Radical assertions that it was necessary for sentimental appeals to be made to Johnson for favors to North Carolina. "Andrew Johnson loved his native State," Holden declared. "It was not necessary to make 'pathetic' appeals to him to influence him to show even special favor to North Carolina."[71]

On May 29 the President issued his two important proclamations. According to its preamble, that of Amnesty was issued "in order that the authority of the government of the United States may be restored, and that peace, order and freedom may be established." With certain exceptions, the President granted "to all persons who have directly or indirectly participated in the existing rebellion," amnesty and pardon, "with the restoration of all rights of property," except as to slaves and legal confiscation proceedings already in court.

Persons thus pardoned must, however, take oath that they would "henceforth faithfully support, protect, and defend the Constitution of the United States, and the Union of the States thereunder"; and would "abide by and faithfully support all laws and proclamations" made during the war regarding emancipation.

Fourteen classes of persons were excepted from this general pardon. These included all civil or diplomatic officers or agents of the Confederate government, United States judges who had resigned to aid the South, all military or naval officers of the Confederacy above the ranks of colonel in the army and lieutenant in the navy; all who had quit Congress to join the South, all officers of the regular army who had resigned "to evade duty in resisting the rebellion," all who had mistreated Federal prisoners of war; all Confederate officers who had been educated at West Point, or Annapolis; all officers of seceded State governments; all citizens of unseceded States who had joined the Confederate forces, and all who, previously having taken the Lincoln oath of December 8, 1863, had violated it.

There was one notable exception, the 13th: All persons who have voluntarily participated in secession, the value of whose property was over $20,000.[72] This last was a special and particular insertion on Andrew Johnson's part, the fruit of his firm beliefs as to the economic causes of the Civil War. He had long been convinced that the rich slave owners had dragooned "the wool-hat boys" into Secession, and was not willing that this class be pardoned, until it showed some evidence of contrition and repentance.

The North Carolina restoration scheme served as the foundation and model for the presidential plan in all thus far unreorganized Southern States, and its provisions accordingly deserve attention.

The North Carolina proclamation was based upon the fourth section of the fourth article of the Federal Constitution, that the United States should guarantee to every state "a republican form of government." It is stated that the President, as constitutional commander-in-chief of the army and navy and chief civil executive officer of the nation, in order to enforce the obligations of the United States to the people of North Carolina, therefore did appoint William W. Holden Provisional Governor of that State.

It would be the duty of this official "to prescribe such rules and regulations as may be necessary and proper for convening a convention, composed of delegates to be chosen by that portion of the people of said State who are loyal to the United States, and no others, for the purpose of altering or amending the constitution thereof, and with authority to exercise, within the limits of said State, all the powers necessary and proper to enable such loyal people of the State of North Carolina to restore said State to its constitutional relations to the Federal government and to present such a republican form of state government as will entitle the State to the guarantee of the United States therefor."

The proclamation carefully set forth the necessary qualifications of a voter. He must "have previously taken the oath of amnesty" prescribed in the Amnesty Proclamation of May 29. In addition, he must be "a voter qualified as prescribed by the Constitution and laws of the State of North Carolina, in force immediately before the 20th day of May, 1861"—that is to say, before North Carolina's secession. The constitutional convention, or the legislature it would set up, "will prescribe the qualification of electors, and the eligibility of persons to hold office under the constitution and laws of the State." Johnson carefully set forth that this was a power "the people of the several States composing the Federal Union have rightfully exercised from the origin of government to the present time."[73] This epochal proclamation was a signal to the prostrate South that Johnson would walk in Lincoln's footsteps. To the country in general it was an omen of the dawn of peace; but to the bloodthirsty Radicals, since it failed to force negro suffrage upon North Carolina, it was a declaration of war.

X. THE TRIAL OF MRS. SURRATT

D URING these intricate political machinations, the apprehension and trial of persons implicated in the assassination of Abraham Lincoln had gotten under way. In the light of fact subsequently developed, the trial of the conspirators by military commission casts a baleful shadow on Andrew Johnson's ill-starred presidency.

Stanton and his assistants made frantic efforts to connect the leading civil officers of the Confederacy with the Booth conspiracy. The Secretary of War employed a shabby troop of self-confessed perjurers to retail venomous scandal to the commission to prove that Jefferson Davis and even General Lee instigated the plot of John Wilkes Booth. But within a brief two years, even while Radical passion was still hot, it became clear that such talk was utterly absurd. No single Confederate of rank was ever brought to trial on the assassination charge.

The truth about the conspiracy may be summed up thus: Assassin though he was, John Wilkes Booth was a very remarkable man. For many years he was remembered as a magnetic personality by the confraternity of the stage. Forty-four years after the tragedy, Sir Charles Wyndham, the noted English actor, described Booth as "one of the few to whom that ill-used term of genius might be applied with perfect truth. . . . Seldom has the stage seen a more impressive, or a more handsome, or a more impassioned actor. Picture to yourself Adonis, with high forehead, ascetic face, corrected by rather full lips, sweeping black hair, a figure of perfect youthful proportions, and the most wonderful black eyes in the world. . . . When his emotions were aroused, they were like living jewels. Flames shot from them."[1]

This ill-starred genius, born in Maryland of a famous actor family, went on the stage as a lad and quickly made a name for himself. Born in the South, surrounded by Southern influences, and as an actor immensely popular in the South, Booth became an impassioned Southern sympathizer during the war. As the Confederate hopes paled, his heart grew dark with anger and something must have snapped in that eerie brain of his. After long brooding over the wrongs of his beloved section, early in 1864, he conceived the daring plan of kidnaping Abraham Lincoln on the streets of Washington, and spiriting him across the Potomac, through the lines of both armies, and into a Confederate prison at Richmond.

Booth quickly realized that he could not carry out such a plot single-handed, and sought to enlist the aid of others willing to go to almost any lengths to aid the South. In January, 1864, the conspirators made their first attempt. Lincoln had announced that he would attend a performance of Edwin Forrest at Ford's Theater. Booth, two former schoolmates named Arnold and O'Laughlin, and an actor named Chester, were waiting for him. But the night was fearfully stormy and Lincoln stayed away.

The madcap actor was bent on enlisting a Confederate agent, one John H. Surratt, in the plot. After being introduced, he cultivated Surratt so assiduously that the latter's suspicions were aroused. When Booth finally revealed his plan, he first peered under the bed, looked in the wardrobe, and then advanced furtively toward Surratt, whispering: "We must be careful; the very walls have ears!" In a moment he added: "It is to kidnap President Lincoln and carry him off to Richmond."[2]

At the outset "aghast" at the "foolhardy undertaking," Surratt, after a few days' thought, concluded that, if only the kidnaping could be effected, it was entirely feasible to carry Lincoln across the Potomac and, by the famous "underground railroad," through the lines of the two armies. Himself willing to do almost anything for Secession, Surratt assented to the proposition. Indeed, if the plan had been executed in 1864, the South could have used the captured President as a hostage through whom to win the release of tens of thousands of captured Confederate soldiers. The length, if not the outcome, of the war might have been affected.

But opportunity was slow, and Confederate fortunes had ebbed to a very low point. On March 16, 1865, it was announced that there would be a benefit performance of "Still Waters Run Deep" at the Soldiers' Home and that Lincoln would attend. Booth's kidnaping band was so well organized that, within three-quarters of an hour of the time he heard of the intended visit, Booth had seven men, all mounted and armed to the teeth, waiting on the road to the Soldiers' Home to capture Lincoln as he came by.[3]

Again chance balked their plans. Lincoln was so busy with his duties that he sent someone else to represent him. When the waiting group peered within the White House carriage and saw not Lincoln but a stranger, their consciences accused them. Thinking their plan discovered, the carriage a decoy and arrest to be staring them in the face, they scattered immediately. But Booth's magnetism was such that he reinspired confidence in most of these misguided youths, and even those who withdrew did not confess.

Two in the crowd which Lincoln had addressed on the night of April 11 had not joined in the rejoicing. John Wilkes Booth, the half mad actor, and Lewis Payne, the half-drunken desperado, co-conspirators in the now abandoned kidnaping plan, could not believe their ears when they heard the President talking about giving votes to "niggers." Only a monster, they thought, would propose such a thing. As Booth and Payne walked away, the actor muttered to his comrade: "This is the last speech he will ever make." At that moment was born their plan to assassinate Abraham Lincoln. Opportunity was not long lacking. At noon, on Friday, April 14, when Booth called for mail at Ford's Theater, he learned that Lincoln would attend the performance there that evening. Booth's chance had come.

Early that afternoon, he called all the conspirators to his room at the Herndon House and proceeded to assign their parts in the evening's enterprise. Atzerodt refused to undertake the assassination of Andrew Johnson. "I went into the thing to capture," he said, "but I am not going to kill." Booth told him he was a fool, adding, "You will be hung anyhow; it is death for any man that backs out." With these words they parted.[4]

That afternoon Booth called at the Kirkwood House to try to sound out William A. Browning, Johnson's secretary, as to the habits of his Chief. But the Vice President and Colonel Browning had been at the Capitol all morning and most of the afternoon. When Browning asked for his key at the hotel desk between four and five that afternoon, the clerk handed him Booth's card with this penciled notation, "Don't wish to disturb you; are you at home? J. Wilkes Booth." Obviously, the actor had in mind assigning someone other than Atzerodt to the murder of the Vice President, and was approaching

Browning, whom he had known when he had played in Nashville before the war, to spy out the land.[5]

It later developed that Atzerodt had actually made some preliminary moves toward kidnaping the Vice President. Between four and five o'clock on the afternoon of April 12, Atzerodt had approached Colonel W. R. Nevins, a guest of the Kirkwood, and asked him if he knew where Johnson was. Nevins showed him Johnson's room and pointed out the Vice President seated in the dining room. Nevins remembered that Atzerodt had looked into the dining room and sized Johnson up. Early on the morning of April 14, he had registered at the Kirkwood House and been assigned to room No. 126, to reach which he had to pass Andrew Johnson's room. After the meeting in Booth's quarters, Atzerodt spent most of the day and the night before the expected assassination in going from barroom to barroom, drinking with anyone who offered to slake his thirst. His courage had failed him, but this did not later save him from the rope.[6]

The tragic scenes at Ford's Theater, the bloody shambles at Seward's home have been described in all their appalling detail by countless pens. Here we are concerned chiefly with the effect of the conspiracy on the career of Andrew Johnson, and with tracing the aftermath of Booth's fearsome deed.

Thrown off his balance by the tragedy, Stanton immediately concluded that the assassination of the President was the result of a great Confederate conspiracy to kill all the leaders of the Federal government, the prime movers in it being Jefferson Davis, his Cabinet and their Canadian agents.[7] This thought soon became a firm conviction with the Secretary of War. He immediately summoned his head detective, Lafayette C. Baker, who glorified in his title of general but was really one of the worst rapscallions of an age in which rascality paid high dividends.[8] The devices to which Baker resorted in securing testimony were so astounding and unspeakable that it seems amazing that such a man could have been the head of the United States Secret Service. In 1867, one of the two minority reports on impeachment presented to the House by the Judiciary Committee, speaking of that committee's examination of Baker, said "it is doubtful whether he had in any one thing told the truth, even by accident. In every important statement he is contradicted by witnesses of unquestioned credibility. To his many previous outrages, entitling him to an unenviable immortality, he has added that of wilful and deliberate perjury; and we are glad to know that not one member of the committee deems any statement made by him as worthy of the slightest credit."

Stanton placed all the resources of the War Department in this man's hands, and Baker plunged into his task of proving that Stanton's theory was right. No sooner had Lincoln's breath left his body than Baker was hard at it. A flood of detectives descended upon Washington and Maryland with peremptory orders to do two things: First, to arrest all suspected of complicity in the crime; second, by "promises, rewards, threats, deceit, force, or any other effectual means," to make the suspects implicate Davis and other high Confederates in the plot.[9]

They moved fast. At two o'clock on Saturday morning, while Lincoln was still gasping out his breath, the detectives burst into Mrs. Surratt's house, displayed to her the bloody coat-collar of the dying president, and demanded to know her son's whereabouts. When it was found that Booth and Herold had escaped on horseback, the livery stable proprietors of Washington were all arrested, and martial law 'was declared over the whole of lower Maryland. Stanton declared vehemently that no actor should every tread the Ford Theater stage again.

Arrests followed quickly. On April 17, Michael O'Laughlin, in Baltimore, and Samuel Arnold at Fortress Monroe, were apprehended. Dr. Mudd, who had set Booth's leg, was arrested for his act of mercy. One Weichman, to whom Mrs. Surratt had been "almost a mother"—the words are his—turned informer. On April 20, Stanton offered a reward of $50,000 for the capture of Booth, and of $25,000 each for the capture of Atzerodt, Surratt and Herold, his proclamation terming them "the above named criminals." On this same day, the drunken Atzerodt was captured in western Maryland; the soldiers who made the captures never collected a cent of this promised $25,-000 reward. Stanton wanted "the criminals tried and executed before President Lincoln was buried," but such speed was out of the question. Johnson could not move so fast.[10]

The prisoners were put upon the Monitor *Saugus*, loaded with double irons and kept under heavy guard. At Stanton's request, the Navy Department issued an order that the prisoners, "for better security against conversation, shall have a canvas bag put over the head of each, and tied around the neck, with a hole for proper breathing and eating, but not seeing!"[11]

On Wednesday of the next week—it was the 26th—Colonel Conger arrived in Washington with the news of Booth's death and Herold's capture. Conger gave Booth's private diary to Stanton, who hid it from the light of day. Booth's body, wrapped in an old army blanket, arrived in Washington the next night. After identification and a hurried autopsy, it was buried in a cellar in an unmarked grave; the door was locked and the key put in Stanton's hands.

Meanwhile Baker and his clever men were making great strides in the second part of their assigned task. They were rapidly building up a towering structure to prove that Jefferson Davis had ordered the assassination. Baker was energetically aided by a branch of the War Department which bore the title of the Bureau of Military Justice, with Joseph Holt, the Judge Advocate General of the War Department, at its head. In 1864, Holt had been among those mentioned for Lincoln's running mate. He had been a Democrat, like Butler, Logan and Stanton. Under the war psychosis, they quickly blossomed into the most rabid Radicals, and Holt became a tool in Stanton's hands for wreaking vengeance on guilty and innocent alike. Colonel Burnett, who had conducted the famous Milligan trial in Indianapolis, was experienced in persuading military commissions to impose sentences of death, and Holt had him ordered to Washington.

Among the spies and informers who flocked to Stanton's door were Richard Montgomery and Sanford Conover, who claimed to have been employed by the Confederates in Canada in 1864 and to have access to the Confederate secrets there. They rushed back and forth to Canada, each time returning "laden with proof" that Jefferson Davis had been the center of the assassination plot. In addition, every man captured was subjected to pressure to make him implicate the Confederate authorities in the plot.[12]

It is not strange that the War Secretary seems to have had an unhallowed influence over the mind of Andrew Johnson during these first weeks, for the relations between Johnson and Stanton had been close and uniformly pleasant. Stanton had written Johnson his enthusiastic letter on March 3. Then, too, the punishment of traitors was a favorite preachment of the President. Again and again he had repeated that, while he desired amnesty for the deluded and misguided followers of Secession, "for conscious and intelligent traitors" hanging was a fate too good. The heinous murder of Abraham Lincoln, a man whom Andrew Johnson sincerely loved, moved him profoundly, and it is not strange that the President allowed himself to be overborne by Stanton's claims of proof of Davis' complicity and his assertions that Washington was a very hotbed of Secession sympathizers, where a civil jury would never convict the conspirators who had plotted Lincoln's death.

When the President asked the Attorney-General for a formal opinion as to the proper mode of trial for the conspirators, Speed had at first inclined to civil trial. But, more closely attuned to Stanton than any of the Cabinet, he soon had his qualms overborne by the vehemence of the War Secretary, and submitted an elaborate opinion to the President, holding that in the disturbed state of the country, with the war not formally proclaimed at an end, a military commission should be formed. Stanton might almost have written the words.

After two weeks of feverish activity, the Bureau of Military Justice let it be known that it was ready to prove its charges, and on May 1 the President ordered a military commission set up to try the conspirators. His proclamation recited that the Attorney-General had given his opinion that the offense was triable before such a commission, and ordered "nine competent military officers" to be detailed thus to serve. Early next morning Stanton wrote Holt that the President desired to be furnished with the list "of the persons late in Canada and Richmond, against whom there is evidence of complicity or procurement" in the assassination.[13]

Holt responded immediately. When the Cabinet met later in the day, Stanton produced a paper from his Judge-Advocate-General implicating Jefferson Davis, Jacob Thompson, George N. Sanders and other Confederate civil officers in the plot to assassinate Lincoln. After giving time for these startling charges to sink in, Stanton submitted and urged the President to issue a proclamation offering rewards for the capture of the Confederate leaders.

In the Cabinet discussion on this, McCulloch and Hunter "went with Stanton without a question." When Welles' opinion was sought, he remarked: "If there is proof of the complicity of those men, . . . they certainly ought to be arrested, and the reward is proper." He added in his Diary, "but I had no facts." [14]

That afternoon Stanton's proclamation was issued by the President. "It appears from evidence in the Bureau of Military Justice," it stated, that the crimes against Lincoln and Seward "were incited, concerted, and procured by and between Jefferson Davis, late of Richmond, Va.; Jacob Thompson; Clement C. Clay; Beverly Tucker; George N. Sanders; William M. Cleary, and other rebels and traitors against the government of the United States, harbored in Canada." Therefore, rewards were issued for their arrests: For Davis, $100,000; for the others, $25,000 apiece, except for Cleary, Clay's clerk, for whom $10,000 was deemed sufficient.

Edward Bates, Lincoln's law officer during most of his term but now practicing law in St. Louis, was amazed at the opinion of his successor as Attorney-General. The forthright old lawyer wrote in his diary that it was "the most extraordinary document I ever read under the name of a law opinion." He added that it was obviously got up to bolster a weak case and that it was "generally denounced by lawyers."[15]

Another who sternly disapproved the Military Commission was Henry Winter Davis. Ardent Radical though he had been, Davis was upset at the proclamation. On May 13 he wrote Johnson from Baltimore of his "conviction that the trial of the persons charged with the conspiracy against President Lincoln and Secretary Seward by Military Commission will prove disastrous to yourself and your administration. . . . It is in the very teeth of the express prohibition of the Constitution, and not less in conflict with all our American usage and feeling respecting criminal procedure, and if it be *necessary to secure conviction*, that confesses the *legal* innocence of the accused."

The Maryland Radical assured Johnson that, "in all the circles of my acquaintance, I have found not one person who does not deplore the form of trial. . . . The only safety is to stop *now*, deliver the accused to the *law*, and let the courts of the United States satisfy the people that the prisoners are either guilty or innocent in law, for the people want justice, not vengeance."[16]

Doubts as to the commission arose within the Cabinet itself. On May 9, Welles expressed his regret that the conspirators were not to be tried by the civil courts, and McCulloch agreed.

But Stanton became almost surly in insisting that the proof was "clear and positive." The rumor got about that the trial was to be in secret, a feature alarming to those conservatively inclined.[17] Carl Schurz disapproved the secrecy of the trial, writing Johnson that it "was very unfortunate" and "quite generally disapproved."[18] The New York papers began to protest against such proceedings and to call Mr. Holt's commission a "Council of Ten." Their criticisms forced a certain modification of the program; the doors of the hearings would not be opened to the public, but "trusty and reliable persons, in limited numbers," might be permitted to attend. Stenographic reports of the proceedings would be taken, and published "in due time." These amendments, Welles conceded, might help somewhat.[19]

The charges against the Confederate leaders had not gone unchallenged. On May 4, George N. Sanders and Beverly Tucker wrote from Montreal to tell Johnson that his proclamation was "a living burning lie, known to be such by yourself and all your surrounders," and challenging the President to select any nine from among twenty-five Federal generals they named to form a court-martial for their trial.[20] Sanders and Tucker denied any acquaintance whatever with Booth or his accomplices and added, with blunt sarcasm, "we have *never seen* or had any knowledge, in any way, any wise, of him or them, and *he has never written us a note, or sought an interview with us.*"

On May 3 the Lincoln funeral cortège reached Springfield. On May 4 his remains were committed to friendly ground. On May 6 the military commission was appointed by the Adjutant General, and ordered to meet on May 8 for the trial of the various prisoners "implicated in the murder of the late President." Even in the order, condemnation was expressed.

On May 9 the commission met. Two of its members asked to be relieved and two other officers were substituted.[21] On Tuesday, May 10, twenty-six days after the assassination, the Military Commission began its trial of the condemned. The same day Jefferson Davis was captured in Georgia. For some strange reason he was not hurried to Washington to be tried for his part in the conspiracy of which he was accused, but was sent by sea to a cell in Fortress Monroe. The very next day Clement C. Clay, similarly accused, surrendered and was sent to the same prison.

The military commission met in the Old Penitentiary. The

nine officers of the court, in full uniform, made an impressive picture. Major General David Hunter, who had sat at the head of Lincoln's coffin as it proceeded from place to place on its funeral train, was its President. A stern, whiteheaded soldier of sixty-three, he was an ardent Radical, and had been a commander of negro troops. The other eight officers were not especially distinguished from a military point of view,[22] but they were, almost without exception, ardent Radicals.

The military law of 1865 was a curious and in some respects an unhallowed thing. Compared with those of civil courts, the safeguards of the accused were negligible. There was no judge, no impartial arbiter establishing law, but a Judge Advocate, who combined the diverse duties of prosecuting the accused persons and of determining the law for the court. It was as if the district attorney in a civil court combined with his duties of prosecution, the powers and responsibilities of the judge on the bench.

Stanton had organized this military commission not to administer justice but to convict the accused.[23] Foul murder had been committed and there was no thought of acquittal. The three prosecutors were Holt, the victor of many a bloody court-martial; John A. Bingham of Ohio, member of Congress and a vindictive, brow-beating lawyer, and Colonel Henry L. Burnett, the "Hero" of the Milligan case. These men were more than prosecutors; they were judges of the law!

At the first session on May 10, six soldiers, heavily armed, brought in the prisoners, seven men and a woman, whose fetters clanked at every step. Heavy handcuffs were on the wrists of the men, in all but one instance connected by a ten-inch bar of iron to prevent the prisoners from clasping their hands. Their legs were weighted with shackles. Huge iron balls were attached to the fetters of Payne and Atzerodt. Mrs. Surratt was not handcuffed, but had iron anklets on her feet.[24]

The charges and specifications were read. The accused had "traitorously" conspired, the charge read, with Booth, Surratt and the various Confederates with them already named, to kill and murder Lincoln, Johnson, Seward and Grant. By this device, Mrs. Surratt's fate was bound up with that of the really guilty assassins, many of whom had already confessed to their parts in the plot.[25] The specifications against Mrs. Surratt charged that she did "receive, entertain, harbor, and conceal, aid and assist Booth and the conspirators, with the knowledge of the murderous and traitorous conspiracy aforesaid, and with intent to aid, abet, and assist them in the execution thereof and in escaping from justice after the murder. . . ."[26]

The prisoners' counsel immediately questioned the commission's jurisdiction, inasmuch as "loyal civil courts, in which all the offenses charged are triable, exist, and are in full and free operation in all the places where the several offenses charged are alleged to have been committed." The Judge Advocate did not even deign to reply with reasons against this contention of the defense, his replication saying simply "that this commission has jurisdiction in the premises." The commission took only a brief recess for discussion, and on reconvening announced tersely that the plea had been overruled. The prisoners then applied for separate trials, this being likewise denied, without consultation. All must be tried together, the guilty with the innocent, Mrs. Surratt with the rest.[27]

The prisoners were permitted to have counsel. General Thomas Ewing, Jr., a brave Union soldier, son of Thomas Ewing and brother-in-law of General Sherman, had been retained by and appeared for some of the accused. The members of the court could scarcely understand how a loyal man could appear in a trial such as this. Ewing was the leading spirit of the defense; and to his credit, he plucked from the bloodthirsty Holt the life of every man whom he represented. Senator Reverdy Johnson, probably the most eminent lawyer then appearing before the United States Supreme Court, appeared as one of the counsel for Mrs. Surratt. Venerable with years, loaded with honors, ennobled by service to his country before and during the war, Reverdy Johnson was truly a conspicuous figure, a man of character and ability unusual in this period.

On May 13 he appeared before the commission. No sooner had he announced his intention than General Hunter read aloud a note he had just received from a member of the commission, objecting "to the admission of Reverdy Johnson as a counsel before this court, on the ground that he does not recognize the moral obligation of an oath that is designed as a test of loyalty." It appeared that General Harris about a year earlier had read some story in a newspaper about Johnson, the Maryland Radicals and the test oath. Based on this recollection, the General now deliberately insulted the gray haired statesman, dean of the bar of the Supreme Court!

Reverdy Johnson was indignant. He had taken the oath of loyalty in the Senate of the United States—"the very oath that you are administering." He had taken it in the Supreme Court of the United States. "It would be a little singular if one who has a right to appear before the supreme judicial tribunal of the land . . . should not have a right to appear before a court-martial." Until the day before, the Senator had never seen Mrs. Surratt. But as she protested her innocence and as she was a Maryland lady, and "because I deemed it right, I deemed it due to the character of the profession to which I belong, and which is not inferior to the noble profession of which you are members, that she should not go undefended," he was there as her counsel.[28]

Reverdy Johnson was admitted, but the commission had destroyed his usefulness in the case. It cannot have been simple spleen or party malice which caused this episode. The members of the commission seemed, by deliberate design, to have "sought to rob her [Mrs. Surratt] of any probable advantage such eminent counsel might procure for her."[29] It paid no attention to him thenceforth.

A few more instances will suffice to indicate the kind of "trial" the prisoners received. One Von Steinacker claimed to have been on the staff of Major-General Edward Johnson, of the Confederate army, and to have seen Booth at Lee's head-quarters in 1863, plotting with the Confederates for Lincoln's assassination. Defense counsel, knowing nothing of him, did not cross-examine. A few days after he had told his perjured tale and left the stand, lawyers for the defense discovered the truth about Von Steinacker. He had once been convicted by a court-martial of an attempt to desert the Union army, and later had deserted. In the Confederate army, he had been convicted of theft. His whole testimony was false. The defense lawyers applied for his recall; they wanted to put him on the witness stand to bring out the truth. The only result was indignation on the part of the commission. General Lew Wallace shouted that the attempt was "very discreditable . . . to the attorneys." The perjuring double deserter was not recalled.

The defense summoned General Edward Johnson. On May 30, when the Confederate officer appeared on the witness stand

in his faded uniform, to tell the truth about Von Steinacker,
General Howe, a member of the commission, launched the following attack on him:

"In 1861, it became my duty as an officer to fire upon a
Rebel party of which this man was a member, and that party
fired upon, struck down and killed loyal men. . . . He comes
here as a witness with his hands red with the blood of his loyal
countrymen. . . . I submit to this court that he stands in the
eye of the law as an incompetent witness, because he is notoriously infamous. To offer as a witness a man who stands with
this character . . . is but an insult to the court and an outrage upon the administration of justice. I move that this man,
Edward Johnson, be ejected from the court as an incompetent
witness on account of his notorious infamy on the grounds I
have stated!"

Thus besmirched, so that his testimony was robbed of
weight with the members of the commission, General Johnson
was allowed to go on the stand.

Among the testimony was that of a telegraph operator at
Charlotte, N. C., "a native of Massachusetts," who claimed,
on April 19, to have delivered to Jefferson Davis a message
from John C. Breckinridge telling of Lincoln's death, and to
have heard Davis remark: "If it were to be done at all, it
were better that it were well done; and if the same had been
done to Andy Johnson, the beast, and to Secretary Stanton,
the job would then be complete."[30]

Since Booth's diary was in Secretary Stanton's hands, it
would seem but just to have placed it in evidence at the trial.
But the prosecution was particularly careful to suppress any
reference even to its existence, for the diary very specifically
showed that the plot originally had been one of abduction; and
that it was in the abduction plot alone that John H. Surratt,
his mother—if at all—and two or three of the minor conspirators were involved, and that they knew nothing about the plot
for the assassination.

The Judge Advocate, in questioning the officer who had taken
the articles from the dead body of Booth, carefully refrained
from asking him any general questions as to what they were.
No diary was exhibited or even mentioned, and the defense
counsel had no inkling of its existence.

The evidence against Mrs. Surratt was tenuous. She
owned an inn at Surrattville, Md., about twelve miles from the

capital, and in October, 1864, had opened a boarding house in Washington. Several of the conspirators had boarded with her, but not Booth—he lived at the National Hotel. To use Andrew Johnson's phrase, "she kept the nest which hatched the egg" of the conspiracy. The chief witnesses against her were John M. Lloyd, who kept her Surrattville tavern, and Lewis Weichman, who boarded with her in Washington. Terrified for their lives, both had readily turned government witnesses.

Some six weeks before the assassination, John H. Surratt, Herold and Atzerodt had ridden to Surrattville and had directed Lloyd, who seemed naught unwilling, to conceal for them two carbines with ammunition and a long rope. At the trial, the tavern-keeper testified that on April 14 Mrs. Surratt had driven out to the tavern and had told him to "get the shooting irons ready"; that they "would be wanted soon."

Weichman, a clerk in the War Department and a former college mate of John Surratt, had boarded with his mother almost from the day she opened her Washington establishment. He had been intimate with Booth, Payne and Atzerodt. On the Tuesday before the assassination, he had visited Booth at the National Hotel to borrow his buggy to take Mrs. Surratt out to her country tavern. On the day of the assassination he again drove Mrs. Surratt to the tavern. His chief testimony was as to Booth's having called on Mrs. Surratt. It came out in the trial that on March 23 Weichman had received a suspicious telegram from Booth. The testimony leaves the impression that Weichman had been in the plot, and to save his own skin sought to implicate Mrs. Surratt, who in his own words, had "been a mother to him."

The third piece of evidence against Mrs. Surratt was an incident of the night of April 17. Troops had come to Mrs. Surratt's boarding house, had arrested her daughter Anna and herself and were about to take them to prison. At that moment a man knocked on the door. The soldiers saw a rough looking fellow, with a gray shirt sleeve on his head, his pantaloons rolled over the tops of his boots and a pickax on his shoulder. When asked what he wanted, he said that he had been employed to dig a gutter for Mrs. Surratt and had come to ask her to show him where to begin the next morning. The man turned out to be none other than the scoundrel Payne. When Mrs. Surratt was confronted with him and asked if she knew him, she answered: "Before God, sir, I do not know this man, and have never seen him, and I did not hire him to dig a gutter for me." Her failure to recognize and acknowledge Payne when thus confronted in the lamplight was held by the prosecutors to be damning evidence of her guilt.

Mrs. Surratt's defense brought forward much testimony to discredit the contentions of all these witnesses. Before the trial, Aiken had asked a government detective if, in his confession, Lloyd had mentioned Mrs. Surratt. The detective had emphatically responded "No." On the witness stand, the sleuth admitted: "Undoubtedly I told you a lie there. . . . It is part of my business. . . ." There was strong testimony to the effect that on her visit of April 14 to Surrattville, when, according to Lloyd, Mrs. Surratt had told him to "get the shooting irons ready," he had been so drunk that he could neither have held an intelligent conversation nor remembered one.[31] It was likewise proved that Mrs. Surratt had made her trip in order to collect some money from a man who had bought 75 acres of her Maryland farm. As to her failure to recognize Payne in his ditch digger's disguise, it was brought out by her best friend that she was so nearsighted that she often passed intimate friends on the street without recognizing them.[32]

Reverdy Johnson's argument was almost exclusively on the constitutional phases of the case. He himself did not appear, but one of his juniors read his paper; its trenchant analysis of the question of jurisdiction was addressed uselessly to a bored and inattentive court. Aiken and Clampitt, of junior counsel, sifted the testimony, and showed that the evidence against their client had only the strength of cobwebs.

Yet it availed not at all. There was no more difficulty about the verdict in Mrs. Surratt's case than in that of Payne. With Spangler alone insufficient connection with the plot was established. All the others were found guilty of the charge as brought. All, the commission found, had been engaged in conspiracy with Jefferson Davis, Clement C. Clay and others to kill Lincoln, Johnson, Seward and Grant. In pronouncing the guilt of the conspirators, the commission likewise pronounced the Confederate leaders' guilt!

The commission next proceeded to fix the sentences, according to military law. The three Judge Advocates were allowed to sit in the secret sentence sessions and to urge upon the members of the commission the penalty of death. The commission was not restrained by any legal limitations as to the sentences it inflicted. Its members possessed full power of justice and full right to extend mercy. There was only one legal limitation—if the death sentence was to be imposed, two-thirds of the commission must so vote.[33]

According to the official record, the commission took up the sentencing in the order of the original charge. There could have been little doubt about the first three. The part taken by Herold, Atzerodt and Payne in the crimes was clear and all three were sentenced to death. In the next three cases, signs of disagreement appeared; the court reported deviations between the charges and the findings, and in the cases of neither O'Laughlin nor Spangler nor Arnold would it decree death by a two-thirds vote.

Next in order in the record was the case of Mary E. Surratt. Doubtless the commission thought her guilty too, but she was a woman. On what theory could Spangler, O'Laughlin, and Arnold be permitted to escape the halter, and Mrs. Surratt be hanged? The court could as easily commute her sentence as those of the three men, and apparently that was what the members made up their minds to do. When the commission held a recess after its first day's task of sentencing, five of the nine officers had expressed unwillingness to impose the death penalty on Mrs. Surratt. Holt immediately communicated this news to Stanton, who was particularly determined that the woman should pay the penalty of death. Was she not the mother of John H. Surratt, next in command to Booth in the band of conspirators?

Stanton conferred with Holt and Bingham, and the three devised an ingenious scheme. If five of the Radical officers were unwilling to doom a woman to the halter, the prosecutors might "suggest" to the court that it formally condemn her, and then have those members of the commission who favored milder measures petition the President to commute the sentence. The bloodthirsty trio counted on the court's forgetting that, through its power to fix sentence, it had the very power to save Mrs. Surratt which they were to petition Andrew Johnson to exercise!

The "suggestion" worked like a charm. Holt denounced the women of the South as greater traitors than the men, and pleaded that an example be made of Mrs. Surratt. Bingham insisted that she was as guilty as her son in the assassination. If "tenderness" had to be shown because of her age and sex, it was not for the soldiers of the murdered Lincoln to show it, but for his successor as president. Through these arguments, one of the five gave way and the vote stood five to four for her death.[34]

Holt and Bingham made one last appeal. The new argument was brought forward that the President would not allow her to be hanged, but that terror was necessary to bring forth her son from his hiding place. His mother's life should be the bait to drag him out. John Surratt would be hanged, and his mother would then go free. Another vote was changed by this argument, and thus six out of the nine concurred in sentencing Mrs. Surratt to be hanged, although not expecting her to be hanged.[35] Thus on June 29, the commission "sentenced the said Mary E. Surratt to be hanged by the neck until she be dead, at such time and place as the President of the United States shall direct, two-thirds of the members of the commission concurring therein."

No sooner had the sentence against Mrs. Surratt been pronounced than Bingham sat down to embody the memorable "suggestion" into a petition for clemency. As he wrote it, "the undersigned" members of the commission besought the President "in consideration of the sex and age" of Mrs. Surratt, if he could, upon all the facts in the case, "find it consistent with his sense of duty to the country, to commute the sentence of death, which the Court have been constrained to pronounce." to life imprisonment. General Ekin copied it on a half sheet of legal paper and together with Generals Hunter, Kautz and Foster and Colonel Tompkins, signed it, Ekin retaining Bingham's draft, doubtless as a memento "of so gentle an executioner."[36] The commission proceeded next in the case of Dr. Mudd and again exercised its own prerogative of clemency, sentencing him to life imprisonment.

It was now noon on Friday, and as Holt announced that there was no further business, the court adjourned *sine die*. General Hunter signed the record, the Recorder countersigned it and General Holt had it carried away. The members dispersed. Their job had been done—and thoroughly done.

There remained one more formality. Under the military law of the United States, all sentences of general courts-martial and of military commissions must be reviewed by the President. It was Judge Holt's task to lay the matter before Andrew

Johnson, and once more this hero of a hundred courts-martial was not lacking in his art.

The commission adjourned on the last day of June. Andrew Johnson was ill at the time—he had had a recurrence of his many attacks of stone or gravel—attacks which caused him excruciating pain and sent him to bed. On this occasion he suffered so much that no Cabinet meeting was held for more than a week.[37] Welles noted in his diary that Johnson was "much indisposed on the 26th, 27th and 30th of June," and there was no mention of a Cabinet meeting in his journal from Friday, June 30, until Friday, July 7. But on Wednesday, July 5, Preston King, the President's closest friend, announced in the Judge Advocate's office that Johnson had recovered sufficiently to sit up.

Soon thereafter, General Holt started to the White House. He did not carry with him the great mass of testimony taken down stenographically during the trial, for it was not then the custom for the President to pore through these verbal depths. The Judge-Advocate-General took with him a brief abstract and report upon the proceedings which he had prepared, along with the Commission's findings and sentences.

Holt sought the private entrance to the White House and was conducted to the second floor, where he met General Mussey, one of Johnson's secretaries, in the hall. After Holt had entered the President's closet, the latter came out to tell Mussey that "he was going to look over the findings of the court with Judge Holt and could see no one." Two or three hours later, Johnson again came out of his room and remarked to his secretary that the papers had been looked over and a decision reached. When Mussey asked what it was, Johnson told him of his approval of the findings and sentences of the court, repeated them as he remembered them, "and said that he had ordered the sentences, where it was death, to be carried into execution on the Friday following." The President also instructed Mussey that he did not desire to see anyone who came on "errands of mercy."[38]

The documents which President Johnson saw on that afternoon of the fifth of July are still in existence. In April, 1929, the author found them under the eaves of the State, War and Navy Building in Washington, wrapped in a crumbling piece of brown paper. The findings and sentences of the commission are written upon a few sheets of legal cap paper, obviously at one time fastened together at the top, for there are several holes punched through them for the insertion of binding ribbons or tape. The pages are now numbered in pencil. On the 16th page thus numbered, comes the entry of the adjournment of the commission. On the same page, half way down, begins the presidential indorsement. The body of the indorsement is not in the handwriting of Andrew Johnson, but in that of Joseph Holt. It is continued over on the back of the page, which is numbered 17, and is signed, in a distinctly different hand and in ink of a different color, "Andrew Johnson, Pres."

The recommendation for mercy is to be found in the file immediately following, not preceding, the page telling of the adjournment and bearing Johnson's indorsement. The recommendation is penciled 18. It is on a different kind of paper, a double foolscap page, hinged at the top. The papers as a whole are pierced by three holes at about the center of the top margin, obviously for the insertion of binding ribbons. At this point on the pages of the petition for clemency the paper is torn out; the tear is a very old one, that might well have been caused by jerking this petition from the general file. The physical evidence justifies the suspicion that, before Holt submitted the findings of the court to President Johnson, he detached the petition for clemency from the file, and returned it to its place after he had won his end.

The petition, as was noted, was written on a different kind of paper. Johnson did not read the papers, but merely glanced at Judge Holt's report about the trial as a whole. This report is vastly significant. The Judge-Advocate-General deemed "it unnecessary to enter in this report into an elaborate discussion of the immense mass of evidence. . . . There were 53 pieces of the evidence and 300 or 400 witnesses. . . . The rights of the prisoners were watched and zealously guarded by several counsellors. . . . The opinion is entertained that the proceedings were regular, and that the findings of the commission were fully justified by the evidence. It is thought that the highest considerations of public justice, as well as the future security of the lives of the officers of the government, demanded that the sentences based on these findings should be carried into execution." The Judge-Advocate-General added that he had been present at all times during the trial and knew whereof he spoke. His recommendation made no reference whatever to any clemency appeal by members of the court.

If this petition was in the file submitted to the President, it was affixed in such a manner as to be easily separated without mutilation. If it had been attached to the record, as the fatal indorsement was being written, if Holt had turned up the page and begun his writing on the reverse side from the bottom down, as had hitherto been done, the petition of mercy would have been "directly beneath the eye of the President."[39] But the careful Holt did not turn up the page from the bottom. The fashion in which the indorsement is continued shows that he turned the whole record over, and continued the writing of the death warrant on the back of the last half sheet of the record, writing from top toward bottom. By this device, the petition was either thrown under the leaves of the record, or, if not bound with it, was left upside down. In either event, it might technically have been "under the eye of the President," without Johnson having been able to make out a single word of its sense.[40]

Having thus finished his writing, Holt pushed it over to Johnson, who signed in a tremulous hand. The "confidential interview" was concluded. Holt took his precious documents and hastened with them to the office of the Secretary of War.

Since June 30 no word as to the fate of the criminals had escaped the War Department. On July 6, this ominous silence was ended by the issuance from the Adjutant-General's office of an order reciting the approval of the commission's findings and sentences, and setting July 7 as the date upon which the executions should take place. Major-General Hancock was commanded to see the order carried out.

At noon that same day, the order was read to Mrs. Surratt. Encouraged during the trial to hope that her life would be spared, she was suddenly confronted with this stern spectre of immediate and infamous death. She protested in faltering accents. She had no hand in Mr. Lincoln's murder. Could not she be given only a few more days to prepare herself for the grave? Harrowed by the sudden shattering of all her hopes, she seemed in danger of insanity; physicians were hastily summoned to keep her alive and sane. The cries of grief and anguish from her daughter in the street outside penetrated even the bleak prison walls and were heard in grim silence by tight-lipped guards. At five the next morning, Mrs. Surratt was moved to a solitary cell on the first floor of the penitentiary, the first step toward the gallows. When it became known in the city that Mrs. Surratt was to die, a chill of despairing terror froze the blood of her relatives and friends, a "thrill of consternation" swept over the city as a whole and dark misgivings disturbed even the most loyal breasts.

Many people hastened to the White House anxious to intercede with Andrew Johnson for the life of Mrs. Surratt. They were not alone the doomed woman's relatives, friends and neighbors, but many strangers, haunted by doubts of her guilt.[41] None of them saw the President. On the day he had signed the indorsement, he had instructed General Mussey, his secretary, that he did not wish to see anyone who came on any such errand and on the next day, he refused to see all visitors. If Mrs. Surratt was guilty at all, he told his aide, her sex did not make her any the less guilty. "I can see no one on this business," he emphasized. "Let them see Judge Holt, and if there is anything new, tell him."[42]

Among those who sought in vain for mercy was the widow of Stephen A. Douglas. She came down from the second floor of the White House, weeping bitter tears. The priests who had testified during the trial to Mrs. Surratt's piety and character likewise sought the Executive Mansion. They, too, were denied interviews with the President and were told to see— ghastly mockery!—Judge Holt.

In agony and anguish, Mrs. Surratt's daughter Anna determined to make a personal appeal. She entered the White House and sought to mount the stairs leading to the President's office on the second floor. Guarding the stairs were Preston King and Senator Lane of Kansas, who would not let her pass. When she tried to make her way by them, they prevented her going up.

In the last extremity, the girl lay down on the bottom steps and sobbed aloud her grief. Invoking the name of Him on high, she appealed to the President and the stair-keepers to listen to her prayer. King and Lane were touched but immovable. Mrs. Martha Johnson Patterson, the President's daughter and mistress of the White House, chanced to come down the corridor. She saw the sobbing girl and stooped to comfort her. "My poor dear," she said, "you break my heart, but there is not a thing I can do." Finally the weeping girl was led away.

Convinced that they could expect no dispensation of mercy, Mrs. Surratt's friends as a last desperate resort, appealed to the civil courts. There still existed a document known as the Constitution of the United States, which contained a safeguard about the writ of *habeas corpus*. On the morning of July 7, they found a judge, Wylie by name, with the courage to issue the writ, which was promptly served on General Hancock. At 11:30 on the morning of the execution, the General appeared before the Judge to make a proper return. He certified that, by order of the President, the writ of *habeas corpus* had been suspended in the District of Columbia. Therefore, by the command of superior authority, he could not obey the mandate of the court. Annexed to his return was a copy of a presidential order dated at 10 o'clock that morning, directing General Hancock to proceed with the execution of Mrs. Surratt.

Washington that day was a city of doom. Bells tolled solemnly, and squads of soldiers tramped through the streets with steady tread. The death march of the doomed men and the doomed woman began. As Mrs. Surratt walked along the prison corridor, her infirmity was such that it required her priest and two soldiers to hold her erect. Dressed in black, bonneted and veiled, she walked between two bareheaded priests. Even the bloody Payne, marching behind her, and seemingly completely indifferent to his own fate, was touched. He burst into rapid words to clear her of all complicity in the assassination plot. Atzerodt and Herold, dumb with fright, followed.[43]

The prisoners entered the execution yard where, on the top of the wall, stood soldiers with muskets in hand.[44] The flags went up, and the assembled newspaper reporters feverishly began to write. The four doomed persons ascended the high scaffold, where they took seats in four chairs, facing the nooses which dangled from above. In full sight were four open graves and the same number of coffins. An aide held an umbrella over General Hartranft as he read the sentence to the prisoners. When he ceased, there came a brief quiet, broken by the cadenced prayers of the priests. Still half supported by the guards, the almost unconscious woman had the noose adjusted about her throat and the three men were similarly fastened. Hoods were drawn over their faces, a signal was given and the scaffold drops fell. The wild justice of vengeance had been done.

After a few minutes of writhing, all signs of struggle ended. Unpitying soldiers glanced coldly at the spectacle while the prison physician pronounced that life was extinct in all four bodies. They were then cut down and laid upon the tops of the coffins. At four o'clock in the afternoon, after hurried autopsies, they were buried side by side in the prison yard. With flourish of trumpet and rapid beat of drum, the executioners then marched away, their task complete. The guilty and the innocent alike had paid the price.[45]

A MONG those to whom the President had shown his North
Carolina Proclamation before its issuance was Carl
Schurz, one of the leading political generals of the Civil War,
who urged him vehemently not to take "any steps that could
not be retracted." When he found the Chief Executive determined upon the Holden appointment, the General sought to
persuade him to eliminate "that one passage limiting the rights
of suffrage."[1]

This importunate presidential adviser, Carl Schurz, was of
German birth. In his youth, he had taken part in the revolutionary activities of 1848 and, following their suppression,
had escaped to the safe asylum of the United States. An alert,
intense, energetic man, keenly interested in public affairs,
Schurz attached himself to the Anti-slavery cause, and soon was
on the road to Radicalism.

Upon the outbreak of the war, Schurz was quickly catapulted into the rank of major general; probably the political
advisability of thus advancing a German-American was no
impediment. Schurz's military career was not impressive and
several of the commanders under whom he served became prejudiced against him. In November, 1862, following McClellan's
various disasters and the Administration's setback at the polls,
the General undertook to instruct the President how to win
the war. The defeat, he wrote Lincoln, had been "the Administration's own fault." It had occurred because Lincoln had
admitted his opponents to his counsels and had put the army
into enemy hands. The Administration "forgot the great rule
that if you are true to your friends, your friends will be true
to you. . . . Let us be commanded by generals whose heart is
in the war. . . ."[2]

Lincoln's answer was a stinging rebuke to the General. "Be
assured, my dear sir," he wrote, "there are men who have 'heart
in it' and think you are performing your part as poorly as
you think I am performing mine." The President continued:
"I must say I need success more than I need sympathy, and
that I have not seen a so much greater evidence of getting success from my sympathizers than from those who are denounced

as the contrary. It does seem to me that in the field the two classes have been very much alike in what they have done and what they have failed to do." As to the question of those who had "heart in it," the President asked, "Who is to be the judge? . . . If I must discard my own judgment and take yours, I must also take that of others, and by the time I should reject all I should be advised to reject, I should have none left, Republicans or others—not even yourself."[3]

Schurz made such a miserable showing in the battles around Chattanooga that he was relieved of his command and sent to Nashville in charge of the recruiting station there, a major general with a major's command. He felt the degradation keenly, and lost no time in enlisting Andrew Johnson's good services to get him reinstated in favor.[4]

Schurz, nicknamed "the Swiss soldier," was a charming fellow. He played the piano, sang "I love thee, O I love thee," beautifully and flattered Andrew Johnson no end. Johnson's appeal to Lincoln in Schurz's behalf was successful.[5] But the General was unable to maintain his new post. Thus on July 13, 1864, Johnson telegraphed the President that Schurz was in Nashville again: "His command is not a very active one. He is anxious to be placed in a position where he can render more service to the country, and distinction and credit to himself." Two weeks later, Lincoln replied: "You can never know, until you have a trial, how difficult it is to find a place for an officer of so high a rank when there is no place seeking him."[6]

Andrew Johnson had sought to aid and favor Schurz in time of need. We shall later see how the Radical General repaid these favors.[7] But on the occasion of this White House interview, Johnson listened so attentively to Schurz's views that the latter felt the President had been convinced. He suggested that the President appoint "some sensible and reliable person to supervise the political action of our military commanders in the South, to work out instructions, to superintend their execution, and to keep the government advised of what was going on," a proposal which, he asserted, pleased Johnson so much that he "even went so far as to ask me whether I would return to Washington at his bidding to aid him in this matter." With his usual capacity for self-abnegation, Schurz agreed to "sacrifice two or three months for this object."

Schurz next heard of the proposed tour after the North

Carolina Proclamation had been published unamended. He was depressed by the political prospect. Delegations of Southern loyalists were crowding into Washington, for whom Schurz had scant respect, but he feared that the President was attracted by their pleas. "The Union men of the South," Schurz said, "are almost all governed by their old prejudices, and no good can be expected from them." He wrote Sumner that the situation urgently demanded the latter's presence. He did not think "any member of the Cabinet asserts his influence in the contrary direction. . . . The President's opinions are unsettled on the most vital points." Schurz proceeded to "entreat" Sumner to see the President "as soon as you conveniently can."

Schurz wrote Johnson more mildly. On June 6 he informed the President that the proclamation was being regarded "as a declaration of policy on your part adverse to the introduction of negro suffrage," an issue sure to provoke "fierce discussion." As soon as "the oath-taking Rebels will have reasserted their influence in the Southern States," the General predicted, it would become the "burning issue."[8]

The German-American General was not the only one disturbed by the North Carolina Proclamation. Indeed, although it met general public approval, the Radical leaders in general were much disturbed by it, and Sumner was widely besought to save the situation. On June 1 Benjamin F. Loan, a Missouri Radical, wrote to ask "what course is best for the Radicals under the circumstances to adopt. Shall we acquiesce with the policies of the Administration, or shall we adhere to our former views that Congress alone is authorized to deal with the subject of reconstruction, and that *our* safety and the peace of the country, requires us to disfranchise the Rebels, and enfranchise the colored citizens in the revolted states . . .?" The Missourian thought it would be "much more disastrous" to abandon "our principles" than it would be to go to war with the President.[9]

A Boston correspondent wrote Sumner: "I . . . do hope and pray for Divine direction and control to be given to the President . . . I do not know what personal influence you have with him, . . . but cannot some direct or indirect influence be brought to bear?" M. D. Conway wrote from London: "For God's sake let the true men of Congress become as *one* man to demand the right thing of the President." J. W. Alden, a

New York Radical editor, warned that "if the Radicals don't wake up and establish a paper either in New York or somewhere else, . . . our cause is lost for another four years at least."[10]

The Radical assault began promptly in Boston. No sooner had the proclamation been issued than Wendell Phillips made a speech to the New England Antislavery Society, in which he termed Johnson's plan of suffrage "a practical surrender to the Confederacy, . . . a practical fraud on the North." Phillips insisted that it would have been better for Grant to have surrendered to Lee than for negro rights thus to be flouted.[11]

On June 1, the day which had been appointed by the President for memorial services for Abraham Lincoln throughout the nation, Charles Sumner delivered a eulogy in Boston. On the Senator's express desire, a negro preacher served as one of the chaplains for the occasion. The speech, as long as was usual with Sumner, was not all concerned with an appreciation of the martyred Lincoln. Its last portion was devoted to Sumner's special subject of votes for negroes. Even Pierce, idolatrous biographer though he was, could not defend it, terming the speech "wanting in artistic unity" and "seriously marred." With Sumner, Pierce admitted, "a moral purpose always overrode artistic limitations," and the Senator seized the opportunity of the Lincoln speech to appeal to the country for the adoption of a plan of suffrage against which Lincoln himself had resolutely set his face.[12]

Even the Boston audience was disturbed at the incongruity. It was felt that "something of the former fascination of Sumner's oratory had gone." The Radicals had mixed motives in this insistence on negro suffrage. The old Abolitionists thought the negro "God's image in ebony" and really far more meritorious than his ex-master. Others conceived universal suffrage as an inescapable element of Democracy as ordained by the Declaration of Independence. A third group deemed negro control of the South proper punishment to the Southern whites; while the fourth and perhaps largest group of all was interested in the political assistance the Republican party would secure from Southern states controlled by negroes.[13]

With the Phillips-Sumner onslaught, the Radicals of the Mid-West began to feel the need of an extra session. J. M. Howard of Detroit foresaw "an open rupture with Mr. Johnson if he persists in this unconstitutional policy. It proceeds

Private

Executive Mansion,

Washington March 26. 1863

Hon. Andrew Johnson

    My dear Sir:

        I am told you have at least thought of raising a negro military force. In my opinion the country now needs no specific thing so much as some man of your ability, and position, to go to this work. When I speak of your position I mean that of an eminent citizen of a slave-state, and himself a slave-holder. The colored population is the great available and yet unavailed of, force for restoring the Union. The bare sight of fifty thousand armed, and drilled black soldiers on the banks of the Mississippi, would end the rebellion at once. And who doubts that we can present that sight, if we but take hold in earnest? If you have been thinking of it please do not dismiss the thought.

            Yours truly,

             A. Lincoln

LINCOLN URGES NEGRO TROOPS

Letter of Lincoln to Johnson, March 26, 1863, Urging the Latter, as Military Governor of Tennessee, to Enlist Negro Troops. Original Owned by J. P. Morgan Library.

from Mr. Lincoln's ill-advised and obstinate conduct in vetoing
Winter Davis' bill." Howard asked "what member of the Cabinet favors this wretched policy? . . . O that we had able men
in the Cabinet! Stanton is my only hope." The Michigan
Radical hinted that it was Johnson's ambition to be "the great
restorer" of the Southern states, adding: "*but we don't want
them back now.*"

Ben: Perley Poore wrote Sumner that he feared Johnson was
"surrounded by a set of corrupt Democratic politicians," and
the editor of a Radical sheet in Indianapolis was "losing confidence in our new President, who *may*, and probably does *mean*
well; but he is a *weak* man."[14]

One New Yorker fulminated to the President "every Rebel
is delighted that you disfranchise loyal blacks"; a second wrote
him, "you are committing the blackest crime of the ages"; and
a third informed him that "as a Northern man," he had learned
he had no business at the White House; "a good Southern
President has no time for Northern men or interests." On
June 10 the Union League Club of New York sent Johnson
resolutions urging a Southern suffrage "equal and just to all,
without distinction of color."[15]

On June 15 the Rhode Island legislature, doubtless under
the promptings of Chase's son-in-law, then Governor of that
State, passed a resolution maintaining that it was the sense "of
the general assembly and the people" that in Southern reconstruction, the federal power and authority should be exerted
"to securing equal rights without respect of color."[16]

At his home in Pennsylvania, Thad Stevens' rage was growing. On June 14 he wrote Sumner: "Is there no way to avert
the insane course of the President on reorganization?" But
Stevens would not be content with attempts to influence Johnson and the Cabinet. He was a practical man. Why not start
a backfire among the gullible folk at home? "Can you get up
a movement in Massachusetts?" he continued in his letter to
Sumner; "I have thought of trying it at our state convention.
If something is not done, the President will be crowned king before Congress meets!"[17]

Acutely alarmed, Sumner sought to enlist everyone he could
to influence the policies of the President, or the sentiment of
the country at large. On June 15 he wrote Schurz, "It is evident that we must create a public sentiment." Four days later,
after he had seen a dispatch saying that Schurz had called on

the President, Sumner wrote to him: "Can you give me any hope?" adding "When shall you speak? We must all speak."[18]

The indefatigable Schurz had conferred with the President on June 15. After complaining that it was hard to get reliable information and that consequently he seemed to be always obliged to act in the dark, Johnson proposed that Schurz visit the Southern states to inform himself as to conditions, give his opinion to the government and make suggestions. As soon as he left the White House, the General hurried to Stanton's office, where the Secretary of War told him it was "absolutely neces-.sary" that he accept. "Even if it did not decide the President's course of action," Schurz's report "would be of the most vital interest in the discussion of the next Congress." The Secretary thought Johnson could not merely put Schurz's report in his pocket, but that his conclusions "would go to the public officials, and could not fail to have some influence."

Stanton warned Schurz that if he declined the commission, "the President would be able later to say to the Radicals, 'I have acted upon the information which was at my command. I wished to send down one of your men to enlighten me about the state of affairs, and give me his advice, but he did not wish to go.' "

Although Schurz wrote to Sumner that "Stanton is right," the General could not forget the monetary side of the question. The next morning he informed President Johnson that he wished to withdraw his resignation from the army so as to make the trip with the pay and appurtenances of a major general.[19] The President could see no legal way to do this.

Schurz explained to Sumner his financial necessities. He was particularly concerned over a large insurance policy which would lapse because of the extra hazards involved if he went South, and which he could protect only by paying a large additional premium. Schurz also suggested that he might supplement his income by writing articles of observation for some Radical newspaper [20] and that Sumner make the necessary arrangements as to frequency and rate of pay. Doubtless he also intimated that such correspondence as he would write would prove helpful in creating the "public sentiment" Sumner so keenly sought.

When he heard the good news of Johnson's proposal, Sumner was much elated. "*You must go,*" he wrote the General. "Let me know the extra premium on your policy. The friends of the cause will gladly pay it. . . . Send me the bill; and do you go at once on your journey."[21] But before he left, Schurz must "make one more effort to arrest the policies of the President. Every step he takes is a new encouragement to: 1, Rebels of the South; 2, the Democrats of the North; and 3, the discontented spirits everywhere. . . . Of course the policies of the President *must break down!*"[22]

As soon as he received these promises of financial subsidy from Sumner, Schurz announced his acceptance. On June 27 he wrote to his helpful friend in Boston: "Your note . . . reached me today. I shall certainly accept the President's proposal."[23] Apparently it was not easy for Sumner to make up his mind as to which paper should print the Schurz dispatches. He quickly employed "the best phonographic reporter in Boston" for the General, but on June 29 wrote the latter, "the newspaper for which you will write is not yet determined." A few days later Sumner selected the Boston *Advertiser* and sent Schurz a copy of the paper, "from which you will see the type of correspondence."[24]

The Radical reception of the President's proclamation has been outlined thus, not because it reflected the dominant attitude of the country, or even that of the Republican party, at the time, but because it shows how the vehement Radicals insisted upon negro suffrage as the crucial point of their political creed. This group was still greatly in the minority in the North.

In making his North Carolina decision, the President finally had the unanimous support of his Cabinet. Stanton "thought he had gone far enough" for his Radical friends, and "submitted without a word." Harlan and Speed likewise came over and took firm position with Johnson.[25] The practical difficulties were such that none could controvert Johnson's conviction "that to prescribe the rule of suffrage was not within the legitimate scope of his power." Even such a hostile critic as James Ford Rhodes comments that "it was an extraordinary demand to make that the President should, by a mere mandatory proclamation, confer the franchise on the negroes." Rhodes recites that at the time all but six Northern states denied the negro the right to vote, that the great majority of the Republican party opposed it, and that "there was no color of law, prece-

dent or custom to justify Johnson in taking the course urged
upon him by Sumner and Chase."[26]

In 1865, the President's military chiefs in the South were
almost a unit against the imposition of negro suffrage. Sherman informed Chase that "to give all loyal negroes the same
political status as white voters will revive the war," and wrote
his wife: "Stanton wants to kill me because I do not favor the
scheme of declaring the negroes of the South, now free, to be
loyal voters, whereby politicians may manufacture just so
much more pliable electioneering material. The negroes don't
want to vote. They want to work and enjoy property." Senator Sherman was frank with his soldier brother. "I admit,"
he wrote on May 16, "the negroes are not intelligent enough to
vote, but someone must vote their political representation in
the states where they live. . . . Who shall exercise this political power?"[27]

During his visit to Raleigh in April, Grant had been impressed with the sad prospect of the South, and wrote his wife
that "the suffering that must exist in the South the next year
. . . will be beyond conception. People who talk of further
retaliation and punishment, except of the political leaders,
either do not conceive of the suffering endured already, or they
are heartless and unfeeling. . . ."[28] A little later Schofield
wrote Grant "of the absolute unfitness of the negroes as a class
to vote. They can neither read nor write; they have no knowledge whatever of law or government; they do not even know
the meaning of the freedom that has been given them, and are
much astonished when they are informed that it does not mean
they are to live in idleness and be fed by the Government."[29]

These views substantially represented the attitude of the
loyal North. Immediately after the proclamation of May 29,
conservative and moderate leaders informed the President by
telegram, letter and interview that they approved his decision
and his course. A little later, party conventions—Republican,
Union, Democratic—throughout the Northern States began
adopting resolutions of similar tenor and tone.

In June William Cullen Bryant's paper declared that Johnson was "already proving himself by his successive acts one of
the most discreet, clear-sighted, upright, and sagacious statesmen of the age";[30] the Philadelphia *Press* lauded his "ardent
patriotism and unblemished loyalty" and Mr. Childs was making good his promise to Blair in almost daily praise in the

columns of his *Ledger*.[31]   The New York *Herald* attacked
Wendell Phillips' Boston speech and characterized its author
as "a man whose mission is to oppose everything.   He first opposed slavery, then the Union, and now he opposes President
Johnson.   Among other things he occasionally opposes himself."[32]

About this time the President's Indiana friend, J. B.
Wright, who had been staying in Vermont, wrote Johnson that
Vermont would indorse his Administration, including his North
Carolina Proclamation.   Shortly thereafter, the Connecticut
General Assembly passed resolutions, urging "a humane and
generous policy" toward the South's "misguided masses."
These declarations stated that the President "has entitled himself to the confidence of the nation," and since of necessity he
was forced to adopt experimental policies of restoration, "he
ought to be sustained in the exercise of the greatest freedom
of action."[33]   A few weeks later the New York *Nation* declared
that Johnson's policy had the "miraculous property of appearing to satisfy all parts and parties of the country."[34]

The chorus of acclaim included declarations from all parts
of the North and South.   In Massachusetts, John A. Andrew;
in Wisconsin, Senator Doolittle; in Indiana, Governor Morton;
in Ohio, Thomas Ewing and Lewis Campbell, and in the South,
military commanders, provisional governors, loyal Unionists
and ex-Secession leaders joined in commendation and good report.   The Radical wrath was at yet but a cloud of a hand's
breadth that in nowise obscured the summer sun.

With the North Carolina edict, Johnson began to hear
words of wisdom from a counsellor of substance and sagacity,
Thomas Ewing of Ohio, a noble, rugged character to whom
Civil War history has done insufficient justice.   In Johnson's
presidential career, there was a backstage drama, with good
and evil counsellors contending for the presidential ear.   On the
one hand, sound and conservative advice by such men as Thomas
Ewing, L. D. Campbell and Francis Preston Blair was offered,
timidly at first and later with bold indignant words.   On the
other side, the plausibility of folly was being stressed by Jeremiah Sullivan Black and many like him.   Johnson's greatest
mistakes occurred when he disregarded the admonitions of such
men as the Ewings and followed the high-sounding phrases of
the Blacks.   On May 29, 1865, the day of the North Carolina
proclamation, Thomas Ewing was writing the President to

urge "a free and full pardon to Stephens of Georgia and Judge Campbell." Such an act of grace, the old Roman believed, would make a most favorable impression on the public mind.[35] A month later he wrote again, warning Johnson against further recourse to military commissions, advice which after the Wirz execution was wisely heeded.

The President's letters during this first summer included many from many of the age and epoch of Thomas Ewing, letters in crabbed and faltering hands, signed with names belonging to the era of Andrew Jackson, Daniel Webster and Henry Clay. One of these was a letter which Duff Green, an able editor in his day, wrote the President on June 25. Even now he wrote with shrewdness.

"Extraordinary efforts will be made," he advised the President, "to organize an unscrupulous opposition to your Administration and your election in '68." There were clear indications that either Chase or Sherman would be the opposing candidate, "and that the vote of the South will control the election in your favor, if you act wisely." The Democrats of the North looked to the South to reinstate them in power. "If you identify yourselves with the ultra-Abolitionists in their warfare on the South, then Democracy will rally on Sherman, and aided as he will be by his brother's influence in Ohio, he will carry the Conservative Whigs and organize the Northwest and the South against New England. . . . Do you ask what the South wants? They want to be reinstated, as loyal, patriotic members of the Union."[37]

Another of "Old Hickory's" fighters to appear in Andrew Johnson's pages was Amos Kendall, who, on July 13, in a very tremulous hand, wrote the President to congratulate him both on refusing the New York merchants' present and on his state suffrage policy. The old Jacksonian applauded the "efforts you are making to purify our government and save its fundamental principles from being swallowed up in the waves of the fanatical revolution."[38]

By July, Seward had recovered his strength, and was throwing all his weight on the side of leniency. On July 23, he told Browning that the effect of hanging would be pernicious, that the Southern people were anxious to and should be permitted to be reconciled. "We have got all we had claimed by the war," he added, "the abandonment of the State right doctrine of Secession, the acknowledgment of the supremacy of

the Government, and the abolition of slavery." As to forcing
negro suffrage upon the South, "this cannot be done, but we
will have to go slowly, . . . probably to wait another election."

On August 24 Senator Dixon of Connecticut gave Johnson
his analysis of the political situation. The Radicals "denounce
your policy in language restrained only by their fears," but on
the other hand, "the thinking, calm, honest, unselfish masses"
approved Johnson's course, "and support it with zeal and energy." The Senator saw proof of this daily. "In the shops, in
the factories, on the farms, everywhere, the first remark is 'Mr.
Johnson is doing right.'" Such, he wrote, was "the almost
universal feeling. I know not whether it reaches you—for the
truth seldom enters the White House—but so it is. . . . You
will be sustained by the people . . . in such a manner as has
never been witnessed, except perhaps in the case of Washington."[39]

The approval thus manifested was not confined to the
letters and oral representations of individuals. Political conventions held throughout the summer and fall indorsed Johnson's policy and pledged cordial support. The Ohio and
Wisconsin proceedings were typical of the rest.

Ohio was the State of Chief Justice Chase, "Bluff Ben"
Wade, Ashley, Giddings and other leaders of Radical thought,
and these worthies felt that the annual state convention of the
Republican party in Ohio would be a good place in which to
commence the fight against the President. But Johnson's
friends were alert. They saw to it that the Radicals did not
pack the convention, and on August 21 Lewis D. Campbell was
able to report to the President: "On this day, we hived the
swarm of Radicals, and your policy was triumphantly approved. I hope you find some comfort in the result." Johnson's friend added a warm indorsement of the President's policy,
especially on the negro suffrage question. "Sensible people
generally are satisfied," he wrote.

But the Chase men would not so easily surrender. Oberlin
was the Radical headquarters—"its population think that when
Oberlin takes snuff, the whole world must sneeze." There the
"Chase guard," as Campbell contemptuously termed them, addressed a letter on negro suffrage to Jacob D. Cox, seeking to
array him against the President. They failed in the effort "as
you will have seen by General Cox's manly letter."

Whatever professions Chase and Beecher might have made

to the President, Campbell warned him as follows: "I *know* that they are preparing to make war on your Administration, and you may expect it. But the great men of the Union party, and nearly the whole of those who have been in the army, will stand by you if you remain firm in your adherence to the present policy. For every Chase Radical who leaves you, at least ten fair-minded Democrats will flock to your standard." Campbell, who had known Chase "intimately for more than thirty years, termed him cold and selfish; he cares for no friendship that cannot be used for his own aggrandizement."[40]

When Senator J. R. Doolittle reached his Wisconsin home, he discovered that the Radicals had been "carried away with the crazy idea that the fertile brain of Wendell Phillips has engendered upon the brains of Sumner and Greeley, *viz* that the States are out of the Union—no longer *States* under the Constitution, but mere conquered territory, and that therefore the government has the right to impose negro suffrage or any other terms upon them." Acting on this theory, the Radicals made a determined effort at the Wisconsin Union State Convention to force through an indorsement of impartial suffrage. Doolittle took the bull by the horns, wrote the majority resolutions report and it "was carried triumphantly." The Radical substitute, "after a pretty warm discussion, was laid on the table by a majority so great they did not call the Ayes and Noes." The platform adopted referred to the Union as unbroken, "not one star obscured, not one stripe erased."[41] Negro suffrage was not indorsed.

In the conventions in a number of States, the Radicals did not deem it worth while even to make verbal protest against the indorsement of the administration. In two, however, their effort was successful—in Pennsylvania, under the leadership of Thad Stevens, and in Massachusetts, with Sumner at the helm. In July, Stevens had sought to browbeat Johnson into giving up his policy. On July 6, he thus addressed the President:

> Sir: I am sure you will pardon me for speaking to you with a candor to which men in high places are seldom accustomed. Among all the leading Union men of the North with whom I have had intercourse, I do not find one who approves of your policy. They believe that "restoration" as announced by you will

destroy our party (which is of little consequence) and
will greatly injure the country.

Can you not hold our hand and await the action of
Congress, and in the meantime govern them by military rulers? Profuse pardoning also will greatly
embarrass Congress, if they should wish to make the
enemy pay the expenses of the war or a part of it.

Stevens signed this letter "with great respect, your obedient servant"—probably a touch of bitter irony. If Johnson
replied to this communication, the answer has not been preserved. His continued pursuit of his policy of Southern justice was the real answer to the Pennsylvania Commoner.[42]

On June 30 the busy Sumner took occasion to send the
President a petition signed by 300 Georgia negroes, asking to
be allowed to exercise the right of suffrage. In his note the
Radical insisted "that the peace and tranquility of the country
require that *they should not be shut out from it.*" Significantly
enough, the petition was on a printed blank and many of the
signatures were written by the same hand.[43]

The inveterate letter writer wrote John Bright that Johnson's plan was "madness." To Francis Lieber he made light
of an educational qualification for negro voting. "We need the
votes of all, and cannot afford to wait," he informed the publi-
cist. Could it be that practical political necessities moved him
as well as lofty idealistic views? He wrote to every member of
the Cabinet with whom he was on good terms, denouncing Johnson's policy. His replies were unsatisfactory. Stanton was
not ready for an open breach. Speed, though a Radical, opposed dictating suffrage conditions to the returning States.
Harlan, the new Secretary of the Interior, addressed a friendly
warning to the Senator. "If our friends all over the country"
should denounce Johnson "and drive him into the arms of the
Copperheads, you will not carry your views by a two-thirds
vote in Congress. . . . We ought to be very careful not to
drive the President over to the enemy."

McCulloch informed Sumner that the President was "intelligent and patriotic," that he was "no lover of slavery, but a
hearty and earnest hater of it," but that none the less, he was
"pursuing the only course which he feels at liberty to pursue
under the Constitution. . . . If it fails, it will not be the fault
of the President." A week later, Sumner's Massachusetts colleague, Henry Wilson, reported Fessenden's opinion that John-

son was "right in sentiment, and sound on all matters pertaining to the negroes except suffrage. . . . We have a President who does not go as far as we do in the right direction, but we have him and cannot change him, and we had better stand by the Administration and endeavor to bring it right."[44] On July 29 Ben Wade wrote that he had "no consolation to impart." E. D. Morgan of New York and Howard of Michigan advised a conciliatory attitude. Henry Winter Davis feared the making of a direct issue with the President on negro suffrage.

The usually Radical New York *Evening Post* termed compulsory action by Congress on negro suffrage "the danger of dangers." The New York *Times* took strong position against it. Charles A. Dana urged the Senator not to break with Johnson, and Forney gave the same advice.[45] It seemed as if Thad Stevens was about the only important leader willing to engage in a fight with the President.

But this Boston Jeremiah was not a man to be deterred by the reluctance of his allies. He kept on writing his letters and in September he had an opportunity to make an important speech. This was at the annual Massachusetts Republican Convention, which met at Worcester on September 14, with Sumner in the chair as President. The controlling theme of his keynote speech was that the work of liberation would not be complete "until the equal rights of everyone once claimed as a slave are placed under the safeguard of irreversible guarantees." The Senator said he heard "one sullen defiant voice" from Southern States seeking to precipitate themselves back into the Union as rapidly as they had precipitated themselves out.[46] He rebuked the presidential policy, insisting that Congress was the proper organ for reconstruction plans. Of the Cabinet, Sumner mentioned Stanton alone as deserving of praise. In his conclusion, the Senator announced that, so far as he was concerned, "my course is fixed. Many may hesitate . . . I shall not." Under this instruction, the convention approved negro suffrage as an indispensable condition of reconstruction.[47]

Stanton, who was in Boston, complimented the speech. When the Senator remarked that it contained pretty strong views, the War Secretary answered, "It is none too strong. I approve of every sentiment, every point, and every word of it."[48]

But everyone in Massachusetts did not agree with Sumner. Representative Henry L. Dawes approved Johnson's plan and

Governor Andrew manifested a sympathetic attitude toward the prostrate South, opposing Sumner's negro suffrage plan. The Dawes defection was so disturbing to Sumner's coterie that Henry Winter Davis wrote the Senator to ask if Massachusetts "would tolerate" Dawes, and Stevens sent a note of warning: "I fear Dawes. Can he be brought right?"

On the eve of the Pennsylvania convention in Harrisburg, a lieutenant of Johnson telegraphed, "Administration will be fully indorsed. Pennsylvania a unit in support of the policies of the President." These expectations were unfulfilled, for the convention adopted Thad Stevens' resolutions expressing mild confidence in Johnson, while virtually condemning his policies. Stevens' "movement" had begun.

The chorus of Conservative praise began to irk the Radicals, particularly when it came from such quarters as the Democratic New York *World*, which but three months before had compared Johnson to Caligula's horse.[49] Northern Democrats were viewed by the Radicals as little more than Northern traitors, "Copperhead" being the usual term employed by the Republicans. Anyone advocating "the Union as it was, and the Constitution as it is," was assailed as a Confederate sympathizer.

Founded as they were upon the old-fashioned Democratic gospel of State Rights, the Northern Democrats acclaimed Johnson's policies, but their leadership was unequal to the crisis. To the consternation of the sensible men in the South, New York's Democracy was full of complaints against the President. Thus, on July 19, Samuel L. M. Barlow of New York, loyal lieutenant of Dean Richmond and Samuel J. Tilden, directors of Democratic affairs in the Empire State, wrote Montgomery Blair of a large Democratic meeting, at which "not a man present was willing to lend his support to the Administration. . . . Stanton and Holt are daily committing Mr. Johnson during peace to a system which could not be followed in England during war for a day without a revolution."[50]

But there came a sudden change in the New Yorkers' attitude. On July 24 Barlow wrote Blair again, saying that Richmond, Tilden and he himself wanted to come to Washington to confer with the President. They wanted the chance to say "earnestly and frankly that the whole party is today a Johnson party; that the South, just as rapidly as his reconstruction plans are carried out, will be a Johnson party, and that nothing can prevent this, unless the President wills it otherwise." Barlow admitted that Blair probably would be surprised at so great a change in his views, and that the principal instrument in his conversion had been Major-General Dick Taylor, of the Confederates—"the brightest, most far-seeing man I have ever met from the South. . . . He says the Southern people are universally pleased with Johnson's course; that his new governors are the very best men in the South for the places. . . . He says Mr. Johnson must be supported at the North, no matter what he may do. . . ."[51] A little later Barlow wrote to another of Johnson's friends in Baltimore, outlining a specific policy, and saying that, if Johnson would adopt it, "he can without difficulty secure constant, earnest, effective support of the Democratic party, North and South. By any other policy he will find himself without a party." Barlow's demands were: First, Johnson must revamp the Cabinet; next, he must "conform generally to our ideas of policy," which, he added defensively, "are his as well as ours."[52]

Tilden, Richmond and Barlow did not get to make their joint call upon the President, but before the date of the New York Democratic state convention Tilden came down alone, had a long talk with Johnson and "returned satisfied." The result was a Democratic indorsement of the President's policy. Soon Barlow began to manifest keen anxiety about patronage. "We shall carry the State," he informed Montgomery Blair, "unless the President unwisely allows the Customs House here, and other Federal patronage, to be exerted against us."[53]

Meanwhile Andrew Johnson, the individual, not as President, but as temporary tenant of the White House, was enjoying perhaps as happy a season as the Tennessee tailor-statesman was permitted to spend in Washington. He had shown a keen desire to be as considerate of the wishes of Abraham Lincoln's widow as possible, and did not enter the Executive Mansion for several weeks after his accession to the presidency. On April 25 Robert Todd Lincoln sent the new executive a note written on stationery with great black borders. "My mother and myself are aware of the great inconvenience to which you are subject," he wrote, "but my mother is so prostrate that I must beg your indulgence. . . . Mother tells me that she cannot possibly be ready to leave here for 2½ weeks."[54]   Four days later, Mrs. Lincoln herself wrote the new President asking that he appoint Alex Williamson, for the last four years the White House tutor of the Lincoln children, to a position with the Freedmen's Bureau.   A week later R. P. French, Commissioner of Public Buildings of the District of Columbia, submitted to Johnson a list of "the White House help," told him of a purchase of china Mrs. Lincoln had made, the bill for which he wished Johnson to approve, and informed the President that Mrs. Lincoln had fixed upon the second Monday following as the time when she would leave the Mansion.

As soon as Mrs. Lincoln had left, the Commissioner proposed "to have all the mourning in the East room removed and sold at public auction, the avails of which would be devoted to the payment of the bills for the funeral expenses."[55]   But the Lincolns did not leave the White House on the day appointed, Mrs. Lincoln departing with great reluctance early in June. Before she left, Robert Todd Lincoln sought to sell the various Lincoln equipages to the new President.   Why he did not buy them, the Johnson files do not show.

When Johnson moved into the White House on June 9, it must have been a dull and cheerless place, for his family was still in Nashville.   At first, the President almost killed himself with work and, during his initial month in the White House, did not leave the mansion a single time.[56]   He was beset again with attacks of kidney troubles and was confined to bed for a week or more at the end of June and the beginning of July.   On July 3 Surgeon-General Barnes warned Johnson not to leave his room, "and on no account to receive visitors."[57]   It was not until the Sunday following Independence Day that Gideon Welles was able to take the President down the Potomac on an outing.   Johnson had a splitting headache, but the trip proved very beneficial to him.   His daughter, Mrs. Patterson, and her two children had by this time reached Washington, and went with the President on this excursion, as did Horace Maynard and two or three of the White House attachés.   Johnson was "pale and languid."   Welles feared "that no constitution would endure such labor and close confinement."[58]

In August a happy scene took place at the Mansion.   Two carriages drove up and the Johnsons were reunited once more. Beloved Eliza, travel worn, travel weary, and worn by disease, was accompanied by a second daughter, Mrs. Stover, and her children, bringing the youthful White House contingent to a total of five. In all, there were now twelve members of the Johnson family in Washington: the President, his invalid wife, his two daughters, Mrs. Patterson and Mrs. Stover, his two sons, Robert, thirty years old, and Andrew, Jr., several years younger, his son-in-law, Senator Patterson, and the five grand-children. Robert Johnson, a colonel in the army, assisted his father as secretary. The other boy entered a Catholic school in Georgetown. The President's wife, too infirm from disease to act as mistress of the White House, soon retired to a quiet bedroom on the southwest of the Mansion, overlooking the greensward of the lawn. Her daughter, Mrs. Martha Johnson Patterson, assumed the duties of mistress of the establishment.

The group of rollicking children transformed the White House, giving it a distinct air of peace and joy, in contrast to the dismal atmosphere of Civil War days following the death of Lincoln's beloved little Tad.[59] Andrew Johnson was immensely fond of children; for them he seems to have reserved most of his infrequent smiles. Indeed, his liking for little folks was often remarked. At one of the White House New Year's receptions, "his affectionate, ample greeting to the children in the throng was particularly noticeable, and was remarked by all. Big-hearted people afterwards remarked, as they gathered in the East Room, that the President's success in putting little peo-ple at their ease was a sure indication of his excellence as a man. . . ." During this first summer, there were many children's parties at the White House, glorious fêtes for the little folk and informal festivities. One youngster, a playmate of young Andrew Patterson, had the high honor of lunching with the President one July day. Preston King was present, a great, pompous fellow, with double chin, deep voice and delib-erate speech. They talked about the fascinating topic of pirates, Jolly Roger and Captain Kidd. And there were smiles and jests about the table. The young visitor remembered, sixty-three years later, how "wonderfully Johnson's face lit up when he smiled."[60]

With the reunion of the family, the children forced the President to work less and play more. He took long walks in Rock Creek Park and drives out to Silver Spring to see the Blairs. The children would take off their shoes and stockings and wade in Rock Creek, frolicking as children will, while the President looked on enjoying their happiness. One such afternoon, as Johnson's cortège was returning from such a drive, there came a sudden thunderstorm and a deluge of rain. The President observed a poor woman on the side of the road, ragged and dripping wet, walking to town with a babe in her arms. He stopped the carriage, put her on the seat facing him, and took the poor creature to her home.

The President had a soft spot in his heart for animals as well as for children. One summer evening he showed Colonel Moore, his favorite secretary, a basket of flour, which had come from a mill Johnson owned at Greeneville, pointing out that the package had been nibbled. The night before, he explained, while he was getting ready for bed, he saw some little mice playing around, and put the basket on the hearth and let them get their fill. "And," he continued, "I am now filling it for them tonight." The next day Moore asked as to his tiny friends. "The little fellows gave me their confidence," the President answered, "and I gave them their basket and poured some water on the hearth for them."[61]

In spite of this unaffected simplicity, the White House ménage was not uncouth and rude. Mrs. Patterson was a woman of fine inherent dignity and taste, as were her mother and her sister: "more sensible or unpretending women never occupied the White House," says Secretary McCulloch.[62] Elizabeth Keckley, Mrs. Lincoln's dressmaker, a former slave, was not greatly impressed with the new White House mistress, for whom she made some elaborate frocks. The seamstress recalls carrying some work to the White House one day and finding Mrs. Patterson busily at work with the sewing machine, a novel sight to Mrs. Keckley, who did not remember that she had ever seen Mrs. Lincoln with a needle in her hand.[63] One of the secretaries says that Mrs. Patterson "made all the butter that was used in the White House during her father's term of office."[64]

Some members of Washington's high society sought rather to patronize the family of the new President, but they succeeded very ill indeed. Mrs. Patterson said with grave dignity, "We are plain people from Tennessee, temporarily in high place, and you must not expect too much of us in a social way." Even so, she never let her patronizing callers forget that she was the daughter of the President and needed no aid from snobs. The demeanor of the White House family greatly pleased the people. "The honor and dignity of the nation lost nothing in the hands of these plain people from Tennessee,"

commented the *Independent*, while Senator Doolittle bore testimony that Mrs. Patterson presided with charm and grace, a
model mistress of the White House.

When his brother William wrote from Texas asking a government position, the President sent him $1,000, urged him to
live frugally, but added that when that was gone, he would send
more. William returned his thanks, but wrote that it was not
money but office he had sought. "I am opposed to appointing
relatives to office," the President replied.[65]

Early in the summer, a group of New York bankers and
merchants opened a subscription to buy the President a span
of horses, a handsome carriage and the requisite accoutrements.
Johnson declined the gift in firm though courteous words which
met with great approval through the whole country.[66] "Nothing
has given more satisfaction to all patriots and thinking men
than your refusal to accept the present," Senator Dixon wrote
from Hartford.[67]

It seems, however, that Johnson did accept a free insurance
policy tendered by the Phoenix Mutual Life Insurance Company.
At that time it was the custom of this company to vote policies
free of cost to the President, the Vice President, and Speaker
of the national House of Representatives. On January 9,
1865, according to the minute book of the Board of Directors
of the Phoenix, "it was voted that the premiums on policies
issued to President Lincoln, Vice President Hamlin, and
Speaker Colfax, be tendered them as a gratuity." On April
17, the minute book records that "the policy of Andrew Johnson was made free for one year." According to the legends of
the company, Lincoln refused, while Johnson accepted, the free
policies.[68]

President Johnson dressed with extreme fastidiousness. His
usual dress consisted of a frock coat, carefully cut trousers,
stiff collar, and well-fitting boots. During his first summer, he
was accustomed to make informal calls on his Cabinet members and friends. Frank Cowan, of Pennsylvania, who had relieved Lincoln of the burden of signing land patents, and, upon
the Tennesseean's accession, continued as a White House secretary, has left us a piquant picture of Andrew Johnson in the
White House. At first Cowan was impressed with the President's "severity." Early and late, he recounts, the President
"was at earnest work" and did not like to be disturbed by

laughter. Cowan thought Johnson's ever present attacks of gravel, with "physical pain amounting to torture" responsible for his grim visage.[69]

During most of his presidency, Johnson was always at work. He rose at six in the morning, in summer; an hour later, in winter. He would write, read or study until ten. For the next hour, he would interview his callers. At eleven he lunched. During the next hour he met his Cabinet or distinguished visitors, if he were not overrun with place-seekers or pardon-hunters. If time availed, at three he would take a walk, but usually the swarm of callers interfered. At four came dinner, a relaxation. At five back to his study, where he would work until midnight, often with a cat and a huge coffee-pot for companions, emerging only at eight for tea with his family. Such was the usual day for Andrew Johnson, month after month and year after year, until his friends wondered that mortal frame could endure it.

Johnson closely resembled Lincoln in his presidential attitude, Frank Cowan, who had served them both, was careful to relate. He felt that the tailor-statesman was a slave to his conception of duty, felt himself a servant of the people and therefore suffered himself "to be bored frequently by Tom, Dick, and Harry, as part of his duty as President of the United States." There was always a curious procession in the busy quarters of the White House, the great men of the country and "the smallest and most contemptible" coming indiscriminately and being alike graciously received. The President was earnest and decided in his ordinary conversation as in his work, and he expected the person to whom he was talking to listen patiently and attentively, as he did himself. When he talked, he would look directly into the eyes of the one to whom he addressed his words.

One day the President thrust his head into the room occupied by several secretaries to ask, "What is the Christian name of Mr. So-and-So?," referring to a Hebrew who frequently consulted him. "He has none, Mr. President," Cowan replied gravely, "he is a Jew." Johnson banged the door. A few minutes later Cowan heard him repeat his inquiry elsewhere in this fashion: "What is the first or given name of Mr. So-and-So, the Jew?" The jocund secretary was properly abashed.

Cowan had another memorable experience with the President. There was a high massive walnut stand in the corner of the secretary's office; Cowan thought it took up too much space, and ordered it removed. When the workmen arrived for the purpose, Johnson looked in at the scene and frowned. Cowan explained what he was doing, and the President burst out: "That desk was General Jackson's. I love the memory of General Jackson,—whatever was Old Hickory's I revere. It is about the only thing in the White House that is a memento of bygone years when the Constitution of the United States was worth more than the paper on which it was printed. I desire that the desk of Andrew Jackson remain in that corner as long as the mantle of its one-time grand possessor is on my shoulders." And so it did.[70]

There were times when Johnson unbent. One night at about eleven, when Cowan was in his room reading the proverbs of Confucius, the President entered, observed the book, sat down by the secretary's side and began to talk of China and the Chinese. Cowan had been studying Marco Polo and other Eastern travellers, but he was delighted at the fund of information and philosophy which rolled from Johnson's lips. "On he talked, fifteen minutes, a half hour, and more till, forgetting himself in far-off Cathay, he cocked his presidential feet upon my writing table, and in mockery of the general ignorance and ridiculous ideas with respect to the 'heathen Chinee' and his history, actually smiled."

In view of the general impression that the Tennessee tailor-statesman was a narrow and almost an unlettered man, the secretary's amazement at Andrew Johnson's fund of information about the Chinese and their philosophy is not surprising. But inspection of a partial list of the books which Andrew Johnson read, quickly dispels the prevalent idea. During the time of his various services in Washington, records were kept by the Library of Congress of the books which the congressmen, senators, and presidents borrowed from the library.[71] Johnson, apparently, had an especial fondness for history. He read Niebuhr's, Rollins', and Ferguson's histories of Rome, to say nothing of John Haywood's "History of Tennessee," Elliott's "Constitutional Debates," Warrington's "History of Wales," Maillard's "History of Texas," Wheeler's "History of North Carolina" and Sabine's "American Loyalists." He was also interested in the biographies of great men. He seems to have been much taken by Vattel and to have read several works on political economy, as well as such philosophical and religious treatises as the works of Jeremy Taylor and James "On the Nature of Evil."

But his interests were by no means exclusively of this character. Although he is not generally thought to have cared much for poetry, he seems to have been a consistent reader of Addison and admired "Cato" especially. He read Byron, Thomas Gray, Macaulay's "Lays of Ancient Rome," Hazlitt on Shakespeare, James' edition of Aesop's Fables, Emerson's poems, Pope's poetical works, Goethe's dramatic works, Dante in translation, and Swinburne's "Atalanta in Calydon."

Nor was he indifferent to the novels of the day. Charged to his name are such books as Tuckerman's "Characteristics of Literature," Madame de Staël's "Corinne," Dickens' "Pickwick Papers," Carlyle's "German Romance," Bulwer-Lytton's "Eugene Aram," "My Novel," and "The Last of the Barons." In the field of humor he enjoyed Rabelais, Samuel Lover's side-splitting "Rory O'More," and Captain Marryatt's "Peter Simple" and "Japhet in Search of a Father."

The President's omnivorous reading was by no means against his inclinations. Indeed, at times he expressed his regrets that he had not been a schoolmaster. "I missed my vocation," he confided to Colonel Moore on one occasion. "If I had been educated in early life, I would have been a school-master . . . or a chemist. It would have satisfied my desire to analyze things, to examine them in separate parts and then unite them again to view them as a whole."

On an occasion when Johnson had recited to him practically all of Gray's "Elegy," Colonel Moore noted in his diary that "the President has a very high conception of language." He repeated again and again the words: "The dark, unfathomed caves of ocean bear," with great relish. They had about them, he said, both grandeur and solemnity.[72]

All in all, the White House seemed to one of the workers in it during Johnson's occupancy "an old-fashioned, hospitable, homelike farm house," one with a work shop, "in which there was at least one hard worker, one severely earnest laborer, early and late, one conscientious devotee before the shrine of duty, and that one the President of the United States himself, Andrew Johnson."[73]

D URING this first summer in the White House, Andrew Johnson had problems a-plenty. It was his task to set up provisional governments in the various States of the South, to watch and nurture their constitutional conventions, to secure information as to Southern conditions and to give attention to the political repercussions of Southern reports on Northern thought—to say nothing of politics, which can never be absent from the mind of an American president. While Schurz, Stanton and Sumner were seeking Radical advantages from the General's tour, the presidential reorganization of the Southern States proceeded apace.

When Gideon Welles returned to Washington early in June, following a jaunt with Dennison to South Carolina, he found the city thronged with loyalists and with conservative leaders from the South. On June 8 a Mississippi delegation headed by Judge William L. Sharkey called on the President. The next day A. J. Hamilton, Lincoln's Military Governor of Texas, "a profuse talker," appealed to the President to be continued in his office.[1] The Secretary of the Navy was very unfavorably impressed with Hamilton, who was known in Texas as "Drunken Jack," but Sharkey seemed "a man of mind and culture" to him.

On June 13 Johnson issued a proclamation appointing Sharkey Provisional Governor of Mississippi; except for the substitution of the names of persons and state, it was a faithful copy of the North Carolina document. On June 17 James Johnson was named for Georgia and, despite protests, Andrew J. Hamilton for Texas.[2] On June 21 Johnson appointed Lewis E. Parsons in Alabama, on June 30 Benjamin F. Perry in South Carolina, and on July 13, William Marvin in Florida.[3]

General Schurz did not conclude his arrangements with Sumner until July, and did not start on his presidential mission of observation until about the middle of that month. However, Chief Justice Chase, his mind occupied with the twin projects of negro suffrage and of a presidential candidacy in 1868, had preceded him.

Chase was writing Johnson from nearly every place he visited. He had written from Beaufort Harbor that nothing would strengthen the President so much as the issuance of a short appeal to the South. "Just say to the people . . . 'I will aid you by enrollment of the loyal citizens; you will not expect me to discriminate among men equally loyal; the men enrolled will vote for delegates to the convention to reform your state constitution. . . . But you may rest on the support of the national government in anything of constitutional expediency.' "[4] From Wilmington, Chase reported that it was of the first importance, if a military commander be appointed, "to have him entirely in harmony with yourself." A few days later, after a speech to an immense throng of freedmen in Charlestown, the Chief Justice wrote Johnson of his observations.

He divided the South Carolina people into three classes,—first, "the old Conservatives who opposed Secession and are now . . . even more opposed to letting the black citizenry vote." The second and as Chase believed, largest class was the "acquiescents" who preferred "the old order of things, would rather dislike to see the Blacks vote, but want peace and means of living and revival of business above all things, and will take any course the government may desire." The third group was the progressives, who knew that slavery was stone dead, who wished that "the blacks made free, will be made citizens, and being citizens must be allowed to vote." These, he added, "are the men of brains and energy, but they are few, and few of the few have been heretofore conspicuous. In the end, however, they will control."[5] On May 17, Chase wrote from Hilton Head pointing out "the absence of all further resistance to the authority of the Union," mixed with the desire to retain "political ascendancy." None the less, the Carolinians "will acquiesce in any plan you think best."[6]

By the time Chase reached Florida, Johnson's friends discovered the real purpose of the Chief Justice's trip. Harrison Reed wrote the President from Fernandina, seeking his "earnest assistance to rescue Florida from the hands of Chase and his corrupt agents. . . . His recent visit was for no other purpose than to revive the efforts to secure the State for his future purpose and against the policy of the administration. . . . He has advised his friends here to organize the colored men, and prepare them to vote. . . ."[7] George Harris observed Chase's visit to Key West,·and informed Johnson of his "conviction that the Chief Justice was looking forward to the vote of Florida one of these days."[8]

These were not the only warnings received as to Chase's journey. R. L. Latham wrote Johnson from Richmond, Va., on June 21, that from Chase he had "more to fear than from any other man in this nation." The President's correspondent termed Chase "a restless, perturbed spirit, whose vaulting ambition knows no bounds this side the fixed stars, and who to gain the presidency will not only use all the influence which his office as Supreme Judge gives him, but who will resort to mean wiles that would disgrace a fool!" Latham claimed to know him as well as any man in the country, and pointed out the Chief Justice's weak point: "He is an unmitigated coward. . . . Besides he is a tyrant, utterly corrupt, and as cold as an iceberg."[9]

The President did not intend to trust to the eyes of Chase and Schurz alone in securing information on the South. He sent three additional trustworthy observers through the region. The first was Harvey M. Watterson, father of Henry Watterson, not yet famous as editor of the Louisville *Courier-Journal*. A little later, his trusted secretary, Major Benjamin C. Truman, made a careful tour. In the fall, General Grant was dispatched on a hurried Southern trip.

Watterson's first report was from Richmond. "The city is as quiet as before the rebellion," the editor wrote. "You may walk the streets for days, and not witness one act of disorder or violence." Watterson found few burning embers of the war and thought Virginia's submission "complete and sincere, one of the most remarkable changes ever known in the history of human opinion."[10]

From New Bern, N. C., Watterson wrote that Secession in that State reminded him of the status of the pig described in the couplet:

> *When it lived, it lived in clover,*
> *And when it died, it died all over.*

"No people were ever more thoroughly conquered and subdued," he stated, "than the North Carolinans." All the President had to do was to point out their path and they would be certain to take it. He thought that a mistake was being made in garrisoning New Bern with negro troops; "the citizens of the town are deeply impressed with the belief that they deserve no such penalty."[11] Watterson thought it very bad policy, for "Boston today is not more loyal than New Bern."[12] From Raleigh Watterson reported to the President that politically, all was well. "North Carolina, like Tennessee, had been literally dragged into the rebellion, and I feel a lively sympathy for the great body of her citizens. The old Secession leaders see that they are politically ruined. God be praised!" Governor Holden was moving forward rapidly and satisfactorily. He had already appointed magistrates in about fifty-five counties out of eighty-five, who would organize the counties and reëstablish civil law. The President could scarce imagine the poverty of these people and Watterson suggested the temporary suspension of the collection of Federal taxes in the State, as the people could not pay them.[13]

On July 8 he sent another dispatch from Wilmington, N. C., confirming his previous report that North Carolina's "future loyalty is as certain as that of any State in the Union. The original Secessionists are surely all dead. . . . Your Administration is growing daily in the confidence of the people of North Carolina. The position that you are now understood to occupy in regard to negro suffrage is more than anything else doing the work." He added that he was warning North Carolina leaders that too prompt action on the President's part towards Southern restoration would be harmful for the South, "because it would array against him an overwhelming majority in both branches of Congress and thus render him utterly powerless to help the South."[14]

General Schurz had not got started before the middle of July and his final report was not rendered to the President until Congress had convened. But he was sending Johnson occasional dispatches of a complaining nature, as well as sending several Radically-tinted dispatches to the Boston *Advertiser* —stories written under a pen name. Schurz conceded that circumstances in the South were unfavorable to the development of a calm public opinion. The returning Confederate soldiers "found themselves not only conquered in a political and military sense, but economically ruined"; they found "their homesteads destroyed, their farms devastated, their families in distress."[15] Even so, the General was irritated by the unpopularity of Northern men in the South and expatiated on it at length. He made much too, of Southern unrepentance.

"Treason does, under existing circumstances, not appear odious in the South," he recited; the people "are not impressed
with any sense of its criminality. . . . The loyalty of the
masses and most of the leaders of the Southern people consists
in submission to necessity."

Schurz, of course, believed that the negro was being mistreated. He reported efforts "to hold the negro in his old state
of subjugation," and thought Federal supervision of the rights
of freedmen very necessary. He paid his debt to Sumner by
insisting on the need for negro suffrage. By forcing their admission to the privilege of the ballot, "in all important issues
the negro would be led by natural impulse to forward the ends
of the government," Schurz predicted. He ridiculed the idea
that of their own free will the Southerners would accord even
a limited franchise to the freedmen, avowing the Radical doctrine that "the only manner in which . . . the Southern people can be induced to grant to the Freedmen some measure of
self-protecting power in the form of suffrage, is to make it a
condition precedent to 'readmission.' "

Sumner kept in close touch with Schurz while the latter was
in the South. On August 28, he wrote to the General: "I fear
that you will make your journey too short," and suggested to
him to "prepare for the future by gathering details and
proofs,"[16] instruction which Schurz gladly carried out.

The General went South with a very definite attitude of
mind which he wished to sustain by his observations. He wrote
his wife from Mississippi, "I found all of my preconceived opinions verified most fully—no, more than that." He was already
planning to "open the eyes of the people of the North" by
publishing his report to the President. A few days later he
wrote to Mrs. Schurz that, if Johnson further opposed the
Radical measures, "he should not be surprised if later I take
the field against him with the entire artillery that I am now
collecting."[17]

The President did not relish Schurz's newspaper correspondence, and hinted to his friends that he might recall the
General from his trip. While Schurz was in New Orleans, a
paper of that city printed a dispatch from Washington to the
effect that he "writes for Northern newspapers his impressions
of what he has seen, and publishes opinions as to what policy
ought to be pursued toward the Southern states, instead of
making his reports direct to the War Department for the in-

formation of the President. . . . It is expected he will be re-called soon."

This "painful surprise" provoked a pleading letter from the General to the President. He admitted that he had "written some letters to newspapers," but he had published nothing that ought to have been kept secret.

"The principal reason why I wrote those letters," he continued, "is well known to the Secretary of War, for I previously informed him of it." The General claimed that what the government paid him was insufficient to meet the expenses of his travel and to support his family at home. Had Johnson only reinstated him as major general, "I should have been above the necessity of doing something for the support of my family while traveling." Schurz added that he had had to pay—he did not reveal that it had been Sumner who paid it—"a considerable extra premium on my life insurance." It annoyed him "to be preceded wherever I go by a public announcement that the President does not approve of my conduct."[18]

Schurz had ample reason to know of the President's dissatisfaction with his conduct. The New Orleans publication, a Mississippi incident and other omens should have checked him in his course. But he remained in touch with Sumner and other Radicals, and carefully prepared his reports so that they would meet the Radicals' political needs.

The General reached Washington about the middle of October and immediately called on Stanton, who told him he must see the President. Schurz went to the White House, and, to use his own words, "waited long and patiently to be admitted. . . . At last the doors were thrown open and I entered with the crowd. The President received me with civility indeed, but with undemonstrative coldness." He did not ask the General for verbal details of his trip. Schurz was again "painfully surprised," left hastily and shook the dust of Washington from his feet.

The next day, the Washington correspondent of the New York *Herald* thus explained the disfavor toward Schurz in the White House: "During his recent trip through the Southern states, ostensibly on Freedmen's affairs, his time was largely spent in efforts to organize the Republican party in that section. . . ." Upon reading this dispatch, Schurz wrote his fellow conspirator Secretary Stanton, that he had examined his conduct in vain to discover anything at which Johnson could have justly taken offense!

Inasmuch as Stanton had forced him to accept the mission, Schurz insisted that the Secretary procure him an "explanation." After his treatment at the White House, he wrote, he could not "apply to the President in person. I never received such treatment in my life . . . I should not like to expose myself to any more of it."[19]

Sumner wrote his consolingly, "It is as I expected." Every step that Johnson took "is toward perdition." Sumner's convictions were stronger than ever: "*The Rebel States* must not be allowed at once to participate in our government."[20]

General Schurz devoted about a month to polishing up his final report. On November 13 he wrote Sumner that he had it ready: "It is quite voluminous, very full in the discussion of all the important points, and has cost me considerable labor." He intended to go to Washington to present it to the President and to ask his permission to publish it at once, "so that it may be before the country when Congress meets." But he doubted securing the permission, and told Sumner that, if Johnson would not give it, the report "will have to be asked for by Congress."[21] As he expected, his appeals to the President to permit publication were unavailing, although he did finally propose that Johnson authorize its issuance with a foreword that "the President has permitted but has not read and so does not indorse" the document.

Reports by such observers were not Johnson's only source of information as to the South. He had his provisional governors and his military commanders to depend upon, as well as a large correspondence with various Southern leaders. Southern delegations came to the White House. Southerners seeking credit to start the business cycle anew found the thirteenth amnesty exception an embarrassment, many being unable to secure the desired credit because of the ban upon them. Early in July, a Richmond group journeyed to Washington, to be met with scant sympathy. "It was the wealthy men who dragooned the people into Secession," Johnson told them. "I know how the thing was done. You rich men used the press, and bullied your little men to force the State into Secession." Precisely this knowledge had led to the insertion of the $20,000 clause. The rich men of the South must show contrition and repentance. The Richmond delegation left the White House with curses on their lips.[22] This address caused wrath in Richmond, but brought "ten thousand thanks" from the United States District Attorney at Alexandria: "It will give joy to the hearts of all true men of this State."

In June Howell Cobb, erstwhile Georgia fire eater, submitted to the Federal commander at Macon a long memorandum as to conditions existing in the State, which General Wilson duly transmitted to the President with the statement that the Georgia people were "completely subjugated and submissive, and only desire to know the will of the government to execute it." A little later, General Steedman reported from Augusta that "everything is moving satisfactorily toward the complete restoration of this State upon a basis that will be perfectly satisfactory to you and the country, as well as a tremendous vindication of the wisdom of your policy." Steedman wrote again a little later to report that Carl Schurz, who had visited Augusta, "was opposed to your policy" and regarded it as premature, if not a blunder.[23] Steedman added that the release of Alexander H. Stephens, "even from parole, would gladden the heart of almost every man, woman, and child in Georgia."

There was "peace, order, and every indication of the return of substantial prosperity" in North Georgia, a citizen of Rome informed the President. "There is no record in history of an erring people manifesting so earnestly a willingness to retrace their steps and help to repair the wrongs they have committed."[24]

From a cell in Fort Lafayette prison there came surprising letters from another Georgian, Benjamin H. Hill, Davis' chosen leader in the Confederate Senate, who sent the President his views as to existing issues and his desire for a pardon. Just before the close of the war, Hill declared, "There was a very general apprehension throughout the Southern States that the existence of these States as States would be ignored, and they reduced to the condition of territories, with foreign government imposed upon them." This feeling, in the last stages of the war had "compelled many to do all in their power to uphold and encourage a struggle commenced in spite of their earnest opposition, and against their lifelong conviction."

These apprehensions were proving unfounded, Hill continued, "It is enough now to know that you have left in the hands of the people of the several States the regulations of the great rights of franchise—have made them the architects of their own future." He then praised Johnson's "wise and noble statesmanship," termed him "the benefactor of the Southern people in the hour of their direst extremity" and said that he was entitled "to the gratitude of those living and of those yet to live."[25]

Evidently Johnson answered the Confederate leader's letter, for on July 4 Hill wrote again, thanking the President for his response and making a fervent plea for pardon. He outlined his own career and case: "Entering politics, originally avowedly to oppose those extreme measures which then endangered the Union; yielding to Secession only from necessity; doing nothing cruel or criminal nor inconsistent with my position during the war; having at no time a feeling or sentiment in common with extreme men South or North, I deem it is clearly not in accordance with your repeated avowals on the subject that I should be selected for exemplary severity."[26] The Georgian's plea proved persuasive, for on July 19 Johnson signed an order for his release from Fort Lafayette and ordered that the government provide him free transportation home.

General Sheridan, commanding in Louisiana, informed the President that there might be malcontents left in that State, but that bitterness was about all that remained to the people. The country was impoverished and the probability was "that in two or three years there will be almost a total transfer of landed property. The North will own every railroad, every steamboat, every large mercantile establishment, and everything which requires capital to carry it on." Sheridan considered the South already "Northernized." Because of these circumstances, he felt that "we can well afford to be lenient to this last annoyance —impotent ill-feeling." It was hard to correct a mental attitude by legislative enactment and, furthermore, "magnanimity is the safest and most manly course."[27]

Harvey Watterson, who had reached New Orleans, reported that the Freedmen's Bureau was more of an obstacle than an asset to Louisiana's restoration. Its administration "has been productive of incalculable evils to both white and black." In addition, the presence of five negro regiments in New Orleans was an annoyance to the people and an encouragement of the negroes to acts of violence. Watterson had heard some sober truths from Texas, too, and declared to the President that

Hamilton was "odious to a large majority of his people and not at all disposed to conciliate them by acts of simple justice." A Kentuckian wrote to Francis P. Blair that the commanders of negro troops and the Stevens Radicals were making tremendous efforts to thwart the President's policy in Kentucky, and that he very much feared "they will contrive in some way to get up an occasion for murdering our citizens and to produce that bloodletting they desire."[28]

One of Johnson's chief problems, because of its reactions in the South as well as in the North, was the question of the trial of Jefferson Davis. When the President brought it before the Cabinet on July 21, the discussion was almost as heated as the day. Seward favored Davis' trial by military commission because he feared a civil court would not convict him. Dennison also favored a commission, "if the proof was clear" that Davis was a party to the assassination; otherwise he would try him for high treason before a civil court. McCulloch counselled delay in prosecution, but preferred a civil tribunal. Despite his certitude two months before that Davis had been implicated in the Lincoln plot, Stanton favored a trial for treason, by a civil court, thus tacitly conceding that his claims as to Davis' part in the assassination had little weight. Gideon Welles was emphatic in his preference for a civil court. Harlan expressed his reluctance to a civil trial unless there was a certainty of conviction. It were better to pardon Davis at once, he said, than to have him tried and not convicted.

Johnson insisted on a definite decision by the Cabinet. Seward proposed that Davis be tried by military commission; but only Harlan and himself voted for the proposal. Another member moved that Davis should be tried for treason. Every member voted aye. Then the question was put as to the proper tribunal, and all but Seward and Harlan favored a civil court.[29]

It was one thing, however, to determine upon a civil trial and another to have one. An indictment of Davis in the district court of the District of Columbia had to be quashed, because the offense of treason, defined with great exactness by the Federal Constitution, had not been there committed. Virginia was the obvious *locus* of Davis' crime, and Virginia was still under the control of the soldiery. The President wished to discover when Chief Justice Chase, to whom had been assigned the Virginia circuit of the United States Circuit Court, would hold court there. Late in August he asked the Chief Justice to come to see him to discuss the matter. Chase declined to hold the conference, being unwilling to be charged, Welles thought, with the responsibility for an acquittal, should one occur.[30]

Johnson was not to be balked so easily. On October 2 he addressed a formal note to Chase. "It may become necessary that the government prosecute some of the crimes and misdemeanors committed against the United States within the district of Virginia," he informed the Chief Justice. The President asked therefore whether the circuit court for the Virginia district "is so far organized and in condition to exercise its functions that you or one of the associate justices of the Supreme Court will hold a term of court during autumn or early winter for the trial of causes." After ten days, Chase replied in the negative. He much doubted the propriety of holding court "in a State which has been declared by the executive and legislative departments of a national government to be in rebellion, and therefore subject to martial law, before the complete restoration of their broken relations in the nation and the supersedure of the military by a civil administration." A civil court in a district under martial law could not act unless by the sanction of the soldiers, and he thought that it did not behoove the justices of the Supreme Court to exercise jurisdiction under such conditions.[31]

In November Governor Morton of Indiana wrote to Johnson to protest against any pardon for the Confederate leader. Such an act would excite intense and lasting indignation. If the President would only promptly put Davis on his trial for treason, his "popular triumph will be complete." If Davis was acquitted, "let the court and jury take the responsibility." But Charles Sumner thought otherwise about it. To him the idea of a civil trial for Davis was "the *ne plus ultra* of folly." "I have never ceased to regret his capture alive,"[32] he wrote his friend Schurz.

During the summer, the Provisional Governors seemed generally to have undertaken their tasks in a spirit of loyalty to the President. By July 17 Holden was able to report to Johnson that he had appointed 3,000 magistrates, mayors and town commissioners in North Carolina; that county courts had been organized and that he was ready to issue a proclamation for a constitutional convention. He sent a draft of his proposed proclamation to the President, who examined it and telegraphed that it was "fully approved."[33]

The report came North that the provisional governors were excluding loyal Southern men from important appointments, preferring the ex-Secessionists, a charge the Radicals used with great effect. Hence, on August 22, the President sent an identical telegram to each of his provisional governors, asking if it were true that "in appointments to offices . . . the true Union men are totally ignored, and the provisional governors are giving a decided preference to those who have participated in the Rebellion." Johnson said he placed no reliance on these charges, recognizing that their object was to embarrass him in reconstruction, but sought to impress on his appointees the importance "of encouraging and strengthening to the fullest extent the men of your State who have never faltered in their allegiance to the government."[34]

There was immediate response. Each governor denied the charge, some with vehemence. Holden telegraphed that he had been very careful to prefer original Union men, that it was his purpose to encourage those who had never faltered in allegiance, and that the Radicals were misrepresenting the truth. Both from inclination and duty, Sharkey said, he had endeavored to avoid the appointment of Secessionists. He was sure that the Union men were satisfied. Georgia's provisional governor had "uniformly given all preference to Union men." When any other had been appointed, it was because the Governor had been imposed upon "or because there is no other application for the place." Hamilton of Texas termed the Radical rumor "a most unmitigated and malignant falsehood." Parsons of Alabama was not so positive. He had appointed Union men "in every instance where one reasonably qualified would accept the office. When such could not be obtained, those least objectionable have been appointed. In no instance has a Union man been neglected or set aside for Secessionists."

The conduct of Governor Perry of South Carolina was giving the President some concern. On July 3, before he had been appointed Provisional Governor, Perry had addressed a public meeting in the court house at his home, Greenville. Upon Perry's appointment, South Carolina correspondents of Radical Northern newspapers telegraphed partial quotations of Perry's speech to the North, and there was a great stir. Among other things, Perry had said that the meeting was "one of deep humiliation and sorrow"; that "we have been deprived of all civil government and political rights," that "now we meet as a disgraced and subjugated people," and that "there is not now in the Southern States anyone who feels more deeply the humiliation and degradation of going back in the Union, than I do." But he immediately added that "I know I shall be more happy and prosperous in the Union than out of it." In the further course of his remarks, Perry made light of the statement that "the South has sustained a great loss in the death of President Lincoln." He said frankly that he did not think so, and that President Johnson was "a much abler and firmer man than Lincoln" and one "in every way more acceptable to the South."

These quotations caused great indignation in the North, and Perry's speech was considered at several Cabinet meetings. When Perry heard of it, he sent the President a copy of his entire address, which put a different light on the matter. Indeed, the sentiments in the speech comport oddly with what is now believed to have been the attitude of Southern leaders at the end of the Civil War. Perry made the bold and definite statement that the heart of the people of the South never had been in Secession or Civil War; that had it been, the South would not have been conquered. He pointed out "the madness and folly of the Southern States in commencing this revolution." The great cause of its failure, he said, was "that the HEART of the Southern people never was in this revolution! There was not a State, except South Carolina, in which there was a majority in favor of Secession. . . . The people themselves were to blame for its failure. They were unwilling to make those sacrifices which were essential to its success."[35] The garbled reports of this speech were made much of by the Radicals. But Perry's response to the President's circular telegram as to appointments of disloyal men was very emphatic. He termed the report "totally untrue," declared that all his sympathies were with the Union men, "but there are many now seeking offices as Union men who were never heard of as such in the Rebellion." . . .[36] There is no record of any response at all from Governor Marvin of Florida.[37]

Doubtless there was some truth in the Radical rumors, for it was difficult to find in the South a sufficient body of men altogether unconnected with Secession to man the multifarious offices of the government. Johnson's Cabinet members had experienced great difficulty in making the necessary federal appointments. When it became necessary to restore the various national services in the Southern States, those of the post offices and post roads, the administration of justice, the various treasury inspections and collections, Dennison, McCulloch and even Speed were perplexed. The statement was made in the Cabinet that, if the test oath were required of all federal appointees, it would be altogether impossible to administer the national laws in the South without the importation of great bands of Northern Carpetbaggers. At first Stanton proposed that if the appointee could not take the whole oath, "to swear to as much of it as he could." Later he suggested appointing the Southerners without any oath at all, because the South as yet technically was still "in rebellion."[38] Some of the Cabinet members cut the Gordian knot by disregarding the Act of Congress, and appointing men of intelligence and integrity, regardless of their Southern sympathy.

About this time, Provisional Governor Sharkey confronted the President with a thorny problem. A white man had murdered a negro. Sharkey wished to try him in a Mississippi court, but General Slocum had refused to honor a writ of *habeas corpus.* "If this be tried by military authority," the irate Mississippian telegraphed Seward, "why not all other crimes, and what is the use of civil government?" Johnson informed Sharkey that the Mississippi civil government was "as yet provisional only," and that it was "inexpedient at present" to rescind the suspension of the writ in that State.[39]

The Mississippi Constitutional Convention assembled at Jackson in August and quickly fell to work. On August 15 the President telegraphed Governor Sharkey that he hoped the convention would amend the Mississippi state constitution without delay, abolish slavery, deny "to all future legislatures the power to legislate that there is property in man" and ratify the thirteenth amendment to the United States Constitution.

The President had a further pregnant suggestion. "If you could extend the elective franchise," he urged Sharkey, "to all persons of color who can read the Constitution of the United States in English, and write their names, and to all persons of color who owned real estate valued at not less than $250.00, and pay taxes thereon, you would completely disarm the adversary and set an example the other States will follow." This suggestion of qualified suffrage bears a striking resemblance to that made by Lincoln in the preceding year to Governor Hahn of Louisiana. Johnson felt the Mississippians could grant this limited franchise "with perfect safety"; that such action by the Southern States would put them on the same basis as the free States, and that by so doing "the Radicals, who are wild upon negro franchise, will be completely foiled. . . ."[40]

The Mississippians unfortunately did not heed the President. Had they done so, the Radicals might have been disarmed completely and the restoration of the Southern States under Johnson might have been undisturbed, thus saving the South from a decade of worse than war. But Mississippi's constitution makers, lacking Andrew Johnson's knowledge of the Northern temper, gave vent to their parochial Mississippi feelings. Every concession was made grudgingly. The Mississippians did not go far enough to spike the Radical guns. They only furnished ammunition for them. By August 28 the new constitution of Mississippi had been agreed upon and forwarded to the President. Suffrage was accorded to "every free white male person of the age of twenty-one years or upward." Johnson's telegram might as well never have been sent. As to emancipation, the Mississippians truculently said, "the institution of slavery having been destroyed in the State of Mississippi," it should never again be established. The Ordinance of Secession was "hereby declared to be null and void." The Convention carefully provided for the pay of its members and for the maintenance of most of the laws in force during the war, and with equal care refrained from repudiating Mississippi's Confederate debt. Though the President had to content himself with Mississippi's grudging action, one can detect a tone of regret in his congratulatory message to the provisional governor.

Sharkey sought to organize a Mississippi militia. Although Johnson advised him to suspend this plan, late in August the Provisional Governor ordered the enrollment of two companies in each county. Acting on a suggestion of Carl Schurz, who had then reached Mississippi, General Slocum issued an order to prevent this. Sharkey protested to the President. It was a critical situation. Committed to the policy of immediate restoration of civil government, the President could hardly have avoided telegraphing sharply to Schurz. In his admonition, the President set forth his presumption that Slocum would issue no order interfering with the civil authorities without first

THE DEATH-BED OF THE MARTYR PRESIDENT, ABRAHAM LINCOLN.

WASHINGTON, SATURDAY MORNING, APRIL 15TH 1865.

THE DEATHBED OF ABRAHAM LINCOLN

From an Old Currier & Ives Engraving Published in 1865. Re-issues of This Print Two Years Later Omitted Andrew Johnson as Among Those Present. The Persons Shown in the Print from Left to Right Are As Follows:

Chief Justice Salmon P. Chase; Attorney-General Speed; Secretary of the Treasury McCulloch; Vice-President Andrew Johnson; Senator Charles Sumner; Secretary Edwin M. Stanton; Secretary Gideon Welles; Robert Lincoln; the Surgeon-General; Abraham Lincoln; Mrs. Lincoln, and her son. (An artist's error, as Little Tad was thirteen years old at the time of his father's death, and is depicted as a boy of five); Miss Harris.

consulting Washington. "The people must be trusted in their government," Johnson advised, adding that "the main object" of Schurz's mission had been to aid in carrying out the presidential policy, and not to obstruct it. A copy was sent to Sharkey, who telegraphed for permission to make it public to "soothe a troubled public mind."

The inauguration of the state government established by the Mississippi convention brought in its wake problems which were to recur in nearly every one of the restored Southern States. The Mississippians chose for their governor Benjamin G. Humphrey, an ex-Confederate brigadier, who undertook to perform his new duties before being pardoned by the President. The latter suspended his functions, as he did those of the other newly elected Southern governors, and directed the provisional appointees to carry on until his "indispensable" terms had been met.[41] In thanking the President for his pardon certificate, Humphreys rather exulted over Mississippi's part in the Civil War, insisted that the people "had been overpowered and exhausted," and now desired "in good faith to return . . . to the protection of the Constitution and the Union." The Mississippi legislature was reluctant to ratify the Thirteenth Amendment. Much disturbed by its dilatory course, the President telegraphed Humphreys that "a failure to adopt the amendment will create the belief that the act of the convention abolishing slavery will hereafter by the same body be revoked."

In Alabama, developments were somewhat more satisfactory to the President. The type of men selected for the constitutional convention even won a good word from General Schurz, who reported to the President that "the most respectable persons seem to have been chosen." When the convention met in September, it quickly repealed the Secession Ordinance. But its division on the ban on slavery aroused grave apprehension among Alabamans in Washington. On September 19 these leaders dispatched a joint telegram to Governor Parsons at Montgomery. While the President earnestly favored Alabama's speedy restoration to all her rights, they declared, yet "if slavery is not abolished and the claim of the right to secede is not fully surrendered, he neither has the power nor the wish to restore us." The convention must not antagonize the President by falling short of the indispensable terms for readmission.[42] Johnson's chart was still the Constitution, but the South was wearing his patience thin.

This warning seems to have been sufficiently effective, for the Convention proceeded to outlaw slavery without equivocation, and made no difficulty about repudiating the Confederate debt. Late in September, Harvey Watterson reported Alabama's "cheerful acquiescence" in the outcome of the war. Johnson telegraphed Governor Parsons of his gratification at the convention proceedings, which had "met the highest expectations of all who desire the restoration of the Union. All seems now to be working well. . . ."

The Federal authorities experienced more trouble with Alabama's preachers than with politicians, editors and business men. The general commanding the Federal troops in the State reported that the clergymen, "especially of the Protestant Episcopal Church, are the most disloyal and mischievous of all the citizens." Bishop Wilmer had suggested to his clergy that they dispense with the usual prayer for the health and safety of the President of the United States, an action of such conspicuous disaffection that the General had been forced to ban Divine services in churches where the proper liturgical prayer was refused. Governor Parsons endeavored to gloss over what he termed the Bishop's "harmless" contumacy, suggesting that what Wilmer sought was martyrdom. The attitude of Bishop Quintard of Tennessee was in pleasing contrast. He wrote the President to join in the hope that the coming Episcopal convention would be marked by a "cordial conservatism such as will heal the seams and scars of war."[43] But when he called at the White House, Johnson gave him "two fingers," and he returned to Tennessee indignant "at having to be patronized that way by a man like Andrew Johnson."[44]

The delegates to South Carolina's convention found that Columbia was "a wilderness of ruins . . . a mass of blackened chimneys and crumbling walls." As every public building had been destroyed, the convention met in the Columbia Baptist Church.[45] Its personnel was largely ex-Confederate, including at least four generals and six colonels. Its leading spirits were James L. Orr, soon to be governor; F. W. Pickens, the first Secession governor; the venerable Alfred Huger and Samuel McGowan, late major general in the Confederacy. There was a sprinkling of "unreconstructed Rebels," for the fire eaters were not all dead, but the general tone was one of resignation to military force.

No sooner had the convention met than a delegate offered

a resolution "that under the present extraordinary circumstances," the State must accept its fate, enduring the evils patiently, and calmly awaiting "the time and opportunity to effect our deliverance from unconstitutional rule." This resolution was generally denounced, chiefly because of its impolicy. General McGowan insisted that South Carolina did not stand "with obedient words on her lip and disloyal spirit in her heart." Finally the resolution was tabled, being even refused printing by the convention. But while Governor Perry's message insisted that the assembly immediately adopt an anti-slavery amendment, it further took the position that "this is a white man's government, and intended for white men only," and termed negro suffrage "folly and madness."

On September 15, South Carolina both "repealed" its Secession Ordinance and passed a resolution asking President Johnson to pardon Jefferson Davis. The convention had its chief debate on the slavery amendment, the delegates being insistent that the phraseology adopted should recite that since the slaves had "been emancipated by the action of the United States authorities," slavery should never be reëstablished in the State. In other words, South Carolina banned slavery, but under duress.[46]

When the South Carolina state elections were held, James L. Orr was chosen Governor, and a legislature was selected which promptly assembled in Columbia. President Johnson watched the deliberations of this body with keen anxiety. On October 31 he telegraphed Governor Perry regarding South Carolina's tardiness in ratifying the Thirteenth Amendment: "If the action of the convention was in good faith, why hesitate on making it a part of the Constitution of the United States?" He appealed to Perry for South Carolina not to defeat the restoration of the Union and not to cause all that had so far been well done to be thrown away.[47] Thus pressed, the legislature ratified the amendment, but it adjourned without repudiating the State's war debt.

North Carolina Unionists had more iron in their souls. The convention which assembled in Raleigh on October 2 contained a very substantial element of thoroughly loyal men. The President of the convention, E. C. Reade, a fine Old Line Whig, expressed the general feelings when he took the chair. "Fellow citizens, we are going home," he said. "Let painful reflections upon our late separation and pleasant memories of our early Union quicken our footsteps toward the old mansion, that we may grasp hard again the hand of friendship which stands at the door."[48]

The convention undid its Secession thoroughly and decisively. Nathaniel Boyden, who proposed the successful phraseology, wanted "the Secession Ordinance buried so deep that even the Day of Resurrection can't find it." And so it was. The Ordinance of 1861, said the Ordinance of 1865, "is now, and at all times hath been, null and void." The ex-Secessionists in the meeting objected to the wording, but the Union men insisted. They wanted to stamp Secession as a wrongful act, and to make public declaration that North Carolina had never left the Union. North Carolina's slavery clause was equally terse and indicative of the temper of the state. "Slavery," it said "and involuntary servitude, otherwise than for crimes whereof the parties shall have been duly convicted, shall be and hereby are forever prohibited within the State." There was no hint that negro suffrage be granted, but a commission was recommended to propose just laws for the freedmen's governance. The great fight of the North Carolina convention was over the repudiation of the Confederate debt. The sessions began with the members determined not to repudiate these obligations. It was necessary for President Johnson to telegraph Holden on the subject before the convention would give way. His dispatch of October 18 that "every dollar of the debt created to aid the rebellion against the United States should be repudiated finally and forever," aroused a furor, but eventually the delegates saw the light and adopted the necessary repudiation clauses.[49]

The Georgia convention met in Milledgeville on October 25. The repeal of its Secession Ordinance, requiring but two minutes' time, was not a declaration of nullity and voidness, but merely a repeal. Georgia's abolition of slavery proclaimed the historical fact, and recited that the action of Georgia was no relinquishment of right for compensation on the part of former Georgia owners of slaves! This likewise was adopted without debate. The chief battles were over a petition for the pardon of Jefferson Davis and the repudiation of the debt. As to the former, a resolution was eventually adopted addressed to the President, saying that if Davis were guilty "so are we; we were the principals, he was our agent. Let not the retribution of a mighty nation be visited upon his head, while we who urged him to his destiny are suffered to escape."[50]

When the Georgians reached the question of debt repudiation in November, there was bitter opposition. Major Truman stopped at Milledgeville and observed the convention, informing the President that "the utmost malignity and meanness and ingratitude was manifested during the entire proceedings."[51] The issue grew so doubtful that the Provisional Governor telegraphed the President, "we need some aid to repeal the war debt." Johnson responded with a blunt warning: "The people of Georgia should not hesitate one single moment. . . . It should be made known at once, at home and abroad, that no debt contracted for the purpose of dissolving the Union of the States can or ever will be paid by taxes levied on the people for such purpose."[52] Under these urgings, by the slender margin of 133 to 117 the convention finally outlawed the Confederate debt. On the following day the Governor telegraphed the President that the convention had adjourned "in good temper." But Johnson's temper was not quite so good. His faith in the good intentions of the Southern leaders was being badly shaken.[53]

The Florida convention seems to have been the least impassioned of them all. It met in October, deliberated in leisurely fashioned, annulled Secession, abolished slavery, repudiated the Confederate debt, and adjourned the following month. Johnson thanked Provisional Governor Marvin, but urged him that the Florida legislature soon to be convened must "without hesitation" ratify the thirteenth amendment to the Federal Constitution.

Under the presidential plan of restoration, the machinery of Southern government moved with amazing alacrity.[54] By the time Congress assembled, North and South Carolina, Georgia, Florida, Alabama and Mississippi had held elections, had amended their constitutions, abolished slavery, undone Secession, and had Senators and Congressmen waiting in Washington to take their seats in the national legislature.

The President had repeatedly urged the Southern people to elect as their Congressmen, and the legislatures to choose as United States Senators only men who could take the prescribed Federal oath. His wishes had been almost completely ignored. Georgia had elected Alexander H. Stephens, late Vice President of the Confederacy, to the Senate not long after he was paroled from Fort Warren prison. His colleague, Herschel V. Johnson, could not possibly take the oath. J. L. Alcorn, a Mississippi Senator, had been a Confederate Brigadier; John L. Manning, of South Carolina had been an officer on Beauregard's staff. Of the four Provisional Governors—Parsons of Alabama, Marvin of Florida, Sharkey of Mississippi and Perry of South Carolina—elected to the Senate, Marvin alone could take the oath. The North Carolina legislature almost unanimously selected for the Senate William A. Graham, who had been in the Confederate Congress.

The House situation was quite as bad. Governor Perry telegraphed the President that he feared South Carolina would not be represented in Congress unless the test oath be modified.[55] Every member "has either held office under the Confederate States, or been in the army, or countenanced in some way the Rebellion." Word came from Georgia's Provisional Governor that not one of its representatives could take the oath: Four out of seven had been in the Confederate Army, two of the other three had held civil office under the Confederacy. None of North Carolina's choice could qualify, save perhaps one man.

There were four Confederate generals in the House membership, several times that number of colonels, many members of the Confederate Congress and of the various Secession conventions.[56] The effect on the Radical Congress of the presence of Confederate applicants in the Capitol lobbies can be easily imagined. James G. Blaine, himself a participant in the Congressional struggles, declares that "the presence of these obnoxious persons inflamed minds not commonly given to excitement, and drove many men to act from anger who were usually governed by reason." Johnson's policies would have been much stronger had these ex-Confederates stayed at home. It seemed to many of the Radicals as if the South were determined to insult the Congress of the United States.[57]

During these Southern events the political situation in the North has been developing rapidly. The Radicals were watching the actions of the Southern conventions with as keen attention as was the President, and with much more satisfaction.

In October Jacob Collamer, a Vermont Radical, informed Johnson that the proceedings of the Southern conventions were unsatisfactory. The failure of any State to adopt the thirteenth amendment, he said, was a distinct implication that such States yet intended to hold themselves in the position to restore slavery at their own pleasure.[58]

In the middle of September Joseph Medill, editor of the Chicago *Tribune*, sent the President a truculent note, warning him not to judge "the political opinions of the twenty millions of Northern people from the columns of the New York *World* or *Herald*. . . ." Johnson might affect to despise the Radicals —"true, earnest men possessing will, nerve, conscience and power,"—"but their votes made you President, their bayonets and principles put down the Southern rebels, and held their allies, the Northern Copperheads, by the throats. . . . They control twenty States in both branches of Congress. Four-fifths of the soldiers sympathize with them. Can you afford to quarrel with their two millions of votes? . . . For God's sake move cautiously and carefully. Don't show so much eagerness to rush into the embrace of the 20,000 Rebels."[59]

The President was not greatly impressed with Medill's advice. On October 6, he wrote James Gordon Bennett a note of cordial thanks for the latter's ability and skill in supporting the Administration. It was the more highly appreciated because it had not been solicited "but voluntarily tendered." Johnson set forth that he had entered upon his high office "with a fixed and unalterable determination to administer the government upon the principles which will bring the people . . . in close proximity with all the acts and doings of the public servants, thereby enabling them to determine understandingly all questions of public policy. So far in public life, the people have sustained me. I have never deserted them, and if I know my own heart I will stand by them now. Hence, in the people's cause I need to ask for aid."

Bennett sent his son James Gordon Bennett, Jr., to Washington with his "sincere thanks to you for your noble letter." The proprietor of the *Herald* wrote that he took a very deep interest in the Administration's success, because Johnson's policy "will lead to reunion and prosperity."[60]

On the whole, political conditions in the North seemed satisfactory to the President. A friend of Secretary Harlan made a tour of political inspection, visiting New York, Connecticut, Ohio, Indiana, Kentucky, Wisconsin and Missouri. He reported to the President on November 21 that in these

States he found "most men ready . . . and anxious to go with us. . . ."[61] Simon Cameron pledged Johnson: "We will sustain your policy, be it what it may."[62]

In October, Senator Dixon reiterated that the President's policy was gaining ground. "Your course," he said, "meets the approbation of a large proportion of the Republican party of Connecticut." It was a pity that the Radicals denounced it, but "the day of Radical fanaticism is over." All the Democrats were with the President, and Dixon hoped that the next Congress would likewise support the President's plan. One thing he thought sure. "If the Southern Senators and Representatives are refused admission to their seats at the next session, the subsequent Congress will be composed of another school of politics. An indignant people will settle the matter right as soon as they can constitutionally act."[63] Connecticut voted on the subject of negro suffrage, rejecting it by a considerable majority. It seemed a portent of the mind of the North.

Late in September George L. Stearns, one of Johnson's former Massachusetts friends, called upon him and was received with the usual politeness. They discussed the political situation for an hour or more.[64] On the subject of Reconstruction, the President was expansive. He told Stearns that he was opposed both to too much power in the State and to too great a consolidation in the central government, and that the elective franchise was not a natural but a political right. As to negro suffrage, "if I interfered with the vote in the Rebel states to dictate that the negro shall vote, I might do the same thing for my own purposes in Pennsylvania." The only safety, Johnson insisted, was "in allowing each State to control the right of voting by its own laws." He added that the country possessed the power to control the Southern States if they should go wrong. If they should again rebel, "we have the army and can control them by it, and if necessary by legislation also." But there was grave danger in any attempt by the central government to control the right to vote in the State. Should the government do so, "it may establish such rules as will restrict the vote to a small number of persons, and thus create a central despotism."

Pleased with the tenor of the President's remarks, Stearns returned to Willard's Hotel, wrote out his remembrance of the interview, and sent it to Johnson for correction. The President read the draft, made some verbal changes and returned it to Stearns. On his arrival in Boston, Stearns called a meeting of the Radicals and read the report of the interview. He was surprised when every one of them opposed his publishing it, probably because they feared it might undo some of their reckless and extravagant claims.

The Radical attitude at the time was better expressed by Wendell Phillips, who on October 17 fired another gun against the President. "You can't trust Andy Johnson," this Abolitionist agitator told his audience in the Boston Music Hall, charging that the President "makes himself ex-Rebel in order that they may be one-fourth Union. . . . The President . . . has put a bayonet in front of every Southern claim, he has spiked every Northern cannon . . . Andy Johnson may not be a traitor, but he is an enemy." It was not long before he was to speak of the President "as an obstacle to be removed."[65]

On October 24 Stearns published his interview, which was hailed "from Maine to Tennessee."[66] The Cleveland *Leader's* comment was typical. "We do not see how Radical men . . . can quarrel with the position of the President. It places him very clearly among the friends rather than the enemies of negro suffrage."

Out in St. Louis, General Sherman was watching the President's policy with considerable pleasure. On November 4 he wrote his brother: "You will observe that Mr. Johnson is drifting toward my terms to Johnston. He cannot help it, for there is no other solution. Any plan will have objections. But that least of all."[67] The Senator promptly answered. He had seen the President several times. "He seems kind and patient with all his terrible responsibility."[68]

Late in November, Sumner started for Washington, stopping on his way in New York, where George Bancroft had a long talk with him and besought him to be sensible about the President, negro suffrage and the South. The historian wrote to Johnson about this conversation. "I did all in my power," Bancroft recounted, "to calm him down on the suffrage question and he admitted fully that the *President* could not have granted the suffrage." Bancroft said Sumner had already prepared an "elaborate" speech, and was determined to get it out of his system, "but was resolved to cultivate friendly relations with you. He told me he would call on you tomorrow night." Bancroft hinted that on foreign relations Sumner agreed with the President exactly. "A little freedom of conversation on your part on our foreign affairs," he suggested, "would conciliate him amazingly. He goes in the main well disposed. Public opinion is all with you."[69]

Sumner did call on the President on the night of December 2. Louis D. Campbell, Johnson's Ohio friend, had arrived in Washington the same day as the Senator, and was at the White House when Sumner called.[70] The interview lasted from eight until eleven o'clock. Bancroft's hopes proved ill-founded. The Senator's conversation was "arrogant and dictatorial"; Campbell thought it "offensive." Sumner charged that by Johnson's official acts, he had "thrown away the fruits of the victories of the Union army, and the Rebellion is not yet subdued."

"Coolly and respectfully," the President asked Sumner to specify the cause of complaint. The latter replied that "the poor Freedmen in Georgia and Alabama are frequently insulted by Rebels," and brought up claims of murder of Freedmen in the South. Campbell was struck by the fact that Sumner "did not in any manner during these three hours of conversation object that the Executive had assumed to start Reconstruction, or that you had improperly taken jurisdiction of the question without convening Congress, nor did he ever intimate that you should have called an extra session of Congress. Sumner's only complaint and the burthen of his tale was that in the North Carolina and other proclamations," Johnson had not enfranchised the negro.

Campbell preserved a vivid recollection of the interview, "and particularly of your replies, some of which were justly caustic." One such colloquy ran:

> The President: Are there no murders in Massachusetts?
> Sumner: Unhappily, yes, sometimes.
> The President: Are there no assaults in Boston? Do men there sometimes knock each other down, so that the police is obliged to interfere?
> Sumner: Unhappily, yes.
> The President: Would you think that Massachusetts on this account should be excluded from Congress?
> Sumner: No, Mr. President, I would not.[71]

In leaving, Sumner warned Johnson that, because of the negro suffrage question, he and his friends meant to make war on him in Congress. This was the last personal interview between Charles Sumner and Andrew Johnson. A day or so later, the Senator wrote a friend that he had left the White House "with the painful conviction that the President's whole soul was set as a flint against the good cause, and that by the assassination of Abraham Lincoln, the Rebellion had vaulted into the presidential chair."[72] A few days later, the Senator disclosed what was running in his mind by sending Gideon Welles a marked newspaper clipping, a memorial to Congress for the impeachment of the President.[73]

O N the last day of November, the Union State Central Committee of Pennsylvania passed resolutions that Johnson's administration "commends itself to the admiration, respect and confidence of the people of the Commonwealth." But such were not the feelings of Thaddeus Stevens, Pennsylvania's Commoner, who came to Washington that same day.[1] Stevens was quite as bitter against Andrew Johnson as was Sumner, but he did not rely on letters and speeches. He brought with him to Washington a campaign plan designed to checkmate the President.[2]

Fertility of resource was characteristic of Thad Stevens, a very practical man. In surveying the career of this Pennsylvania Caliban, it is hard to repress a feeling of admiration for his brutal realism. Sumner never dropped his pose of statesmen, never admitted that other than the loftiest idealism animated his every act. Stevens did not stoop to self-deception; he knew what he wanted, was cynically frank in admitting his true motives, and did not scruple as to means.

In some respects the career of Pennsylvania's Great Commoner bore striking resemblance to that of the President whom he so bitterly maligned. Stevens was born in Vermont in 1792. Malformed from childhood with a clubfoot, and born in dire poverty, he was embittered in character. From his earliest recorded years, Stevens' attitude of mind was grim, unrelenting and severe. What education he had was due to the self-denial of his mother, who worked night and day to get the money to send him first to school and then to Dartmouth College.

In 1815 he was graduated from college and went to Pennsylvania to teach school. A few years later he was admitted to law practice at Gettysburg and became a jury lawyer par excellence, his biting words and acid phrases having great effect upon the talesmen of Gettysburg and Lancaster and York. Stevens' first incursion into politics was characteristic. At the beginning as at the end, he was an apostle of proscription and hate. He was elected to the Pennsylvania legislature on the anti-Masonic ticket in 1833, and comported himself accordingly.[3]

Upon the break-up of the Whigs, Stevens became an ardent Free Soiler. In 1848 he was elected to Congress, and in his first session delivered a bitter philippic against slavery. Upon the advent of the Republican party, he attached himself heart and soul to its cause. He was out of Congress from 1853 to 1859, but in the latter year returned as a stalwart Republican, and remained member from the Lancaster district from that day until his death. In the 37th Congress Stevens became almost a despot. As chairman of the all powerful Ways and Means Committee of the House, his word was law and his rule was almost undisputed. As a parliamentarian, he was almost without peer in former or in succeeding congresses. As a leader of men, he had unusual gifts—but perhaps the word leader is badly chosen. He did not lead men—he drove them, with stinging words and harsh rebuke, and with wit which cut like the lash of a whip. Lincoln had little love for Thad Stevens and Stevens little for him. The Commoner was one of the first to assert the exclusive right of Congress to control Southern Reconstruction. He was an ally of Henry Winter Davis and Ben Wade.

In the first year of the war, Stevens worked out his theory of the status of the Southern States, and thereafter continually propounded it with brutal frankness. He scoffed at Sumner's cobweb spinning; no "state suicide" for him. The Southern States had seceded; they were no longer in the Union and were no longer American States. Therefore they had no color of title to any of the rights of States. They were foreign powers; when occupied by Federal troops, they were merely conquered provinces, and as such the United States could deal with them as it saw fit. Slaves could be freed. The Southerners' property could and should be confiscated. It was folly, Stevens contended, to think of States in a state of suspended animation. They were merely territories which might or might not be admitted into the Union, as Congress might prescribe.

Stevens' appearance expressed the virulence of his views. Tall, thin and cadaverous, he had hatred stamped upon his brows. His "long and pallid" face was crowned with a dark brown wig. His brows were beetling, his eyes gleaming and insolent, his under lip protruded "defiantly."[4] The mouth was one "of unexampled cruelty."[5] Even his fellow Radical, James

G. Blaine, terms him "somewhat unscrupulous as to political methods, somewhat careless in personal conduct, somewhat lax in personal morals."[6]　Toward his own race he was "misanthropic."

But this is no complete picture of this "Lord Hategood of the Fair," for it does not reveal the characteristics which made him a force. He had unusual ability. He would cut through oceans of wordy debate to the kernel of controversy in a flashing sentence. A student and a cynic, he talked brilliantly, but did not like to listen. His speech displayed an amazing economy of words. His sentences stung like those of Dean Swift. He was unmerciful to his antagonist. So smarting were his rebukes that most of the members of Congress would endure almost any contumely rather than offend or cross him. Indeed, he was the Czar of the Radicals, the autocrat of the House.[7] His voice was devoid of music, but his wit flashed like lurid lightning. In the midst of a diatribe, Stevens seemed to sweat venom from every pore.[8]

No sketch of Stevens would be complete without reference to other personal traits. In his younger days, he had been a most ambitious drinker. All his life he was an inveterate gambler. At the close of the day in Congress, he was wont to wander down the Avenue from gambling den to gambling den, taking several hours to reach his Washington abode. There is a story of one such expedition. A committee from a church in Lancaster which was building a new steeple came to Washington to solicit a contribution. They found Stevens just coming out of a gambling establishment. The Commoner had "made a killing" and had a hundred dollar bill in his right trousers' pocket; a dollar bill was in the left. Old Thad heard the request, did not remember which bill was in which pocket, rammed his hand down in the right and drew forth the hundred dollar bill, giving it to the ecclesiastic. As soon as he saw the denomination of the note, Stevens, chagrined, remarked sarcastically, "God moves in mysterious ways his wonders to perform," and hastened up the street.[9]

Stevens never married. Yet today, the inquiring visitor to Lancaster, if properly discreet, may be shown in a certain parlor a portrait of "Miss Smith," Thad Stevens' negro mistress—"housekeeper" is the euphemistic phrase the Lancasterians sedulously employ. By his own request, Stevens was buried in a negro cemetery at Lancaster. There was no hypocritical pretence about this arch-Radical, this Caliban of the House.

When Stevens came to Washington in December, 1865, just before the assemblage of the Thirty-ninth Congress, he had thought out and brought with him a plan of campaign. He knew that as yet neither the North nor the Republican party had yielded to the Radical views on reconstruction and negro suffrage, and he was prepared to have his way through stratagem if he could not have it otherwise. The first need was to prevent the admission to House and Senate of the newly elected Representatives and Senators from the Southern States. If Johnson's policies were to be checkmated, Congress must do it, and with the Southerners seated, the Radicals would lack the necessary votes.

Regarding the qualification of members of the two Houses of Congress, the United States Constitution declares specifically that each house shall be the judge of the eligibility of its members. If this express direction were allowed to control, it was foreseen that, under Stevens' direction, the House would refuse seats to the Southerners, but that the Senate, with no leader lashing the others with a whip of scorpions as Stevens did, might admit members from the Southern States. Stevens had devised a scheme to fit this situation.

The first step was a caucus of Stevens' Radical associates. At this meeting in Washington on Friday, December 1, about thirty of the most "advanced" attended. The subject of discussion was how to thwart the President. Stevens was named the chairman of a committee to prepare resolutions to pledge both House and Senate not to admit members from the South until the other House had thus agreed.[10] The next day the Republican party as a whole held a caucus. A committee was named, again with Stevens as chairman, to consider what should be done with the claimant members from the Johnson States. The Commoner had his resolutions in his pocket, produced them, carefully refrained from hinting of the previous evening's meeting, and his plan for a joint resolution was adopted without a single dissenting vote.

The caucus was no mere Radical rally, but was attended by Conservatives and Moderates as well as by the Stevens-Sumner-Wade contingent. It is hard to understand how Henry J. Raymond, chairman of the Union National Committee and thus far a staunch defender of the presidential views, who was present at the caucus, could have permitted the Stevens resolution to be adopted without a fight. It was a signal illustration in American politics of the value of careful planning and of the consequences which may follow when a leader is asleep on the job. Raymond might have been hero of the Baltimore Convention, but on the present occasion his goldheaded cane, spats and monocle proved poor equipment in a contest with Stevens' keen and bitter brain.

The Pennsylvanian likewise put through the caucus a resolution under which its members would be bound by any caucus action. Thus Stevens tied the hands of Moderate Republicans in advance of the call of the Clerk. By this bit of political legerdemain, he had undone the patient work of Andrew Johnson and his Cabinet.

The Presidential advisers learned of Stevens' *coup d'état* when it was too late. On December 3 Welles told the President that the caucus action "was in conflict with the spirit and letter of the Constitution, which gives to each House the decision of election of its own members, . . ." a blow to our governmental system. But Johnson was not much upset. "There would be a representative from Tennessee who had been a loyal member of the House since the war," he told Welles, referring to Horace Maynard, a man who "would so state the case that he could not be controverted."[11]

The opening scene in the House of Representatives on December 4 was dramatic. The galleries were crowded with spectators expecting to witness the reunion of the States. The Clerk of the House was one Edward McPherson, a Stevens henchman and a resident of Stevens' section of Pennsylvania, indebted to the Commoner for his clerkship and thoroughly imbued with Old Thad's views. McPherson manfully did his duty to the Radicals.[12] It was the task of the Clerk of the House to prepare and call the temporary roll of the House. Usually this was a purely perfunctory clerical act, with the names of all regularly elected members appearing on the temporary roll. But when McPherson read his list not a single name of a Southern man appeared—not even that of Horace Maynard, Congressman-at-large from Tennessee.[13]

When McPherson read the roll, omitting Maynard's name, the Tennessean jumped to his feet and insisted that his name be called. There was no answer. Then he demanded a chance to be heard by the House. The Clerk remained silent. "Does the Clerk decline to hear me?" shouted Maynard. The Clerk did decline to hear. At this, James Brooks of New York, the Democratic leader, took a hand in the debate. "If Tennessee is not in the Union and has not been in the Union, and is not a loyal state, and the people of Tennessee are aliens and foreigners to the Union, by what right does the President of the United States usurp a place in the White House?" he asked. The Radicals did not trouble to answer this query. "I wish to know when the matter of admitting Southern members will be taken up," Brooks continued. McPherson looked to Stevens for orders. "I have no objections to answering the gentleman," Stevens curtly said, "I will press the matter at the proper time." Then he resumed his seat, his wig awry, a sardonic smile on his face.[14]

Schuyler Colfax, whom Johnson thought "admirably fitted to keep a grocery store at some crossroads," and of whom Lincoln had remarked to Welles, "Colfax is for Colfax, under any and all circumstances," was then reelected Speaker. In his response, the Speaker hinted at the Radical program. "The attitude of Congress is as plain as the sun's pathway in the heavens," he said. "The door having been shut in the Rebel faces, it is still to be kept bolted. . . . Establish a Republican form of government and put the Rebel states anew on such a basis of enduring justice as to guarantee every safeguard and protection to the loyal people."[15] The Radicals applauded loudly. Congress refrained from appointing the usual committee to call on the President, a deliberate Radical snub.[16]

Immediately upon the conclusion of this ceremony, Stevens introduced his joint resolution for a committee on reconstruction to which all credentials should be submitted. Immediate objections was made by a Wisconsin congressman. Stevens moved to suspend the rules to receive it, and his motion was carried by a vote of 129 to thirty-five. A Pennsylvanian then asked whether it would not be fitting to postpone the resolution until after President Johnson's message on the state of the nation had been received. The Radicals brushed this suggested courtesy aside in contempt.[17] This first day of Congress, the *Independent* exulted, was "A Victory of Liberty." Theodore Tilton's Radical organ thought Stevens' plan "wise, brave and satisfactory," and that on its success, the whole country had drawn "a long, free, joyous breath!"[18]

Under the terms of Stevens' resolution, the joint committee of fifteen was charged with considering "the condition of the so-called Confederate states and with reporting by bill if any were entitled to be represented in Congress," adding ominously that "until that time, no member be received into either House." Sumner offered a similar resolution in the Senate, but that body struck out a further provision requiring a joint vote for admission, for Fessenden did not see the justice of that clause. The House consented, and the deed was done. The resolution was more drastic than any adopted before or since in the halls of Congress. It was a declaration of war on Andrew Johnson. By its terms Old Thad had made himself the real director of the United States. The six Senators selected for the committee were Fessenden, Howard, Harris, Grimes, Johnson and Williams. The nine Representatives were Thad Stevens, Washburne, Morrill, Grider, Bingham, Conkling, Boutwell, Blow and Rogers. But Thad Stevens, although not its chairman, dominated its sessions. Caliban had won the day.

Johnson had set to work upon his message to Congress in October. He had already worked out his ideas on the state of the nation, and wished to employ competent literary assistance to impart stylistic polish to this important public document. He therefore enlisted the aid of George Bancroft, the famous historian, who was then living in New York and watching with admiration the President's direction of affairs. Shortly after Johnson's entry into the presidency, Bancroft had written to recall their pleasant associations during Polk's administration —Bancroft had been a member of Polk's Cabinet—and to assure Johnson that his speeches as President "have won you friends everywhere."[19]

During the summer the intimacy deepened, and Bancroft became more and more attached to the presidential policies. In the fall, Johnson turned to the historian as a literary draftsman for his message. He could not have made a better choice. Outlining his views to Bancroft, Johnson kept in close touch with him during the fashionings of the message. On October 29, he pencilled a note to the historian, enclosing two excerpts for consideration for the message. The first, from a Jefferson inaugural, concerned foreign policy, and this Johnson termed "one of the best expositions ever made of democracy." The second, from a speech of Charles James Fox, the President thought notable because it was "thoroughly imbued with the spirit of democracy." "You will see the best use to make of these references, if any," Johnson continued, "and will dispose of them accordingly."

On November 9, Bancroft reported to the President: "My work will be done tomorrow, but as no one knows what I am about—as I am my own secretary—I must ask a day or two more for a careful revision and for making a clean copy, which must be done with my own hand. I will send it early, very early, next week." The literary amanuensis assured the President that "no pains have been spared to express your ideas with exactness."[20]

The fruit of this joint labor was the message which the President sent to Congress on December 5. House and Senate listened reluctantly to cogent words which the country read with admiration and gratitude. In its first sentence, the message adopted a lofty tone and throughout was couched in words of informed and elevated wisdom.

"To express gratitude to God in the name of the people for the preservation of the United States," Johnson began, was his first duty. The assassination of his predecessor had cast upon him "a heavier weight of cares than ever devolved upon any one of his predecessors." To fulfill his trust, Johnson needed the support and confidence of his associates in the various departments of government and the support and confidence of the people. He knew of only one way to gain this necessary aid: "To state with frankness the principles which guide my conduct and their application to the present state of affairs."[21]

The Constitution was the chart for his policies. Its authors intended the American Union to last as long as the States themselves might last. The hand of Providence was never more apparent in mundane affairs than in its framing and adoption.

The government thus established "is a limited government, and so is every state government a limited government." The States, with proper limitations of their powers, are essential to the life of the United States Constitution. The assent of the States gave vitality to the Union, and "the perpetuity of the Constitution brings with it the perpetuity of the States; their mutual relation makes us what we are, and in our political system their connection is indissoluble. The whole cannot exist without the parts, nor the parts without the whole. So long as the Constitution of the United States endures, the State will endure. The destruction of the one is the destruction of the other; the preservation of the one is the preservation of the other."

The President thus explained his views of the mutual relations of the Constitution and the States, because they made plain the principle upon which he had sought to overcome the "appalling difficulties" which confronted him. "It has been my steadfast object," Lincoln's successor declared, "to escape from the sway of momentary passions, and to derive a healing policy from the fundamental and unchanging principles of the Constitution."

The first question he had to decide was whether or not the territory lately in rebellion should be held as conquered territory by military force. He traced carefully the arguments against any such policy. Military governments, unavailing to suppress discontent, "would have envenomed hate rather than have restored affection." No limit could be put upon them after their establishment. Their expense would have been "incalculable and exhausting." Plunderers would have followed in the train of the army, seeking profit from the miseries of their erring fellow citizens. The patronage such governments would have put in the hands of the President was greater than "unless under extreme necessity, I should be willing to entrust to any one man."

But these were not the most serious considerations. Such a policy would imply "that the States whose inhabitants may have taken part in the Rebellion had by the act of those inhabitants ceased to exist." The "true theory" was that all pretended acts of Secession were, from the beginning, without force or effect. "The States cannot commit treason," he emphasized, and those the inhabitants of which had sought to do so had had their vitality "impaired but not extinguished, their functions suspended but not destroyed." Whenever a State neglected or refused to perform its offices, there was all the more need that the Federal government should maintain all the State's authority and cause it to resume the exercise of all its functions. On this principle he had gradually and quietly, "and by almost imperceptible steps," endeavored to restore the rightful energy of the Federal and the state governments. He recited what had been done:

Provisional governors had been appointed, conventions called, governors elected, legislatures assembled, Senators and

Representatives chosen. The United States Courts, "as far as could be done," had been reopened so that federal law could be enforced. The blockade had been removed, custom houses reopened, the post-office department had renewed its ceaseless activity. With a sense of justifiable pride, the President philosophized: "The courts bring security to persons and property; the opening of the ports invites the restoration of industry and commerce; the post office renews the facilities of social intercourse and of business." And he asked if it were not a happy augury for them all that, "after all that has happened, the return of the general government is known only as a beneficence?"

The President was not unaware that risks attended this policy; its success depended upon "at least the acquiescence of the States which it concerned," but it was a risk which must be taken, the smallest risk of all. To diminish it, he had exercised freely the power of pardon conferred upon him by the Constitution. In doing so he had taken every precaution "to connect it with the clearest recognition of the binding force of the laws of the United States and an unqualified acknowledgment" of the change brought about by emancipation of the slaves.

The better to secure this reconciliation, the President had invited the Southern States to ratify the federal amendment abolishing slavery, as an evidence of their sincerity in the future maintenance of the Union. Until the amendment was adopted, the past could not be forgotten, but the adoption "reunites us beyond all power of disruption; it heals the wound. . . . It makes us once more a united people."

After the Thirteenth Amendment had been ratified, the States would be entitled to have their representatives resume their places in House and Senate "and thereby complete the work of restoration." The next sentence was aimed by inference at Thad Stevens' recent resolution. It was the duty of the members of the House and of the Senate, the President emphasized, each to judge "for yourselves of the elections, returns, and qualifications of your own members,"—advice most displeasing to Radical ears.

An important section of the message discussed negro suffrage. The President explained that the Constitution itself had counselled him against attempting "to make the freedmen electors by the proclamation of the executive." He called attention to the diversity of electoral qualifications in the several states. He could not extend the vote to the Southern negro without extending it to all colored men, wherever found. The matter must be referred to the individual commonwealths, which "can, each for itself, decide on the measure, and whether it is to be adopted at once and absolutely, or introduced gradually and with conditions." Johnson's judgment was that, by showing patience and manly virtues, the negroes would sooner win the vote through the States than through the general government, even if the latter had the power to intervene. But while he doubted the Federal competence to interfere in the extension of franchise, yet good faith required securing the negroes in their freedom and property, in the right to work and to claim the just return of their toil. He was not impressed with enforced colonization schemes, but sensibly urged that the two races be encouraged "to live side by side in a state of mutual benefit and good will." He sympathized with the zeal of sincere philanthropy, but pointed out that time was always an element in reform.

The remainder of the message summarized the conditions of the chief federal services and made specific recommendations for new legislation for their improvement, for the unthrottling of trade, the reduction of army and navy, the liquidation of the gigantic war debt and the sharp reduction of public expenditure. The only feature deserving special note was the President's financial recommendations.

"Sparing economy" was necessary. The country must prepare for a recovery "from the ever increasing evils of an irredeemable currency," and must do so without causing panic and without undue delay: National Banks empowered to issue notes based on government bonds must be chary in their issuance. Public and private enterprises must be alert "to liquidate debts contracted in a paper currency," and thus aid the return of a gold standard. "The gradual reduction of the currency is the only measure that can save the business of the country from disastrous calamity." There must be "no favored class" in tariffs and taxation, which must be distributed so as not to fall unduly on the poor, "but rather on the accumulated wealth of the country." Annihilating Jay Cooke's facile phrase, he insisted that "we should look at the national debt just as it is—not a national blessing, but as a heavy burden on the industry of the country, to be discharged without unnecessary delay."

"Who will not join with me," the President concluded, "in the prayer that the Invisible Hand which has led us through the clouds that gloomed around our path will guide us onward to a perfect restoration of fraternal affection that we of this day may be able to transmit our great inheritance of state government in all their rights, of the general government in its whole constitutional vigor, to our posterity, and they to theirs through countless generations?"

This magnificent message won instant praise for Andrew Johnson throughout the United States and Europe. The President's mail was heavy with congratulations. Bancroft was especially delighted, as well he might have been. "In less than twenty days," the historian predicted, "the extreme Radical opposition will be over. *All* of all parties approve the ground you have taken. The extreme friends of the South are gratified at the total want of asperity and passion. The Radicals are compelled to approve . . . All approve." Henry Myers of St. Louis likened the measure to the balm of Gilead. In all his life Governor Holden had never seen a document of which he so heartily approved.

Oliver P. Morton was in New York, where he found financial leaders united in hearty commendation. "I can't be mistaken," he wrote the President, "the great body of the people of the North will indorse your doctrine and policy, and this the Members of Congress will find out before they are ninety days older." The Indianan advised Johnson to use every power and instrumentality in his hands to sustain his policy, and to aid the friends who favored it. General John A. Dix had read the message "with unqualified gratification." D. H. Cadwalader of New Albany, New York, thanked "our eternal Father for a chief ruler that knows neither North nor South."

The Northern Democrats were delighted with the tone of the message. Barlow wrote a friend that his party was "fully and absolutely committed" to the President's plan of reconstruction, "regardless of disposition of patronage." The message reminded many throughout the country of Andrew Jackson. Southern opinion likewise glowed with approval. William Crutchfield, a Chattanooga Unionist, informed the President that "the South looks upon you as a pillar of cloud by day and of fire by night." A former Arkansas Senator assured Johnson of the coöperation of the entire South. Ben Truman reported from Memphis that "the whole people are determined to do precisely what you want them to do."

The responses of newspapers and their editors were notably commendatory. Parke Godwin of the New York *Evening Post*, impressed with the President's "frank, dignified, direct and manly" policy, wrote him that he had chosen "a true Democratic method. . . . I trust you will adhere to it in the face of any hostility. . . . The old parties are disintegrated and new parties must inevitably grow up." George W. Childs of the Philadelphia *Public Ledger* wrote Colonel Robert Johnson that the President "has the confidence and love of the people, and the politicians cannot injure him." He asked for a cue as to any publicity Johnson wanted in his paper's columns. The New York *Times* termed Johnson's views "full of wisdom." The *Tribune* doubted "whether any former message has contained so much that will be generally and justly approved, and so little that will or should provoke dissent." The *Herald* indorsed it heartily, while the *Nation*, struck by the omen for Democracy that such a message could come from this tailor from Tennessee, termed it "one which any Democrat as well as any American may well read with pride."

When he read the message in far-off London, Charles Francis Adams wrote his cousin Sidney Brooks that it, and McCulloch's financial report, had "raised the character of the nation immensely in Europe. I know nothing better in the annals, even when Washington was the chief and Hamilton his financier."[22]

The judgment of present day historians is in line with this contemporary praise. It is now generally recognized that the restraint, the conservatism, the lofty patriotism and enlightened program of Johnson's first message established it as one of the great state papers of the American presidents. Even a critic so habitually unfriendly as James Ford Rhodes concedes that the message was in the spirit of Lincoln's Second Inaugural.[23] But the Radical leaders, far from being pleased with the moderate and considered judgment of the message, deemed it therefore all the more dangerous, and needing immediately to be counteracted. Blaine referred to Johnson's "gentle, persuasive, insinuating" words as a menace the Radicals must check.[24]

On December 8 Sumner called upon Secretary Welles to

denounce Johnson's Southern policy "as the greatest and most criminal error every committed by any government." As to reestablishing the Union, he said that Congress had all the powers and the President none. He attacked Welles as having been responsible, with Seward and McCulloch, for involving Johnson in this "transcendent error." Seward and Welles were "foully, fatally culpable." Although Welles knew that Sumner's vanity and egotism were enormous, he could hardly believe his ears. He told the Senator that Johnson's policy was correct, and that, aside from a few Radicals, the country approved it; did Sumner imagine there was opposition to it in the Cabinet?

"I know Stanton is opposed to it," replied the Senator, and seemed surprised that Welles did not know this. Then Sumner told of Stanton's emphatic and unequivocal indorsement of his speech to the Worcester Republican convention on the last of September.[25] Welles immediately related this conversation to the President, who heard it with keen attention but without being moved from adherence to his adopted policy.

When Sumner called on Welles again a week later, he was almost beside himself on the policy of the Administration, which he "denounced with great bitterness." Welles told him that there were two lines of policy before the country, one harsh, cold and distant, the other conciliatory, kind and inviting. "Which will soonest make us a united people?" he asked. Sumner hesitated and would not make a direct reply, but denounced the provisional governors, and told Welles that the majority of Congress was determined to overturn Johnson's policy. Welles also reported this interview to the President, and warned him that there was a deep and extensive intrigue afoot against him, hinting that it extended even into the Cabinet, that the executive patronage was being used to defeat the executive policy and that one or two mischievous men ought to be removed. Johnson agreed with him, but did not act.

At the next Cabinet meeting, Postmaster-General Dennison brought up the matter of some appointments he wished to make, appointments recommended by the Congressmen in the districts affected. Welles inquired if he knew the position of the recommenders on the pending issues. When this was answered in the negative, Welles asked "if the time has not arrived when we should know who is who and what we are doing to

276 THE AGE OF HATE

fortify ourselves and the cause of right." Johnson said he thought this was their duty.[26]

About this time the rumor got about that Stanton had determined to quit the Cabinet. Seward knew Stanton's duplicity, and thought this a move which should be furthered. After the Cabinet meeting on December 23, he remained behind to ask the President if there was any truth in the report. Johnson answered that it was only rumor, that he had heard nothing lately, and that "we might as well keep on for the present without any fuss." Seward's vague warning thus went unheeded.[27]

Unfortunately Andrew Johnson was afflicted with the fatal vice of hesitation. Thomas Ewing gravely reprehended this trait in the President. "He never acts," Ewing wrote, "until he is compelled by an external force. His great vice is tardiness in action—procrastination."[28] This habit of indecision and delay in action cost him dear. Even in the fall of 1865, there could have been no doubt about Stanton's double-dealing, but Johnson hesitated until it was too late.

The Secretary of War was reckless in his conduct toward the President. From the day of Johnson's accession, he kept him surrounded by detectives and spies and made the most of this espionage. Whatever the President said to a White House confidant, would probably be carried straightway to Stanton, who continually betrayed the measures and purposes of the President to the Radicals and concocted schemes against the Administration with them. The President had ample knowledge of this treachery, yet he permitted Stanton to remain. One cannot but feel in Andrew Johnson's career that his fatal procrastination was responsible for much of the sorrow he had to endure.

Early in January Sumner told Welles that only three of the Cabinet supported Johnson's policy, "the greatest mistake which history has ever recorded"; that three others opposed it and "one of them has advised and urged me to prepare and bring in a bill which should control the action of the President and wipe out his policy. It has got to be done. Half of the Cabinet, as well as an overwhelming majority of the two Houses of Congress, are for it, and the President must change his whole course."[29] Welles was much disturbed at this news. He suspected Stanton was the man.

Following the President's message, the moderate Republicans showed a disposition to avert open war with the White

House. But although Welles knew that many Republican Congressmen were voting against their convictions, he also saw how "party discipline, cunningly kept up with almost despotic power," prevented them from doing what they knew was right, and he did not see how open conflict could long be avoided. He could only hope that when it came, the Moderates would take courage from their conscience, break away from caucus rule and support the President.

Strange as it may seem, the Radicals still claimed that they were supporting the President and were urgent in demanding appointments. Nor was Johnson properly chary in making them—another instance of his faulty judgment. He did not cease to make Radical appointments until the government service had been filled with Radical opponents to his policies. When, too late, he began to change his course, a law had been passed to protect his enemies from discharge.

Stevens, Sumner and other Radical leaders, apprehensive over their followers' new attitude of friendliness toward the President, proceeded without delay to acts of war. Sumner introduced a resolution calling on the President to send to the Senate the reports made to him by Carl Schurz and John Covode on their Southern journeys. The Senate quickly adopted the resolution, and Sumner awaited with impatience the arrival of this ammunition with which he expected to arouse the North against the South.

In the House Thad Stevens threw down the gauntlet almost immediately. On December 18, he made a bitter speech in which he frankly confessed his partisan purpose. "The Republican party and it alone," he declared, "can save the Union." A question was hurled at him! Did he admit the partisan purpose of his schemes? "I do," he succinctly responded. The Republican party must control Congress. Southern members must be excluded if Republican control was to be preserved. Thus alone could the country—and the Radicals—be saved. Stevens knew the figures. There were thirty-nine Republicans and eleven Democrats in the Senate; 140 Republicans and forty-three Democrats in the House. If the Southerners were admitted, twenty-two Democratic Senators and fifty-eight Democratic Congressmen would come in. There were some weak-kneed Republicans who showed evidences of supporting the President. Thus Congress might pass into "Copperhead" control if the Southern States were not kept out. And so

Thad Stevens set his face like a flint against letting them come in.

He was contemptuous of the new Southern constitutions. The Southern States "will not and ought not to live up to the Thirteenth Amendment." Stevens cynically admitted that the whites of the South should "scorn and disregard their present constitutions forced upon them in the midst of martial law. . . . No one who has any regard for the freedom of elections can look upon these governments forced upon them in duress with any favor."[30]

The Pennsylvanian's plan was this: The Southern States should be reduced to territories and no attention should be paid to their ratification of the Thirteenth Amendment. By a constitutional change, House representation should be based upon actual voters rather than upon population. Measures must be passed to give a homestead to every negro, to protect the freedmen by a new body of laws insuring equal civil rights, and giving them the vote.[31] The Pennsylvanian had gone Edmund Burke one better. The English statesman had said he did not know the method of drawing up an indictment against a whole people. Stevens did.

Old Thad ended by declaiming that the doctrine of a white man's government "is as atrocious as the infamous sentiment that damned the late Chief Justice to everlasting fame, and I fear to everlasting fire."[32]

This Radical declaration of war greatly distressed the administration. Johnson's advisers were anxious that it be answered before the Christmas recess, and by a stalwart Union Republican rather than by a Democrat or Copperhead. Therefore, on December 21, Henry J. Raymond was scheduled to deliver a reply. Unfortunately for Johnson's defender, Finck of Ohio, a Vallandigham disciple, seized the floor ahead of Raymond to offer a Democratic defense of the President more damaging to Johnson than an attack would have been. Thus chagrined at the outset, Raymond had first to castigate the Democrats before he turned to the flagellation of the Radicals. His chief theme was to deny Thad Stevens' contention that the Southern States were dead States. He did this with eloquence and force, but without affecting the Radical bloc.

Immediately after the recess, the reconstruction debate was resumed and several advanced men sought to answer Raymond, chiefly among them Shellabarger of Ohio, who upheld Stevens' opinions and was applauded by nearly every Republican in the House. The following day Daniel Voorhees of Indiana noted Democratic orator, offered resolutions terming the President's message "able, judicious and patriotic," referring to the policies therein portrayed as the safest and most practicable available, declaring that States could not withdraw from the Union and thanking Johnson, on behalf of Congress and the country, "for his faithful, wise and successful efforts to restore civil government, law and order to the States lately in rebellion." The resolution could not have come from a more unfortunate quarter. It lent color to the Radical contention that Johnson had the support of the enemies of the Administration, to Stevens' charge that Copperheads and not loyal people made common cause with him. John A. Bingham of Ohio immediately proposed a substitute motion damning the President with faint praise, and this was adopted by a vote of 107 to 32. Only one other Republican voted with Henry J. Raymond in favor of Voorhees' text. It was a bitter disappointment to Raymond, and a turning-point in the relations between the Radicals and the President.

On the day of Stevens' speech, Johnson reluctantly responded to the Senate's resolution by transmitting the Schurz report. He accompanied it with a brief report from General Grant, who had just completed a Southern journey, and sent a message of his own. He recited that "the Rebellion has been suppressed," that the Southern aspect of affairs was more promising than they had a right to expect. The Southern people had evinced a laudable desire to renew their allegiance and to repair the devastations of war. True, there were occasional disorders, local in character, and infrequent. But this was inevitable, due to many readjustments. "Systems are gradually developing themselves under which the freedman receives the protection to which he is justly entitled." The President's information induced him to believe that sectional animosity was surely and rapidly merging into a spirit of nationality. He transmitted Schurz's report, as requested by the Senate, and invited that body's attention to the report from Grant.[33]

Well advised in advance as to the tone and tenor, background and circumstance of Schurz's purposes, tour and report, the Radicals received it with high acclaim. But Grant's letter aroused their indignation. The General was satisfied "that the mass of thinking men of the South accept the present situation in good faith." Southern leaders actually believed the decision a fortunate one. They were anxious to return to self-government within the Union; "they are in earnest in wishing to do what is required by the government, not humili-.ating to them as citizens, and if such a course was pointed out, they would pursuit it in good faith."[34]

Johnson's message and Grant's report aroused Sumner to impetuous violence. To Welles they seemed to have made him demented.[35] On December 20 the Massachusetts Senator made a speech in which he termed Johnson's message "whitewashing," and compared it to Franklin Pierce's letter on the Crime of Kansas. He referred to "sickening and heart-rending outrages where human rights are sacrificed and Rebel barbarism received a new letter of license."[36] Doolittle of Wisconsin criticized the use of the word "whitewashing," but Sumner refused to withdraw it. He had "nothing to modify, nothing to qualify, nothing to retract. In the former days there was one Kansas that suffered. . . . There are now eleven Kansases suffering as one; therefore, as eleven is more than one, so is the enormity of the present time more than the enormity of the days of President Pierce."[37] Such was the Radical tone. Schurz had given them the Gospel. Grant and Johnson were anathema.

The so-called "black codes" being adopted in the Southern States added fuel to the Radical flames. Viewed from the distance of sixty years, while they seem a blunder, they are at any rate understandable. But in the wake of Appomattox they seemed to Northern eyes merely brazen efforts to reenslave the black millions who had just been freed. Nearly every Southern legislature adopted a code of this type. Mississippi led the way in October. When her action was reported in the Northern papers, it caused an outburst of indignation, and added ammunition for Sumner, Stevens and their followers.

In the fall of 1865 and the winter of 1866, the mass of Northern Radicals had not yet committed themselves unreservedly to the demand for negro suffrage. Many of their leaders recognized that this privilege was still denied the colored man in the majority of Northern states, and that it was "illogical and unwarrantable to expect a more advanced philanthropy, a higher sense of justice from the South than had been yet attained by the North."[38]

And yet the North was much concerned that the negro be accorded certain civil rights for his protection. James G. Blaine indicates the important measures as including for the negro the full protection of the law of marriage with its privileges and obligations, the benefit of laws to assure him the wages of his labor and to confer upon him the right to acquire and hold property on the same terms which white persons enjoyed. A third need was some provision for "the rudimentary instruction of colored children, in order that they might learn the mechanical arts." These things Radicals and Moderates felt essential for the advancement of the freedmen, and upon this Northern attitude of mind, the Southern legislatures catapulted their "black codes." Under the Mississippi apprentice law, for example, all negroes under eighteen years of age must be apprenticed by the probate court to some white person, the negro's former owner to have the preference in securing the right to his toil. The master or mistress must make a bond to the State to furnish the servant with food and clothing, treat him humanely, give medical service and teach him to read and write. The master also was given the power "to inflict such moderate corporal chastisement as a father . . . is allowed to inflict on his child." If the apprentice should run away, he might be pursued, recaptured and put in jail. If any person enticed the apprentice away from his master, the offender was guilty of a high misdemeanor.[39]

Even more drastic was the same State's enactment as to vagrancy. All negroes found on the second Monday of January, 1866, without employment or "unlawfully assembling themselves together," and white persons thus assembling with negroes, would be deemed vagrants, and fined or sent to jail. If the negro could not pay the fine—of course almost none of them could—the sheriff should "hire out" the negro "to any person who will, for the shortest period of service, pay the fine and costs," the preference again being given to the negro's former employer. Another section of this act levied a poll tax of a dollar a year on every negro. Anyone who failed to pay it would therefore be deemed a vagrant, and subject to fine, sentence and binding out as such.

Under the Mississippi Civil Rights statute, enacted during this same legislature, negroes might sue and be sued, acquire property and transmit it, but no negro could "rent or lease any lands or tenements except in incorporated cities or towns." The negro must have a lawful home and must carry with him an officer's certificate stating it. Otherwise, he was liable to arrest. Any negro who, after making a contract to work for a white employer, quit his job before his contract period had expired thereby forfeited all his wages. The law provided for his arrest and return to his employer. Mississippi likewise forbade negroes (except those in the United States Army) to keep firearms, dirks, or bowie knives. Negroes could not ride in a first class passenger car used by white persons, unless traveling with their mistresses as maids.

All the Southern legislatures seemed to the Radicals to have been proceeding deliberately to inflame Northern public opinion against them. Some Southerner made use of the unfortunate phrase widely current a decade before, following the Dred Scott decision, that the negro possessed "no rights which a white man was bound to respect"; the Radicals convinced themselves that this represented the general Southern attitude. They thought it outrageous that an act which was no offense if committed by the white man became a misdemeanor or a felony if committed by a negro. They looked with anger upon labor laws and vagrancy statutes seemingly aimed at the negro race alone. "The truth was," Blaine declared, "that his liberty was merely of form and not of fact, and the slavery which was abolished by the organic law of the nation was now to be revised by the enactments of the State."

Alabama's black code declared to be a vagrant "any stubborn or refractory servants," as well as "servants who loiter away their time." Any such person might be haled before a justice of the peace, fined $50.00 and, if he could not pay it, be hired out for six months labor. The Radicals believed that the effect and the direct intent of this law was to reduce "the helpless negro to slavery for half a year—a punishment that could be repeated whenever desired, a punishment sure to be desired for that portion of the year when his labor was specially valuable in connection with the cotton crop, while for the remainder of the time, he might shift for himself. . . . There may have been more cruel laws enacted, but the statute books of the world might be searched in vain for one of meaner injustice."[40] The language of these statutes did much to bear out the Radical contention that such laws were framed so as not to

Edwin M. Stanton

A CABINET MARPLOT

Edwin M. Stanton, Johnson's Secretary of War, and
One of the Most Interesting Figures of the Age of
Hate.

be limited in specific words to negroes, but were confined to that race in execution. The Radicals thought this deceptive form a signally dishonest feature.

The South Carolina code, enacted on December 21, 1865, at the height of the Radical fervor in Congress, provided for enforced apprenticeship, the master to have the right to the profits of the apprentice's labor and authority to inflict "moderate chastisement," the adjective not being defined. It required contracts for service, defined the principals thereto as "master" and "servant"—the words have the flavor of slavery —and carefully defined what constituted proper service for a farm hand.

The hours of farm labor were from sunrise to sunset. Servants "shall rise at the dawn in the morning, feed, water, and care for the animals on the farm, do the usual and needful work about the premises, prepare their meals for the day, if required by the master, and begin the farm work or other work by sunrise." The servant was to be accountable for all property lost, damaged or destroyed by his negligence, dishonesty or bad faith. He might not leave the premises without permission from the master. If he quit the job, he forfeited all wages due him. But he might legally quit his job if he did not receive wholesome food, or if he were the victim of an "unauthorized" battery upon his person, or for similar causes.

The South Carolinians went further and passed a statute that, without first obtaining a license from the judge of his district court, good for a year only, no negro could pursue the craft or trade "of an artisan, mechanic, or shopkeeper, or any other trade or employment besides that of husbandry." He had to pay a license of $100 per year to be a merchant or a peddler. He must pay a license fee of $10.00 a year to pursue the most rudimentary mechanical craft, though no such fees were exacted of white men similarly circumstanced.

Such enactments gave the Radicals a strong basis for contending that the South had deliberately closed their avenues of improvement in the face of the colored man.[41] It is not to be wondered that the Moderate as well as the Radical North was irritated. Even the Conservatives were disturbed. Welles thought this course of the South quite as rash, unreasonable and impracticable as was that of the Northern Radicals.[42] The Northerners could not realize that such laws had not been altogether passed in spirit of defiance, that they were the fal-

tering steps of the Southern peoples to establish a system for
the government of a race which for generations had been in
bondage; a race which, although freed, had neither the education nor experience nor as yet the capacity to exercise equal
civil rights. The negroes did not know what to make of this
new freedom; their ideas of it were pitiful. They thought it
meant that the government was going to give each one of them
"forty acres and a mule," and Northern sharpers drove a
thriving business by selling these ignorant freedmen four little
blue-pointed pegs which they told the negroes they could drive
on any forty acres of their former master's lands and that they
would then own the land thus pegged. The negroes flocked by
thousands to the cities, where they lived in vagabondage and
want. Many of the planters found it almost impossible to
secure workers for the crops. The vagrancy laws represented
in part the South's endeavor to insure the raising of corn and
cotton, but they were passed in total disregard of their effect
on the North, with perhaps a large touch of defiant unconcern
as well.

The Southern leaders, in the considered opinion of James
G. Blaine, had no excuse for adopting these codes. The Radicals at the time contended that the purpose of the Southern
legislatures was a deliberate resolve to prove that the negro
"was fit only to be a chattel"; that slavery was his "normal
and natural state," and that he had lost rather than gained by
his emancipation.[43]

When such legislation for the negro was superadded to the
acts of the Southern conventions, which the Radicals charged
had been inspired by irreconcilable hatred of the Union, the
men who followed Stevens and Sumner were given almost irresistible arguments with which to draw into their camp the
Moderates who hitherto had hesitated at interfering with the
rights of the Southern States. The Radicals pictured to the
country the generosity accorded the South following Appomattox. "Never had any rebellion been followed by treatment
so lenient, forgiving, and generous, on the part of a triumphant
government," they proclaimed, and yet observe the fashion in
which this forbearing generosity was met. "Ineffable folly,"
Blaine termed the Southern attitude.

Such was the background in which the Freedmen's Bureau
bill came to be written. Senator Lyman Trumbull of Illinois,

its author, was in some respects very much of a man, in other ways a blind fanatic. Almost as great a student as Sumner, rather dour, and a zealous believer in the necessity for protection for the negroes, he was fundamentally a sound, honorable, courageous man. As Chairman of the Senate Judiciary Committee, he assumed the task of protecting the safety of the freedmen in the South, which he determined could best be secured by the use of the existing machinery of the Freedmen's Bureau and the enlargement of its authority and power.

This agency, as a bureau of the War Department, with General Oliver O. Howard as commissioner, had been established in March, 1865, to afford some agency to handle the multitudes of homeless and wandering negroes freed by the advance of the Northern armies. Trumbull himself described it as an agency "only designed to aid these helpless ignorant unprotected people . . . until they can provide for and take care of themselves."[44]

The extension of the powers of the Freedmen's Bureau which Trumbull contemplated was unprecedented. Two sections of the bill sought to guarantee civil rights to the negroes, "equal and exact justice before the law." If any negro were not accorded thorough equality, an agent of the Freedmen's Bureau, one of whom was to be named for each Southern county, could act as a court to impose a fine or prison sentence on the persons who had deprived the negro of his right. This extraordinary extension of federal authority was not to be achieved through due process of law, but through the military arm. On January 11, Trumbull reported this bill from the Judiciary Committee. After two weeks' debate, it passed the Senate by a strict party vote. In the first week in February, it passed the House similarly, and then was presented to Andrew Johnson to sign or disapprove.[45]

The first week in February, Sumner, Stevens and Wade summoned to Washington a group of negro leaders, with Frederick Douglass, a negro orator and agitator at their head, and carefully coached them in the details of a White House interview to embarrass the President. When they reached the White House, Johnson "shook hands kindly" with each of the negroes. The delegation spokesman then informed him that "we are not satisfied with an amendment prohibiting slavery, but we wish it enforced with appropriate legislation." The negroes expected the Federal Government to secure full enfranchisement for them.[46] Douglass told the President that he had the power to save or destroy the negroes, to bless or blast them.

Johnson seems not to have realized that the purpose of the interview was to embarrass him rather than to secure his views. He told the negroes frankly that, while he was a friend of the colored man, he did not wish to pursue a policy which would "end in a contest between the races, which if persisted in will result in the extermination of one or the other." He urged them to turn their minds from high-sounding theoretical talk about the Declaration of Independence to the conditions which actually prevailed. One of these was that the States were the depositories of their own political power, governing their suffrage, and that it would be tyrannical in him to attempt to force negro suffrage on them in opposition to their wish.

"It is the people of the States that must for themselves determine this thing," he added. "I do not want to be engaged in a work that will commence a war of races." He wished so to prepare things that, in each community, if the negroes acted well, the States would give them every possible advantage. If done by the volition of the States, the result would be harmony. But forcing suffrage upon the negroes "will result in an injury of both races, the ruin of one or the other." He wished that the things the delegation desired "could be done in the twinkling of an eye, but it is not in the nature of things, and I do not assume or pretend to be wiser than Providence, or stronger than the laws of nature."

Douglass attempted to argue with the President, expostulating so loudly and frequently that the latter was forced to tell the negro that he would not enter into a controversy, that he had merely done them the courtesy of indicating his own views. In concluding the interview, Douglass remarked "the President sends us to the people, and we go to the people." The negroes immediately busied themselves in denunciation of the President. That very day the delegation wrote the President an open letter terming his views "entirely unsound." The following evening, Frederick Douglass made a "grossly abusive and insulting" speech in Philadelphia.[47]

The negro leader was unfair to Andrew Johnson in seeking thus to give the impression that he was hostile to the blacks. The truth was that the President was deeply interested in the negro's welfare, and warmly seconded southern efforts to that end. Not long after Douglass began denouncing him, he received an Episcopalian minister from Columbia, S. C., who unfolded a plan of the Episcopal diocese to establish a school for negro children at Charleston. The President warmly applauded the project, and offered the aid of his Administration. More, he said, "I will send you a check for $1,000, my subscription to the good work." Soon thereafter, his check was received.[48]

But such deeds as this did little to counteract the vigorous Radical propaganda that the President was the enemy of the freedmen. None the less, the leading officers of the army staunchly took the President's side during the early months of the struggle. Typical of the attitude of Hancock, Meade, Schofield and Thomas was a letter from General Sherman informing the President that he was telling all Senators and Representatives he met "that the extreme Radical measures of Sumner and Stevens were calculated to lead to a result that they ought not to desire—the everlasting estrangement of all the people of the South."[49] About this time he warned John Sherman that measures were "being pushed beyond the Rule of Right. . . . To place or attempt to place the negro on a par with the whites will produce new convulsions. . . . It will take ten years for the South to regain full prosperity with the negro free."[50]

From St. Louis, Edward Bates, outraged at Trumbull's "Bill of Enormity," wrote the President "a plain, downright letter about the duties of his position and what the nation expected of him"—a veto![51] By the middle of February, encouraged by such remonstrances, and much concerned over the Radical plots in Congress, Johnson informed Welles that "the unmistakable design of Thad Stevens and his associates is to take the government into their own hands, and to get rid of me by declaring Tennessee out of the Union." They planned a sort of French Directory and were going to remodel the Constitution.[52] Thus, when the President and his Cabinet examined the Freedmen's Bureau bill, most of them were startled at the Radical designs. Welles termed it a "terrific engine," more like a "decree emanating from despotic power than a legislative enactment by Republican representatives." General Fullerton, an assistant commissioner of the existing Freedmen's Bureau, also thought the bill a very bad one, and advised a veto.

Johnson submitted his veto draft to the Cabinet on February 19. Seward, McCulloch and Dennison warmly indorsed it.

"Stanton was disappointed, Speed disturbed, and Harlan apprehensive," but no one of the three dissented. The President was emphatic and unequivocal in his discussions, making a speech of about twenty minutes, in which he reviewed the Radical intrigues in Congress, and exposed Thad Stevens' committee of fifteen and its secret sessions. He was firm in his refusal to let the Radicals dictate the policy of the Administration or to force him to abandon his attitude of peace and good will toward the conquered South. The veto would be an open rupture with the Radicals, but the President had his duty under the constitution and would not shirk it.

While he shared with Congress their desire to secure to the freedmen full enjoyment of freedom and property and entire independence and equality in making contracts for labor, the veto message stated, the President's examination of the bill had disclosed provisions unwarranted by the Constitution and unsuitable for the accomplishment of the desired end.

He objected to the military jurisdiction established and to the penal provisions against any white person charged with depriving a freedman "of any civil rights or immunities belonging to white persons," without definition of these rights. He thought it remarkable that such offenses should be judged not by civil courts, but by agents of the Freedmen's Bureau under regulations of the War Department. He pointed out that the punishment would not be defined by law but imposed by court-martial, and that there would be no appeal from the decision of these tribunals, not even to the United States Supreme Court. The President could not reconcile such military jurisdiction with the language of the Constitution. Likewise, the power of patronage conferred on the President was such "as in time of peace certainly ought never to be entrusted to any one man."

Nor could he discover in the condition of the country anything to justify the need for an extension of the rights of the existing Freedmen's Bureau. What was the necessity for unlimited federal aid to the negroes? "A system for the support of indigent persons . . . was never contemplated by the authors of the Constitution."

A vital objection was that the bill would not help, but would hurt those whose interests it was intended to advance. The negroes would be encouraged to a state of uncertain expectation. There was no need for any such extraordinary bulwark. The negro lived in a section where his labor could not be spared. Economic necessity would bring him justice. Let the laws of supply and demand do their work. The freedmen had received their freedom with moderation and forbearance, and they would soon demonstrate that they were self-sustaining and could establish themselves by their own efforts. Finally, such a measure was a very dubious public policy. It would array section against section and would cause the reanimation of the hatreds of the war. The measure had been enacted by a Congress in which eleven States had not been represented. While the President did not wish to interfere with the discretion of Congress in regard to the qualification of its members, yet he had a plain duty to represent the people of all the States and sections, and as such he held it his duty to recommend, "in the interests of peace and the interests of Union, the admission of every State to its share in public legislation when, however insubordinate, insurgent and rebellious its people may have been, it presents itself not only in the attitude of loyalty and harmony, but in the persons of representatives whose loyalty cannot be questioned under any existing constitutional or legal tests." Therefore, "in accordance with the Constitution," he returned the measure, earnestly hoping that a bill of such importance be not made a law, "unless upon deliberate consideration by the people it shall receive the sanction of an enlightened public judgment."

The veto occasioned the profound sensation Johnson's Cabinet had expected. Conservatives the country over were rejoiced, while the wrath of the Radicals was greatly intensified. The next day, jubilant New York Moderates met in Rochester and indorsed the veto, the secretary of the meeting writing Johnson that "nothing so good or important has in our opinion occurred since Lee's surrender. The veto message . . . is perfect." Jeremiah Sullivan Black felt that the presidential negative "has made millions of good hearts glad and grateful, for it has saved the nation." To Orville H. Browning, Lincoln's Illinois friend, the veto was "patriotic and statesmanlike." Had Johnson signed the bill, "the restoration of the unity and harmony of our unhappy country would thereby have been made impossible." In Cincinnati the veto caused a "sensation," and brought the *Commercial* to the President's support. In New York there was a great meeting of civic leaders, and a committee numbering such men as Mayor John T. Hoffman,

William B. Astor, William M. Evarts, Moses Taylor, John Kelly and Charles G. Cornell was appointed to go to Washington and confer with the President to receive suggestions from him as to what the New Yorkers could do to aid the success of Johnson's policies.[53]

Radical wrath was great, but its manifestation more covert. Carl Schurz had come to Washington as head of Greeley's bureau, and was "poking sticks at" the Conservative Senators every chance he had. Grant was being worked on to recant his Southern report, and the Radicals about had him won over.[54] An effort was made to repass the bill over the veto, but while the Radical numbers in the lower house were plenty, they lacked the two-thirds in the Senate, and therefore the veto stood. Dixon, Doolittle and Norton had gone with the President. King Caucus was not so despotic in Senate as in House.

The Administration's friends made Washington's Birthday the occasion for a national demonstration of confidence in the President. In a great meeting in New York, David Dudley Field presented the resolutions, and Seward, Dennison and Henry J. Raymond spoke. The Board of Aldermen of that city applauded Johnson's "conservative, liberal, enlightened and Christian policy." Similar meetings were held in Philadelphia, Baltimore and Buffalo. A great rally was planned for Washington.

The Radicals likewise took advantage of the day, both branches of Congress adjourning for a memorial service for Henry Winter Davis, Lincoln's foeman, who had recently died. As an intimate of Stevens, Wade and Sumner, "extraordinary honors" were paid to the memory of the Maryland Radical. The program for this memorial was copied almost literally from that in memory of Lincoln. Seats were assigned to the President and Cabinet, the Supreme Court and Ambassadors, for this "burlesque." Scandalized at the honors thus paid "this distinguished 'Plug Ugly' and 'Dead Rabbit,'" Welles believed that the Radicals "wished Davis to be considered the equal or superior of Lincoln."[55]

That evening, the President's supporters—all "Copperheads," the *Independent* sneered[56]—gathered at a Washington theater and indorsed his veto of the Freedmen's Bureau bill. Then they adjourned to the White House lawn to present their resolutions to the President. Bands played and there were demonstrations of rejoicing. Earlier that day McCulloch and

Doolittle had both urged him not to speak extemporaneously, and Johnson had responded for them not to be troubled. "I have not thought of making a speech, and I shan't make one. If my friends come to see me, I shall thank them, and that's all."[57] When the crowd of several thousand called vociferously for the President, Johnson finally yielded, and addressed the throng in the manner which had served him so well back in Tennessee.

By the light of a guttering candle, he read his speech. The day, he said, was singularly appropriate for the consideration of the maintenance of the "glorious Union." He recounted the wrongs and sufferings inflicted upon him during the war, and reiterated his views that treason was a crime. None the less, whole communities and States must not be made to submit to the penalty of death. Hence the President had freely exercised his power of pardon. Hence he was earnestly endeavoring to restore the entire Union to prosperity, happiness and peace.

However, now there had come a new usurpation. The slavery rebellion had failed, but now there was an attempt "to concentrate all power in the hands of a few." Power of a most extraordinary character had been assumed "by an irresponsible central directory . . . without even consulting the legislative and executive departments of the government." The President elaborated on the enormity of Stevens' reconstruction committee, which had virtually negatived the Constitution by taking away from the two branches of Congress the right to rule on the admission of their own members. For four years the nation had been struggling to prove that a State had neither right nor power to leave the Union. And now that it had won its battle, "this committee turns around and assumes that they are out and that they shall not come in."[58]

"When the States that attempted to secede," he continued, "comply with the Constitution, and give sufficient evidence of loyalty, I shall extend to them the right hand of fellowship, and let peace and union be restored. I am opposed to the Davises, the Toombses, the Slidells, and the long list of such. But when, on the other hand, men—I care not by what name you call them—are still opposed to the Union, I am free to say to you that I am still with the people." He spoke with deep feeling and emotion. An auditor four feet away noted his angry determination to make his position clear.[59]

At this point there were several shouts from the crowd: "Name them!" Johnson hesitated before replying. "Suppose

I should name to you those whom I look upon as being opposed to the fundamental principles of this government, and as now laboring to destroy them," he said, giving the names of Thaddeus Stevens, Charles Sumner and Wendell Phillips. A voice shouted "Forney!" Johnson responded contemptuously, "I do not waste my fire on dead ducks."[60] A shout went up from the throng.

The President did not intend to be governed by real or pretended friends, or to be bullied by enemies—"an honest conviction is my sustenance, the Constitution my guide." He knew it had been claimed he was a usurper. Of what usurpation had he been guilty? The only one was that of "standing between the people and the encroachment of power." "They may talk about beheading," he said, referring to hints of impeachment and assassination, "but when I am beheaded, I want the American people to be the witness. . . . Are those who want to destroy our institutions . . . not satisfied with the blood that has been shed? . . . Does not the blood of Lincoln appease the vengeance and wrath of the opponents of this government?" He did not fear assassins, and yet, if his blood was to be shed because he vindicated the Union, let it be so. "Let an altar of the Union be erected, and then, if necessary, lay me upon it, and the blood that now warms and animates my frame shall be poured out in a last libation as a tribute to the Union."

Lincoln's successor told of a talk he had had with Lincoln shortly before his second inauguration. The Emancipator had advocated "an amendment to the Constitution which would *compel* the States to send their Senators and Representatives to the Congress of the United States." Such had been the view of the martyred President. Today Congress wished to compel the South to stay out. "It is now peace," he added, "and let us have peace. Let us enforce the Constitution. . . . I tell the opponents of this government, and I care not from what quarter they come—East or West, North or South— you that are engaged in the work of breaking up this government are mistaken. The Constitution and the principles of free government are deeply rooted in the American heart." His closing apostrophe had the ring of his speeches on the eve of Fort Sumter. "I intend to stand by the Constitution," he said, "as the chief ark of our safety, as the palladium of our civil and religious liberty. Yes, let us cling to it as the mariner clings to the last plank when the night and the tempest close around him."

WHEN Andrew Johnson thus boldly "named the traitors," he created a great sensation. Even the moderate *Nation* believed that "anyone whose moral sense was not offended by it the minute his eye lighted on it" was quite past redemption. But although shocked at "such a disregard for decency," and keenly conscious of the President's "terrible mistake," Godkin counselled patience: "Andrew Johnson has in times past been tried and not found wanting in patriotism, in devotion to the Union, in faithfulness to his obligations."[1]

But the Radicals were delighted at their new opportunity. The *Independent* expressed its horror at the spectacle. In Congress and the Departments, word was passed that Andy had been intoxicated when he made the Washington's Birthday speech. "Last Thursday," one of the clerks of the House of Representatives wrote to a friend: "Andy made one of the most disgraceful speeches at the White House ever made in this country. He has been drunk for a week, and was when he vetoed the Freedmen's Bureau bill last Tuesday."[2] With such canards as evidence, historians generally fix February 22, 1866, as the beginning of Johnson's downfall.

This is not altogether correct. There were many—and loyal Unionists at that—who applauded Johnson's boldness and indorsed every word he had said. Conservatives generally were greatly delighted, and the President received many letters comparing him to Old Hickory.[3] Thurlow Weed thanked the President "with my whole grateful heart for that glorious speech of yesterday." Seward's preceptor felt that it "vindicates and saves our government and our Union. The people will rally to the support of the administration. Faction is rebuked and traitors will seek hiding places."[4]

The common council of Utica resolved that Johnson deserved the gratitude of the American people. Veto and speech had thrilled and electrified the country, wrote the editor of the Louisville *Courier;* "your appeal to the people will not be in vain." Johnson's speech struck a responsive chord in Tennessee, A. O. P. Nicholson writing that it was "fully equal to any of your best popular addresses."[5] The Maryland legislature indorsed the Johnson program. Sumner and Stevens "would have made another Civil War inevitable," General W. T. Sherman wrote his brother. "As I am a peace man, I go for Johnson and the veto. I recollect that Congress is but one of three coördinate branches of the government. I want to hear the Supreme Court manifest itself. Let Johnson fight it out with Sumner." A little later, he reiterated that, "Of course I agree substantially with the President. If we do not design to make a complete revolution in our form of government, but rather to preserve it, you must, sooner or later, allow representation from the South, and the longer it is deferred, the worse will be its effect."[6]

Several of the President's friends, in addition to congratulating him, pressed him to reorganize his Cabinet. Browning came to the White House on the morning of February 23 to say that "a change would have to be made in the War Department." "It must come," Johnson answered, whereupon Browning pressed Thomas Ewing for Stanton's successor.

To counteract this widespread feeling that the President had been justified in his philippic, the Radicals initiated a widespread propaganda that Johnson had betrayed Lincoln's policies. Lincoln's devoted friend and companion, Ward H. Lamon, was disgusted with these wild assertions. "Among the numerous allegations made against you by the ultra-Abolitionists," he wrote Johnson, "I hear none repeated so often as this: That you have deserted the principles upon which you were elected, and turned aside from the path in which your lamented predecessor would have walked if he had lived."[7] It seemed to be believed by some that Lincoln could have been used by the Radicals for all their purposes, including the destruction of the government, the overthrow of the Constitution and the indefinite postponement of union or harmony among the States.

Such a suggestion was a libel both on the martyred President and on the party which had nominated the Lincoln-Johnson ticket. In 1864, the party members were "sincerely attached to the Union, and devout believers in the Constitution," Lamon continued; its members "everywhere asserted that the object of the war was to reestablish the Union with the least possible delay, and one of the resolutions of the Baltimore convention pledged you both to restore the permanent authority of the Constitution in all the States."

It was true, he continued, that "some of the malignants

hated the Union and tried to destroy it before the war began, and their pretended love of the Union during the war was more than suspected to be insincere and hypocritical." But to the best of Lamon's knowledge, Thad Stevens had been "the only leading man in the party shameless and impudent enough to avow his hostility to the Union. He was not the exponent of our views, and represented not even a fractional part of the honest millions who cast their votes, spent their money and shed their blood to bring back the government of their party." As to Lincoln himself, Lamon "came here with him as his special friend, and was marshal of this district during his whole administration. Down to the date of his death I was in the most confidential and intimate relations with him. I knew him as well as one man can know another; I had many and free conversations with him on this very subject of restoration." Lincoln had repeatedly declared to him that "he would exert all his authority, power and influence to bring about an immediate pacific reconciliation between the two sections of the country. As far as depended upon him, he would have had the Southern States represented in both houses of Congress within the shortest possible time. All the energies of his nature were given to the 'vigorous prosecutions of the war' while the rebellion lasted, but he was equally determined upon a 'vigorous prosecution of peace' as soon as armed hostility should be ended."

Lincoln had not been unaware of the Radical attitude. He knew their "base designs . . . to keep up the strife for their own advantage, and he was determined to thwart them, as he himself told me very often. . . If that inscrutable Providence whose ways are past finding out, had permitted his life to continue until this time, there can be no doubt that the Northern disunionists would now be as loud in their denunciation of his policies as they are of yourself. Mr. Stevens' demand for the head of 'that man at the other end of the avenue' would not have been a whit less ferocious." Lamon pronounced the claim that Lincoln would have signed the Freedmen's Bureau bill "a foul slander on his memory." Lamon had loved Abraham Lincoln and revered his memory; and so, "if there be any insult upon his reputation which his true friends should resent more indignantly than another, it is the assertion that he would have been a tool and an instrument in the hands of such men as those who now led the heartless and unprincipled contest against you."

But some of the more cautious Conservatives had begun to manifest alarm even before the President's speech. Among these was James Gordon Bennett of the New York *Herald*. On the morning of February 23, the *Herald* had come forth with an editorial advocating General Grant for president in 1868. A letter to the President from W. B. Phillips, chief editorial writer of the *Herald*, bared the secret reasons of the Commodore in this new move.[8]

It seemed that the appearance of the editorial on the morning after Johnson's speech had been merely a coincidence. Bennett had sent for Phillips on the night of February 22 and had outlined a "new program" to him. Bennett estimated that the Radical strength in Congress was so formidable that the contest would be long and fierce, the grounds of opposition being really political, with the next presidential election in mind. Thus the "true way" to aid Johnson in bringing peace to the country was to advocate General Grant! Bennett had a high opinion of Grant and a not less exalted opinion of Johnson himself, Phillips wrote the President. "He would be as ready, and perhaps more ready, to go for you," if political conditions should then be favorable. Bennett deemed it good policy to keep Grant attached to Johnson. Phillips himself was delighted both with the veto and the Washington Birthday speech.

Some Conservative leaders sought to work out a pacification between the President and the more moderate of the Republicans in Congress, efforts which at first met an encouraging response. Among those who endeavored to act as peacemaker was Senator Sherman of Ohio. The Ohio Senator had known Johnson many years, admired and respected him and believed that the President was really proceeding on sound and patriotic lines. Likewise, Sherman knew the political purposes of the chief enemies of the President.

The very day that Lamon wrote the President, Sherman addressed the Senate in a pacificatory vein. He could imagine no calamity more disastrous than for the loyalists, by their division, to surrender the powers of the government to the late public enemies; anyone who contributed "in any way to this result deserves the execrations of his countrymen." The creation of such divisions, he warned the Radicals, might result from "thrusting upon the President new issues, on which the well known principles of his life do not agree with the judgment of his political associates." Likewise, they might be caused "by irritating controversies of a personal character," or might arise from the President turning his back upon those who had entrusted him with high power. But the Senator expressed "an abiding confidence that Andrew Johnson will not and cannot do this." His warning was addressed to the Radicals and not to the President.[9]

What would be the freedmen's fate if the Radicals persisted in their policy? "Will you," Sherman asked, "by your demand of universal suffrage, destroy the power of the Union party to protect them in their dearly purchased liberty? Will you, by new issues upon which you know you have not the voice of the people, jeopard those rights which you can by the aid of the Union party secure to these freedmen? We know that the President cannot and will not unite with us upon the issues of universal suffrage and dead States, and will never agree to. No such dogmas were contemplated when, for his heroic service in the cause of the Union, we placed him side by side with Mr. Lincoln as our standard bearer. Why then present these issues? . . . The curse of God, the maledictions of the mass of our people, and the tears and blood of the new-made freemen will, in my judgment, rest upon those who now for any cause destroy the unity of the great party that has led us through the wilderness of war."

As to the President himself, Sherman had no qualms. In his mind's eye, he saw Andrew Johnson "yet surrounded by the Cabinet of Abraham Lincoln, pursuing Lincoln's policies. No word from me shall drive him into political fellowship with those who, when he was one of the moral heroes of this war, denounced him, spit upon him, and despitefully used him. The association must be self-sought, and even then I will part from him in sorrow. . . ."

Sherman's calm and sensible words gave a new feeling of hope to Conservatives through the country. Many of the Moderate Republicans felt the same way. On March 9, Grimes of Iowa told Gideon Welles that Stevens was "an unscrupulous old fellow, unfit to lead any party, . . . a debauchee in morals and politics," and that Sumner was "a cold-blooded, selfish, and dangerous man."[10] Two days after Sherman's speech, Thurlow Weed wrote him that he had spoken boldly and at the right time. It would "help save the Union . . . if fanatics and despots will allow it to be saved."[11]

But when addressed to Sumner, Wilson, Wade or Stevens, such counsel fell on deaf ears. The House followed the Pennsylvania Commoner "to any length in abusing the President." It quickly adopted an attitude of studied disrespect and deliberate insult to Andrew Johnson. His messages would be pushed aside without reading. Whenever his name was mentioned, objections would be made that he was merely a Vice President acting as President. Almost every day some member would send to the desk a villainous newspaper clipping assailing the Chief Executive, and the Clerk would read it amid Radical jeers and catcalls.[12]

On March 10 Stevens staged a deliberate and venomous bit of buffoonery intended to insult and enrage the Chief Executive; "a blackguard and disreputable speech," Welles termed it.[13] It was an ironical tribute to Johnson's "integrity, patriotism, courage, and good intentions." Doubtless through prearrangement, Stevens was asked if he was the same Thaddeus Stevens mentioned in Johnson's Washington Birthday speech, whereupon he informed the House "confidentially" that the speech referred to had really never been delivered; that it was a gigantic hoax. "I am glad," he said, amid the laughter of the Radicals, "to have at this time an opportunity (although I do not wish the matter to go before the public, for they might misunderstand my motive) to exonerate the President from ever having made that speech." The claim that such a speech had been made was a "cunning contrivance of the Copperhead party, who have been persecuting our President since the 4th of March last. Why, sir, taking advantage of the unfortunate incident which happened on that occasion, they have been constantly denouncing him as addicted to low and degrading vices."

Then "Old Thad" sent to the clerk's desk a treasured clipping from the New York *World* of March 7, 1865, and had the clerk read the editorial in that paper describing Andrew Johnson as "an insolent drunken brute, in comparison with whom even Caligula's horse was respectable." Stevens called this a "vile slander," got up by the Copperheads, and added "if these slanderers can make the people believe the President ever made that speech, then they will have proved their case."[14]

Under these promptings, the Pennsylvania Union State Convention of March proved almost a hand-picked Stevens rally, which the Radicals sought to make even more one-sided by packing the floors with 200 plug-uglies "who cheered, yelled, and voted, and hissed everybody they did not want to hear."[15] Conservative Pennsylvania men were amazed at the Radical frenzy.

The acclaim with which Caliban's words were received and the growing restlessness in the North led Thurlow Weed to revise his estimate of the political future. In March he warned Seward that "reckless and headstrong as the Radical leaders are, they will keep the people with them if any serious mistakes are committed. The danger comes from extremists, South and North. The President's reconstruction policy is sound. There should however be some punishment for the redoubtable traitors, for 'treason' *is* a 'crime.'"

About this time the Wisconsin legislature passed a resolution that, while it remembered Johnson's part in the war, it gratefully indorsed and approved the action of those of their Senators and Representatives who had supported the Freedmen's Bureau bill. From California came warnings that the Union party had turned upon the President and that its leaders almost to a man were denouncing Johnson, while the Democrats were supporting him. "Every federal office holder is bitterly opposed to the President."[16]

The Democrats were making "desperate" efforts to convince the President that there was no use in his trying to secure support from the Republicans. Edwards Pierrepont of New York wrote him that the leading Republicans were not and never would be with the President, that at the most they merely pretended to be so "for the retention of offices and for the sake of power until the fall elections. If they carry them, no further pretensions will be needed." The New Yorker assured the President that "we can bring the loyal Democrats and Conservative Republicans to your cordial support," if only he would build a bridge over which they could lead the mass of the party. And by building a bridge he meant the appointment of some such conspicuous Democrat as General John A. Dix to a Cabinet post.[17]

The story of the President's position in regard to Congressional developments, described in this chapter, and the attitude of the Members of his Cabinet toward them and him, are of such importance in the study of Andrew Johnson that they are treated separately elsewhere.[18] Suffice it to say here that, while the President was delaying and procrastinating in the matter of a thoroughgoing reorganization of his Cabinet, his enemies in

Congress were pushing ahead with malignant zeal. The vote
on the Freedmen's Bureau bill had shown them the weak spot
in their situation. They now knew what they had to do. They
possessed more than the required two-thirds majority in the
lower House, but in the upper chamber they had narrowly
escaped the necessary two-thirds. If they were to expect triumph in the contest with the President, they must strengthen
themselves in the Senate.

Two methods presented themselves. The first was to increase the number of Radical senators by the admission of new
States into the Union. The second was to decrease the number
of Johnson supporters by turning them out of the Senate
whenever pretext could be had. The first method presented
an inherent difficulty; it involved the adoption of an Act of
Congress which the President would veto, necessitating the
mustering of a two-thirds vote in each house for it to be repassed. But the need was so desperate that both plans were
tried. The Radicals struggled several times for the admission of Colorado and of Nebraska. But the cases of both
were so inadequate that the Radicals could not command their
own full strength in either of them.

Colorado's population was much too small. In the summer
of 1864, under Congressional authority, a proposed state constitution had been drafted; on its submission to a vote, her
people had rejected it by three to one, in a total vote of 6,192.[19]
Without any further Act of Congress, some Colorado Radicals
held a convention of their own in 1865, adopted a "constitution,"
submitted it to the voters and secured an asserted ratification
by a majority of 155, out of a total of 5,895. In December of
the same year, a legislative election under this pretended constitution sent two senators to Washington. But in view of the
irregularities in procedure and the paucity of the vote, President Johnson refused to proclaim that the Colorado territory
was a State.

To the dismay of the practical Radicals, who were looking
with eager eyes upon the two votes Colorado would add to their
columns, Charles Sumner vigorously objected to its admission
as a State. The Colorado constitution makers, in adopting
suffrage qualifications had used the word "white." Sumner
could not stomach the qualifying adjective, even though it
would give the votes needed for Andrew Johnson's overturn:
He made a speech about it, exposing with merciless scorn every

weak point in the Colorado claims. He confronted his enraged fellow Radicals with the illegality of the second convention election, with the pitiful population figures—hardly 25,000, when the existing ratio for a member of Congress was 127,000—and with the discrimination against the negro. Thus betrayed in the house of its friends, the first Colorado bill collapsed.[20]

But Sumner was quite willing to decrease the President's strength in the Senate by ousting a regularly elected member. An opportunity speedily arose in the case of Senator John P. Stockton of New Jersey. The Commodore's son had been elected by the legislature of that State in the spring of 1865. There had been no protest as to the regularity of his election at the time. When Congress opened in December, his credentials had been presented to the Senate, and he was sworn in, his right to his seat being unquestioned. By request, Cowan of Pennsylvania later presented a protest signed by several members of the New Jersey legislature, which was tabled without reading and referred to the Judiciary committee. On January 30 Trumbull, as chairman of that committee, recommended a resolution declaring Senator Stockton entitled to hold his seat. Every member of the committee except one signed this report, and that one made no other protest than withholding his signature.[20]

This had been before the President had vetoed the Freedmen's Bureau bill. After the veto, some shrewd Radical minds discovered in the New Jersey protest a method to pluck out a Johnson vote. Accordingly the Judiciary committee's report was called on March 22, and Clark, the one dissentient, moved to substitute for Trumbull's resolution another declaring Stockton not entitled to his seat.

The difficulty was solely technical. Under its constitution, the New Jersey legislature was to hold "joint meetings" to appoint certain state officers. For many decades the legislature had had a mode of procedure for governance in joint meeting. In 1865 it was made up of a senate of twenty-one members and an assembly of sixty, the joint ballot being eighty-one. There had been a death in its membership; therefore when the legislature first met on February 15, 1865, it adjourned to March 15, so that the vacancy might be filled. The Senate was made up of thirteen Democrats and eight Republicans, the assembly was evenly tied, thirty to thirty. On a joint ballot the legislature was Democratic by five majority. Nine of the Democrats refused to go into a caucus and to vote for Stockton after the caucus had nominated him.

At the first session of February 15, the joint committee amended its existing rule requiring a majority of votes cast to elect, substituting one requiring a majority of all members elected to the legislature. This made a deadlock certain, so upon the legislature reconvening on March 15, its first act was to rescind the rule of February 15, and instead to adopt a rule "that any candidate receiving a plurality of the votes of the members present should be declared duly elected."[21]

The Republicans in the legislature had maneuvered this change on the assumption that it would result in the election of a Republican Senator. But when the ballot was taken, Stockton had forty votes to thirty-seven for the Republican aspirant. In obedience to the joint rule thus adopted, "with the unanimous acquiescence of the assembly—not a single protest, objection, or even a dissenting murmur being heard," the presiding officer declared Stockton duly elected. The legislature in joint meeting then adjourned *sine die*. The "protest" was a much belated afterthought, of which nothing was heard for several months. Indeed some of the signatures to it were not secured until November, within a month of the meeting of Congress, when the Radical-Conservative battle was foreseen and when it was known that the next New Jersey legislature would be Republican in joint meeting.

The report of Trumbull's committee pointed out these facts, and set forth its conclusion that, "in the absence of any law either of Congress or of the State on the subject, a joint meeting of the two houses of the legislature, duly assembled and vested with authority to elect a United States senator, has a right to prescribe that a plurality may elect; on the principle that the adoption of such a rule by a majority vote in the first instance makes the act subsequently done in pursuance of such a majority vote its own," an obvious and a fair statement of the parliamentary law and the essential justice of the case.

But considerations of law or justice meant little to the Radicals. Senator Clark, the one committee member who had refused to sign, opened the debate, the implication of political necessity running between the lines of his thin legislative argument. Senator Hendricks annihilated the Radical reasoning with a pithy paragraph. "The joint committee agreed to elect by a plurality," the Indiana Democrat said. "They did so elect. The presiding officer announced the result and there was no objection to it. The convention proceeded to other business on the result being announced and by silence acquiesced. I say that is conclusive upon the question." But to Charles Sumner it was not a matter of fairness or justice. If there was doubt in the matter, the benefit of the doubt should be given to "the law of the majority." For the benefit of the Radicals, he quoted a rule of Hoyle: "If you are in doubt, take the trick." In other words, it was justifiable to do anything to get rid of a Johnson vote.

The Radicals began pressing for a vote on Clark's resolution. Several of the Conservatives were not able to attend the session. Dixon of Connecticut was sick, Foot was dying, and Wright, Stockton's New Jersey colleague, had gone home gravely ill. Before going home, Wright had arranged a pair with Morrill of Maine upon this specific question so that his absence would not injure his colleague's rights.

When the matter approached a vote, Morrill let it be known that he was debating whether he would disregard the pair with Wright. Stockton telegraphed his absent colleague, and the next day an answer came from Wright that he was very ill, could not be in Washington until the middle of the next week and that he trusted Morrill would keep his word. The Maine Senator sought to salve his conscience by taking counsel with Sumner and Fessenden, whom Blaine ingenuously terms "safe mentors," and both, of course, urged him to vote.[22]

Under these circumstances the vote was taken on Clark's resolution; it resulted in nineteen yeas, twenty-one nays. Apparently, the Radicals had lost, but they were not willing to let the matter drop. A vote next was called for on the resolution recommended by Trumbull's committee, affirming Stockton's right to his seat. This vote was closer, with twenty-one voting aye, twenty no. Senator Wilson, who had not voted before, now voted with the Radicals.

A disgraceful episode ensued. Thus far, Morrill had kept his word to Wright and had not voted. Now Radicals throughout the senate chamber began to shout to him to vote. Nye was vehement. Above the tumult the hoarse cry of Sumner was heard: "Vote! Vote! Vote!" At last Morrill weakened, sacrificed his troth to his Radicalism, told the clerk to call his name and voted no.

At this juncture, Stockton made his great mistake. The vote was now a tie—both sides having twenty-one votes. The resolution had not carried affirmatively, but neither had it failed to carry, while the resolution denying him a seat had been lost by two votes. Had he kept silent, he would have remained a member of the Senate. But Morrill's bad faith had roused his anger. He jumped to his feet, told the Senate of the pair between Morrill and Wright, of the telegrams about it, and that Wright had insisted that Morrill keep his agreement, otherwise he would not have gone home. Stockton then directed the Secretary of the Senate to call his own name, and voted Aye. The result was announced—yeas, twenty-two, nays, twenty-one. Stockton had voted for his own seating and the resolution had been passed by one vote.

The victory was only temporary. By this last action the New Jersey Democrat had supplied the Radicals with ammunition. They held caucuses throughout the week-end, and by Monday had mapped out their program. Sumner undertook the task of redeeming "the honor of the American Senate," moved that Stockton's vote be stricken out as null and void, and made a lengthy speech condemning the New Jersey man for voting in his own case. Stockton finally agreed to withdraw his vote, the Senate reconsidered its resolution, and another vote was due.

The minority made an impassioned attempt to secure delay in this new vote on Stockton. Wright was making desperate efforts to get to Washington. Dixon, gravely ill, was willing to endure the dangers of being carried to the Senate chamber, but his physicians advised against it. Another Conservative, Morgan of New York, had been added to the sick-list. The efforts for delay merely added to the insistence of the Radicals. Nye blurted out the truth about it. "The Senate should act promptly upon it," he said. "It is a thing perfectly well known that the Legislature of the State of New Jersey has held on now for no other purpose than, if the vote of this body is such as to relieve Mr. Stockton from further duty here, that they may elect a man in his place."

Under these urgings, the Senate set the next day for the vote. And thus on Tuesday, March 27, the galleries were crowded with spectators awaiting the ousting of President Johnson's friend. Wright sent a telegram begging the Senate to delay until Thursday. A Radical objected that if he could

be there Thursday, why not today. Whereupon another telegram was read that Wright's physician had warned him that
he must not start so soon. But appeals for fair play meant
nothing to the Radicals. They insisted on the roll call. The
result was preordained. Stockton was denied his seat and
ousted from the Senate of the United States by a single perjured vote.[23]

One of the chief reasons why the Radicals had been so determined to vote on the Stockton case before Wright could
return was a rumor which had spread through the Senate that
morning that a veto of the Civil Rights bill was on its way from
the White House. They were determined to repass this measure over the objections of the President.

On the day on which he had introduced his Freedmen's
Bureau measure, Trumbull had likewise offered a bill "to protect all persons of the United States in their civil rights, and to
furnish the means of their vindication." On January 11 the
Judiciary Committee gave it a favorable report, and debate
commenced. Finally, on February 2, the Radicals pushed it
through by a vote of thirty-three to twelve, and it went to the
House.[24] This body welcomed this new Radical undertaking,
adding an amendment that nothing in the bill should be so construed "as to affect the laws of any state concerning the right
of suffrage." After having thus protected Northern discrimination against the negro, while penalizing Southern discrimination, the House passed the bill, and on March 18 it was
submitted to Andrew Johnson for approval or veto.

The measure thus enacted was drastic. It declared all
persons born in the United States (except Indians not taxed)
citizens of the United States. Such citizens, "of every race
and color, without regard to any previous condition of slavery
or involuntary servitude," should have the same right, in every
state and territory of the United States, "to full and equal
benefit of all laws and proceedings for the security of person
and property as is enjoyed by white citizens, and shall be subjected to like punishment, pains and penalties, and to none
other."

Anyone depriving a negro of such equal rights would be
guilty of a misdemeanor, punishable on conviction by a fine of
not more than $1,000, a prison sentence of not over a year, or
both. Federal district courts were given jurisdiction in such

cases, and federal district attorneys, marshals and commissioners, officers and agents of the Freedmen's Bureau, and others were specially authorized and required, "at the expense of the United States," to institute legal proceedings against any and all who violated the provisions of the act. Any federal official refusing thus to act, or to do so with due diligence, would be fined $1,000, this sum to be paid to the person upon whom the infraction was alleged to have been committed. Other provisions of a similar tenor sought to make the act enforceable.[25]

By the time this measure reached the President, many of his theretofore staunch defenders were seeking shelter from the Radical storm. Several of Johnson's advisers pled with him to sign the bill, not because it was right or proper but because it would be expedient. Typical was the attitude of Henry Ward Beecher, the magnetic preacher-orator, who hitherto had given warm support to the peace and reconciliation policies of the President.

In the preceding October Beecher had written Johnson an enthusiastic letter. "I feel that God has raised you up for such a crisis," he said. "Indeed, you unite the ability and disposition to serve the nation, rather than yourself or any mere party, and your renown will be in having your name intimately associated with the nation, the grandeur of whose history even the most lively imagination cannot estimate or conceive."[26] Later he had gone so far as to print a pamphlet in Johnson's defense, bringing down on his head the wrath of Wendell Phillips and angry resolutions from Congregational meetings in New England and elsewhere. While he did not back water precipitately—that might have been too undignified— Beecher quickly hauled in his sails, and prepared to shift his course. On March 17 he wrote the President that, unless the latter should be "withheld by the most substantial reason, it is exceedingly to be desired that you should sign the Civil Rights bill—the thing itself is advisable. But aside from that, I am persuaded that it would go far to harmonize the feelings of men who never should have differed, or permitted a difference."[27]

"Having suffered as being a friend of the President," the pastor of the Plymouth Church felt himself in a position to perceive "the deep tide of moral feeling," and that for several months the effort had been made "to detatch [*sic!*] from you the sober and reflecting class of men. The passage of this bill will in a great degree frustrate the influence of those who have sought to produce the impression that you had proven untrue to the cause of liberty and loyalty."

Beecher had "strongly and to my own personal inconvenience (for the present), defended both your wisdom in those things, and your motives, and I feel most profoundly how the signing of this bill will strengthen the position that I have defended in your behalf."

Ex-Governor Andrew, who had generally sustained Johnson's Southern course, informed him on March 18 that the country was unanimous in one thing. "The rebellious States ought not and could not return into the Senate and House without conforming to some certain arrangement made necessary by the rebellion itself." Oliver P. Morton, just back from Europe, went to Washington to urge compromise on the President. If he did not sign the Civil Rights bill, all hope for harmony would be gone.[28]

Governor Jacob D. Cox, of Ohio, sought to inform the President as to the sentiment of the Middle West. It was a difficult situation to handle because of a sensitive jealousy lest in some way the gains of the war be lost by mistaken statesmanship. Even intelligent people failed to appreciate "the wisdom and necessity of handling the Southern States kindly as well as firmly." Cox advised Johnson to conciliate this Mid-Western feeling whenever it could be done without a sacrifice of principle, and insisted that the Democratic leaders were hypocritical in their pretense of supporting his policy. He urged Johnson to sign the Civil Rights bill, advising that, if the Southern legislature were wise, they could easily pass laws to make the Civil Rights bill "of little practical moment. . . . The bark of the law, would, I think, be infinitely worse than its bite." If only he could sign the bill, he would be "fully master of the situation." Senator Cowan, however, wrote: "Don't hesitate for a moment to veto the Civil Rights bill. To do otherwise would be fatal."

In some way, the idea had gone abroad that Johnson would withhold a veto. The importunings of political weathervanes, the known views of some of the Cabinet, and a certain ambiguity in the President's casual remarks led to the belief that he would sign. Indeed, Senator Sherman made a speech in Connecticut in which he assured his audience of his certainty that the Civil Rights act would be approved."[29] Of the Cabinet,

Welles alone was adamant against the bill; to him it was "very centralizing and objectionable."[30] If the bill were carried into effect, he told the President, it would "subvert the government."

On March 26 Johnson assembled the Cabinet to ask the opinions of his advisers. Seward thought the bill unconstitutional in many respects, but that it might be well to have a law declaring negroes citizens; McCulloch made no argument, but hoped the President could conscientiously sign the bill; Dennison thought it had faults, but should be signed; Harlan did not like the second section, but urged signature. Stanton, after a long argument as to objectionable features of the bill, advised that "under the circumstances it should be approved."[31]

The arguments of expediency did not, however, persuade the President that he could in conscience approve a measure which he believed broke the Constitution into bits. He read his veto message to the Cabinet, which made no further objection, and then transmitted it to Congress. Even the hostile Rhodes, while terming the Civil Rights bill "reasonable," and Johnson's policy "dogmatism run mad," admits that the veto message was "remarkable for its moderation and careful reasoning."[32] It was couched in calm and dignified language. It made its points with irrefutable logic. It did not rant or appeal to passion but appealed to the Constitution.

The President pointed out the minor absurdities as well as major objections to the bill. It accorded citizenship to the Chinese on the Pacific Coast as well as to the negroes. It made everyone a citizen of the United States, without conferring State citizenship. Did Congress imagine that the 4,000,000 ex-slaves possessed the qualifications to entitle them to all the privileges and immunities of American citizenship? He would not go so far as to say that the bill repealed state laws forbidding the intermarriage of negroes and whites, but he believed that it did, an obvious objection to it.

The machinery for the enforcement of the Act was unprecedented and unnecessary. Adequate judicial remedies could be found without invading the immunities to legislators. The means seemed to him not only anomalous but unconstitutional. "For the Constitution guarantees nothing with certainty if it does not insure to the several States the right of making and executing laws in regard to all matters arising within their jurisdiction," a right restricted only by the Constitution of the United States.

Whence did Congress derive its power to transfer to federal tribunals the trial of cases of state offenses, he asked, showing by historical citation that it had no such power. He pointed out the imperfect machinery set up by the measure, and pronounced the details of the bill "fraught with evil." It frustrated the readjustment of Southern relations and fomented discord. It was a step toward centralization. Its tendency must be "to resuscitate the spirit of rebellion." While he fully recognized the obligation to protect and defend negroes whenever and wherever it should become necessary and to the full extent compatible with the Constitution, and while he would "cheerfully coöperate with Congress in any measure that may be necessary for the protection of the civil rights of the freedmen," yet in conformity with the provisions of the Constitution, he was compelled to withhold his assent from the bill.[33]

Johnson had the logic, but the Radicals, with Stockton ousted, believed they had the votes. Indeed, they had an added vote, for the venerable Foot of Vermont had died, and the Governor of that State, with Radical impetuosity, had appointed George F. Edmunds his successor, had given him his credentials, and Edmunds had appeared in Washington almost before his predecessor's body had grown cold.[34] The Senate, however, must adjourn in respect for the departed statesman, so its great effort to repass the vetoed measure was delayed a little while.

When the day finally came, Wright of New Jersey had been brought to Washington "at the peril of his life." Dixon had suffered a relapse, but had himself brought on a stretcher to the Capitol. There was an appeal for further delay. Ben Wade sprang to his feet in brazen protest. "I will tell the President," he thundered, "and everybody else, that if God Almighty has stricken one member so that he cannot be here to uphold the dictation of a despot, I thank Him for His interposition and I will take advantage of it if I can."

It was the critical moment. If the veto failed to be overridden, the slow dissolution of Radical strength in Congress would probably ensue, and Johnson might maintain his restoration governments in the South. Although the Conservatives had made the most strenuous effort to count every possible vote, rumors became current of defections from the President's sustainers. On April 5 Welles noted that "Stewart of Nevada has persuaded himself that it is best to desert and go with the majority. . . . There are some vague intimations that Morgan is equivocating and may go with Stewart, but I discredit it." Father Gideon immediately had the New York Senator in to tea and questioned him as closely as senatorial dignity would permit. When he told Morgan that Bingham of the House had committed himself in precise terms to the President, the Senator "expressed himself highly gratified,—he had feared Bingham was wavering." Welles thereby deduced that Morgan would prove true. But when the vote came to be taken, the rumors proved more truthful than the Senator's own words. Morgan had been unable to stand the pressure. Welles termed his vote "one of calculation, not of conviction."[4]

Upon Morgan's Aye, the galleries burst into loud applause, and Theodore Tilton could not contain himself for joy. The result was thirty-three votes for overriding the veto, fifteen against it, and one vote absent. The veto had been overridden by a single vote. The Civil Rights bill had been enacted into law, the President's objections to the contrary notwithstanding.

The veto vote had first been taken in the Senate. There was no question of the result in the House. It was repassed in that body on the following Monday amid such scenes of exultation that Speaker Colfax directed his own name be called, voted Aye with great gusto, and then declared that, by authority vested in him by the Constitution, the bill had become a law. There was shouting and stamping of feet.

This was a new constitutional departure, and not precisely a happy one. It was the first important measure ever repassed by Congress over a Presidential negative. Even in the fiercest fights of "Old Hickory" and the Whigs, things had never gone so far. It was an omen of unbridled political passion—the Radicals cared little more for Constitution or Supreme Court than for the President. They had the votes and the power, and intended to rule.

One day during the height of the Radical clamor, Colonel Moore, the President's secretary, was in Johnson's bed-chamber, drinking a glass of claret with him. The President, in deep thought, was pacing the floor. Suddenly he turned on Moore, with a look of deep determination, and said: "Sir, I am right. I know I am right, and I am damned if I do not adhere to it."[35]

Following their triumph, the Radicals again undertook to bring in Colorado as a State. At the time of the initial failure, Wilson of Massachusetts had entered a motion to reconsider. On April 17, following the defeat of "that man at the other end of the Avenue," Wilson brought the subject up once more. In view of the existing emergency, he was willing to forego his feelings as to the word "white" in Colorado's Constitution, "because we need her two votes in the Senate." But he reckoned without Charles Sumner, to whom the word "white" was as much an objection as ever. The Senate was startled when Sumner exclaimed: "It is whispered that we need two more votes on this floor. Sir, there is something that you need more than two votes." The Senate, however, passed the bill by a vote of nineteen to sixteen, and a little later the House carried it by eighty-one to fifty-seven; the slender majorities were omens that the expected presidential veto could not be overcome.

The sentiment of the Conservative Republicans in Congress began to change, when the President started decapitating some of the most obnoxious of his critics in the executive service and replacing them with men willing to uphold his views. This was the one thing which the Conservative Republicans could not countenance. They had not minded Johnson's vetoes. Some of them had supported the vetoes; others who had rejected them had none the less admired Johnson for his courage, and had privately agreed with him. But now that it appeared that the President meant to reward his supporters, whether Democratic or Republican, with public office, and to rebuke his traducers by removal, even John Sherman could not tolerate it. Differences of opinion on public policies were endurable, but "turning out good men merely because they adhered to their party convictions is simply an unmitigated outrage."[36]

The Radicals maneuvered to persuade the President not to veto the Colorado bill. The two Senators-elect addressed a joint letter to Johnson's secretary, denouncing as entirely untrue the assertion that they "had sold out to the Radicals." In an interview with the President, the Coloradans made several tricky promises, but Johnson informed them bluntly he did not think it well for the future of the Union to admit two more Radicals into the Senate to perpetuate schemes for disunion. A veto message went in the same day, and the Radicals could not muster Senate votes to repass the bill.

In the meantime the Reconstruction Committee had finished
its time-consuming hearings, burdened chiefly with biased testimony as to dangers to life and liberty of negroes and Northerners sojourning in the South. On April 30 the committee
reported its plan for a constitutional amendment and for two
statutes to supplement these proposed changes in the national
organic law.

This was not the first amendment which the committee had
reported. As soon as this Directory of Fifteen started its
secret deliberations, the political menace of according the
Southern States a Congressional representation based on full
population, if the full population was not allowed to vote, was
paraded. Under the Constitution of 1789, representation in
Congress had been based upon the full number of free inhabitants plus three-fifths of the slaves. Immediately upon
emancipation, the Southern population had been increased by
two-fifths of the number of negroes. Blaine termed any such
result "a mere mockery of justice."[37]

Other matters prominent in the Reconstruction Committee
debates were: to exclude ex-Confederates from the right to hold
office, even though they had been pardoned by the President; to
make sure that pensions should be forbidden to Confederate
veterans, and to deny, under any circumstances, any repara-
tion even to loyal holders of slaves emancipated by the war.

There was another consuming care. On all sides it was admitted by the Radicals that Representatives from the Southern
states must be kept out of Congress, because their admission
would endanger Radical control. As a leading member phrased
it, if the President's plan should be followed, involving the instant admission of Senators and Representatives, "these Constitutional changes could not be effected, because the party
desiring them would no longer control two-thirds of both
House and Senate."[38] With his usual pungency, Thad Stevens
said it was no more proper to admit Southerners to a voice in
the solution of Southern problems than it would be to authorize
"the criminal to sit in judgment when the extent of his crime
and its proper punishment were under consideration."

On January 22 the committee submitted to House and Senate
a proposed constitutional amendment providing that the future
basis of apportionment should be the number of persons in each
State, but "that whenever the elective franchise shall be denied
or abridged in any State on account of race or color, all persons

of such race or color shall be excluded from the basis of representation." If, on account of color, South Carolina should
exclude a single negro from the vote, none of her colored population should be counted in her representation basis. During
the extended House debate on the amendment, a further clause
to define citizenship so as to make negroes as well as whites
citizens of the United States and to accord them equal civil
rights, was offered; the language was taken from Trumbull's
Civil Rights bill. On January 31 the House adopted the
amendment substantially in the form cited, but when it reached
the Senate, to the dismay and irritation of the more practical
Radicals, the doctrinaire Sumner opposed it.

He insisted that the Constitution must not be "defiled" by
incorporating in its text so patent an acknowledgment of racial
discrimination. His wrath was without limit—his speech filled
forty-one columns of the *Congressional Globe!*[89] The Radicals
had scant patience with his plea for the ballot, "the great guarantee," and Fessenden testily annihilated Sumner's rhetoric as
well as his logic. But even the annihilation of the annihilator
failed to give the amendment sufficient strength to pass.

The amendment, proposed in the report of April 30 contained five distinct clauses. The first section repeated and re-
stated the equality guaranties written into the Civil Rights
bill. The second based representation in Congress on the
actual population of states, and provided that any State which
discriminated against anyone on account of race, color or
previous condition of servitude should have its representation
reduced by the proportion such excluded citizens represented
to the whole. By the third clause, all persons who had voluntarily sustained the South in the war were excluded from voting
until July 5, 1870. The fourth section prohibited the payment
of any Confederate debt. The final clause conferred enforcement power upon Congress.

The two accompanying bills were of similar tenor. The
first provided that when the proposed amendment had been
ratified by the required three-fourths of the States, and any
State lately in rebellion had ratified it, the Senators and Representatives from such States, if properly elected to Congress
and if able to take the "ironclad" oath, would be admitted.
The second bill recommended that five groups of ex-Confederates[40] be rendered ineligible to federal office.

The amendment seems to have been a compromise. The

Stevens Radicals disliked it because it did not invalidate the State governments established under the Johnson plan. "Old Thad" told the House he thought the third section much too lenient, the product of "a morbid sensibility sometimes called mercy," the punishment inflicted by it "the mildest ever inflicted upon traitors."[41] Sumner and his followers were indignant because impartial suffrage had not been made an indispensable condition for the reëntry of States. But all of the Radicals dissembled their fears because they applauded the four year ban on ex-Confederates, realizing that it would postpone the restoration of the Union and maintain the Radicals in power for many years. Far from being a scheme for restoration, Dixon and other Conservatives saw that it was a scheme for the perpetuation of discord and hate.[42]

Under Thad Stevens' lash, the amendment resolution was quickly pushed through the House,[43] but the Senate was more attentive to its verbal form, and several caucuses of Radicals had to be held before difficulties could be ironed out. Finally a substitute for the disqualifying clause was agreed upon, eliminating the general four year ban on voluntary Confederates, and making ineligible for state or federal office any person who, having held an office before the war which required him to take the constitutional oath, had supported the Southern enterprise.[44] Reverdy Johnson told the Senate that this clause embraced perhaps nine-tenths of the gentlemen of the South, but this was precisely what the Radicals wanted it to embrace.

On June 4 the Senate resumed its study of the amendment, and debated it for five days. The Radicals rejected all suggestions from the Democrats and Conservatives of modifying the amendment so as to make it acceptable to the South; they neither expected nor desired the South to ratify. On June 8 the necessary two-thirds majority was secured to send the amendment to the legislatures of the several States.

It may have been regrettable that the Fourteenth Amendment was not ratified by the South in 1866. It is difficult to accept Rhodes' view that it was "an act of care and foresight," combining "reasonableness with justice." But it is true that it did not forcibly impose negro suffrage on the Southern States, merely penalizing any State refusing impartial suffrage by reducing its Congressional representation and its strength in the electoral college. Yet the amendment's scope seemed too extensive even to the Radical mind of Chase, who wrote his associate, Judge Field, that he feared it was too large a contract; he did not approve the disfranchisement or the Civil Rights provisions.[45]

"Of all proposed solutions of the question of negro suffrage," Rhodes declares, "none was so wise as the section of the Fourteenth Amendment."[46] Had the South accorded impartial suffrage, it would have had seventy representatives; if it had excluded the negro, it would have had forty-five. But in either event, it would have been placed under no constitutional compulsion to accord the colored man the vote; and its representation in both branches of Congress would have been great enough, added to the Northern Conservatives and Democrats, to have prevented the initiation of further amendments or the repassage of statutes over presidential vetoes.

The difficulty was a practical one. Conservatives and Democrats, Northern and Southern, put no faith whatever in Radical promises. They were convinced that the real mainspring of the Radical maneuvers was not concern for negro rights, but a deliberate desire to keep the Southerners out of Congress under any and every pretext, so that Radical control would not be endangered. Neither the President nor the South could afford to trust the inferential promises of the Stevens committee. They were sure that after, accepting the amendment, still further and more humiliating—even deliberately unacceptable—conditions would be proposed. Thus, while Rhodes may term the Fourteenth Amendment "magnanimous in a high degree," it seemed another case of Greeks bearing gifts.

As much proof of Radical insincerity as the Conservatives needed was furnished by the fate of the companion measures suggested by the Reconstruction Committee. Sumner introduced an amendment making it a further condition of readmission that the State in question should strip her constitution of every vestige of negro disfranchisement. Although the bill itself never came up in the Senate, it was languidly debated in the House, where the Radicals admitted that they would not restore any State which had not established impartial suffrage.

Another Freedmen's Bureau bill was now introduced, extending the life of that institution for two years, a measure even more rigorous than the one the President had disapproved in February. Johnson's veto of the new bill was of no effect, but the message did destroy Radical expectation of laying grounds for the impeachment of the President because of his hoped-for refusal to enforce the Civil Rights bill. In the message he said that "the Civil Rights bill, now the law of the land, will be faithfully executed as long as it shall remain unrepealed and may not be declared unconstitutional by courts of competent jurisdiction."[47]

The Radicals were impetuous to get the amendment ratified. Governor Curtin of Pennsylvania addressed a circular letter to the governors of the States suggesting extra sessions for ratification, and several Radical state executives called such sessions. Connecticut, the first to ratify, did so on June 29. New Hampshire followed on July 6. But the Radicals had turned their eyes not to New England but to Tennessee. "Parson" Brownlow, now Governor of Andrew Johnson's beloved State, was as bitter a foe of the President as Thad Stevens himself. The Fighting Parson had never liked Andrew Johnson. In their race for Congress in 1845, Brownlow had let loose his billingsgate on his competitor, his charges and innuendoes running the gamut from illegitimacy to atheism. His attitude in 1866 was quite as hostile.[48] No sooner had Congress submitted the amendment than Brownlow called a special session of the General Assembly of the State.

The Conservative legislators knew what was planned, and many of them refused to come. Enough Senators assembled to secure a quorum, but it was extremely hard to get together two-thirds of the House. Some resigned, but Brownlow refused to accept their resignations. Others did not resign, but took the position that they would not attend until the amendment had been submitted to their constituents and voted on by them. Governor Brownlow asked General Thomas for troops to awe the legislature, whereupon Thomas telegraphed the War Department for instructions.[49] Stanton delayed three days before presenting this dispatch to the President, who, irritated, said that if Thomas "had nothing else to do but to meddle in local controversies," he had better be sent somewhere else. Stanton now saw a chance to turn Thomas, a friend of the President, against him and asked the latter if he should add his remark to the orders to Thomas. "My wish is," Johnson answered, "that the answer should be emphatic and decisive, not to meddle with local parties and politics. The military are not superior masters."[50]

Although Brownlow did not get Federal bayonets to force ratifications, by other high-handed methods he finally managed, on July 19, to get together fifty-four members of the House, only two less than a quorum. Two other members were then in Nashville; the Governor had the Sergeant at Arms seize them bodily and drag them into the House; while guards held them by force, the speaker counted them present, the vote was taken and the amendment declared ratified.[51]

The Parson immediately telegraphed "the good news" to Congress. His official notification to the Secretary of the Senate was in these words: "We have fought the battle and won it. We have ratified the constitutional amendment in the House, forty-three voting for it, eleven against it, two of Andrew Johnson's tools not voting. Give my respects to the dead dog of the White House!"

This scurrilous and offensive telegram was received and published "with joyful acclaim" by the Radicals. The next day Cowan remarked that "this is the first time in the history of the Senate, unquestionably, that such a dropping as this has fallen from so foul a bird into this chamber, and it is the first time I think, in the history of this chamber, where members of this body would sit patiently by and not vindicate themselves from the charges of being accessories to such vituperation." On the contrary, prompt measures were taken to admit the Tennessee members into both Houses of Congress, as a reward to the vituperative Parson. A joint resolution was immediately introduced, declaring Tennessee now "restored to her proper practical relations to the Union and again entitled to be represented by Senators and Representatives. . . ."

Stevens thought this was moving a bit fast—he could not forget that one of Tennessee's Senators was the President's son-in-law. But the resolution passed the House. When it reached the Senate, the Radical doctrinaires joined to it a preamble reciting the Civil War and Reconstruction history of Tennessee and the recent exceptional circumstances justifying its admission, and asserting that no other Southern State could "be restored . . . without the consent of the law-making power of the United States." The House concurred and the resolution was sent to the President.

The Radicals wished the mode of admitting Tennessee to be so repugnant to the President that he would be forced to veto the resolution admitting into full legislative membership the delegation from his own State; the form of the resolution was purposely offensive. Several of the President's friends feared he would veto it. Doolittle, Cowan, Dixon, Hendricks and Guthrie called on him on the evening of July 23 to urge him not to do so. Their fears were groundless. The President was equal to the emergency. He met it like a statesman rather than a doctrinaire. He did not veto the resolution, but signed it the morning after its presentation.

The preamble was objectionable, he notified Congress, but it "simply consists of statements, some of which are assumed, while the resolution is merely a declaration of opinion. It comprises no legislation nor does it confer any power which is binding upon the respective Houses, the Executive or the States." The resolution "does not admit to their seats in Congress the senators and representatives from the state of Tennessee, for, nothwithstanding the passage of the resolution, each House, in the exercise of the constitutional right to judge for itself of the election, returns, and qualifications of its members, may, in its discretion, admit them or continue to exclude them." None the less and despite the "anomalous" character of the resolution, Johnson approved it, warning that his signature should not be deemed acknowledgment of any right in Congress to pass laws preliminary to the admission of duly qualified members from any State.[52]

Thereupon, the eight Representatives presented themselves to the bar of the House and were sworn in, and the Senate admitted the Radical Joseph S. Fowler without hesitation. The other Senator-elect, Judge David T. Patterson, was under the unfortunate stigma of being the husband of a daughter of the "man at the other end of the Avenue." Patterson's fidelity to the Union had been proved in the crises of the war. He had been arrested and imprisoned by the Confederates, banished from home and driven into the mountain forests as a hunted wanderer. But he was Johnson's son-in-law. Radical senators who had gone to desperate lengths to oust Stockton from the Senate could not look without alarm on the prospect of adding to their body one so intimate with the President.

Sumner found a flaw in Patterson's record, and objected to

his induction.[53]   While Sumner pursued this path, Wade endeavored to add two more Radicals to the membership by bringing Nebraska into the Union as a State.   But the constitution of that territory, like that of Colorado, had the word "white" in its suffrage qualification.   There were only about fifty negroes in Nebraska, but the practical aspect did not swerve Charles Sumner.

He assailed Wade's project with stinging words.   Indeed, though not for these reasons, it was an outrageous enterprise; Nebraska was still a wilderness, its population no more than 40,000, and its purported constitution had been adopted most irregularly.   Despite Sumner's opposition, the Senate passed the bill.   Johnson had no need to veto it, as it had been passed so tardily that the adjournment of Congress prevented its becoming a law.

In the midst of this Nebraska debate the Patterson committee reported, upholding completely the loyalty of the President's son-in-law.   Even Clark, who had forced Stockton from the Senate, declared there was not a shadow of doubt in the mind of any who heard Patterson before the committee, "that he had been throughout a Union man; and not only a Union man, but such a Union man as would put some of us to shame that we should be admitted into the Senate because we were Union men and he should be put out."   In the final hours of its session, the Senate declared him entitled to his seat.   In an impassive silence, without faltering or tremor, the President's son-in-law swore the full ironclad oath.

D URING the exciting scenes just described, the President was beset on all sides. In both Houses of Congress his enemies had built up such majorities against him that, whenever agreed among themselves, they could override his vetoes. Although elected as the candidate of the National Union party and faithfully carrying out the declared policies of that party, Johnson had been largely deserted by its politicians and was being forced to depend upon Democrats for support. This he did reluctantly, for the Southern Democrats were impenitent and impotent; while the Northern ones, too often deserving the appellation of "Copperhead," seemed more interested in filling Federal offices than in sustaining the President. The Southern legislatures were adding to Johnson's troubles, the Northern Conservatives were quailing before the storm, and to cap it all, four of the Constitutional advisers of the President were giving him grave concern.

As far back as March 3, Gideon Welles—who never hesitated, equivocated or faltered in his forthright support of his chief, and whose judgment, courage and loyalty made the latter affectionately term him "a perfect brick"—became apprehensive that there was "treachery to the President" in the Cabinet.[1] He thought Johnson was aware of it, but that he was unwisely giving his ear to the temporizers. Upon nearly every issue which was discussed in the Cabinet, Dennison, Harlan, Speed and Stanton advised a course of action which would play into the hands of the Radicals.[2]

Dick Taylor came to Washington in the spring and had many long interviews with General Grant.[3] Both approved Johnson's policy and both agreed that, to succeed in it, the President must get rid of Seward and Stanton. They called at the White House and put their views frankly before the President, who "responded to them favorably, earnestly, and decidedly."

To Grant's amazement, Stanton called on him at his home the next day, and informed the General that he was ready to join him and Taylor in backing Johnson, even to the point of abandoning Seward. Much puzzled, the General of the Armies told the story to Taylor, who hastened to the White House to

tell the President they had been betrayed; that Stanton knew
of their plans and was ready to go with them if he could keep
his post. This, the Ex-Confederate assured Johnson, was out
of the question, as Stanton was absolutely untrustworthy.[4]

From an analysis of the votes in Congress on the vetoes, it
was observable that the members attached to both Seward and
Stanton had failed to support the President in his vetoes. In
the case of the Civil Rights bill, "all of Stanton's pets were
active in opposing the veto," and of the Seward contingent only
Raymond had not deserted. Theodore Tilton was writing from
Washington to reassure the Radicals that Stanton would not
resign, but would "occupy his present premises until served
with a formal writ of ejectment."[5]

To Johnson's more observant friends, this condition of affairs was ominous. On the night of April 12 Senator Doolittle
of Wisconsin called on Welles to urge action by the President,
before it became too late. Doolittle felt that if Johnson's
Cabinet had properly supported him with its persuasion and
influence, the veto would not have been thrust aside. The
President must do something positive; the idea was growing
that he could do nothing for himself.

Welles felt there was some truth in this; it was not that
Johnson lacked courage, but that he disliked "to break with
those who elected him." Doolittle was importunate: Both
Speed and Stanton were hurting the President. The Attorney
General was without stamina, power, or character as a lawyer;
he was "the laughing-stock of the court."[6] Stanton should be
turned out and Grant assigned temporarily to the War Department. The Wisconsin Senator earnestly besought Welles
to press these essential changes on the President.

When the Secretary of the Navy related Doolittle's misgivings to the President, the latter was much disturbed. It
exceedingly annoyed and discouraged him "to witness so good
a man as Doolittle desponding, and especially on the subject
of removals and appointments, when he himself is not prepared
to take or recommend action, even in his own State." Johnson
frankly discussed the Cabinet problem. "It is true that my
Cabinet is not in all respects what I wish," he said, "but I have
taken it as I found it." He supposed Harlan, who "could
never look you in the face" was out of line with his policy,
but surely "delicacy and propriety would seem to prompt him
to resign." Yet Harlan had given no sign. Speed he con-

sidered of no account. "His wife is the better man of the two." And yet Speed "was manifestly in harmony with the Radicals, advising with and encouraging them," but he too had made no motion to resign. Johnson was aware that Stanton was claimed by the Radicals, and yet "Stanton has given me no intimation of that character, except in some general criticism on one or two measures, in which he finally yielded and acquiesced." To have an open rupture with him now, without plain cause, would be embarrassing, and Stanton had made no move to leave.

The President thought he had reason to expect his Cabinet to act as gentlemen, and to respect the delicacies and proprieties of the situation. If the members of his political family were men of proper character, those who did not agree with his policies would retire of their own volition. If Harlan, Speed and Stanton disapproved his policy, they had not informed him of it. Radical papers made much of their apostasy. "Still they hold on here," Johnson added bitterly, "and some of them likely report our proceedings. I do not, however, know the fact. What, then, can I do? Are these men to whom I give my confidence hypocrites, faithless, insincere, treacherous? The time has not arrived for a decisive stand. With mischievous Radical leaders, who appear to have little regard for the country, it is not a proper time to take upon ourselves other quarrels nearer home." He would act at the proper time, but his friends must let him be the judge as to when that time had come.[7]

When Welles reported Johnson's words to Doolittle, the latter was much disappointed. There must be no further delay, he repeated; "the President must act promptly." The next day Horace Maynard suggested to Welles that Johnson adopt a bold, almost revolutionary course. He wished the Southern Representatives and Senators to come to Washington, to meet with the Democratic members from the North, make a numerical majority, constitute themselves the true Congress and organize as such. Many Northern Democrats urged the same scheme, but the President resolutely rejected it.

None the less, Andrew Johnson was not the man to quail before the Radical storm. Whatever evils may have resulted from his ill-fated procrastination, his public course was brave and manly. His demeanor and his words reflected his trust in the propriety of his acts. A day or so after Stockton had been ejected from the Senate, Johnson countered by issuing a proclamation of peace, formally terminating the legal state of war in all the late insurgent States, Texas alone excepted, and declaring the restoration of civil law.[8]

On the evening of the day upon which the Senate overrode his veto of the Civil Rights bill, the President, accompanied by his two daughters, attended a large public reception given by General Grant.[9] The Welleses, Montgomery Blair and a few other of the President's friends were there, but Radicals chiefly attended, exultant at their triumph in the Senate and eager to dazzle Grant. Upon being confronted with an Andrew Johnson more courtly and assured than ever, the Radicals were taken aback. Even Thad Stevens, "though a brave old stager, . . . showed himself discomfited."[10]

A little later, when a delegation of soldiers and sailors called at the White House, Johnson announced his unyielding determination to maintain his position. His speech was a bold defiance of his persecutors, men who, when he had been battling for the Union in the Senate and in Tennessee, "were lolling in ease and comfort." He did not care for them—"the whole pack, Tray, Blanche and Sweetheart, little dogs and all, coming along snapping at my heels."[11]

The President continued to receive signs of approval from Conservative leaders throughout the country. When A. J. Drexel, the Philadelphia financier, returned from Europe in the spring, he wrote the President of his interviews with influential men throughout Europe: "I found all to approve of your policies, think it the only one that can restore peace and Union to the country."[12] Ex-President Franklin Pierce wrote the Tennessean to thank him for his "brave devotion to the Constitution," and the Democratic members of Congress called upon him in a body to pledge their support. The expressions of approval were not altogether theoretical. Conservatives in Indiana began to organize Johnson Clubs and to nominate independent tickets to oppose the Radicals. This activity looked promising in Schuyler Colfax's district, and at the beginning of May, the Indiana situation generally was "most cheering."

But the welcome news was interspersed with reports of political treachery and evil doing. A Nevada Conservative informed Johnson that Senator Stewart of that state, who had pretended to be a supporter of the Administration, was using Nevada

Federal patronage against the President. Stewart, he warned, was "incapable of keeping faith," a statement which had proved true before the letter reached the President. San Francisco's Federal officeholders were "viciously opposed" to Johnson's policies. If he hoped for California, patronage must go to friends, not enemies. When Provisional Governor ("Drunken Jack") Hamilton of Texas visited New Orleans, General Gordon Grainger found that he had "gone over bag and baggage to the Radicals." Evidence of Stanton's unfaithfulness kept piling up. Instance after instance was furnished Johnson, for example, of the fashion in which the official advertising of the War Department was given to Radical newspapers, chiefly to those "infamous" in their abuse of the President.[13]

A further problem, though not a new one, was Jefferson Davis, still imprisoned at Fortress Monroe. In the spring of 1866, discussion of the desirability of Davis' immediate trial for treason was resumed, but it was observed that the public tone had altered. One eminent New York lawyer wrote the President as to the "extreme impolicy" of a trial. To arraign the head of the late Confederate States would reopen the whole subject as a constitutional question. "If Davis should be acquitted, he would be purged of all crime, and all Rebels would be adjudged innocent."[14]

It was determined not to indict the Confederate leader for high treason, but for a milder crime, and at the May term of the United States District Court for Virginia an indictment was returned to the effect that Davis, "owing allegiance and fidelity to the United States of America, and not having the fear of God before his eyes, . . . but being moved and seduced by the instigation of the devil," and in order to effect his "traitorous compassings, imaginings and intentions, on the 15th day of June, in the year of our Lord, 1864, in the city of Richmond . . . with a great multitude . . . most wickedly, maliciously, and traitorously did ordain, prepare, levy and carry on war against the United States."[15]

Immediately upon the finding of this indictment, Charles O'Conor, the famous New York lawyer who had been employed to defend the accused ex-Confederate, called on Chase to discover if the latter would admit the prisoner to bail, the Attorney General accompanying him to represent the Government. But the Chief Justice was no more willing now to hold court in Virginia than he had been in the previous fall. He

Charles Sumner

CHARLES SUMNER

Senator from Massachusetts, and One of Andrew Johnson's Bitterest
Antagonists in the Battles of Reconstruction.

had noted the President's peace proclamation, and also that it had been followed by other orders from the President through the War Department inconsistent with the interpretation that the writ of *habeas corpus* had been fully restored. Until the danger of military intervention against civil process was fully removed, he would not sit in the district courts in the South. No application for bail could be made to him. Davis' release was not yet to come from Chase.[16]

To add to his official perplexities, the President was confronted with a sad personal problem. His son, Colonel Robert Johnson, had become a hopeless inebriate, and the son's habits were a basis for Radical slurs upon the father. Henry Ward Beecher had word from Senator Pomeroy that the latter had called at the White House and found the President, his son and his son-in-law all drunk and unfit for business.[17] When questioned about it, Pomeroy denied having said he had seen the President drunk, but he had seen Robert Johnson very much so.

Johnson consulted physicians about his son's infirmity, and was advised that it might be possible to reclaim him. Welles doubted this, but because it was "important, for his father's sake, and the country's, that the President should in these days be relieved of the care and anxiety which his [Robert's] excesses and passions involve," he arranged a sea voyage on the U. S. S. *Chattanooga*, then ready to sail for Liberia and other distant waters. The anxious father approved the project, but wanted Robert to have something to do on the trip. Welles accordingly consulted Seward, who entered into the plan with a good spirit, and commissioned the young man, who was capable and attractive when sober, to look into the African slave trade.[18] When the vessel departed on its private-public mission, the paymaster had a check of the Department of State to pay Robert's expenses, but no part of the amount was to be spent without the "express sanction" of the Commander of the vessel.

More pressing and perplexing than the defections of postmasters or Congressmen, or even the inebriety of a beloved son, was the President's disquietude as to the loyalty and faithfulness of the members of his Cabinet, and particularly of Edwin M. Stanton, the evil genius of his presidency.

As a youngster, Stanton had been eager to write a book on "The Poetry of the Bible."[19] Benjamin Lundy, the famous

Abolitionist, was a frequent visitor at his father's house in Steubenville, Ohio, but Stanton imbibed no conscientious scruple to prevent his joining the Democratic party and accepting election to office at its hand. His duplicity began early. In 1842, just before his selection by a strict party vote to a lucrative position by the Democratic legislature, he told Salmon P. Chase of his "entire accord" with the latter's anti-Slavery views.[20] None the less, Stanton continued publicly to espouse the Democratic party. In 1849 he moved to Pittsburgh, where he built up a valuable law practice; among the Pennsylvania friends who aided him was Jeremiah Sullivan Black, to whom Stanton unburdened himself anent the Abolitionists, flaying them for "their hypocrisy, their corruption, their enmity to the Constitution, and their lawless disregard of the rights of States and individuals."

In the middle 50's, Stanton first met Abraham Lincoln, a gangling Springfield lawyer who had been associated in an important patent case. When Lincoln showed up at Cincinnati for the trial, Stanton was shocked at his appearance and asked: "Where did that long-armed baboon come from?"[21]

When the reorganization of Buchanan's Cabinet in December, 1860, had sent Judge Black to the Secretaryship of State, that President drafted Stanton for attorney-general. The new member nauseated both Black and the President with his gratitude and flattery. During the seventy-two fateful days in which State after State left the Union, Stanton sat quietly by. Black has given us a picture of Stanton's attitude at this time, of language "habitually deferential," of behavior "free from insolence," of a fervor of personal devotion to chief and colleagues.[22]

But this was not the only side of Stanton's conduct while attorney-general. Seward, who was then in Washington as chief of the Senate Republicans, relates how "immediately after Mr. Stanton took office, he put himself into direct communication." In January, 1861, Stanton called on Sumner at one o'clock in the morning, to describe to him an alleged scheme of the Secessionists to capture the National Capital.

Upon Lincoln's accession to the presidency, Stanton stayed on in Washington, writing Buchanan letter after letter describing the mistakes of the "gorilla" in the White House. "Why should Paul du Chaillu have to go to Africa for an ape?" Stanton inquired. "He has a better specimen in Washing-

ton."[23] After the first Battle of Manassas, he wrote Buchanan
that "the imbecility of this Administration culminated in that
catastrophe," a result "of Lincoln 'running the machine' for
five months."[24] Not without knowledge of Stanton's attitude,
but with his usual greatness of mind where personal dislikes
were concerned, upon Simon Cameron's resignation, Lincoln
selected Stanton to take the post left vacant.

Nearly every biographer of the Great Emancipator de-
votes many pages to outlining Lincoln's forbearance to his
busybody secretary, despite countless instances of insubordination and gross insolence. Lincoln would not have endured such
contumely had not Stanton been in many ways a man of genius.
As an organizer and administrator, the Pennsylvania lawyer
displayed unusual capacity. His aptitude for work was amazing, his mastery of detail prodigious, his energy and resource-
fulness were matters of constant surprise. These qualities
were of real value in the conduct of the war. Even so, Lincoln
often found the situation intolerable, and at times reprimanded
his subordinate with brusque sternness.

With his accession to Lincoln's Cabinet, Stanton became a
Radical of the Radicals. No more did he treat his friends of
the Buchanan days with deference; now he termed them "Copperheads" and "traitors." He gathered around him a coterie
of unscrupulous partisans, men of the stripe of Joseph Holt
and Lafayette C. Baker. Upon the assassination of Abraham
Lincoln, Stanton seemed to consider himself acting President.

President Johnson knew of Lincoln's dependence upon Stanton despite the outrageous attitude of the latter, and was
loath to believe Lincoln's War Minister unfaithful. Yet as
early as April 22, Browning had noted in his diary his belief
that Stanton and Johnson would not agree, that the President
"is determined to be master," and that the Cabinet would be
reorganized in thirty days. Similarly, in the clear eyes of
Gideon Welles, there was no illusion as to the Pennsylvanian's
loyalty.

The Secretary of the Navy deemed him "more violent than
vigorous, more demonstrative than discriminating, more vain
than wise." Stanton hungered for power; he was drunk with
the lust for it. When Russell of the London *Times* first saw
him, that shrewd reader of character in countenance deduced
that Stanton, excessively vain, aspired to be thought "a rude,
rough, vigorous Oliver Cromwell sort of man," and that no one

could expect from him courtesy of manner or delicacy of feeling.
Rhodes terms him "incapable of generosity to a prostrate foe,"
and John T. Morse, Jr., calls attention to Stanton's "arbitrary,
harsh, bad tempered and impulsive" nature.   He was often
cruel and unjust, and almost never made amends.[25]

Stanton was "double-faced, tyrannical, with an inordinate
desire for office" and his personal appearance hinted at these
traits of character.[26]   Of medium height, and stocky body, he
had "a head which Titian would have loved to paint, so massive were its proportions and so sweeping were its long locks
and beard."[27]   An obstinate mouth, a large nose and beetling
brows completed Stanton's physiognomy.   His nervousness
was proverbial, giving an air of excited irascibility to his every
movement.

By August, 1865, Welles had been partially convinced that
Stanton had arrived at a "full understanding" with the Radicals.   As the months wore on, this belief turned to conviction.
By April, the Secretary of the Navy was determined that Stanton be forced to show his colors. He must be either for the President or against him.   He could not be allowed to continue his
double dealing any longer.

When the "Central Directory" reported its proposed constitutional amendment, it precipitated a further crisis in the
relations of the President and his Cabinet.   Realizing that the
whole purpose of Old Thad's scheme was "party ascendency,"
Johnson felt that he must have the support of an undivided
Cabinet, and the very next day brought the Stevens report
before that body.

There was an impression abroad, he informed his Constitutional advisers, that they were divided in their counsels, and
that he was not sustained by them.   He "had determined to
avail himself of the report of the Committee of Fifteen as a
suitable and proper occasion for an explanation with his Cabinet."   Johnson added that he desired to know whether he was
sustained by the members of the Cabinet, and also that he intended to make public the result of the conference.[28]

As a resolution constitutionally passed by both Houses by
greater than a two-thirds vote, the President said he was not
called upon to approve or veto any such proposed amendment.
But it was an important public matter and should be thoroughly
discussed.   The President was opposed to "all conditions precedent to the admission of loyal representatives from the

Southern States, in the shape of amendments to the Constitution or the passage of laws." What did his advisers say? He then asked for the views of the members of the Cabinet in the order of their official rank.

Seward expressed himself at length as opposing the Radical plan. Before he could finish, Stanton broke in upon him. The Secretary of War was vociferous in his pleasure that the President has brought the matter up; claimed that "he had been strongly inclined to do it himself, and had been restrained only by a sentiment of delicacy, thinking it would come more appropriately from the President." At first, Stanton said, he had differed with the rest on negro suffrage, but after reflection he had conformed to the others' views, and had "approved the policy of the President from the beginning." He used "the strongest and most decided terms" in favor of the Johnson policy. Despite the loud emphasis of these declarations, Welles took note that Stanton had expressed no opinion favoring or opposing the Stevens plan.

McCulloch decidedly opposed the amendment, but was not hopeful as to the result. Dennison interjected that he thought it premature to express an opinion. When the President reached Stanton's turn, the latter was silent, wishing to have his vehement but ambiguous remarks, out of order, taken as indicating his view. Johnson then said that he had brought the subject forward that he might have the views of each member, a desire which the watchful Welles said was very proper, adding: "I trust each will state his opinion; I think it is due to the President." With these words, Welles looked toward Stanton, and Johnson too turned toward him. At that, the Secretary of War said he did not approve the committee plan in the present form, thought it could be amended and improved, and made some enigmatic remark about reconciling the President to Congress. Stanton had again eluded the effort to smoke him out.

There was no ambiguity about Gideon Welles. He said the plan was an "outrage"; he favored no Constitutional amendment in the existing condition of the country, and he knew of no right of Congress to pass amnesty laws, or to prescribe terms to the States. Stanton sneered that Welles opposed any terms to Congress. "You have not only fifteen-inch guns leveled against Congress, but you are for running your prow into them." Harlan, "very reserved," stood back and said nothing, very much embarrassed. Speed was not there.

This heated session lasted nearly four hours; every man who wished to state his views had the amplest opportunity to do so. The President spoke twice, at considerable length, expressing his usual objections to all conditions precedent to admitting loyal members to their seats. The discussion revealed plainly that both Dennison and Harlan were not in harmony with Johnson, and that Stanton, while equally hostile, was determined so to conceal his attitude—at least, to the President—that the latter would have no definite occasion to demand his resignation.[29]

The President caused a synopsis of the Cabinet discussion to be prepared and had it furnished to the *National Intelligencer* for publication the next morning. The Cabinet Radicals were taken aback when they saw their views, as offered to the Chief Executive, thus broadcast to the world. It was a shrewd move, doubly embarrassing to the Radicals. Johnson's friends would now see that Messrs. Dennison, Harlan and Stanton were not squarely behind the President. The Radicals, who were daily claiming these three worthies as their own in plan and policy, now knew their Cabinet agents for double dealers, facing two ways.

Welles thought this a shrewd move of Johnson, who had shown "tact and sagacity." Stanton's Radical friends were incredulous as to his position, yet Stanton must "content himself with the exposition made, or openly deny it. He can no longer equivocate or dissemble." This was Johnson's expectation. "We must know," he informed Welles, "whether we have a united or divided Cabinet." Seward remarked that, if asked, while he naturally would say nothing as to what other Cabinet members had declared, he would declare that he himself had not been misrepresented in the *Intelligencer's* account.[30]

At the next Cabinet meeting, the Secretary of State twitted Stanton. Inasmuch as the *Intelligencer* had said its account had come from a Cabinet minister, and as "there is no interest felt as regards anyone else but you," he said Stanton must have written out the account. After adding playfully that there were other indications of Stanton's authorship, Seward opened his snuff-box, took a pinch of snuff and walked away, smiling sardonically. But Stanton scowled; he was far from amused at the jest. He was in a ticklish situation. One or two of his Cabinet associates hinted that the War Minister must make a decided statement, because it was wrong "that a

Cabinet Minister should occupy a false or equivocal position on such a question at such a time." It had been the Radical habit to assert that their course was justified, and that the best evidence thereof was in the President's Cabinet, where Stanton was leading the opposition to Johnson's policy. Radical speakers and papers had "eulogized" and magnified Stanton to an enormous proportion.[31] Even now some denied that his views were those given in the *Intelligencer's* report. But Stanton himself did not dare deny the account.

The Colorado matter came before the Cabinet on May 8, and characteristically, Stanton advised the President to let Colorado in so as to avoid further trouble, while Harlan argued for admission so strongly as to convince the wavering Dennison. Seward, McCulloch and Welles remained unyielding against the admission of a State "with a population below the ratio for one representative."

When the confrontation of the Cabinet Radicals had failed to produce the hoped-for resignations of Dennison, Harlan, Speed and Stanton, Johnson was still more perplexed. Every day developments were making it more certain that he could not depend upon any support from the friends and followers of the Cabinet Radicals. Every day the President's friends and supporters grew more critical of his indecisiveness. Unless he was prepared to fight the Radicals vigorously, with appropriate Cabinet reorganization and recognition by patronage to supporters, with its denial to opponents, his advisers saw little hope for the future. Even Lewis D. Campbell sent suggestions of caution, urging his friend to sign the *habeas corpus* bill, conveying Henry Stanbery's similar advice, and adding that a veto "would give the Radicals great capital, and alienate many of our cherished friends."

James Gordon Bennett, whose support was valuable to any national figure, was becoming more and more impatient, not with the framework of the Presidential policies, but with the lack of vigor in adopting practical methods to carry them to success. On May 19 he told his lieutenants that the only way Johnson could sustain himself was to make terms with the Democrats, turn patronage over to them and strike a bold blow at the Radicals in the place where it would hurt most. Thereupon Bennett's lieutenant wrote the President a word of warning. Bennett believed the Radicals would carry the timid and wavering Conservatives with them, "because you are not decisive and bold enough in using the patronage in your hands against them, and in favor of those who support you." The Commodore had told him that "Johnson is gone, unless he takes the boldest and most decisive course."

Phillips warned the President that unless he adopted bold measures, the Bennett papers might alter their attitude and oppose the entire presidential program. ."The *Herald*, as you are aware, goes with the strongest, or with the party it believes to be the strongest, and, Hercules-like, it will help those who do and can help themselves." A few days later, he repeated the warning; there was still cause for alarm as to the policy of the paper, particularly because of the attitude of young Mr. Bennett, "who is very self-willed and not very steady or comprehensive in his views." The *Herald* sometimes made "extraordinary somersaults."[32]

Under the pressure of such warnings and under the steady insistence of Dixon, Cowan, Doolittle and the few Conservatives in Congress, backed up by Gideon Welles, the President finally yielded, and decided that the time had come to organize a new political party, a real National Union party, founded on the principles which had underlain his policy toward Congress, the Constitution and the South. Thus, late in the Spring, a National Union Club was organized in Washington, with A. W. Randall, former Governor of Wisconsin and then First Assistant Postmaster-General, a man much under Seward's influence, taking the lead. A little later another organization, under the name of the National Union Johnson Club, was set up under Democratic sponsorship, Montgomery Blair, Ward H. Lamon, Charles Knapp, T. B. Florence, of Pennsylvania, and Charles Mason of Ohio being active in its initiation.[33] In May the two organizations merged under the name of the former and began actively to organize for projecting the National Union Party into the coming Congressional elections.

This Club now took upon itself the task of smoking out the Radical Cabinet members. It announced that it would serenade the President and each member of the Cabinet on the night of May 23, so that each man would have a chance publicly to make known his views. Welles did not approve of serenades, deeming these methods of calling out public men undignified. He had repeatedly urged both Lincoln and Johnson not to talk on such occasions. On this one, with rare restraint, Johnson did not make a speech to the serenaders, confining himself to a word of thanks to the Club for its approbation of his policies. When the crowd of perhaps a thousand, with a band at its head, appeared before Welles' door, Father Gideon declined to speak, and would only say, briefly and gruffly, that he approved the policies of the Administration, and stood for the Union and the rights of the States.

McCulloch also was emphatic in indorsement of the President. Seward was not at home, but there was no uneasiness as to his views; his New York speech had committed him. It was the Radicals whom the serenaders wished to quiz.

Of these, Dennison "acquitted himself with credit," making a soothing speech to the effect that "everything was lovely" in that circumstances were bringing the President and Congress rapidly together. The other Radicals conducted themselves characteristically. Speed "ran away," sending the committee a letter claiming that the pressure of public business prevented his speaking. Harlan, too, wrote a letter, and did "not show himself."

But Stanton had a long address in his pocket, carefully prepared in advance, and read it from his door, "a man standing on each side of him with a lighted candle."[34] Stanton's remarks were framed in such fashion that the President could find nothing specifically offensive in them, yet their tenor was such that the Radicals would be reassured that the Secretary of War was ready to do whatever they should demand.

After referring to the circumstances of the conclusion of the war, Stanton said that "no one better than Mr. Johnson understood the solemn duty imposed upon the national executive to maintain the national authority vindicated at so great a sacrifice, and the obligation not to suffer the just fruits of so fierce a struggle to slip away. There was no disguise of his purpose to secure the peace and tranquility of the country on just and sure foundations."[35]

The President's messages, he continued, "received the cordial support of every member of the Cabinet." The point of difference was that of whether the negroes should vote or not. Stanton had thought that they should, "but after calm and full discussion, my judgment yielded to the adverse arguments resting upon the practical difficulties encountered in such a measure, and to the President's conviction that to prescribe the rule of suffrage was not within the legitimate scope of his power." The North Carolina plan, Stanton continued, represented the President's principles.

As to admission to Congress, the Secretary recited the Constitutional provision that "each House shall be the judge of the elections, returns, and qualifications of its own members." He commented thereon that the President "in emphasizing this fact, has conformed to the plain letter of the Constitution." He cunningly counteracted this sop to the Administration party by adding that the obligation was implied on each House of Congress to take testimony, weigh evidence and decide questions of membership, but "of course the President, in thus referring the question of its own members to the judgment of each House of Congress received, and continues to receive, my cordial support."

Stanton next analyzed the problem of the freedmen, quoted from Johnson's annual message to Congress on the subject, and said that "these views of the President . . . received and continue to receive, my hearty concurrence. They have guided the action of the War Department." He termed the Freedmen's Bureau bill an honest desire on the part of Congress to conform to them, said he had advised the President to sign it, but that, inasmuch as it had been vetoed, it was no longer a living measure and no longer needed comment from him. He was similarly evasive as to the Civil Rights bill, saying that as Congress had passed it over the veto, it had "ceased to be the subject of debate."

"I have not been able to give my assent to the proposed Fourteenth Amendment," he said. He objected to the provision binding Congress for four years to exclude from the ballot "all persons who voluntarily adhered to the late insurrection, giving it aid and comfort." Whatever might be the condition of the country and whatever proofs of present and future loyalty might be offered, there would be this absolute constitutional bar for four years. Stanton pointed out that "elements of change are now at work, stimulating on one side to loyalty, and on the other tending to continued hostile feelings. In my judgment, every proper incitement to Union should be fostered and cherished, and for Congress to limit its own power by Constitutional amendment for four years might be deplorable in its result."

Such were Stanton's views—in public. Such were the

equivocal words he used to lull the President and his friends into a false sense of security. Yet the shrewder of these knew well that Stanton was engaging in intentional duplicity—and so did Andrew Johnson. But in his anxiety to remain in the Cabinet to aid the President's enemies, Stanton had a powerful ally—Johnson's fatal procrastination. The President could not persuade himself to discharge the marplot minister.

Shortly after this ineffectual serenade, much pressure was brought in on the President to come to an agreement with Congress. Sumner, Stevens and the extreme Radicals "have at length been induced to coöperate in a judicious scheme of reconstruction with the Conservative Republicans," John Binney of New York wrote the President on June 16. The plan adopted did not consider negro suffrage for the present, and Binney urged that it would be deeply gratifying to the nation if the President would coöperate with Congress in carrying forward "this wise and practical scheme." If he would do so, "you will rise in immortal renown as one of the greatest statesmen in the world."[36]

The Union State Convention of Ohio adopted a platform urging the President to support the proposed amendment and Governor Cox of that State wrote Johnson to point out that the convention resolution "does not advocate or advise negro suffrage. It does not indorse any specific act of Congress whatever, but simply and solely the amendment as it stands, and makes it a party measure in Ohio to vote for it." Except for its disqualifying clause, Cox himself heartily approved of the amendment. He had coincided thoroughly with Johnson's program, had been deeply grieved at the obstacles thrown in its way, but thought the friends of the Administration should not quarrel with the Ohio resolution or with the proposed amendment.

A different aspect of the Ohio meeting was revealed by Lewis D. Campbell. At least a third of its delegates had been revenue collectors, clerks, assessors, and other treasury appointees, "all picked by Chase from extreme Radicals, and postmasters of the same type, who were there to prevent any expression in your favor, on the pretext that it would prevent harmony." Campbell was greatly discouraged "because your most active and vindictive opponents are permitted to hold the Federal patronage. If this cannot be remedied, we shall make a poor fight in Ohio."[37]

The serenade had left Cabinet matters little better than before. Johnson's enemies remained on in the Cabinet, and seemed as determined as ever to stick. Meetings of the Constitutional advisers of the Chief Executive were changing from frank forums for the discussion of public questions to occasions where tension and distrust were such that important matters went undiscussed. Indeed, Welles believed that trifles were brought forward by the Radicals expressly to exclude more important subjects. As he and McCulloch left the meeting on June 5, they compared notes on the unpleasant condition of affairs, and concluded that it was a matter of plain duty for them to tell the President their views as to the want of frankness and freedom in the Cabinet and as to the general status of affairs. They were sure that the Republican party was being used by the Radicals to destroy the President, and that his great mistake was in endeavoring to prevent a break with the Radicals.

Seward, too, gave them concern. A number of Johnson's friends, notably the Blairs, insisted that the Secretary of State was also betraying the President, and that he and Stanton had a secret understanding. Welles did not entirely agree with this, believing Seward "less false to the President than adhesive to the Secretary of State." It was not that he did not like Johnson, but that he feared the Democrats and felt himself identified with the Republicans, indeed was the father of the party. On their part, the Democrats had no faith at all in Seward, looking on him as a Mephistopheles whom they never would trust.

But the President, while feeling that Seward was a per-- plexing study, and never ceasing to wonder at the Secretary's "equanimity under all circumstances," maintained the most implicit confidence in "the Old Roman," as he affectionately called him.

At one time, he told Browning, he had thought Seward a trickster, but that was wrong, for the Secretary of State was "able, faithful, firm and reliable, . . . a truly great man, unselfishly devoted to the interests of the country." None the less Johnson's faith in Seward was beginning to beget a general distrust of the Administration. The Conservatives commented that none of Seward's fast friends—"men who under Weed breathe through his nostrils—had sustained the President."[38] Stanton's anxiety to retain his place in the Cabinet was still more disheartening to McCulloch and Welles. The War Secretary's relations with the Radicals were more intimate than they were with the President or with any of the Cabinet, and yet Stanton studiedly conformed to Johnson's decisions.

One Friday evening McCulloch and Welles called at the White House by appointment and spoke bluntly to the President. After an hour's conversation, they concurred that it was impossible to have in mind much longer the preservation of the Republican party, because the Radicals were using the organization to harm the President. It was no longer justifiable to repel Democrats so as to court the Sumner-Stevens group. The President expressed his amazement that, under existing conditions, Harlan and Speed should stay on in the Cabinet. "Aren't there others among us as objectionable and more harmful?" Welles inquired. McCulloch interjected that he did not think Seward faithless; Welles agreed to this, but referred to Stanton's hold on the Secretary of State,[39] pointing out how steadily the Seward men had voted with the Radicals. Johnson was reluctant to give Seward up, suggesting a conference and explicit understanding. As to Stanton, he knew not how to act.[40]

Johnson's "want of spirit and decision" in permitting Stanton to remain, was inexplicable to McCulloch. The Secretary of War "attended the Cabinet meetings, not as an adviser of the President, but as an opponent of the policy to which he had himself been committed, and the President lacked the nerve to dismiss him." In the considered opinion of the Secretary of the Treasury, Johnson's failure "to exercise his undoubted right to rid himself of the Minister who had differed with him upon very important questions, had become personally obnoxious, and whom he regarded as an enemy and a spy, was a blunder for which there was no excuse."[41]

On the evening of June 11, a group of Conservative leaders called at the White House. The President told them that his only ambition was to restore all the States, and to give unity, tranquillity and prosperity to the country; then he wanted to retire. But this could not be done with the Radicals controlling Congress; their schemes were revolutionary, and would ruin the country. "We must rescue the power from their hands," he exclaimed. "I am willing to put in all the capital I have. I will give $20,000 in cash and all the influence I have as President. . . ." All the group agreed that "a convention of the friends of the country" must be called.[42]

On June 15 Doolittle breakfasted with the Secretary of the Navy. The two unswerving Conservatives were firmly agreed that the time had come when Johnson must make a pronounced and definite stand against the Radicals. They went to the White House, the President indorsed their views, and once more suggested calling a national convention of the true friends of the Union. The Wisconsin Senator agreed to draw up the call, proposing that it be signed by the members of the Cabinet. This Welles unfortunately opposed. Had it been done, Stanton would have been forced to sign or resign. But the Secretary of the Navy had a rigid view of the proprieties for Cabinet Members, and combining in such a call was not the sort of things of which he approved.

The Democrats also had such a convention in mind, for which Francis Preston Blair was writing a call. Apprehensive of Seward's control of the President, the Democrats at first conditioned their coöperation on Johnson's ridding himself of his Secretary of State—they "would rather give up Johnson than retain Seward."[43] But Doolittle drafted his call so as to secure approval of Seward. Henry J. Raymond, still titular chairman of the National Union committee, approved it, as did the President.

On June 18 the Senator showed Welles a preliminary draft of his call. The Secretary objected; it put too much restriction on the men to be admitted; there was "too much fear that we should have men we did not care to fellowship with, although we might agree on present issues." Again, it did not present the real issue, the objection to the proposed Constitutional amendment. Welles wanted the call to sound an alarm to arouse the people against any such alteration of the national organic law.

Despite these objections, the Secretary of the Navy was unable to have the call modified. Doolittle, Cowan, Orville H. Browning, Randall, Welles and some other members of the National Union Johnson Club gathered at the White House on June 21 to give a final scrutiny to the appeal. Once more, Welles sought insertions of the Constitutional objection, was overborne, and went home "desponding and unhappy."[44]

At a Cabinet meeting a day or so later, it was apparent that Postmaster-General Dennison had been "tampered with" by the Radicals, and had definitely joined them. McCulloch remarked to the President that as there were now four of the Cabinet in opposition, he did not see how they would get along. "Yes," Johnson answered, "from what we now see of Dennison, and if we count Stanton after his patched up speech; but it is uncertain where he wishes to place himself"—an uncertainty which existed in the mind of none but the President. Welles could not understand why Johnson should cling to Stanton when his insidious treachery had become obvious.

Welles awaited the issuance of the call with apprehension, fearing that Johnson's interests had been sacrificed to those of Seward. Whatever had been the intention of Seward and Weed, Welles was pleasantly disappointed in the result, for the call met with an immediate and hearty response. Issued on June 25 in the name of the National Union Club, it was signed by A. W. Randall, President of the Club, by Senators Doolittle and Cowan, by Orville H. Browning, Charles Knapp and Samuel Fowler, and indorsed by four other Senators—Norton, Nesmith, Dixon and Hendricks.

It was addressed to all who agreed that the Union was indissoluble and perpetual and the Constitution supreme and constant; that the rights, dignity and equality of the States, "including the right of representation in Congress," were solemnly guaranteed by the Constitution, and that both the secession of States and the exclusion of members from Congress were unauthorized; that slavery was abolished and could not be reestablished; that each State "had the undoubted right to prescribe the qualifications of its own electors, and no external power can rightly question, or ought to dictate, control or influence the free and voluntary action of the States in the exercise of that right," but the maintenance of the rights of the States was essential; that the purpose of the war had been to preserve the Union, and that since this had been attained, harmony and concord should be encouraged and the States promptly restored to the full exercise of their constitutional powers.[45]

Those subscribing to these views throughout the Union were asked to select two delegates in each Congressional district to assemble at Philadelphia on Tuesday, August 14,—delegates who, "in a spirit of patriotism and love of Union, can rise above personal and sectional considerations." The convention would refuse to admit any delegate who did not "loyally accept the national situation" and who was not attached "in true allegiance to the Constitution, the Union and the Government of the United States."[46]

Contrary to apprehensions, Democrats determined generally to give a hearty support to the convention. True, the New York *World* opposed it, but this gave a good flavor to the proceedings. War Democrats generally welcomed the opportunity to support the President, and Doolittle was overwhelmed with offers of aid and counsel.

The movers of the convention were careful to address letters of invitation to each member of the Cabinet. This had the effect of finally smoking out the three open Radicals. On July 11, the Postmaster-General sent in his resignation, which was immediately accepted by the President. Attorney-General Speed tried to hold out, but by the middle of the month he could dissemble no longer and resigned. Speed's note was curt, almost discourteous. Harlan, however, was a thorny problem. On July 20, the President told Browning that he felt "that it was indecent for him to remain," but that he further realized that the Methodist Church was a powerful body, and he was anxious to avoid its hostility. When hints failed, the President took things into his own hands, and on July 27 asked Harlan to resign. The latter did so, courteously but reluctantly.

Secretary Stanton too, had received an invitation from Senator Doolittle to attend the convention, or failing that, to indorse its purposes. On July 16 Stanton drafted this response to Doolittle: "The within letter is returned to the person by whom it purports to be addressed to me. I do not choose to recognize him as an organ of communication between the public and myself on any subject; and because moreover I am in favor of securing the civil rights of all citizens in the United States in the States lately in rebellion, and in favor of equalizing the representation in Congress so as to give the loyal States their due weight in the legislative branch of the government, and am also in favor of repudiating the Rebel debt. . . . These being objects of the proposed amendments to the Federal Constitution adopted by the Congress, I am in favor of these amendments."[47]

Stanton continued that he understood the object of the approaching Philadelphia convention "to be the organization of a party consisting mainly of those who carried on the war (Rebellion) against the government and undertook to destroy the national life by war in the rebel States, and those in the Northern States who sympathized with them," and added, "I do not approve the call of that convention. So far as the terms of the call and the purposes and objects of the convention are designed to oppose the Constitutional authority of Congress, I heartily condemn them."

Such were the sentiments of Edwin M. Stanton in his secret heart. But after he had set on paper this condemnation of the course of the President in whose Cabinet he served, his inherent duplicity and double-dealing reasserted themselves, and he filed the letter away, unsent, making no response at all to the communication he had received. Had he then sent this letter, he could not have remained in the Cabinet another day. But he was determined to defeat the plans of the President, and so this Constitutional adviser of the Chief Executive remained at the head of the War Department to embarrass and betray the man it was his duty to serve and aid.

This statement is made not without authority. It is based not alone on inferences and internal evidence, but on a revelation made in the public speech of a Radical Congressman from Michigan. This Representative told his constituents that, before leaving Washington, he had called on Stanton, who had assured him "that he fully sympathized with the Radicals in Congress, and was remaining in the war office for their benefit." The Congressman—his name was Driggs—had urged Stanton to stay in the Cabinet, telling him "it is best to have someone in that office in whom Congress can depend in case of trouble with the President."[48]

At last the President had been able to force three of his enemies from his Cabinet and he made excellent appointments to replace Speed, Harlan and Dennison.[49] The choice of Henry Stanbery as Attorney-General was a happy one, for the Cincinnati lawyer proved a man of capacity, integrity and unflinching loyalty to his chief. Orville H. Browning, Lincoln's friend from Illinois, became Secretary of the Interior. In ability perhaps equal to Stanbery and quite superior to Harlan, Browning had been a little dubious in some of his dealings in the courts, but no suspicion has attached to his official conduct. Randall, prime mover in the machinery of the approaching convention, was promoted from Assistant Postmaster General to full Cabinet rank. Politically, his task was the most arduous in the government, certain to arouse criticisms and attack, and particularly so in Johnson's Administration, with its wholesale official decapitations made necessary by the President's effort to build up a party. Yet on the whole Randall seems to have filled his post reasonably well.

As July progressed, the mind of the country politically turned more and more to the Philadelphia Convention. "Old Line" Conservatives were delighted with the prospect; the meeting would be the great movement of the day. Never had Senator Dixon been "so sure of the salvation of the country." The Missouri Conservatives were rallying to the defense of the President; Lincoln's Attorney-General, Edward Bates, informed him that they were organizing, "fully resolved to fight the battle for the Constitution . . . under your banner." Sam Randall had hopes of carrying Pennsylvania and desired a Cabinet member appointed from that State to help out in the fight. The personnel of the delegates elected in Connecticut pleased Gideon Welles.

In the beginning, the convention plan did not particularly impress Commodore Bennett; it might be very well in its way, he wrote the President, but the election of the next Congress was vital, involving "momentous consequences not only to you but to the future of the country." The *Herald* deliberately sat on the fence until the success of the convention seemed assured. But by the middle of July Bennett was convinced, and began to commend and sustain the approaching Union meeting enthusiastically.

Of the political problems aroused by the coming convention, perhaps the most thorny was that of the admission or nonadmission of Northern Democratic Copperheads, men of the stripe of Vallandigham and Fernando Wood. The names of these men had become gravely obnoxious to the mass of the Northern people. Moderate Unionists as well as Radicals felt that it had been far more heinous to betray the Union in the free States than it had been to serve in the armies of Johnston and Lee. While they might welcome the spectacle of the opponents in arms burying their differences, they could not forget or forgive the leading spirits in the Knights of the Golden Circle.[50]

The apprehension of the Conservatives increased. The United States District Attorney at Pittsburgh, a Johnson appointee, informed the President that he feared the convention was to be filled with men "distinguished for little else than in-

veterate malignant hostility to the War. . . . The country will
not take counsel of these men."[51]

Both Vallandigham and Wood had themselves elected delegates to the Philadelphia meeting, and angry mutterings ensued.
Leaders in the Union movement hinted broadly that, should the
conspicuous Copperhead leaders present themselves, they would
not be admitted. Thereupon Fernando Wood wrote the President in anger: "We represent those who ask no offices or official
favors. We give you our support only because you are right.
Myself and others here have been elected by the *people* delegates to this convention, and we do not intend to be excluded."[52]

None the less, the plans for the convention proceeded. Elections were held throughout the country and delegates of character and standing selected in each of the 36 states. It seemed
that the convention was sure to be a great success.

A great hall was specially built in Philadelphia to house
the convention, and an application was made to Stanton for
bunting with which to decorate the convention hall. On August
7 the Secretary of War brought the matter up before the
Cabinet, saying with a sneer, "I have none for them; I will turn
them over to the Navy."

Welles bristled at this slur. "My bunting has always been
promptly shown," he informed Stanton, "it would be well were
you now to let us have a sight of yours." The Secretary of
War flushed and replied that he had no bunting available for
the convention.

"Oh, show your flag," Welles continued impatiently.

"You mean the convention?" Stanton now said. "I am
against it."

Welles said he was sorry to hear, but glad to know Stanton's
opinion. "You did not answer the inquiry like the rest of us."
The War Minister answered that he did not choose "to have
Doolittle or any other little fellow draw an answer from me."

That evening, Father Gideon went to the White House to
see the President. He asked Andrew Johnson if he had noticed
Stanton's remarks that day about the convention; "probably
you knew his opinions previously."

"I had not known them before. It was the first intimation
I had received," Johnson responded.

"This is wrong," Welles said. "We cannot get along in this
way."

"No," the President answered, "it will be pretty difficult."

T HE campaign of 1866 affords the only instance in American political history in which a Congressional election was deemed so important that four great political conventions were held to influence its results, and a president stumped the country to forward the fortunes of his friends only to be met with insults and indignities.

Had Andrew Johnson triumphed in this election, or had he even decreased the Radical strength in either House or Senate so that the Radicals would have had less than a two-thirds majority in either branch, the whole course of American history might have been altered, and altered for the best. As Blaine admits, there would have been no further amendment to the Constitution, there would have been no conditions of reconstruction. The South would have escaped ten cruel years of rule by carpetbagger and scalawag. The "Solid South" would never have been formed.

Andrew Johnson staked everything on an appeal to the people. It was his habit to trust in the commonalty, to believe that, when properly informed, the people would decide honestly and wisely. And so this year, betrayed by trusted Constitutional advisers, ignored by fanatic Radicals in Congress, and opposed by the Big Business of the day, which for its own ends had thrown its weight to the Radicals, Andrew Johnson determined to carry his case to the people for a verdict at the polls.[1]

The first step in this great appeal was to be the approaching Union meeting at Philadelphia, upon which great hopes were set by the Conservatives. Only two weeks before the date set for this meeting, the bright anticipations of Johnson's friends were dampened by a fearful riot in New Orleans. Following so closely upon the Memphis troubles, the New Orleans tragedy was a body blow to the prestige of Johnson's policies in the North.

The Memphis outbreak had been caused by trouble between the garrison of Third United States colored artillery and the city police, largely Irish in its personnel. On the afternoon of April 30 the colored gunners indulged in the dangerous pastime of jostling the Irish policemen off the sidewalks; fights broke

out and a riot resulted. The next day the police, aided by a
white mob, attacked the negro population of Memphis. In the
resulting riot, which lasted for two days, forty-six negroes were
killed and many more injured; twelve negro school houses and
four churches were burned.

The Northern Radicals proclaimed Memphis as fresh evidence of the South's unregeneracy. The riots supported their
contention that, unless protected by Union bayonets, the negro
was not safe in the South, and that the President's desire to
readmit the Southern states was naught but a scheme virtually
to reënslave the freedmen.

But Memphis troubles were dwarfed by those which occurred in July in New Orleans. Taking advantage of Abraham
Lincoln's ten per cent plan, Louisiana had held an election in
1864, a constitutional convention had assembled, a new organic
law for the State had been adopted, and the government had
been reorganized from top to bottom. After Appomattox, the
pardoned Confederates had recovered control of Louisiana's
government, occupying every important office except that of
governor. This position was filled by the Radical J. Madison
Wells, a shabby vacillating scoundrel. These Conservative
gains in Louisiana were displeasing to the Radicals, who began
to scheme about how to repossess themselves of control of the
state. Instigated and directed by Radicals in Washington, the
Louisiana conspirators undertook to initiate negro suffrage
and thus vote themselves upon the throne.[2]

When Louisiana had adopted her constitution in 1864,
negroes had not been given a vote. During the sessions of the
convention, President Lincoln had urged upon Provisional Governor Michael Hahn that qualified suffrage be given to educated
negroes and to those who held property, but the convention had
ignored the hint. At the close of its labors, the constitution-
making body of 1864 had adopted a resolution adjourning, not
sine die, but subject to the call of the president of the convention, a provision generally regarded as having been beyond its
right and power.

In 1866, the Radicals determined to make use of this clause
to call back the defunct convention and have it declare impartial suffrage the rule of the State. Although they could not
persuade the president of the convention to issue the call, nothing daunted, they issued the call themselves, asking the dele-

gates of the old convention to assemble in the Mechanics Hall in New Orleans on July 30.

These high-handed plans aroused the indignation of the Conservatives, who deemed the alleged convention little short of a mob without legal power or right, and determined by law to prevent its assembly. Governor Wells displayed great irresolution in meeting the crisis, refusing to sanction the convention and likewise refusing to forbid it.

State Attorney-General Herron and Mayor Monroe of New Orleans, took the lead against the meeting. They made repeated efforts to persuade the Federal troops stationed in the city to prevent the assemblage of the "conspirators." General Sheridan, district commander, was away in Texas, and General Baird of the Freedmen's Bureau was commanding in his stead. On July 25 Mayor Monroe interviewed Baird, and urged him to take steps to prevent trouble. On July 27 the Mayor again saw Baird and informed him that, should the convention assemble, the New Orleans grand jury would indict its members and the sheriff would arrest them. The General told Monroe that he would telegraph the War Department for instructions, and suggested that the Mayor likewise telegraph his fears and plans to Washington.

On this same day, the Radicals were busy in New Orleans. A great crowd of negroes had gathered before the City Hall and was addressed by one Dr. Bostie, a Radical leader, appropriately described as a "white scoundrel." "I want the negroes to have the right of suffrage," this incendiary told the assembled mob of blacks. "We have 300,000 black men with white hearts. Also 100,000 good and true Union white men who will fight for and beside the black race against the 300,000 hell-bound Rebels. With these forces we cannot only whip, but exterminate, the other party. . . . We want brave men and not cowards Monday. . . . There will be no such puerile affair as at Memphis. . . . If we are interfered with, the streets of New Orleans will run with blood."[3] The inflamed negroes shouted back that they would be on hand.

Under these circumstances a certain Judge Abell took it upon himself to charge the New Orleans grand jury. He told the grand jurors that the reassembly of the 1864 convention was unlawful, and that the mere gathering together of the delegates without authority and for unlawful purposes was an overt act. He read to the inquisitorial body the declaration of a legal authority that "the mere assembly of persons to do an unlawful thing is a disturbance of the peace."[4]   Thereupon the grand jury proceeded to indict the members of the convention, warrants were issued for their arrest and turned over to the sheriff to serve.   When the Federal military authorities heard of what Judge Abell had done, they arrested him.

As suggested by Baird, Mayor Monroe and the Attorney-General had telegraphed the President.   On July 26 Herron wished to know Johnson's feeling about the convention scheme. The next day he informed the President that the whole matter was before the grand jury, but that it, would be impossible to execute civil processes without the certainty of riot.   "It is contemplated," the Attorney-General's telegram continued, "to have the members of the convention arrested under process from the criminal court of this district," and he asked: "Is the military to interfere to prevent the process of court?"

Baird had telegraphed Stanton of the troubles looming and of the proposed arrests; he informed the Secretary of War that he had "given no orders on the subject, but have warned parties that I could not countenance or permit such action without instructions to that effect from the President.   Please instruct me at once by telegraph."[5]   Stanton received this dispatch on July 29, but carefully refrained from transmitting it or showing it to Andrew Johnson, and the President had no knowledge that General Baird had asked for instructions until ten days after Baird's telegram had reached Stanton's hands.[6]

On July 28, Johnson responded to the inquiries from the New Orleans civilian officials.   "The military will be expected," he telegraphed, "to sustain and not to obstruct or interfere with the proceedings of the court."   On the same day the President addressed a sharp inquiry to the Louisiana governor, asking him by what authority he had resummoned the 1864 convention, and by what authority that body assumed to represent the whole people of Louisiana.   Wells answered that he had not convened the convention.[7]

Mayor Monroe showed the President's wire to General Baird, who took note of it, and who was greatly disturbed at not receiving definite orders or instructions from the War Department.   The General announced that, as he had had no instructions from the President through official channels, he would arrest any officer interfering with the delegates.   Mayor Monroe then turned the task of policing the city on the day of the convention over to General Baird, the latter promising to have troops on hand for the purpose.

At noon of the day appointed, the delegates assembled at the Mechanics Hall without disturbance. Neither police nor soldiers were observed in the vicinity of the convention hall. There was no quorum of the pretended convention, and so adjournment was taken until 1:30 in the afternoon.

During the recess, a mob of negroes armed with clubs and pistols made for the convention hall. During the disorderly progress of the blacks toward the hall, a white boy was either knocked or shoved off the sidewalk. The police interfered, no doubt with undue readiness, to arrest the negro who had pushed the boy. In the scuffle, the negroes fired one or two shots and a call went out to the police reserves to quell the disturbance.

The police had armed to the teeth beforehand and, with a large mob of white citizens, immediately advanced against the negroes. The blacks ran for safety to the convention hall. When a white flag was displayed from a window of the hall, the police advanced to make the arrests; but at this juncture, some negroes inside the hall fired on the police outside. Maddened passions did the rest. The angry whites broke into the building and a scene of fearful butchery ensued. About two hundred negroes were killed, many others wounded and a race warfare raged throughout the city. Federal troops did not reach the scene until the fury of the slaughter had been spent.

The Radicals proclaimed the New Orleans butchery as a direct outcome of what Thad Stevens called "universal Andy Johnsonism." First terming it a "rebel riot," Greeley's *Tribune* later changed and said it was not a riot at all, but "cold-blooded murder."[8] Senator Sumner informed an English friend that he might judge the President "by the terrible massacre in New Orleans." Stanton had "confessed" to him that "Johnson was its author"![9] It was not difficult for Sumner, Stevens, Ashley and Wade to convince the North not only that the New Orleans riots were an evidence of the imperfect operation of "universal Andy Johnsonism," but to carry the charge a step further and hold the President personally responsible for the riots. "This man aided and abetted the New Orleans mob," declared the *Independent*. "He doubly inspired the murderers." His course was "utterly without palliation," the *Nation* insisted. There was "scarcely an act of usurpation . . . he has not committed, and such usurpations will no longer be tolerated."[10]

This news was a bombshell to the President. As soon as word came of the trouble, he had taken prompt action and ordered General Sheridan to keep the peace in New Orleans, to investigate the cause of the disturbance and report. The General's initial telegram placed blame on the Radicals as well as on the Conservatives. A little later, he altered his tone and fastened complete responsibility on the Conservatives. On learning of this shift, Welles concluded that the General had been "coached" by the Washington Radicals. Sheridan finally urged that the Governor and the Mayor be removed from office. The whole matter came up for Cabinet discussion on August 3, when Stanton read his correspondence with Sheridan —but *not* with *Baird!*—to his associates, who observed his "marked sympathy with the rioters." The President still did not know of Baird's telegraphic request to Stanton for instructions. But by this time Welles had formed the opinion that the Louisiana Radicals whose acts had incited the troubles had been initially instigated by Congessional Radicals in Washington; "Boutwell and others had said sufficient to show their participation"; it was "part of a deliberate conspiracy, and was to be the commencement of a series of bloody affrays through the States lately in rebellion." Frantically excited, Stanton referred to the Attorney-General of Louisiana and the Mayor of New Orleans, as "pardoned Rebels who had instigated the murder of the people."

When Sheridan's ouster plea was brought before the Cabinet, it was immediately noted that the President had no constitutional or statutory authority to displace civil officials in the States. During the ensuing debate on the subject, Stanton did not say a word.

The President did not learn of the existence of the telegram from Baird to Stanton until about the middle of August, when it was much too late for it to be anything but a memento of deliberate unfaithfulness on the part of his Secretary of War. Johnson was indignant that this important dispatch had been withheld from him, and Stanton was hard put to it to explain why he had not shown it to the President. The best he could do was to make the lame excuse that he did not think it called for any answer, because he did "not understand from the wire that force or resistance was to be used to break up the convention"![11]

Amid sneering Radical suggestions to postpone the meeting,

lest the effort to "hold up the President's hands . . . reveal that they are red with blood," the delegates to the National Union Convention gathered in Philadelphia.[12] The sessions were to be held in a great frame hall which had been erected at the corner of Girard Avenue and 20th Street, a building able to house 10,000 people. Though Stanton had not furnished it, there was bunting in abundance, the national flag and the national colors being aflame in every part of the hall. An arch of thirty-six sections rose above the speaker's platform, each section carrying the shield of a State, and every State of the Union being represented, South, North, West, and East.

Postmaster-General Randall went early to Philadelphia to observe the course of affairs for the President. On August 11 he reported to Johnson that it was "an extraordinary gathering." Men were there from every section of the country and, best of all, there was "a universal feeling of good will toward each other, and toward yourself, cropping out everywhere."

The next day things continued favorably, except for the insistence of Clement L. Vallandigham, chief of the Ohio Copperheads, "bent upon mischief and determined to rule or ruin," to be admitted as a delegate.[13] Randall wrote the President that "our friends the Southerners are endeavoring to persuade him to get out of the way. . . . I hope Vallandigham will be magnanimous enough to stand aside." The convention was determined to expel him if he dared claim a seat. The general feeling was to stand fast by the President; the Southerners were "acting nobly and with a good sense which annoys the Radical reporters here. . . . If we can pass through without discord, it will be the most remarkable turn in the history of your administration."[14]

One of Johnson's secretaries sent him word that "men never came together in a better temper of mind. There seems to be complete harmony of views and purposes." The only cloud upon the horizon was the Ohio Copperhead, who was "actuated by the intensest selfishness, and had rather this grand effort in behalf of the country should fail than it should succeed without glorifying him."

Amid scenes of great enthusiasm, the sessions opened at noon on August 14. Bands intermingled the patriotic airs of North and South, "Rally Round the Flag, Boys," "The Star Spangled Banner," and "Dixie." As the chief signer for the call of the convention, Randall called it to order, pounding the desk with a gavel made from the tough oak of the famous frigate Constitution. A telegram from Andrew Johnson was read to the convention: "The people must be trusted, and .the country will be restored."[15]

General John A. Dix was made temporary president. Every one of the thirty-six States was represented, the delegates being "reasonable, intelligent, well-known and influential citizens."[16] At the head of the Conservative Republicans were such figures as Montgomery Blair, Weed, Raymond, Dix, Cowan, Doolittle, Browning and Dixon, but the Radicals claimed, and with some truth, that the convention's personnel was "overwhelmingly" Democratic.[17] Among leaders of the latter at the Philadelphia meeting were Samuel J. Tilden, Dean Richmond and Sanford E. Church of New York; John P. Stockton and Joel Parker of New Jersey; William Bigler, Asa Packer and David R. Porter of Pennsylvania; James E. English of Connecticut; Robert C. Winthrop and Josiah E. Abbot of Massachusetts; William B. Lawrence of Rhode Island and Reverdy Johnson of Maryland.

"Will they turn out the Vallandighams and Woods?" This question was on everyone's lips as the chairman's gavel fell. But the outcome was fortunate. Fernando Wood withdrew from the New York delegation and Vallandigham was persuaded to give up his seat. There was no breach of the peace by the Copperheads. On the contrary, harmony almost of a saccharine nature prevailed.

Federal and Confederate officers buried belligerence in friendship, a harbinger of better days to come. Major-General Couch, a Federal soldier at the head of the Massachusetts delegation, walked up the aisle of the convention hall arm in arm with Governor Orr of South Carolina, head of the delegation from the cradle of the Confederacy. It seemed an omen of better days. When the convention saw this spectacle of amity and concord, all burst into uproarious applause. Radical newspaper correspondents had first dubbed the gathering "the bread and butter convention," but they now gave it the sobriquet of "the Arm-in-Arm Convention," and sought to make this spectacle of reunion odious to the people of the North.[18]

Radical wits scoffed at this scene of reconciliation, quoting the verse of Genesis describing the entry of the various animals "two by two," into Noah's ark, "of clean beasts, and of beasts that are not clean, and of fowls, and of every thing that creep-

eth upon the earth."[19] With such shrewd quips, embellished
by appropriate cartoons by Thomas Nast and the vulgar buf-
fooneries of Petroleum V. Nasby, the President's supporters
were later made to regret their "arm-in-arm" dramatization of
renewed concord.

Senator Doolittle was made permanent president of the
gathering, while Henry J. Raymond guided the Resolutions
committee in preparing an address to the country. During the
deliberations of this body, when Raymond read the first line of
the seventh resolution, "Slavery is abolished and forever prohibited," Judge Yerger of Mississippi, ejaculated, "Yes, and
nobody wants it back again." Raymond eagerly took note of
the interruption, declaring "if we can say *that* on behalf of the
South, and on the authority of its delegates, it will strengthen
our case very much." The Mississippian said to go ahead.
Governor Graham of North Carolina added that it was true of
his State and of the entire South. Thereupon Raymond added
the words, "and there is neither desire or purpose on the part
of the Southern States that it [slavery] should ever be reestablished upon the soil or within the jurisdiction of the United
States."[20]

These resolutions were presented by Senator Cowan on
Friday and unanimously adopted, amid great enthusiasm. In
general they followed the spirit of the convention call. They
hailed the return of peace, set out that the war had sustained
the Constitution and had "preserved the Union, with the equal
rights, dignity and authority of States perfect and unimpaired." Representation in Congress was a constitutional
right abiding in every State, and neither Congress nor the General Government possessed authority or power to deny this
right to any State. Therefore, the convention appealed to the
country to elect to Congress "none but men who admit this
fundamental right of representation."

The resolutions recited the abolition of slavery, denied that
there existed either desire or purpose in the Southern States for
its reestablishment, demanded that the freedmen "in all the
States of the Union should receive, in common with all their inhabitants, equal protection in every right of person and property." But as to the proposed constitutional amendment, the
convention insisted that in ratification, "all the States of the
Union have an equal and an indefeasible right to a voice and a
vote thereon." Andrew Johnson had proved steadfast in his

devotion to the Constitution, unmoved by persecution and undeserved reproach. In him the convention recognized "a chief
magistrate worthy of the nation, and equal to the great crisis
upon which his lot is cast," and tendered its profound respect
and assurances of cordial and sincere support.[21] Such was the
Philadelphia convention, a presage of peace, an omen of a
nationwide approval of President Johnson's policies toward the
South.

At its conclusion, General Dix, who had been the Temporary
President, wrote Johnson enthusiastically that the convention
"was the most able, harmonious and enthusiastic body of men
of such magnitude I have ever known in my long acquaintance
with public affairs." Dix could not be mistaken; "it insures the
success of your patriotic and unwavering efforts to heal the
breach between the two great sections of the Union."

On August 17, Doolittle and Browning returned to Washington from the convention, "overflowing with their success and
the achievements of that assemblage." Accompanied by Secretary Welles, they called on the President, who was much gratified by their report. Among other things, they told him that
it was "the strong and emphatic voice of the convention" that
Stanton must leave the Cabinet.

The next day, the imposing committee which had been selected at Philadelphia to present the convention's resolutions
to the President, gathered in the East Room of the White
House. General Grant stood on the right hand of the President, and Gideon Welles on his left, as Senator Reverdy Johnson of Maryland, chairman of the committee, addressed the
Chief Executive. The absence of Secretary Stanton was conspicuous.[22]

The Maryland Senator's address was "courtly." The
President received it with unaffected pleasure and General
Grant smiled approval.[23] "If you could have seen the men of
Massachusetts and South Carolina coming into the convention
. . . hand in hand, amid the rapturous applause of the whole
body," the Maryland Senator said, "you would have felt, as
every person present felt, that the time had arrived when all
sectional or other perilous dissensions had ceased, and that
nothing should be heard in the future but the voice of harmony
proclaiming devotion to the common country, or pride in being
bound together by a common Union." He added that, in the
measures which the President had adopted for restoring the

Union, the convention "saw only the continuance of the policy which for the same purpose was inaugurated by your immediate predecessor"; and that, having been on the ticket with Lincoln, Andrew Johnson would have been false to obvious duty if he had not endeavored to carry out the same policy.

The President was much affected by these words. He responded, in a quiet, almost conversational tone. He pointed out that the nation was in peril. It had just passed through a bloody ordeal, and was not yet free from difficulties and dangers. In the restoration of peace, there were still greater and more important duties to be performed. So far as the Executive was concerned, the effort had been made "to restore the Union, to heal the breach, to pour oil into the wounds which would consequently open the struggle and (to speak in common phrase) to prepare, as the learned and wise physician would, a plaster healing in cure and coextensive with the wound."

Such had been the desires of the Executive, but as the work had progressed and the country was becoming reunited, "we found a disturbing and warring element opposing us."[24] "We have witnessed," he continued, "in one department of the government every endeavor to prevent the restoration of peace, harmony, and union. We have seen, hanging upon the verge of the government as it were, a body called, or which assumes to be, the Congress of the United States, while in fact it is a Congress of only a part of the States. We have seen this Congress pretend to be for the Union, when its every step and act tend to perpetuate the disunion and make disruption of the States inevitable." This Congress had been gradually encroaching upon the Constitution, and day after day and month after month had violated fundamental principles of government. This minority "usurped powers which, if permitted, would result in despotism or monarchy itself."

Little did Andrew Johnson realize, as he uttered these words in a quiet tone, that he was committing an act which two years later Thad Stevens' House was to call "a high misdemeanor," an offense for which he should be impeached. Nor did any of his auditors perceive the heinousness of the words. Gideon Welles had been much pleased; the President, he noted, had "replied extemporaneously, but happily and well."[25] The crowd in the East Room greeted his words with cheers and cries of "That's right," "Glorious"; a band played, "Hail to the Chief," and the ceremony was at an end. That evening Johnson at-

tended a dinner Seward gave in honor of Queen Emma of
the Sandwich Isles, "a very agreeable body of good bust and
pleasing face."

The Radicals were alarmed at the initial success of the
Philadelphia meeting.[26] They promptly countered by a con-
vention of their own, also held in Philadelphia, on September 3,
the call being issued by Southern "loyalists." The leading
Northern Radicals responded readily, such men as "Dead
Duck" Forney, Governor Curtin, Horace Greeley, Morton of
Indiana, (now a "galvanized" Radical), Carl Schurz and Zach
Chandler taking leading parts. The Southern representation
was somewhat sparse but it made up in virulence what it lacked
in character. "Drunken Jack" Hamilton of Texas, young
Henry C. Warmoth, the Louisiana firebrand, and "Parson"
Brownlow of Tennessee, who had now made up his mind that he
"would rather associate with loyal negroes than with disloyal
white men," were conspicuous examples of the type of "loyalists" who had come from the South.

The convention hall was garnished with such mottoes as
"'There can be no neutrals—only patriots or traitors'—S. A.
Douglas"; "'When the wicked are in authority, the people
mourn'—Isaiah," and with ironic sentences from Johnson's
own speeches of 1864.[27]

After assemblage, the body split in two, a Northern and a
Southern meeting being called. James Speed of Kentucky,
chairman of the latter, repaid the President's forbearance by
an offensive address. "Whenever you have a Congress," Speed
shouted, "that does not resolutely and firmly refuse, as the
present Congress has done, to act merely as the recording secretary of the tyrant of the White House, American liberty is
gone forever."[28]

The "Loyalists" issued an address to the country and "an
appeal for protection and justice." The President's hands,
they charged, had been "laid heavily upon every earnest loyal-
ist of the South. . . . He has removed the proved and trusted
patriot from office and selected the unqualified and convicted
traitor. . . . He has corrupted the local courts by offering
premiums for defiance of the laws of Congress. . . . He has
pardoned some of the worst Rebel criminals. . . . His policy
has wrought the most deplorable consequences."

There were two more conventions during this unparalleled

by-election campaign. The Administration sought to demonstrate that its course had the support of the soldiers through a convention of ex-service men which met in Cleveland on September 17. Many conspicuous officers took part in the meeting, including such men as General Thomas Ewing, Jr., Gordon Granger, General Custer, McClernand of Illinois and Steedman of Ohio.

The venerable General Wool, the oldest major general in the army, who presided, denounced the Abolitionists in scorching words, as "revengeful partisans with a raging thirst for blood and plunder, who would leave their country a howling wilderness for want of more victims to gratify their insatiable cruelty."

One of the fruits of this meeting was a round-robin signed by Generals Wool, Granger, L. M. Rousseau, Thomas Ewing, Jr., S. Meredith, Thomas Kilby Smith, Edward S. Brass, J. W. Denver and McCook, reciting that "in discharge of a duty which we owe to you, to the country and to ourselves, we beg leave to say that the Honorable E. M. Stanton, Secretary of War, does not possess the confidence politically or otherwise of any considerable number of your friends, or of the supporters of your policy, and that his continuation in that position greatly tends to weaken your administration."[29] About the same time, a committee of Washington Irish also asked Stanton's speedy removal.

The country could not understand why Johnson did not discharge the faithless Secretary. Radicals were as amazed as Conservatives. Queer rumors began to be passed around to explain it. Doolittle wrote the venerable Francis Preston Blair of a rumor so damnable that Blair sat down immediately to present it to the President, to force the latter to act.

"For six long months," Doolittle had written, "I have been urging the President to call on Grant temporarily to do the duties (of the) War Department, so that he could be called to council and be fully identified and committed with all his moral support to our cause.

"But Stanton remains, and so the report has spread all over the State, that there is something sinister. It started through the Milwaukee *Sentinel* printing the letter of a correspondent from Washington, which says that Stanton is not removed because it is rumored and believed that Stanton has testimony to show that Mr. Johnson was privy to Lincoln's assassination; and in the midst of all the excitement raised by the representation and misrepresentation of the President's speeches, it gains currency and produces such a state of frenzy and insane madness, that no man can read the future. . . . I cannot close my eyes to what we lose by this long delay in making the Cabinet a unit. . . . I begin to have my fears that it is too late."[30]

Hope that the President would realize the impossibility of Stanton's remaining would not die. Not long after Doolittle's letter, Samuel J. Randall urged the President to "push on. Relieve the people of their suspense. Bring Sherman to Washington as speedily as possible. The people will indorse Stanton's removal."[31] A few days later he advised the President that he had secured information that Stanton would not leave: "It is given to me in a reliable shape that the Radicals insist on his remaining." But still Johnson did not act.

The Radicals countered with a soldiers' convention of their own at Pittsburgh, on September 25, led by that distinguished military commander, General Benjamin F. Butler, "the Hero of Fort Fisher." General Hartranft, who had been marshal at the execution of Mrs. Surratt, was likewise conspicuous.

In the excitement of the moment, the permanent president, General Jacob D. Cox, indulged in a bitter speech. The citizen-soldiery of the North, he said, recognized Congress "as a representative government of the people. We know and all traitors know that the will of the people has been expressed in the complexion and character of the existing Congress." He indorsed the pending Fourteenth Amendment, and said that, in standing by it, the soldiers followed the flag they had fought for in the war. The resolutions, drafted by Ben Butler, indorsed the amendment as "wise, prudent, and just," and denounced the President's restoration policy with "a tempest of anger."[32]

Exciting and dramatic as were these four conventions, they seem but minor incidents in comparison with the tumultuous scenes of the "Swing Around the Circle."[33] Its immediate occasion was a journey of the President to Chicago to take part in a great memorial to Stephen A. Douglas.

In 1866, the Douglas Memorial Association, which had been established to do reverence to the memory of the ill-fated "Little Giant," completed the construction of a great memorial shaft in Chicago. The unveiling was set for September, and the Association undertook to make the ceremony notable. A pressing invitation was given to Andrew Johnson to make the chief speech at the Chicago unveiling. Since the Douglas ceremonial would afford the President an opportunity to pay tribute to a great Conservative, to a man who had ventured much in support of the Union under the Constitution, Johnson accepted the invitation. Trusting implicitly in the people and in his own power to present the truth, Johnson determined to use the occasion to present his case to the American court of last resort.

Seward made the arrangements for the tour. The Secretary of State wished General Grant and Admiral Farragut to be members of the presidential party, particularly to prevent disorder, which he especially feared in Philadelphia. In these reckless and violent times, Gideon Welles apprehended that "some rash and ruffianly partisan may place obstructions on the railroad track" and urged the President to take Stanton along. The Secretary of War had favored and urged the excursion; if he were on the train, the Radicals "would not endanger or hurt him." But the President was indifferent to the suggestion.[34]

Three days before the party was due to leave, several cases of convenient illnesses or other excuses developed. McCulloch thought he could not leave because "business is so pressing." Stanton, "who had been urgent, now regrets that he cannot go, his wife is ill." Browning, Randall and Stanbery had reasons of their own. Seward, however, was a good soldier and Father Gideon made no excuse or evasion.

The party departed on August 28 on a special train. The group included the President, his daughter, Mrs. Patterson, and her husband; Colonel Moore, his faithful secretary; Gideon Welles, his wife and her two sons; General Grant and General John A. Rawlins, his chief of staff; Admiral and Mrs. Farragut, and Generals Rousseau, Custer, Steedman, Stoneman and Crook.[35] The itinerary planned included stops at Baltimore, Philadelphia, New York, West Point, Albany, Auburn, Niagara Falls, Buffalo, Cleveland, Toledo, Detroit, Chicago, Springfield, Alton, St. Louis, Indianapolis, Louisville, Cincinnati, Columbus, Pittsburgh, Harrisburg, and then back to Washington. It was a gigantic undertaking for any man, no matter what

OLD THAD

A Striking Likeness of Thaddeus Stevens, of Pennsylvania, the Caliban of Andrew Johnson's Presidency.

seasoning he had had as a "stumper" in the political battles of his state.

It had been Andrew Johnson's custom at the beginning of a Tennessee canvass of the State to work up a single, long and forceful speech, which he would repeat from Sullivan to Shelby. Tennessee's newspapers were then so comparatively few in number and so restricted in circulation, that Johnson could use the same speech again and again without causing comment. He had expected to do this in his Swing Around the Circle, but he was to find himself badly mistaken. Furthermore, in Tennessee Andrew Johnson had been speaking to "home-folks." Everywhere he had devoted partisans, and even his enemies admired his courage and his strength. But in the North it was quite different. Through their propaganda, which had been spewed forth through newspapers, cartoons, lectures and sermons for many months, the Radicals had alienated much of the rank and file from him. Andrew Johnson had faced hostility before. He had climbed up the ladder by convincing men against their will. It may be said, even of this ill-fated Swing Around the Circle that Johnson swayed those who heard him. Time after time he faced a hostile crowd and converted it into a friendly one. But while he was convincing a hundred thousand, the Radical correspondents, in reporting his speeches, so distorted and misrepresented them that they turned three millions against him.

Some of Johnson's closest friends were apprehensive of the outcome of this personal appeal. They feared that the President would be led into traps by interruptions, or would be carried off his feet into unwise words by the intoxication of extemporaneous oratory. Some of them warned him in advance of these dangers, among them the sagacious Doolittle of Wisconsin, who wrote the President, "in the spirit of that true friendship which enables me to speak in all frankness," that it was most important that Johnson should not "allow the excitement of the moment to draw from you any *extemporaneous speeches.* You are followed by the reporters of a hundred presses who do nothing but misrepresent. I would say nothing which has not been most carefully prepared, beyond a simple acknowledgment for their cordial reception."

"Our enemies, your enemies," the Wisconsin Senator sapiently added, "have never been able to get any advantage from anything *you ever wrote.* But what you have said extem-

poraneously, in answer to some question or interruption, has given them a handle to use against you." The day before he left, both McCulloch and Browning urged the President "to make no speeches" during his tour.[36]

This wise and timely warning seemed unneeded at the outset. The "ovation" to the President was "very fine all the way from Washington to Buffalo."[37]   In Baltimore, a hundred thousand turned out to greet the President; cannon thundered, and the throng raised cheer after cheer.   Several mechanics broke through the crowd to grasp Johnson's hand, amid great applause.   When Seward, who acted as master of ceremonies throughout, presented Grant and Farragut, they were "wildly cheered."   But Republican politicians were conspicuous by their absence.   The party reached Philadelphia without untoward incident; the Radical city authorities meanly refused to participate in the occasion, but the President was given a "splendid reception," the party being met at the station and escorted to its hotel by a great and joyous throng.   In New Jersey there were similar outpourings, the party being met by girls with flowers and by committees with ponderous but respectful welcomes.   All along the route, Rawlins noticed that "the enthusiasm was unbounded."

The train arrived in Jersey City at 11:30 on the morning of August 29 and was met at the station by an impressive committee, including such merchant princes as A. T. Stewart and Henry Clews, many public officials and the full membership of the Manhattan Club.   Guns thundered as the party landed at the Battery to begin a monster parade up Broadway to the City Hall.[38]   More than twenty regiments of New York troops were in the line of March; from Battery to City Hall, the street was jammed, "every window was filled with happy smiling faces, roofs were crowded, . . . every window was white with cambric waved by fair hands."[39]   Even the dour Welles was touched and asked the President, "What do you think of that, sir?" Johnson responded, "It's wonderful."   The New York ovation had "never been excelled in this country," General Rawlins believed.

That evening there was a great banquet at Delmonico's,[40] followed by speech-making.   The President was introduced amid great applause.   His speech ran along familiar lines. After the war had been fought to keep the States in the Union, a department of the government had declared "that the government was dissolved, and the States were out of the Union."   It was a violation of the "sacred charter of Liberty" to deprive any State of its representation in Congress. The question before the voters was: "Will the American people submit to this practical dissolution?" Johnson's appeal for his and their Southern fellow countrymen was dramatic and effective. "They are our brethren. They are part of ourselves. They are bone of our bone, and flesh of our flesh. . . . We have come together again; and now, after having understood what the feud was, and the great apple of discord removed; having lived under the Constitution of the United States in the past, they ask to live under it in the future."

Amid great approval he projected his concluding lines. "I fought those in the South who commenced the Rebellion," he said, "and now I oppose those in the North who are trying to break up the Union. I, am for the Union. I am against all those who are opposed to the Union. I am for the Union, the whole Union, and nothing but the Union." Every phrase was punctuated with prolonged applause. The President continued that the cup of his ambition had been filled to overflowing, except for one thing: "I find the Union of these States in peril. If I can now be instrumental in keeping the possession of it in your hands, in the hands of the people; in restoring prosperity and advancement in all that makes a nation great, I will be willing to exclaim, as did Simeon of old of Him who had been born in a manger, that I have seen the glory of Thy salvation, let Thy servant depart in peace. . . . I would rather live in history in the affection of my countrymen, as having consummated this great end, than to be President of the United States forty times."

The party proceeded up the Hudson upon the *River Queen*, the same vessel which Lincoln had delighted to use. At West Point the President reviewed the cadets; crowds assembled at every village and town along the shore to cheer the passing party. At every stopping place, Johnson would close with perorations like this: "Take the flag, take the constitution, take the Union into your hands. In your hands they are safe."[41]

In Albany the President was received with dignity, but Secretary Seward was openly insulted by the New York Senate, which, in its resolution of welcome, deliberately omitted his name from the list. Again, when the party was introduced at the Capitol, Governor Fenton first presented Andrew Johnson and then called for Grant to come forward, ignoring Seward. Cut to the quick, the Secretary of State stepped to the desk and said: "I am here among old friends and familiar scenes and require no introduction from anyone. Here are men and objects that I have known in other days, and have honored and been honored here."[42] In Albany Thurlow Weed took the President aside to suggest "that men . . . were little flies, and that more of them could be caught with honey than with vinegar." Seward's *alter ego* urged Johnson to model his speeches on Choate's "glittering generalities"; it would win more votes.[43]

From Buffalo, General Rawlins, Grant's chief of staff, wrote his wife that he was "now more glad than ever that Grant had made the trip. Everywhere along the route thus far, enthusiasm had been unbounded." The President made "innumerable speeches every day, and the people cheer him lustily." Fidgety, at first, the General of the Armies had come to enjoy the proceedings very much; Farragut took everything admirably, and General Rawlins was all admiration of Seward, whom he termed "a man unequalled in tact and shrewdness to manage an assemblage of men opposed to him in politics."[44]

Thus far, Radical hostility had taken the form of declining to extend courtesies to or to participate in receptions to the President, in which cases, Welles noted, "the people . . . took the matter in hand and were almost unanimous in the expressions of their favorable regard and respect for the Chief Magistrate." But by the time this "triumphal procession," this "continuous ovation," reached the Ohio border, the reports of the President's success had greatly alarmed Stevens, Ashley, Wade and other Radicals of their vengeful kind. The President was carrying his case to the common people and it seemed as if the common people were hearkening to his words.[45] It was a disastrous development. The Radicals could not permit the President's trip to be successful. If this "ovation" continued, Andy would carry the North that fall!

Therefore, as the Johnson party approached Cleveland, the Radicals prepared a warm reception. "An enormous crowd" gathered in front of the Kennard House, where the Presidential party had put up, and shouted for Johnson to show himself. The President had no intention of making a speech; but finally he stepped out on the balcony to thank the crowd for its welcome.[46]

Unfortunately, after his first few words, Johnson warmed up and began to review his own policies, asserting that the Radicals would have assailed Lincoln similarly, had he lived. "Who is he that can come and place his finger upon one pledge I ever violated?" he asked, "or one principle I ever proved false to?" At this point, little groups of toughs, interspersed through the crowd by Radical prearrangement, began to interrupt and heckle the President. One voice shouted "New Orleans"; another, "Why don't you hang Jeff Davis?" a third, "Hang Thad Stevens and Wendell Phillips."

Taking up the words of the heckler, as was his unfortunate habit to do, Johnson countered: "Hang Jeff Davis?" and the crowd responded: "Give us an opportunity." "Haven't you got the court?" he went on. "Haven't you got the Attorney-General? Who is your Chief Justice who has refused to sit on this trial? I am not the Chief Justice! I am not the Attorney-General! I am no jury! But I'll tell you what I did do. I called upon your Congress that is trying to break up the Government. . . ."

Before the President could finish his sentence, Radical plug-uglies burst into loud hisses and shouted, "A lie, a lie." The crowd grew disorderly and the scene became almost a riot. It would have been better had Johnson stopped right there, but this was not his custom. "This eye," he once had said, "has never seen the face which this heart has feared"; and so, at Cleveland, the victor of many such Tennessee combats stood his ground, determined to face it out. He appealed to his listeners, "to your common sense, your judgment, and your better feeling, not to the passion and malignancy in your hearts." Would they hear him for his cause and for the Constitution of the country?

Would anyone point out when or where or in what circumstance, not only as President but in any capacity, he had "ever deserted any principle or violated the Constitution." By this brave appeal he cowed the rowdies and won cheers from the great majority of his listeners. "I have been fighting the South," he shouted, "and they have been whipped and crushed, and they acknowledge their defeat and accept the terms of the Constitution; and now, as I go around the circle, having fought traitors at the South, I am prepared to fight traitors at the North. . . . Are you for dividing this country?" When the crowd shouted "No," Johnson added: "Then I am President, and I am President of the whole United States."

"A preconcerted effort to insult him had been agreed upon by a few bigots," the *Plain-Dealer* declared, and Johnson knew it. One man cried out, "Traitor!" Johnson looked in the direction from which the cry had come. "I wish I could see that man. I would bet you now that if the light fell on your face, cowardice and treachery would be seen. Show yourself. Come out here where I can see you. If you ever shoot a man, . . . you will do it in the dark." The tough did not dare to show himself and temporarily subsided.

"I love my country," Johnson added. "Every public act of my life testifies that it is so. . . . And what is my offending?" One voice shouted "Veto!" and another, "Because you are not a Radical." Johnson continued: "I tell you, my countrymen, that though the powers of hell, death, and Stevens . . . combine, there is no power that can control me save you . . . and the God that spoke me into existence. . . ."[47]

In closing, he asked his auditors, "with all the pains this Congress has taken to poison the minds of their constituents against me—what has this Congress done? Have they done anything to restore the Union of these States? No; on the contrary, they have done everything to prevent it; and because I stand now where I did when the Rebellion commenced, I have been denounced as a traitor. . . ."[48]

The evidence seems clear that the Cleveland interruptions were carefully arranged for from Washington by the Radical leaders. Cleveland was the home city of Ben Wade, a politician accustomed to employ almost any means to win his way. Welles was struck by the "concerted plan to prevent the President from speaking."[49] A few days after the outrage, the President learned the facts as to the origin of the disturbance. "These men, some thirty or forty in number, were *hired* by notorious Abolitionists in this vicinity for the purpose of disturbing you," a friend who had carefully investigated the matter wrote him, "and were paid for their services out of the Union League funds."[50] During the speech, when the President had turned upon his most vituperative heckler, a friend had worked his way through the crowd towards the heckler and identified him as a disreputable fellow, the black sheep of the well-known Sterling family, whose "fitness for the particular task evidently assigned him was beyond dispute."[51] The *Leader*, Cleveland's Radical organ, exulted over the speech, terming it "the most disgraceful ever delivered by any president of the United States."[52]

The next morning the party continued on to Chicago, where, on September 6, the President delivered the chief address at the unveiling of the monument to the "Little Giant." If only Andrew Jackson or Stephen A. Douglas were aware of what was now happening in the country, he said, "they would shake off the habiliments of the tomb, and declare 'the constitution and the Union, they must be preserved!'" The Chicago reception was "magnificent," but Radicals flaunted banners bearing the legend "No Welcome to Traitors" and had bands parading the streets, playing the "Dead March."[53] Abraham Lincoln's widow was so anxious not to be in the city during the President's visit that she left hastily for Springfield.[54]

The party proceeded to Springfield and to Alton, where they were met by thirty-six steamers—one for each State—and carried to St. Louis. The vessel bearing the President was named the "*Andy Johnson*." The greeting in the Missouri metropolis was warm and affectionate, yet in this city occurred one of the most unfortunate episodes of the journey.

A great civic banquet had been planned for the President, on the night of September 8, at the Southern Hotel. While Johnson and his party were waiting in a hotel parlor for word to enter the banquet hall, a great throng had gathered in the street and was importunately demanding to see the President. Remembering Cleveland, Johnson refused, but the cries from outside became louder and louder. Members of the St. Louis committee finally urged him to go out "and say a few words, at any rate." Despite his reluctance, the President said he was "in the hands of friends," and went out on the balcony and began to say just a few words.

But the temptation was too great. The Tailor-Statesman went on and began to discuss the issues. A Radical planted in the crowd hurled the taunt at him: "New Orleans." Goaded by these words, Johnson answered:

> Go on, perhaps if you had a word on the subject of New Orleans you might understand more about it than you do. . . . When you read the speeches that were made and take up the facts on the Friday and Saturday before that convention sat, you will find there that speeches were made . . . exciting . . . the black population to arm themselves, and prepare for the shedding of blood. You will find that a convention did assemble in violation of law, and the

intention of that convention was to supersede the organized authorities in the state government of Louisiana . . . and every man engaged in that rebellion
—in that convention . . . was a traitor to the
Constitution of the United States, . . . You will find
that another rebellion was commenced, having its
origin in the Radical Congress.

The determination of the Radicals in Congress to establish
a Radical Louisiana government on negro votes was the "origin
of the blood that was shed," he charged; "every drop of blood
that was shed is upon their skirts and they are responsible for
it."[55]   Johnson had said more than enough already; he should
have stopped right there. But when he began making a speech,
an oratorical intoxication seemed to suffuse his veins and he
could not stop.

A Radical voice shouted "Judas," an indignity the sensitive
President would not endure without replying. "There was a
Judas," he declared, "and he was one of the twelve apostles.
. . . The twelve apostles had a Christ. . . . If I had played
the Judas, who has been my Christ that I have played the
Judas with? Was it Thad Stevens? Was it Wendell Phillips?
Was it Charles Sumner?" Amid mingled hisses and cheers, he
continued: "These are the men that stop and compare them-
selves with the Savior; and everybody that differs with them
. . . is to be denounced as a Judas."

Johnson concluded by placing himself upon the ramparts
of the Constitution. It had been his peculiar misfortune to
have fierce opposition because he had always struck his blows
direct, "and fought with right and the Constitution on my side."
"Let us stand by the Union of these States," he concluded, "let
us fight the enemies of the government, come from whatever
quarter they may. My stand has been taken."

Whatever good the Swing Around the Circle had accomplished, or might have been hoped to accomplish, the Cleveland
and St. Louis incidents undid. Obviously, it was a gross breach
of the dignity of the office of President thus to bandy words
with heckling toughs, and Johnson's blunt retorts laid him open
to answering billingsgate from the crowd. Worst of all, here
was fuel for the flames of Radical newspaper misrepresentation.
It was doubtful if the words of any President of the United
States have ever been so distorted, deliberately misquoted and
misconstrued as were Johnson's words on this tour.

A large corps of newspaper correspondents accompanied the party, most of its members devoting their efforts to portraying the President as a vulgar demagogue, and by innuendo and broad hint creating the popular impression that the trip was nothing but a drunken orgy. The claim was made that the President had been "dead drunk" when he made his Cleveland speech, although it was later proved at the impeachment trial that this charge was a slander. The only man who drank heavily on the tour was General Grant. Indeed, at Cleveland, Grant had been so intoxicated that he had been put on a Detroit-bound steamer to conceal his shame; this was not the only such incident affecting Grant upon the tour.[56] A St. Louis newspaper proprietor discharged, for plain mendacity, his reporter who "covered" the Johnson St. Louis speech. History has unfairly judged the President on the Swing Around the Circle. The interruptions undoubtedly were the result of Radical stratagem, in many instances paid out of Union League funds. The President was the victim of subsidized toughs who goaded him and of hostile journalists who printed lies about his trip.

The type of thing that the Radical press had to say about this President of the United States shows to what low estate journalism had fallen. Editorially and in their news columns, such papers as Joseph Medill's Chicago *Tribune* and Horace Greeley's New York *Tribune* gave vent to vituperation which a decent man would be ashamed to apply to a convict. The *Independent* was quite as bad. In this religious journal for religious folk, Johnson's eyes were called "deep-set, lascivious," and he was further described as having "the face of a demagogue, the heart of a traitor. . . ." Those who heard his speeches, the *Independent* said, "give thanks to God that the basest citizen of the republic, even though its chief magistrate, is unable to destroy, but only to disgrace it." This "trickster," this "culprit," this man "touched with insanity, corrupted with lust, stimulated with drink," should take warning at the side of Douglas' grave "how a Chief Magistrate who betrays his country shall become a handful of dishonest dust."[57] To the *Nation*, it was "a melancholy tour."[58]

The Radicals made the most of the political purposes of this trip to honor Douglas. Nasby described the tour as one undertaken "to arouse the people to the danger of concentrating power in the hands of Congress instead of diffusing it through one man." The Radical dubbed Johnson's program

"My Policy," and made those words a hissing and a byword from one end of the country to the other.[59]

The return journey from St. Louis was equally calamitous, or even more so. Grant left the party after the St. Louis episode, giving as excuse his desire to visit his father near Cincinnati, but confiding to Rawlins that he did not "care to accompany a man who was deliberately digging his own grave."[60] By now the Radicals were even better organized. Wherever the President stopped, there was evidence of deliberate Radical prearrangement. Governor Morton fled from Indianapolis to avoid the President, imitating the action of the Governors of Ohio and Pennsylvania, Illinois, Missouri and Michigan. There were riots in the public square and a man was killed. When Johnson showed himself, bullies shouted: "Shut up!," "We don't want to hear from you!," "We want nothing to do with traitors."

After the Radical turmoil had continued a short while, the President retired without attempting to speak. Gideon Welles termed this treatment in the Indiana capital the result of "an extreme Radical conspiracy to treat the President with disrespect and indignity."[61]

From Indianapolis the party proceeded to Louisville, where it had "a grand reception." Thence they pushed on to Cincinnati and Columbus. At Cincinnati, it became apparent that one result of the Radical maneuvers had been the alienation of General Grant. Grant felt a keen hatred of Copperheads. He was particularly annoyed by a leather-lunged Democratic Congressman named Hogan, who pushed himself forward. "I can stand a Rebel, but a Copperhead like Hogan I cannot forgive."[62]

At Pittsburgh, banners inscribed with former Johnson phrases, such as "We must make treason odious," were flaunted in the President's face. He tried to speak, but the mob—it was little less—would not hear him. It would only cheer Farragut and Grant.[63]

Just outside Louisville, Seward had been taken very ill with an attack of cholera and sent home on a special train. When the rest of the party reached Harrisburg, word reached them that Seward was gravely ill in a car at the station and might not last through the night. The President quietly withdrew from the dinner table and hastened to the bedside of the Secretary of State for what he apprehended might be a "last interview."

Seward grasped his hand and whispered: "My mind is clear, and I wish at this time to say that your course is right, that I have felt it my duty to sustain you in it, and if my life is spared I shall continue to do so. Pursue it for the sake of the country, —it is correct."[64]

Seward's seizure threw a damper on the party, the speaking was cut short and the pilgrims hastened home. On Saturday, September 15, they reached Washington, where they were greeted with the greatest enthusiasm. The Washington City Council had arranged a mammoth demonstration of confidence in the President. Pennsylvania Avenue was lined with a cheering throng, and the President stood up in his barouche and waved his hat all the way up the Avenue to the White House.[65] Mayor Wallach delivered the address of welcome; the throng had come out, he said, "to cheer you in your effort to restore eleven States to their places in the Union." Johnson replied briefly and appropriately, and the Swing Around the Circle was at an end.

XVII. BAYONET RULE BY ACT OF CONGRESS

THE 1866 campaign did not end with the Swing Around the Circle. Although the events of the tour and Radical misrepresentation of them probably rendered the outcome hopeless from Andrew Johnson's point of view, the campaign proceeded for six weeks longer. During this time the chief Radical effort was to express hatred of the South and its people, to exaggerate the Memphis and New Orleans riots, and to charge that the President had personally instigated them.

The powerful influences concentrated against the President in this election were well summarized thus: "An almost united party *as a party;* control largely of telegraph and railroads; of the moneyed, manufacturing and other business interests of the country; of a powerful and audacious press; of an organized religious fanaticism; of all the departments—legislative, executive and judicial—of every State government except two, and the benefit of the influence and the votes of nearly the whole body of Federal office-holders. The President has no party *as a party* to support him, and no instrumentality of power except his patronage."[1]

In addition to this, the Northern industrial leaders had determined that a protective tariff must be maintained for their self-protection, and that greenbacks must be retired. For these reasons, the great financial interests of the North, save those of merchants and importers, were cast practically solidly against the low-tariff, currency inflationist Democratic president.

But if any chance had existed of repairing the damage done at Cleveland and St. Louis and of overcoming the influences just mentioned, the Democrats perversely destroyed it. Johnson had hoped that a combination of Conservative Republicans and Democrats would furnish the necessary majority to sustain his course. But the latter, far from availing themselves of the Radicals' errors, conducted their campaigns so as to repair the rents in the Radical armor. "Instead of openly and boldly supporting the President and the policy of the Administration,

showing moderation and wisdom in the selection of candidates,"
to quote a notation of Secretary Welles, the Northern Democrats were "pressing forward men whom good Unionists, remembering and feeling the recent calamities of the War, cannot
willingly support," and so they put in jeopardy the Administration cause. The Democrats and the South had lost an
opportunity; had there only been "prudent and judicious management," disaster would not have stared them in the face.[2]

The disingenuous support which the Northern anti-War
Democrats gave the President caused it to be generally accepted by the people that Andrew Johnson was "leagued with
the traitors and Copperheads." At last, when it was too late,
the President's shrewdest advisers began to see that the Northern people were not ready "to place the government in the
hands of the Copperheads, or even of Democrats who were cold
and reserved during the War." But the Democrats, with their
"selfish, narrow adherence to the organization, their avarice
for power, their exclusion and their arrogance," had refused to
make common cause with the Conservative Republicans, and to
nominate candidates inoffensive to the Northern mind.[3] "The
Democracy are irreclaimable and unmitigated fools," Thomas
Ewing wrote his son.[4]

In November, with hindsight to guide him, Welles again
passed judgment on the campaign. False issues had prevailed
and the real question had nowhere been discussed. The Radicals had proposed to reëstablish the Union through a program
of "passion, prejudice, hate of the South." Their papers and
speakers had demanded to know if the North "would consent to
have the Rebels who had killed their fathers, brothers, sons
. . . brought into power?" The President had been denounced
as a traitor because he had not persecuted the South. The
Democrats, on their part, forgetful of the true interest of the
country and seeing only the weakness and wickedness of the
Radicals, "strove to install their old party organization,"
unaware that it had "made itself odious by its anti-War conduct and record." The consequence was that, instead of winning, they had entrenched the Radicals in power. "Never was
a political campaign so poorly managed." It had been an election "without any test, statement or advocacy of principles,
except the false one that the Radicals had forced." The President had had many friends in the country anxious to sustain

him, "if they could get at the question, but a large portion of them would not vote to restore the old obnoxious Democrats to power on old issues."[5]

With the election returns in from the two States voting in September, it became obvious that Johnson's appeal to the people had been in vain. Vermont increased its Republican vote by many thousands, while the Republican candidate for governor of Maine triumphed by the unprecedented majority of 28,000 votes. The whole result in New England was thus foreshadowed. Senator Dixon of Connecticut wrote the President that "in Massachusetts, our cause is hopeless. Connecticut is the only New England State in which we have any hope of success."

As might have been expected, James Gordon Bennett was disquieted by the outcome of the September elections. Immediately upon receiving the news from Vermont and Maine, Commodore Bennett had determined upon "a new course" hostile to the President. Unable to prevent it, Phillips hastened to write to Johnson: "The *Herald* cares nothing for party, and likes to 'pitch in' (to use its own particular expression) to all parties in turn. Nor does it care about individual public men —like the London *Times* in this respect—but its course is directed more by capricious moods or personal feelings than by large and liberal views or fixed principles.

"Yet at the bottom, Mr. Bennett is not without patriotism or generous sentiments, nor are these apparently fitful moods without a motive. While he is naturally disposed to change with the changing tide, . . . he makes this subservient to his business interests. His business is in the midst of a mercurial and an excitable people, and he attracts attention to his paper by doing startling or exciting things. Young Mr. Bennett . . . is more changeable than his father, while his judgment is more defective and his information limited."

The September elections had convinced Bennett "that the whole of the States will go the same way this fall, that in fact the majority of the Northern people is in favor of the Republicans and the Republican organization. . . . He thinks your trip to Chicago was unfortunate. . . . He says you have done all you could to restore the South, and that now you should leave it to Congress, and no longer make an issue with that body on the subject." The President should forget the South and take up public finance or foreign affairs.[6]

At the very first Cabinet meeting after the ill-fated tour, Stanton presented a plea of Judge-Advocate-General Holt for a Court of Inquiry, to "vindicate him against charges of subornation of perjury in the assassination trials of the year before. All the Cabinet except Stanton opposed it. Browning suspected it "a political trick of Holt and Stanton to reopen agitation just on the eve of the election."

About this time, some of the Radicals in the departments mustered up courage to resign in order to sustain the assault on the President. On September 29 the Auditor of the Treasury Department for the Post Office insolently addressed the President: "Believing you are today exerting your vast power in the interest of traitors, and that your policy should be overthrown at the ballot box, that the Republic based on liberty and justice may live, I retire from office that I may more freely and effectually aid in that overthrow."[7]

The mere taste of victory makes small men dangerous. Soon George Boutwell of Massachusetts began talking of impeachment and told the Boston correspondent of the *National Intelligencer* that the House would prefer such charges early in its next session. After canvassing Rhode Island and Connecticut, Ben Truman informed Johnson "that the long-haired men and cadaverous females of New England think you are horrid. I had a conversation with an antique female last night in the course of which she declared that she hoped you would be impeached." Truman asked her what the President had done. "Well," she replied, "he hasn't done anything yet, but I hope to God he will."[8]

The Radicals made a great effort to enlist the Fenians in their cause. Phillips of the *Herald* learned on unimpeachable authority, "that there is an understanding between the Radical leaders and some of the Fenian leaders." He informed the President that it was intended "to get up another armed expedition to invade Canada, not of course with any expectation of taking Canada, but to place you in a dilemma. The Radicals expect you will be compelled to execute the laws and prevent the invasion or the pretended attempt to invade Canada, and then they would denounce you and your administration."[9]

Richard Oulahan of Washington informed Johnson that a Colonel Kelly, a deputy of James Stevens, was in the Capital urging the Irish of the District of Columbia to join in opposition to the Administration, because of the way Irish-American officers had been treated in Ireland by American diplomatic representatives. Oulahan added that unless the President made it known distinctly "that American citizens shall be protected abroad, these returned officers are determined to stump the State of New York against your Excellency on that issue alone."[10]

Early in October the Radicals concocted a canard—"a stock-jobber's telegram," Welles termed it—against the President, palming it off on a Washington correspondent of the Philadelphia *Public Ledger*, who made a great story out of it to the effect that the President had submitted five questions to the Attorney-General for study and report. They were carefully outlined:

> 1. Was the present Congress such a Congress as the Constitution requires, or is it an illegal and unconstitutional assembly?
> 2. Would existing circumstances justify the President in sending his next annual message to an illegal and unconstitutional assembly pretending to be the Congress of the United States?
> 3. Does the Constitution making each House the judge of the qualifications of its own members give to the present Congress the right to exclude the members from ten States or to impose unconstitutional terms upon their admission?
> 4. Does the President's oath of office require him to enforce those provisions of the Constitution which give to each State an equal right of representation in Congress?
> 5. What steps does the Constitution and his oath of office require the President to take in order to secure the assemblage of a Constitutional Congress?

Johnson immediately repudiated the story as a lie out of whole cloth. George W. Childs of the *Ledger* was greatly humiliated at the way in which his paper had been made the vehicle for this Radical slander. But the damage had been done. This falsehood, added to the great body of other Radical lies about New Orleans and Cleveland and St. Louis, had its part in turning the Northern Conservatives away from the President.[11]

About the middle of October, one of Chase's Ohio lieutenants wrote the Chief Justice that "in the Radical counties our majorities are steadily increasing, while our Conservative counties are as weak as they were ten years ago. . . . In the Reserve counties, some of our speakers have openly advocated impartial suffrage, while in the other places, it was thought necessary not only to repudiate, but also to oppose it. . . ."[12] Ben Butler—"who, by the way, is in training for the presidency"—had been well received in Ohio, and had met with all the manifestations of great popularity, but much of this was due to Southern attacks on him and to his originality, which drew crowds to hear him. "In many places he was greeted as 'the next president,' and loudly cheered as such." But Chase's ally, with little confidence in the soundness of Butler's conversion, "still looked to Chase as the Radical Moses."

Already, however, the Radicals were beginning to talk to Grant about the Presidency, and the General to hearken to the siren song. On October 25, Rawlins, Grant's Chief-of-Staff and political brains, called on Browning to lament these developments. At this time, Rawlins was with the President, and felt annoyed and provoked at Grant's attitude. "Grant is thoroughly Conservative," Rawlins remarked, but "he knows how to do nothing but fight. . . . The Radicals are anxious to use him as a candidate, and they are making some impression upon him." Rawlins suggested Sherman be brought to Washington to keep Grant straight; let Stanton be dismissed, and Sherman become Secretary of War.[13]

On the eve of the October elections in Pennsylvania, Ohio, Indiana, and Iowa, Welles was convinced that the issues of the campaign had been poorly stated and were not well drawn up. For this he blamed Seward's irrepressible associates, Raymond and Weed, who had "over-refined and irreparably injured the cause of the Administration." Even so, Welles was not convinced that the Radicals would be as triumphant as they boasted they would be. After six weeks' campaigning in Pennsylvania, Montgomery Blair believed that State would go Conservative.

But carrying Pennsylvania was proving a vexing problem to the President's chief prop and supporter in that State, Senator Edgar Cowan, from whom came a cry of distress. He was making the best fight he could, "but we must have *some money,* as it is impossible to contend with the Radicals, who have thrown $13,000 into my Congressional district to elect Covode over me and my influence." Cowan recited that he was poor himself, but he had found a possible way to raise the fund. A certain Major Hall wanted to be a paymaster, and one Wharton White to be a second lieutenant in the Regular Army, "and they all agreed to give, for the purpose of the election, $2,000 each; this will enable me to pay the expense of speakers who have been speaking day and night, and to pay canvassers and wagons to bring out the votes of two or three close districts in this State."[14]

On election night, several telegrams revealed strong Conservative gains in Philadelphia, and there was jubilation at the White House. If this trend were general over the rest of the State, the Conservative candidate for governor would be elected. The President was in great spirits, though Welles thought he hoped too much, "for there is a good deal of bad material and much political debauchery in Pennsylvania."[15]

But the final results were gravely disappointing. General Geary was swept into office in Pennsylvania by a large majority, and 18 Republican Congressmen were selected against six Democrats.[16] The Republican State ticket in Ohio had 43,000 majority; out of nineteen seats in Congress, only three were won by supporters of the President. Indiana's Radical majority was not so great—only 15,000—but the Democrats won only three Congressmen there. In Iowa, the Republicans carried every Congressional district. These results were ominous for November.

Among the worst of the Radical schemes was their illegal effort to control the Maryland election. New election commissioners had been chosen in regular form in that State, but the Radicals denounced these new officers as Revolutionists, had them put into prison and kept in the old Radical set, so as to steal the election if it were at all close. The Conservatives appealed to the President to prevent the riot and bloodshed which they felt sure the Radicals intended for election day.

Johnson watched these developments with indignant apprehension. On November 2 he telegraphed the Maryland Executive that "the Constitution and the laws must be observed. Riots and insurrection, if possible, must be prevented, peace and order preserved."[17] That same day, he directed the Secretary of War to have forces ready to put down insurrection in Maryland. "Whilst I am averse to any military demonstration that would have a tendency to interfere with the free exercise of the elective franchise in Baltimore," he wrote, "I feel great solicitude that should an insurrection take place, the government should be prepared to meet and promptly put it down."

Fortunately, however, the Radicals' illegal methods did not bring them victory. After the Conservatives had carried the State, the judges ordered the legitimate election commissioners released from jail.[18]

New York's campaign was the most exciting in the country and interest in it was intense. Here again the Democrats made the mistake of emphasizing their party purpose, and General John A. Dix "foresaw the inevitable result" as soon as the Albany convention was held and the Democratic mistake stood revealed.[19] Both parties made desperate efforts to collect campaign funds and to exercise all the arts of electioneering. The followers of Johnson received large sums from New York merchants, some of whom likewise assuaged the financial needs of the Radicals. The manufacturers opened their money-bags alone to the Radicals.[20]

At times, the outlook was encouraging. On October 28, a lieutenant reported to the President that "things here look *promising*. Greeley told me this afternoon that he thought it very doubtful whether he could carry this State." The agent added that he was "spurring these church-going Germans on to vote."[21]

In 1864, Lincoln's majority in the Empire State had been less than 7,000, but in this campaign, Fenton, the Republican nominee for reëlection as Governor, defeated his Democratic rival by twice that margin, and the Radicals won two-thirds of the Congressional districts. In the West they won not victory but overwhelming triumph. Michigan went Radical by 39,000, and every Congressman was Republican. In Illinois, the Radical lead was 56,000; in Wisconsin, 24,000; and similarly on the Pacific Coast. In the Northern States as a whole, the Radicals had majorities aggregating 390,000 votes. The combination of extemporaneous stumping, the New Orleans riots, and Radical lies had proved too much for Andrew Johnson.[22]

The election determined that the next Senate would be made up of forty-two Republicans and eleven Democrats, the next House of 143 Republicans and only forty-nine Democrats. The Radicals had increased their narrow Senate majority into a very substantial one. The effect of the election had been to remove the last vestige of the authority of the Presidential veto.[23]

The Radicals returned to Washington lusting for vengeance on the defeated President. It was planned to receive them with a great demonstration, but the ovation shrivelled into a ludicrous negro parade.[24] Thad Stevens was on hand early to have the Radical program ready when Congress opened on December 2. He convulsed the House with his "wit," by announcing "I was a Conservative in the last session of this Congress, but I mean to be a Radical henceforth." He contended that the election had given him a mandate to inflict vengeance on the South and he intended to carry it out; he was determined to sow the wind, caring not whether the nation reaped the whirlwind.

On November 7 Simon Cameron made a speech at a banquet of "the Boys in Blue" at Harrisburg, indicating the attitude of the triumphant Radicals. "There is not on record such a body of disinterested and able men as Congress," this shifty politician declared. "I believe they did nothing wrong. And if they find it necessary to impeach the bad man who represents the government, let them do it." Cameron was a candidate for the Senate, and no language was adequate to express his contempt for the unpopular Chief Executive. "I did not believe the *low* white of the South was fit to become President," he said. "Educate him a hundred years, and you would not lift him to a place of honor. Why suffer him to remain there if we can put him out? I am no lawyer, but if I were there, I would be the first to impeach him and put him out."[25]

When Congressman George S. Boutwell of Massachusetts reached Washington on December 3, Stanton sent for him immediately, and solemnly assured him that he was "more concerned for the fate of the country than at any time during the war." The apostate Cabinet Member went on to charge that Johnson had issued orders to army officers as to which neither Stanton nor Grant had been informed. "There is danger. . . ." Thereupon Boutwell sat down, and Stanton dictated to him an amendment to the Army Appropriation Act limiting the power of the President, requiring him to issue his army orders through the Secretary of War or the General of the Army, and making null any orders issued otherwise.[26]

Such was the mental attitude with which the Radicals returned to the House and Senate in Washington. Their minds were made up to strip the President of the powers of the office of Chief Executive by carefully designed statutes, and, if he should rebel at these indignities, the Radicals would not hesitate to use the impeachment process to remove this obstruction from the path of their vengeance on the South.

Wild ideas were also afloat among Johnson's supporters. Clingman of North Carolina informed Duff Green of a great organization which he was getting up—"a revolutionary movement," Green described it to the President—based upon Johnson's well-known *ante-bellum* advocacy of a Constitutional amendment to cause the election of the President by direct popular vote. Clingman's scheme was for the President to incorporate in his message to Congress a renewal of this recommendation; and, if Congress should refuse to pass it, "the people shall nevertheless hold an election, and organize an army of 500,000, who shall go to Washington and inaugurate the President thus chosen."[27] Offers of armed assistance began to come to the President. "If you have need of a regiment of good fighters, I can raise the men," an ex-Confederate wrote from Baltimore. "It may appear to you desirable to have some men under your control who would know no law but your will."[28]

But the President rejected these unwise counsels and continued in the even tenor of his way. When his annual message to Congress, still in draft form, was read to the Cabinet on November 15, Stanton lamented the President's failure to indorse the pending Fourteenth Amendment. No one supported him, all others indorsing "manner and matter" of the message, until Stanton likewise said he fully approved of both. The message, which went in unchanged, did not yield an iota in the positions hitherto assumed, but it indulged in no unseemly language. Written in simple, straightforward English, as was the case with almost every one of Johnson's public papers, the message made its points with calm and irrefutable logic, and without passion presented the evil state of the nation to the chief authors of its woes.

On the matter of the admission of members from Southern States, the President was again emphatic in his language. He knew "of no measure more imperatively demanded by every consideration of national interest, sound policy and equal justice than the admission of loyal members from the now unrepresented States. This would consummate the work of restoration and exert a most salutary influence in the reestablishing of peace, harmony, and fraternal feeling."[29]   He mercilessly exposed the unconstitutionality of the exclusion.

The nation was then undergoing "its most trying ordeal," which could best be endured by the revival of fraternal relations.   In concluding, he appealed for mutual endeavors to preserve harmony between the coördinate departments of the government, "that each in its proper sphere may cordially coöperate with the other in securing the maintenance of the constitution, the preservation of the Union, and the perpetuity of our free institutions."

Once more Conservative opinion was charmed with the temperate tone and sober good sense of the message.   Most of Johnson's enemies and some of his friends were surprised at the restraint of his language.   Acquainted with the President's combative nature, his old friend, Sam Milligan, had feared that Johnson would, "under the storm of wanton abuse . . . be betrayed into some intemperance in the message."   But when Milligan marked its calm, dignified and dispassionate spirit, he rejoiced at this "offspring of a mind conscious of its own rectitude."[30]

But the Radicals were derisive and contemptuous of the President's sober words of expostulation.   In the *Tribune,* Greeley termed the message "a dreary, lifeless document," no more worth reading than those of Franklin Pierce.[31]   The *Nation* remarked that, now that the Chief Executive had been "reduced to a cipher," Congress would make him understand his "future insignificance."[32]   On the first day of the session, the House repealed a section of an act of 1862 which had authorized the President to proclaim amnesty to those who had taken part in Secession, the avowed object of the repeal being to narrow the Executive's prerogative, and thus to bring him closer to the borders of impeachment.[33]

Congress first whittled away and then committed major surgery on the President's power and legal authority, hedging it about by harsh laws, divesting him of constitutional prerogative and making it impossible for him to govern even his own Cabinet.   The next step was the enactment of a statute establishing continuous sessions of Congress.   This measure was boldly proclaimed as designed to have Congress "always on guard" to

checkmate the President.   According to Welles, Grant and
Stanton urged the passage of this scheme![34]

Before the Senate had been in session an hour, Sumner introduced and demanded immediate consideration for a bill to
give negroes the right to vote in the District of Columbia.   Any
election officer rejecting a black man's vote was to be liable, on
conviction, to a fine of up to $5,000, imprisonment up to a
year's duration, or both![35]

Sumner pleaded for the passage of this misshapen measure.
Not only was right involved, but political expediency.   "As
you once needed the muskets of the colored men," he told the
Senate, although his remarks were really addressed to Radicals
everywhere, "so now you need their votes."   Their voting negro
suffrage in the District would serve as a good example to the
States.   On December 14 the bill passed House and Senate, and
it was transmitted to Johnson for his scrutiny.   The Radicals
little doubted that he would veto it; and they did not care.

But while men of the Sumner stripe laid great store by
negro suffrage for the District, their more practical fellows
were planning two major assaults on Johnson and the South.
Thad Stevens' Reconstruction Committee undertook to work
out two projects; the first a plan to abolish the government
of Johnson in the Southern States, replace them by military
rule, and through the soldiery force negro supremacy upon
the prostrate whites; the second sought to take from the President his power of removal of subordinate executive agents of
the government, unless he had previously secured the Senate's
consent.   With this two-headed hydra in incubation, Stevens
was well satisfied to let Sumner say his pious words.

But the Senator from Massachusetts could not refrain
from savage exultation over the President's impotence.   "What
do you suppose the vulgarian of the White House thinks of his
'fight with treason at this end of the line' by this time?"
Sumner wrote a friend early in January.   "How very contemptible he must appear just now even in his own villainous
eyes.   Our only purpose in retaining him a day longer is simply
to compel him to fill the measure of his shame by draining to
the very dregs the cup of bitter-blasting humiliation that shall
be held remorselessly to his lips, until, together with his own,
he complete the degradation of his own accursed section by

executing the high behest of that body he presumed to denounce, and affected to despise. . . .

"I must pray for him, that of late he has learned his lesson, and promises to become a very dutiful scholar. How pleasant he must find it. . . . We have been a little surprised, to say the truth, to see how very quietly, since the rod had been raised over him, he *yields* even his dearest and most unquestionable Constitutional privileges."[36]

Such was the prevalent psychology with which the Radical apostles of hate awaited the inevitable presidential negative. On January 4, Johnson read his veto, a document of considerable length, to the Cabinet. It somewhat disappointed Welles because of its defensive attitude. With the exception of Stanton, all the members of the Cabinet approved the veto, while Grant, who had been especially invited to attend, was very emphatic and termed it "very contemptible business for Members of Congress whose States excluded the negroes," to vote them suffrage in the District.

When the veto was submitted, it made its points with the unimpassioned clearness usual in Johnson's writings. The *Nation* commented that the message was "temperate," although Godkin termed its reasoning mere "sophistry."[37] Yet to the Radicals in Congress, any sort of veto from the White House was unendurable. By a strict party vote, both Houses of Congress immediately overrode it. In the House of Representatives, partisan fanaticism ran wild. The half-mad Ashley of Ohio, who was angered by the President's daring in further opposing his negative to the sovereign word of the Radicals, introduced a resolution of impeachment. Personally unscrupulous, almost mentally unbalanced, the Toledo Congressman was a willing tool for Stevens and Ben Wade. His impeachment resolution was referred by the usual party vote to the Judiciary Committee for investigation and report.[38]

By early January the Stevens Military Reconstruction bill had advanced legislatively to such a stage that Johnson thought the time ripe to learn the opinions and views on it of each of his constitutional advisers; if united, it would carry weight in Washington and in the country; if divided, weakness would result. On January 8 he brought the matter before the Cabinet for discussion. The members were taken by surprise, and Seward sought to minimize the possibility of success for Stevens' scheme, but declared that, under no circumstances, would he ever concede "that a sovereign State had been destroyed, or can be reduced to a territorial position." McCulloch was equally decided.

Stanton made a long and carefully worded declaration. "Here in the Cabinet," the War Secretary said, "I have assented to and cordially approved of every step that has been taken to reorganize the governments of the States which rebelled, and I see no cause to change or depart from it. I have not seen and do not care to see Stevens' proposal—it is one of the sort that will end in noise and smoke. I have conversed with one member—Mr. Sumner, and that was one year ago—when Sumner said he disapproved of the policy of the Administration, and intended to upset it. Never since have I conversed with Sumner, nor anyone else. I do not concur in Mr. Sumner's views, nor do I think a State would or could be remanded to a territorial condition." He had approved the restoration policies of both Lincoln and Johnson; it was the President's duty to reconstruct the States as he did, and in no other way could he have saved them from anarchy. The existing governments were lawful, and he was opposed to the Congressional scheme.[39] For once, Welles concurred with Stanton, as did Stanbery and Browning.

Despite the fate which had attended prior efforts to increase Radical strength in the Senate by according statehood to Colorado and Nebraska and enlisting Radical Senators therefrom, the measures were introduced again, this time with negro suffrage inserted. They were promptly passed, Sumner now voting Aye.[40] When Johnson laid these two bills before the Cabinet, all but Stanton advised prompt and emphatic disapproval. On January 28 the President sent in his negative on the Colorado bill, reciting that the "obvious intent of the Constitution was that no State should be admitted with a less population than the ratio for a representative at the time of application," and exposing with merciless scorn the ineffable folly of admitting as a State a territory with less than 30,000 population.[41] Colorado's case was so thin that the Radicals made no effort to override the veto. The next day the Nebraska bill was returned, similarly disapproved, but here the Radicals had a slightly better case, and repassed the bill.

With Congress every day taking further steps to reduce the President to a nullity, and with their noisome committee airing every vicious scandal of the past twenty years, the spirits of the President's friends grew low. McCulloch and Welles were greatly discouraged. Although Andrew Johnson "is in many respects one of the best and most single-minded executives we have ever had," Welles felt sure that the Radicals would displace him by Ben Wade, so as to secure the appointing power, pass a bill increasing the number of Supreme Court justices, and thus convert the Supreme Court into a Radical agency.

During all this "wild delirium," the President held firm. The *Independent's* correspondent noted that in his intercourse with the Radicals, the President "has of late been good natured. Let him have the credit of his courtesy." He manifested no uneasiness over the impeachment proceedings and abated none of the presidential courtesies, a typical instance being his call on George Peabody at his hotel, "as a mark of respect to one who had made such liberal provision for the cause of education in the South."[42]

Believing he could assuage the Radicals, Seward was "dancing round Stevens, Sumner, Boutwell, Banks and others." He would run to the Capitol and seat himself by Stevens in the House and by Sumner in the Senate. Both were flattered by these attentions, but did not for an instant relax their assault.[43] Radicals sneered at the conduct of the Secretary of State, terming him an "apostate" who stood with "the vilest politicians the country contains."[44]

The impression must not, however, be given that the President or the Conservatives were standing idly by during these hectic Radical advances. Late in January Johnson sought to work out a compromise, a constitutional amendment mutually satisfactory to North and South. On January 30 Provisional Governors Orr of South Carolina, Marvin of Florida and Parsons of Alabama, together with two North Carolina Conservatives, consulted the President on the project. They thought that if the Southern States would present a united front for it, it would "operate as a flank movement and defeat the Radical program."[45] It was planned for the North Carolina legislature to adopt a series of resolutions, offering an amendment that no State should retire from the Union, that none should be excluded from it, or deprived of its constitutional right of representation. The scheme pleased Welles and other White House advisers, but the Radicals received it with disdain.[46]

Early in January General Sherman wrote his brother that "if the President be impeached and the South reduced to territories, the country will, of course, relapse to a state of war, or quasi-war, and what good it will do passes my comprehension."[47] A little later, the latter responded; he wanted the General to advise the Southerners to make the best of a bad bargain, and believed the South would gladly heed his words. "Three years ago they hated you and Johnson most of all men; now your advice goes farther than any two men of the nation."[48]

Indeed, Southern conditions were rapidly growing worse, so much so that such a Radical as Sickles told Browning that the Freedmen's Bureau "had filled the South with tyrants, knaves and robbers" and was doing a great deal of harm. Such conditions caused many Southerners to look to General Sherman to save the situation. William Lowndes of South Carolina wrote the President that if he would authorize the General to do it, the latter would "yet restore the Union under the Constitution." The President must not yield to an "unprincipled body." To do so would mean the sacrifice not only of himself, but of "the Constitution, State and individual rights, the Union, and both the general and the private welfare" of the whole country. "Lift up the dishonored flag of your country," the South Carolinian adjured the President,—"tear it from the sacrilegious grasp of Butler and Brownlow, and the people will rally to your support." Duff Green believed that "the refusal of the Radical Senators to admit the Senators from the Southern States" was a sufficient cause for the President to refuse to recognize the sitting body as the Congress of the United States. Jeremiah S. Black felt sure that the real fundamentals of the controversy had not yet been apprehended by the public, and wanted Johnson to issue a solemn appeal to the people, stating the issue in his own words. Black offered his services to compose such an invocation, "with the understanding, of course, that my intervention is a confidential secret not to be known even to the members of your Cabinet."[49]

Francis Preston Blair urged a *coup d'état* on the President, a complete change in his Cabinet, an idea which haunted Blair's mind and those of other Conservatives. Blair's suggested Cabinet was: Secretary of State, John A. Andrew; Secretary of the Treasury, George Peabody; Postmaster-General, Horace Greeley; Secretary of the Interior, Governor Cox of Ohio; Attorney-General, Edgar Cowan of Pennsylvania; Secretary of the Navy, *ad interim*, Admiral Farragut; Secretary of War, *ad interim*, General Grant. "No patriot," Blair declared, "can refuse to you his aid in your effort to lift the government above revolutionary faction, to save the Constitution."[50] The venerable Conservative pleaded for the change, but the President "could not see the point."[51]

Some of the Radicals also hoped that a change in the Cabinet would ameliorate the struggle between the President and Congress. On February 14 N. P. Banks of Massachusetts called at the White House to suggest Horace Greeley for Postmaster-General, his idea being that there should be someone in the Cabinet who could be a link between the President and the Radicals. After he had gone, Colonel Moore mentioned the matter to the President, who said it would not take him long to send for Greeley, and that he did not see that any member of his present Cabinet would give him strength with the country.

"By appointing Grant as Secretary of War, Farragut as Secretary of the Navy, Charles Francis Adams as Secretary of State, and Greeley as Postmaster-General," Johnson remarked, "I could settle the question in two hours." But to do so would cause harsh feelings in the present Cabinet, "to some of whom I am much attached." Moore asked if there was no way in which he could carry out such a program. Johnson shook his head, "I do not know that there is." As the subject was obviously painful to the President, the Secretary let it drop.[52]

The wildest charges were being made on the floor of Congress. W. B. Allison of Iowa told the House that Johnson had appointed dishonest men to office over the protest of the Secretary of the Treasury. The latter wrote Allison indignantly that he knew "of no case in which the President has appointed dishonest men to office, nor has any officer held a position connected with this department against the protest of the Secretary of the Treasury; nor has any appointment been made by the President against my protest."[53]

On February 15 another incident in the Cabinet showed Stanton's treachery. Congress, on January 8, had called upon the President for any facts which might have come to his knowledge in regard to failure to enforce the Civil Rights bill. When the resolution reached him, on Stanton's suggestion it was referred to the Attorney-General, who was to forward copies to the heads of Departments for answer.

This was done, and all members responded promptly, except the Secretary of War. Stanton, realizing that the purpose of the resolution was to furnish ammunition for the Radicals, asked General Grant and General Howard, head of the Freedmen's Bureau, to report. Grant replied tersely, but Howard sent in a voluminous document, a veritable scavenging of every rumor and charge of negro trouble in the South. There were 400 such exhibits! It seemed to Welles "an *omnium gatherum* of newspaper gossip, rumors of negro murders, neighborhood strifes and troubles . . . vague indefinite party scandal."

When this sinister production was laid before the Cabinet, the secretaries were astonished and disgusted; several expressed surprise at the documents; Stanbery wanted to know what this mess had to do with the President's inquiry. Browning termed it "mean and malicious," and intended to embarrass. Welles was scathing. Taken aback at this reception, Stanton admitted "there was no doubt that Members of Congress had seen this— likely had copies." In other words, he had already furnished them with this villainous concoction. It was part of the Radical effort to convict the President of not executing laws, and the President's own constitutional adviser was aiding in the plot.

After this episode, Welles once more pointed out Stanton's treachery to the President, who agreed with him but failed to take action. Welles concluded "that Seward has the ear and the confidence of the President, and is the man who, by his efforts and representations, retains Stanton. These two men have sacrificed the President. He has permitted it, and thereby made his Administration impotent."

Meanwhile the Tenure-of-Office and the Reconstruction bills were steadily going through the legislative mill. Stevens' "Central Directory" had reported the Reconstruction measure on February 6, and on February 13 he pressed it through the House, allowing but a week's consideration to a bill to wipe out "the pretended state governments" of Virginia, North Carolina, South Carolina, Georgia, Florida, Alabama, Louisiana, Mississippi, Texas and Arkansas!

The diplomatic and other galleries were crowded to hear Old Thad's final speech on the bill. It was listened to "in perfect silence," no one daring to challenge his words. A Radical correspondent wrote admiringly that the Commoner conferred with no one and never stopped an instant to consult. When he finished, years seemed to have dropped from Stevens' shoulders and his eyes sparkled. Quoting "good old" Laertes, "Heavens rules as yet, and there are gods above," he demanded a roll call, and the hypnotized Radicals passed the bill by 109 to fifty-five.[54]

In the view of the *Independent*, "it was an excellent measure, it puts the whole South under military rule."[55] The territory was to be divided into five military districts: 1. Virginia; 2. North and South Carolina; 3. Georgia, Alabama and Florida; 4. Mississippi and Arkansas; 5. Louisiana and Texas. Each district should be commanded by an army officer of the grade of Brigadier General or higher, this functionary being clothed with practically unlimited powers. As proposed by the House, the military governors were not to be named by the President, although he was commander-in-chief of the army under the Constitution. They were to be picked by the General of the Army—that is, by Grant, whom the Radicals were sure they had now taken over, through whom the President had by law been instructed to issue all Army orders. These generals were clothed with the "right" to dismiss governors, suspend elections, annul orders of court, and in fact rule in absolute despotism throughout the "so-called States."

The Senate could not stomach the Stevens bill unamended, although Sumner undertook to force it through, and carried the Republican caucus with him. But the minority was fighting the battle of its life. Its leaders were Hendricks, Saulsbury, Garrett Davis and McDougall for the Democrats, and Cowan and Doolittle for the President. Saulsbury refused to "touch, taste or handle the unclean thing." McDougall asked how anyone could suppose intelligent white people would allow themselves to be governed by negroes "as ignorant as a horse in a stable about all things that belong to government." Doolittle called the bill a declaration of war against ten States, a bill which if enforced would cause "such a horrible state of things as no language could describe." John Sherman took the lead in the effort to modify it somewhat, and was largely followed.

Because Sherman's substitute was slightly less offensive than the Stevens measure, Sumner was violently abusive, swearing savagely when the substitute prevailed and rushing out of the Senate.

The Senate bill made these changes in the House bill:

First, in describing the States, it termed them "not legal," rather than "pretended." Second, the President, and not the General of the Armies, was to select the military commanders. Third, a method was provided by which the States could free themselves from bayonet rule and resume their full national authority. To begin with, the Fourteenth Amendment must become part of the Constitution of the nation. Next, the State in question must adopt a constitution drafted in a state constitional convention elected by all citizens without distinction of color; this constitution might disfranchise the ex-Confederates, but it must give the vote to the negro. This constitution would have to be submitted for ratification to an electorate identical to that which elected the convention. If ratified, Congress must examine it. If Congress thereupon approved the state constitution, that State must ratify the Fourteenth Amendment. And finally, the Senators and Representatives elected must be able to take the ironclad oath.

Surely this plan of the Senate was sufficiently stringent. But the House was outraged at Senatorial mollification of the measure for bayonet rule of the South, and would not concur. To Sumner's despair, the Senate, suddenly stubborn, refused a conference. As the end of the term was approaching and the whole measure was in jeopardy, Stevens reluctantly accepted the Senate substitute, adding to it, however, further amendments stiffening the terms of readmission. One declared that no person rendered ineligible for office under the terms of the pending Fourteenth Amendment should be eligible to vote in the reorganization "of the Rebel States." A further amendment provided that, until these States were admitted to Congress, any government in them was provisional only and could be abolished or revised at any moment by Congress. The Senate accepted these added conditions and on February 22, "An Act to Provide for the More Efficient Government of the Rebel States" passed both Houses of Congress and was laid before the President.

"To the astonishment of everybody," a Radical correspondent wrote, "Reverdy Johnson wheeled around at the last moment in support of the bill. . . . He made an able argument against it, and then voted for it."[56] The Maryland Conservative attempted to palliate his course by a curious argument of expediency. He knew and declared that the bill was unconstitutional and wrong;.but he pretended that if the

terms contained in it were not accepted, the Radicals, in their
fury, would impose even harsher terms. "Senatorial trimmer,"
Welles termed him on doing so, and the reason was not long in
showing itself. Reverdy Johnson's son-in-law was a candidate
for United States Attorney of Maryland. Were the President
to nominate him, he would have to be confirmed by the Senate.
There must be special reasons to induce confirmation. In any
event, Senator Johnson voted for the bill, and at one o'clock
on the morning of March 4, a letter from the apostate Mary-
lander was brought the President, requesting that his son-in-
law be appointed to the post. "As cool a piece of assurance
as I have ever witnessed," Andrew Johnson remarked, but he
nominated the Senator's son-in-law, none the less, and the
Radical Senate confirmed the choice.[57]

While the Military Reconstruction bill was swiftly advancing to enactment, equal progress was being made with the
Tenure-of-Office bill. While this measure lacked the social
significance of the Act of Congress which reduced ten states of
the Union to military serfdom, yet so far as the fortunes of
Andrew Johnson were concerned, the Tenure-of-Office bill had
equal if not greater importance.

Few of the President's "offenses" seemed more heinous in
Radical eyes than his removal of unfriendly Federal officeholders. On his Swing Around the Circle, Johnson had contemptuously threatened "to kick them out," a remark which
rankled with the Republican politician. They began to insist
vehemently that the President's patronage power be emascu-
lated.

This Executive prerogative includes the right to appoint
and the right to remove. The first is explicit in the Constitution, but in most instances its exercise is subject to the check
that the nominations must be made "with the advice and consent of the Senate." By virtue of this clause, the Radicals already possessed the whip hand over new appointments. If Johnson's nominees were of the wrong politics, the Senate could
refuse to confirm them.

As to removals, the matter was not so plain. The Constitution said nothing, negatively or affirmatively, about it. Yet,
since the very foundation of the Federal Union, it had been
accepted in Constitutional construction that the right to remove was an inherent and fundamental part of the right to
appoint. From the days of John Adams, presidents had made

free use of this power, the last conspicuous example being Abraham Lincoln, who, when he became president, had made almost a clean sweep of government offices to provide provender for the hungry Republican place-men.

The whole matter of Tenure-of-Office had come up for debate, in the first Congress, and such giants as James Madison, Fisher Ames, James Monroe, Albert Gallatin, Spencer Roane and others of equal note, familiar with the purposes of the makers of the Constitution, had threshed it out. The emphatic decision had been that the President had the unquestionable power to remove. Recognized later judicially as an authoritative construction, this had been followed until Andrew Johnson's days, when the Radicals' political necessities impelled them to upset the precedents of nearly eighty years. Williams of Pennsylvania frankly disclosed the necessity to the House. "If you would impeach successfully, . . . no glittering bauble must be allowed to dazzle the vision, or tempt the cupidity of or ambition of either the prosecutor or the judge. No army of stipendiaries must be allowed to surround his person and depend upon his will."

In the first session of the Thirty-Ninth Congress, the matter had been sketchily discussed and submitted to a Joint Committee on Retrenchment for inquiry and report. With the December term, this body brought in a bill, the first section requiring the Senate's consent to the removal of all officers as to whose appointment the Constitution required confirmation by the Senate, excepting only members of the President's Cabinet. Upon challenge of this exception, the House sustained it by a narrow vote; they had not yet progressed to the point of enacting that the Chief Executive must harbor a traitor among his constitutional advisers. A second section of the bill empowered the President, during recesses of the Senate, to suspend any civil officer for misconduct, disqualification or incapacity, and to designate someone to fill the duties of the office thus vacated. However, within twenty days after the Senate had met, the President must report to that body the suspension, together with the reasons for it; if the Senate concurred, the suspended officer could be removed by the President and another named for confirmation to the vacant post. If the Senate refused to concur, the suspended person was thereby immediately reinstated.

When this measure came before the Senate on January 10,

Senator Edmunds, who had it in charge, was asked why Cabinet officers were excepted from its operation. It had seemed to the committee "after a great deal of consultation and reflection," he answered, that it was due to the President that he should have "persons personally agreeable to him" as his "confidential advisers"; he should be able to place entire confidence and reliance in his Cabinet officers, and whenever relations between the Chief Executive and a Cabinet member "had become so as to render this relation of a confidence and trust and personal esteem inharmonious, . . . he should in such cases be allowed to dispense with the services of that officer." Howe of Wisconsin challenged this view; it was not the President's Cabinet, but "the Cabinet of the people." This maladroit Radical claimed that he had "not the slightest reference to the person of the present incumbent," but everyone saw that he had, and not a single Senator supported him in his stand.

By January 14 Radicals began to change their attitude and Williams of Oregon came to Howe's defense, quoting Alexander Hamilton in the *Federalist* that the Senate's consent "would be necessary to displace as well as to appoint" and decrying Madison's adverse opinion. But Reverdy Johnson made mince-meat of the Senator from Oregon by showing that Hamilton had altered his view after becoming Secretary of the Treasury. This tilt led to an exhaustive discussion of the debates of the first Congress, in which Buckalew of Pennsylvania annihilated the contention of the Radicals with overpowering authority. Sumner's contribution to the debate, as usual, was an appeal to the higher law. The proposal was the outcome "of the exigency of the hour. . . . That is its strength and merit. We shall pass it . . . in order to meet a crisis. We all feel its necessity." To the mind of the statesman from Massachusetts, the President "ought to be deprived of the extraordinary function which he has exercised." His speech occupied three days and was entitled, "Protection against the President."[58]

In the second day's installment, he insisted that protection against the President had become the duty of the hour; their senatorial predecessors had had no such duty "because there was no President of the United States who had become an enemy to his country."[59] When he uttered these words, a Conservative called Sumner to order, but Ben Wade, in the chair, sustained him, and on appeal to the floor, the Senate did so likewise. Far from being out of order to term the President a public enemy, the Radicals acted as if Sumner had deserved a vote of thanks.

He returned to the charge on the following day, dwelling at length on Johnson's "treason." The President had become "the successor of Jefferson Davis." Sumner was not greatly concerned over his "beastly intoxication" when inaugurated, nor over his maudlin speeches, nor over reports of "pardons sold, or of personal corruption." But the President had usurped the powers of Congress and had become "a terror to the good and a support to the wicked." Reverdy Johnson was aghast. How could a Senator so express himself with impeachment proceedings pending in the House? So far as Sumner was concerned, "what sort of a trial . . . would the President of the United States have?"

A little later, Howe warned Congress that it "assumed a grave responsibility" if, knowing there was a probability of Stanton's being removed, "they allowed it to be done when they could prevent it." Despite this appeal, by a vote of twenty-seven to thirteen, the Senate left Stanton to Johnson's tender mercy and then passed the bill.

The House did not get to the Senate's Tenure-of-Office bill until February 1, by which time a great change had come over the temper of the House. It immediately struck out the Cabinet exception, and then passed the Senate bill. But the Senate Conservatives were still unwilling to fasten an unfriendly Cabinet member on the President. John Sherman opposed such a scheme with blunt vigor. It was a question of propriety rather than of Constitutional law. He did not see how any gentleman could hang on to office against the will of his Chief, "yet if we adopt the amendment . . . we compel the President to retain in office . . . any man who has not courtesy enough to retire." The Ohio speaker felt sure that "any gentleman fit to be a Cabinet minister who receives an intimation from his Chief that his longer continuance in office is unpleasant to him would necessarily resign. If he did not resign, it would show he was unfit to be there. I cannot imagine a case where a Cabinet officer would hold on to his place in defiance of and against the wishes of his Chief; and if such a case should occur, I certainly would not by any extraordinary or ordinary legislation protect him in that office."[60]

By a vote of twenty-eight to seventeen, the Senate refused

to yield its exception of Cabinet members. The House insisted on a conference. As an outcome, a provision was agreed on and reported back to the two Houses striking out the Cabinet exception and substituting the declaration that Members of the Cabinet "shall hold their offices respectively for and during the term of the President by whom they may have been appointed, and for one month thereafter, subject to removal by and with the advice and consent of the Senate."

When this change was reported back to the House, its members believed they had won a victory. General Schenck declared it to be "in fact an acceptance by the Senate of the position taken by the House." It was otherwise considered in the Senate. Senator Williams explained that it left an incoming President with free hands to select his Cabinet. In addition, he did not doubt "that any Cabinet Minister who has a particle of self-respect . . . would decline to remain in the Cabinet after the President had signified to him that his presence was no longer needed. . . . Whenever the President sees proper to rid himself of an offensive and disagreeable Cabinet Minister, he will only have to signify that desire, and the minister will retire." Sherman took the same view. No gentleman with any sense of honor would stay in the Cabinet after the President wished him out, "and therefore the slightest intimation on the part of the President would always secure the resignation of a Cabinet officer."

Senator Doolittle, Johnson's staunch advocate, gave a lesson in grammar to the Radicals, reciting the exact language of the conference substitute, and showing how, under the actual circumstances, no member of the Cabinet who had been appointed by Lincoln was protected by the Tenure-of-Office law. He was specific as to Stanton: "The Secretary of War was appointed by Mr. Lincoln during his first term; he has never been appointed since. . . . Mr. Johnson has given him no appointment, but he has held over." Similarly as to the Secretaries of State and Navy, all three of whom, "according to the terms of this provision, may be removed by him tomorrow." Doolittle's exposition was challenged or questioned by no Senator, and Sherman declared, with heat, "we do not legislate in order to keep in the Secretary of War, the Secretary of the Navy, or the Secretary of State."

Upon Doolittle's taking up the point, Sherman again responded that Doolittle had himself shown "and argues truly that it would not prevent the present President from removing the Secretary of War, the Secretary of the Navy, and the Secretary of State. And if I supposed that either of these gentlemen was so wanting in manhood, in honor, as to hold his place after the politest intimation by the President of the United States that his services were no longer needed, I certainly, as a Senator, would consent to his removal at any time, and so would we all."

After these plain words, which went unquestioned, the conference report was agreed to by the Senate. The House had previously accepted it. On February 18, the Tenure-of-Office bill was sent to the President.[61]

On February 22 the President laid the two bills before the Cabinet, but only the Military Reconstruction measure was considered that day. As to it, "there was," says Welles, "the usual uncertainty. No one of the Cabinet advised the President to approve the bill but Stanton." The Secretary of War quoted Reverdy Johnson as example and authority for favoring the measure; as for himself, had it been his task, he would have framed it differently. He thought the President should approve it. Welles and Browning bluntly urged a veto. The others, as if dazed by Stanton's course, said little. Johnson also asked what his Cabinet would advise him to do, should the Radicals impeach and attempt to arrest and depose him.

The Monday following this Cabinet scene, Welles called at the White House on another matter, and Johnson referred to the pitiful exhibition the Secretary of War had made of himself. "I wonder if he supposes he is not understood," the President remarked, and Welles noted that "the sparkle of the President's eyes and his whole manner betokened intense though suppressed feeling. Few men have stronger feeling; still fewer have the power of restraining themselves when evidently excited."[62]   Welles replied that Stanton's act had only been part of the drama which had long been enacting, and inquired what would be done if impeachment were pressed and an attempt made to arrest the President.

Francis Preston Blair advised the President not to veto the Reconstruction bill, but to refuse to execute it. A veto, he said, "is in effect to make it a law by executive action." The bill had been rushed through Congress under duress. Every delay the Constitution made possible ought to be interposed to arrest such proceedings. He thought the best plan would be to make a "clean sweep" of the Cabinet, as a concession to the discontent of the country.[63] But Henry Ward Beecher, H. B. Claflin and other New York Conservatives urged approval of the measure; it would be a calamity if he did not approve it, for Stevens' bill was "regarded by people of all parties as the most sane and reasonable bill likely to be passed."[63]

But Johnson had not for a moment thought of approving the bill. Rather than sign a measure which would deprive an American citizen of the right of *habeas corpus,* he told Colonel Moore, "I would sever my right arm from my body."[64] He determined to address his veto more to the country than to a heedless Congress, and to make it a message to awaken the people to the unprecedented and revolutionary step proposed. In its composition, the President availed himself of the services of Jeremiah Sullivan Black, as skillful an advocate, as careful a logician and as keen a legal mind as the Conservative ranks possessed. For several days the Pennsylvania lawyer worked assiduously in the President's office, with Johnson and the surefooted Stanbery aiding and supervising. The paper was written and rewritten until it met the President's approval, but it was not submitted to the Cabinet, as had previously been done with other vetoes.

The Tenure-of-Office bill came before the Cabinet at a session subsequent to that which considered the Reconstruction bill, when it met general condemnation, in which Stanton was "more earnest and emphatic in the expression of his objections than any member of the Cabinet." "No man of a proper sense of honor," the Secretary of War remarked, "would remain in the Cabinet when invited to resign." Upon these words, Johnson did his best to make Stanton understand that his resignation would be most acceptable, but the War Secretary brushed aside even the broadest hints.

After this fruitless effort, the President said he was so overwhelmed with other pressing matters that he wished Stanton to prepare the veto message, but that worthy refused, saying he could not do so "on account of the rheumatism in his arm." Stanbery, too, was gravely pressed by other business. Johnson next turned to Seward, who agreed to assume the task if Stanton would help him.[65] This the War Minister agreed to do. On March 1 the veto, the joint work of the two Secretaries and bearing Stanton's impress throughout, was presented to

AN UNSIGNED STANTON LETTER

This Letter of Edwin M. Stanton, Marplot Member of Andrew Johnson's Cabinet, Written on July 16, 1866, Reveals the War Secretary's True Feelings Toward His Presidential Chief. Significantly Enough, It Was Never Sent. Original in Stanton Papers, Mss. Div., Library of Congress.

the President. On March 2 he sent it to Congress, along with the veto of the Military Reconstruction bill.

In disapproving the Tenure-of-Office bill, the message based its arguments upon the firm foundation of the precedent of 1789, beginning with James Madison's opinion that the clause of the Constitution providing that "the executive power shall be vested in the President" covered the power to remove. The message followed up the course of subsequent controversies over the subject, including those under Andrew Jackson, the remarks of Justice Story, Chancellor Kent and Daniel Webster, and concluding with a reference to Lincoln's own wholesale removals.

"Under these circumstances," the veto continued, "as a depository of the executive authority of the nation," the President did not feel at liberty to unite with Congress in thus reversing the hitherto undisturbed construction of the Constitution. At an early period he had accepted the Constitution in regard to the executive office in the sense in which it was interpreted with the concurrence of the founders, and he found in the present Radical contentions insufficient ground to change. He concluded with an appeal for adherence to the letter and the spirit of the Constitution and for making changes in the organic national law through the agencies prescribed by it rather than by unconstitutional and unnecessary acts of Congress.

The veto of the Military Reconstruction bill was a more formidable document, consisting of some 20,000 words or more. The President had examined the bill with care and anxiety; his reasons for vetoing it were so grave that he hoped the outline of them might "have some influence on the minds of the patriotic and enlightened men with whom the decision must ultimately rest."[66] The bill "placed all people of the ten States therein named under the absolute domination of military rulers." The language of the preamble of the bill, which undertook to justify such measures, failed to justify them. The preamble had asserted that, in the States in question, legal government did not exist, and that life and property were not adequately protected. The President denied that this was true in point of fact. The ten States had actual and existing governments, quite as properly organized as those of other States, and administering and executing laws concerning their local problems. As to the protection of life and property, all the information of the President had convinced him "that the masses of the Southern people and those who control their public actions, while they entertain diverse opinions on questions of federal policy, are completely united in an effort to reorganize their society on the basis of peace."

The Reconstruction bill, he continued, showed on its face that its real object was not the establishment of peace and good order. Its fifth section set out the steps which States must take to be readmitted into the confraternity of the Union, and it was thus revealed in the very text of the Act that it sought to establish military rule, "not for any purpose of order, or for prevention of crime, but solely as a means of coercing the people in the adoption of principles and measures to which it is known that they are opposed, and upon which they have an undeniable right to exercise their own judgment." Did not Congress realize that such an act, in its "whole character, scope and object, was without precedent and without authority," in open conflict with the plainest provisions of the Constitution, and "utterly destructive to those great principles of liberty and humanity for which our ancestors . . . have shed much blood?"

He analyzed the powers of the military commander of a district, as being those of an absolute monarch. "His mere will is to take the place of all law. . . . Being bound by no State law, and there being no other law to regulate the subject, he may make a criminal code of his own. . . . He is bound by no rules of evidence; there is indeed no provision by which he is authorized or required to take any evidence at all. Everything is a crime which he chooses to call so, and all persons are condemned whom he pronounces to be guilty." Such authority "amounts to absolute despotism," and to make it even more unendurable, the district commander could delegate it to as many subordinates as he wished. For more than 500 years, no English monarch had ruled with such power, in that time no English-speaking people "have borne such servitude." The whole population of ten States would be reduced "to the most abject and degrading slavery."

What was the excuse for this unprecedented enormity? Congress has passed this bill in time of peace. There was neither war nor insurrection raging in any of the States. Both State and Federal courts were open and functioning. The excuse that life and property were not protected was threadbare. As to "martial law," Johnson quoted from the Supreme Court's recent decision in the famous Milligan case to prove that martial law could only constitutionally exist where there was actual invasion or warfare. The message pointed out that the Federal Constitution guaranteed that "no person shall be held to answer for a capital or other infamous crime unless on presentment by a grand jury." And yet this measure laid every person in ten States who was not a Federal soldier subject to sentence on the whim of a military commander.

The whole purpose of the bill, he charged, was to alter the structure and character of the government of Southern States. Congress had no constitutional, legal or moral right to undertake such coercion. Especially did a Congress from which the members of the States affected had been excluded possess no right to undertake to enact any such unconstitutional and oppressive system. The men from the South were entitled to a hearing upon measures concerning "the destiny of themselves and their children." This was a measure vitally important, "not only during the life of the present generation, but for ages to come." It had been passed while the ten States chiefly affected were denied representation. He adjured Congress in conclusion that this fact and others adduced "should induce us to pause in the course of legislation, which, looking solely to the attainment of political ends, fails to consider the rights it transgresses, the law which it violates, or the institutions which it imperils."

Congress listened to these vetoes in disdainful silence, and immediately repassed the two measures over the presidential negatives, the results in both instances being greeted with great applause. Thus an act to rob the Chief Executive of his constitutional prerogatives and a companion measure to force the people of ten States into humiliating subjection to a military satrapy became laws. Of the latter, Rhodes declared: "No law so unjust in its policy, so direful in its results, had passed an American Congress since the Kansas-Nebraska Act."[67]

But contemporary critics had no such sober viewpoint. The *Nation* thought the President's argument against the Reconstruction Act one of "extraordinary fatuity." If he believed the bill's consequence to be as his message describing it declared, "he will be one of the worst and meanest of men if he allows himself to be the instrument of putting it in force." But if he faltered in so doing, Godkin trusted there would be "neither hesitation nor delay in bringing him to justice."[68] Theodore Tilton exulted in the *Independent* that it was a day "to make the blood merry in a Radical man's pulse," and insisted that the first great duty of the new Congress was that of "removing a traitor from the chief magistracy."[69]

XVIII. THE FIRST ATTEMPT AT
IMPEACHMENT

A NDREW JOHNSON's impeachment had been in the minds of
the leading Radicals ever since it had become plain that
he would not be bullied by Congress into forcibly imposing
negro suffrage on the South. In February, 1866, William Lloyd
Garrison had informed a Brooklyn audience that, were he then
in Congress, he would deem it a "patriotic duty" to impeach
the President. Thenceforward, whenever Andrew Johnson did
something to displease them, similar threats came from leading
Radicals. Following their triumph at the polls in the fall of
1866, many Radicals returned to Congress with the firm intention of ousting the occupant of the White House.

On December 17, James M. Ashley of Ohio introduced a
resolution into the House looking to impeachment, but it failed
to secure the necessary two-thirds majority. Gideon Welles
viewed the Toledo Congressman as "a calculating fanatic,
weak, designing, fond of notoriety." But despite the shabby
authorship of this first resolution, Welles believed that the conviction of the President of impeachment charges was a Radical
necessity, for unless they achieved this, "they cannot carry out
their plans of dwarfing the States under the torture of Reconstruction, with the judiciary opposition to their revolutionary
schemes."

Indeed, the attitude of the United States Supreme Court
was commencing to give the Radicals great concern. On December 17 the court made public the full text of its opinions in
the famous Milligan case.[1] The nine justices were unanimous
that the Indiana military commission which President Lincoln
had authorized had been unlawful. Five of them, with Justice
David Davis, Lincoln's devoted personal friend, announcing
their views, went further, in holding that the Constitution of
the United States could not "be suspended during any of the
great exigencies of government. . . . Martial law can never
exist where the courts are open, and with the proper and un-
obstructed exercise of their jurisdiction." Chase, however,
expressed the views of himself, Miller, Swain and Wayne, that

under certain circumstances Congress did have power to provide for military trials.

Immediately upon the announcement of the opinion, the Radical attacks upon the court were quite as savage as those made when the justices had determined the Dred Scott case. The Indianapolis *Journal* stated that the decision was "intended only to aid the Johnson men, and is so clearly a forerunner of other decisions looking to the defeat of Republican ascendency and to the restoration of Southern domination, that the indignation against the court is just and warranted." The Cleveland *Herald* termed it " judicial tyranny," while to the *Independent* it was "the most dangerous opinion ever pronounced by that tribunal."[2]

John W. Forney, editorial apostle of the Radicals, contributed the most scathing of the attacks to his Washington *Chronicle*. "The hearts of traitors," Forney's organ fulminated, "will be glad by the announcement that treason, vanquished upon the battlefield and hunted from every other retreat, has at last found a secure shelter in the bosom of the Supreme Court." Again he wrote: "Time and reflection have only served to strengthen the conviction of the partisan character of the decision and the apprehension that it is the precursor of other decisions in the interest of unrepentant treason in the support of the apostate President."

This chorus of denunciation of a decision now generally regarded as one of the bulwarks of American individual liberty, greatly overshadowed the applause which Conservatives and supporters of Johnson accorded the words from the high bench. The *National Intelligencer* pointed out that the decision meant that "They are disloyal, who, under the pretense of preserving the liberties of the citizen, have disregarded the applications of the organic law. They are Disunionists, who, claiming to fight for the Union, have trampled upon its fundamental bond. . . . It is not the crime of treason which is shielded by this memorable decision, but the sacred rights of the citizen that is vindicated against the arbitrary decisions of military authority. Above the might of the sword, the majesty of the law is thus raised supreme."

A voice like this was but a feeble whisper in the shrill shriek of Radical wrath. When Congress reassembled after the Christmas holidays, many of its leading Radicals had made up their minds that they would no more permit the Supreme Court to interfere with them than they would permit the President to do so. They would impeach Andrew Johnson and fill the White House vacancy with a Radical president who could change the constituency of the Supreme Court and thus safeguard Radical measures for vengeance against the prostrate South. On January 3 the *Independent's* Washington correspondent pointed out this necessity.[3] Early in January William Lloyd Garrison contributed two articles to the *Independent*, demanding Johnson's impeachment. The resort to this grave constitutional process "should have been the first motion made after the organization of the House," he insisted. "The honor, the safety of the country, and the integrity of the Constitution imperatively demand it."

The views of the Liberator met with the complete indorsement of Theodore Tilton, who declared in his editorials that Congress had a treble duty: "First, to impeach the President of the United States; second, to expunge and obliterate every usurping State government he has created; third, to secure the political rights of the negro whom he has sought to trample in the dust." Irritated at the decisions of the Supreme Court, Tilton editorially warned the membership of the nation's highest judicial body that "the same people who triumphed over Taney, and stamped his unjust judgment with infamy, are again aroused to battle. . . . The victory will be sure."[4]

The President's veto of the District of Columbia suffrage bill—"wantonness," Tilton termed it—aroused House Radicals almost to madness. Even before the message had been read, a Missouri Radical named Benjamin F. Loan made a bitter and vituperative speech submitting a resolution providing for "the impeachment of the officer now exercising the functions pertaining to the office of President of the United States, and his removal from said office upon conviction of the high crimes and misdemeanors of which he is manifestly and notoriously guilty."[5]

On a point of order, this resolution was referred to the Joint Committee on Reconstruction. But when the President's veto had been read, there was a tumultuous outburst. Ashley of Ohio could be restrained no longer. He rose "to perform a painful but nevertheless to me an imperative duty," none other than the impeachment of Andrew Johnson, "Vice President and acting President of the United States," of high crimes and misdemeanors.

Amid Radical applause, the Toledo fanatic continued: "I charge him with usurpation of power and violation of law;

"In that he has corruptly used the appointing power;

"In that he has corruptly used the pardoning power;

"In that he has corruptly used the veto power;

"In that he has corruptly disposed of public property of the United States;

"In that he has conspicuously interfered in elections, and committed acts which, in the contemplation of the Constitution, are high crimes and misdemeanors."

Thereupon Ashley offered a resolution directing the House Judiciary Committee to examine Johnson's official conduct and to report if he "has been guilty of acts which are designed or calculated to overthrow, subvert or corrupt the government of the United States or any department or office thereof." This resolution was adopted by a strict party vote, to the joy of the Radicals and the consternation of the country.[6]

Such tirades against the President were not uncommon in the House. On January 24 Benjamin Loan made the open charge that Andrew Johnson had caused Abraham Lincoln's death. In the beginning, the Missouri Radical said, the assassination had been thought the deed "of a reckless young man rendered desperate by the failure of the cause to which he was devoted. But subsequent developments have shown it to have been the result of deliberate plans adopted in the interests of the Rebellion. The appeal to arms on the part of the Rebels had failed. The only alternative left them upon which they could hope for success was fraud and treachery. . . . Such agencies could not be successfully invoked so long as the incorruptible Lincoln guided the destinies of the Republic."

But next to Lincoln stood Andrew Johnson, a Southern man, a life-long pro-Slavery Democrat, a man "powerfully influenced by all the grossest instincts of his nature, without moral culture or moral restraint, with a towering ambition." Therefore the Confederate leaders "were quick to understand the chances given them by such a person occupying the second office in the government. . . . But one frail life stood between him and the chief magistracy of the Republic. . . . An assassin's bullet wielded and directed by Rebel hands and paid for by Rebel gold made Andrew Johnson President. . . . *The price that he was to pay for his promotion was treachery to the*

Republicans and fidelity to the party of treason and Rebellion!"[7]

Most of the Radicals approved the Missourian's frenzy, but one New York Congressman made a point of order which Speaker Colfax overruled, and Thad Stevens broke in approvingly with, "The decision of the chair is all right." Upon the objector demanding proofs, Loan answered that he was determined "to pursue this matter in my own way. . . . The course which this resolution will take will carry it before the proper tribunal to inquire into this matter, and there, in a legitimate way, the proofs I presume will be furnished to the gentleman's satisfaction."

The Judiciary Committee quickly got under way for this epoch-making investigation, with James F. Wilson of Iowa as Chairman. In earlier years the new inquisitor had been friendly with the President, and even now while he had become a thorough Radical in his political views, he had scruples none the less, and drew a clear distinction between political offenses and those of an impeachable character. George F. Boutwell of Massachusetts, also a member of the committee, was "a fanatic, ardent, industrious and ambitious, but narrow-minded, impulsive and partisan." There was but one Democrat on the sub-committee. Thomas Williams, another Radical member, who had at one time been a law partner of Stanton at Pittsburgh, was "vindictive, remorseless, unscrupulous."[8] The House thought so little of Ashley that he was not named, but yet this public servant pursued the impeachment with unflagging zeal, acting as unofficial prosecutor before the committee and endeavoring almost frantically to purvey thin scandal from the witness stand.

The Committee and its successor sat spasmodically from February to December. The more carefully it went into Johnson's conduct, the more certainly did its members become convinced that the President had committed no high crime or misdemeanor to render him triable by impeachment. Had there been anything in his career as Chief Executive which could even have been subject to suspicion of a taint of illegality or treason or corruption, the Committee would have brought it out. For Ashley was not the only bloodhound on the scent. Boutwell, Ben Butler, Wade and Sumner gave every assistance of which their eager souls were capable. There was a "regular understanding" that, if the Committee could not find enough testimony for impeachment, it would manufacture it.[9]

The Committee's proceedings, according to an official judgment upon it by two Democratic members, were "unparalleled." They described the character of the evidence thus:

"A dragnet has been put out to catch every malicious whisper throughout the land, and all the vile vermin who had gossip or slander to retail, hearsay or otherwise, have been permitted to appear and place it upon record for the delectation of mankind. Spies have been sent out all over the land to find something that might blacken the name and character of the Chief Magistrate of our country. Unwhipped knaves have given information of fabulous letters and documents, that, like the *ignis fatuus,* eternally eluded the grasp of their pursuers, and the chase resulted only in aiding in the depletion of the public treasury. That most notorious character, General L. C. Baker, chief of the detective police, even had the effrontery to insult the American people by placing his spies within the very walls of the Executive Mansion. The privacy of the President's home, his private life and habits, and most secret thoughts have not been deemed sacred or exempt from invasion; the members of his household have been examined and the chief prosecutor has not hesitated to dive into loathsome dungeons and consort with convicted felons, for the purpose of arraigning the President on the charge of infamous crimes."[10]

The notorious Lafayette C. Baker, the first witness heard, set the tone for the entire proceedings. According to Baker's tale, Andrew Johnson, in the last month of the war, when he was Military Governor of Tennessee, had written Jefferson Davis accepting proposals of the Confederate President for Johnson to betray the Union and go over to the Southern side. Baker claimed that this letter had been lying on Johnson's desk in Nashville, that one of the sons of Parson Brownlow had employed a negro to enter the room and steal the letter, and that Brownlow's son had thereupon turned the letter over to John W. Adamson of Nashville, who had tried to sell it to Baker.[11] But the most frantic efforts of the Committee to develop this precious document failed miserably, and it soon appeared that there was no such letter in existence, that there was no such person as John W. Adamson in Nashville, nor had there been for twenty years, and that Baker's whole tale was a tissue of lies.

Stanton's detective also made an effort to involve the President in selling pardons. From July, 1865, Johnson had been granting pardons to ex-Confederates with prodigal liberality. In proclaiming general amnesty, he had excepted certain classes, and persons falling within these classes were urged and encouraged to apply for pardon, so that legally the war and its consequences could be quickly liquidated. Evils had grown up about this business, and certain notorious characters set themselves up in Washington as pardon-brokers, preying on the ignorance of ex-Confederates by making claims of their power to get the President to grant pardons, for a consideration, pardons which Andrew Johnson would have granted much more readily had they been brought to him in normal course.

The President's anterooms were crowded with a milling throng of people seeking favors at his hands. Andrew Johnson took the position that the President must see all people who called upon him, regardless of their character or conduct. One of those who most frequented the public rooms of the White House was a lady of easy virtue, one Mrs. Lucy L. Cobb. The officious Baker, becoming suspicious that Mrs. Cobb was making money by selling pardons, laid a trap for her. One of his detectives impersonated an ex-Confederate, swore out an application for amnesty, and insisted on paying Mrs. Cobb for her services and taking a receipt. She presented the application to the President, who referred it to the Attorney-General; it was examined, and a pardon was duly issued. Thereupon, in the dead of night, Baker arrested Mrs. Cobb, snatched the pardon from her hand and rushed to the White House to confront the President with the evidence of her guilt!

Baker's testimony, *verbatim*, as to subsequent developments, reads: "I directed one of my men to go to the door of the White House, and if Mrs. Cobb came there, to tell her she could not go into the building. . . . My man went down there, and had been there about an hour, when she came and wanted to go into the White House. He said, 'No, you can't go into the building.' She wanted to know by whose orders she was prohibited. She went around the back way, entered the grounds, passed the conservatory, came into the kitchen, got upstairs, and went to the President's room. After a few minutes, the President sent for the man whom I had stationed at the door, and wanted to know by whose orders he was guarding the doors of the White House. This man's name was S. S. Jones. Mr. Jones told the President he was there by my orders. The President said, 'Tell General Baker I want to see him immediately.'" Baker continued that Jones had informed him that "the President is very furious, and that he was a little drunk and that I had better not go down there then." The detective none the less went to the White House, and Baker declared that, in the ensuing interview, the President shook his fist in his face, abused him loudly, told him to take himself off, and added that "you can tell your friend Stanton what I say."

How much credit could be attached to this flimsy tale was shown by the testimony of Jones himself. On May 17 he went on the witness stand and talked freely. Asked directly, "Did you know of any improper influences that were used by persons having cases at the White House, in order to obtain pardons?," he answered emphatically in the negative. Asked if he had reported to General Baker any improprieties he saw going on about the White House, he likewise emphatically denied this. As to the Baker interview, the testimony reads:

Q: Did you tell General Baker that the President was furious and a little drunk?

A: No, I do not know that I did.

Q: Was he drunk at the time?

A: I never saw the President drunk.

Q: Then you did not tell General Baker that he was drunk?

A: No, sir, I never told him, for I had no reason to tell him. I never saw the President drunk. He always treated me like a gentleman all the time I was there.

Q: You spoke of seeing Mrs. Cobb at different places in the White House frequently. I wish to ask you whether the White House was not open to the public?

A: To everyone who wished to go there.

Q: Nobody is excluded?

A: No, sir, not to my knowledge. The doors are open at fixed hours, and everybody has a right to go into the rooms which are public rooms.

Q: I ask you if hundreds do not go there to the Executive Mansion that the President never sees, and knows nothing of their presence?

A: Thousands of them.   They are going there every day.

Q: I ask you whether objectionable persons might not go there without his knowing anything about it or having any control over it?

A: He would not know anything about it.

Q: Is it not the custom of the President, so far as he can, to see everyone who calls to see him on business?

A: Yes, sir.   I have been there when the doors were thrown open, and 25 or 30 or 40 people would come in.   He would shake hands with them and answer a great many foolish questions that I thought nobody ought to detain the President to ask.   He would then ask if there were any more.   If he was told that there were 25 or 30 more waiting, he would say, "Let them come in," and he would go through the same performance of shaking hands and answering their foolish questions.

Q: I ask you if, during the time you were there, you ever saw any impropriety of any kind whatever on the part of the President?

A: I never did.

Q: And you also said that you never saw him intoxicated or under the influence of liquor?

A: I never did.   I never saw any liquor in the house, nor anything approaching to intoxication.   He always treated me very kindly.   He took me down once to see a new carriage that he had just purchased. I never saw anything on his part that was not gentlemanly and proper.[12]

As to Baker, a committee report later declared that "it is doubtful whether he has in any one thing told the truth, even by accident.   In every important statement he is contradicted by witnesses of unquestioned credibility.   And there can be no doubt that to his many previous outrages, entitling him to an unenviable immortality, he has added that of willful and deliberate perjury, and we are glad to know that no one member of the committee deems any one statement made by him as worthy of the slightest credit."[13]   So much for the testimony of General Lafayette C. Baker, and, in general, for the character of the testimony brought before the Committee.

Several hundred pages of the testimony were taken up with an inquiry into the return by the government, after the war, of the Nashville, Chattanooga and Northwestern Railroad property to the stockholders of the road.[14]   The implication was that, because President Johnson had owned $40,000 worth of bonds of the State of Tennessee and bonds of this Railroad guaranteed by the State, he had caused the return of the railroad in order to benefit himself financially, a thin story mercilessly exposed by the testimony of none other than Edwin M. Stanton.

Another charge the Committee attempted to sustain by testimony was that the President had sought to bribe politicians in the campaign of 1866.   In their effort to lend color to this charge, the "low villains"—such was Jeremiah Sullivan Black's estimate of the Committee—haled before them the cashier of the First National Bank of Washington, where Andrew Johnson kept his personal account, and forced him to expose to the public gaze every check the President had given since he had become Chief Executive.   When the banker objected at his first appearance, the impeaching Committee was elated; they thought that at last they had found some "pay dirt."   But on the witness' next appearance, he took the wind out of their sails by relating that he had gone to the White House to inform the President that the Committee had demanded a list of all his checks, with other private financial data as to Johnson's bank account.

"The President did not make any objection to its production?" a Committee member inquired.

"None whatever," the witness answered.   "He smiled, and said he had no earthly objection to have any of his transactions looked into, for he had done nothing clandestinely, and desired me to show them anything I had relating to his transactions."[15]

The impeachers showed great zeal also in seeking to establish the complicity of the President in Abraham Lincoln's assassination.   There was no document more thumbed over than the diary of John Wilkes Booth, all the more fascinating because some of its pages were mysteriously missing.   Incidentally, although in 1866 officials of the War Department had exhibited this gory relic to Theodore Tilton, Andrew Johnson had never heard of its existence until it was brought before the impeachment body.[16]

The Radical theory was that the missing pages had contained memoranda of Booth showing Andrew Johnson's instigation of the assassination. The Committee sought valiantly to persuade some one who had seen the diary to imply as much, and to hint that the President or one of his friends had torn out the missing leaves.[17] But although Lafayette C. Baker had already testified to having seen a letter from Andrew Johnson to Jefferson Davis agreeing to commit treason, he did not dare help the Committee out as to the diary. His nephew's testimony was equally unproductive. Colonel Conger, who had taken the diary off Booth's body, could add nothing.

Stanton testified that he saw the diary on the day it was first brought to town, and "examined it carefully," before turning it over to Holt. He had "read over all the entries in it, and noticed that the leaves had been cut or torn from it at the time." It was precisely in the same condition when he first saw it as it was then. Immediately it came to his hands, Holt testified, he had examined the diary with the greatest care and "there was nothing in the diary which I could conceive would be testimony against any human being."[18] Therefore, he continued in his testimony, "I did not offer it to the Commission."

So far as its actual historical importance is concerned, the testimony at the investigation deserves little attention. Yet there were many interesting incidents, such as one in Grant's testimony. Examined as to his objection to the trial of General Lee for treason, Grant became indignant at some of the questions. "I am not quite certain," he said, "whether I am being tried, or who is being tried, by the questions asked."[19] All of Johnson's Cabinet Members and ex-Cabinet Members, all those suspected of preparing or aiding in veto messages, his private secretaries, and even his son, Colonel Robert Johnson, were summoned. Stanton testified four times, Lafayette C. Baker, six times. High and low, the great and the humble, villains and heroes, succeeded one another indiscriminately on the stand.

The Committee hearings were in secret, and the President and his friends were naturally anxious to be kept in touch with the new charges that were being concocted against "the criminal in the White House." Allen Pinkerton, a friend of the President, undertook to see what he could do, and through his instrumentality, the President and his friends were every day informed as to the secret deliberations of the men trying to impeach him.[20]

As they went along, even the more ardent impeachers could see that instead of constructing a case against the President, the testimony was constructing a case in his behalf. It was obvious that impeachment could not succeed unless some real evidence could be secured. To such a man as Ashley, impeachment must be carried out regardless of the facts. If there was no evidence to convict Johnson, evidence must be made. Ashley took upon himself the task of having evidence manufactured to prove that Andrew Johnson had inspired the plot to assassinate Lincoln.

One of the men whom the fanatic Ashley believed he could use as a tool to damage the President was John H. Surratt, son of the woman who had been hanged for participation in Lincoln's assassination. John H. Surratt, evading apprehension in April, 1865, had fled to Canada and thence to Europe. In the spring of 1866 he was discovered as a soldier in the Papal Zouaves at Rome. Stanton and Holt seemed somewhat negligent in their efforts to secure his return for trial. When the Papal authorities finally acted on their own responsibility and arrested Surratt, the prisoner broke away from his captors and made his way to Egypt. He was again taken into custody at Alexandria. On December 21, 1866, the United States naval vessel *Swatara* sailed for America with Surratt on board, heavily ironed.

Before the *Swatara* arrived with her prisoner, the President had begun to suspect Radical efforts to connect him with Lincoln's assassination, and he feared that Ashley or some of his fellow scavengers might suborn Surratt into any sort of lie to save his own neck. Late in January Johnson summoned Welles to the White House to tell him of his fears. "The man's life is at stake," the President said; "the more reckless Radicals, if they could have access to him, would be ready to tamper with and suborn him." Johnson wished orders given that "unauthorized persons be kept from seeing the prisoner."[21] Johnson's apprehensions were well-founded. No sooner had Surratt been lodged in the Old Capitol Prison at Washington than Ashley and his agents began making overtures to him.

A second tool in this subornation of perjury against the President was sought in the person of Sanford Conover, *alias* Dunham, a shabby and perjuring scoundrel employed by Stanton in 1865 to implicate Jefferson Davis and the Confederates in Canada in the assassination plots. His testimony proved to be a tissue of lies so infamous that Conover was indicted for perjury, tried and convicted, and sentenced to several years' imprisonment. At the time when Ashley began his search for fresh "evidence," Conover was incarcerated in the Old Capitol Prison, awaiting court order to go to the penitentiary to begin his sentence.

On February 25 one of Ashley's aides, the Rev. W. B. Matchett, approached Dr. William Duhamel, the physician to the Old Capitol Prison, and asked him if he often saw John H. Surratt. Duhamel answered that he did in a professional way. Matchett then asked the Doctor to tell Surratt that "there is a means by which he can save his neck, have the shackles struck from his arms, and his mother's name rescued from odium." Surratt had only "to give the name of someone high in position who might have prompted the assassination."[22] Duhamel, who was the President's friend, wrote him of this overture.

Ashley's endeavors to persuade Conover to save his own skin by implicating the President in the Lincoln plot bore more fruit, but again the President was not without information of this perjured enterprise. In the cell with Conover was one Dr. Cleaver, a friend of Conover's who was awaiting trial for rape and murder, and a third prisoner, who overheard these two rascals discussing their plot. "Their intention is to have President Johnson implicated with or knowing to Mr. Lincoln's death," the eavesdropper sent word to the White House: "Conover tells me tonight that he will be out of jail . . . in a few days, and that it will be brought about by Ben Butler and Ashley, of Ohio. Butler and Ashley, he says will be here to-morrow evening to see him again. They have both been here several times, and had private interviews with him last week."[23]

On March 27 Dr. Duhamel sent the President news of further developments in the Radical plot to entrap Surratt. Miss Anna Surratt had asked him to prescribe for her, a pretext to enable her to tell the Doctor that Butler and Ashley had sent for her, but that after she had told them that she would be interviewed only in the presence of her lawyer, they had declined to see her. Duhamel spoke to the girl "of the infamous attempt to implicate the President by evidence of her brother John," and she answered earnestly that John "knew nothing in that case against the President . . . and could not be induced to swear away his own soul." Duhamel was treating a patient living next to Ashley's rooms, and informed the

President of his personal observation that Ben Wade has seen Ashley "every day, and very often Mr. Sumner was with him."[24]

In May a guard at the Old Capitol Prison told the father of Colonel Moore, the President's secretary, that Ashley had had several interviews at night with Conover in his cell. The guard had asked Conover what Ashley wanted with him so much. Was it Surratt? "No, it is higher game than that," the convicted perjurer had replied.[25]

On May 10 Conover's cellmate made an affidavit and dispatched it to the President, that soon after February 20 Conover's wife had conveyed to him an offer from General Ashley . . . that "if he would make deposition in order to implicate the President, Andrew Johnson, in the conspiracy to assassinate the late President Abraham Lincoln, the deposition to be used as evidence before the Judiciary Committee in order to impeach the President," Ashley and others would secure the perjurer's release. When Conover was asked by his fellow prisoner, William Rabe, if he in fact knew anything about President Johnson's implication in the conspiracy to assassinate the late President Lincoln, he answered that he did not, but that Cleaver knew more about Andrew Johnson, and that he would use Cleaver as a tool, "if it should come to extremities. . . ."[26]

After much backing and filling with Butler and Ashley, Conover finally concluded that the Radicals wanted to use his evidence without securing his pardon. He then determined to betray the impeachers to the President. On July 29 he sent the latter a long petition for pardon, in which he exposed "the atrocious plot of Ashley & Company." The Radicals had sought his pardon, the petition declared, in order that "they might use me as an instrument to accomplish their devilish designs." Ashley had carefully explained to him the kind of evidence he wanted Conover to concoct against the President: "First, that Booth had, on several occasions, paid you familiar visits at the Kirkwood. This it was hoped I might be able to induce some of the old servants to testify to. . . . Second, that you corresponded with Booth. . . . Third, that the placing of Atzerodt with weapons at the Kirkwood was only a sham. . . . Fourth, that Booth, just after the 4th of March, stated to an intimate friend in New York . . . that he was acting with the knowledge of the Vice President. That it had been arranged to kill Lincoln on the day of the inauguration, which would account for Mr. Johnson's strange conduct on that occasion."

Conover admitted assuring Ashley that he would have no difficulty in finding witnesses "of good standing and moral character to prove these matters." He gave an earnest of his ability to procure this testimony by manufacturing some parts of it, which he turned over to Ashley. These the latter altered slightly, better to fit the needs of the case, and then returned it to the perjurer's cell![27]

With the printing of Rabe's affidavits and Conover's confession, the plot to implicate the President in Lincoln's assassination came to an end, but not without a final exposure of the half-mad Ashley. On November 23, on the summons of the Democratic members of the Judiciary Committee, he was called to the witness stand and asked what he meant by telling Members of Congress that he had evidence that the President was implicated in Lincoln's assassination, and why he had not presented it to the Committee. "Because it was not of that legal character which would have satisfied me in presenting it," he answered. "It was not that kind of evidence which would satisfy a great mass of men, especially the men who do not concur with me in my theory about this matter. I have had a theory about it. I have always believed that President Harrison and President Taylor and President Buchanan were poisoned, and poisoned for the express purpose of putting the vice presidents in the presidential office. In the first two instances it was successful. It was attempted with Mr. Buchanan and failed. . . . Then Mr. Lincoln was assassinated, and from my standpoint I could come to a conclusion which impartial men, holding different views, could not come to. It would not amount to legal evidence." Members of the Committee were anxious to know how Ashley could make so grave a charge against the Chief Executive on "bare suspicion," a question he was unable to answer.[28]

The proceedings of the Judiciary Committee have been described as a whole, for the sake of unity. There were, however, actually, two investigations, the first by the Judiciary Committee of the House of the 39th Congress, which ended with the legal life of this body on March 4, 1867, and the second by the Judiciary Committee of the House of the new, or 40th Congress, which began functioning immediately after noon of that same day.

The result of the inquiry of the initial month had been very thin. On February 28 the eight Republicans on the Committee joined in a report that, owing to the magnitude of the task, the Committee had not been able to conclude its labors or to submit a definite and final report. While the charges had not been "so entirely negatived as to admit of no discussion," enough testimony had been brought forward "to justify and demand a further prosecution of the investigation."

A. J. Rogers, the lone Democrat, declared there was "not one particle of evidence to sustain any of the charges. The case is wholly without a particle of evidence upon which an impeachment could be founded; with all the effort that has been made, and the mass of evidence that has been taken, the case is entirely bald of proof." Most of the testimony was "such as would not be admitted in a court of justice." Rogers could see "no good in the continuation of the investigation."[29] But Ashley was determined that his project should not die. On the third day of the new Congress, he secured the floor of the House on a matter of personal privilege, to indulge in by far the worst vituperation addressed against a President in a hall of Congress. The abuse was so coarse that even "Smiler" Colfax called Ashley to order. Andrew Johnson had entered the White House "through the door of assassination," he charged. The President was guilty of "black and infamous crimes." He was a "loathing incubus" [*sic!*]. He had blotted the history of the country with "its foulest blot."[30]

The Democrats were rather elated at this outburst. Sam Randall asked if there were a lunatic asylum in the neighborhood. Other Democrats pleaded with Colfax to let Ashley go on, as his speech would help the President. But the House quickly adopted Ashley's resolution for a continuance of the impeachment investigation by the Judiciary Committee, and with this renewed authority, the impeachers continued their scavenging, the results of which we have already seen.

While these savage attacks were being made against his public and private character, the President was conducting himself with remarkable moderation and self-restraint. In January he began to take countermeasures, and had had the Adjutant General of the Army search the files for Butler's official record and also report if Ashley had ever endangered himself in his country's service. This Ashley had not done. Indeed,

Johnson was informed from New York that the Ohio Radical might have moved the impeachment more with a view to influence the stock market than to oust the President. A New York banker of high standing disclosed to one of Johnson's friends his personal knowledge that $50,000 in cash had been given Ashley by a clique of gold operators to introduce the impeachment charges.[31]

With the first rumbling of impeachment, the President had had Charles G. Halpine busy himself to array the New York papers against it, and the Irish humorist succeeded surprisingly well with Horace Greeley, who promised that he would "take strong grounds against General Butler and the whole impeachment policy."[32] But Halpine's persuasive Irish tongue had no effect on Commodore Bennett. Upon Ashley's resolution, the *Herald* again adopted "a new course" and began shouting impeachment as vehemently as any Radical sheet.

Phillips wrote the President that this was not his doing; he had done his best to prevent it,—it was Mr. Bennett's deliberate act. The Commodore "makes everything—yes, the public welfare and everything else—subordinate to what he supposes may promote his interests as proprietor of the paper. . . . The question of impeachment is an exciting one, a new and startling sensation, which may occupy the public mind some time and help to give life and circulation to the paper. That is one of the controlling motives of the *Herald's* course, unworthy as it may be . . . Mr. Bennett does not believe your impeachment or removal would be attended with any serious consequences. . . . His mind is so constituted that it is not difficult for him to believe what suits his purpose. He appears to be firmly persuaded that your impeachment and removal is determined upon. . . . He believes that party will accomplish its object. It is, he believes, one of the inevitable phases of the revolution the country is passing through. He doubtless favors this revolution, because he has always been in favor of a strong consolidated government. . . . Besides, the *Herald* always endeavors to go with the stronger party. . . . Should the Radicals push their measure to an extreme that will create a revulsion in the public mind, and a consequent political reaction, the *Herald* will take another tack."[33]

Despite such desertions, Johnson was not to be deterred from what he conceived to be his duty. In March Welles wanted to know what the President planned to do if, after the

House should vote impeachment, it should next vote to order his arrest. If not prepared to submit to arrest, was he prepared to meet it? In whom could he confide and what officer of the army would stand by him against an order issued by Congress under the signature of the Chief Justice? The President evaded answering, and his faithful and blunt-tongued friend noted in his diary for the day: "It has been the misfortune, the weakness, the great error of the President to delay—hesitate before acting. It has weakened him in public estimation, and given the impression that he is not strong in his own opinions. Yet I know of no man who is more firm when he has once taken a stand. But promptness, as well as firmness, is necessary to inspire public confidence."[34]

At the next Cabinet meeting, after the scheduled business had been disposed of, McCulloch reached over the table and began talking to the President. The Secretary had a suggestion to make to check the impeachment enterprise. Johnson flared up angrily: "Let them impeach and be damned," he said bitterly. "I am tired of being threatened. God Almighty knows I will not turn aside from my public duties to attend to these contemptible assaults which are got up to embarrass the Administration."[35]

Yet Johnson did not often permit his calm to be ruffled by these attacks. One of his secretaries recollects that the President never seemed so happy and cheerful as during these trying days. If it were fated that the Radicals take his official life because he had done his duty, so be it.[36]

On March 5 the President accorded General Halpine an interview, which was widely republished, declaring that he was unmoved by the "slights and indignities" Congress had attempted to put upon him, except as they impaired the high office which he held. There would come a day of wiser thought and sounder estimate, to which he looked "with perfect confidence."[37]

One smiling day in May, a lady who wrote letters for Theodore Tilton wandered up the steps of the Treasury. From this vantage point, she saw Andrew Johnson come from the White House onto the lawn, and was startled to find that his appearance was not that of a fiend in human form. The President "does not look tired at all," she wrote. . . . "His step was strong and comfortable and slow; . . . a smile brightened the clogged lines of his face; in his happier moments, it is not an unkind face." The Chief Executive was dressed "like a gentleman of leisure, with a scrupulous nicety"; and this feminine Radical described with surprise "this elegantly attired gentleman, gloved, caned, his iron-gray hair rolled smoothly under, walking placidly on the green grass under the trees."[38]

In truth the Chief Executive had no need for concern over the proceedings of the House Committee. After a few weeks of testimony, it had become apparent to every sensible man that Andrew Johnson had committed no impeachable offense. From March until December, it was obvious that impeachment would be resorted to only as a political necessity and not as a judicial act. Indeed, the impeachment investigation became little more than a rough barometer of the temperature of the Radicals against the President.

Although Tilton might fulminate that "Andrew Johnson has become an offense to the nation," the general view was well expressed by Godkin in the *Nation:* "Impeachment, whether it succeed or fail, will prove a great and lasting calamity. Public opinion . . . seems decidedly against it."[39] On March 7 John Sherman wrote his brother: "The impeachment movement has, so far, been a complete failure. . . . The President has only to go forward and enforce the laws as they stand, and he is safe."[40] The *Independent* admitted on the same day that if Johnson would execute the Reconstruction law with vigor, Congress might safely adjourn. It was only if he failed to do so, "and especially if he exhibits any of his constitutional obstinacy," that he would be impeached and removed as "an obstruction to the reconstruction of the rebellious States."

On March 9 the Republicans caucused on the impeachment problem and Butler, Ashley and their friends were beaten on two points. Ashley declared he "had no doubt of the guilt of the President," but Spaulding, an Ohio Radical retaining some glimmer of common sense, termed the impeachment enterprise "an act of consummate folly." The "Hero of Fort Fisher" made a fight for the formation of a select committee of thirteen to prosecute impeachment, but the caucus preferred letting the Judiciary Committee of the new House go ahead. Butler also wanted Congress to remain in continuous session, but this, too, was voted down.[41]

On March 23 the *Independent's* Washington correspondent sorrowfully expressed his belief that an impeachment bill "will never be reported for the Committee." The Committee was merely going to assail Johnson politically in its report. "The elevation of Mr. Wade to the presidency of the Senate," Tilton lamented, had proved a check on impeachment.[42]

There was a flare-up in May, when Jefferson Davis was released on bail. But feverish investigation by the Judiciary Committee showed that the President had been the only one to remain firm in insisting on Davis' trial.[43] Johnson had perforce to be acquitted of blame for this failure; Chase, if anyone, was at fault. By May 24 impeachment had again been given up, "even by the original impeachers."[44] By July prospects of impeachment had grown so dim that Tilton began to insist that the country must not make support of impeachment a test of Republican fealty. Chase, it seemed, regarded the move as "impolitic."[45] Upon the veto of the second supplementary Reconstruction bill, the demands of Boutwell, Butler, Thomas, Williams, Schenk and other for impeachment went unheeded.

In July a rumor that Johnson planned to remove General Thomas from command in Tennessee, caused more talk of impeachment. "If he were to make such an attempt, his impeachment would surely follow," a Radical declared. "If he goes on quietly about his duty, and executes the law, impeachment is dead."[46] When the House ordered a recess in the Spring, the Judiciary Committee had been directed to report upon its impeachment investigation immediately upon the reassemblage of Congress in July. On July 10 Chairman Wilson announced that the taking of evidence must be continued, and that the Committee could not report until October 16. Boutwell stridently but unavailingly insisted on an immediate report.

In August, after Stanton's suspension and Sheridan's removal, the Radicals renewed their demand that this "brigand," this man "long the chief enemy of the republic," be impeached. The *Nation* lamented the resurgence of the agitation, because it might reestablish the reputations of the impeachers, a group "as little qualified to inspire or direct a great public movement in troublous times as any set of men who have ever secured places in the government of a free country."[47] But Tilton asserted editorially that the two removals would "prove sufficient to incite an easy-going and amiable Congress to the stern duty of deposing the traitor in the White House. . . . We have demanded and shall continue to demand that this Aaron Burr, this Benedict Arnold, this

Andrew Johnson shall be put out of the way of injuring the government which he first disgraced, then betrayed, and would willingly destroy."[48] Thomas Ewing thought it "almost certain" that Johnson would be impeached that winter.[49] Late in the fall, after the election returns proved favorable to the Conservatives, the Radicals got what comfort they could from the belief that Johnson, "in his elation over the so-called 'Reaction,' would commit further outrages which Congress cannot overlook."[50] But this was merely whistling through the woods. Impeachment was dead—unless the President did something which could be construed as a crime.

Between the July recess and the reassemblage of Congress, John C. Churchill of New York, who had hitherto sided with Chairman Wilson, turned a sudden somersault and united with the extreme Radicals. Since Boutwell's views now commanded the votes of five of the nine committee members, he determined to recommend to the House that the President be impeached.[51]

His report was laid before the House on November 27. Upon announcement that perhaps ten hours would be required to read it, reading was dispensed with, and the resolution of impeachment was laid before the House.

Signed by Boutwell, Williams, Francis Thomas, William Lawrence and the turncoat Churchill, the majority report sought to make impeachment appear a political, not a legal process. The five Radicals claimed that the practice of the President, even in the use of rights of appointment and of veto constitutionally entrusted, had been illegal and impeachable. His offending has all grown out of "the one great overshadowing purpose of reconstructing the shattered governments of the Rebel States in accordance with his own will, in the interests of the great criminals who carried them into the Rebellion . . . restoring their lands and hurrying them back—their hearts unrepentant, and their hands yet red with the blood of our people—into a condition where they could once more embarrass and defy, if not absolutely rule, the government which they had vainly endeavored to destroy."

Boutwell recited the familiar steps of Presidential Reconstruction as if each were a link in the chain of a great criminal conspiracy. He viewed with exceeding suspicion the return of Southern railroads to their legal owners, seeking to make much of Andrew Johnson's relations with Michael Burns and to charge financial impropriety on the part of the President. It was also contended that, in restorations of confiscated and abandoned land and property, "the acts of the President were not less arbitrary and unwarrantable." Charges of dereliction were brought against Johnson's exercise of the pardoning power, which had resulted in an "obstruction of public justice, in sheltering the violators of the law from the just punishment which is awarded to their crimes."

The majority condensed their "facts" into seventeen precise statements, of which the seventh is typical: "That he has abused the pardoning power conferred on him by the Constitution, to the great detriment of the public, in releasing, pending the condition [conclusion?] of the war, the most active and formidable of the leaders of the Rebellion, with a view to the restoration of their property and means of influence, and to secure their services in the furtherance of his policies; and, further, in substantially delegating that power for the same objects to his provisional governors." The concluding statement of "fact" was that the President "has been guilty of acts calculated, if not intended, to subvert the government of the United States, by denying that the 39th Congress was a Constitutional body, and fostering a spirit of disaffection and disobedience to the law and rebellion against its authority, by endeavoring, in public speeches, to bring it into odium and contempt."

After this review of the "facts," the report undertook to contend that such "offenses" were high crimes and misdemeanors in the Constitutional sense. To build up his case, Boutwell went back to Tacitus' study of the Germans, and proceeded with remarkable laboriousness, through ten centuries of English authorities, all contending that impeachment was a political remedy for political differences, and "not necessarily a trial for a crime." Having proved to his own satisfaction that England in the days of the Plantagenets so regarded impeachment, Boutwell pleaded that America proceed on this precedent.

After this preamble, "and upon the fullest consideration of the facts disclosed," the Radicals "do solemnly pronounce and declare it as their deliberate judgment that Andrew Johnson, as President of the United States, is guilty of high crimes and misdemeanors within the meaning of the Constitution, in the exercise of his great office, of so grave a nature as to demand his immediate arraignment and trial therefor; and they do accordingly, in behalf of the loyal people of the United States, whose rights and interests he has betrayed, and whose government he has endeavored to subvert; in vindication of the law that he has violated, and the justice that he has contemned; and in the name of the thousands who have died in order that the Republic might live, recommend and respectfully insist that he be impeached, and held to answer therefor before the Senate of the United States."

James F. Wilson, chairman of the Committee, filed a dissenting recommendation, in which another Radical Republican committeeman, F. E. Woodbridge, joined; while the two Democrats filed a separate report substantially agreeing with Wilson's views. If Boutwell's 59 pages of labored straining seems but sorry rant, Wilson's document affords a gratifying surprise. Both signers of this report were ardent Radicals, political enemies of the President, but in approaching the question of impeachment, they declared that they had laid aside the feelings of partisanship, because "the interests of the Republic, as they are measured by its Constitution and laws, alone should guide us." They were pained at the "tone, temper and spirit" of the majority report, and proceeded to demolish it bit by bit.

At the very outset, the chairman tumbled over Boutwell's house of cards that impeachment might be for a political offense by reciting Section 2, Article II, of the Constitution: "The President . . . shall be removed from office on impeachment for, and conviction of, treason, bribery, or other high crimes and misdemeanors." The House might impeach a civil officer, "but it must be done according to law. It must be for some offense known to the law, and not created by the fancy of Members of the House." Thus there could not be an impeachment for a political difference. It must be for a crime. Had Andrew Johnson committed a crime?

The Wilson report next skillfully analyzed Ashley's various charges against the President. The first, "usurpation of power and violation of law," was based upon Johnson's Reconstruction policy. The minority sapiently noted that "the Reconstruction policy of the President cannot succeed except through an approval by Congress. Such an approval would destroy every element of crime involved in it, for it would then be the act of the government of the United States. If it do not receive the sanction of Congress, it cannot present a perfected crime. The present Congress will continue until the close of the President's term of office. Success in his alleged crime is thus rendered impossible."

The charge that Johnson had "corruptly used the appointing power" was disposed of with equal ease, as was the third charge, that the President had corruptly used the pardoning power. Wilson's report carefully exposed the failure to prove this charge. The Executive's use of pardons might have been unwise, impolitic, or dangerous, but it had been neither corrupt nor criminal; "the testimony does not disclose a crime or misdemeanor as known to the law in its exercise." Ashley's fourth indictment, "that the President has corruptly used the veto power," was effectually demolished, as was the charge of corruptly disposing of public property.

After thus in detail reducing the vainglorious charges of the Toledo Radical and Boutwell's magniloquent oratory to unworthy dust, Wilson and Woodbridge told the House of what stuff the testimony before the Committee had been. A great deal of it was "of no value whatever. Much of it is mere hearsay, opinions of witnesses, and no little amount of it utterly irrelevant to the case." Very little would be admissible in a trial before the Senate. All of the testimony concerning Jefferson Davis, Lincoln's assassination, the missing pages from Booth's Diary, Lucy Cobb, "the alleged correspondence of the President with Jefferson Davis . . . is not of the slightest importance. . . . Strike out the stage effect of this irrelevant matter and the prominence given to the Tudors, the Stuarts, and Michael Burns, and much of the play will disappear. Settle down upon the real evidence in the case . . . and the case in many respects dwarfs into a political contest."

While the two Radical dissentients thus stoutly maintained their views that the President had committed no high crime or misdemeanor subject to impeachment, they wanted it clearly understood that politically—not legally—they condemned Andrew Johnson. "He had been blind to the necessities of the times," they declared, "but the day of political impeachments would be a sad one for this country. Political unfitness and incapacity must be tried at the ballot box, not in the high court of impeachment." Let the Judiciary Committee be discharged from the impeachment investigation and the subject laid on the table.

The two Democrats agreed with Wilson and Woodbridge as to the impeachment itself, but disagreed with the political condemnation. Their opinion was a closely reasoned and compelling defense of the President's entire policy, and an excoriating condemnation of methods used in the impeachment hearings. They declared that, in view of the belief of thousands all over the country, "that it would be a righteous act to get him out of the way by any means, fair or foul, and when he has been hunted down by partisan malice as no man was ever hunted and hounded down before, it is really wonderful that so little has been elicited that tends in the slightest degree to tarnish the fair fame of the President. The American people ought to congratulate themselves, for the sake of the reputation of their country, that this failure has been so emphatic and so complete."[52]

The matter thus being before the House, Boutwell endeavored to have his report accepted and the proceedings undertaken. But Wilson's exposition of its imperfections had been too thorough.[53] On December 7 the enterprise was laid to rest by a vote of 108 to fifty-seven, two-thirds of the votes against it being cast by Radicals. "The impeachment humbug has gone by," Thomas Ewing wrote his son, "and in passing covered with disgrace the parties most active in getting it up."[54]

Only a few seconds after the gavels sounded the death knell of the Thirty-Ninth Congress, they struck again to call the Fortieth Congress into being. "Thanks to the firmness of the Northern people and the follies of Andrew Johnson," the *Nation* declared, the personnel of the new Congress was substantially that of its predecessor.[1] Although in strict fact there was hardly a minute's interval between the two sessions, all the forms of organization of a new legislative body were carefully complied with. The opening was full of color. The galleries were so crowded that the members' cloak-rooms were opened to the ladies, and the staid Congressional sofas were quickly filled with billowing loveliness.[2] The initial scenes of the new session were faintly reminiscent of those which had marked the beginning of the preceding one: Edward McPherson, Thad Stevens' clerk, called the roll, omitting the names of the Southern members—save that now the members from Tennessee were called—and James Brooks, the minority leader, a melancholy, scholarly looking man, somewhat resembling Charles Sumner in appearance, made a protest which he knew would go unheeded.

No attention was paid to Brooks' objection to the organization of the House with ten States absent. "Smiler" Colfax was immediately reëlected speaker and the new members from the Northern States went forward to take the oath. Among them was a new representative from Massachusetts, elected by the voters of a Congressional district in which he did not live, none other than Benjamin F. Butler, the "Hero of Fort Fisher," now as blatant in his Radicalism as any in the House. His visage startled those unaccustomed to it. "Make the best you can of it," wrote a correspondent who witnessed his induction into the House, "it is a terrible face; it looks like a pirate's —a strong, unscrupulous, cruel face, a low wide head, the crossed eyes, the hatchety Roman nose, the thin lips, make a combination powerful and pitiless."[3] Aside from the addition of Ben Butler, the House leadership was substantially the same as before. But it was a leadership which caused the *Nation* a little later to remark that "this is not a time to legislate under the guidance of . . . persons who are more anxious for victory than for either truth or justice."[4]

There were many changes in the personnel of the new Senate and, without exception, they were favorable to the Radicals. The President's staunch Pennsylvania friend, Edgar Cowan, had dropped out, and Simon Cameron had taken his place, the change reducing the number of Johnson Republicans in the Senate to four.[5] Two Democratic Senators, McDougall of California and Nesmith of Oregon, had been defeated, reducing the Democrats to seven, of whom only two came from the North. Several of the more Conservative Republicans had been replaced with extremists: Harris of New York had given way to Roscoe Conkling, "with his Saxon curls";[6] Foster, president *pro tem* of the Senate in the last Congress, had been replaced by Ferry. Drake, one of Missouri's most ferocious impeachers, had taken the place of Brown of that State. James S. Harlan, late of the President's Cabinet, had been elected to the Senate by the Radical Iowa legislature. Oliver P. Morton, once a supporter of Johnson, now a fugleman for the Radicals, and soon to be Thad Stevens' successor as the autocrat of Congress, entered the Senate. From Kansas came a meek looking little man named Ross, the successor of Johnson's friend, Jim Lane, who had committed suicide. Nebraska's two new Senators were "men of the right sort," Ben Wade pledged. By these shifts, the Radical roll in the Senate had grown to forty-two, an overwhelming majority.

With Foster's departure, the Senate had to elect another of its members president *pro tempore*. At 10:30 on Monday morning, the retiring Senator bade farewell to his associates, who proceeded forthwith to the election of his successor. The changing temper of the majority was indicated by the choice they made. No longer did such men as Fessenden or Trumbull appeal to them. For, with all their active Radicalism, both Fessenden and Trumbull were men of conscience and of high standards of public duty. In December, 1865, at the beginning of the Thirty-Ninth Congress, had Foster not been elected, majority choice would have fallen upon the able senators from Maine or Illinois; but by the summer of 1866, the Radical temper had changed and Gideon Welles made note that the Radical program was "to make Wade president of the Senate, then to impeach the President."[7]

In March, 1867, the Radical Senators saw even more clearly

the possibility of a new president in the White House, and they picked Ben Wade of Ohio—"Bluff Ben"—for the job. "You know I am not a parliamentarian," Wade warned them.[8] They knew it full well, but they had not picked the Ohio Radical for a parliamentarian. They had picked him because if there were to be a new president in the White House before March 4, 1869, they wanted him to be one of their own.

Although Wade had served in the Senate for a dozen years or more, his mien and character could appeal only to men ready to win their way by any means. His appearance, though less startling than that of Ben Butler, was sufficiently rough. His head was "most savage," his forehead high and steep; shaggy eyebrows beetled from a "perceptive brow." He had a "rough-hewn" nose, a mouth resolute and dogged, a broad and "immovable" chin.[9] By his election, the *Independent* declared, "the Senate has honored itself"; but the country felt otherwise, as did many of the Conservative Republicans in both Houses. The idea got abroad that Ben Wade was even more unfit for the presidency than was Andrew Johnson, and his election as president *pro tem* was to deliver a body blow to the first attempt at impeachment.

The first sitting of this new Congress continued until March 30, the time being occupied with the debate and passage of a Supplementary Reconstruction Act. No sooner had the first one been passed, vetoed and reenacted over the presidential negative than the Radicals determined to amend a fatal defect in the law. The processes by which States should secure their readmission into the Union had been set forth in the initial measure with great particularity, but either by inattention or design the framers of the bill had failed to provide for the initiation of the processes. No one was charged with the duty or clothed with the power to take the first step, the election of delegates to a constitutional convention of the State. The Military Reconstruction Act carefully prescribed the constituencies which were to select the new constitution-makers and the qualifications of the members, but it failed to indicate the authority which should call the convention or supervise the election of its members.

This lapse was probably the result of design rather than of negligence. Many in the Thirty-Ninth Congress were unwilling that the Southern States be coerced against their will into adopting these processes, but desired that such terms be

held out to the South as a "boon" which the South could accept
or reject. Furthermore, a substantial group of the Radicals
was not anxious for the South to adopt the steps for readmission. They were quite willing for military rule to continue
—so long as it did, Radical control of Congress would not be
challenged—and they thought, with probable truth, that the
South would prefer bayonet to negro rule.

But the new Congress had a different tone. More Radical
than the old one, its majority was determined that something
be done at once towards restoring the Union. As soon as it
had been organized, steps were taken to repair the omission of
initiating authority in the first Reconstruction bill. The result
was the supplementary Military Reconstruction Act, which
directed the district commanders to have a complete registration of the qualified voters of each State made before the first of
September of that year. They were next directed to fix a day
for the election of delegates to the state constitutional conventions and otherwise to arrange for the initiation of the steps
provided for in the original act.

One new, distinct addition was made to the prescribed
steps by which a State could secure a new constitution. The
majority of votes cast for holding a convention was to be
ignored unless a majority of all registered voters should have
voted in the election. Similarly, no state constitution should
be considered as having been ratified unless at least half of all
the registered voters should have taken part in the ratification
election.

The House gave but two hours to this measure, putting
a gag on debate, apparently "because it loves to apply the gag
to Democrats." But the Senate took a week for debate, and
the bill did not finally pass until Tuesday, March 19.[10] It then
became necessary for the Radicals to remain in session until
the Constitutional time given the President for approving or
disapproving measures should elapse. Since the Radicals had
no especial further business to press through, the wait for the
inevitable veto passed rather slowly. The House desultorily
debated a project to accord government aid to the destitute of
the South, irrespective of their attitude during the war. In
this discussion an exciting colloquy took place which was to
influence the fortunes of the President.

John A. Bingham of Ohio was supporting the bill; during

his advocacy, he wandered over to the Democratic side of the House, and Ben Butler taunted him that he had "got over on the other side not only in body but in spirit." Enraged at this palpable hit, Bingham assailed the General in scathing terms. "It does not become a gentleman who recorded his vote fifty times for Jefferson Davis, the arch-traitor in this rebellion, as his candidate for President of the United States, to undertake to damage this cause by attempting to cast an imputation either upon my integrity or my honor. I repel with scorn and contempt any utterance of that sort from any man, whether he be the Hero of Fort Fisher not taken or of Fort Fisher taken."

But Butler was in nowise at a loss for a crushing reply. "I have never concealed that before the war, I . . . voted fifty-seven times for Jefferson Davis for President," he told the House. "I thought him the representative man of the South, and I hoped by his nomination to prevent threatened disunion. . . . The difference between me and the honorable gentleman from Ohio is this: While Jefferson Davis was in the Union, a Senator of the United States, and claiming to be a friend of the Union, I supported him; but now he [Bingham] supports him when he is a traitor."

Butler next referred to his own war record. Bingham had had the bad taste "to attack me for the reason that I could not do any more injury to the enemies of my country. I agree to that. I did all I could, the best I could, . . . and because I could not do more, I feel exceedingly chagrined. . . . But the only victim of that gentleman's prowess that I know of was an innocent woman hung upon the scaffold, one Mrs. Surratt. And I can sustain the memory of Fort Fisher if he and his present associates can sustain him in shedding the blood of a woman tried by a military commission, and convicted without sufficient evidence. . . ."

Driven wild by this sudden blow beneath the belt, Bingham lost control of himself and responded almost in gibberish—so much so that a few days later, he asked leave to revise his remarks for the record. When he did so, Butler returned to the charge, expanding his indictment of Bingham.

The Hero of Fort Fisher adverted at great length to Booth's Diary, which had just been uncovered by the Judiciary Committee. He was exercised over the leaves which had been torn from it, which, he contended, must have contained evidence of a startling nature; the same hands which had suppressed the Diary thus far might have torn the pages from it to suppress the evidence contained. By all means this document should have been produced at the trial of Payne, Herold, Atzerodt and Mrs. Surratt, he charged, for it proved two things: First, that Booth's original plot had been to abduct President Lincoln, and only at the last moment had it been changed from kidnaping to murder. Therefore, "if Mrs. Surratt did not know of the change of purpose, there is no evidence that she knew in any way of the assassination. Second, the people of the country had a right to know every bit of evidence available as to the assassination conspiracy, so as to find who were all the accomplices of Booth; to find who it was that changed Booth's purpose from capture to assassination; who it was that could profit by assassination who could not profit by capture and abduction of the President; who it was expected by Booth would succeed to Lincoln if the knife made a vacancy."

"Who spoliated that book?" Butler asked dramatically, "who suppressed that evidence? Who caused an innocent woman to be hung when he had in his pocket the diary that states at least what was the idea and purpose of the main conspirator in the case?" Butler quoted Booth's statement that he proposed to return to Washington and give himself up "and clear myself from this great crime." How then, asked Butler, could Booth clear himself: "By disclosing his accomplices? Who were they? Who spoliated this book after it got into the hands of the government, if it was not spoliated before?" He sought to imply the answer to his questions: Andrew Johnson had been Booth's accomplice and had mutilated the Diary in order to suppress the evidence of his own guilt.

Upon the utterance of this charge, Bingham returned to the encounter, this time as a defender of the President. "Such a charge," he said, "is only fit to come from a man who lives in a bottle and is fed with a spoon."[11]

Congress did not have to wait the expected ten days for the Presidential veto. On March 23 Andrew Johnson returned the Supplementary Military Reconstruction bill with his disapproval. The general tone of his message was that of the veto of the original act, but to the Radicals, it was "one of the strangest messages ever written." One striking paragraph read:

"When I contemplate the millions of our fellow citizens of the South, with no alternative left but to impose upon themselves this fearful and untried experiment of complete negro enfranchisement—and white disfranchisement, it may be, almost as complete—or submit indefinitely to the rigor of martial law, without a single attribute of freemen, deprived of all the sacred guarantees of our Federal Constitution, and threatened with even worse wrongs, if any worse are possible, it seems to me that their condition is the most deplorable to which any people can be reduced."[12]

Neither House paid any attention to the veto, not even according it the distinction of angry remonstrance, but immediately passed the bill over the veto. With this action the business of the session was concluded. But the Members of Congress were by no means agreed as to the fashion in which and the date to which they should adjourn.

Blaine wished the recess to be from March 26 to November 11, but Ben Butler objected strenuously to a seven months' suspension. He recalled that in ordering this March session of the new Congress, the previous one had declared "that Andrew Johnson was a bad man, and that this House and the Senate should sit here and take care of his acts." Furthermore, impeachment should not be postponed eight months. Blaine responded that the public was not anxious for impeachment. The question had already been settled in the negative. With this, Old Thad turned his scorn upon Maine's Representative, asserted that the growing reluctance to impeach arose from Ben Wade's selection by the Senate, and declared that Blaine had told the House, "there will be no impeachment by this Congress; we would rather have the President than the scalawags of Ben Wade." Blaine hotly denied this, maintaining that he had said that Fessenden was a safer man for President, while Stevens angrily reiterated his charge.[13]

The Senate, too, was divided on adjournment. Trumbull wished to suspend until the constitutional date in December. But Sumner and other extreme Radicals were vehemently opposed to this. "Our President is a bad man," said Sumner, "search history and I am sure that you will find no ruler who, during the same short space of time, has done so much mischief to his country . . . and now, I ask, can Congress quietly vote to go home and leave this bad man without hindrance of any kind?" Senator Nye declared that the Supreme Court

WILLIAM H. SEWARD

A Revealing Pose of Lincoln's and Johnson's Secretary of State.

might hold the Reconstruction measures unconstitutional the very next month. Where would Congress then be, unable to meet this situation until its reassembly in December?

After much controversy the two Houses finally agreed to adjourn until the first Wednesday in July, "when the roll shall be called and the presiding officer of each House shall inform the presiding officer of the other whether or not a quorum is present, and if a quorum of the two Houses shall not have appeared, they shall adjourn the two Houses without day." Thereupon Congress adjourned.

During these difficult days in Congress, the President had not been inactive. The passage of the original Military Reconstruction bill had imposed several important executive duties upon him. Even though he deemed the measure a gross violation of the Constitution, he still felt it his duty to undertake its enforcement, until the Supreme Court should have declared it a contravention of the Federal charter.

Questions of the construction and interpretation of the initial Military Reconstruction act quickly came before the Cabinet. Exactly what were the power and jurisdiction of the military governors and department commanders to be put over the Southern States? If the President must enforce an unconstitutional law, Welles early hinted to him that it was most important to pick the right men for military governors. After several such hints, it became apparent that Johnson intended to make one further effort to trust Stanton; Welles was alarmed when he saw that the President was consulting only Grant and Stanton about the governorships, and predicted "he will have trouble." At the Cabinet of March 12 Johnson said nothing on the subject, but took the Secretary of War aside for a private talk for a quarter of an hour, at the close of which "Stanton was unusually jubilant, . . . and could not suppress his feelings."[14] On the next day the list was announced in the newspapers, this publication being the first hint of the personnel to several Members of the Cabinet.[15] "The slime of the serpent," Welles felt, "is over them all." It might not have been easy to find five men among the army generals in whom to put confidence, Father Gideon agreed, but in yielding to Stanton the President had named two undependable men, particularly hostile to him: Sickles to command the two Carolinas, and Sheridan for Louisiana and Texas.[16]

Late in March, Cabinet asperities over the proper interpretation of the acts of Congress were lessened because of the interest in the political campaign in progress in Connecticut. It was beginning to be suspected that the sentiment of the voters of the North was not nearly so Radical as had been indicated by the 1866 election. At a by-election in Iowa, a Johnson candidate won by a majority of over 500 votes, and George H. Parker of Davenport telegraphed, "We are indebted to the uncompromising firmness of the President for this result." If the Connecticut outcome were to bear out the tendency observable in Iowa, the assault of Congress on the South might be checked.

The Radicals were intensely anxious over this New England test. On March 21 the *Independent* fulminated editorially: "If Connecticut shall vote the wrong way on the first of April, she will reincite Andrew Johnson to further usurpations, and reanimate the Rebellion to further defiance. A vote cast for the Democratic party of Connecticut is a plaudit to Jefferson Davis and a laurel to General Lee."[17]

The Radicals made the usual charges that the Johnson men "spent money like water." In any event, the result of the election was a Conservative triumph up and down the line. The Democratic candidate for governor, James E. English, was elected by a handsome majority, and the voters of the Nutmeg State strongly disapproved the admission of negroes to the ballot box. The *Independent* entitled its editorial on the outcome "O! Backsliding Connecticut," and reflected sadly that "the States that now need reconstruction are the Northern."

The result created a sensation in Washington, bringing confusion to the Radicals and joy to the White House. Johnson interpreted it as the harbinger of the "inevitable doom" of the Radicals. With mock generosity, the *Independent's* Washington correspondent declared, "Everybody will excuse the President for excessive delight, for it is the first crumb of comfort he has had since he turned traitor."[18]

The attention of the country now turned to two judicial involvements. These were the release on bail of Jefferson Davis, and the unavailing attempt of Southern State governments to bring the Military Reconstruction Acts before the Supreme Court for adjudication by that body.

The President of the late Confederate States had been incarcerated at Fortress Monroe since the summer of 1865. Why

had he not been put on trial for treason? This question had
been raised again and again in and out of Congress, but President Johnson had not been responsible for the delay. Repeatedly he had sought to have Davis brought to the bar of justice.
The government had hired eminent counsel to take charge of
the case, with William M. Evarts as the principal. An indictment had been returned by the Federal Grand Jury sitting at
Norfolk, but Chief Justice Chase remained unwilling to hold
circuit court in Richmond, and both the United States attorney
at Richmond and Mr. Evarts were unwilling to bring Davis
to trial before District Judge Underwood when the Chief Justice was not sitting with him.

In the meantime Northern sentiment toward Davis had become more forgiving. Charles O'Conor, perhaps the most
eminent member of the New York bar, had volunteered to act
as Davis' counsel. Conover's trial and conviction had proved
that Davis' implication in the plot to assassinate Lincoln had
been on perjured testimony, and public sentiment reacted in
his behalf. Dr. Craven's account of Jefferson Davis' prison
life, showing how harshly the Confederate president had been
treated, caused the North further to relent. Horace Greeley,
John A. Andrew, Senator Henry Wilson and other Radicals
began to advocate better treatment for Jefferson Davis. The
President and the Attorney-General had insisted all along that
humanity be practiced in his incarceration while the strict letter of the law be observed at the trial.

Late in April, 1867, Judge Underwood of Richmond determined to bring Davis to the bar. On May 7 Stanton submitted to the Cabinet a letter which L. H. Chandler, United
States Attorney for Virginia, had written the War Department
asking for "an order upon the commandant at Fortress Monroe, directing him to surrender Jefferson Davis to the United
States Marshal, or his deputies, upon any process which may
issue from the Federal Court." When the President inquired,
"Well, Mr. Secretary, what recommendation have you to make
in this case?" Stanton replied, "I have no recommendation to
make." After Stanton's evasion of responsibility, Johnson
directed the application to be returned to the Secretary of
War, "who will at once issue the order requested by District-
Attorney Chandler."

Stanton "is playing the same old trick," the President told
Colonel Moore that evening. "If it had not been for the in-

fluence of the War Department with this damned extreme gang during the past session, . . . all this trouble would long since have been brought to a close."[19]

At any rate, on May 13, Jefferson Davis was. brought into court at Richmond, entering on the arm of General Burton. Charles O'Conor was there to conduct his case, and Mr. Evarts was on hand to represent the government. When the case was called, it was announced that the government was not ready, whereupon O'Conor asked that the prisoner be admitted to bail. Judge Underwood questioned whether the offense of treason was bailable. No objection being made by the government, the judge gave his opinion that, as the indictment had been returned under the act of 1862, the court could use its discretion as to whether the offense was or was not bailable. He held that it was bailable and set the bond at $100,000.

Waiting in the court room were Horace Greeley and a number of other distinguished Northern citizens. The editor of the New York *Tribune,* whose excoriation of Davis while President had been unsparing, was now preaching universal amnesty as well as universal suffrage, and he had come to Richmond to sign Jefferson Davis' bond. Along with him were Augustus Schell and fourteen other wealthy and distinguished men. After the document had been signed, the judge announced: "The marshal will discharge the prisoner." This was done amid "deafening applause, huzzas and waving of hats." A Radical newspaper correspondent declared that the ovation expressed the city's heart, "jubilant and defiant."[20] After an informal levee, the President of the late Confederate States made his way to Canada, where he remained until the next episode in the attempt to try him for treason took place in 1868.

While Horace Greeley had signed Davis' bond, his act by no means represented the general attitude of the Radicals. The *Independent* denounced the act with "regret, indignation and scorn."[21] Greeley was made to feel Radical anger, for the circulation of the *Tribune* diminished by many thousands almost over night, and the sale of Greeley's "American Conflict" shrank suddenly to a negligible amount. After the "arch-criminal of all times" had been admitted to bail, the languid proceedings of impeachment investigation flared up in fitful vigor, only to die down again when it became apparent from the testimony of Stanbery, Evarts, Judge Underwood, the United States Attorney and others that President Johnson

had been about the only man consistently desirous that Davis
be tried.[22]

Another legal measure which attracted great public attention was the attempt of Provisional Governors Sharkey of
Mississippi and Jenkins of Georgia to bring the Military Reconstruction Acts before the Supreme Court. With the passage
of the two acts the Southern people were appalled at the prospect before them. It was hard for them to realize that the
North was determined to exclude intelligence from Southern
governments and to enforce the rule of the most ignorant
class upon those unhappy States. The President apparently
was impotent. The Northern voters had not listened to his
appeal. But there remained a third department of the government, the judicial. It was no Radical body. Its decisions in
the Milligan, Garland and Cummings cases afforded a faint
hope that there was still a Constitution in the land.[23] Before
giving up in black despair, the South would appeal to the
Supreme Court.

On April 5 Governor Sharkey, Alexander H. Garland and
Robert J. Walker, representing the State of Mississippi, asked
leave to file a plea to have the Supreme Court perpetually enjoin Andrew Johnson from "executing or in any manner carrying out" the Reconstruction Acts.[24] On the same day the President brought the matter before the Cabinet, and Stanbery was
instructed to appear before the Supreme Court and object to
the Mississippi motion—"Sharkey's new rebellion," a Radical
journal termed it—on the ground that the President, as representative of the United States, could not be sued. Doubtless the Radicals were somewhat surprised to find Andrew
Johnson's attorney-general appearing before the high court
and endeavoring to prevent the judicial overthrow of these last
measures which Andrew Johnson himself had gravely reprehended as unconstitutional. But the Tennessee tailor-politician
was just the man to do his duty, no matter what anguish of
heart it cost him.

Senator Trumbull appeared as special counsel for the government. Stanbery made a forcible presentation of the government's position, Charles O'Conor argued the Mississippi
motion and the court took the matter under advisement.[25]

Before its decision was handed down, Provisional Governor
Jenkins of Georgia made similar application to the Court. On
April 10 Jenkins issued an address to the people of his State,

pointing out that of the three departments of the Federal Government, two were in direct antagonism regarding the constitutionality of the Military Reconstruction measures. There yet remained, however, the third department, the judicial, "the great conservator of the supremacy of the Constitution, whose decrees, unlike the executive veto, cannot be overridden by the Congress. That court has not yet spoken. Should it be found in accordance with the executive, this usurpation will be arrested."[26] Jenkins avoided Mississippi's error by seeking to enjoin, not the President, but the Secretary of War, the General of the Army, and the Department Commander assigned to the Georgia command.

Unhappily for the Southern people, the Supreme Court was unwilling to accept jurisdiction in either of these applications. On April 15 an unanimous court, the Chief Justice speaking, denied the Mississippi petition, lack of jurisdiction being given as the cause. In May the Georgia petition was also rejected. Prudence rather than judicial judgment seems to have influenced the court's determination in these two cases. In the Mississippi case Chase gave this explanation: "The Congress is the Legislative Department of the government. The President is the Executive Department. Neither can be restrained in its action by the Judicial Department; though the acts of both, when performed, are, in proper case, subject to its cognizance." The Chief Justice pointed out the "impropriety" of such interference as had been sought by limning its possible consequences. "Suppose the plea filed and the injunction prayed be allowed," he recited. "If the President refused obedience, it is needless to observe that the court is without power to enforce its process. If, on the other hand, the President complies with the order of the court and refuses to execute the acts of Congress, is it not clear that a collision may occur between the executive and legislative departments of the government? May not the House of Representatives impeach the President for such refusal? In that case could this court interfere, in behalf of the President, thus endangered by compliance with its mandate, and restrain by injunction the Senate of the United States from sitting as a court of impeachment?"

The court had refused to take jurisdiction in the Mississippi case because no question of person or property was involved, the only matter at issue being the rights of putative governments. As soon as its decision had been announced, Mississippi's counsel made desperate efforts to be permitted to amend their application so that they could involve person or property in the case and thus meet the Supreme Court's definition of the types of cases it felt properly to be within the province of its decision. The application was reargued and, by a four to four decision, Justice Grier being absent, the plea was disallowed.[27]

Thus the South's last hope to prevent the forcible imposition of negro domination had proven vain. The President had been unable to stop the Radical onslaught, and the Supreme Court, fearful of its own fate, appeared unwilling to interpose its protecting hand between the Radicals and the prostrate South. "We have fallen on evil times," lamented ex-President Buchanan. "What is to become of the Supreme Court of the United States?" And the Radicals mixed their exultation and relief with warnings; Congress would find the means "to carry out its purposes if the Supreme Court puts itself in the way"; the Court had better beware "the risk of amputation!"[28]

Long before the Supreme Court dismissed the Southern petitions, the President began to have trouble with his district commanders in the South. His unwisdom in allowing Stanton to name the men assigned to the five military districts quickly became apparent. Eight days after assuming command of the fifth district, Sheridan, under his own interpretation of his powers as granted by the Reconstruction Act, abruptly removed A. S. Herron, Attorney-General of the State of Louisiana; J. S. Monroe, Mayor of New Orleans, and Edwin Abell, Judge of the First District Court of that city. A few days later he removed the Board of Levee Commissioners. When questioned by Washington about these summary actions, Sheridan almost insolently contended that he had the right and power to remove whomsoever he saw fit without authorization by the President. In Alabama, General Pope had removed the Mayor of Mobile, and there was trouble under way in Georgia.

After a series of such episodes, McCulloch, Secretary of the Treasury, could contain himself no longer. Early in May he went to the President to tell him bluntly, face to face, that he had brought his troubles on himself. His hesitating course was responsible for the Administration's evil days. He had retained in his Cabinet a man "notoriously opposed to his

Administration, a man who from the beginning had been an embarrassment; that there was never any free interchange of opinion when that member was present. . . . Yet in many of the important measures and movements, that false member had a controlling voice and often was the only person consulted." McCulloch thrust the instance of the selection of the military governors up to the President, selections "made without consultation with any Member of the Cabinet, save the false and unfaithful one." Johnson listened to McCulloch's reproaches and agreed that the Secretary of the Treasury was right. But this was all.[29]

None the less, Andrew Johnson pushed ahead on the task ahead of him, examining with the most careful detail every one of the multifarious problems presented. The President was acutely dissatisfied with conditions in the internal revenue bureau of the Treasury Department. This unit had at its head Commissioner Rollins, an arrant Radical, and its conduct was a source of great scandal under Lincoln, Johnson and Grant. Secretary McCulloch was peculiarly blind to Rollins' treachery to the President and to the frauds of the Federal Revenue being committed by the Commissioner's subordinates. The President asked again and again for reform, but McCulloch consistently defended the Bureau. On May 6 he wrote Johnson: "If there be honest men in the country, they are at the head of the office of Internal Revenue. Great demoralization pervades the country and great frauds are being unquestionably committed upon our revenue, particularly . . . in the illicit distribution of liquor. But I assure you that earnest efforts are being made to prevent them."[30]

In this same month came an invitation which must have seemed to the harassed Chief Executive an opportunity for temporary escape from the heart-breaking problems of the Presidency. A monument to Jacob Johnson was to be unveiled at Raleigh on June 4, and Governor Jonathan Worth invited the President to be present at these exercises and to attend the commencement of the University of North Carolina at Chapel Hill. Mayor Dallas Haywood of Raleigh also urged the President to visit his birthplace. On May 22 Johnson answered: "I accept the invitation of my native city to be her guest and, deeply grateful for the respect in which they hold my father's memory," will be present.

Another invitation, this one to take part in the dedication

of the great Masonic building in Boston, came to the President. Remembering the sad experiences of the Swing Around the Circle, his apprehensive friends sought to restrain him and, on May 24, Thomas Ewing wrote: "Do not, I pray you, go to Boston. The occasion is not a propitious one. There are yet anti-Masons as well as Masons. . . . Besides, there will be fifty lying scamps dogging at your heels who will circulate more fresh slander than can be corrected in six months.

"Your proposed trip to Raleigh is well, the occasion warrants it [but] I hope you will meddle not at all with politics, even in private conversation, and let all who honestly or dishonestly inquire as to your opinions and purposes find them in your official papers. Foolish friends and crafty enemies will publish their version of what you say, alike to your injury. . . . He who is a President must in his intercourse with the public forget that he is a man."[31]

Fortunately, Ewing's apprehensions as to untoward incidents on these presidential journeys proved unfounded. Johnson greatly enjoyed them both and was treated with great respect by the public.

Upon his return to Washington from Raleigh, the vexing problems of Reconstruction again imperatively presented themselves. On June 10 General Sickles sent the President his views of the responsibility of commanders. "I regard these States," he wrote, "as having been placed under your control as commander-in-chief by Congress, which assume that the United States have paramount and exclusive jurisdiction. Your control as commander-in-chief is exercised through district commanders appointed by yourself. These commanders are subject to your orders. You may revoke or suspend any order they give. You may control their action by general or particular instructions. You may relieve or supersede them."

About this time Sickles' suspension of execution of an order of a civil court aroused the Southern Conservatives to fever heat, and drew an opinion from Attorney-General Stanbery that the General's procedure was illegal and an usurpation.

On June 19, smarting under Stanbery's sharp words, Sickles asked to be relieved from the command of his department and demanded a court of inquiry on his conduct, that "I may vindicate myself from the accusations of the Attorney-General." But the General did not secure his wish. The President, who disliked him, and remarked, concerning him, "A conceited cuckold is an abomination in the sight of God," liked neither his Carolina conduct nor his attempts to embarrass the Administration. Accordingly he directed the General to retain command and declined to order the court of inquiry.[32]

About this same time Sheridan went a step further and removed Governor Wells of Louisiana from office. This aroused even greater furore through the South, and on June 20, General J. B. Steedman telegraphed the President from New Orleans that "want of respect for Governor Wells personally alone represses an expression of indignation felt by all honest and sensible men at the unwarranted usurpation of General Sheridan in removing the civil officers of Louisiana. It is believed here that you will reinstate Wells. He is a bad man and has no influence. I believe General Sheridan made the removal to embarrass you, believing the feeling at the North would sustain him. My conviction is that on account of the bad character of Wells and Monroe, you ought not to reinstate any who have been [ousted] because you cannot reinstate any without reinstating all. But you ought to prohibit the exercise of this power in the future."[33]

In view of such impetuous proceedings on the part of the military commanders, the President determined to do what he could to assuage the asperities of the Reconstruction Acts by careful administration. He made a written request of Attorney-General Stanbery for that officer's considered and careful legal opinion as to the meaning of the Reconstruction Acts. On May 24 Stanbery had furnished his views on the Reconstruction Acts' provisions regarding qualification of voters in the Southern States. On June 12 he supplemented this first opinion with one of considerably greater length dealing with this and other phases of the Acts.

On June 18 the President brought the whole matter before the Cabinet. Stanbery proposed that a record be kept of the ensuing Cabinet deliberations and that the vote of each member on each point be recorded. Welles looked askance at this new departure, but the President, "nervous and apprehensive," was anxious to have a written record of this important discussion.

At the outset, Welles said that the Reconstruction Acts were "so abominable, so flagrantly unconstitutional, that I do not feel inclined to have anything to do with them." His chief objection to Stanbery's opinion was that the Attorney-General had endeavored to raise an edifice with no foundation; he had sought so to interpret the Reconstruction Act as to enable the South to endure it. Indeed, Stanbery "had done more for popular rights, under a law which despotically deprived the people of their undoubted guaranteed rights, than I had supposed possible."[34]

The Secretary of the Navy considered the President in an extraordinary and embarrassing position; he had sworn to support the Constitution and had also taken oath to see the laws faithfully executed. The two were incompatible. When Johnson had appointed military governors, he had done all that could be expected of him. But now that the governors disagreed and sought instruction, he had quite properly asked the law officer of the government for his opinion. But let it be sent out merely as the Attorney-General's construction and not as a binding order. In this Welles agreed with Stanton, whose temper and attitude during the four days' debate—indeed, from the very moment of the passage of the Tenure-of-Office Act over the veto Stanton had prepared for the President— had become surly, rude and overbearing. The Secretary of War insisted that Congress had intended to strike down civil government in the South and to establish military dominion, and that the President had no right or authority to temper the process.

On June 19 the President submitted a list of nineteen interrogatories which he had prepared, remarking as he did so upon "the necessity for uniformity of opinion in the Cabinet."[35] Stanton objected to any such mode of procedure, demanding time for written answers. The Attorney-General answered that the questions were very plain and such as he himself could answer at once. Seward and McCulloch said they were ready. Still protesting, Stanton yielded, but first read a paper he had written the night before, disclosing his Radical attitude toward the acts. Though his paper was condemned by every one of his associates, he did not reply. Then the Attorney-General began the interrogatories. Of the nineteen questions, twelve produced no dissent. On the seven remaining—and they were the important ones—all members agreed except Stanton, who dissented from each, at times with insolence.

The President wished to know if the power was vested in him "to see that the Reconstruction Acts are faithfully executed," and all but Stanton answered yes. But the latter referred to "the limitations and qualifications . . . of the Act of Congress." Another question was whether the President had the right of supervision over the military commanders, and whether they were bound to perform their duties in conformity with his instruction. All answered affirmatively save Stanton, who declared that "the duties assigned to the military commanders . . . are specifically entrusted to them, and they are not bound to perform these duties in conformity with his [the President's] instruction unless they are in accordance with the Acts of Congress."

Johnson desired to know whether unlimited power had been given the military commanders "to abolish, modify, control or supersede the laws of the State," to which question all responded in the negative except Stanton, who said that "the military authority is paramount," and that a commanding general "has unlimited power to abolish, modify, control or supersede the State law." It was all too apparent that the attitude of subservient submissiveness which he had displayed prior to the Tenure-of-Office Act had been hypocritical. Stanton had at last removed his mask.

None the less, Johnson determined to issue Stanbery's rulings to the military commanders, and after some dispute as to the form of the preamble, a draft was adopted, reciting that several commanders had sought instructions, that the Acts and the Attorney-General's opinions thereon "have been carefully considered by the President in conference with the heads of the respective departments" and that the President "has concluded that the following is the correct and practical interpretation of the acts . . . and directs the same to be transmitted to the said commanders for their information, in order that there may be uniformity in the execution of the said acts."

The important portion of Stanbery's opinion concerned the registration of voters. The Attorney-General gave the South all the leeway the strict letter of the law allowed. Whenever an applicant for registration as a voter took the oath prescribed by the Supplementary Reconstruction Act, Stanbery ruled, "his name must go on the registry. The Board of Registrations cannot enter upon the inquiry whether he has sworn truly or falsely."

This opinion angered and alarmed the Radicals, who immediately began to agitate for quorums to be present in July in both Houses of Congress to annihilate the Attorney-General's views. General Sheridan telegraphed from New Orleans to Grant: "Mr. Stanbery's interpretation is practically . . . opening a broad macadamized road for perjury and fraud to travel on." "The little fellow" gave out for publication this dispatch, highly disrespectful to the President. The latter resented it keenly, and rumors began to be bruited about that Sheridan was to be removed.[36] These led the *Independent* to declare that "the people would throw a thousand Andrew Johnsons into the sea sooner than permit one Phil Sheridan to walk the plank."

With the publication of this opinion, Radical demand for the July session of Congress became so insistent that there was no doubt that quorums would be present when the designated July date arrived. Some of the Radicals affected surprise that "the President would do so stupid a thing as to interfere with the successful operation of the Reconstruction Act."[37] But the extremists in both Houses of Congress set to work with a vengeance to annihilate the opinion given by the Attorney-General.

In the House debate, Ben Butler startled the Radicals by informing them that "in the opinion of some of the ablest lawyers of the country, some of the points in Mr. Stanbery's opinion were well taken." Therefore, he argued, the act which Congress now would pass must be made so distinct and so clear that misinterpretation of it would be impossible.[38]

The bill finally enacted conformed to Butler's specifications. It authorized the commanders of the military districts, in so many words, to suspend or remove any official in the "pretended governments" of the "Rebel States" and to fill vacancies thus created. These acts were to be reviewed not by the President but by the General of the Army. Such removals were not merely permissive but mandatory. It was made the duty of the district commanders to oust "all disloyal persons."

This measure reached the President on July 14, and on July 19 he returned it with his veto. Even Andrew Johnson's patience was approaching a breaking point. Congress had had the insolence to declare that none of the officers or military commanders should "be bound in his action by any opinion of any civil officer of the United States," a direct endeavor to remove all authority from the President. In his message, Andrew Johnson spoke sternly about this new usurpation of executive authority by Congress.

"Within a period of less than a year, the legislation of Congress has attempted to strip the Executive Department of some of its essential powers. The Constitution, and the oath provided in it devolve upon the President the power and duty to see that the laws are faithfully executed. The Constitution, in order to carry out this power, gives him the choice of agents, and makes them subject to his control and supervision. But in the execution of these laws the constitutional obligation upon the President remains, but the power to exercise that constitutional duty is effectually taken away. The military commander is, as to the power of appointment, made to take the place of the President, and the General of the Army the place of the Senate; and any attempt on the part of the President to assert his own constitutional powers may, under pretense of law, be met by official insubordination. It is to be feared that these military officers, looking to the authority given by these laws, rather than to the letter of the Constitution, will recognize no authority but the commander of the district and the General of the Army."

Nor was this all. While he remained President, he informed Congress, and "whilst the obligation rests upon me to see that all the laws are faithfully executed, I can never willingly surrender that trust or the powers given for its execution. I can never give my assent to be made responsible for the faithful execution of the laws, and at the same time surrender that trust, and the powers which accompany it, to any other office, high or low, or to any number of executive officers."

When the Radicals promptly repassed the bill over the veto, these sentences gave rise to excited comment. Here was further proof that the President was a bad man, an enemy of the country, who must be impeached. But calmer counsels prevailed and impeachment once more was pushed aside. Congress adjourned to the November date already set.

It was observable, however, that while the Radicals were keenly determined on further restricting the presidential power, their lust for presidential appointments was as keen as ever. None showed their willingness to sacrifice alleged principle for patronage more clearly than Senator Pomeroy of Kansas. This Radical scoundrel had a candidate for the postmastership at Leavenworth, to whom he furnished the following letter: "Dear Legate—I want you to see the Postmaster-General in person, and ask him for the Post Office at Leavenworth, and if he will

give it to you today, he may count on my support for his nominations, and should either himself or the President get in trouble,
even if it be impeachment, they can count on me to aid in getting them out by word or vote, and you may say so to him.
Don't go along without making the trial and make it in earnest.
I sent for you last night but could not find you. Burn this as
soon as you have read it."³⁹

In the meantime, Johnson's difficulties in the execution of
the Military Reconstruction laws, had been, if anything, increasing. He had objected to General Sheridan's registration
regulations because the time allotted for registration was so
short. The General was unwilling to lengthen it, but on June
24 General Grant telegraphed Sheridan that the order of the
President to extend the time of registration in Sheridan's district on the first of August had "probably" better be complied
with.⁴⁰

"It will silence all charges of attempting to defeat the
Attorney-General's construction of the Reconstruction Acts,"
Grant declared, adding that Sheridan need not publish the
order of extension until a few days before the expiration of
the time already allotted, because in the meantime, "the Congress may give an interpretation of their own acts differing
possibly from the one given by the Attorney-General." Furthermore, the form of Stanbery's opinions was not such as to
entitle them to the force of orders, and if Grant were district
commander, he "would not be controlled by them further than
I might be convinced by the argument."

Thus beset by insubordination, Johnson's thoughts once
more turned to the removal of Sheridan and perhaps of Sickles
and Pope. Throughout July he took counsel with the Cabinet
on the matter and received divided opinions. At length, however, the report came to him that Stanton had personally
drafted the Supplementary Reconstruction Act which Congress
had just passed.⁴¹

Thereupon, on the first of August, the President determined
to go to the seat of the trouble and remove Stanton as Secretary of War. He called in Grant, informed him of his intentions and of his desire that the General act as Secretary of
War. Startled at the President's decision, Grant sought to
persuade him to change his mind. Most of Stanton's enemies,
he declared, had opposed the war. There were many claims

pending in the department of which he knew nothing, and he entertained serious doubts of his ability to pass upon these. Stanton's removal would be impolitic.

Johnson answered that he was sure it could not be said that his own policy had been to oppose the war. His action was not based upon any personal enmity to Stanton, but upon "public considerations of a high character." Any claims that pended might be settled by a special commission, or passed on to Congress. He did not wish to place the General in the attitude of one seeking the place. "I will not shrink from the performance of any public duty that may be imposed upon me," Grant answered, but reiterated his views as to the impolicy of the contemplated step.

But Johnson's mind was made up. At last, his long period of indecision and hesitation had come to an end. As soon as Grant had left, the President summoned Colonel Moore into his office, remarked that "for a year past Mr. Stanton must have seen that his resignation would at any time have been acceptable to me," and dictated this terse note, directing that it be held until he wished it presented:[42]

> Sir: Public considerations of a high character constrain me to say that your resignation as Secretary of War will be accepted. Very respectfully yours,
>
> ANDREW JOHNSON.

At the Cabinet meeting that day, as at most of the Cabinet meetings for the past year, the feeling that there was a traitor in their midst was so strong that little discussion of important topics took place until after Stanton had left. The President remarked that as those who remained could now freely speak their views, he wished their opinions on Sheridan's removal. McCulloch thought it would be injudicious. It would strengthen the ultra-Radicals and discourage the Conservatives. It might reanimate impeachment. Browning wished the Radicals to be given a free hand. "Let them go on with their violent and obnoxious measures—their usurpation and tyranny—and it will break them down." Such counsels of tame submission irritated Welles. The Administration could not afford to do nothing while great wrongs were being committed by the military governors. Surely the Executive had some duties to perform besides temporizing with corruption. Sheridan ought never to have been appointed and should have been removed long ago. Randall excitedly advocated Sheridan's dismissal.

The President warmed up under these remarks, and his eyes flashed. "What have we to expect from longer keeping quiet?" he asked. "Will the Republicans, the Conservative portion of them, come into our views? They are always promising, but they never perform. It may be said this will enrage them, and that they will then go forward and impeach me. If they would impeach me for ordering away an officer who, I believe, is doing wrong—afflicting and oppressing the people instead of protecting and sustaining them—if I am to be impeached for this, I am prepared."

McCulloch again reprehended the removal. Sheridan was so popular that disturbing him would bring down a Radical avalanche on the President's head. The Secretary of the Treasury told of a talk he had had with Wilson of Iowa, Chairman of the House Judiciary Committee, before the latter had gone home. Wilson had said that if Johnson were to do nothing rash and not disturb Sheridan, "all will go along well, and the extreme Radicals will be defeated; a division will certainly take place." This argument irritated the Secretary of the Navy. "What if Sheridan should proceed to hang some of the prominent and best men of Louisiana who differ with him," he asked McCulloch, "would Wilson expect, or you advise that he should still be continued?"[43]

McCulloch was so much disturbed by the danger involved in the case that he called on Welles early the next morning and besought him to see the President and prevent hasty action. Father Gideon told him to do so himself. He himself thought Sheridan must be removed. In his mind there was no question that the people of Louisiana and Texas deserved to be rid of an officer "who has so little discretion, such unformed judgment in civil matters, and who knows so little how to exercise power." Indeed, the law itself was an outrage, "a violation of the Constitution, and Sheridan outrageously administers it, removing and making appointments at will." None the less, Welles did go to see the President and mildly urged that it might be inexpedient to remove "the little fellow." It would undoubtedly lead to a renewal of Radical assaults, "more vindictive and ferocious" than before.

"What have I to fear?" Johnson answered, "what to gain

or lose by keeping this man who delights in opposing and counteracting my views in this position? . . . If Congress can bring themselves to impeach me, because in my judgment a turbulent and unfit man should be removed, and because I, in the honest discharge of my duty to my country and the Constitution, exercise my judgment and remove him, let them do it. I shall not shun the trial, and if the people can sanction such a proceeding, I shall not lament the loss of a position held by such a tenure."

This provoked Welles to remark that Sheridan was really but a secondary personage in the business. He would not have dared take the course he had without prompting and encouragement from others from whom he had advice, if not orders. "There is no doubt of that," the President answered, "I am giving that subject some attention," and he told of his interview with Grant. He then went to his desk and dug out a letter which Grant had written him following their talk.

In it the General remonstrated against the proposed removal, and referred to "the great danger to the welfare of the country should you carry out the designs thus expressed. . . . It certainly was the intention of the legislative branch of the government to place Cabinet Members beyond the power of executive removal, and it is pretty well understood . . . it was intended specially to protect the Secretary of War."[44]

Welles was surprised that Grant should have written such a letter—it was neither discreet, judicious nor excusable, even from his own point of view. When he had finished reading it, he remarked, "Grant is going over." Johnson answered: "Yes, I am aware of it. I have no doubt that most of these offensive measures have emanated from the War Department."

The Secretary took occasion to chide the President for his long hesitation. "If you had been favored with an earnest and sincere supporter of your measure in the War Department," he pointed out, "the condition of affairs in this country would this day have been quite different. It is unfortunate, perhaps, that you did not remove all of the Cabinet soon after your Administration commenced; certainly some who have made it a business to thwart and defeat your measures ought to have been changed." The President agreed, with evident emotion, but said he doubted whether he could have got rid of Stanton. "It would be unpleasant to make the attempt and not succeed."

Welles did not believe Stanton would persist in holding on when asked to resign.

At this point, the case of Mrs. Mary E. Surratt again impinged upon Andrew Johnson's life. The trial for Lincoln's murder of her son, John H. Surratt, captured in Egypt, brought back to the United States and made the target of Radical efforts to secure evidence of President Johnson's complicity in Lincoln's assassination, had begun in Washington on June 10 before a civil court. The Supreme Court's decision in the Milligan case had made further recourse to military commissions impossible. The case was long-drawn out.

On August 1, in the course of argument to the jury, one of Surratt's lawyers attempted to bring out into the open the truth as to the rumor about the petition to the President in the case of Mrs. Surratt. "Where is your record?" he inquired, referring to the record of the Military Commission which had tried the Lincoln conspirators two years before. "Why didn't you bring it in? Did you find at the end . . . a recommendation of mercy . . . that the President never saw?"

Disturbed by this attack, Edwards Pierrepont, chief of the attorneys for the prosecution, sent posthaste to Holt for the original record, which the Judge-Advocate-General himself brought into court, privately relating his version of its history to Pierrepont. The following day, when Joseph Bradley, another of Surratt's lawyers, renewed the taunts of the prosecution over their failure to produce the record in the earlier trial, Pierrepont felt ready to respond. With the record in his hands, he declared:

> President Johnson, when the record was presented to him, laid it before his Cabinet, and every single member voted to confirm the sentence, and the President with his own hand wrote his confirmation of it, and with his own hand signed the warrant. No other one touched this paper, and when it was suggested by some members of the Commission that in consequence of the age and sex of Mrs. Surratt it might possibly be well to change her sentence to imprisonment for life, he signed the warrant for her death with the paper right before his eyes—and there it is.

This plain and explicit declaration by the leading government counsel in this trial proved a sensation for the Sunday morning papers; their accounts went to the White House, where the President read them with amazement. The very next morning Johnson instructed Colonel Moore to deliver to Mr. Stanton in person the letter asking him to resign. The date was changed from August 1 to August 5 and the title, "The President of the United States," was added beneath Johnson's signature. Moore departed on his errand. On his first call he did not find Stanton in his office, so he went back again at about 10:15; he found the Secretary with a caller, handed him the letter without comment and retired.

A little later that same morning Johnson sent for the record in the Surratt case. Grant was in Stanton's office when the message came, and heard the Secretary of War send for the ranking officer of the Bureau of Military Justice, in Holt's absence, and direct him to take the original records to the White House.

When the document came before Johnson, he accorded it a "careful scrutiny." As soon as he discovered the clemency recommendation in it, "the President very emphatically declared that he had never before seen the recommendation. He was positive that it had never before been brought to his knowledge or notice."[45]

At last Andrew Johnson realized that he had been duped into signing the death warrant for the woman.[46] He remembered with great distinctness that Holt had brought the record in the case to him privately; that Holt had written out the body of the order of Presidential approval; that Holt had made not the slightest reference to any clemency petition, and that he had not seen it; and that the Judge-Advocate-General had carefully carried away the record as soon as the President put his name to the death warrant.

The harassed and indignant Chief Executive could come to no other conclusion but that Holt had played a shabby trick upon him—not only Holt, but Stanton, for the Secretary of War undoubtedly had either suggested or acquiesced in the imposition. Stanton had full knowledge of the existence of the clemency petition, and a direct subordinate of such a master of detail as the Secretary of War would not have dared perpetrate "so deadly a fraud" without his immediate Chief's knowledge.

Stanton returned no answer that day to the President's note. When Welles called at the White House, Johnson remarked: "I have dropped Sheridan for the present, and gone to the fountain head of mischief. . . . I have this morning sent a note to Stanton requesting him to resign. It is impossible to get along with such a man in such a position, and I can stand it no longer. Whether he will send in his resignation is uncertain. What do you think he will do?"

"I think he will resign," answered Welles, "and not intrude himself upon you and longer embarrass you; and yet his friends are the ones who have tried to tie your hands."

"Yes, and he instigated it," Johnson commented. "He has, I am satisfied, been the prolific source of difficulties. You have alluded to this but I was unwilling to consider it—to think that the man whom I trusted was plotting and intriguing against me."

Welles was afraid it was too late. He did not see how Stanton could refuse to resign, and yet he noted in his diary that he would not be surprised if Stanton did refuse. Andrew Johnson had been passive so long that he was powerless. "I do not perceive any benefit to himself by removing Stanton at this time. One year ago it would have been effective, and he would have retained Grant and the army; he would have had a different Congress; the country was then with him, and would have continued so. But the conspirators and intriguers have bound him hand and foot; he has permitted his prerogative to be despoiled, the Executive authority and rights to be circumscribed; until he is weak and powerless."

At 11:45 on Tuesday morning, Stanton's answer was received at the White House. Bearing date of August 5, it fulfilled the President's sharpest apprehensions, for it said:

> Sir: Your note this day has been received, stating that public considerations of a high character constrain you to say that my resignation as Secretary of War will be accepted.
>
> In reply, I have the honor to say that public considerations of a high character, which alone have induced me to continue at the head of this department, constrain me not to resign the office of Secretary of War before the next meeting of Congress.
>
> EDWIN M. STANTON,
Secretary of War.

When Andrew Johnson read this paper, Colonel Moore took note that he "did not evince much, if any surprise." The President said that Stanton's course was one which neither he nor his friends could sustain before the country. "I will leave Mr. Stanton hanging on the sharp hooks of uncertainty for a few days," he said, "and then suspend him from office."[47]

At that day's Cabinet meeting Welles was shown the note from Stanton and was very much disturbed. The other Cabinet Members were equally amazed. Seward asked when Stanbery would be back so as to give his advice as to the next step. Welles noted that the President seemed embarrassed as to how to act. The following day, however, Johnson had about made up his mind, as to his course. He would suspend Stanton and order Grant to take charge *ad interim*.

On August 9 the whole matter again came up before the Cabinet. The course of the Tenure-of-Office bill from its inception was reviewed, Senator Sherman's remarks in the debate were recited, and Stanton's own part in the preparation of the veto was discussed. Welles suggested that the time might be fitting to strike a body blow against the Radicals. The President could arouse the South and the better portion of the whole country "by sweeping out the whole batch of generals who are governing the States of the South in violation of the Constitution." Why should the President be the instrument for enforcing an unconstitutional act? He would be justified in declining to do so any longer. True, the Radicals in the House might prefer impeachment articles, and the Senate, "in its partisan violence," might convict. But in any event, the fundamental issues involved would be brought forcibly to the attention of the country, and if the President were convicted, "he would be sacrificed for adhering with fidelity to the Constitution. . . . His historic record would be worth more than any office."

Johnson listened attentively and approvingly to these urgings and occasionally interrupted Welles with expressions of contempt at threats of impeachment. "The President seems much relieved by the course he has taken," Colonel Moore noted in his diary of that day.[48]

On Sunday, August 11, the President and General Grant had "a pleasant, social, and friendly interview." Johnson and Grant came "to a mutual understanding," and Grant "seemed pleased with the proposed arrangements."[49] The President had definitely informed the General that he had made up his mind to suspend Stanton, that the place thus made vacant must be filled, and the question in his mind was whether it would not be better for the General to be made acting secretary than for a stranger to be named. As Commanding General of the Army, Grant understood the wants and interests of the service. If appointed, would Grant take the place?

"With the hectic smirk peculiar to him," the President noted, General Grant replied, "I will, of course, obey orders." Johnson next said he thought he had the right to ask if there were "anything between them." He had "heard it intimated that there was," and would really like to know. Grant answered that he knew of no personal unpleasantness between them, "and merely alluded to the difference of opinion" between the President and himself as to the Reconstruction Acts.[50]

After the General had departed, the President directed Colonel Moore to deliver to Stanton a letter already prepared, informing him that he was suspended from his office. Johnson told his secretary he was strongly inclined not merely to say "you are hereby *suspended* from office as Secretary of War," but, "you are hereby suspended and *removed* from office as Secretary of War." Moore did not deliver the letter until the following day.

"By virtue of the power and authority vested in me as President, by the Constitution and laws of the United States," Johnson's note informed Stanton, "you are hereby suspended from office as Secretary of War, and will cease to exercise any and all functions pertaining to the same. You will at once transfer to General Ulysses S. Grant, who has this day been authorized and empowered to act as Secretary of War *ad interim*, all records, books, papers and other public property now in your custody and charge."[51]

The President also addressed a formal note to Grant, in which the General was notified of Stanton's suspension, of the General's being authorized and empowered to act as Secretary of War *ad interim*, and directed at once to take up these duties. After Stanton had called on him and "wheedled him,"[52] Grant addressed to the secretary a copy of the President's letter notifying the General of his "assignment" in Stanton's stead, and added: "In notifying you of my acceptance, I cannot let the opportunity pass without expressing to you my appreciation of the zeal, patriotism, firmness and ability with which you have ever discharged the duties of Secretary of War."

The suspended minister responded immediately to Grant,

claiming that he was compelled by a "sense of public duty" to deny the President's right to suspend him, but that, inasmuch as the President had assumed to do so, and as Grant had notified him of his acceptance, "I have no alternative but to submit, under protest, to the superior force of the President." The note added a word of appreciation "of the kind terms" Grant had used in his letter, and of Stanton's "cordial reciprocation of the sentiments expressed."

Stanton's "furious, blustering" answer to the President was as insolent as he knew how to make it.[53]   He wrote: "Under a sense of public duty I am compelled to deny your right under the Constitution and laws of the United States, without the advice and consent of the Senate, to suspend me from office as Secretary of War.   But, inasmuch as the General commanding the Armies of the United States has been appointed *ad interim,* and has notified me that he has accepted the appointment, I have no alternative but to submit to superior force."[53]

When the President received this insubordinate communication from a Constitutional adviser, he read it with a frown, turned to Colonel Moore with an expression of feeling in his face beyond any his secretary had ever seen there before, and said, "The turning point has at last come; the Rubicon is crossed.   You do not know what Mr. Stanton has said and done against me."[54]

XX. GENERAL GRANT BREAKS HIS WORD

SHORTLY after Stanton's suspension, Thomas Ewing regretfully informed his son Hugh, American Minister to the Hague, that it was "almost certain that the President will be impeached this winter," and advised the diplomat to make his plans for recall upon Ben Wade's entry into the White House.[1] But the Old Roman's apprehension proved over-keen. The general temper of the Northern people was probably expressed by Godkin in the *Nation;* he looked to the Stanton matter "to furnish entertainment during the next two or three months." In suspending his War Minister, Johnson "has completely lost his head," but it was not at all likely that he hoped or intended "to effect any real change in the government of the South." The editor thought that the President merely hoped "to annoy a number of people who have annoyed him."[2]

While Stanton received encouraging messages from a few Radicals, the contumacious minister must have been disappointed at the small number of such letters and at the comparative insignificance of their signers.[3] The truth is that Stanton's removal did not greatly grieve the Radicals, the Army or the country; this "Carnot of the Civil War" was nowhere popular.

The day after the suspension, a Pittsburgh friend informed the President that his supporters were delighted with his action "in regard to 'Black Bull' Stanton. Nothing has done you so much harm as your Cabinet." Johnson's exhibition of vigor had caught the fancy of James Gordon Bennett, who again took "a new course" and began to support the President. Regarding Stanton's conduct "as unprecedented in a Cabinet officer, and tending to be revolutionary," the Commodore did not see how the President could escape the issue without degrading his high office. But Johnson should not let Stanton be the single martyr; he should change the entire satrapy in the South. In truth, the President was surprised to find how few really cared· about Stanton. Pleased with his new position, General Grant immediately began attending the Cabinet meetings, and his "very obvious" self-satisfaction was a matter of general remark. At the second meeting with the General present, Browning noted in his diary that Grant "had been stuffed for the occasion," and that his manner was one of "ridiculous arrogance."[4] None the less, the administration of the Army proceeded smoothly, and Radical ebullitions died down in a few weeks.

The two main concerns of the President now were to secure more endurable treatment for the South, and to endeavor to carry the State elections in the North that autumn. The chain of events ending in Stanton's suspension had had its beginning in General Sheridan's amazing conduct in Louisiana. On August 1 the General had made further wholesale removals of New Orleans civil officials and by this repetition of offensive acts had determined the President to remove him. Although Johnson first went to the fountain head of disaffection and suspended Stanton, his original purpose as to Sheridan was unchanged. No sooner had Grant been firmly placed in his new position than the President informed him that he wished Sheridan removed and General George H. Thomas put in his place.

On August 17 Johnson dictated an order for these changes and sent it to Grant with an accompanying personal note: "Before you issue instructions to carry into effect the enclosed order, I would be pleased to hear any suggestion you may deem necessary respecting the assignment to which the order refers." The President commented to Colonel Moore that if there were any good reasons against the order, Grant would call upon him to state them; but to his surprise, the Secretary of War *ad interim* answered in writing.[5] "In the name of the patriotic people who have sacrificed hundreds of thosands of loyal lives and thousands of millions of treasure to preserve the integrity and union of this country," Grant remonstrated that Sheridan must not be removed. He had performed his civil duties "faithfully and intelligently." It was "unmistakably the expressed wish of the country that General Sheridan should not be removed. . . . This is a Republic where the will of the people is the law of the land. I beg that their voice may be heard."[6]

"While cognizant of the efforts that have been made to retain General Sheridan in command," the President replied to Grant, "I am not aware that the question has ever been submitted to the people themselves for determination. It certainly would be unjust to the Army to assume that, in the opinion of the nation, he alone is capable of commanding the States of Louisiana and Texas." Johnson contrasted Thomas' record as a department commander with that of Sheridan; the former "has not failed, under the most trying circumstances, to enforce the laws, to preserve peace and order, to encourage the restoration of civil authority, and to promote as far as possible a spirit of reconciliation." But Sheridan had rendered himself "exceedingly obnoxious" by his exercise of the powers conferred by Congress, "and still more so by a resort to authority not granted by law or necessary to its faithful and efficient execution. His rule has in fact been one of absolute tyranny . . . and is alone sufficient to justify a change." This was indeed a republic, the Chief Executive informed the General, but one based "upon a written constitution" which made the President the Commander-in-Chief of the Army and Navy, and which directed that "he shall take care that the laws be faithfully executed." In response to this constitutional obligation and in the discharge of the duty thus required of him "by the will of the nation," the President had directed the removals.[7]

As soon as Grant read this communication, he hastened to the White House, and after a brief talk with the President, acquiesced in the removal of Sheridan, who, he said, would do admirably in an Indian command. Grant then related a rumor abroad that first Sheridan would be removed, then the other district commanders, and finally Grant himself! Johnson smiled, reminded the General that long ago he had wished him to act in Stanton's place. "Yes, I see no use of a civilian as Secretary of War," Grant answered.[8]

The President's first desire had been to send Hancock to Louisiana; he had named Thomas because the choice would occasion less criticism. Thomas objected strenuously to his new assignment, sending a surgeon's certificate that it would be dangerous for him to go to New Orleans. Upon this plea, Johnson promptly substituted Hancock.[9]

It had by this time become apparent to the President and his Cabinet that, while General Grant had been a fine soldier, he was a child in civil affairs, and been almost completely taken in by the Radicals. At the Cabinet meeting of August 23, there had been some discussion of modes of appointment, and the clause of the Constitution declaring that Congress "may by law vest the appointment of such inferior officers as they think proper in the President alone, in the courts of law, or in the heads of departments," had been read. Grant had actually argued that the commanders of military districts were the heads of departments in the meaning intended by the Constitution! He had likewise insisted that the satraps should not be corrected from Washington, because "such interference must tend to lessen their influence in their commands."

But it was high time for such correction, as the course of General Sickles additionally emphasized. On April 11 he had promulgated his famous Order No. 10. In intention, much of it was well designed for the betterment of Southern economic conditions. Its second section declared that "judgments or decrees for the payment of money, or causes of action arising between the 19th of December, 1860, and the 15th of May, 1865, shall not be enforced by execution against the person or property of the defendant. Proceedings in such cases of action now pending shall be stayed; and no suit or process shall be hereafter instituted or commenced for any such causes of action."

In June, Chief Justice Chase had gone to Raleigh to hold Circuit Court in North Carolina. In the sessions, he gave judgment against certain defendants, and execution writs were issued and given to the marshal of the court to serve upon their property. But in view of Sickles' stay law, the military commander at Wilmington, where the property was situated, expressly forbade the execution of the process of the Federal Court. Chase was not in North Carolina when this action was taken, but had he been there, he later wrote, "the judicial authority would have been maintained. I hardly think General Sickles would have arrested me for directing the commencement of the usual criminal proceedings against the officer who resisted the process. Certainly no fear of the consequences would have deterred me."[10]

There was one man at least in the country whose devotion to the Constitution and to the supremacy of law exceeded that of Chase—none other than the President. On August 17 Sickles telegraphed the army authorities that "if the United States courts in the rebel States be allowed to control the military authorities, the execution of the Reconstruction Acts will for obvious reasons soon become impracticable. Some of these courts will begin by declaring those acts of Congress void."[11] When the President showed this dispatch to Welles, he became highly indignant at "King Sickles," and advised Johnson to make short work of him. The President signified his displeasure that a military officer should obstruct the processes of federal court, and Grant sent Sickles a telegram to cancel his "stay-order." But the Secretary of War *ad interim* was vacillating. No sooner had he disapproved Sickles' act than he withdrew his dispatch, telegraphing instead, "Follow the course of action indicated by you as right."[12]

On August 23, when the Sickles matter came before the Cabinet, Stanbery was not present but Assistant Attorney-General Brinckley was on hand at the President's invitation, and expressed amazement that General Sickles, who was a lawyer, should have put himself in opposition to Chief Justice Chase. Grant said that at first he had sent an order to Sickles not to obstruct the United States Court, but after reflection had concluded that Sickles might have his reasons for his conduct, and had therefore countermanded his order. "Congress has put in my hands," the General continued, "the execution of this law, and I intend to see it is executed, but I am willing to see Mr. Brinckley's opinion when it is made out." Despite these overbearing remarks, the Attorney-General responded coolly that he had supposed that the General had expected to execute the Reconstruction laws "in subordination to law and authority."[13]

Such incidents were convincing Welles and others in the Cabinet not only that Grant was ignorant and obtuse, but also that he had become so anxious for the presidency that he would follow the Radicals in every move. By the last of August, Welles' confidence in Grant had almost been destroyed. Not yet did he believe him a bad man, but an insincere one; the General, without political experience or familiarity with the Constitution or even with "the elementary principles of civil government," had allowed himself "to be flattered, seduced, and led astray by men who are bad. Unless he can be extricated, and that soon, he will be made an instrument of evil."[14]

On August 26 the President had issued his modifying order retaining Thomas at the head of the Department of the Cumberland, assigning Hancock to New Orleans, Sheridan to the Department of the Missouri, removing Sickles and putting Canby in his place as Commander of the Second Military District. At the Cabinet meeting the next day, Grant adopted a surly attitude. He began by saying that the Military Reconstruction laws placed in his hands the task of their execution. He had not been consulted before receiving the orders the President had issued the day before, and they counteracted some of his own instructions. "While I have not wished to come in conflict with anyone," he continued, "I have a duty to perform. I must see the Reconstruction law executed."

This declaration was obviously premeditated and deliberate, doubtless prompted by some of Grant's Radical advisers. But the President met the test calmly and firmly. "General Grant will understand," he remarked unemotionally but with determination, "that it is my duty to see that the laws are executed, and also that when I assign officers to their duty, my orders must be obeyed. I have made this arrangement and performed this work deliberately, and it will go with as little delay as possible."[15]

Upon this "great rebuke," Grant seemed humbled and abashed, and immediately changed the subject, taking up Sickles' removal, admitting that the General's orders had been unauthorized and agreeing to Canby taking Sickles' place. In a very subdued manner, Grant said that while he wished to discharge his duties as Secretary of War *ad interim*, he was no politician, preferred not to be mixed up with political questions, and would like to be allowed not to sit at Cabinet consultations. The President replied that the General might act in this matter as he wished, and Grant immediately retired.

About three o'clock that afternoon, the President received from Grant a letter, dated August 26, protesting against the military assignments. In it he declared that the laws devolved certain duties upon him, and that he would not consent to yield any of the authority legally vested in him, but would insist upon exercising it. Admitting the President's right to assign district commanders, he none the less thought that he should be consulted. Furthermore, he said, whether the country judged rightly or wrongly, this act of the President would be interpreted as an effort to defeat Congress' plan of Reconstruction.

After reading this communication, Johnson turned it over to Colonel Moore, who noted that the President had been more than usually excited by its contents. After Moore had read the document, his chief remarked to him that it was insubordinate and that if published, it would condemn its author in the minds of all sensible persons. The President determined not to answer in writing, but sent for Grant the next morning and pointed out to him his error in writing such a letter. He was surprised at this communication, he told Grant, and, without meaning offense, he meant to speak plainly about it. The letter could do the President no harm, and if published with an answer it would play into the President's hands.

"At yesterday's Cabinet meeting," Johnson reminded the General, "you asked to be excused from attending Cabinet sessions, as you did not wish to participate in political discussions. . . . It now seems that while you were making this suggestion, this very letter, which amounts to a sort of political essay, was being copied for your signature at army headquarters." The President further suggested that if every order he gave was to provoke a political essay from Grant, it would be impossible for them to work together; the General must know that certain persons had an interest in creating misunderstandings between them. After some further blunt exposition by the President of Grant's fallacies, the crestfallen General asked if he could withdraw the paper, said he would issue the order as instructed by the President, and a little later sent a note to the White House withdrawing his insubordinate communication.[16]

Radical papers were angry at Grant's "surrender." Asserting that not a single member of the Cabinet had supported the removals, the *Independent* alluded to Grant's "dangerous position"; he had become Johnson's "cat's-paw." He had better beware.[17]

Following Sickles' removal, that Radical General once more demanded that a court of inquiry be ordered to judge his conduct in command of the Second District, his contention being that the dispute over the Chief Justice's writ was a collision of coördinate federal authorities. But the acting Attorney-General of the United States in a formal opinion denominated it a much less important conflict, actually "the mere misdemeanor of an unfaithful executive agent, who, having offended against the lawful power of the judiciary, has rendered himself liable to prosecution according to law." But Grant did not see why Sickles' demand for a court of inquiry should not be met. He seemed unable to perceive that what Sickles desired had no connection with military conduct, that the General was displeased with the views of the Attorney-General and with his removal by the President, and that he really wanted a court of inquiry to try the President and Attorney-General for having disapproved his conduct.[18]   The President saw clearly what Grant did not, and sternly refused the demand for a court.

It must not be thought, however, that these controversies with his obtuse and obstinate Secretary of War *ad interim* were the President's only, or indeed his chief trouble.   He was greatly concerned over the state elections scheduled for October and November.   If their outcome were to be the triumph of the Conservatives, or even a substantial gain of Democratic strength at Radical expense, it would be a virtual indorsement of the President's course by the Northern people, a great reversal of the verdict of the ballot box of the year before.

Immediately after Stanton's suspension, and with a view to bettering the Conservative position in the coming elections, pressure was brought on the President to make a general change in his Cabinet, the special targets of attack being Seward, McCulloch and Randall.   The country was filled with rumors of a general upheaval, and the *National Intelligencer,* an almost personal Johnson organ, ran a series of articles on the impending Cabinet changes.   Seward's feelings should be salved by sending him as Minister to England, while Charles Francis Adams or David Dudley Field should take his place.

To Francis Preston Blair, the fight between the President and the Radicals had resolved itself into an appeal for the support of the people of the North at the elections of that Autumn and of the next year, and "nothing but the most perfect organization on our side, and a discipline upon a plan equal to those of an army, can save us."   He appealed for a Cabinet reorganization which would bring "men of standing and enthusiasm" to Johnson's support.   Let Seward be sent abroad, he urged; "your fate is nothing to him."[19]

"It is wholly useless," E. G. White wrote the President from New York, "for your friends and those of the Constitution to struggle for success . . . while they are impeded by the odium and prejudice which attaches to various Members of your Cabinet, who have lost all standing before the country."

"The people trust in you," J. B. Stoll, editor of a Democratic paper at Ligonier, Indiana, informed the President, "but they utterly despise your Cabinet.   Tell me, Mr. Johnson, have you more than two true friends in the Cabinet?   What is Seward, Randall, McCulloch doing for you?"   Of the executive

GENERAL ULYSSES S. GRANT

A hitherto unpublished photograph taken soon after his inauguration in 1869.

subordinates in the editor's district, only one was supporting the Administration, a fact which he thought proved the unfaithfulness of McCulloch and Randall. Why would Johnson not surround himself with friends?

The various Cabinet Members under fire were not ignorant of the attacks being made upon them, and several indicated verbally to the President their willingness to relieve him of embarrassment, despite the Tenure-of-Office Act, if he would but hint his wish. Seward went a step further. On August 23 he formally tendered his resignation in writing. In his note he assured the President of his "sincere acknowledgment of the consideration and confidence with which you have honored me," of his "earnest desire for the success of your arduous labor in conducting public affairs of the country in this unfortunate crisis, and for your personal welfare and happiness."[20]

While the President was realistic in his estimate of Seward's value to the Administration—occasionally he admitted to intimate friends that the Secretary of State was a great political handicap and not a tower of strength—he seems to have concluded that no great good would be accomplished by a change; furthermore, Johnson had learned the workings of Seward's mind and had developed a real affection for him. The resignation was not accepted, but the President filed it away, doubtless with a feeling of pleasure at Seward's act of grace, contrasting so sharply with Stanton's uncivil stand.

Johnson's estimate of McCulloch was not quite so favorable; indeed, the course of the Secretary of the Treasury in appointing Radical after Radical to important offices, and in maintaining them despite their most vindictive attacks upon the President, must have been irritating to the latter. On the other hand, McCulloch was reluctant to protect loyal Johnson men against removal on trumped up charges. "Whenever I secure an influential man to go to work in your behalf," N. P. Sawyer of Pittsburgh complained to Johnson, "Members of your Cabinet, if in their power, strike me in some way or other."[21]

And yet McCulloch, within his limitations, was a valuable public servant; honest, attentive to duty, an able financier and economist, he was personally convinced of the rightness of Johnson's course, and even though timidity and irresolution led him to permit Radical intrigues in the Treasury, he was perhaps the best secretary available whom the President could secure. McCulloch's fellow Indianan, Senator Hendricks, bestirred himself to prevent a change in the Treasury; he interceded personally and had Dan Voorhees and other Indiana Democrats do likewise. In any event, the President decided to retain McCulloch.

The only actual vacancy in the Cabinet was that of Secretary of War. General Grant was merely filling the position *ad interim* until a successor should be appointed. Johnson consulted freely as to the man he should select to take Stanton's place. It was obvious that he should appoint a man not personally objectionable to the Radical Senate majority, for they must confirm him. At the same time, the new Secretary of War must be a man willing to execute the orders of the President without friction or contumacy. Governor Jacob D. Cox of Ohio was strongly urged for the appointment, as were General Frank Blair and Thomas Ewing, Senior, the choice of the latter being considered particularly desirable because he was General Sherman's father-in-law, and if he were Secretary of War, his influence and that of Sherman might keep Grant straight. But by the first week in October, the President became sure that Grant had completely gone over to the Radicals, and he decided to do nothing about a new Secretary of War for the time being.

Thus, despite the almost frantic urgings of supporters throughout the North, President Johnson entered the campaign of 1867 without amending a Cabinet politically disadvantageous to his cause.[22] This was only one of his handicaps in his great effort to secure indorsement at the polls. In 1866 the National Union Party had been projected as a great national political organism to embrace both Conservative Republicans and Democrats of every shade and, by a thorough union, to oppose and defeat the Radicals. But the Conservatives had had little Democratic assistance in constructing it, the Democrats seeming to prefer defeat to effective combination. After the disasters of September, October, and November, 1866, the National Union Party was no more.

In 1867 President Johnson could have his Conservative policies upheld at the polls only by the triumph of the Democrats in the state elections, but the Democratic leaders adopted a course of deliberate dissociation with Johnson and his Administration. They were pretending to do battle for the principles of free government for which the Tennessee tailor-statesman was contending even to the point of facing impeachment, and yet the Democratic leaders were loath to rally to the President's defense, or to indorse his dauntless patriotism.

On September 1, William Cassidy, editor of the Albany *Argus*, and a prominent up-state leader of the Democratic party in New York, wrote Montgomery Blair that he was disposed to disclaim all connection with the Administration.[23] This attitude gave the Administration much concern. The New York Democratic leaders of the day, in Welles' judgment, were small men with slight patriotism or sagacity, and he greatly feared that their lust for power and place would redound to the advantage of the Radicals. On September 12 the New York *World* sought to clear the skirts of the Democratic party of all responsibility for President Johnson—he was a problem for the Republicans, not for the Democrats. This attitude was the key of the policy of the Northern Democracy. In the resolutions adopted at the New York Democratic state convention, the President's name was not mentioned, the omission being a deliberate effort to dissociate the Democrats from the ranks of Johnson's supporters.

Despite this Democratic unwillingness to battle squarely for the vindication of the policies of the Administration, the President and his supporters did what they could to help the Democrats carry the fall elections. H. A. Smythe, Collector of the Port of New York, came to Washington, conferred with Johnson and went back to Manhattan to awaken the Conservative editors to their responsibilities. He aroused Thurlow Weed, who now was publishing the *Commercial Advertiser*. The managers of the *World* apologized for past misconduct and promised thenceforth to support the President. But Smythe's most important interview was with Bennett, who said he was "in for it now, and would not change his course." Bennett thought the whole Cabinet should resign, thus enabling the President to retain only those whom he wanted; then things would be better.[24]

One step which Johnson took, not alone with a view to influencing the elections but also as an act of peace and concord, was the issuance of a proclamation of general amnesty. Some of his advisers had urged against it, Jeremiah Sullivan Black going so far as to predict that if such a proclamation were issued, it would overwhelm the President's friends in Pennsylvania. The document was drafted with great care by Seward, with suggestions by Welles, and was carefully rewritten by the President. In the outcome, it was received with general approval except by the extreme Radicals. There was again a fitful revival of talk of impeachment, but it died down again before very long.

William Thorpe, a shrewd political observer whom the President had sent through the Middle West, reported improving conditions. As good an index as could be found in Michigan was the conduct of Zachariah Chandler, Radical Senator from that State, whose anxiety was so great that he "could be seen at all hours of the day running after men in the streets and exhorting them in the most fervent manner." The chief obstacle in Michigan, Johnson's agent reported, was the attitude of the Radical Federal officeholders, but prospects looked much better.

Conditions in Illinois were likewise improving. Thorpe was astonished at the great efforts the Radicals were making in Ohio. Among their speakers were Senators Patterson of New Hampshire and Chandler of Michigan, Representatives Bingham, Spalding and Ashley, and Chief Justice Chase! The Conservatives were not extending themselves thus, but the tide seemed to be turning in their direction. From New York, Halpine advised the President that he might rely on that State in November.

The October outcome in Ohio and Pennsylvania seemed to Welles "hardly credible." The overturn of the results in those same States the year before had been startling in the extreme. Although the Conservatives did not carry their state ticket in Ohio, they lost it by less than 3,000 votes out of a total of 284,000, and with a little greater activity probably would have won. But the great Ohio test was on the adoption of an amendment inserting negro suffrage in the state constitution; this proposal was rejected by a majority of 50,269. Despite Black's apprehensions, the Democratic candidate for Governor of Pennsylvania was elected.

These October results occasioned a great outburst of joy from Conservatives; it was a "signal triumph" for the President; "impeachment died at the polls," Conservative newspapers thundered. "We are transported with joy," General McClernand telegraphed from Illinois, while Lewis D. Campbell exulted that "the party that planted itself squarely on negro suffrage in Ohio was overwhelmingly beaten wherever the issue was squarely made."

Thomas Ewing informed the President that Ohio was "absolutely in the power of Conservative men, who will allow neither party to run the country. It has convinced the Radicals that they have not the country in a sling, and the vote on the negro question has shown them the handwriting on the wall."[25] He wrote his son in Holland that the election had settled two things: there would be no impeachment, and the next President would not be an extreme Radical.[26] In addition, he issued a powerful address to the country, pointing out the great repudiation of Radical doctrine, and indicating that a dire fate awaited the Radicals if they sought further to breach the Constitution of the United States.

These results in the October States were good indices of the general temper of the voters. Throughout October the Radicals made violent efforts to avert this virtual repudiation of their policies. Some of their Senators were becoming uneasy at the criticism that it was unbecoming for a member of a body which might soon serve as the court to try the President to declare in advance their certitude of his guilt. One of these was Chandler of Michigan, who prepared an article for Forney's *Chronicle* contending that "senators cannot be precluded from sitting in judgment on the President because they may have expressed an opinion that if he had done such and such things, he ought to be convicted." The *Chronicle*, however, was unwilling to print this letter, for the zeal of the impeachers had been dampened by the fears of the Northern capitalists.[27]

From coast to coast, the results were favorable to the President. The New York election, Thomas Ewing wrote, had created a sensation, and because of it "the Radical Congress is on its last legs."[28] There was an overturn in California; the Radical majority of 23,000 registered in that State in 1866 had been transformed into a Democratic lead of 8,000 votes. Conservatives carried two of California's three congressional districts and elected a Democratic legislature. Major Benjamin C. Truman wrote to the President from San Francisco that Stewart of Nevada, now the most Radical of the Radicals, was demoralized, while Senator Conness of California, "who fled around like a galvanized grasshopper before the election, hasn't been signalled since."[29]

The shift in the vote between 1866 and 1867 was startling.

In the former year, the total vote cast for Radical candidates in nineteen Northern States had been 1,741,135. That for Democratic and Conservative candidates in the same States had been 1,457,146, a Radical lead of almost 300,000. In 1867, however, the Conservative strength had increased to 1,628,183, and the Radical vote had shrunk to 1,578,748.[30] Of the States which voted in 1867, the Radicals had, in the year before, carried California, Connecticut, Iowa, Kansas, Maine, Massachusetts, Michigan, Minnesota, New Hampshire, New Jersey, New York, Ohio, Pennsylvania, Rhode Island, Vermont, West Virginia and Wisconsin. But in 1867 California, Connecticut, Kansas, New Jersey, New York and Pennsylvania went Democratic, the Democratic majorities in Kentucky and Maryland were greatly increased, and the Radicals were able to win in Minnesota, New Hampshire, Ohio and Massachusetts by the barest possible margins. Ohio was not the only Northern State to repudiate "Impartial suffrage." In November, both Minnesota and Kansas rejected a similar negro suffrage amendment, while in New Jersey, where the issue was indirectly presented, it was dismissed by a large majority.[31]

Following the election, the President expressed his gratification in a public speech, the first after a long silence. Before he made it, Browning urged him "to do nothing more than congratulate the country on the result—to criticize nobody and to say no harsh words." Johnson followed this advice so faithfully that sneering enemies wrote: "This time, his friends, knowing his weakness, persuaded him to put his speech on paper; the result was a very tame speech, and a disappointed audience. It was a sorry sight to see the Tennessee lion in chains."[32]

The Democrats undertook to chide the President because his appointees had not more ardently supported him. "We have gone through a great contest," Horatio Seymour wrote, "the results of which in this and other States have cheered your heart. In this conflict you had a deeper personal interest than any living mortal. It was in effect a struggle on the part of the defenders of constitutional liberty to rescue you from the assaults of the Radical leaders, who were resolved, if sustained by the popular vote, to oust you from official station, and regardless of constitutional prohibitions to put their Ohio champion in your place."[33]

Under such circumstances, Seymour had been provoked "to

encounter in this vicinity the secret and generally the open influence of the national government appointees. We were entitled at least to their tacit support. Their voices and means
were used against us. The Internal Revenue, the Post Office,
the Customs House, are all filled with these Radical partisans.
. . . Some influence should be brought to bear upon the heads
of departments at Washington to insure a selection of subordinates who are not your enemies. We care nothing about
their being Democrats, but we do ask that they may be *your*
friends. I speak earnestly and with a feeling of indignation
inspired by victory achieved in spite of the opposition of this
army of federal appointees. Is there no remedy for this
evil?"[34]

In the coterie of Radical leaders in Washington, the effect
of the election was to increase their anxiety to impeach the
President. Following the October elections, when Charles
Sumner visited Milwaukee to deliver a lecture, a friend asked
him if Pennsylvania and Ohio had not disposed of impeachment.
"In what respect?" inquired Sumner.
"The elections have gone against the Republicans," his
friend answered, "and the voice of the people is against impeachment.".
"Those elections only show more imperatively the necessity
for impeachment,"[35] Sumner replied.
In the House, Boutwell, Butler and Thad Stevens were unflagging in their zeal for the trial of the President. The proposal was again bruited that not only should the President be
impeached, but also that Congress should pass a law suspending him from office during his trial, a possibility which greatly
disturbed Johnson. His friends advised him variously. Governor Bradford of Maryland held that resistance would be
unwise; "what the Radical leaders most desire," he wrote, "is
the assurance that the President would resort to force to defeat
such legislation," for it would "reunite their now discordant
followers and bring back those who are leaving them." If
suspension were attempted, the President should resign and let
Ben Wade take hold. The Radicals would then quickly disgust the country.[36]
After writing this sound advice, Bradford determined not
to send it. This was perhaps just as well, for the President
was in no temper to listen to it with patience. He felt that to

be impeached was one thing, to be suspended from office, perhaps imprisoned while on trial before the Senate, another. He deemed the latter flagrantly unconstitutional, and had made up his mind to resist it.[37]

On October 8, Browning predicted to the President that Congress would impeach him. Should Congress pass a law that, in all cases of impeachment, the accused should be deposed and arrested during trial Browning asked, what would Grant do about it? Such a law would be clearly unconstitutional, Johnson answered, but Grant "would not deem it his duty to pass upon its constitutionality, but would obey it." The President thought, however, that the Supreme Court would be in session, the law could be immediately adjudicated, and Grant would abide by the Court's decision.

Two days later, Welles earnestly advised his chief to have a frank and unreserved understanding with Grant. The President on several occasions had been able to convince Grant of his errors, and perhaps he could do so again. If Grant could be detached, the Radicals could not move. In any event, the President was entitled to know what Grant would do in the event of an attempt at arrest. Johnson called on General Grant the next day.

Johnson began by saying that the General could not be ignorant of the schemes and threats being made against the Chief Executive, and must also be aware that it was the President's duty to vindicate the rights of the Executive.[38] What were the General's views as to the course Stanton would pursue to obtain possession of his office, if the Senate should not concur in his suspension. Grant replied, "Mr. Stanton will have to appeal to the courts to reinstate him," and illustrated this view by citing the position he had taken in the case of the Baltimore Police Commissioners. The President expressed his desire to keep Stanton from returning to the office of Secretary of War, whether the Senate should sustain the suspension or not. Grant then said that he had not looked particularly into the Tenure-of-Office bill, "but what I have stated is the general principle, and if I should change my mind in this particular case, I will inform you of the fact"; and he added that he would do so in ample time for the President to make his arrangements.[39]

Since the President's "sole object" in the interview had been to ascertain what Grant would do if Stanton sought to

reoccupy the place of Secretary of War, he was much pleased
at Grant's frank answers, and the interview terminated with
the "distinct understanding" that if, upon reflection, Grant
should not wish to become a party to the controversy, he was
to return the office to the President prior to the Senate's decision, so that the President, if he desired to do so, might
designate someone else to succeed the General as Secretary of
War *ad interim*. After Grant's explicit declaration, Johnson
believed he could safely rely upon him, and Welles too felt sure
that the General would make good his word.

In a further effort to keep Grant from going over completely to the Radicals, the President summoned General Sherman to Washington. The two Generals were great friends;
Sherman sympathized with the President and had a mortal
antipathy to Stanton, but Welles feared that "the stubborn
will and selfishness of Grant will overpower the yielding genius
and generous impulses of Sherman."

These two Generals, whose roles were so important during
the Johnson Administration, afforded a curious contrast in
their abilities and their habits. Sherman had the gift for self-
expression and vivid—almost clairvoyant—analysis and pre-
vision. Grant was dull and sodden, his stolidity being mistaken
for firmness and force. Sherman abhorred politics; Grant was
fascinated by its lure. Sherman was eager to be serviceable to
his friends; Grant moved most cautiously to aid them. The
contrast in smoking habits of the two Generals was indicative
of their general temperamental difference. Sherman was a
"passionate" cigar smoker, putting energy and zeal into it.
After one cigar was but half consumed, he would throw it
away, and light another. His old stumps were known in the
Army as "Sherman's old soldiers." Grant's favorite occupation also was smoking; he would "lean back comfortably, in his
chair, body and soul sunk in deepest peace." From Johnson's
standpoint, and that of the reconstructing South, it might be
regretted that Sherman, rather than Grant, was not then the
General of the Army.[40] In the present instance, Sherman did
the best he could to convince Grant that Radicalism was wrong,
but it was too late. "The Hero of Appomattox" had the White
House in mind for himself.

Despite the failure to detach Grant from the Radicals,
Johnson's advisers were buoyed up by the election, and many
of them urged the President to carry the war into Africa. On

November 25 Jeremiah Sullivan Black wrote that there was no mistake about the public mind, the mass of the people were determined to compel respect to the Constitution, and would not consent to put its keeping into colored hands. The people were likewise indignant at the frauds on the Treasury. To make himself a great name, Black urged, the President need only to plant himself firmly on these three propositions, and "your ship will ride triumphant in the wave which submerges Chase and Grant both. Remember that on these great principles you have no rival before the Nation. Let Chase spend his money and Grant beat his drums to all eternity—the truth has got a start."

Black had been working on a draft of Johnson's message to the Congress shortly to assemble. The document he had drawn up, he informed the President, "is plain, as you had it prepared when I saw you, and plain speaking is exactly what is needed. It is respectful, too, in its tone and language. Let them see if they can find you guilty of not violating the Constitution."[41]

On November 30, Colonel Moore read the message to the Cabinet, where it was received with general approval, Welles terming it a "sound, strong document."[42] At the President's request, Black had also drafted some questions to be laid before the Cabinet as to what should be done if an attempt were made to suspend or arrest the Chief Executive before conviction of impeachment charges. This memorandum was carefully revised by Johnson before being presented. The questions, as phrased by the Pennsylvania Conservative, were:

> 1. Whether a change in the Executive Department can be legally accomplished by decree of the two Houses of Congress, or either of them?
>
> 2. Whether an order of one or both of the Houses to arrest and imprison the President and transfer the executive authority to some other person would be legalized merely by the previous finding of articles of impeachment by the House of Representatives and their presentment to the Senate?
>
> 3. Whether it is or is not the duty of all citizens and especially of all officers civil and military to obey the lawful orders of the President and Commander-in-Chief until his term of office is lawfully brought to a close?
>
> 4. Whether an attempt to change the government

by a forcible deposition of the President would or
would not be levying war upon the United States and
therefore an act of treason by all who engage in it?

5. Whether such deposition or arrest of the Presi-
den and the transfer of his official functions to another person would be more or less a violation of an
organic law if done with the consent of Congress
than if it proceeded from private parties?[43]

The President went over this draft with unusual care, and
when Colonel Moore read it to the Cabinet on November 30, its
phraseology had been much changed and the second of Black's
questions altogether omitted. Seward, McCulloch, Grant,
Welles, Browning, Randall and Stanbery were present, and
this minute was entered upon the questions in the President's
hand and signed by him. "The above paper was submitted
to the Cabinet this day, and after a full and free discussion
was unanimously approved, dispensing with the necessity of
requesting written answer."[44] Welles noted in his diary that
the Cabinet Members were all agreed that if the House preferred articles against the President, he should submit to be
tried, and all were likewise agreed that he should not consent
to be arrested or suspended before conviction. Grant said that
such a measure "would be revolutionary and ought to be resisted; the President ought not to submit to it; a mere law of
Congress would not justify such a step; an amendment to the
Constitution would be necessary.[45]

The President was much gratified at this united front on
the subject and, after his advisers had left, remarked to his
secretary, "The day has produced great results. The time
for mere defense is now past, and I can stand on the offensive
in behalf of the Constitution and the country."[46]

In November Thomas Ewing came to Washington to remain during the winter, "and do what I can to aid in bringing
things right. I do not know where we shall land. We are in
the sight of the breakers."[47] Late that month Johnson's apprehensions had been increased by Representative Churchill's
sudden switch to the Boutwell group of the committee, thus
giving the Massachusetts Radical a majority of the House
Judiciary Committee willing to urge impeachment. Thus, when
the House refused to bring the articles against the Chief Executive, there was a general feeling of relief on the part of the

Conservatives the nation over. None the less, Thomas Ewing regarded it as important for the President to report Stanton's suspension to the Senate, and prepared a rough draft of a message Johnson could use. Ewing believed the public should be reminded immediately of the manner in which the President was obstructed in the performance of his public duties.[48]

Stanbery, too, was anxious for the President immediately to communicate to the Senate his reasons for suspending Stanton, and prepared "a very elaborate paper" on the subject. The President himself had written a brief and dignified report, which he believed was all the matter required. But Stanbery was insistent that a thorough discussion be given in the message, and that the occasion be seized for Johnson to vindicate himself.

On December 12 the President read his revised message to Welles, Stanbery and Browning; they thought it an able document, but Welles suggested that he add a paragraph reciting Grant's economy and acceptable performance of duty in Stanton's place. This was done.[49] But even after the message had gone to the Senate and had been made public, Johnson thought his own summary the best that could have been sent in, although several Senators told him of their pleasure at the message; among other things, they said, it contained the only sound exposition yet made of reasons for the New Orleans riots and of Stanton's suppression of the Baird telegram.

Later that week, the President drafted a message to Congress regarding General Hancock. That officer had signalized his assumption of command of the Fifth Military District by issuing an order which evoked the glowing approval of Conservatives throughout the country. Peace and quiet, he said, reigned in the department, and he intended to maintain the civil authorities in their power. "The great principles of American liberty still are the lawful inheritance of this people," he announced; free institutions "always furnish the strongest inducements to peace and order." Whenever insurrectionary force had been overthrown and civil authorities "are ready and willing to perform their duties, the military power should cease to lead, and the civil administration resume its natural and rightful dominion."[50] None was more pleased at this order than Andrew Johnson. Early in December he sent a copy of Hancock's proclamation to Congress—the same Congress which in July had adopted votes of thanks to Sheridan, Sickles and

Pope. In his message, the President declared that to Hancock belonged "the distinguished honor . . . of being the first officer in high command south of the Potomac since the close of the Civil War who has given utterance to these noble sentiments in the form of a military order," and therefore "respectfully" urged Congress that "recognition of General Hancock's patriotic conduct is due, if not to him, to the friends of law and justice throughout the country." Such a resolution sat poorly with the Radicals. They contemptuously ignored Hancock's order, but passed instead a resolution "utterly condemning the conduct of Andrew Johnson, acting President of the United States," in removing Sheridan.

The effect on the public mind of the Stanton message was good, but that as to Hancock less satisfying. Welles found that the Radicals were "striving to retain their usurped power by outrageous measures and violence," with Chase remaining their candidate for the Presidency; but that the Conservative Republicans, or at least those who, because of their views were not as extreme as the extreme Radicals, seemed Conservative in contrast, were daily inclining more and more to General Grant, who, on his part, was "not only willing, but grows daily more and more anxious; his aspirations . . . are equal to and even surpass those of the Chief Justice." None had been more surprised by the election results than Grant, who had already committed himself to the Radicals, and it was too late for him to change.[51] The Secretary of the Navy noted the estimate he had finally and regretfully made that "Grant may prove a dangerous man. He is devoid of patriotism, is ignorant, but cunning, yet greedy for office and power."[52]

The chief cause of irritation in the Cabinet was Grant's support of the district commanders in the South in their imposition of oppressive measures on that unhappy section. In August the President had rid himself of Phil Sheridan, and General Hancock had quickly won the respect and admiration of the Conservatives by his liberal attitude at New Orleans. In the Carolinas General Canby was a great improvement on Sickles. But Johnson had much cause to regret that he had not removed General Pope from suzerainty of the Third Military District. Pope was ardently loyal to the Radical Reconstruction measures, and "convinced of the importance of suppressing the old political leaders in Georgia, Alabama, and Florida."[53]

This Radical General asserted that the advance of the negroes in "education and knowledge" was "marvelous"; and that,
if it should continue, within five years the intelligence of Georgia would shift from the whites to the negroes. When he had
announced his assumption of command of the district, he had
declared that he would permit the existing officers of the state
government to continue in office until their terms expired and
would interfere only if the state tribunals failed to do equal
justice to all persons; a little later he added that he would
likewise remove any state officer who interfered with or opposed
Reconstruction methods.[54]

Pope's conduct was irksome to the Georgia Conservatives.
His opinions and personal character gained for him the general reputation of a tyrant, a reputation his official acts do
not altogether justify. Georgia's Constitutional Convention,
ordered by the Reconstruction Acts, had assembled and had immediately levied a tax to defray its expenses; but receipts from
the tax were slow to come in, and Pope greatly irritated the
Georgia people by issuing a peremptory demand upon the State
Treasurer that he immediately advance the money to pay them.
The State Treasurer took legal counsel on the subject and informed the General that there was no authority in the laws of
Georgia or its Constitution to permit him to make any payment without warrant drawn upon him by the Governor, that
he was under bond to conduct his office in accordance with the
Constitution and the laws of the State, and that he must refuse.
Pope threatened his immediate removal, and took the matter
up with Governor Jenkins, who refused to issue the desired
warrant. Interchanges between the two grew rather warm and
Pope made repeated threats to remove Jenkins and State Treasurer Jones.

Pope's course in Alabama likewise aroused indignation, and
John M. Forsythe of Mobile wrote the President imploring him
to relieve the people of that State from Pope's oppression and
misgovernment. When Johnson brought this communication
before the Cabinet on December 20, Stanbery told Browning
he was glad to see it; that the President must not move a finger;
let the Radicals go on and they would kill themselves. Browning agreed, but Welles raised emphatic protest. What was to
become of the people of Alabama? Would the President be
discharging his duty and the Cabinet Members theirs, if they
quietly witnessed these wrongs without trying to prevent them?

In December, when the Georgia controversy had reached a crisis, Jeremiah Sullivan Black urged the instant removal of the General, while Thomas Ewing insisted that the President "relieve General Pope at once before he has time to do further mischief, and give as a reason that you can permit no military officer to rob a state treasury for the benefit of any man or set of men, not even to apply the funds for the purpose of Reconstruction, without the special and distinct direction of Congress to that effect."[55] On December 27, Henry S. Fitch appealed to the President to "save the people of Georgia from this last humiliation, the filling of all state and municipal offices with those admirably adapted to prostitute and disgrace them." The cry was heeded, and an order was issued removing Pope from command and placing in his stead General George Gordon Meade, who, Johnson hoped, would follow a less Radical course.

These political troubles, however, were far from being the only cause for distress in the South. Throughout the fall, reports of suffering came from the late Confederate States, where the combination of a bad économic situation and unparalleled political disturbance had proved gravely detrimental to the welfare of white and black alike.[56] Conditions were indeed deplorable. The President of the Memphis and Charleston Railroad wrote the President that "such a state of demoralization I could never have conceived as exists in Mississippi and Alabama. . . . The fall in cotton has brought ruin upon the planter and the merchant. . . . The negroes are beginning to feel the pinch of cold and hunger; he must rob, murder or steal. This has already commenced and will end in bloodshed or anarchy, unless the government takes active steps to prevent it."[57]

With Pope's removal, Thomas Ewing believed that "the President had Congress on the hip." During December the Radicals had taken no action upon the President's notification to the Senate of his suspension of Stanton. Late that month Stanton had returned to Washington, but was there chary of public appearance because of fear of personal chastisement from people whom he had insulted or wronged while in office.[58] Following the Christmas holidays, with the return of Congress to the Capital, the Senate Committee on Military Affairs, to which the President's message on Stanton had been referred, resumed its task. The Radicals generally agreed that they must reinstate Stanton, and that in doing so, they must make

as good a showing for Stanton as they could. Howard of
Michigan undertook the task of answering the President.

The latter determined to be ready for eventualities, and on
January 7 Colonel Moore prepared both a brief letter removing
Stanton and a short message to the Senate to inform that
body of Stanton's definite dismissal. Johnson wished these
papers ready for his signature at any moment, so that they
could be acted on as soon as the Senate disapproved Stanton's
suspension. Colonel Moore asked his chief about the newspaper
report that General Grant had said that, should the Senate
reinstate the suspended Secretary, he would turn the Department back to Stanton. The President told Moore of Grant's
promise that his action would be limited to withdrawing from
the Department, thus leaving it in the President's hands. Johnson continued that perhaps it might be as well for the Senate
to reinstate Stanton, because "Grant has served the purpose
for which he has been selected, and it is desirable that he should
be superseded in the War Office by another."[59]

On Friday, January 10, the Senate Committee reported a
motion that "having considered the evidence and reasons given
by the President in his report of the 12th December, 1867, for
the suspension from office of Secretary of War, Edwin M. Stanton, the Senate do not concur in such suspension."[60] On Saturday Senate Democrats denounced the Howard report at
such length that a vote could not be had until Monday; the
Radicals listened in silence to these attacks. That same day
Grant decided that he would not remain Secretary of War if
the Senate should disapprove Stanton's suspension, and told
Sherman of his decision. The latter urged him promptly to
inform the President of his determination, and Grant accordingly went to the White House, where he had a "protracted"
conversation with the Chief Executive.[61]

Grant said that he had recently examined the Tenure-of-
Office Act and had concluded that it left him no discretion as
to what he should do; that he did not want to be subject to
the fine or imprisonment which the act provided as penalties
for its infraction. The President told him that he had not
suspended Stanton under the Tenure-of-Office Act, but under
the authority given him by the Constitution. This same authority did not preclude his reporting the suspension to the Senate
as an act of courtesy. But inasmuch as Grant had been appointed under the President's constitutional authority and not

under the Tenure-of-Office Act, he should not be governed by
the latter. So far as the penalties of the law were concerned,
the President would be glad to undergo the fine and imprisonment in Grant's stead. The General maintained that the law
was binding upon him, whether constitutional or not, until set
aside by the proper court.

After they had debated their divergent views for more than
an hour, Grant said that, as had been agreed in their former
conference, he would either return the office to the President's
possession in time to enable the latter to appoint a successor
before the Senate had reinstated Stanton, or would remain as
Secretary of War *ad interim* "awaiting a decision of the question by judicial proceedings." If "he could not properly resist the action of the Senate, he would at least leave the office
. . . in the condition in which it was when he was appointed to
that position." With the understanding that there should be
another conference on Monday, at which Grant should inform
the President of his final decision, the General left.[62]

Another important matter discussed that Saturday related
to General Pope's successor, General Meade, who had inherited
the latter's quarrel with the Governor and the State Treasurer
of Georgia. To Johnson's disappointment, Meade's attitude
was almost as Radical as Pope's; Meade informed the authorities at Washington of his purpose to oust the governor and
the treasurer and to install two army officers to perform their
duties. After a discussion, General Grant promised the President that he would not permit General Meade to carry this out.

The next day—it was Sunday—Grant was "greatly concerned," and busied himself with consultations with Senator
Reverdy Johnson of Maryland, General Sherman and others.
Adam Badeau, his secretary and biographer, asserts that the
General was not keen to have Stanton restored; that Grant
"felt that . . . the workings of the government would be need-
lessly thwarted by the intrusion of an unwelcome Cabinet officer upon the Head of the State." Sherman and Grant both
thought that the President should immediately nominate a
Secretary of War who would be acceptable to the Radicals,
and Sherman suggested Jacob D. Cox as the man whose name
should be sent in. Grant caught at the idea and begged Sherman to go to the White House and convey this advice to the
President. This Sherman did.[63]

That evening Thomas Ewing wrote Johnson that he had

"assurance" that if he would nominate Cox on Monday morning, "he will be confirmed at once, and no direct vote will be taken on Stanton—indirectly this will sanction his removal. . . . It must be done tomorrow morning, or the occasion will have gone by. It will avoid unpleasant complications, of which we have had as many as the country can well endure."[64] Yet despite his promise of Saturday, Grant took no steps to tender his own resignation as Secretary of War *ad interim* so that the President might place in that position another, of firmer character, to force Stanton to resort to law and thus bring the constitutionality of the Tenure-of-Office bill before the United States Supreme Court.

Late on Monday afternoon the Democrats were talked out, and the Radicals brought the reinstatement resolution to a vote; it was adopted by a vote of thirty-six to six, thirteen not voting.[65] Early Tuesday morning General Grant went to the Secretary's office, bolted one door on the inside, locked the other on the outside, handed the key to an Adjutant-General and announced, "I am to be found at my office at Army Headquarters."[66] Apparently Stanton was already in the building, for the Adjutant-General "then went up stairs" and handed the key to Stanton, who forthwith resumed possession of the vacant office.[67] His first act was to send a curt message to Grant informing him that "the Secretary of War wanted to see him," an action which seemed to Grant purposely offensive, in sharp contrast to the General's courtesy to Stanton in August, when the situation had been reversed.[68]

Monday night Grant had attended a ball at the White House, but said nothing further to the President of the Stanton affair. Johnson did not know of General Grant's failure to make good his promise until after the General's hasty relinquishment and Stanton's immediate repossession had become accomplished facts. Even so, on the night of the 13th, when he received notice of the Senate's action, the President was alarmed by his failure to receive from General Grant his resignation in accordance with the latter's pledge.

The next morning, one of Grant's aides brought the President a note from the General, enclosing a copy of the official notice from the Senate of its action, and declaring "according to the provisions of Section 2, of 'An Act Regulating the Tenure of Certain Civil Offices,' my functions as Secretary of War *ad interim* ceased from the moment of the receipt of the enclosed notice."[69]

When he had read this letter, Johnson became highly indignant at "Grant's duplicity."[70] He told Colonel Moore of his interview with Grant on the Saturday before, and of Grant's promise that if he came to the conclusion that he could not resist the action of the Senate, he would immediately resign as Secretary *ad interim*. That morning the President had learned of another instance of General Grant's deception. Despite his promise not to permit General Meade to remove Governor Jenkins of Georgia, the removal had been announced in that morning's papers.[71]

President Johnson immediately summoned Grant to the Cabinet meeting, and the General responded. As soon as Grant entered the Cabinet room, he was addressed as "Mr. Secretary," a title which he haltingly disclaimed, saying that he had notified the President that he could no longer serve in that capacity. Johnson seemed "excited and indignant," but Browning noted the way he "maintained perfect self-control."[72]

In the presence of the entire Cabinet, the President expressed his surprise at the course Grant had pursued, and then put three questions to the General. First he asked if, in their conversation several months before, the General had not agreed either to remain at the head of the War Department and abide judicial proceedings if the Senate should reinstate Stanton; or, if Grant wished to avoid such involvement, "to put me in the same position with respect to the office as I occupied previous to your appointment, by returning it to me in time to anticipate such action by the Senate?" Grant sought to avoid answering the question directly, admitted that some time before he had promised to give the President notice before giving up the office, but maintained that when he had thus declared himself, he had not closely examined the penalty sections of the Tenure-of-Office Act, and was not willing to suffer five years' imprisonment, or to pay a fine of $10,000.

The President then asked him a second question, whether at their conference on Saturday he had not requested the General to state what he intended to do, "and whether, if, in reply to that inquiry, you had not referred to our former conversations, saying that from them I understood your position, and that your action would be consistent with the understanding which had been reached?" To this question Grant again reluctantly replied in the affirmative. Johnson then asked him if it had not been understood, at the close of their talk on Saturday, that "we were to have another conference on Monday, before final action by the Senate in the case of Mr. Stanton?"[73]

"Was it not our understanding," the President asked him, "did you not assure me some time ago, and again on Saturday, that if you did not hold to the office yourself, you would place it at my hands that I might select another?"

"That," the General replied, "was my intention. I thought some satisfactory arrangement would be made to dispose of the subject. Mr. Reverdy Johnson and General Sherman spent a great deal of time with me on Sunday. Didn't Mr. Johnson come to see you? I sent General Sherman yesterday after talking the matter over. Didn't you see Sherman?"

The President said he had seen both of them, but he did not see what these interviews had to do with carrying out Grant's promise. "Why did you give up the keys to Mr. Stanton and leave the department?" he demanded. Grant answered that he had given the keys to the Adjutant-General and had sent word to the President by his aide.

"Yes," the President answered, "but that, you know, was not our understanding."

After one or two further mumbled attempts at apology, Grant stammered, hesitated, said he had intended to call on the President on Monday, and hurriedly left.

During this scene, the General was "humble and hesitating," and had "an abashed look never to be forgotten." His entire appearance and conduct produced the impression on the Cabinet Members that "he had acted with duplicity—had not been faithful and true to the man who had confided in and trusted him. . . . His mien, never very commanding, was almost abject, and he left the room with less respect . . . from those present than ever before."

The President displayed calm and dignity, although manifestly displeased and disappointed. While unable to conceal his chagrin, Johnson used no harsh expression, nor committed anything approaching incivility, yet Grant "felt the few words put to him, and the cold and surprised disdain of the President, in all their force."[74]

Thus Stanton was back in the office of Secretary of War, and the President had been prevented from securing a test in the court of the constitutionality of the Tenure-of-Office Act by General Grant's breaking his word to the President.

XXI. THE IMPEACHMENT OF THE PRESIDENT

E ARLY on the morning of January 15 Generals Grant and
Sherman called upon the President. Disturbed at an
account which the *National Intelligencer* had that morning
given of the events in the Cabinet the day before, Grant wished
to protest the publication. Johnson received them "promptly
and kindly." "Whoever gave the facts for the article of the
Intelligencer this morning," Grant began, "has made some
serious mistakes." Johnson interposed: "General Grant, let
me interrupt you just there. I have not seen the *Intelligencer*
of this morning, and have no knowledge of the contents of any
article therein." Grant continued that the idea was that he
had not kept faith. He then recalled again their conversation
of the last summer and said: "I remember . . . I did say that,
like the case of the Baltimore police commissioners, I did suppose Mr. Stanton could not regain his office except by a process
through the courts." Johnson said he remembered this conference and Grant resumed: "I said, if I changed my opinion,
I would give you notice, and put things as they were before
my appointment as Secretary of War *ad interim*."[1]

Sherman thought the explanations "full and *partially*
satisfactory." A general friendly conversation then ensued,
in the course of which Grant offered to call on Stanton and tell
him that "the good of the service required his resignation."[2]
As he was taking his leave General Grant turned at the door
to say, "Mr. President, you should make some order that
we of the Army are not bound to obey the orders of Mr. Stanton as Secretary of War," and Johnson intimated that he
would.

As soon as the two generals had left, the President had
Colonel Moore read him the article in the *Intelligencer*, and he
pronounced it substantially true. When Welles called, he ratified that judgment, adding his regret that someone had not
been present at the Cabinet meeting on Saturday to record
the exact words and more especially, "to paint Grant's confusion of face and manner." The General, Welles added, had "acknowledged everything the President said in regard to the

understanding between them, and when the conversation was through, slunk away to the door in a manner most humiliating and pitiable."³

After Sherman had returned to the War Department, Stanton, "all very loving," sent for him and sought to flatter him about "how much he respected me and admired me." The General was waiting for a chance to advise Stanton to resign, an opening which that canny gentleman carefully avoided giving. Sherman believed that the condition of affairs would sooner or later bring about a direct collision, after which Congress would impeach the President. "I feel for Mr. Johnson," the General wrote his wife, "but must say, for his experience, he has made some fatal mistakes."⁴

On the 18th, the President again sent for Sherman, and after the interview, the General wrote his wife somewhat impatiently: "I do not see why he and Grant both count on me somehow to cut the present Gordian knot. I believe Stanton ought to quit, but it is dangerous for the President to begin any fray. I thought by his disregarding my advice an Sunday he had a plan of action of his own, but from his conversation of today I find he has none but wants me to do it for him. I will think it over."⁵ Sherman immediately had a talk with Grant, and wrote the President that the General would call at the White House the next day, "and offer to go to Mr. Stanton to say, for the good of the service and of the country he ought to resign."⁶

Indeed, it seemed to be the general expectation that Stanton would resign. Before the Senate's action on January 13, the *Independent* had declared "Mr. Stanton declines to go back into the Cabinet except constructively. He desires to have the Senate vindicate him . . . and he will resign."⁷ A little later the same journal reported that "Mr. Stanton is warmly urged to remain in his office until the close of Mr. Johnson's term, and he may reconsider his decision and consent to do so."⁸ Even so, Stanton's eager reoccupancy of the War Department had seemed in bad taste to all except the most extreme Radicals. Seward told the President that he had expected Stanton's resignation before then. But after the Senate's "vindication," although he carefully refrained from issuing orders to the Army, Stanton showed no signs of resigning.

On the 19th, Grant went to see him. Having advance information of the reason for the call, and understanding how to overawe the General, Stanton started off in a great voice about other matters, talking vehemently, while the General listened in silence. After he had waited for some time for Stanton to subside and had sat quietly in his chair smoking his cigar for half an hour, Grant saw no diminution in Stanton's "imperious and angry look," nor in his "loud and violent" speech, so that he got up and left "without daring to make known the object of his mission." He wrote the President after this "interview" that the attitude of the Secretary of War had led him "to the conclusion that any advice to him of the kind would be useless."[9]

On the same day, before leaving for Richmond for a meeting of the Peabody Fund trustees, Grant called at the White House and in the course of the conversation remarked on the insignificance to which Stanton could be reduced. The President referred to the law creating the office and answered, "Yes, the Secretary will amount to nothing more than a clerk." When Grant responded that he would not obey Stanton's orders unless he knew they emanated from the President, Johnson replied that the General was right in pursuing such a course; that he did not consider Stanton authorized to act as Secretary of War, since he had suspended him and did not intend to recognize him.[10]

While in Richmond, Grant told General John M. Schofield, a friend of long standing, that Stanton's conduct was "intolerable" to him, and emphatically declared that he intended to demand either Stanton's removal or the acceptance of his own resignation.[11]

But upon Grant's return to Washington, a distinct change of purpose seems to have come over him. Rawlins, who at times had a commanding influence over the General, had determined that political necessities demanded an open and irrevocable breach with the President. Grant had not been back in Washington two days before he declared war on Andrew Johnson.

At the interview of January 15, Grant had requested the President to issue an order to relieve the Army from the necessity of obeying orders by Stanton. On January 19, he had reiterated his unwillingness to obey Stanton. These expressions had led Johnson to believe Grant's dislike such that, in the operation of the Army, he would tie Stanton's hands completely and make a formal order unnecessary. The President told Colonel Moore he did not think he would give the order, that Grant has been restive under Stanton, evidently was glad to get rid of him, had let him back into the war office and now he would make them fight it out.[12]

But on January 24, the General addressed this note to the President: "I have the honor, very respectfully, to request to have in writing, an order which the President gave me verbally, on Sunday the 19th inst., to disregard the orders of the Hon. E. M. Stanton as Secretary of War until I know from the President himself that they were his orders."

On receipt of this brusque note, Johnson realized that Grant had gone over. completely. He could expect no aid there. He must dismiss Stanton or endure him. An order for Stanton's removal had been written out on January 5; it was still resting on his desk. He now determined to make use of it and to appoint General Sherman Secretary of War *ad interim.*

So, on the same day, the President informed General Sherman of his wish and asked whether he would accept the appointment. Sherman was much troubled. While he thought Stanton should be removed, he did not wish to be the agent of removal. He promised to think it over and to consult with Thomas Ewing, his father-in-law.

In writing the Old Roman for a letter to help him "to escape this dilemma," Sherman insisted that he did not want the place, that it was not to his interest to replace Stanton, and that Stanton's removal by force would play into the Radicals' hands. "*Now* Stanton can give no order to the army," the General wrote, "and therefore can do no mischief. . . . If the President wants to make an issue to go to the Supreme Court, why not let the Secretary of the Treasury refuse one of his [Stanton's] warrants, and deny that Stanton is Secretary of War."[13]

Accordingly, on January 25, the sagacious Ewing wrote his son-in-law of his belief that it was inexpedient for the President to take any further action as to Stanton. In so far as Johnson's interest was concerned, "things are in the best possible condition. Stanton is in the department, not *his* secretary, but the secretary of the Senate, who have taken upon themselves his sins, and who place him there under a large salary to annoy and obstruct the operations of the Executive. . . . He is a stench in the nostrils of their own party. I thought the nomination of Cox at the proper juncture would have been wise as a peace offering. But perhaps it would have let off the Senate too easily from the effect of their arbitrary act.

"Now, the dislodging of Stanton and filling the office even temporarily, without the consent of the Senate, would raise a question as to the legality of the President's act, and *he* would belong to the attacked instead of the attacking party. If the war between the President and Congress is to go on, as I suppose it is, Stanton should be ignored by the President, left to perform the clerical duties which the law requires him to perform, and let the party bear the odium which is already upon them for placing him where he is."

As to Sherman himself, Ewing advised him to avoid political complications. "I do not think the President will require you to do an act of doubtful legality. Certainly he will not without sanction of the opinion of the Attorney-General, and you should have time in a questionable case to consult with him before called upon to act. . . . The appeal is to the people, and it is better for the President to persist in the course he has for some time past pursued—let the aggressions all come from the other side."[14]

Two days later, Sherman transmitted Ewing's letter to the President, along with three pages of printed matter, containing the rules of army administration which Sherman thought Johnson should issue as an executive order to General Grant. If the President would do so, "they would so clearly define the duties of all concerned that no conflict can arise."[15]

In truth, Stanton's position was giving the Radicals about as much concern as the President. To such burning flames as Theodore Tilton, Stanton's situation was really infamous. "Mr. Stanton is said to be Secretary of War," Tilton fulminated in an *Independent* editorial on January 23. "This is not true. He is sitting in his old seat, but not wielding his old power. All official promulgations of the War Department are necessarily signed 'by order of the President.' As yet, however, the President has given no order to Mr. Stanton, has held no communication with him, has made no recognition of him."

Tilton insisted that Johnson's cool contempt of Stanton furnished ground for impeachment. "Of course it follows that, as the President refused to obey the Act of Congress which restored the Secretary to his secretaryship, Mr. Johnson must be impeached. Unless the President consents to act *through* Mr. Stanton, and instead of acting *over* him, he violates both the letter and the spirit of the law. . . . Mr. Stanton must be accepted as a *bona fide* Secretary of War, or else the President . . . must be blotted out of official life forever."

But neither the advice of cautious Conservatives nor the outbursts of rage of Stanton's friends altered the President's desire to get rid of his hostile Secretary of War. Nor would he abandon hopes of enlisting Sherman's aid. On January 27 he again summoned the General, to tell him that he could not execute the office of President any longer with Stanton pretending to be Secretary of War. "For the purpose of having the office administered properly in the interest of the Army, and of the whole country," he tendered that position to Sherman.[16] The General asked why the lawyers could not make up a case and avoid bringing him into the controversy. The President answered that it had been found impossible, but that "if we can bring the case to the courts, he [Stanton] would not stand half an hour." Sherman again hesitated, and said he wanted his father-in-law's advice.

Accordingly, on the 29th, Ewing again adjured the President to calmness. "It will not do to adopt rash measures," he wrote. "It is better to let Stanton alone. Public opinion is against him and his backers, and by an imprudent act you may turn it in his favor. I cannot advise Sherman to take his place, and he is not willing to do it. There is indeed no object to be gained by it. Reconstruction will dispose of itself in spite of the act of any persons you may place in the department. . . .

"It is important that you sever the connection which the practice of the military presumes between you and the Secretary of War by a *written* order. Draw it up carefully and submit it to your Attorney-General, and let him see that you fall into none of the traps they have laid for you. They evidently are preparing to resume impeachment, but it must be on some new pretense, and if they have any plausible pretense, and carry it out, it will have a bad effect on the country, on *you*, and what I should not much lament, on them. It is at present wise to bear and forbear. Some of the Democratic leaders whom I know are eloquent orators but most dangerous counsellors."[17]

Ewing's advice as to the need for written instructions to

prevent orders Stanton might issue as coming from the President from being acted upon as such seems to have determined Johnson. On January 29 he set himself to the task of answering Grant's note of January 24. "I have tried to be decent," Johnson remarked to Moore, "but I will be damned if some things have not gone about as far as they are to go." Accordingly an indorsement was placed on Grant's insolent communication. "As requested," the General was instructed, in writing, "not to obey any orders from the War Department, assumed to be by the direction of the President, unless such order is known by the General commanding the armies of the United States to have been authorized by the Executive."[18]

But the President would not be swerved from his appeals to Sherman by the blunt words of the General's father-in-law. On January 31 he again pressed the War Office upon the General. Sherman replied that although it was against his interest, his desire, his personal wish, his official wish, if Stanton should simply retire, he might be willing to undertake the task. For a moment, Johnson thought that Sherman had agreed. Then the soldier asked: "Suppose Mr. Stanton do not yield?"

"Oh! he will make no objection," the President answered, "you present the order, and he will retire."

When Sherman expressed his doubts as to this, the President remarked: "I know him better than you do; he is cowardly."

Again Sherman asked for time. He sympathized with the President, but had an unconquerable aversion to living in the capital and to political controversy. A little later he wrote firmly declining the appointment. He did so, however, not on the ground that he disapproved the President's course, but because he did not want to live in Washington, this "political maelstrom;" this city "full of spies and slanderers."[19]

While the hard-pressed Chief Executive was thus vainly seeking a suitable man to put in Stanton's place the moment he was removed, General Grant was waging epistolary warfare with great vigor. On January 28 he addressed a lengthy communication to the President. Grant took Johnson's delay to reply to his note of the 24th as the excuse for his letter. Until written instructions were received, he wrote, he would "suspend action on your verbal ones." He had been compelled to ask written instructions because of "the many and gross misrepresentations affecting my personal honor . . . purporting to come from the President."

His letter reviewed the occurrences at the Cabinet meeting of January 14 and flatly declared: "I did not agree to call again on Monday, nor at any other definite time. . . . From the 11th to the Cabinet meeting on the 14th inst., a doubt never entered my mind about the President's fully understanding my position."[20]

He further asserted that, in the Cabinet meeting, he had "in no wise admitted the correctness of the President's statement of our conversation, though, to soften the evident contradiction my statement gave, I said . . . the President might have understood me the way he said, namely, that I had promised to resign if I did not resist the reinstatement. I made no such promise."

Before the President could prepare his reply to this denial by Grant of what had been obvious to all who had witnessed the scene on the 14th, another contumacious note came from him, acknowledging Johnson's instructions in response to his note of January 24, and saying "that I am informed by the Secretary of War that he has not received from the Executive any order or instructions limiting or impairing his authority to issue orders. . . . While this authority for the War Department is not countermanded, it will be satisfactory evidence to me that any orders issued from the War Department are by direction of the President or authorized by the Executive." Johnson had directed the General not to obey any orders issued by Edwin M. Stanton in the name of the President, and Grant had refused to obey the President!

In his answer to the General, dated January 31, the President reviewed the interview with Grant in October, discussed their conversation of January 11, and made the definite statement that it had been understood at that meeting "that there would be a further conference on Monday, by which time I supposed you would be prepared to inform me of your final decision. You failed, however, to fulfill the engagement."

As to the General's statement about the Cabinet meeting of January 14, "my recollection of what then transpired is diametrically the reverse of your narration." After stating what he remembered of the occasion, the President wrote that he was so anxious to be correct in his statement that he had that day read his words "to the Members of the Cabinet who were then present. They, without exception, agreed in its accuracy."

When he received the President's letter of January 31, Grant was troubled; perhaps his memory was plaguing him; perhaps he was troubled over the statement that five Cabinet Members had scrutinized and indorsed the accuracy of the Executive's account of the meeting. At any event, the General prepared a draft of a reply again admitting the possibility of his words having been such that the President had misconstrued them.

In his draft, he gave a significant detail. "After our conversation on the 11th instant," Grant wrote, "I meditated seriously how I could leave the President free to resist the Tenure-of-Office bill himself as he chose, without making me a party to the action." The plan which the General had determined upon "was to notify the President, as soon as relieved by action of the Senate, and when notified by Mr. Stanton of his readiness to assume the functions of his office, to forward that notice to the President. Inasmuch as Mr. Stanton had requested me to notify him, in writing, of my acceptance of the office of Secretary of War *ad interim*, after he had received officially notice of his suspension and my appointment, I supposed he would extend the same courtesy to me."[21]

Grant submitted the draft containing this admission to his shrewd Chief of Staff. A politician by nature and versed in public affairs, Rawlins saw quickly that this letter would not further Grant's march to the White House. "This will not do," he chided, "it is not enough." Thereupon he took the draft and rewrote it, eliminating all note of explanation and apology, and making its important passages direct contradictions of the President's word and defiance to him.[22]

This letter reiterated Grant's statements of the 28th, made light of the testimony of the Members of Johnson's Cabinet, declared bluntly that "you know that we parted on Saturday . . . without any promise on my part," and gave an entirely new version of the reasons why he had agreed to serve in Stanton's stead.

The President must have known, Grant's letter stated, that he had accepted the appointment of Secretary of War *ad interim* to prevent the office being filled by someone "who would, by opposition to the laws relating to the restoration of the

Southern States . . . embarrass the Army in the performance of duties specially imposed upon it by these laws." He had not accepted the office "for the purpose of enabling you to get rid of Mr. Stanton."

In concluding, he said that "when my honor as a soldier and integrity as a man have been so violently assailed, pardon me for saying that I can but regard this whole matter . . . as an attempt to involve me in the resistance of law. . . . I am in a measure confirmed in this conclusion by your recent orders directing me to disobey orders from the Secretary of War—my superior and your subordinate—without having countermanded his authority to issue the orders I am to disobey."

The President promptly laid this letter before the Cabinet, which heard it with "indignation and ridicule." When Moore began his reading, there were frowns, but at the close, "there was a laugh which was heartily joined in by all." Browning termed the letter "a very extraordinary production—weak, petulant, false and disreputable." Stanbery was astounded at its tone, McCulloch condemned it, adding that "Grant was so drunk at the Cabinet meeting that it would be hardly surprising if he did not recollect what he said." Welles thought it "highly discreditable to Grant's integrity, honor, ability and truth."[23] The question arose as to how the President should reply, if at all. Stanbery believed that Johnson's private secretary should acknowledge it, and Welles urged that Colonel Moore inform the General "that his last letter was of such extraordinary tone and character that no further communication or correspondence could be had with him on that subject."

But the President concluded that, on the whole, it was best to reply. After this decision, Stanbery earnestly urged him that, as the question had become one of veracity, the Members of the Cabinet be called upon to put in writing their remembrances of the interview, and to accompany his answer with them. This the President determined to do.[24]

That evening Welles called at the White House to discuss this letter and to express his apprehensions of impending calamities. The duty confronted them all, he said, of preparing for extraordinary emergencies, as the unprincipled men in Congress were preparing for extreme and unconstitutional acts. Was the President prepared for this crisis? If the Radicals should seek to arrest him and to seize the government, what course would he pursue? In whom could the President confide?

Upon these questions Johnson became very much excited, arose from his seat and paced the floor. He admitted that he still thought of General Sherman. Before the General had left Washington he had been more emphatic in his support. Might it not be a good plan to make Washington a new Military Department and to order Sherman to its command? He believed Sherman would accept. But Welles feared that while Sherman was well disposed towards Johnson, in any collision with Grant, he would yield.[25]

On February 6 Johnson carried out his plan and issued an order creating the Military Division of the Atlantic, with headquarters at Washington and with General Sherman in command. He told Moore that this order would "set some persons to thinking."

An hour before Grant's letter of February 3 had been delivered at the White House, Hubbard of West Virginia—one of Stanton's henchmen in the House—introduced a resolution calling upon the Secretary of War for copies of any correspondence between Grant and the President. Stanton immediately responded, including in his communication a copy of Grant's letter of February 3, thus demonstrating that it had been in Stanton's possession before it reached the President.[26] So it appeared that, while General Grant had been telling Johnson he thought Stanton should resign, he had at the same time been in collusion with the latter in the war against the President.

The correspondence produced a sensation such as had not occurred in the House for many years. At the outset Grant seemed to have won his case, but during the reading of Johnson's letter of January 31, Grant's friends grew less certain. While the concluding sentences were being pronounced, "a pin . . . might have been heard to drop on the carpeted floor."[27] Thad Stevens' spirit rose perceptibly. Two weeks before, to a friendly writer, he had seemed "a broken old man, who has lost his faculty of hope but can never relax his nerve of courage." With the Grant-Johnson letters at hand, Old Thad sniffed impeachment from afar.[28] When the reading had been finished, a Radical went up to him and asked: "Won't it do now to let Grant into our church?"

Stevens smiled sardonically and replied: "Yes, open the doors and let him in. He is a bolder man that I thought him to be."[29]

Radical papers made the best they could of Grant's letter-writing—the *Independent* proclaiming that the General "has driven his pen through the President like a spear" and insisting that "the people will believe nothing that Mr. Johnson or Mr. Browning or Mr. Seward may say against General Grant." In the epistolary record of the General's duplicity, the Congressional extremists sought to find evidence of an impeachable offense on the part of the President. A resolution was rushed through the House to refer to Stevens' Reconstruction Committee the earlier "evidence" collected against Johnson. On February 6 the Radicals held a caucus to debate how he could best be deposed. A sub-committee of the House Reconstruction Committee began examining witnesses. Under examination, Stillson of the New York *World* revealed that it had been Postmaster-General Randall who had termed Grant "a liar and a sneak."

The President's response to Grant's letter of February 3 completed the demolition both of the General's reputation as a truthful man, and also of the renewed impeachment threat. Johnson's answer, dated February 10, was likewise communicated to Congress. The "extraordinary character" of Grant's last letter, the President said, "induced me to take this mode of giving, as a proper sequel to the communications which passed between us, the statements of the five Members of the Cabinet who were present on the occasion of our conversation on the 14th ultimo. . . . These gentlemen heard that conversation, and have read my statement. They speak for themselves, and I leave the proof without a word of comment."

Johnson sharply called attention to the fact that Grant, in giving the "history" of his "connection," had admitted that, from the very beginning, he "intended to circumvent the President. It was to carry out that intent that you accepted the appointment. . . . It was not, then, in obedience to the order of your superior, as has heretofore been supposed, that you assumed the duties of the office. You knew it was the President's purpose to prevent Mr. Stanton from resuming the office of Secretary of War, and you intended to defeat that purpose. You accepted the office, not in the interest of the President, but

of Mr. Stanton. . . . You not only concealed your design
from the President, but induced him to suppose that you would
carry out his purpose."

Grant's refusal to obey the President's orders of January
29 was duly noticed. Johnson wrote: "The President issues an
order to you to obey no order from the War Department purporting to be made 'by the direction of the President,' until
you have referred it to him for his approval. You reply that
you have received the President's order and will not obey it,
but will obey an order purporting to be given by his direction,
if it comes from the War Department. You will not obey the
direct order of the President, but will obey his indirect order.
. . . You refuse obedience to the superior out of deference to
the subordinate."

The final paragraph of this letter must have stung General
Grant. "Without further comment upon the insubordinate
attitude which you have assumed," it read, "I am at a loss to
know how you can relieve yourself from obedience to the orders
of the President, who is made by the Constitution the Commander-in-Chief of the Army and Navy, and is, therefore, the
official superior, as well of the General of the Army as of the
Secretary of War."

Appended to this stinging rebuke were copies of letters
from the five Cabinet Members addressed to the President.
Welles' recollection "corresponds with your statement." Mc-
Culloch had "no hesitation in saying that your account . . .
substantially and in all important particulars accorded with
my recollection of it." Reciting the three questions which the
President in his letter of January 28 had said he had put to
Grant, Randall said, as to the first, "this General Grant admitted"; to the second, "to these questions General Grant replied
in the affirmative"; and as to the third, "General Grant replied
that such was the understanding." Browning, who kept a diary,
gave an elaborate account of what happened. It sustained the
President throughout.

Seward displayed an obvious desire to uphold the President
and at the same time not to offend General Grant. He recol-
lected that Grant's initial admission of his promises was "indirect and circumstantial." Seward recited the President's
claim that Grant had promised on Saturday that the President
understood his views and that his proceedings thereafter would
be consistent with what had been so understood. He said,

THE OLD ROMAN

Thomas Ewing of Ohio, One of the Shrewdest of Johnson's Friends.

"General Grant did not controvert" this, but he sought to give the General a loophole by adding, "nor can I say that he admitted this last statement." But Seward did state unequivocally: "Certainly General Grant did not at any time in the Cabinet meeting insist that he had in the Saturday's conversation either distinctly or finally advised you of his determination to retire from the charge of the War Department otherwise than under your own subsequent direction. He acquiesced in your statement that the Saturday conversation ended with an expectation that there would be a subsequent conference . . . on Monday."

When the Cabinet letters were read in the House, the Radicals affected ironic laughter. And indeed, Seward's letter made it obvious to them "that the wily Secretary of State intended to stand as well as he could with the President and the General."[30]

The President's letter and the Cabinet missives with which it was buttressed silenced Grant as to the issue of veracity. The next day, "without admitting anything in these statements where they differ from anything heretofore stated by me," he disclaimed "any intention, now or heretofore, of disobeying any legal order of the President, distinctly communicated."

The Committee was disappointed in the lack of evidence of impeachable offenses to be found in this correspondence. But Stanton was goading them on, and Stevens, implacable as ever, strove to stem the tide now running against the voting of impeachment. "There is enough evidence anyway to enable us to get rid of Johnson," he declared, yet when the first vote was taken in the Committee, not a single member, not even Boutwell, supported him.[31]

Two days later, Stevens told his Committeemen that the testimony as to the Grant correspondence did not matter. There were plenty of proven charges, and impeachment should be instituted "without further palaver." But Bingham moved to table Stevens' resolution. The Commoner lashed the Committee as "a pack of wincing politicians," but his motion was voted down none the less by six to three. After this last defeat, the *World* correspondent found Stevens' irritation unassuaged. Old Thad had said there was "enough evidence to impeach a dozen men" in the first part of the Grant-Johnson correspondence.

"Damn it," he continued, "don't both the President and

General Grant subscribe to this vital fact, that Grant had first considered and that Johnson had insisted upon the proposition that Grant should help Johnson keep Stanton out of office . . .? What the devil do I care about the question of veracity, as they call it, between Johnson and Grant? That's nothing to do with the law. Both of them may call each other liars if they want to; perhaps they both do lie a little, though the President has the weight of evidence on his side. . . . If they want to settle the question, they may both go out in my back yard and settle it alone. . . . Grant may be as guilty as the President . . . but Grant isn't on trial; it's Johnson." The correspondent asked Stevens if Johnson would ever be impeached. "I shall never bring up this question of impeachment again,"[32] he answered.

But if Stevens had despaired, Theodore Tilton had not. Following the collapse of the Grant correspondence as a pretext for impeachment the *Independent* asked: "Is the President *about* to violate the laws? His fate hangs on his conduct. If he ventures for an instant into open resistance to the laws, his fate is sealed." If Johnson "lifted a hand against Mr. Stanton," he would be impeached "in half an hour!"[33]

On February 11 Welles told the President that there was need in the War Department of an Adjutant-General in sympathy with the President, for one not overawed by the imperious Stanton. Johnson "caught promptly and at once to the suggestion," and said he would order General Lorenzo Thomas, still titular Adjutant-General, to his former rôle. The next day the President issued orders for Thomas to resume his position and duties as Adjutant-General and also renewed his order as to the Department of the Atlantic.[34] The following day he sent to the Senate his nomination of Sherman "to be general by brevet in the Army of the United States for distinguished courage, skill and ability displayed during the War of the Rebellion."[35]

Sherman had gone back to St. Louis, congratulating himself on escaping the Johnson-Grant "outburst." Now the "danger . . . has come upon me like an avalanche," he bewailed. He was unconquerably opposed to coming to Washington to take the command of this new department. He wrote and telegraphed his objections to the President, going so far as offer to resign. He wrote his father-in-law, Thomas Ewing, that "I am out of it, and shall keep out," and he pleaded with his brother, the Senator, for the latter to induce the Senate not to confirm his undesired brevet rank.   After these strenuous efforts on Sherman's part and after the Senate's failure to confirm his rank, Johnson reluctantly abandoned his dependence upon the General, and telegraphed him that he had withdrawn the assignment.[36] Johnson now thought of bringing General George H. Thomas to Washington, but that plan also failed.

One by one, the men in whom the President had hoped for help in his emergency, proved unwilling to give their aid. Some of his strongest friends—Stanbery in particular—urged that any plans for removal be abandoned.   But Andrew Johnson's mind was made up.   He would endure Stanton in the War Office no longer. His self-respect demanded Stanton's removal, he told the faithful Moore.   "If the people do not entertain sufficient respect for their Chief Magistrate to uphold me in such a measure, then I ought to resign."   If he could not secure Sherman or George H. Thomas as temporary replacement for Stanton, he would appoint some *locum tenens* for the place.

On Sunday, the 16th, Moore went to church with the President, and, on their return, read Addison's "Cato" aloud to him.   Johnson descanted at length on Cato's character; he "would not compromise with wrong, but, being right, died before he would yield."   Moore saw clearly that the President felt himself to be pursuing a Catonian course.[37]

The next day, John Potts, chief clerk of the War Department, was summoned to the White House and told of the President's intention to remove Stanton and to appoint him Secretary of War *ad interim*.   If Stanton should refuse to yield, let the case be brought into the courts.   Potts pleaded not to be put in such a situation, and the President had to seek another.

After this failure, Johnson told Moore that the minute he could find a proper person to act as Secretary *ad interim,* he would settle the question of the War Department.   The next day he thought of using his new Adjutant-General, Lorenzo Thomas, in the emergency.[38]   Moore urged him to wait, and Johnson admitted that Thomas' appointment would carry no weight.   But his mind was made up.   On the morning of February 21, when the President entered his office, he instructed

Colonel Moore immediately to prepare four papers: the first for the removal of Stanton; the second, a note to Lorenzo Thomas, notifying him of his own appointment as Secretary *ad interim;* the third, a message informing the Senate of these actions, and a fourth, a nomination for the appointment of General George H. Thomas as General by brevet. The Adjutant-General was promptly summoned. After Moore had read the notices of removal and appointment, the President showed the General the laws upon the subject, and told him, "I shall uphold the Constitution and the laws, and I want you to do the same." Thomas answered, "I will, and I will obey your orders." The President then gave him the Stanton papers to deliver and told him to take along a witness.

Thomas forthwith proceeded to his task. He did not do so reluctantly, but with considerable feeling of vanity and pride, for in addition to being weak, he was a vain and foolish old man. Accompanied by a brother officer as witness, Thomas called on the recusant Secretary. They bade each other good morning, and the Adjutant-General handed Stanton the letter of removal, saying, "I am directed by the President to hand you this." Stanton sat down on the sofa, read the paper, and asked the General:

"Do you wish me to vacate the office at once, or will you give me time to remove my private property?"

"Certainly," Thomas answered, "act your pleasure." Then he showed Stanton his own order to serve as Secretary *ad interim.*

General Grant entered the room at the moment and Thomas exhibited his authority to him. Stanton then asked for a copy of the order, and Thomas left the room to have one made. When he returned with a copy and handed it to Stanton, the latter remarked: "I want some little time for reflection. I do not know whether I will obey your instructions, or whether I will resist them." Apparently, while Thomas was out of the room, Grant had said something to Stanton which caused Stanton to change his mind as to obeying the order of the President.[39]

After this incident Thomas returned to the White House and told the President what had occurred. Johnson listened carefully and then said to the General: "Very well, go and take charge of the office and perform the duties." A little later, following the routine of the Cabinet meeting, Johnson informed the Members that he had that morning removed Stanton and had appointed Thomas to officiate *ad interim*. Welles asked if Stanton had surrendered the place and Thomas taken possession. Johnson replied that Thomas had informed Stanton, that the latter seemed "calm and submissive," and that there had been no difficulty. Welles believed that the removal would impel the Radicals to impeach; "the President is vigorous and active, but too late, and has attempted too much at once."[40]

While these scenes had been taking place in the ugly red brick building which housed the office of the Secretary of War, the excitement on Capitol Hill had been intense. Upon receipt of the President's notice of Stanton's removal, there was a great hubbub in the Senate; at 2:30 it went into executive session. An unfriendly correspondent reported how the Senators "all went into the Senate chamber and sat there alone, with no human being except a confidential clerk and a confidential doorkeeper to do them reverence," and worked themselves into such a fever heat that "between five and six o'clock, fiery flames seemed to be issuing from all the Senate portals. Every time one of them opened, a Senator came forth fit to set the Republic ablaze with indignation."[41]

Senator Wilson of Massachusetts offered, and the Senate by a strict party vote adopted a resolution declaring that "under the Constitution and the laws," the President "has no power to remove the Secretary of War and to designate any other officer to perform the duties" of that office. Thus, in advance of any impeachment, the Radical Senators adjudged the President guilty of violation of the Tenure-of-Office Act. By this vote, they beckoned to their fellow partisans in the House and said: "Impeach Andrew Johnson! We have already adjudged that he has violated the law."

While the Senate was determining the President's guilt beforehand, the House had become an open and public forum for denunciation of the "criminal," the "tyrant," the "usurper," the "bad man" in the White House. A Radical caucus was hastily summoned and selected four Senators—Conness, Cattell, Cameron and Thayer—to hasten to the War Department to strengthen Stanton in the faith. The four Senators begged Stanton to stand by, some of them shedding tears. Stanton lachrymosely responded that never would he forsake Congress, which had never forsaken him.[42] A laconic note was thrust in Stanton's hands:

United States Senate.

Hon. Edwin H. Stanton:
Stick!

CHARLES SUMNER.

The Radicals of the House made preparations to vote immediate impeachment. The more histrionic of their leaders seized upon the fact that the next day was February 22; it would be a dramatic gesture to vote the impeachment of the President on the anniversary of George Washington's birth. Stevens gave notice that the House Reconstruction Committee would meet the following morning, and the House ordered a session upon the holiday.

No sooner had Thomas left Stanton's presence than the latter was energized into feverish activity. He prepared a formal message to Congress notifying it of the President's action. He wrote a formal order to Thomas commanding him to issue no orders as Secretary of War. He sent private notes to various Senators beseeching their aid. One such was a joint note to Senators Fessenden, Howard and Edmunds, informing them "that Adjutant-General Thomas is boasting at the hotels that he intends to take possession of the War Department at nine o'clock tomorrow morning. If the Senate does not declare its opinion of the laws, how am I to hold possession?" A little later he wrote Senator Conness, "I am at the War Department, and mean to continue in possession until expelled by force."

He ordered Grant to station a guard about the building and in front of his office. He was going to resist force by force. Nay, he did more. For several weeks, his office in the War Department became his permanent abode. He ate there and he slept there, and with the guards about him and Radical Congressmen in almost a continuous attendance, Stanton maintained a state of siege.

The President's new Secretary of War *ad interim* saw neither Stanton nor Johnson again that day, but his hours did not pass without incident. During the early evening, Thomas talked to an old crony, to a reporter and to a chance acquaintance, and expanded to them all what he intended to do the following morning. When his friend Walter Burleigh, a Dakota delegate, called, he found the General dressing to attend a masked ball. Burleigh wished to leave, but his boastful friend insisted upon talking of the eventful day. When the caller asked him when he would assume the duties of the office, Thomas replied the next morning at ten o'clock, and invited Burleigh to come and see the performance.

"You are going to take possession tomorrow?" inquired Burleigh. Thomas answered affirmatively. "Suppose Stanton objects to it—resists?" Burleigh continued. "Well," the garrulous old man answered, "I expect to meet force by force." The Dakota delegate wanted to know what Thomas would do if Stanton barred the doors. "I will break them down," Thomas declared with gusto.[44]

That same evening, the General told a newspaper man that if Stanton should refuse his demand for possession, he intended to "apply to the General-in-Chief of the Army for a force sufficient to enable him to take possession of the War Department," adding that he did not see how Grant could refuse his demand. Nor was the General yet done with boasting. He met the reporter again at Willard's Hotel and repeated his bold threats.· Thence, he went to the masked ball, where he bragged that he was going to take possession of the War Department and open all its mail.

These boasts of the preening old General were straightway carried to the barricaded Stanton, who was thrown into a sweat of anxiety. Late that evening, while Thomas was dancing at the famous ball, Stanton prepared an affidavit, reciting the report that Thomas planned forcibly to remove him, that this was a violation of the Tenure-of-Office Act, and that Thomas was therefore "guilty of a high misdemeanor." On this showing, Stanton sought a warrant for Thomas' arrest, that the Adjutant-General might be "dealt with as the law and justice in such case appertains." The papers were addressed to David K. Cartter, Chief Justice of the Supreme Court of the District of Columbia, a fervent Radical and Stanton's willing tool. The Judge was found, the warrant ordered, and the clerk of Cartter's court aroused from bed to affix the seal to the warrant. In his haste and excitement, Stanton had done the very thing Andrew Johnson had been prayerfully seeking—he had brought into the courts the question of the legality of his own possession of the office of Secretary of War.

Thereupon, early the next morning, before he had his breakfast, General Thomas was waited upon by officers of the law and was informed that he was under arrest. The General asked Marshal Gooding, who had served the warrant, if he would be permitted to see the President. He wanted to tell him of his arrest. The Marshall said yes, but he must not lose sight of the prisoner for a moment. The officers went along with Thomas to the White House and into the President's room, where Thomas informed his Chief that he had been arrested.

"Very well," Johnson remarked, "that is the place I wanted him—the courts." Then he told Thomas to call on the Attorney-General and tell him what had occurred. So the General and the Marshal went to Stanbery's office and repeated the information. Stanbery, however, did not offer to represent Thomas, but told him to go ahead to the court. It seems strange that Stanbery did not immediately grasp the importance of Thomas' arrest, and the possibility it afforded of a *habeas corpus* application to bring the constitutionality of the Tenure-of-Office Act before the Supreme Court, but he did not. The General and the Marshal proceeded to Justice Cartter's court, where Thomas was required to give $5,000 bail and was discharged.

With no one there to counsel or advise him, the poor old General seems to have been much befuddled. He asked Judge Cartter what it all meant, and the Judge told him to present himself in the court at 10:30 the next Wednesday morning. "Does this arrest suspend me from any of my functions?" Thomas then inquired. "No," the Judge answered hastily, "it has nothing to do with them."[45]

At midnight, on the 21st, Moore was awakened with the news that Thomas had been drunk at the Grand Ball, and that the President wished him to straighten Thomas out. He said he would do so the next morning. But by that time, the arrest had been made, and Moore's plan of refusing bail and seeking *habeas corpus* was too late. Thomas had already made bond.[46]

Still without breakfast and in some anxiety on that account, Thomas once more visited the White House to tell the President he had given bail. The latter answered, "Very well, we want it in the courts." The General proceeded to the War Department, where he found his own office locked. He then went up to the office of the Secretary of War, where he found Stanton, with a group of six or eight Radical politicians clustered about him in a semi-ellipse, Stanton at the apex.

Thomas said, "I do not wish to disturb any of these gentlemen, and will wait." Stanton answered, "Nothing private here. What do you want, sir?" The Secretary of War *ad interim* demanded the surrender of the office, Stanton refused this, ordering him back to his room as Adjutant-General. Thomas refused, saying, "I claim the office of Secretary of War, and demand it by the order of the President."

Stanton now requested one of his Radical friends from Capitol Hill to take careful note of the conversation. The Congressman has recorded it thus:

> Stanton: I deny your authority and order you back to your own office.
>
> Thomas: I will stand here. I want no unpleasantness in the presence of these gentlemen.
>
> Stanton: You can stand there if you please, but you cannot act as Secretary of War. I am Secretary of War. I order you out of this office and to your own.
>
> Thomas: I refuse to go and will stand here.
>
> Stanton: How are you to get possession, do you mean to use force?
>
> Thomas: I do not care to use force, but my mind is made up as to what I shall do. I want no unpleasantness though. I shall stay here and act as Secretary of War.
>
> Stanton: You shall not, and I order you, as your superior, back to your own office.
>
> Thomas: I will not obey you, but will stand here and remain here.
>
> Stanton: You can stand there as you please. I order you out of this office to your own. I am Secretary of War and your superior.

After this last refusal on Stanton's part, Thomas left the room and went across the hall into another officer's quarters, where he began issuing orders. Accompanied by some of his Congressional witnesses, Stanton entered the room, and handed Thomas the written order he had prepared the day before; it recited that Thomas' "conduct and orders are illegal, and you are hereby commanded to abstain from issuing any order other than in your capacity as Adjutant-General."

After this paper had been thrust upon the General, there was a further dialogue:

> Stanton: I am Secretary of War, and I now order you, General Thomas, out of this office to your own quarters.

Thomas: I will not go. I shall discharge the functions of Secretary of War.

Stanton: You will not.

Thomas: I shall require the mails of the War Department to be delivered to me, and shall transact
the business of the office.

Stanton: You shall not have them, and I order
you to your own office.[47]

Honors were about even in this verbal conflict, but the
boastful old General had not secured possession of the War
Department. It is noticeable however, that all of his fine
threats of force and of breaking down the door and of demanding soldiers of Grant to oust Stanton had evaporated in the
sunlight of the day. Nothing was farther from Thomas' mind
than the actual use of force or violence to secure possession of
the office the President had directed him to take. The conflict
quickly changed to *opéra bouffe.*

As soon as this dialogue had been concluded, Thomas
turned facetiously to Stanton and said: "The next time you
have me arrested, please do not do it before I get something to
eat," lamenting that he had nothing to eat that day. Stanton
arose, came over to the General, put his arm around his neck,
ran his hand through Thomas' hair, dispatched a messenger to
his home for a bottle of whiskey, turned to General Schriver
and said, "Schriver, you have got a bottle here; bring it out."

That officer went to a medicine case and brought out a
bottle with a little whiskey in it. Stanton took two glasses,
measured the whiskey evenly, and he and Thomas drank in
unison. In a minute the messenger arrived with another bottle,
the cork was pulled, the antagonists took larger, but still equal
drinks, Thomas remarking, "Now this, at least, is neutral
ground." Thereupon he left.[48]

The Adjutant-General returned immediately to the White
House and reported Stanton's refusal to surrender the office.
The President was surprised and perturbed at Stanton's change
of attitude within one day. Welles and Stanbery called at
about this time and the President told them of developments.
It was his intention, he said, to nominate Thomas Ewing, Sr.,
for Secretary of War. What did they think of that?[49] He
himself believed the Conservative statesman was sound and right
on the questions before them, and trustworthy as well. After

all had agreed, the President had Colonel Moore write out
Ewing's nomination, he signed it, and Moore took it to the
Capitol to give to the Senate.[50] The issue was demanded by
his self-respect, Johnson told his callers. If he could not be
the President in fact, he would not be the President in name
alone. "What advantage," he asked, "would it be for me to do
wrong? I have taken a step which I believe was right, and I
intend to abide by it. I do not want to see this government
relapse into a despotism. I have battled for the rights and liberties of the people, and I am now endeavoring to defend them
from arbitrary power."[51]

During this conversation, Welles told the President of an
incident which had occurred the night before and which had
caused the Secretary of the Navy great alarm. Edgar Welles,
the Secretary's son, had attended a party given by a Mrs.
Ray, at which an orderly in uniform had appeared to require
all officers of the Fifth Cavalry to appear at headquarters.
Soon after, a second orderly had brought word for all officers
under command of General Emory, the Washington post commander, to report at headquarters.

When Edgar the next morning told his father of this
occurrence, the Secretary hastened to the President to ask if he
had given these orders. He had not. "Someone has," Welles
went on. "Who is it and what does it indicate? While you,
Mr. President, are resorting to no extreme measures, the conspirators have their spies—have command of the troops. Either
Stanton or Grant or both issued orders which were proclaimed
aloud, and peremptorily at this large social gathering." Johnson was very much disturbed at this news. Could it be that the
Radicals had filled the town with troops to arrest him and
thrust him into jail?[52]

Colonel Moore immediately sent a note to General Emory,
asking him to call. When the General arrived, the President
told him of his information that various changes had been
made among the troops there, which had not been brought to
his notice or reported to him, and wanted to know what they
meant. Emory explained that the orders had come through
the General of the Army. He called the President's attention
to a General Order of the War Department issued on March
14, 1867, publishing for the information of the army the
Congressional enactment that "all orders and instructions re-

lating to military operations issued by the President or the Secretary of War shall be issued through the General of the Army."

After the President had read this order, he said to the half insolent, half respectful officer, "This is not in accordance with the Constitution of the United States, which makes me Commander-in-Chief of the Army and Navy, or of the language of the commission which you hold." After Emory had made some noncommittal answer, Johnson asked: "Am I to understand that the President of the United States cannot give an order but through General Grant?" Emory answered that such was the opinion of some of the leading lawyers of the country. When Johnson asked who they were, the General gave a name or two, and retired.[53]

An arrant Radical, General Emory immediately reported the conversation to the politicians, representing the President as having demanded that he violate orders, rather than as having inquired whether as President he had not the constitutional right to give him an order direct. The most fantastic rumors spread through the city, and Stanton told newspaper correspondents that the President had sent for Emory and ordered him to detail soldiers to eject Stanton, that Emory had refused to do so, and that the President had then asked Secretary Welles for a company of marines to thrust him out.[54]

Even more exciting scenes were going on at the other end of the Avenue. With the break of dawn on Saturday morning, there had been a rush for the Capitol. The hotels, which had been thronged with thousands, were empty, while the streets were crowded with people moving to witness the great scene. Early in the day the House Reconstruction Committee went into session, the only question before it being the form in which to report a resolution recommending impeachment. Bankers, politicians, newspapermen, gathered in the corridor outside the committee room anxiously awaiting word as to the result.[55] The proprietor of the *Independent* sent his card in to Thad Stevens and informed that statesman that "the country will sustain you in this last great effort to purge the nation of its criminal Head Center." Old Thad grinned. Word came out that the Committee stood seven to two for impeachment.

A multitude had packed the galleries and the corridors, and the scene was tumultuous and picturesque. The crowd was so dense that it took newspaper correspondents an hour to thread their way through it. A little before noon, Speaker Colfax entered the House, "smiling, bowing, shaking hands."[56]   At high noon, two flags were run up above Congress. The Senate immediately adjourned, and all the Radical Senators hastened to the House Chamber to witness the impeachment of the "great criminal" they were to be called upon to try! Sumner looked "dignified and calm," Chandler "as bold as a lion," while Ben Wade ascended the speaker's platform, sat there beside the smiling Colfax, and surveyed the situation "with evident satisfaction."[57] Washington's birthday "was to be the criminal Johnson's death day." After the Chaplain's prayer, an unterrified Democrat with a sense of humor offered a resolution that Washington's Farewell Address be read to the House, and that the House then adjourn in honor of the day.   Mr. Eldridge was himself almost impeached for this scornful jest.

Shortly after two o'clock the Committee on Reconstruction filed into the Senate Chamber, Stevens hobbling at its head. Colfax demanded silence, and then asked that no approval or disapproval be expressed on the report shortly to be made. Then Old Thad arose, "haggard and trembling."[58] The House was still as death while the Commoner offered his committee's terse report: "Resolved, that Andrew Johnson, President of the United States, be impeached of high crimes and misdemeanors."

"I am ready for the vote without debate," he declared. "But if the other side must speak," he claimed the right to close the debate.

The "other side" did wish to speak. The Democrats in the House understood full well that their resistance would have no effect whatever on the outcome, that impeachment would be ordered by a party vote. But none the less they took up the battle. The debate lasted so long that adjournment had to be taken until Monday. The Radicals, unwilling to surrender Washington's birthday as the day for impeaching the President, set back the clock of the House in order that Monday should appear on the House journal as Saturday, February 22.[59]

During these tumultuous and unprecedented scenes, Andrew Johnson, coolly surveying the arrangements being made to thrust him out, was probably the calmest person in Washington. On Saturday evening, the President tendered the Democatic National Executive Committee a formal dinner which lasted until ten o'clock, and the President and his guests sat at the table "blandly indifferent" to the turmoil on Capitol Hill. During Sunday his self-possession did not leave him, for the President, although subject to fits of indecision, was resolute by nature and in this emergency courageous and buoyed up by a calm belief in fate.

On Sunday he prepared a message to the Senate, disapproving that body's resolution of the day before denying his power to remove Stanton. In this message, which was transmitted on Monday, the President recited his views on the subject, and concluded with words which proved exceptionally offensive to the Radicals bent on impeachment. Although he had been advised by every member of the Cabinet that the Tenure-of-Office Act was unconstitutional, he wrote, he had sought to proceed "with the greatest circumspection." He had acted only in cases in which he had been impelled by the "solemn obligations which rest upon me to sustain inviolate the powers of the high office committed to my hands." Such a case was that of Mr. Stanton.

"Therefore, whatever may be the consequences merely personal to myself, I could not allow them to prevail against a public duty so clear to my mind and so imperative. If what was possible had been certain, if I had been fully advised when I removed Mr. Stanton, that in thus defending the trust committed to my hands my own removal was sure to follow, I could not have hesitated."[60]

But while Sunday was calm at the White House, it was a day of great excitement in the hotel lobbies and other gathering-places of the politicians throughout the city. The wildest rumors filled the air, rumors of troops marching on Washington, of Maryland Conservatives clad in Confederate gray approaching the city to thrust Stanton forth. It was a day of extreme tension, with everyone expectant of what the morrow would bring forth.

Monday morning witnessed another great rush of the populace for the House galleries. By nine o'clock, they were filled to overflowing, the entire Capitol police and a force from the city being needed to preserve order. By Radical prearrangement, Ashley led off, Boutwell combed the heavens with his rhetoric and Thad Stevens closed the performance. The principal Democratic speech was that of Judge Woodward of Pennsylvania.

At 4:30 in the afternoon, Stevens walked feebly to a chair placed on the platform behind the speaker's desk. The fire of his implacable spirit gleamed from his sunken eyes, and his lips curled with a half smile of triumph. The Radicals quivered with suppressed excitement. Members flocked around him from all parts of the House, and a Radical correspondent termed it "a beautiful, touching and solemn picture."[61]

"Eloquent almost to inspiration," and speaking "as from the very brink of the grave," Stevens began; soon he had to sit down. A clerk finished the reading of his speech. Finally the fated hour of five o'clock arrived. Debate ceased. The speaker read the resolution Stevens had offered on Saturday, and called for a vote.

The House and the galleries were still as death. The sound of "a raging storm" outside was plainly heard above the reading clerk's metallic voice, calling the first name of the roll.[62] "Aye" rang out the answer. As the roll call proceeded, murmurs were heard: "The President is impeached." The galleries were orderly during the procedure. When the result of the vote was announced—for impeachment, 126; against impeachment, forty-seven—there was not the expected wild demonstration. It was a strict party vote. Not a Democrat had voted Aye, not a Republican Nay. The Radical Republican Party had impeached the President of the United States.

Immediately after the mild applause had died down, Stevens moved that a committee of two be sent to inform the Senate of the action of the House. Thad Stevens and John A. Bingham were chosen for the task.

At ten minutes past one, on the following day, this announcement committee entered the main portals of the Senate. Old Thad advanced, pallid and ghastly, leaning upon Bingham's arms. The Senate doorkeeper announced loudly, "A message from the House of Representatives," and every Senator whirled about to face the messengers.

Stevens straightened himself up, melodramatically threw his hat on the floor behind him, handed his cane to the doorkeeper and slowly drew a piece of paper from his pocket. In tones of sepulchral solemnity, Old Thad informed the Senate that "The People of the United States" had impeached Andrew Johnson, for high crimes and misdemeanors.[63]

"The Senate will take order in the premises," responded Ben Wade, sitting in the President's chair.

About six o'clock on Monday evening, word came to Andrew Johnson that the House had voted his impeachment. He received the news "very coolly, and was not at all excited." He turned to Colonel Moore, whom he had asked to dine with him, to remark: "I think many of those who have voted for impeachment feel more uneasy as to the position in which they have thus placed themselves than I do as to the situation in which they have put me."[64]

"$\mathbf{B}$EN WADE will be President in a fortnight from today."
While Andrew Johnson would be allowed several days to
prepare his defense, "the trial, once begun, will be speedily
ended." Such were the hopeful words of the *Independent's*
Washington correspondent at the outset, and such was the full
expectation of the Radicals. When the Senate was debating
its resolution of February 21, the hitherto Radical Fessenden
warned his colleagues that they were proposing "a very unwise
resolution," an open bid to the House to impeach, refused to
vote for it, and wrote home that his friends were "acting like
fools, and hurrying us to destruction."[1]

The haste of the impeaching members, both in House and
Senate, was in line with Fessenden's words. On February 25,
immediately after Stevens and Bingham had given notice of the
impeachment, the Senate appointed a committee of seven to
draft rules for the trial. On February 26, Senators Howard
and Edmunds, two Radical members of this committee, called
on Chief Justice Chase to inform him that their committee was
preparing rules for the procedure of the trial, and invited suggestions from him; indeed, they would be pleased to have him
attend their sessions. They also asked Chase if he considered that
he had a right to vote in the Senate court about to be organized.
He said he had not thought much about it, but supposed that
he would be a member of the court and as such would have a
right to vote—although, as he was replacing the Vice President
in ordinary impeachment trials, his vote might be limited to
deciding a tie. The two Radicals let him know that they denied his right to vote in any case.

After carefully examining impeachment precedents, the
Chief Justice formed the definite opinion that, until the Senate
should be organized as a court of impeachment, it had no
right to take any action relative thereto other than to receive
the notice from the House. On the 27th he wrote Howard this
conclusion, but received no response.[2] The Senate majority
pressed forward, determined to expedite the proceedings.
Overriding the objections of the Democrats, they prepared and
adopted twenty-five rules to govern all possible crises of pro-

cedure in trial, vote and judgment. Chase watched these proceedings with anxiety. On March 4 he indicated his disapproval to the Senate by a terse letter, setting out that it seemed unquestionable that when the Senate sat for a trial of impeachment it sat as a court, that its organization as a court must precede the House's actual announcement of the Articles of Impeachment; and that the court itself should adopt the rules for its governance and not the Senate as a legislative body. This letter created a storm among the Senate Radicals, who proceeded straightway to ignore its counsels by immediately receiving the House to present its Eleven Articles.

These debates were not without their alarums. Within a week after the vote of the House for impeachment, Speaker Colfax, for once not smiling, read the House a letter he had that morning received. It was from the Chief of Police of New York, reciting that a great quantity of nitroglycerine had mysteriously disappeared from Manhattan, and that he did not know where it could be going unless to Washington. The Radicals were thrown into a panic. Additional police were excitedly ordered, and the House adjourned instanter. But poor Stanton could not adjourn. Nitroglycerine or not, he must hold on to the War Department. His former Cabinet associates laughed grimly over the resulting "fortifications and entrenchment of the War Department," and over the redoubling of Stanton's guard.[3]

Even without this incident, it had not been easy for the House to evolve its bill of indictment. On February 24 a special committee was selected to report the impeachment articles to the House. Desiring to expand their scope, the committee summoned Thomas' interlocutors of the night of February 21, to elicit their recollections of the boastful General's verbose threats. They had General Emory detail his interview with the President on February 22. Then the committee set themselves to debate, and after great travail, the mountain labored to bring forth a mouse.

On Saturday, February 29, they reported to the House ten articles, framed and phrased so as to win the assent of every phase of opinion of Senate Radicals. The first charged Johnson with Stanton's removal, contrary to the Constitution and the Tenure-of-Office Act. The second recited the President's letter to General Thomas, and held it to be a violation of the Constitution and the law. The third was substantially the same as the second, except that reference to the Tenure-of-Office Act was lacking. The next five articles charged conspiracy, stating that Johnson and the Adjutant-General had plotted "by intimidation and threats" to prevent Stanton from holding his office, thus violating the Constitution and the Conspiracy act passed in 1861; that they had sought "by force" to hinder execution of the Tenure-of-Office act, and that they had conspired "by force to seize" government property. The ninth was a repetition of the second and third, charging additionally the President's illegal intent to control public funds appropriated for the War Department. The tenth, based upon the Emory interview, charged that the President had been guilty of a "high misdemeanor" by giving illegal instructions to that General.

When these were laid before the House, one of the prevalent Radical slurs at the Chief Executive was settled at once. It had been their custom to proclaim doubts that Johnson was President and to term him "Acting President." When Boutwell now affected to hold these doubts, Bingham scattered them to the winds. "I was not aware," he declared, "there was a member of that committee who had the slightest doubt that Andrew Johnson was the President of the United States. . . . If he be not President, then the people have no President, then you can pass no law. If he be President, then let him be called President upon your records." Thus the Radicals were forced to give Johnson his true title before they could proceed to snatch it from him.

Thad Stevens was disgusted at the mildness of the articles. Never had "a great malefactor been so gently treated," he sneered. The bill of indictment charged "the most trifling crimes and misdemeanors." He then offered an article of his own, reciting Stanton's suspension, Johnson's submission of his reasons for it, and charging that, while the Senate was considering these reasons, the President had formed a deliberate design to prevent Stanton from resuming his office, and, with conscious intent to violate the law, had issued the letter to Thomas directing its violation.

"If there be shrewd lawyers," he challenged, "as I know there will be, and caviling judges, and, without this article, they do not acquit him, they are greener than I was in any case I ever undertook before a court of quarter sessions." But if this article were inserted, he called attention to the fact that

the Senate had voted four times in favor of the Tenure-of-Office
Act, and "let me see the recreant who will now dare tread
back upon his steps and vote upon the other side."[4]

On Monday, the Committee brought back another version
of its articles, the changes being chiefly verbal, except that one
of the conspiracy articles was dropped. Ben Butler now offered a pet draft of his own. Suspected of opposition to
Grant's nomination for the Presidency, the "Hero of Fort
Fisher" had been left off the drafting committee, but he was
a man who could not easily be silenced. The article he proposed was based upon three of Johnson's speeches, the one
of August 18, 1866, in the East Room of the White House, in
which he had termed Congress a body "hanging on the verge
of government," a Congress "of only a part of the States";
second, the Cleveland speech on the Swing Around the Circle,
in which Johnson had charged that Congress was "trying to
break up the government"; and again, the President's unfortunate comparison in his St. Louis speech of Thad Stevens
to Christ. Butler had vainly presented this article to the committee. Now he submitted it to the House which, by a vote of
seventy-four to forty-eight, also turned it down. Thereupon
the nine articles as reported by the committee were adopted
without change.

The articles as adopted were far from satisfactory to intelligent Radicals. A few days after the House had voted
them, Joseph Medill, from his Chicago sanctum, informed General Logan that "a grave and terrible blunder" had been committed. "If Johnson can't be impeached and ousted from office
for violating the Tenure-of-Office law," the editor of the
Tribune declared, "he will never be put out for anything he
said. . . . We are in danger also of causing a reaction in the
popular mind against Congress and the Republican party by
dragging in this extraneous and unnecessary matter. . . . I
shall thank God if the affair has not been botched." Two
weeks later he wrote that "we are all nervous about delaying.
. . . Like an aching tooth, every one is impatient to have the
old villain out."[5]

But the other Radicals were no more impatient to "get the
old villain out" than the Conservatives were determined to
leave no stone unturned to acquit him. One matter was immediately repaired. For several months, Reverdy Johnson
had been the only Senator from Maryland. Philip F. Thomas,

whom the Maryland Legislature had elected for the second seat, had presented his credentials, but had long been held under consideration by the Radical majority. Finally, on February 19, he had formally been refused admission by the Senate, its resolution charging that he had "voluntarily given aid, countenance and encouragement" to the South during the war. With the House's vote for impeachment, the increased importance of every Senate vote brought a quick solution to the situation. Thomas resigned and the Conservative legislature at Annapolis immediately selected George Vickers, a staunch Democrat of Chestertown, and one in whose war record not even a minor blemish could be found, to fill the vacant seat.

So anxious were the Marylanders to have their new Senator in Washington in time to qualify as a judge of the impeachment court that their great ice-breaker was sent up the icebound Chester river to bring Vickers to Baltimore, from which city a special train rushed him to Washington. Reverdy Johnson presented his new colleague to the Senate on March 9, but Sumner immediately objected to the administration of the oath, claiming that Maryland, under its new constitution, did not have "a republican form of government," as contemplated by the Federal Constitution, and therefore had no title "at this time to elect and commission a Senator of the United States." The offer of this resolution having afforded him the opportunity for a diatribe against Maryland, Sumner announced that he had accomplished his purpose, withdrew his objection, and Vickers took the oath.[6]

The seven Managers of Impeachment for the House, agreed on at a Radical caucus immediately after the vote of the 24th, were formally elected the next week. They were Bingham, Butler, Wilson, Boutwell, Thomas Williams, Logan and Thad Stevens.[7] When the prosecuting attorneys had been selected, the House notified the Senate of the fact and that it was ready to exhibit the Articles of Impeachment, and adjourned.

But the next day, when the Senate sent word that it was ready to receive them, the House was not ready to attend. At the moment Butler was again pressing his rejected article upon his colleagues. Finally he had his way. At the same time an eleventh article was agreed upon. Its authorship was attributed to Thad Stevens, but it differed in many respects from the one the Commoner had urged the day before. This new article was an *omnium gatherum*, a sweeping together of all the charges of the other articles, commencing with the contention that Johnson's speech of August 18, 1866, was a denial of the constitutionality of Congress, that he had sought to defeat the ratification of the Fourteenth Amendment and that he had conspired against Congress, the Constitution and the laws by his attempt to remove Stanton and put Thomas in his place. It was obviously contrived in this vague and voluminous form to afford a vehicle upon which doubtful Senators could overcome their conscientious scruples and vote for conviction. Senator Buckalew remarked that, "as an article on which to convict, its strength consists in weakness—in the obscurity of its charges and the intricacy of its form."[8] After these last two articles had been hastily drawn up, the House resolved itself into a Committee of the Whole, and accompanied its seven managers to the Senate Chamber.

The Radicals were much impressed with the dramatic possibilities the day afforded. There had been much reading of Lord Macaulay's essay on the impeachment of Warren Hastings, and many were the efforts to stage the American scene in rival splendor and solemnity to the great English legal drama. The result was heavy farce. Eight luxurious arm chairs had been removed from the Vice President's room and set in front of the President's desk for the Managers of the Impeachment. Logan placed himself in front of one of these, "in the grandiloquent attitude of a Choctaw Chief in council." Supported on his cane, Thad Stevens, feeble as he was, stood erect until exhaustion forced him to sit. Ben Butler solemnly hung his bald head and, with his hat clasped in both hands beneath his paunch, seemed "an overgrown schoolboy on the stool of repentance."[9] By invitation, Speaker Colfax took a seat beside Ben Wade, who still presided.[10] Bingham's reading of the articles required about half an hour; while the tenth article was being read, quoting Johnson's St. Louis speech, in which he had asked if Thad Stevens was the Christ he had betrayed, Stevens was observed to "grin horribly a ghastly smile." The House having retired, the Senate appointed a committee of three to wait upon the Chief Justice to give him notice of the trial and request him to attend.

On the following day, the Senate galleries were packed with spectators anxious to see the show. Every newspaper of importance in the country had correspondents on hand, to say nothing of artists and cartoonists by the score. A hush fell over the hall upon the entry of the Chief Justice, clad in the trailing robes of his office. He was accompanied by Associate-Judge Nelson, who immediately administered to Chase the oath: "That in all things appertaining to the trial of the impeachment of Andrew Johnson, President of the United States, now pending, I will do impartial justice according to the Constitution and laws: So help me God." By this bold initial stroke of having himself sworn with the oath of the Court, the Chief Justice served notice on the Radicals that he considered the Senate an Impeachment Court and that he would so conduct it. He then proceeded to administer the oath to the Senators.

When Ben Wade's name was reached, Senator Hendricks made a protest. The Senator from Ohio was the President *pro tempore* of the Senate. If Andrew Johnson should be found guilty of the impeachment charges, under the existing law Ben Wade would become President of the United States. Therefore Hendricks questioned that Wade was competent to sit as a member of the court, both because "the Constitution does not allow him to preside . . . because of his possible succession," and further, because "he is interested, in view of his possible connection with the office, in the result of the proceedings."[11]

Sherman, Wade's Ohio colleague, immediately challenged this view, and the Radicals, one and all, ran to Bluff Ben's defense. Under the Constitution, Sherman declared, Ohio was entitled to two Senators. That was all there was to it. The Senate must submit to Wade's conscience as to how he would vote.

This debate was continued the following day, and Wade's "rights" were rather roughly handled by Hendricks, Reverdy Johnson, Dixon and others. Finally Hendricks withdrew his motion, having probably raised it primarily to emphasize to the country Wade's great personal interest in conviction. Thereupon the man who, if the impeachment should be upheld, would succeed the accused President, advanced to the bar of the Senate and swore to "do impartial justice"! After all the Senators had taken the oath, Chase declared the Senate "now organized for the purpose of proceeding to the trial of the impeachment," and Senator Howard moved that the House managers be notified.

Before he would put the question, the Chief Justice made

plain the status of the body now organized. It was, he pointed out, a distinct body from the legislative Senate, and "the chair conceives that rules adopted by the Senate in its legislative capacity are not rules for the government of the Senate sitting for the trial of an impeachment, unless they be also adopted by that body." Thereupon he put the question as to whether these rules already affirmed should not be readopted to govern the proceedings of the impeachment court, and upon a general affirmative response, he declared such should be ordered. The Chief Justice had again served notice on the Radicals that, so far as he could control them, the proceedings would be those of a court.[12] The Senate then ordered the President to appear before it at one o'clock on March 13, to answer to the articles.[13] On March 7, the Sergeant-at-Arms of the Senate served this summons at the White House. The President, Colonel Moore noted, "deeply felt the solemnity of the matter."

After the release on bail of the unfortunate Thomas on February 22, he had employed a clever lawyer, Richard T. Merrick, to represent him, and the President retained another, Walter S. Cox, to get the Stanton-Thomas case before the Supreme Court of the United States. At first the attorneys hoped that *quo warranto* proceedings could be instituted, but it developed that it would take at least a year for the Supreme Court to reach such a suit. Thereupon the lawyers determined to surrender Thomas to the District of Columbia court on the day the case was set, to refuse to renew bail for him, and to swear out immediately an application for a writ of *habeas corpus*.

Thomas was accordingly surrendered into custody on the day appointed. Stanton's lawyers were horrified at the thought of a *habeas corpus*, Judge Cartter refused to receive Thomas into custody and instantly dismissed the charge against the Adjutant-General, thus forcing the General—and the President—out of court. "The trick," the New York *World* commented, "is transparent and disgraceful, and humiliating to both Stanton and the Court."[14]

Stanton himself remained on in the War Department, carefully maintaining a state of siege. He slept upon a lounge in his office, and his meals were brought in three times a day. Mrs. Stanton came to see him every day. He would leave the building only for a short promenade, under guard, on the walk outside.[15]

During these trying days, the President's intimates were surprised and some of them a trifle nettled at the calm with which Johnson met the crisis. Indeed, the tailor-statesman, as has been seen on many an occasion, was never calmer than in dire trouble; never did he present so noteworthy a figure as when his enemies were gathering about him, eager to pronounce his doom. Such emergencies seemed to steel him to exceptional courage, calmness and dignity.

Thus, during the two days following the vote in the House, to the surprise and almost the consternation of the Radicals, Johnson and his daughters unexpectedly attended one of Chase's Wednesday Evenings, a favorite social event of Washington Radicals. The extremists among the company were amazed and disturbed when the doors were thrown open and "The President of the United States" was announced. The Chief Executive took occasion to look the world straight in the eye and to show that he was not afraid. After the usual greetings and civilities, the President left, but his brief appearance caused great agitation among the Radical papers. Did this mean that the Chief Justice was going to be a traitor to the cause, as Andrew Johnson had earlier been?[16]

If the mass of congratulatory telegrams and letters which Johnson received as soon as the news of Stanton's removal became known, be an index, the President had no cause to feel downcast over the attitude of the public toward him. The verdict of most historians seems to be that the removal of the recusant Minister occasioned universal anger, and that the swift vote of impeachment was followed by a general chorus of joy. But this is only a partial view of the matter. The extreme Radicals, to be sure, everywhere rejoiced. But the Democratic masses were appalled, and while some of the Democratic leaders secretly hoped that the impeachment would succeed, they did so only because of their firm belief that this success would ruin the Republicans, just as the passage of the Alien and Sedition laws had spelt the death-knell of the Federalists. The Conservative Whigs, of whom Thomas Ewing was a good example, were aghast at the disclosure of the willingness of the Radicals to employ the great engine of impeachment for mere party ends. Even the milder body of the Republican party, which had been carried along unresistingly in the current of the two amendments and military reconstruction, was beset with increasing qualms at the spectacle the extremists of House and Senate were making of themselves.

"The hostility you are meeting from many of our representatives," read a letter to the President from Ohio, "leaves us, the people, no other way but to approach you personally and assure you of our sympathy and approbation." There were scores of such letters. "If you require brave hearts and stout arms to aid you," wrote a leading Democrat in Indiana, "give the word, and the friends of Liberty and Union will respond." M. H. Beaumont of Perth Amboy, N. J., tendered the "service of thousands at a moment's notice." Charles W. Carrigan of Philadelphia telegraphed that the people "are with you, peaceful or forceful, with ballots or bullets, for the maintenance of the Constitution and the law." From Warrenton, Va., W. G. Douglas informed the President he could have 30,000 Virginia men to help him by force of arms. Seventy-five stalwart men of Omaha offered themselves. "For the sake of God and liberty, stand firm," exhorted Editor Stoll, "eject Stanton and do not allow yourself to be arrested. If you want troops, let us know. This county will furnish a regiment in ten days. We have captains, colonels, and generals who are anxious to rally to your support."

Meetings were held throughout the country to indorse Johnson's course. "Stand firm, the people will sustain you," came a telegram from a monster mass meeting at Columbus, Ohio. "If he would but stand firm," Pennsylvanians were "ready and eager to sustain him," a Member of Congress from that State declared. From Boston, J. M. Lincoln telegraphed the President, "stand by the Constitution of our country, and God will sustain you, and the people also."[17]

The Radicals in Washington may have affected to think the impeachment a party question, but it was not generally so regarded in the country. The *Nation*, while not regretting the impeachment of this "sore trial to the nation for the last three years," derided the rhetoric hurled at the President, and wondered ironically why he had not been compared to Philip II or Alva; Editor Godkin pointed out that "the terms of the law are such that the unfortunate man was unable to test its constitutionality without exposing himself to impeachment."[18] But the advice and indirect admonition which General Sherman sent his Senatorial brother pretty well represented the feeling of thoughtful men: "the vote in the House, being a strictly party vote, looks bad, for it augurs a prejudiced jury. Those who adhere closest to the law in this crisis are the best patriots."[19]

Had Andrew Johnson sought an appeal to arms, without doubt he could quickly have provoked a formidable civil war, with a stirring battle cry—"Protect the Constitution; restore the prostrate South." But Johnson paid no heed to talk of violence. It was not his mode to defend the national charter by breaking it. The procedure of impeachment, while basely partisan, was regular in form, and did not contemplate suspending him. He could endure this trial by his enemies; posterity would decide aright.

At the Cabinet meeting on February 25, a general feeling of doubt and sadness was noticeable. While the President was calm and made no complaint, it was obvious that he felt "the wrong and outrage of the conspirators." Johnson's friends began to make the best they could of the situation, and to look for encouraging circumstances. John Bigelow reported that "the large Conservative force in the Senate, with the Chief Justice, looked with repugnance and horror to the accession of Wade." The President's friends derived solace from the knowledge that the whole proceeding was cheap politics. On the 27th, Woodbridge of Vermont, of the House Judiciary Committee, came to see Welles to say that he "regretted that he was compelled to vote for it under party command. . . . It would have been death for him to have resisted. He voted with reluctance and against his wishes and convictions, for the President he knew to be honest and patriotic." The Secretary noted this confession as added evidence that "the whole impeachment scheme is a piece of party persecution."[20]

On February 28, without invitation of the President, and over Seward's objection, Browning brought before the Cabinet the question of counsel. It was "unanimously agreed" that Attorney-General Stanbery should take the lead, with two other eminent counsel associated. For these two, the President's advisers properly felt that he should have the most distinguished lawyers in the United States, men who by reputation, ability and character possessed the confidence of the country. The name of Benjamin Robbins Curtis of Boston, a former justice of the United States Supreme Court, immediately suggested itself. Curtis' dissenting opinion in the Dred Scott case had given him deserved fame. In his private practice, he had subsequently increased this high repute. A man of the greatest dignity of demeanor and of the highest professional and public standards, Curtis' retention as counsel was properly esteemed as highly beneficial to Andrew Johnson's cause. The suggestion was immediately accepted by the whole Cabinet, with the President's emphatic approval.[21] Johnson did not know Curtis personally, but a high sense of public duty induced the latter promptly to accept the case. It was intimated that the President was unable to offer compensation for the service; but Curtis—and the other distinguished lawyers of Johnson's counsel—represented him without fee because of the great importance of the public issues presented by the trial.[22]

In addition to Judge Curtis, Charles O'Conor was suggested, but McCulloch objected that O'Conor had been counsel for Jefferson Davis, and so would arouse Radical hostility. William M. Evarts, another great leader of the bar, perhaps not so sound as Curtis but far more brilliant, was next suggested. A Republican and almost a Radical, his selection, it was held, would tend to balance the Conservative O'Conor or Jeremiah S. Black. It was determined that Stanbery should confer with Evarts, and that, if Evarts should be willing to "enter heartily and conscientiously" into the case, he should be employed.

When the Cabinet came together again on Saturday evening to discuss the matter of counsel, Stanbery announced that Curtis had already been secured and would arrive in Washington early the next week. Stanbery wanted to resign as Attorney-General immediately, so as to devote his whole time to the defense of the President, a cause upon which he had deeply set his heart. The others of the Cabinet, however, all opposed such a step unless he were compelled to it. Next, a discussion as to Black's desirability in the case followed. Hendricks had told McCulloch that Black's appearance for the President would be injudicious, maintaining that the Senate Democrats would be amenable, but that the Republicans were hostile to the Pennsylvanian. McCulloch urged that Black be left out; but Welles thought it was both unwise and impolitic not to have a Democrat among the counsel. The President's legal representatives should embrace all the great sections of public opinion. Something more than a mere lawyer was wanted; there was need as well for a politician and a statesman who had studied the Constitution and public affairs.

On Monday Welles called at the White House to advise the President of his considered opinion. Although there was opposition to Black, yet if the Pennsylvanian had the President's confidence, Welles believed that Johnson should not allow himself to be dissuaded from naming him. The President thanked him, and said that he had decided to name Black, and had so informed Seward the night before. Evarts and Black were added to the list, and the President also made a personal selection, Judge T. A. R. Nelson, from his home town of Greeneville.

Curtis arrived at Washington, a day or so later, and immediately went into conference with Stanbery. To his brother, George Ticknor Curtis, who came to the capital to aid him, the Boston jurist stated that, at their first meeting, "the calm honest sincerity of Mr. Johnson" had aroused his admiration. Curtis wrote to his uncle, George Ticknor, the historian: "The President is calm, cheerful and self-sustained. He firmly believes he has been and is right, he knows he is honest and true in his devotion to the Constitution. If he is expelled from office, he will march out with a firm step and a strong heart." While the ex-Justice had taken the case because of the public importance of the cause, he quickly became impressed with and attached to the individual defendant. "My respect for the moral qualities of the man is greatly enhanced by my knowledge of him," he wrote a few days later. "He is a man of few ideas, but they are right and true, and he could suffer death sooner than yield up or violate one of them. He is honest, right-minded, and narrow-minded; he has no tact, and even lacks discretion and forecast. But he is firm as a rock; and if he should be convicted, he will go out with a firm reliance that the time will come when a 'black line' will be drawn around that senatorial record, by the command of the people of the United States." None of the counsel had any thought of advising the President's resignation, but, Curtis wrote, "if everyone advised it, the President would not listen to such advice."[23]

There were suggestions that he make a deft use of patronage to secure acquittal. His Tennessee friend, Colonel Edmund Cooper, was irritated at Johnson's obstinate refusal. "Impeach me for violating the Constitution! Damn them!" the President exclaimed to Colonel Moore. "Have I not struggled ever since I occupied this chair to uphold the Constitution which they are trampling under foot? I suppose I made Colonel Cooper mad with me today. He wanted me to use the patronage of my office to prevent a judgment against me by the Senate. How would I feel after acquittal if I had bought it? How would I feel if my conscience told me I owed my acquittal to bribery? I will do nothing of the kind. I will not seek to use any unfair means of vindication."[24]

A Radical agent brought a proposition to Seward that, if he would do nothing to interfere with the success of impeachment, Ben Wade would retain him as Secretary of State. "I will see you damned first," Seward indignantly told the Radical emissary, "the impeachment of the President is the impeachment of his Cabinet."[25]

By March 10, Stanbery had definitely determined that he must resign; unless he did so, the Radicals would charge that he was being paid out of the public treasury while defending the President. After the trial, if the Senate would permit him, he would resume as Attorney-General. The next day he submitted his resignation, "that I may perform a duty, which, under the circumstances, seems to me a paramount obligation."

The lawyers at times found their high-placed client rather trying. He was determined that his defense be made not alone for the Senate, but even more directly for the people of the country, so that they might know the truth about his policy as President.[26] On one occasion he told the lawyers that "after all, the defense he desired to make was for the people," and that he "would care nothing for conviction by the Senate if he stood acquitted by the people." On another, he threatened his counsel if they would not conduct his defense according to his views, he would appear in person before the Senate and defend himself. "Then, if I should be convicted, I alone can be blamed if it follows as a result of plain speaking." These threats seem to have brought the counsel to time, and thenceforth they gave heed to the President's views of what should be done in his behalf.[27]

About this time, Alexander H. Stephens visited the President and shed bitter tears over the impeachment. "I have served with you in Congress ten years," the Georgian said, "I have been in your canvasses, I know you as well as you are known by any man, and now let me counsel you, as I would a brother, to make your own defense. No one can do it as well as yourself, and I believe your safety demands it."[28]

But while Johnson allowed himself to be dissuaded from taking a personal hand in his defense, he found it difficult to conquer his habit of giving interviews to Washington correspondents, a habit which often plunged him into trouble. Some of the correspondents grossly misquoted his statements. Even worse, the President at times revealed matters which his counsel greatly wished to be kept from the public gaze. On March 9, Johnson accorded an interview to Stillson of the New York *World* in which he paid his respects to his Secretary of War. "Mr. Stanton was a marplot," the President remarked. "I forbore until forbearance ceased even to seem to be a virtue."

In this interview he also revealed a matter which one of Seward's clerks, in hunting precedents, had discovered,—that in 1800, President John Adams had summarily removed Timothy Pickering as Secretary of State, over Pickering's protest, while the Senate was in session, a case quite parallel in form to that of Stanton. Johnson's counsel had been relying largely on this precedent, which had been kept a studied secret until the President proclaimed it to the world.

On March 12, at a special Cabinet meeting, the Attorney-General's resignation was considered and accepted. Stanbery was about to leave the room when he stopped, turned to the President and said: "You are now, Mr. President, in the hands of your lawyers, who will speak and act for you, and I must begin by requesting that no further disclosures be made to newspaper correspondents." Referring then to the *World* interview and the printing of the Pickering precedent, he chided: "This is all wrong, and I have to request that these talks or conversations be stopped. They injure your case and embarrass your counsel." Browning backed up Stanbery. The President was taken aback and sought to apologize, but no one attempted to excuse him, and while he "evidently did not relish being muzzled," there were fewer exclusive interviews thenceforth.[29]

The next day had been set for the President's formal appearance at the bar of the Senate, in response to the notice served on him. After the Sergeant-at-Arms of the Senate had announced the service of the summons on the President and the Chief Justice had directed him to call the accused, a clarion voice rang out: "Andrew Johnson, President of the United States; Andrew Johnson, President of the United States, appear and answer the Articles of Impeachment exhibited against you by the House of Representatives of the United States." An impressive silence ensued. The Radicals hoped against hope that the Chief Executive would appear in person, thus lending dignity to their proceedings. But Johnson would be represented only by counsel. Presently Stanbery, Curtis and Nelson entered and took their seats.

"Mr. Chief Justice," Stanbery began, "my brothers, Curtis, and Nelson, and myself, are here this morning as counsel for the President. I have his authority to enter his appearance, which, with your leave, I will proceed to read." The President's brief statement, addressed to the Chief Justice, said that through his counsel, Henry Stanbery, Benjamin R. Curtis, Jeremiah Sullivan Black, William M. Evarts and Thomas A. R. Nelson, he entered his appearance, these gentlemen having his warrant and authority to represent him. The appearance likewise asked for forty days' time for the preparation of his answer to the Articles of Impeachment.

In support of this application, Stanbery read a statement which all the counsel had signed, setting out the need for this length of time. The articles involved many questions of law and fact. In prior cases, Judge Chase had been allowed thirty-two days to answer eight articles, and Judge Peck fifteen days for a single one. Surely the President was fairly entitled to more time than was allowed in either of these cases. "It is seldom that a case requires such constant communication between client and counsel as this," the statement continued, while "such communication can only be had at such intervals as are allowed to the President from the usual hours that must be devoted to his high official duties." The lawyers concluded that, in a case of such magnitude, so out of line of usual professional experiences, they were entitled "to ask for themselves such opportunity to discharge their duty as seems to them to be absolutely necessary."[30]

The Radicals treated this application with derision. It had already been more than a fortnight since Johnson had been impeached, and Ben Wade was not yet in the White House. Bingham insisted that, under the rules the Senate had adopted, the appearance of Johnson's counsel constituted an answer, and that the case should immediately proceed upon the general issue. When Curtis expressed his amazement at this attitude, Manager Wilson insisted on immediate trial.

Stanbery's ire was aroused by the managers' attitude. "The objection," he informed the court, "is so singular that in the whole course of my practice, I have not met with an example like it. A case like this, Mr. Chief Justice, in which the President of the United States is arraigned upon an impeachment presented by the House of Representatives, a case of the greatest magnitude we have ever had, is, as to time, to be treated as if it were a case before a police court, to be put through with railroad speed on the first day the criminal appears!"

All the President's counsel were not yet on hand, he pointed out; one had not yet reached the city. The managers had made much of English precedent, but English fair play always gave fair time. "Give us the opportunity that even in common civil cases is allowed to the defendant. . . . Give us time; give us a reasonable time; and then, with a fair hearing, we shall be prepared for that sentence, whatever it may be, that you shall pronounce."

This forceful protest took Bingham aback and he somewhat modified his earlier insistence. The Senate immediately retired for a two hour debate and consultation. Upon its return, Bingham moved that the trial "proceed forthwith." The eagerness of the Radical Senators to use "railroad speed" in the case was shown when this motion failed to pass by but a single vote. Butler then informed the Senate that "the state of the country, the interests of the people, all seem to require that we should urge the speediest possible trial." He insolently inquired, "Who is the criminal?" and answered himself by saying that he was the Chief Executive, with all the executive power in his hands, and that "in any hour of passion, of prejudice, of revenge for fancied wrong in his own mind, he may complicate your peace with any nation of the earth, even while he is being arraigned as a respondent at your bar." Butler made much of the "mischiefs of delay," prating that it had taken the Almighty but forty days to destroy the world by flood. Other managers insisted that the country had a right to quick relief, and the greater part of the Senators were obviously of the same belief.

Finally, the President was allowed ten days to draft his reply to the Impeachment Articles. It was likewise ordered that the trial should proceed immediately after the House should have answered the President's replication. Bingham promised boastfully that the House's replication to Johnson's answer would be made the day following the deliverance of the answer. The managers considered the impeachment trial worthy of no loftier methods than "a horse case"—Ben Butler's phrase—and sneered at all the pother about forms and precedents. There had already been too much delay in throwing the President out.

The President's counsel set immediately to work on the preparation of the answer. The eleven articles raised a myriad questions of fact and of law, of the constitutional powers of the Chief Executive, and of the intent of his mind. Stanbery, Curtis and Evarts toiled ceaselessly at their task, while Nelson busied himself checking up citations, seeking precedents and arranging rebutting proof to the charges of the House. Although Black gave less and less attention to the consultations, for reasons presently to appear, the others abandoned all other engagements, their courts, cases and clients, and devoted every hour to the preparation of the answer. It was a laborious and exhausting task, and the document was in final form only a few minutes before the appointed hour on March 23.[31]   Stanbery, whose health was not good, undertook a course of physical training and had a man rub him down every morning and evening, to keep him in trim for his great fight.

On the morning of March 16, Stanbery entered the White House library, where he found Johnson worried over the situation. "Don't lose a moment's sleep, Mr. President, but be hopeful," the lawyer urged his Presidential client. "When some things are done, we cannot tell if they be for good or evil. I confess I felt a misgiving about this act of impeachment when it was first done; but now that it has been done, and the whole matter is to be considered, I see in it nothing but good. It gives you a great opportunity to vindicate yourself as President against every charge made against you . . . not only before the American people, but before the entire world . . . . . to show whether you are a traitor or not; to show whether or not your policy, when contrasted with theirs, is not the policy of wisdom. . . .

"Why, Mr. President, they call you a traitor to the party which elected you. When I put the question to myself as to services, I find that I am far behind you in good works, for what did I do? All that I did was without loss or peril, while what *you* have done, has been in the face of all sorts of dangers and difficulties. . . .

"I have watched you day and night; I have been with you under all circumstances, and have been consulted by you upon

every subject, from the beginning to the end of my connection
with your Administration, and I have seen nothing which, had I
been in your place, I would not have done myself. . . . Mr.
President, if I can only keep well for this trial, I will be willing
to be sick during the balance of my life. I know, Sir, that you
will come out of it brighter than you have ever shone."[32]
Throughout the preparation of the answer, Johnson was in
consultation. It was evident that he felt deeply. "Too bad;
too bad," he constantly remarked. It was as difficult to
satisfy him of the perfection of responses as it was to satisfy
any of the counsel. But this was by no means his only occupation. Radical Senators began to intimate to him that he could
save himself from conviction by making a change in his Cabinet.
On the evening of Stanbery's glowing tribute, Senator Pomeroy
of Kansas—the same who in 1867 had offered, in writing, to
exchange his impeachment vote for the Leavenworth Post Office
—summoned R. W. Latham, one of Johnson's friends, and
authorized him to inform the President that, as matters then
stood, "Conviction is a dead certainty, but that the resignation
of the entire Cabinet will place him in a position, if he will act
promptly—say not later than Thursday—to kill impeachment." Pomeroy had a new Cabinet slated, with Banks of
Massachusetts for Secretary of State, Robert J. Walker for
Secretary of the Treasury, and F. P. Stanton for the Secretary of the Navy. He had not yet fastened on new men for the
Post Office and Interior Departments, but felt sure that the
present heads should be removed.

Stewart of Nevada, "the bitterest man in the Senate," told
Latham that such a move would "destroy impeachment entirely." If he were in Johnson's place, Stewart said, he
would even "put Butler in one of these offices rather than stand
in his present position." Pomeroy emphasized that he and
many other Senators deemed impeachment a *political* rather
than a *legal* matter, and would be compelled to vote for it, unless the President gave some excuse to change. "We are not
satisfied with Stanton; we are not satisfied with our position in
respect to him. We would be glad to have an excuse to get
rid of him in some way, and there must be a general change in
the Cabinet before that can be done. The country is not satisfied with Stanton's position, and the President is entitled to
have his friends in the Cabinet."

The next morning, Latham came to the White House to

bear Pomeroy's proposal, and as Johnson was busy with his lawyers, he informed Colonel Moore of the offer. When the President was told of it, he was highly indignant and said, "I will have to insult some of these men yet."[33] On the 18th, Pomeroy himself appeared at the White House and sought a confidential talk with the President. The Senator was "very friendly" in his manner, and was obviously waiting for Johnson to bring up the matter, but Johnson would not indicate that he had even heard of the proposition and Pomeroy did not dare to suggest it himself. In leaving, the Kansan suggested broadly that he would be pleased to receive from the President "any suggestions that might tend toward producing a good effect in the present condition of affairs."[34] None ever came to him.

Manager Logan also sent word to the White House that the President "could do nothing that would aid him more in this impeachment matter than to send some good name to the Senate for McCulloch's place," and that the Secretary of the Treasury was doing the President "serious injury." The Conservative T. W. Egan wrote the President that he knew "of several Radical Senators who would esteem it a compliment to be consulted by you, and who could and would be of great service." Egan pleaded with Johnson not to "neglect any means of defense, no matter how distasteful they might seem." The impeachers, he said, were going on in fear and trembling, and "looked for death in triumph." He related how, a few days before, Senator Sherman "cut to the quick by thoughts of your undeserved persecution . . . actually shed tears."[35] But the President was still unwilling to seek to influence his senatorial judges by such means.

During the week, Jeremiah Sullivan Black withdrew as counsel for the President. The latter's refusal to be forced into executive action in the Alta Vela claim, a private case in which Judge Black was counsel, led to the break. Title to Alta Vela, a small guano island in the Caribbean Sea, off the Dominican Coast, was claimed both by Santo Domingo and by the United States. The Dominican Republic had leased the guano rights on the island to some Americans, who were working it. Asserting that the island was American rather than Dominican, Patterson, Murguindo and Company, of Baltimore, claimed right and title to exploit its guano. Jeremiah Sullivan Black and his son Chauncey were lawyers for the American claimants,

THE STANTON-JOHNSON EMBROGLIO IN CARTOON

Upper: Andy Discharges His Right at His Secretary.
Lower: Stanton Puts in His Tenure of Office and Draws Blood from the President.
From old water colors of the day.

and on their behalf were vigorously seeking government aid to
put them in possession of the rich little island. They had petitioned for an American naval vessel to be dispatched to seize it.

The President had at first listened with some sympathy to
the application, which on its face seemed just. But when he
turned it over to the Secretary of State for investigation,
Seward found that when Black had been Attorney-General, in
the last part of Buchanan's Administration, a similar guano
island title case had been presented to him for decision, and he
had decided against the American claims. Seward thought
the precedent Black himself had set should be persuasive as to
Alta Vela. The President accepted his report, and so informed
the Judge. This, be it remembered, was prior to impeachment.

"Go ahead—keep your father at work," one of the Baltimore claimants wrote Chauncey Black on February 14. "Let
him see the President whenever the occasion requires." As soon
as the impeachment was voted, there came a further suggestion
from Baltimore that the Blacks endeavor to secure from leading movers in the impeachment "expression of opinions favorable to the claim" for Alta Vela.

About this time, Johnson had overborne the remonstrances
of some of his advisers, and had engaged Judge Black for
counsel; when he did so, the President later said, Judge Black
accepted, "Knowing full well my views and determinations re-
respecting Alta Vela." Black thanked him "cordially" for the
selection.[36]

Nevertheless, the Black firm fell to work on their guano
clients' suggestion with readiness, and on February 28 reported
to Murguindo that Colonel J. W. Shaffer, of the Black firm,
would try to secure such opinions from the impeachers, but that
"he cannot of course expect to get them to ask a favor of
Johnson."

Shaffer, who during the war had been an aide on General
Butler's staff, set to work to enlist the assistance of the Managers of the impeachment. On March 6, the Baltimore claimants to Alta Vela assigned to Black and his partners, "one and
one-half percent on all their rights, title and interest in and
to the deposit of guano on the Island of Alta Vela in trust, to
disburse . . . in aid in the prosecution of the claim."

The document of the Black firm did not disclose to whom
this percentage was to be disbursed, but three days later Ben
Butler accommodated his former aide by addressing a letter to

him which declared: "I am clearly of the opinion that under the claim of the United States, its citizens have the exclusive right to take guano from Alta Vela. I have never been able to understand why the Executive did not long since assert the rights of the government, and sustain the rightful claims of its citizens to the possession of the island in the most forcible manner consistent with the dignity and honor of the nation."

Possessed of this document, Shaffer approached General Logan, another of the impeachment Managers, who wrote on it: "I concur in the above opinion expressed by General Butler." James A. Garfield, though not a Manager yet an ardent Radical, similarly concurred. After a copy of Butler's letter had been made, Thaddeus Stevens and John A Bingham indorsed and signed their concurrence upon it, as did three other Republican Congressmen, James G. Blaine, J. K. Moorehead, one of Stanton's witnesses to the scene of February 22, and W. K. Koontz. On the 10th Butler's original letter was sent to the White House, to be followed the next day by the copy bearing Stevens' and Bingham's indorsements.

Johnson was amazed at the proceedings. "Thus four of the seven men selected by the House to prosecute me," he told Colonel Moore, "come to me to ask me to prosecute an award, doubtless that each might secure to himself a half million, or, it may be, a million, of dollars. The whole land seems to be rank with corruption. *Judge Black won't do!*"

About this time, Chauncey Black reported to his clients that the President was studying Alta Vela, "but it requires an awful pressure to make him act in the present ticklish condition of affairs." A persistent campaign was being directed against the President. On the 10th, Simeon Johnson, a writer on the *National Intelligencer* and a close friend of the Blacks, had seen the President; "father is with him now . . . Mr. Dawson will see him tonight. Mr. Winder will try to get Phelps and Archer to go up during the day." In his visit, the elder Black "pressed the claim on personal considerations," an appeal which the President regretted.[87]

Johnson might have been "studying Alta Vela," but the effect of this amazing campaign on him was what anyone acquainted with his mind might have expected. He was not a man who could be seduced by bribes or coerced by threats. Though his initial feelings had favored Black's petition, this unseemly proceeding aroused his ire, and word went to the firm that no warship would be sent.

Accordingly, on March 14, Jeremiah Sullivan Black informed the President that he would "be literally compelled to decline to act as the President's counsel if he refused to grant the claims."[38] "Please don't understand me as making any condition," Black wrote. "I am so connected with this business that as long as it is pending, I cannot desert my robbed and ruined clients. I am compelled to take the misfortune of your adverse action, or inaction, coupled with the superadded calamity of retiring from the impeachment case. I am perfectly sure this will not influence you, for I don't want any decision in the case that is not founded in your sense of right and justice, and duty to the law of the land."[39]

The very actual threat of this letter, despite its verbal disavowal, in no degree altered Johnson's determination not to be driven into an act he did not believe had been clearly demonstrated to be right. Rumors of differences became noised about, Black ceased attending the consultations of counsel in the White House library, and mutual friends of the President and the lawyer bestirred themselves to persuade Johnson to yield.

From the waste-paper baskets of the White House, the Managers had secured a note Black had written the President: "Unless you can do something for your friends, it is useless for me longer to apply my personal and professional powers where defeat stares us in the face."

Thus given an inkling of the President's new troubles, on March 18, Forney's *Chronicle* appeared with an apparently inspired article saying that "Jerry Black said today very freely that he has no hope of the acquittal of the President, and that he so informed him yesterday." That same morning Black had a "strange talk" with Welles as to the guano island. The Secretary, displeased at the lawyer's "half threat" against the President, advised delay, which did not suit Black in the least. The next day he saw Welles again, to ask if the latter had received any order from the President as to Alta Vela. The Secretary had not, and Black left in an angry mood. An hour or two later, Simeon Johnson came to Welles and charged that Johnson had gone back on his word. But the Secretary remarked that if the lawyer "thinks to take advantage of the President's necessity . . . he is mistaken in his man. The President is about the last man who would be moved under compulsion of such circumstances."[40]

After learning from Welles that no action had been taken by the President, that afternoon Black thus wrote the latter:

"Your determination to determine nothing for the relief of the owners of Alta Vela makes it impossible for me to serve you longer as counsel in the impeachment case. They cannot allow their rights to be trifled with, and I cannot advise them to submit in silence to the outrage perpetrated upon them. They must seek elsewhere for the justice which you deny them. . . . Mr. Seward's little finger, it appears, is thicker than the loins of the law.

"My retirement from your cause will not probably diminish the chances of its success. . . . But to me it is cause of sincere grief that I cannot aid in the struggle you are making for truth, justice and the Constitution of your country. I do most devoutly believe that the accusation now made against you by the House of Representatives is unfounded in fact and law, and that your defense must be regarded as conclusive by every impartial mind. I know it will be presented with consummate ability.

"I hope you see plainly that I have adopted the only possible mode of relieving myself from embarrassments and complications which would be wholly unendurable if I did not get rid of them in some way."

Johnson was indignant at Black's conduct.[41] A few days after the resignation, the President said to Colonel Moore: "Because I did not consent to send a vessel of war to Alta Vela to oust one set of Americans in favor of another, and thereby produce a collision in the Dominican Republic, Judge Black refuses to act as my counsel. He had made a poor record— one which will do him far more injury than it can me." Johnson referred to efforts being made to cause him to send for Black, and said he would never do so. "I would rather be put to death than submit to such humiliation." A few days later, he reverted to the topic, and said sadly: "Many seem to have supposed that, as I was now in trouble, I might be forced to do things that I would not do under other circumstances. They will find out their mistake."[42]

If there be in the record of any President of the United States, a finer illustration of calm courage and of devotion to a rigorous conception of duty than the foregoing, it has not been brought to public attention. Andrew Johnson's conduct in the Alta Vela case approached closely to Immanuel Kant's categorical imperative. Here was the President of the United States, impeached for high crimes and misdemeanors. Here was one of his counsel upon whom he placed great reliance and trust, pressing for the adoption of his own views in an obscure private claim. Here were four of the seven impeachment managers urging that Black's plea be granted. Here was the threat of a lawyer that if the President refused, he would withdraw from the case. Upon any such withdrawal, word would go forth to the country—as it did —that Andrew Johnson was so guilty of the charges brought against him that, after the facts had carefully been examined by a distinguished Conservative lawyer, the latter abandoned hope of successful defense and dropped the case. And if Johnson were to yield, harm would be done to none except to the impotent Republic of Santo Domingo, rent by revolution. For a practical man, every argument concurred to urge yielding to Judge Black. But for Andrew Johnson, right was right and wrong was wrong, and it was as wrong to violate the rights of Santo Domingo as it was to twist the British lion's tail. Here was a President willing to be convicted of impeachment rather than to save himself by doing an act which he did not believe right.[43]

Deprived though they were of Black's assistance, the President's counsel were able to complete their answer to the Articles of Impeachment, and on March 23 to the day, they appeared in the Senate to present their response. Stanbery prefaced the reading of the document by a statement of the difficulty and haste attending its preparation and of the counsel's "profound regret" that the court had not given adequate time. Stanbery and Evarts divided the task of reading the response, which made detailed answer to the charges brought, and set forth the President's conduct along lines with which the reader is now familiar. At the conclusion of the reading, the Senate took order for it to lie upon the table until the replication of the managers had been received.

At this juncture General Logan injected a lengthy speech purporting to be based upon the answer, but actually made for the delectation of his Illinois constituents. While he was speaking, his brother managers hung their heads, the Senators smiled contemptuously, and although his constituents may have enjoyed it in print, his audience did not.[44]   A debate ensued as to how much time would be allowed, after the replication of the House, for the President's counsel to prepare for trial.   Thirty days was asked, was sternly voted down, and an immediate opening of the trial was directed.

The replication of the House managers was immediately forthcoming. On March 24, the terse assertion was entered that the House "do deny each and every averment in said several answers . . . which denies or traverses, the acts, intents, crimes or misdemeanors charged against said Andrew Johnson," and reiterated that the President "is guilty of the high crimes and misdemeanors," the House being "ready to prove the same." "The greatest case in history" was proceeding at railroad speed!

THROUGHOUT their revolutionary attempt to put the bottom
rail on top in the South, the Radicals feared the Supreme
Court quite as much as they hated "the bad man in the White
House." After the Court's decision in the Milligan case, the
extremists were keenly apprehensive lest the nation's high
judiciary interpose to overthrow their plans. In March, during the height of the impeachment fervor, their fears were re-
doubled by the famous McCardle case. "The Radicals are
becoming ferocious," Thomas Ewing wrote his son. "They are
about to strip the Supreme Court of its power, or attempt to
do so—but it is doubtful whether the Court will consent to the
operation."[1]

McCardle, a colonel in the Confederate army, after the war
became editor of a newspaper in Vicksburg. Thoroughly disapproving of the reconstruction measures, in the fall of 1867
he published editorials protesting against the policy of Congress, and criticizing the official conduct of General Ord, in
whose district Mississippi lay. Irritated by these critical articles,
General Ord on November 13 had McCardle thrust into military prison, and announced his intention of having him tried
for his "crime" by a military commission. Ord would permit
the prisoner neither bail nor privileges. The editor sought a
writ of *habeas corpus* from the United States Circuit Court
for Mississippi, but the application was denied. As McCardle
languished in his cell, awaiting whatever justice Ord's military commission might mete out to him, his lawyer had a brilliant thought. In one of the Reconstruction laws, there was a
provision authorizing an appeal from the United States Circuit
Court to the United States Supreme Court "in all cases where
any person may be restrained in his or her liberty, in violation
of the Constitution or of any treaty or law of the United
States." It had been passed to protect federal officials and
other "loyal persons"—a term which the Radicals used to
cover carpetbaggers and scalawags—from punishment by
Southern state courts. This device to bind the South more

firmly was now seized upon by McCardle and his counsel as a weapon by which to release the South from her bonds.

The editor appealed to the Supreme Court. He charged that the Military Reconstruction Laws were "in violation of the Constitution," that he was "restrained in his liberty" under its provisions, and asked the Court to have him set free.

The alarmed Radicals sought to persuade the Attorney-General to resist the editor's application, but Stanbery resolutely refused. He announced in open court that, inasmuch as he had previously advised the President that the Reconstruction laws were unconstitutional, he would not now stultify himself by seeking to convince the Court that they were sound. The War Department thereupon engaged Senator Trumbull of Illinois to oppose the suit, while Jeremiah Sullivan Black took up McCardle's side.

On January 10 Black moved that the case be advanced for a speedy hearing. A week later the Court granted the motion and set the first Monday in March for the argument. Alarmed at this new hazard to their plans, the Radicals busied themselves to block it. A bill was hastily prepared in the House to narrow the Court's authority to hold an Act of Congress unconstitutional. If this measure had been enacted, the Court would have been forbidden thus to decide unless two-thirds of the justices concurred. The Radicals hoped in this way to prevent further five-to-four decisions such as had come down in *ex parte* Milligan.[2]

Although Conservative members assailed this proposal as "revolutionary" and "dangerous," an instrument "brought forward to subvert and destroy the institutions of our country," a "confession of guilt on the part of the majority," the House passed it by a vote of 116 to thirty-nine, thus evoking the applause of the Radical press. The *Independent* went so far as to proclaim that "the Supreme Court is at this hour the guilty confederate of Andrew Johnson. The country will rejoice to see it checkmated." Forney's *Chronicle* urged that this remedy for "the new peril of the Republic . . . be applied without waiting or shrinking."

Other leaders of the dominant faction affected unconcern over the Court's impending decision. "They hoped by that time," a Republican journal said, "to have affairs in such condition in the States of Mississippi and Alabama that, even if the

Court decides the Reconstruction acts unconstitutional, it will not seriously impede the work in those States."[3]

When the House bill reached the Senate, Doolittle alluded sharply to the motives which had inspired it, and charged that the entire proceeding was an outrageous effort to prevent the voiding of the Reconstruction laws, which, he hinted, five of the nine justices agreed were unconstitutional. Trumbull took violent umbrage at this remark. "If it be true," he said, "then I say these five judges are infamous, and should be impeached tomorrow."[4] Fortunately for the Court, the Senate did not pass the House bill.

On January 31 and on February 1, there was vigorous argument before the Court as to its right to hear the McCardle case. A few days later it upheld its jurisdiction, and on March 2 the unconstitutionality of the Military Reconstruction laws was argued before the Court. Trumbull and his associate counsel boasted that they had "rattled the bones" of the justices, but from the expressions and questions of the judges, the Radicals were fearful that a majority of the Court believed the law unconstitutional.[5] So they secretly determined to pass a law removing the McCardle case from the Court's jurisdiction, although it had already been received, argued and briefed!

The House had before it at the time a measure sent over by the Senate, designed to extend the Supreme Court's appellate jurisdiction to include cases involving customs and revenue officials. The Democrats were thrown off their guard when General Schenck of Ohio, Chairman of the Republican Congressional Committee, informed the House that the bill was a mere routine matter. Without explanation or debate, Manager Wilson immediately offered an amendment to repeal the Supreme Court's appellate jurisdiction under the *Habeas Corpus* Act of 1867—the act under which McCardle had taken his appeal—and to prohibit the court from exercising any jurisdiction on any appeals which *had been* or might be taken under its terms! The Democrats did not scrutinize the amendment, it was accepted without objection or comment, and went to the Senate for that body's prompt concurrence.

Then, for the first time, the Conservatives discovered that they had been tricked. Boyer of Pennsylvania charged Schenck with deceit in smuggling through this device to prevent the test of the Reconstruction Acts by the Court. Thus challenged, Schenck boldly avowed that such had been his intention; he had lost confidence in a majority of the Supreme Court; "they usurp power whenever they dare to undertake to settle questions purely political in regard to the status of the States. If I find them . . . attempting to arrogate to themselves jurisdiction under any statute that happens to be upon the record from which they claim to derive that jurisdiction, and I can take it away from them by a repeal of that statute, I will do it. . . . I hold it to be not only my right, but my duty as a representative of the people, to clip the wings of that Court."[6]

After the measure had gone to the White House for action by the President, it burst with a shock upon the country that, without debate, Congress had sought to tie the hands of the Court. Welles commented that the Radical conspiracy was "designed to overthrow not only the President but the government. The impeachment is but a single act in the drama." The New York *Herald* lamented that "the country is in the hands of Congress." For the Radicals, the *Independent* exulted at the way in which "that little bill" had "put a knife to the throat of the McCardle case. . . . Congress will not abandon its Reconstruction policy to please any Court."

Although undergoing trial and expecting conviction, the President was still as ready to defend the rights of the Judiciary as those of the Executive. On March 25 he sent to Congress his veto message. The bill, he pointed out, "established a precedent which, if followed, may eventually sweep aside every check on arbitrary and unconstitutional legislation." Thus far during the existence of the government, the Supreme Court "has been viewed by the people as the true expounder of their Constitution, and in the most violent party conflicts, its judgments and decrees have always been sought and deferred to with confidence and respect. . . . Any act which may be construed into, or mistaken for, an attempt to prevent or evade its decisions on a question which affects the liberties of the citizens and agitates the country, cannot fail to be attended with unpropitious consequences. It will be justly held by a large portion of the people as an admission of the unconstitutionality of any act on which its judgment may be forbidden or forestalled."

The motion for the bill's repassage called forth the Senate debate, hitherto avoided. Trumbull was bold and uncandid enough to inform the Senators that there was no case then pending before the Supreme Court which would be affected by the repeal of the statute. If there were no such cases pending, Doolittle asked witheringly, "why undertake to take away the jurisdiction of the Court? The truth is, and we may as well look it square in the face, it is because men know that these acts will be decided to be unconstitutional." When Stewart came to Trumbull's aid by a malignant assault upon the Court's integrity, Hendricks taunted the "brave Senators" who were "afraid of the decision of the Court," and Reverdy Johnson and Buckalew further exposed the partisan purposes of the measure. But on March 26 the Senate, by a vote of thirty-three to nine, and the day after the House, by 115 to fifty-seven, repassed it over the veto. Thus Congress warned the Supreme Court that evil days might be in store for it if it resisted the will of the Radicals.[7] Let the Justices consider the President's predicament, and pause.

Three days after Congress had "clipped the wings of that Court," the impeachment farce resumed the boards. On March 30 the House began the presentation of its "evidence" against Andrew Johnson. The case of the Managers of the Impeachment was opened by Ben Butler in a four hour speech, outlining the charges of "the people of the United States."

It was not entirely by chance that this evil-looking demagogue made the opening argument. He had made up his mind at the outset to take the lead in the trial, and had ingeniously worked matters to do so. The seven managers had chosen Thad Stevens as their chairman, thus according the Commoner the closing argument. Butler thereupon innocently inquired: "But who is to make the opening argument, and put the case in form for presentation in the Senate? There are less than three days in which to prepare it. Who is anxious for that place?" When silence greeted his question, he declared, "Very well, I suppose, as usual, the opening of the case will fall upon the youngest counsel, and that is myself." Relieved, the other managers asked if he would undertake it. He agreed with seeming reluctance, "and thus," to quote his own words, "I became the leading figure of the impeachment, for better or worse."[8]

The next three days proved "the hardest labor" of Butler's life. During the entire time he had only nine hours' sleep; no other manager offered aid in any shape. A brief of the legal authorities on impeachment, prepared by an Ohio Congressman, William Lawrence, represented the sum of outside assist-ance. But the "Hero of Fort Fisher" assembled a corps of faithful stenographers, dictated hour after hour, revised and elaborated, and had the speech rushed into type. Then it was mailed and telegraphed to newspapers throughout the country, to be held awaiting its delivery. It is of note that the version thus dispatched in advance was sprinkled with marks of "ap-plause," and "prolonged cheers."[9]

The speech, such as it was, was ready for delivery on the afternoon of March 30. Ben Butler endeavored to attract attention with his attire as well as by his oratory, appearing in an evening suit with a white necktie.[10] But he read his speech and, inasmuch as he was "the worst reader in Congress," it proved a bore to his audience. Senators who knew Butler's relations with the Emancipator smiled broadly when he essayed pathos about the "sainted martyr" Lincoln. Wilson, Colfax and Sumner snickered at Butler's "humor" in reviewing John-son's "Swing Around the Circle." But otherwise, the end of the speech was welcomed with relief by all.

As legal argument, Butler's remarks are worth only pass-ing attention. But as an exhibition of the Radical insistence that the President did not need to be guilty of a crime to be convicted of impeachment, they are of compelling significance. Was the Senate a court or a political inquest? Need the Sena-tors who had taken solemn oath to do impartial justice to Andrew Johnson be bound by their oaths? What was an im-peachable offense? Could the Senate convict Johnson because they disagreed with his politics, or must he be proved guilty of wrongful intent in the commission of a specific act as charged by the Impeachment Articles of the House? These were the questions at issue before the Senate—these the Manager sought to meet.

First Butler defined what, to the Managers, constituted an impeachable high crime or misdemeanor. It was "one in its nature or consequences subversive of some fundamental or es-sential principles of government, or highly prejudicial to the public interest, and this may consist of a violation of the Con-stitution, of law, of an official oath, or of duty, *by an act committed or omitted, or, without violating a positive law, by the abuse of discretionary powers from improper motives, or for any improper purpose.*"[11]

After seeking by citations to give color of authority to this astounding declaration, Butler broached the question as to whether the body trying impeachment was "the Senate . . . or a court." "This tribunal has none of the attributes of a judicial court," he insisted. "The fact that Senators are sitting for this purpose on oath or affirmation does not influence the argument." It was the duty of the Senate "to inquire into and determine whether Andrew Johnson, because of malversation in office, is longer fit to retain the office of President of the United States, or hereafter to hold any office of honor or profit." The Senators were "bound by no law, either statute or common, which may limit your constitutional prerogative. You consult no precedents save those of the law and custom of parliamentary bodies. You are a law unto yourselves, bound only by the natural principle of equity and justice; and the safety of the people is the supreme law."[12]

He next set up the claim that the Chief Justice had no right to aid the Senate in its determination, even though he attended in his robes of office. Their proceedings, he continued, were merely "an inquest of office," and therefore it was impossible that Senators should not have already formed definite opinions as to the guilt of the accused. He did not think that a preconceived opinion was any bar to the competency of a Senator to cast his vote; indeed, the Senator's "seat and vote belong to his constituents, and not to himself."

Having thus set forth that the President should be convicted, although he might have violated no law, that impeachment was a political and not a legal proceeding, and that Senators should give heed to their constituents rather than to their consciences, Butler discussed the Impeachment Articles themselves, putting forward the familiar Radical charges against the President. He insisted that the question of whether the Tenure-of-Office Act was constitutional or unconstitutional was "totally irrelevant," because the President must execute any law of Congress, no matter how patently unconstitutional it might on its face appear, until the Supreme Court had held it so.

Butler sought to build a great edifice to sustain the claim that the speeches on the "Swing Around the Circle" constituted impeachable offenses. "It may be taken as an axiom in the affairs of nations," he ponderously proclaimed, "that no usurper has ever seized upon the legislature of his country until he has familiarized the people with the possibility of so doing by vituperating and decrying it." He set up the instances of Oliver Cromwell and Napoleon Bonaparte to support his view. But then he himself unintentionally destroyed his own foundations by admitting that the impeachment article in question "does not raise the question of freedom of speech, but of propriety and decency of speech." The President was to be thrust forth because of impropriety of speech; "we rest upon the scandal of the scene. . . . It is the noise and disturbance in the neighborhood that is the offense."[13]

"By murder most foul," Butler charged, Andrew Johnson had become President; but "our frame of government gives us a remedy for such a misfortune. . . . We can remove him—as we are about to do—from the office he has disgraced, by the sure, safe and constitutional method of impeachment." The President's offense was that he "not only endeavors to thwart the constitutional action of Congress, and bring it to naught, but also to hinder and oppose the execution of the will of the *loyal* people of the United States. . . . He used his veto power indiscriminately to prevent the passage of wholesome laws."

"If Andrew Johnson go quit and free this day," his peroration concluded, the people of this or any other country, never again "can by constitutional checks or guards, stay the usurpations of executive power. . . . The future political welfare and liberties of all men hang trembling on the decision of the hour."[14]

With the conclusion of this appeal to the Senators not to do impartial justice to Andrew Johnson, the managers began the presentation of their evidence. The first mass of evidence was documentary, beginning with certified copies of Johnson's presidential oath and the Chief Justice's certificate that he had administered it. Next came Lincoln's nomination of Stanton for Secretary of War in 1862, and the Senate's confirmation. Johnson's message to the Senate in December, 1867, reciting his reasons for Stanton's suspension, was introduced, to be followed by the journal entry showing the Senate's nonconcurrence. The message of February 21, 1868, and the Senate's resolution of the same day denying that Johnson had power to remove Stanton were next put of record.

Manager Wilson, who began the presentation of these documents, was so awed by the occasion that his hand trembled visibly. Butler then took the papers, finished their introduction, and thenceforward, by self-appointment, became the leader of the prosecution. There was no awe in the mind of the "Hero of Fort Fisher." "I came to the conclusion," he said, "to try the case upon the same rules of evidence, and in the same manner, as I should try a horse case, and I knew how to do that. I therefore was not in trepidation." This mode of procedure did not please the other managers, who seemed to be "a good deal cut up," and expostulated that "this is the greatest case of all the times, and it is to be conducted in the highest possible manner." "Yes," Butler answered, "and that is according to law; that is the only way to conduct the case." Finding him incorrigible, they left him to his own devices.[15]

The presentation of evidence at the trial consumed a total of twenty-three days. But two-thirds, if not three-fourths, of this time was occupied by argument between the House managers and the President's counsel over the admissibility of evidence. In general, the Senate voted to admit all evidence Butler offered against the President and carefully excluded any vital matters the defense lawyers sought to introduce.

The House founded its case on documentary evidence, placing its human witnesses—chiefly clerks, attachés, and newspaper men—on the stand to prove the accuracy of the documents or to amplify the statements they contained. It is worthy of note that the testimony which the managers offered on behalf of the House was not directed to sustain the charge contained in several of the Impeachment Articles, that the President had purposefully, deliberately and with evil intent, violated the Tenure-of-Office Act and the Constitution of the United States. Although witnesses were put on to regale the court with all sorts of shabby tattle, no direct evidence as to Johnson's intent was offered. In making the claim that the President had directed Lorenzo Thomas to use force to expel Stanton, Butler carefully refrained from putting Thomas himself on the stand, but relied upon the recital of Thomas' boasts by those who had heard the General on the night of February 21. For this purpose, Burleigh, the Dakota delegate, Moorehead, Stanton's stand-by, Wilkeson, the newspaper correspondent and others were put on. Under skillful cross examination by Evarts and Stanbery their grandiose stories of Thomas' threats of force quickly crumbled into mirthful recitals of the garrulities of a foolish old man.

Another witness for the House was one George W. Karsner

of New Castle, Delaware, the town and State from which Thomas hailed. This foolish fellow had gone to the White House on March 8 to catch a glimpse of the great and near great, and had seized upon Thomas when he made exit from the Cabinet meeting. He introduced himself, claimed acquaintance with the General many years before, and informed him: "General, the eyes of all Delaware are upon you, and they expect you to stand fast." Amused, Thomas responded, "Certainly I shall stand fast," and turned to leave. His clamorous fellow citizen from New Castle seized his hand again and repeated that he expected Thomas to stand fast. Thomas, even more amused, raised himself on tiptoes and asked, "Why, don't you see I am standing firm?" Karsner then inquired: "When are you going to kick that fellow out?" With the words put in his mouth by his interlocutor, the old General replied, "Oh, we will kick him out by and by." Then Thomas had broken away and left. The managers now put the yokel from New Castle on the stand to show Johnson's determination to expel the patriotic Stanton by force. But when the story of what really happened came out, even the Radicals rocked with laughter and "The eyes of all Delaware are upon you" became a stock jest of the day.[16]

General Emory was next put on the stand to tell the story of his interview with the President on February 22, the basis of the charges in the ninth article. Under cross-examination, the great story of a plot was punctured, for it was made clear that there was nothing to the charge, and Article IX immediately collapsed.

During Burleigh's examination, Stanbery objected to one of Butler's questions to the witness. "The Chief Justice thinks the testimony is competent," Chase ruled, "and it will be heard unless the Senate think otherwise." A Radical Senator took exception to the Chief Justice's action in offering even a preliminary ruling, and an excited debate ensued. To the manifest delight of extremist Senators, the Managers insisted that Chase had no such authority. The Chief Justice with great dignity responded that "in this body he is the presiding officer; he is so in virtue of his high office under the Constitution. He is Chief Justice of the United States, and, therefore, when the President of the United States is tried by the Senate, it is his duty to preside in that body; and, as he understands, he is, therefore, the President of the Senate sitting as a court of impeachment." After the question had been debated for several hours, a motion was made that the Senate retire for consultation, and when the vote was taken, it resulted in a tie.

"On this question the yeas are twenty-five, and the nays are twenty-five," Chase immediately announced. "The Chief Justice votes in the affirmative. The Senate will retire for conference." Then he arose from his chair, and led the way into the conference room, the crestfallen Radicals following, with maledictions on their lips. In the conference, Sumner submitted an angry resolution that the Chief Justice "is not a member of the Senate, and has no authority under the Constitution to vote on any question during the trial, and he can pronounce decision only as the organ of the Senate, with its assent." After debate, this was voted down, as were several similar Radical motions designed to restrict the Chief Justice's powers.

The next day, in public session once more, Sumner offered a motion that "it is hereby declared that, in the judgment of the Senate," the casting vote by the Chief Justice the day before "was without authority under the Constitution of the United States." When this Radical recital was defeated by a vote of twenty-one to twenty-seven, it began to be apparent that all the Republican Senators had not adopted Ben Butler's theory that it was not a trial but a political inquest.

This vote upon an important preliminary question alarmed the impeaching Senators, indicating as it did a perceptible weakening of party lines and discipline among the more conservative Republicans. It occasioned a great flare-up of Radical feeling. Newspapers, politicians and officeholders clamored that Johnson must be removed "to save the life of the party." General Grant took public ground for the conviction of his official superior, the Commander-in-Chief of the Army and Navy.

Greeley's *Tribune* had a great double-leaded article proclaiming that the General had found it "not inconsistent with his duty as a soldier to announce it as his opinion that the only hope for the peace of the country is the success of the pending impeachment trial. He feels that the national security demands the removal of the President."[17] Grant believed he had a right, "in so grave an emergency," to "support the weak and confirm the strong," and lobbied zealously with wavering Senators.

Nor was Grant above low intrigue. He had a trusted negro servitor work on a negro janitor at the White House, until the latter began turning over to agents of the Radicals all the waste-paper scraps from the Executive Mansion. But unfortunately for the Manager, little evidence of an impeachable nature was found in the scraps.[18]

Grant's activity was typical of the Radicals' campaign. From the outset of the trial, they had been unbelievably aggressive. As early as March 5, the *Independent* delivered a thinly veiled warning to all Republican Senators. "There are crotchety men, weak men, corruptible men, in every legislative body," it declared, "and the President will try to seduce the corruptible. He will aim to get at the sympathies of the weak, and to raise objections to confuse minds which are not easily suited. . . . One fact will have some weight with genuine Republicans—the fact that if Mr. Johnson is acquitted, Reconstruction and the Republican party are destroyed together."

Accordingly, the paper's proprietor appealed to his readers to bring pressure. "The Senators are the judges," he wrote, "but *you* are the attorneys for the prosecution. Speak, therefore speak to the Senate. Speak by letter by thousands and tens of thousands; speak in convention; speak in mass meetings; speak in the newspapers; speak in the pulpit; speak everywhere; SPEAK NOW; I pray you, or forever after hold your peace."

Every day, Horace Greeley in New York and Joseph Medill in Chicago, and Radical editors elsewhere too numerous to mention were making similar appeals. In consequence, the doubtful Senators were deluged with demands from their constituents.

Fessenden's case was characteristic. The Maine Senator had never liked nor admired Andrew Johnson. As chairman of the Joint Committee on Reconstruction of the thirty-ninth Congress, he had sponsored the Fourteenth Amendment and other important Radical measures. But a man of the strictest integrity, Fessenden's high conception of public duty would not allow him to disregard his trial oath. The demands of his constituents seemed to strengthen his determination to do his duty. Impeachment, the result of yielding to the advice of "bad men and unwise men," had led the party "to the brink of a precipice," he wrote a friend; he was determined to keep his oath, "if my wishes and prejudices will permit me to do so, and to take all the consequences."

It is not to be wondered that a man so constituted found it "hard work to behave decently." "If anyone avows his determination to keep to his oath," he complained to a friend, "villains and fools set him down as a friend of the President. . . . Whatever I may think and feel as a politician, I cannot and will not violate my oath. I would rather be confined to planting cabbages for the remainder of my days. . . . Cowardice has led us to follow bad counsels because the majority so determined; as far as I can go, I prefer tar and feathers to lifelong regret."[19]

After Fessenden's conservative votes on the preliminary questions, he began to receive threats through the mails. "Any Republican Senator who votes against impeachment need never expect to get home alive; so take notice," read one warning. General Neal Dow, Maine's great prohibitionist, urged Fessenden to "hang Johnson up by the heels like a dead crow in a cornfield, to frighten all his tribe."

"I wish you, my dear sir, and all others of my friends and constituents," the Senator angrily answered, "to understand that I, and not they, am sitting in judgment upon the President. I, not they, have solemnly sworn to do impartial justice. I, not they, am responsible to God and man for my action and its consequences. The opinions and wishes of my party friends ought not to have a feather's weight with me in coming to a conclusion. You, as a friend, should advise me to do my duty fearlessly, regardless of the opinions and wishes of men and of all consequences to myself, and you should add to that advice your prayers that no outside clamor, either of the press or of individuals, no prejudice or passion, no hope of benefit or fear of injury to myself, no just indignation against the individual on trial, no consideration of party, no regard for those I am most anxious to please, should induce me to swerve from the straight line of impartial justice according to the Constitution and the laws."[20]

But not all the waverers were of Fessenden's tough texture. Under the enormous pressure, several who had expressed uncertainty as to the President's guilt resolved their doubts and pledged to vote for conviction.

When Chase's impartiality had become manifest, a torrent

of invective descended upon him. His mail was filled with
abusive letters. Spies watched his house. Politicians threatened him with political annihilation. Sumner had been anxious
for Chase to be the Republican nominee for President. Now he
shook his head and said sadly, "Alas, poor Chase!"[21] The
Chief Justice was daily denounced as an apostate and a traitor,
and the social recognition which he loved was denied him.[22]
Yet he stood firm. We have had occasion to note the conduct
of Salmon Portland Chase before this time, his intrigues
against Abraham Lincoln while within his Cabinet, his setting
up a Presidential candidacy against his Chief. His tour of the
South in 1865 has been painted as almost a bid for delegations
for a presidential nomination. It has not been a wholly pleasing picture. But Chase's course during the impeachment trial
was that of an altogether different man. The politician was
forgotten while he wore his judicial robes. One may be sure
that Chase did not contemplate the death of his political hopes
without anguish of spirit. That he withstood the temptations
steadfastly is all the more to his honor as a man.

On March 10 the Chief Justice wrote to a friend: "Whatever I may have formerly thought, or even desired, in connection with the Presidency, I wish now to have my name completely disconnected from it." He anticipated that in the
coming trial he would be obliged to pass judicially upon important questions, "and I cannot be a party judge, I must
express an honest opinion of the Constitution and the law. I
must do my duty without fear and without favor. . . . Hence
I prefer to keep clear of all personal interest in political contests. . . . I prefer to dismiss every thought which might
incline the scale of judgment either way."

To a correspondent who questioned him as to the report of
"the Chief Justice being the ally of Mr. Johnson," he replied
that the charge was an "absurdity," and carefully explained his
position: "My duties are judicial. What I honestly believe
the Constitution and laws to sanction or condemn, that I must,
fearless, sanction or condemn. I am of no party on the bench.
If I believe an act, or part of an act, of a Republican Congress to be unconstitutional, I must say so. If a man whom
Republicans would gladly see condemned has rights, and I
must judge, the rights shall be respected. And so of the
Democrats. I expect to please neither at all times. But, God

helping me, I will do my duty, sorry only that limited powers do not allow me to do it better." He would permit "neither clamor nor imputation" to move him from doing impartial justice; all he wanted was "strength, wisdom and courage, for whatever duty reason and conscience show to me." He recognized the peculiar difficulties of his position. He felt and was felt as a foreign element in the Senate. When Sumner had made his motion, the Chief Justice had silently pondered the self-addressed question, "What will be my duty in case the Senate, by denying to me the casting vote, which belongs to the President of the Senate," thus refused "in effect to recognize my right to preside?" He had been relieved in spirit when he was not compelled to decide the point.[23] Had the Senate denied his right, it is not beyond the bounds of possibility that he would have declared the Court adjourned and the trial at an end. Happily for the country, and unhappily for historians eager for dramatic moments in the drab weavings of political chicanery, Chase was not confronted with the need to choose.

In lieu of actual evidence as to Johnson's intent to break the law, the House managers had the effrontery to insist to the Senate that that body, when it had adopted its resolution on February 21, had already pronounced judgment of guilt upon Andrew Johnson, that the documents and evidence themselves exhibited the President's breach of the law, that further testimony was unnecessary, and that whatever proof of intent the defense might adduce was immaterial to the great central fact that Andrew Johnson had written the order removing Stanton as Secretary of War. It was not alleged that Stanton had been removed. He remained in office. The Tenure-of-Office Act did not make it a high crime or a misdemeanor unsuccessfully to attempt to remove an officer without the Senate's consent, but yet the President must be removed because he sought in vain to get rid of an unfaithful Cabinet Member.[24]

The testimony for the prosecution was concluded on April 9, the last witness being a postmaster at Augusta, Ga., who had been suspended by the Postmaster-General because of indictment for perjury, a suspension which the Radicals thought highly culpable. After this man had told his story, Butler announced that he was done with other evidence, and the presentation of the case for the President began.

Judge Curtis first outlined the case for the Chief Executive, in an address which was a masterpiece of reasoning and presentation. "It is due for the truth of history to say," Ben Butler stated later, "that after he had presented the case of his client, in my judgment nothing more was said in his behalf, although . . . much *else* was said."[25]

Dressed in simple black, the former Justice presented an impressive figure, the "incarnation of dignity, self-possession, repose." His mien was impassive, his eyes were confident and serene. When he arose, there was a slight murmur of applause. Some of the Radical Senators regarded him uneasily, but Sumner sprawled in his chair, in an attitude of exaggerated lounging, adopted to express the scorn of one who had made up his mind and had neither ears nor tolerance for opposing argument.[26]

At the outset Curtis' voice was low, but it soon gathered volume and was heard throughout the room. He spoke from voluminous notes, and he frequently consulted and read from a pile of law books resting by his side. Two or three times he interspersed his sober recitation of facts with exhortation "which gave to his aspect an inspiring majesty and glow." In his opening sentence, the great jurist brushed from the eyes of the Senators all possibility of the trial being a mere political inquest. "Mr. Chief Justice," he began, "I am here to speak to the Senate of the United States sitting in its judicial capacity in its court of impeachment, presided over by the Chief Justice of the United States, for the trial of the President of the United States. . . . Here party spirit, political schemes, foregone conclusions, outrageous biases can have no fit operation. The Constitution requires that here should be a 'trial,' and in that trial an oath, which each one of you has taken, to administer 'impartial justice according to the Constitution and the laws.' . . . The only appeal which I can make in behalf of the President is an appeal to the conscience and the reason of each judge who sits before me. Upon the law and the facts, upon the judicial merits of the case, upon the duties incumbent on that high officer by virtue of his office, and his honest endeavor to discharge that duty, the President rests his defense."[27]

This impressive opening shook the more conservative of the Republican Senators and gave a new tone to the nation's press. Curtis insisted that the Senators give their close attention to the articles, both as to manner and form. He separated them into two groups, the first eight substantially charging that Johnson had violated the Tenure-of-Office Act in removing Stanton, and the last three being connected with the alleged commission of other alleged crimes.

He read the specific provision of the Tenure-of-Office law covering members of the President's Cabinet, which set out that these officers "shall hold their offices respectively for and during the term of the President by whom they may have been appointed, and for one month thereafter, subject to removal by and with the advice and consent of the Senate." What was the meaning of the language "for and during the term of the President by whom they may have been appointed," in its relation to Johnson and Stanton? Stanton had been appointed by Abraham Lincoln in 1862, in Lincoln's first term, which had expired on March 4, 1865. In the eyes of the law, Lincoln's second term was a different term, quite as much as if Lincoln had been a different individual. Stanton had not been recommissioned by Lincoln at the beginning of the latter's second term. He had merely held on at the pleasure of the President.

But Lincoln had been assassinated and Andrew Johnson had taken his place. What sort of term was Andrew Johnson serving? Was he filling out Lincoln's term, as the managers contended, or was he a president serving his own term? Curtis very clearly demonstrated that the term of the president was not a fixed and finite space of four years. It had other limits, "conditional limitations," one of which was death. Upon the end of a president's term by death, the office devolved upon his successor, and the successor's legal term was not the remainder of the predecessor's, but until the new president had been elected and inaugurated. "There is no more propriety," he continued, "under these provisions of the Constitution . . . in calling the time during which Mr. Johnson holds the office of president that was devolved upon him a part of Mr. Lincoln's term, than there would be propriety in saying that one sovereign who succeeded another sovereign by death holds a part of his predecessor's term."

Thus Stanton did not come under the Tenure-of-Office Act. He had been appointed by Lincoln; under the terms of the Act, his tenure expired on April 4, 1865, and thereafter and in strict conformity with the Tenure-of-Office Act itself, Stanton could have been discharged at any time. Judge Curtis buttressed this keen legal argument by quotations of words of

General Schenck in the House, and Williams and Sherman in the Senate, at the time the Tenure-of-Office bill was up. He then pointed out that the sixth section of the Act declared removals "contrary to the provisions of this Act," to be high misdemeanors, but that no such removal had taken place.

Yet Curtis was far from resting his case upon the inadvertence of Congress in the enactment of the law. His propositions were fourfold: First, that the law did not cover Stanton. Second, that if the law did cover Stanton, which he denied, it had not been violated, because Stanton had not been removed—there had only been an unsuccessful attempt to remove him, and the law provided penalties only for removals and not for attempts to remove. Third, admitting that Stanton had been removed, it was not an unlawful removal, because the Tenure-of-Office Act was not valid and binding legislation, being in clear violation of the national Constitution. And last, again conceding for the sake of his argument that the law was constitutional, the Articles of Impeachment had charged the President with intentionally misconstruing and violating the Act, and so it was necessary for the House to prove that Johnson had willfully broken the law. On the contrary, Curtis insisted, the Chief Executive had not violated the Act, except upon the advice of his constitutional advisers that the law was void.

In making his argument, Curtis reviewed exhaustively the debates of the first Congress of 1789, demonstrating conclusively that the Tenure-of-Office law was in contravention to the implied constitutional powers of the national executive. He easily disposed of the prosecution's argument that it was the duty of the President to obey the law, even though it were unconstitutional. This might be true, he said, in cases where the President himself was not constitutionally affected. If a third party were injured, he could take the case into court. But if the President himself were affected, he was in duty bound to resist, so as to bring it before the court; he was the only person who could do so, and if he did not, it never could be judicially determined.

After the second, third, and fourth articles had been treated with similar careful analysis by the Boston jurist, it seemed pretty obvious to all that if the removal of Stanton was legal, the appointment of Thomas in his place *ad interim* could have no color of crime attached to it. As to the conspiracy articles,

Curtis pointed out that the House had presented no testimony
to prove the President's bad intent, or, indeed, any intent at all.
"The articles had charged a conspiracy between Johnson and
Thomas to employ force, threats, intimidations. What they have
proved against the President is that he issued these orders, and
that alone." As to the ninth article, based on the Emory interview, he pointed out that it appeared from Emory's own statement that there was nothing whatever to it.

The tenth article, charging various high-sounding offenses
based upon Johnson's "Swing Around the Circle" speeches,
presented to Curtis the question as to what, under the Constitution, was an impeachable offense. He did not need to go to
the Middle Ages for authority on this point. He went to the
Constitution, which spoke of "treason, bribery, and other high
crimes and misdemeanors" as matters for impeachment. A
man's speeches did not come within this category.

Curtis concluded his presentation by annihilating Butler's
contention that the Senate sitting on impeachment was not a
court, was bound by no law, and should follow political rather
than legal precedents. "Far different," he said, "was the understanding of the fathers of the Constitution on this subject."
In the impeachment process, in the words of the Constitution
itself, "there is the trial of a crime, a trial by a tribunal designated for the Constitution in place of court and jury, a conviction if guilt is proved; a judgment on that conviction; a
punishment inflicted by the judgment for a crime; and this on
the express terms of the Constitution itself. And yet, say the
Honorable Managers, there is no court to try a crime and no
law by which the act can be judged."

After Curtis' speech, the Radicals finally began to appreciate that perhaps it would not be quite so easy to convict
Andrew Johnson as they had hoped. It became apparent
indeed that Stanton was not covered by the Tenure-of-Office
law and that Andrew Johnson had not even committed a technical infraction of an unconstitutional law.

The evidence offered by Johnson's counsel was of three
general sorts. Witnesses were put on the stand to rebut statements of fact incorrectly made by the prosecution; a number
of witnesses were offered to introduce new facts as to the
occurrences covered by the articles; a third group was presented to prove the lawful intent of the President. Such

charges as that in the second article, that Andrew Johnson
"did, with intent to violate the Constitution of the United
States" do certain acts, made it important, Stanbery and his
colleagues insisted, for the President's intent to be taken
into consideration. Did Andrew Johnson knowingly and deliberately violate the Constitution, or did he receive advice that
the purported law which he ignored was unconstitutional?
Was his dismissal of Stanton a flouting of the Constitution, or
an earnest attempt to maintain it by bringing before the high
court of the land the question of the validity of the law?

Lorenzo Thomas was the first witness for the defense. His
ingenuously frank explanations completed the demolition of the
prosecution's charges as to Johnson's plans to use force in
ousting Stanton. When Thomas told the story of the events
in Stanton's office on February 22, and of Stanton's running
his fingers through the General's hair affectionately and tossing
off drink for drink with him, another aircastle of the Radicals
crumbled to the ground, amid the laughter of the spectators,
and to the discomfiture of the Radical Senators. Ben Butler
blustered mightily in an effort to confuse the witness, but far
from shaking him as to the main issue, succeeded only in disgusting the spectators by the viciousness of his assaults.

When General W. T. Sherman took the stand, the House
Managers quickly objected to his answering questions as to
what the President had said to him about wanting to take the
Stanton matter into the courts. The battle over the admissibility of this conversation proceeded an entire day; finally, by
almost a party vote, the Senate excluded the question. The
next day, however, Sherman was recalled, and Senator Reverdy
Johnson sent the Chief Justice a written question which, as a
member of the court, he desired put to the witness. Again there
was objection, but for some unaccountable reason, by the
margin of a single vote the Maryland Conservative's question
was ordered asked. Thus Sherman was given an opportunity
to tell of a conversation with the President in which the latter
had expressed his hope to get the matter into the courts.

Buoyed up by this unexpected success, the counsel for the
defense soon offered Gideon Welles as a witness. He was permitted to tell of the Emory incident, and by slow degrees was
then brought to the point where he could be logically questioned
as to what had occurred in the Cabinet, in the Spring of 1867,
when the President asked his advisers whether he should ap-

prove or veto the Tenure-of-Office bill. Butler immediately demanded that the question be reduced to writing, and Evarts did so in these words:

> We offer to prove that the President, at a meeting of the Cabinet while the bill was before the President for his approval, laid before the Cabinet the Tenure-of-Office bill for their consideration and advice to the President respecting his approval of the bill; and thereupon the Members of the Cabinet then present gave their advice to the President that the bill was unconstitutional, and should be returned to Congress with his objections, and that the duty of preparing a message, setting forth the objections of the constitutionality of the bill, was devolved on Mr. Seward and Mr. Stanton; then following by proof as to what was done by the President and Cabinet up to the time of sending in the message.

The most important debate, perhaps, of the entire trial now ensued. It was vital to the managers to keep this evidence out, for otherwise their whole contention that Johnson had deliberately and purposefully violated the laws would fall to the ground. Ben Butler's argument was characteristically demagogic. He set up a straw man to be knocked down with violent declamation. He charged that Evarts was seeking to introduce a new principle of law that the advice of Cabinet Ministers could shield their Chief from blame for wrongful acts which he committed. Practically all Butler's argument was devoted to this contention, which Evarts demolished in short order. The question was not as to whether advice from a Cabinet Member could shield the President; it was as to what had occurred in the Cabinet to indicate that officer's purpose, his attitude of mind, his intent.

"It is not to be forgotten," Evarts set forth, "that in the matter of defense, the bearing of all circumstances of intent and of deliberation and inquiry and pursuit of duty, on the part of the great official to arrive at and determine what is his official duty, under an apparent conflict between the Constitution and the law, forms a part of the general issue of impeachment and defense." The counsel for the defense contended that whatever had been done, had been done "upon the President's judgment of his duty under the Constitution of the United States, and after that deliberate and responsible, upright and sincere effort to get all the aid and light on the subject of his duty that was accessible within his powers." Among the most important of such aids was advice from the constitutional advisers of the President.[28] Certainly, the testimony of these advisers as to what opinion they gave the President was valuable in determining the President's intent.

Under these sledge-hammer blows, the Radicals were observed to become very anxious. Sitting idly in the witness chair, Welles observed a whispered conference among their leaders and that notes were being passed back and forth. Party discipline was being invoked to produce an immediate adjournment of the Senate as a court, so that overnight stern measures could be applied to the weak-kneed members to keep this testimony out! "I saw it whispered," Welles noted that night to his diary, "and notes passed from one to another. Judges! O, what judges!"[29]

As Welles had suspected, there was great party drilling and caucussing that night, to line up the votes by which his testimony should be excluded. The next day, Senator Howard of Michigan at the outset propounded a written question. "Do not the counsel for the accused," it read, "consider that the validity of the Tenure-of-Office bill was purely a question of law, to be determined upon this trial by the Senate; and, if so, do they claim that the opinion of the Cabinet officers touching that question is competent evidence by which judgment of the Senate ought to be influenced?" But Curtis pointed out that in the first three articles of impeachment, instead of saying "it is wholly immaterial what intention the President had; it is wholly immaterial whether he honestly believed that this Act of Congress was unconstitutional; it is wholly immaterial whether he believed he was acting in accordance with his oath of office to preserve, protect, and defend the Constitution when he did this act," the House had charged that the President acted "with an intention to violate the Constitution of the United States." Therefore evidence on the question of intent was extremely necessary.

The validity of the Tenure-of-Office bill, he said, answering Howard, depended upon a comparison of the Constitution with the law. As to whether that question was to be determined in the pending trial by the Senate, he could not answer. The Senate could only determine that itself. If it should find that Stanton's case was not within the law, then no such question would arise. Furthermore, if it should find that Stanton's case was within the law but that the intent of the President had not been bad and that he did honestly believe the law unconstitutional, then it was immaterial whether the law was constitutional or not. As to claiming that the opinion of the Cabinet officers as to the constitutionality of the law was evidence which should influence the Senate's judgment, that was not at all the point. The counsel for the defense sought testimony from Welles and the other Cabinet Members to purge malice and improper intent from the President's acts.

When the debate had ended, the Chief Justice gave his ruling. The determination of this question, he said, made it necessary first to determine what was charged in the Articles of Impeachment. He pointed out that the first article charged that the President had issued his order removing Stanton on February 21, "with intent to violate the Tenure-of-Office Act, and in violation of the Constitution." Intent was the subject of much evidence on both sides; "and the Chief Justice conceives that this testimony is admissible for the purpose of showing the intent with which the President has acted in this transaction."

Chase added that if any Senator desired, he would submit the question to the Senate. Howard promptly called for the ayes and nays, and by a vote of twenty-nine to twenty, the Senate rejected the question. Among those who favored admitting the evidence, in addition to the Democrats, were the Presidential Conservatives, Norton, Dixon and Doolittle, and seven regular Republican Senators, who hitherto had generally worked with the Radicals—Fessenden, Fowler, Grimes, Henderson, Ross, Trumbull, Van Winkle and Willey. It was an omen of the break within the Radical ranks.

Indeed, the refusal of the Radical majority to admit this clearly proper and admissible evidence as to the intent of the President was destined to be a contributing factor in saving the President from conviction on impeachment. Two regular Republicans, outraged at this partisan refusal to admit the testimony, and convinced Johnson had been deprived of a fair trial, thereupon determined to vote to acquit him.

Among those not voting on the question was Senator Sumner. During most of the progress of the trial, he had been sitting in bored inattention, negligent of whatever testimony might be offered in the case. In the Senate and out of it, he had expressed his deliberate opinion that Andrew Johnson was guilty as charged, and should and would be thrust out. Sumner cared nothing about the evidence. He deemed the trial an empty formality, purely a waste of time. Why not let the President's lawyers put in all their evidence? What difference did it make? The Senate was going to convict the "great culprit" anyway. A few days earlier, he had offered a resolution that the Senate admit any and all testimony that might be offered on either side. The other Radicals, somewhat more concerned with the public response to allowing the President to put his side into evidence, promptly voted Sumner's resolution down. But now at this critical test, at this offer of the President's counsel to disclose the advice of the Cabinet Members, Charles Sumner faltered. Henderson sardonically sent him a note paraphrasing Sumner's to Stanton a few weeks before: "Stick, Sumner, stick."[30] But he was not willing to admit the President's case into evidence, and was registered among those carefully absenting themselves from the vote upon the question. With Sumner, justice was a gesture only to be made when it did not benefit the "great criminal," the "public enemy" in the White House.[31]

"Greatly disappointed and pained" at the Senate's refusal to admit the testimony from Welles, the Chief Justice wrote Gerritt Smith the next day: "I could conceive of no evidence more proper to be received, or more appropriate to enlighten the court as to the intent with which the act was done. . . . The vote, I fear, indicated a purpose which, if carried into effect, will not satisfy the American people, unless they are prepared to admit that Congress is above the Constitution." It was the Senate's "greatest and most injurious mistake."

Indeed, to Chase the whole business seemed wrong, and if he had had any option under the Constitution, he would not have taken part in the trial. "Nothing is clearer to my mind," he wrote, "than that Acts of Congress, not warranted by the Constitution, are not laws. In case a law believed by the President to be unwarranted by the Constitution, is passed, notwithstanding his veto, it seems to me that it is his duty to execute it precisely as if he had held it to be constitutional, except in the case where it directly attacks and impairs the Executive power confided to him by that instrument. In that case, it appears to me to be the clear duty of the President to disregard the law, so far at least as it may be necessary to bring the question of its constitutionality before the judiciary tribunals. . . .

"How can the President fulfill his oath to preserve, protect and defend the Constitution, if he has no *right* to *defend* it against an Act of Congress sincerely believed by him to have been passed in violation of it? To me, therefore, it seems perfectly clear that the President had a perfect right, and indeed, was under the highest obligation, to remove Mr. Stanton, if he made the removal not in wanton disregard of a Constitutional law, but with a sincere belief that the Tenure-of-Office Act was unconstitutional, and for the purpose of bringing the question before the Supreme Court.[32] Plainly it was the proper and peaceful, if not the only proper and peaceful, mode of protecting and defending the Constitution."[33]

With the Senate's refusal to hear Welles, the defense's case was quickly concluded. There was no use for Johnson's counsel to offer Seward, McCulloch, Browning or any other of the President's constitutional advisers, for the Senate had emphatically declared its refusal to hear what advice they had given the President. The mummery of "evidence" had now been finished. But before taking the vote, there must be the semblance of argument and consideration. Accordingly, the Senate sitting on the trial of impeachment adjourned until April 22, on which day the lawyers' speeches would commence.

The evidence of the House, Thomas Ewing wrote his son, "was a miserable failure, but it does not therefore follow that there will not be a conviction."

A TRUE picture of the trial requires the depiction of a shabby episode in which Ben Butler held the center of the stage. In the midst of the introduction of defense testimony, Stanbery, the President's counsel-in-chief, had been taken ill. His services had been of inestimable value in the trial; by virtue of his labors as Attorney-General, he was intimately acquainted with the details of the President's defense; he knew the pertinent documents, he had examined the witnesses, he had directed the cross-examination. When illness forced his absence, the remaining counsel were embarrassed. Although Evarts took up the burden, he was anxious for Stanbery's return to complete all details of defense. But the Ohio advocate's recuperation was very slow. "We have reached a point," Evarts therefore told the Court on April 16, "at which it will be convenient to us that we should not be required to produce more evidence today."

This request produced a violent outburst from Ben Butler. "The case must go through," he shouted. "The whole legislation of this country is stopping. . . . Larger, higher, greater interests are at stake than any such questions of ceremony. . . . The interests of the people are greater than the interests of any one individual."

Butler proceeded to wave the Bloody Shirt. "Gentlemen of the Senate," he shouted, "this is the closing up of a war wherein 300,000 men laid down their lives to save the country. In one day we sacrificed them by tens and twenties of thousands on the field of battle, and shall the country wait now in its march to safety because of the sickness of one man?" He declared that he held in his hand "testimony of what is going on this day and this hour in the South." When Curtis and Evarts objected to the relevancy of its introduction, he replied grossly that "the relevancy of it is this, that while we are waiting for the Attorney-General to get well, and you are asked to delay this trial for that reason, numbers of our fellow citizens are being murdered day by day. There is not a man here who does not know that the moment justice is done on this great criminal, these murders will cease. . . . We are asked

566

'Why stand ye idle here?' by every true man in the country.
. . . While we are being courteous, the true Union men of the
South are being murdered, and on our heads and on our skirts
is this blood if we remain any longer idle."

The fuming demagogue proved the truth of Lincoln's description of him—"as full of poison gas as a dead dog"—by
continuing to charge that Johnson was mixed up in the corrupt
gold ring, and that "for the safety of the finances of the people,
for the progress of the legislation of the people, for the safety
of the true and loyal men, black and white, in the South, . . .
for the good of the country, for all that is dear to any man
and patriot, I pray let this trial proceed." From Johnson
came "all this corruption, and all these murders, and in the
name of Heaven let us have an end of them." He said that
threats of assassination were being made every hour, and that
while "we have not the slightest fear of these cowardly men-
aces," all such threats would cease "when this man goes out of
the White House."

This unspeakable outburst evoked joy among the Radical
Senators. Conness offered a motion to move the hour for the
Senate as a Court from noon to eleven in the morning. Not
satisfied with that, Sumner offered a substitute for the Senate
to sit from ten A. M. until six P. M. upon the trial. It is
really a matter for wonder that they did not order the suspension of all arguments and direct an immediate vote for the
conviction of the President. After listening to Butler's remarks with ill-concealed disdain, Evarts remarked, "I have
never heard such a harangue before in a Court of Justice, but
I cannot say that I may not hear it again in this Court." The
Managers, he said, protested greatly over delay by the defense,
but whenever the defense wished to introduce really competent
testimony, "hour after hour is taken up with debates on the
production of our evidence. . . . And now twenty minutes by
the watch with this harangue of the Honorable Managers about
the Ku Klux Klan." Senators had not objected to Butler's
verbal villainy, but Cameron arose to inquire whether Evarts'
apt description of it as "harangue" was in order! Conness'
motion for an eleven o'clock opening was carried by the usual
Radical vote.

When the President read this interchange, he was outraged
at Butler's effrontery, and was angry at Evarts' mild response.
"All Mr. Evarts had to say," Johnson told Colonel Moore,

"was that it was a *harangue,* and I believe he thinks he did a most smart and dreadful thing. . . . Then was the chance to have administered a rebuke that would not only have told upon the Senate but upon the whole country. . . . The Managers allude to me as a 'criminal.' Why has that not been replied to by my counsel?" The President seemed particularly dissatisfied with Evarts, and considered telling him he had mismanaged the case.[1]

None the less, in Evarts, Ben Butler had tackled a formidable foe. A student of the law, he was also a practical man. His wit was proverbial. At a course dinner given in his honor, a friend observed him drinking the wines and the liqueurs served with every course, and leaned over to remonstrate, "Mr. Evarts, it will hurt you to drink so many different wines." In a flash the great lawyer responded, "It isn't the different wines that hurts me—it's indifferent wine." One Sunday, during the impeachment trial, he went to Sumner's house for dinner and complained of the work he had done that Sabbath Day. When someone chided him for such efforts on Sunday, Evarts inquired, "Is it not written that if thine ass falleth into a pit, it is lawful to pull him out on the Sabbath day?"[2]

In addition to being a wit, Evarts was no mean politician. In 1860, he had presented Seward's name to the Chicago Republican Convention. During the early part of Johnson's presidency, Evarts had been inclined to play with the Radicals, and when he reached Washington to represent the President, his acquaintance and friendship with certain Radical leaders was not without its advantages. It quickly became apparent to him that if the Senate were to convict Johnson, it would not be because of any belief by two-thirds of the Senators that he was guilty of specific allegations of the articles of impeachment. It would be because certain moderate Republican Senators, who knew that Johnson was not guilty under the specific articles, could not rid their minds of fears that, if he were to be acquitted, he would begin a new war against the Radicals, and that an intolerable situation would result. Evarts shrewdly concluded that if the President could send in to the Senate the nomination of a Secretary of War in whom the moderate Republican Senators had trust and confidence, these apprehensions on their part would be assuaged, and they would decide upon the law and the evidence rather than upon their fears. He talked the matter over with Johnson, discussing the name

FIRM AS THE ROCKS OF MAINE

William Pitt Fessenden, United States Senator from the State of
Maine, and One of the Gallant Seven Whose Votes Saved Andrew
Johnson from Conviction of Impeachment.

of General John M. Schofield, and the President authorized Evarts to summon the General to Washington. Although Schofield was "a cold and selfish man," Johnson remarked to Moore, he was competent, and much to be preferred to Stanton.

On April 21, in response to a written invitation from Evarts, Schofield called on the lawyer in his room at the Willard. Evarts quickly told the General that he wanted his consent to allow the President, at any time before the close of the trial, to send in Schofield's nomination for Secretary of War. When the latter, surprised, asked the purpose of this nomination, Evarts proceeded to enlighten him.

During his explanation, it was announced that Grant was at the door asking for Schofield. When General Schofield arose to depart, he asked Evarts if he could mention the subject to Grant. Evarts at first objected, but finally assented. On Schofield's broaching the matter to Grant, the latter did not like the idea of Johnson thus extricating himself from embarrassment, but finally said that while there was "no reasonable doubt of the President's removal," yet he would be glad to have Schofield as Secretary of War, for Wade would have difficulty in making up a Cabinet.

With this grudging assent, Schofield returned to Evarts' room, and the latter once more went into the proposition. He informed Schofield he was sure that Johnson would not be convicted on the evidence, and, if removed, it would be altogether because of supposed party necessity; that this was the belief of "a considerable number of the ablest lawyers and statesmen among Republican Senators"; that these Senators were anxious "to remove the apprehensions of the Republican party as to what the President would do in the case of acquittal," and that this could only be done by placing the War Department "in a satisfactory condition in advance."

Evarts expressed his judgment that the majority of Republicans in both House and Senate regretted that they had begun impeachment, but that the serious question with them now was "how to get out of the scrape." A judgment of conviction against Johnson "will be ruinous to the party and will cause the political death of every Senator who votes for it, as soon as the country has time to reflect upon the facts and appreciate the frivolous character of the charges upon which the removal must be based." It would be a fearful precedent, and the emergency was great. While Evarts thought the

Democrats in the Senate would vote to acquit Johnson, they really hoped for his conviction, feeling "confident that it would cause the overthrow of the Republican party and the defeat of General Grant."

Schofield was convinced by these arguments, but wanted to see Grant once more. When he went to the General's house at eleven o'clock that night to outline the proposition, Grant heard him with displeasure. If Johnson were acquitted, he said, as soon as Congress adjourned "he will trample the laws under foot and do whatever he pleases." None the less he told Schofield that, under the circumstances, he had better accept.

Having gained Grant's grudging consent, Schofield saw Evarts again the next morning and promised to accept, subject to the solution of one remaining difficulty in his mind. Schofield did not like some of the President's recent acts, such as the creating of the Military Division of the Atlantic. Evarts answered that this had grown out of the Stanton imbroglio, and would disappear with Stanton. The lawyer did not see how the General could satisfy himself on this point without a talk with the President, and he thought such a talk would be inadvisable. The General, realizing the force of this remark, said that he expected no pledge from the President, and would not see him in advance. He would definitely accept the office, with the understanding that Johnson should be informed that he did so in the interest of peace between the President and Congress and that, as Secretary of War, he would give "a just and faithful administration of the laws, including the Reconstruction Acts." This was satisfactory to Evarts, and Schofield returned to Richmond.

On April 24 the President sent to the Senate his nomination of Schofield as Secretary of War. Although it was not acted upon, it had an immediate effect upon the moderate Republicans, and Judge Curtis sent word from the Capitol that "impeachment has gone rapidly astern." This fact alarmed Grant, and on the 25th he wrote Schofield a very confidential letter protesting with great vigor against the General's accepting the post. But the latter stood firm to his word. He wrote that Grant's change of mind had come too late. He would not decline.[3]

At eleven o'clock on April 22, the day which marked the fruition of Evarts' negotiations with Schofield, the Managers

of Impeachment launched their formal plea for the conviction
of the President. George S. Boutwell of Massachusetts delivered the opening argument. An admiring claque occupied the
galleries of the Senate to cheer him on. The ladies' galleries
were packed to suffocation. Boutwell strove manfully to live
up to the occasion, but his lengthy speech was deadly dull.[4]
The object of the trial, he began, was not "the punishment of
the President, but the safety of the State." Senators had already found that the issues of record in the trial "were technical and limited." The House had met them, its evidence being
"bright, clear, and conclusive." The Senate need only determine whether, in attempting to remove Stanton and appoint
Thomas, Johnson "has violated the laws or the Constitution of
the country."

As to the claim that the President had a right to disregard
an unconstitutional law, Boutwell maintained that to the President, "all laws are alike. He can enter into no inquiry as to
their expediency or constitutionality. All laws are presumed to
be constitutional, and whether in fact constitutional or not, it
is the duty of the Executive so to regard them while they have
the form of law." Senators likewise, he continued, had no
right to be governed in their votes on the articles by their
beliefs as to the validity of the law. He took a fling at the
President's counsel, terming them men whose intellects had
been "sharpened but not enlarged by the practice of the law."[5]

"Never in the history of any free government," he charged,
"has there been so base, so gross, so unjustifiable an attempt
upon the part of any executive . . . to destroy the just authority of another department of the government. . . .
Nothing, literally nothing, can be said in defense of this respondent. . . . There are no limits to the consequences of this
man's evil example. . . . Caius Verres is the great political
criminal of history. For two years he was prætor and a
scourge of Sicily. The area of that country does not much
exceed 10,000 square miles, and in modern times it has had a
population of about 2,000,000 souls. The respondent at your
bar has been the scourge of a country many times the area of
Sicily, and containing a population six times as great . . .
40,000,000 of people . . . look to this tribunal as a sure defense against the encroachments of a criminally-minded chief
magistrate."

Then Boutwell soared into the empyrean. "In the Southern

Heavens," he said, "near the Southern Cross, there is a vast space which the uneducated call a hole in the sky, where the eye of man, with the aid of the powers of the telescope, has been unable to discover nebulæ, or asteroid, or comet, or planet, or star or sun. In that dreary, dark, cold region of space . . . the Great Author of the celestial mechanism has left the chaos which was in the beginning. If the earth was capable of the sentiments and emotions of justice and virtue, . . . it would heave and throw . . . and project this enemy of two races of men into that vast region, there forever to exist in a solitude eternal as life. . . ."

After having proposed this novel punishment for Andrew Johnson, Boutwell concluded by demanding "justice for the people" and by telling the Senators that "the case of the Republic is in your hands. Your verdict of *guilty* is *peace* to our beloved country."

T. A. R. Nelson opened the argument for the President. Slight in stature, lame in one leg, and limping when he walked, Nelson was somewhat nervous over the occasion, and the Radical papers derided his defense of his fellow townsman. But there is little ground for the scorn heaped upon his speech. T. A. R. Nelson was no backwoods bumpkin. Although his practice had been on a rural circuit, he had sharpened his wits in legal combats with several great lawyers and he was a shrewd and an able man. His style was laden with poetic quotations, in the manner of Tennessee, but what he said had moment. Did not some of the judges present recall the days of '60 and '61, he asked, days when treason was rife in the Capitol, and when Andrew Johnson was "standing here, almost within ten feet of the place in which I stand now, solitary and alone"? It was this man "who has periled his life in a thousand forms to put down treason," who now was "stigmatized and denounced as a traitor!"

He was a Democrat, was Johnson, "a Democrat of the straightest of strict constructionists; an old Jacksonian Jeffersonian Democrat." Throughout his career, in every emergency, they would find him clinging to a strict construction of the Constitution. While there might have been a difference between him and the Radicals as to the interpretation of the Constitution, "attribute the difference, if you please, to the training, to the education, to the habits of thought of his

whole life; but do not, in the absence of proof attribute it to
unworthy, base, mean, dishonorable motives, as you are asked
to do on the other side."

In the course of his speech, Nelson took up one of Boutwell's charges. The Manager had described the President as
"a man of strong will, of violent passions, of unlimited ambition, with capacity to employ and use timid men, adhesive men,
subservient men, and corrupt men, as instruments of his design.
. . . He has injured every person with whom he has had confidential relations, and many have escaped ruin only by withdrawing from his society altogether. He has one rule of life:
he attempts to use every man of power, capacity or influence
within his reach. . . . He spares no one." To this Boutwell
added the charge that "already this purpose of his life is
illustrated in the treatment of the gentleman who was of counsel for the respondent but who has never appeared in his behalf." The Massachusetts Radical was flaunting the withdrawal of Jeremiah Sullivan Black as an argument against
the President.

Nelson addressed himself to this unworthy insinuation. "I
regret that this topic has been introduced here," he began, "but,
as it is brought forward, I must meet it." He then recited the
whole story of the Alta Vela case, including Black's effort to
coerce the President, Ben Butler's letter, dated March 9, after
the trial had begun, and the concurrence in it by Logan, Stevens
and Bingham, and Black's refusal "to appear further as his
counsel in this case." So far as the President was concerned,
Nelson stated, "the head and front of his offending hath this
extent—no more."

Through it all, Johnson had acted like a noble-hearted man.
"He was determined not to be used . . . as an instrument in
the hands of anybody, or any set of men under Heaven to carry
on a speculation which he believed might be carried on with dis-
honor to the government, or with disgrace to himself if he
consented to be concerned with it." The President was a man
of a peculiar temperament. By careful management he might
gently be led, but "no power under the Heavens can compel
him to go one inch beyond what he believes to be right."

There was an aftermath to this plain exposition. On April
28 Ben Butler arose, recalled Nelson's remarks, and said that
he "felt called upon to notice the insinuating calumny." He
denied stoutly that he had written a letter to Shaffer on the

date the letter set forth, asserted that he had given it several months before, and that Nelson's statement "contains every element of falsehood," producing an affidavit from Chauncey Black to buttress his denial.

Nelson arose with fire in his eyes. He hurled back Butler's imputations "with indignation and with scorn. . . . I treated the gentleman on the other side with courtesy and with kindness. He has rewarded me with insult and with outrage in the presence of the American Senate. . . . So far as any question that the gentleman desires to make with me is concerned, this is not the place to make it. Let him make it elsewhere, if he desires to do it."

Upon a Radical Senator calling him to order, the Tennessean said he hoped that the Senators would pardon him for repelling the strong remarks made by the gentleman on the other side. He reiterated the truth of his statement as to the Alta Vela course, and asked permission to lay before the Senate the originals of Butler's letters. "I trust not," Butler interjected, "until they are shown not to have been mutilated!"

The next day Sumner sought to discipline the Tennessee lawyer, by offering a motion reciting Nelson's words and saying that "whereas such language, besides being discreditable to these proceedings, is apparently intended to provoke a duel or to signify a willingness to fight a duel, contrary to law and good morals; therefore be it ordered that Mr. Nelson, one of the counsel for the President, justly deserves the disapprobation of the Senate."

This was a little too much for John Sherman, who forced the resolution to go to the table for a day. Butler said he hoped no further action would be taken. Nelson sought to read the Butler letters to the Senate. After objection and some confused debate, he was permitted to go on. "The remarks," he said, had been "made under the heat of what I esteemed to be very great provocation. I intended no offense to the Senate in what I said."

In view of Butler's willingness to drop the matter, Nelson said he desired to say nothing more of a personal character. But he did exhibit Butler's original letter, and reiterated that, "in that paper, from beginning to end, there is no date but the 9th of March!"

When Sumner's resolution of censure came up, he demanded a vote, and Reverdy Johnson moved to table. Thereupon Anthony asked if it had been Nelson's "intention to challenge Butler to mortal combat." The Tennessean answered with winning frankness. He had regarded Butler's remarks as charging him with dishonorable conduct. In the heat of the discussion, he had used language to signify that he repelled Butler's charge and that he would answer it "in any way in which the gentleman desired to call me to account for it. I cannot say that I had particularly the idea of a duel in my mind, as I am not a duellist by profession; but nevertheless, my idea was that I would answer the gentleman in any way in which he chose to call upon me for it. I did not intend to claim any exemption on account of age or any exemption on account of other things that are apparent to the Senate." After these candid words, the Senate proceeded to table Sumner's censure by a vote of thirty-five to nine.

Nelson was followed by William S. Groesbeck, the Ohio lawyer who had taken Black's place at the President's counsel board. Because of his brevity, clearness and force, his presentation won the admiration of the Senate and of the country. Groesbeck thus defined the act for which Andrew Johnson had been impeached: "He tried to pluck the thorn out of his very heart, for the condition of things in the War Department, and consequently in his Cabinet, did pain him in his heart. You fastened it there, and you are now asking to punish him for attempting to extract it. What more, he made an *ad interim* appointment to last for a single day. You could have terminated it whenever you saw fit. You had only to take up the nomination which he sent to you—which was a good nomination —and act upon it; the *ad interim* appointment vanished like smoke. He had no idea of fastening it upon the Department. . . . The thing was in your hands from the beginning to the end. . . . Surely this is no crime."

"I do hope you will not drive the President out," he concluded, with a note of pathos. "I hope this not merely as counsel for Andrew Johnson; for Andrew Johnson's administration is to me but as a man, and himself as nothing in comparison with the possible consequences of such an act. No good can come of it, Senators, and how much will the heart of the nation be refreshed if, at last, the Senate of the United States can, in its judgment upon this case, maintain its ancient dignity and high character in the midst of storm and passion and strife."

On Monday the Senate listened to a voice almost from the

grave. It was Thad Stevens' last great effort. In March, the President had scoffed at a rumor of Old Thad's death.[6] Stevens, he said, was a human Vesuvius. When you thought him extinct, it was a temporary paralysis, which soon would be succeeded "by a flow of living passion." This prediction proved correct. Stevens was determined to strike another blow at Johnson. Throughout the trial, the Commoner had needed to be carried up the stairs to his seat. "I wonder, boys, who will carry me when you are dead and gone," he remarked to the youths who carried him.[7]

Thus far he had taken but a minor part in the trial. Too infirm himself to take the reins, he had been forced to endure Ben Butler's antics. Had Stevens been five years younger, wielding the bitter lash of his whip of scorpions upon the Senate, one might wonder if the outcome would not have been different. But the old man was sustained only by the intensity of his hate. His eye was bright, but his face bore the crooked autograph of pain. After he had talked a few moments, he sank to his chair. Then Butler took the manuscript and finished it.

Stevens appealed to the Senate to turn out this man who had defied it. How could "this offspring of assassination . . . escape the just vengeance of the law? Wretched man, standing at bay, surrounded by a cordon of living men, each with an axe of the executioner uplifted for his just punishment." "Every Senator now trying him," he proclaimed, had, with the exception of a few Democrats and Johnson men, already voted for the Senate's resolution of February 21, thus pronouncing the President's "solemn doom."

"Will any one of them vote for his acquittal on the ground of its unconstitutionality?" he asked—or rather, Butler asked in his behalf. "I know that Senators will venture to do any necessary act if indorsed by an honest conscience or an enlightened public opinion; but never for the sake of the President nor anyone else would one of them suffer himself to be tortured on the gibbet of everlasting obloquy. How long and dark will be the track of infamy which must mark his name and that of his posterity! . . ." Stevens was followed by Manager Williams, one of the most ferocious and least able of the impeaching group. Neither his words nor his thought deserves report.

In brilliant contrast to Williams' dullness, Evarts' speech was "almost a model of forensic eloquence."[8] Evarts did not chop with the butcher's cleaver but thrust with a fine Milan blade. He had a clear voice of great penetration and power, a pleasing delivery, which often rose to eloquence, and carried conviction by his comprehensive grasp of the great issue at stake. His large blue eyes often seemed to look not at outward objects but introspectively, as if he were seeking the depths of his own mind.[9] Judge Curtis had been firmly anchored to the Constitution. Evarts fastened himself to the hearts of living men.

"All the political power of the United States of America is here," he began. "The House of Representatives is here as accuser; the President of the United States is here as the accused; and the Senate of the United States is here as a Court to try him, presided over by the Chief Justice, under a special constitutional duty attributed to him."

Suppose they were to acquit the President? Then all things would be as before, and the government and its Constitution would receive no shock. But if he should be condemned, a new thing would have occurred to the country, and "a great nation whose whole frame of government, whose whole scheme and theory of politics rested upon the suffrage of the people, will be without a President, and the office sequestered will be discharged by a member of the body whose judgment has sequestered it!"

Passing now to the points at issue, he reminded the Senate of the oath which the President had taken. It was not the simple oath to discharge faithfully the duties of his office, as if the principal duty of the office were to execute the laws of Congress. No, it was a greater oath, one to preserve, protect and defend the Constitution itself, an oath which no officer except the President had to take. It was not to Congress, but to the people of the United States. To keep this oath was Andrew Johnson's duty and obligation, and the people were determined that the President should not take the oath in vain.

Evarts warned the Congress that it was not above the Constitution, and that the People "are converts of no theories of Congressional omnipotence. They understand none of the nonsense of the Constitution being superior to the law except that the law must be obeyed and the Constitution not. They know their government and they mean to maintain it; and when they hear that this tremendous enginery of impeachment, of trial and threats of conviction and sentence . . . has been brought into play . . . they wish to know what the crime is that the President is accused of. . . . Whether the President has betrayed our liberties or our possessions to a foreign State, . . . whether he has delivered up a fortress or surrendered a fleet, . . . whether he has made merchandise of the public trust and turned authority to private gain. And when informed that none of these things are charged, imputed, or even declaimed about, they yet seek further information, and are told that he has removed a Member of his Cabinet!"

They would ask how the removal of a Cabinet Member came to be a crime, and would be told that Congress had passed a law to make it so. Then they would ask if the Secretary of War was removed and would be informed that he was not; he was still Secretary and in possession of the department. Was force used? No, it was all on paper. The people saw and felt that Congress was putting forward "a claim of right and in exercise of what is supposed to be a duty to prevent the Supreme Court of the United States interposing its serene judgment in the collisions of government and of laws."

The people would not be "slow to understand, without the aid of the very lucid and very brave arguments of these Honorable Managers," he said, with infinite scorn, "that it is a question between the omnipotence of Congress and the supremacy of the Constitution of the United States!" and on that issue, from the beginning of their liberty, the people "have had a clear notion that tyranny was as likely to be exercised by a parliament or a congress as by anybody else." In the formation of the Constitution, he recalled, "inordinate power which should grow up to tyranny in the Congress was more feared, more watched, more provided against, than any other extravagance that the workings of our government might be supposed possibly to lead to." The people were unwilling that any department of the government should "claim to be too strong for the restraints of the Constitution." Whatever advance parliamentary theories of government might have made with the Radicals, they had made none whatsoever in the hearts and the heads of the people of the United States.

With cutting satire, Evarts rocked an unfriendly Senate in

unwilling laughter and brought fear to the hearts of the managers. He alluded to Boutwell's "astronomical punishment" for the President. Cicero had said that a lawyer should know everything, for sooner or later all kinds of knowledge might be apposite to his arguments. But Evarts confessed himself painfully sensible of his ignorance; alas, he belonged to a profession which "sharpens and does not enlarge the mind." Thus he could admire without envying Boutwell's exhibition of his own immense store of facts. The Manager "had discovered an untenanted and unappropriated region in the skies, reserved, he would have us think, in the final councils of the Almighty, as a place of punishment for convicted and deposed American Presidents."

At first, Evarts confessed, he had thought that the Massachusetts Manager had ignored the Constitutional penalty of "removal from office." But after reflection, he had concluded that Boutwell was right, for the Constitution put no limit to the distance of the removal, and so the instant transportation to the skies was constitutional after all. However, as Boutwell alone knew the constellation reserved for Johnson's punishment, he should take into his own hands the execution of the sentence.

"With the President made fast to his broad and strong shoulders," Evarts proceeded, while the Senate shook with laughter, "and, having already essayed the flight by imagination, better prepared than anybody else to execute it in form, taking advantage of ladders as far as ladders will go to the top of this Capitol, and spurning then with his foot the crest of Liberty, let him set out upon his flight, while the two Houses of Congress and all the people of the United States shall shout *'sic itur ad astra!'!'*"

But here a distressing thought struck the speaker. How would the Manager get back? Already he would have gone far beyond the law of gravitation, "and so ambitious a wing as his could never stoop to a downward flight." When Boutwell had reached this space beyond the power of Congress, how could he return, and how could be decided the contest, there become personal and perpetual, between the impeacher and the President? "In this new revolution, thus established forever, who shall decide which is the sun and which is the moon?" During this exhibition of the deliberate scorn of a great lawyer for a petty one, Boutwell seemed "almost suffocated."[10]

For three days, the Senate attended Evarts' words, in rapt attention. When he was done, so far as the law and the Constitution were concerned, the impeachment case was dead. The President was now greatly pleased with the handling of the case, and especially so with Evarts' work.

Stanbery had been back only a few days after his serious illness, and was still weak and feeble. The day before his scheduled appearance, he received a call from Browning, who found him in bed, looking "more dead than alive," but busily arranging his notes for the morrow. The next morning, against the advice of his physician, he arose to make the final argument in behalf of the President. It might seem an indiscretion "amounting to temerity," he began, "that in my present state of health I should attempt the great labor of this case. . . . But, Senators, an irresistible impulse hurries me forward. . . . Unseen and friendly hands seem to support me. Voices inaudible to all others, I hear, or seem to hear. . . . They say, or seem to say, to me 'Feeble champion of the right, hold not back; remember that the race is not always to the swift nor the battle to the strong; remember in a just cause a single pebble from the brook was enough in the sling of the young shepherd.'"

He had not proceeded long before it was necessary for him to ask the Senate to adjourn to the next day, for his strength was giving out. His argument is chiefly of interest because of the tribute which he paid to Andrew Johnson, a tribute which came from a noble heart. "There may be among you Senators who cannot find a case of guilt against the President," he began. "There may be those among you who, not satisfied that a case for impeachment has yet arisen, are fearful of the consequences of an acquittal. You may entertain vague apprehensions that, flushed with the success of an acquittal, the President will proceed to acts of violence and revolution. Senators, you do not know or understand the man."

Let them attend the words of one who perhaps understood Andrew Johnson better than they did, for his opportunities had been greater. Stanbery had responded to the President's call two years before "under a sense of public duty. I came here almost a stranger to him and to every Member of his Cabinet, except Mr. Stanton. We had been friends for many years. . . .

"From the moment that I was honored with a seat in the

Cabinet of Mr. Johnson, not a step was taken that did not come under my observation, not a word was said that escaped my attention. I regarded him closely in Cabinet, and in still more private and confidential conversation. I saw him often tempted with bad advice. I knew that evil counsellors were more than once around him. I observed him with the most intense anxiety, but never in word, in deed, in thought, in action, did I discover in that man anything but loyalty to the Constitution and the laws. He stood firm as a rock against all temptation to abuse his own powers or to exercise those which were not conferred upon him. Steadfast and self-reliant in the midst of all difficulty, when dangers threatened, when temptations were strong, he looked only to the Constitution of his country and to the people."

Nor was that all. "I have seen that man tried as few have been tried," he told the very men who tried him. "I have seen his confidence abused. I have seen him endure, day after day, provocations such as few men have ever been called upon to meet. No man could have met them with more sublime patience. Sooner or later, however, I knew the explosion must come. And when it did come, my only wonder was that it had been so long delayed.

"Yes, Senators, with all his faults, the President has been more sinned against than sinning. Fear not, then, to acquit him. The Constitution of the country is as safe in his hands from violence as it was in the hands of Washington. But if, Senators, you condemn him, if you strip him of the robes of his office, if you degrade him to the utmost stretch of your power, mark the prophecy: the strong arms of the people will be about him. They will find a way to raise him from any depths to which you may consign him, and we shall live to see him redeemed, and to hear the majestic voices of the people 'Well done, faithful servant; you shall have your reward!' "

John A. Bingham of Ohio closed the case "for the people of the United States" with a carefully prepared stump speech. The galleries, well packed with Radicals, were somewhat disappointed at what Bingham had to say. His three-day address seemed a tremendous drop from the heights which Evarts and Stanbery had attained. Bingham's concluding peroration adequately indicates the character of the speech: "I speak before you this day," he said, "in behalf of a violated law, pleading for the violated majesty of the law, by the graves of a half-million martyred hero patriots who made death beautiful by the sacrifice of themselves for their country, the Constitution and the laws, and who, by their sublime example, have taught us that all must obey the law; that none are above the law; that no man lives for himself alone, but each for all; that some must die that the state may live.

"I demand, in the name of the House of Representatives and of the people, judgment against the accused for the high crimes and misdemeanors in office of which he stands impeached, and of which before God and men, he is clearly guilty."

To Mrs. Ben Wade, sitting hopefully in the gallery, the last word was earnest and impressive, and she wrote to a friend in Ohio that, the moment it had passed Bingham's lips, "there was a perfect storm of applause in the galleries." The claque that had been arranged was doing its work. The Chief Justice "in an angry voice, ordered the galleries cleared, and then the applause burst forth once more."[11]

The Radical Senators looked with pleasure upon this part of the drama, and when the Chief Justice announced that, if the cheers were repeated, the Sergeant-at-Arms would clear the galleries, some of the Senators are said to have joined in the hisses greeting his remark. Cameron was so irritated at the interruption to the claque that he insisted that the reporters' gallery likewise be cleared.

After this scene, the Radicals made known their desire to proceed to a final vote, after a brief "consultation." But Fessenden objected in a bland speech. He wished "an opportunity quietly and at home, to reëxamine the argument and evidence."[12]

When should the vote be taken? The Radicals were not unwilling to secure more time in which to exert pressure upon recalcitrant Senators. The debate as to the day for the vote lasted the rest of the day, and the next day as well. Finally it was agreed that on the following Monday the Senate should meet to afford each Senator who wished it a chance to make a fifteen-minute speech giving his opinion. The vote would be taken, without debate, at high noon, the day following this oratorical free-for-all.

F ROM the first of May, the newspapers were filled with the most contradictory predictions as to the outcome of the trial. The Washington correspondents polled and repolled the Senate and filled the columns of their papers with discordant prophecies.

Mathematically, the question was simple enough. The Senate contained fifty-four members. Of these, forty-two were Republicans, nine were Democrats, and three—Doolittle of Wisconsin, Dixon of Connecticut, and Norton of Minnesota— were Johnson Conservatives, elected Republicans who had followed the President and therefore had been excluded from their party membership. Under the Constitution, a verdict of guilty to be pronounced by the Senate upon the trial of an impeachment required the concurrence of two-thirds of the members. To eject Andrew Johnson, the Radicals need only muster thirty-six votes for conviction upon any single impeachment article. If nineteen Senators should vote for acquittal on each of the eleven articles, the President would go free.

Thirty Senators, Thomas Ewing estimated, "will vote for conviction quite irrespective of law and fact. There are twelve Democratic and Conservative Senators, who, as there is no case made, are certain for acquittal Then there are twelve Republican Senators who are too tall to be overawed and driven to judicial perjury by threats or party clamor—in these is our hope. Seven of them are sufficient to save the case."[1]

Long before Bingham had made his final appeal, the Radical Senators began their campaign to convict. As early as April 21, the faithful Moore noted in his diary that "managers of States and others are here to manage Senators who are suspected of leanings to the side of the President." The Radicals recognized that the votes of the three Johnson Republicans were hopelessly lost. They realized that, although several of the nine Democrats might secretly hope the President would be convicted, because of the general Democratic expectation that the political effect of Johnson's ejection would bring disaster upon the Radicals at the polls, every Senator of the minority party would uniformly vote to acquit. Thus the President was sure of twelve votes. If to this number should be added the votes of seven Republicans, "the great criminal of the age" would go free. Nay, more, if Ben Wade should unexpectedly exhibit a sense of honor and refrain from casting an interested vote, six Republican Senators could acquit the President.

In March the list of doubtful Republicans had run as high as twenty, for most of the moderate Senators had qualms of conscience at the whole impeachment farce. But throughout April the party lash was ruthlessly applied, and by May 1 the intentions of only eleven Senators remained in doubt: Fessenden, Trumbull, Grimes, Fowler, Van Winkle, Sprague, Anthony, Ross, Edmunds, Henderson, Willey and Morrill of Vermont.[2]

Early in May, the Radical Senators began holding daily caucuses at Pomeroy's house. Young Theodore Tilton temporarily quitted the sanctum of the *Independent* for Washington to assume the management of the campaign—a "carpet-bag lobbyist," the *World* called him.[3] About twenty Senators generally attended, as did Butler, Bingham and other leading Radicals of the House. Elaborate plans were made to ascertain in advance the views of each Senator upon each of the eleven articles. The Radicals meant to leave nothing to conscience or to chance.

The eleven doubtful Republicans were the object of the fevered attention of the caucus. Their personalities were studied and their blind sides catalogued. Willey was a great Methodist—the Radicals would set Bishop Simpson on his trail. Fowler was a Brownlow man—they would stir up the Parson, back in Tennessee. Trumbull was a crank on equal rights for negroes—could not some new tale of Ku Klux outrage be scraped up to prejudice his mind? Henderson had always been susceptible to his constituents—let telegrams be poured in upon him from the folks back home. Ross was weak and pliable—he might weaken under a bribery charge. Sprague was the son-in-law of the Chief Justice and Anthony was Chase's devoted friend. They might be impressed with the evil consequences to the Chief Justice's ambitions if they should fail the Radicals upon this crucial test.

Thus these Senators who had taken oath "to do impartial justice to Andrew Johnson" busied themselves to dragoon their more honorable colleagues of the impeachment Court. Soon the members of the caucus found that a daily meeting was insufficient, and began to meet twice a day.

Their drastic methods were having effect. Sprague had been counted on by the President because of the influence of Mrs. Sprague and her father; but these proved "frail staffs," for the ambitious politician regretfully concluded that the country needed his services in the Senate for another term, and capitulated to the Radicals.[4] Anthony became alarmed over the threats against Chase. Bishop Simpson, "the high priest of the Methodists," worked with Senator Harlan, an elder of the church, to bring Willey into line.[5]

But help was to come from an unexpected quarter. The Spiritualists seemed to have adopted Andrew Johnson as their patron saint.[6] The leading mediums of the country moved to Washington, established their "batteries"—as they termed their establishments for projecting thought—throughout the city, and set to work to invoke the eerie world to influence the Senate in the President's behalf. One of the most energetic of these batteries was established by Mrs. C. A. Coleman, directly opposite the house of Chief Justice Chase.[7]

Johnson's more practical friends countered the efforts of the Radicals in a political rather than a spiritual way. Reverdy Johnson, Colonel Moore, "Sunset" Cox, and W. W. Warden took charge of the presidential counter-offenses. Warden's special assignment was to keep in touch with moderate Senators. Every night he would go to the White House to report. The President would always begin with the quizzical question: "Well, what are the signs of the Zodiac today?" whereupon Warden would outline the developments of the day.

Warden discovered that the chief danger was that Conservative Republican Senators would be affected by the predictions that if the "great criminal" were acquitted, he would "go on in his excesses." A few doubtful Republican Senators hinted to Reverdy Johnson of such apprehensions. When the Maryland Conservative asked what they would suggest to relieve their doubts, they urged that the President "get himself heard publicly in some form denying such intention." But Senator Johnson pointed out that, with the trial under way, any such declaration was out of the question.

One day Grimes called Reverdy Johnson aside, and after a short talk it was confidentially agreed that it should "so happen" that the President and the Senator from Iowa might meet "casually," so that the Executive might give his own assurances. Accordingly, Warden tendered the President a pressing invitation from Reverdy Johnson to pay him a brief visit on the following evening, and the Senator from Maryland himself invited Grimes. When Johnson and the Iowan were brought together, their greeting was cordial. After some pleasant jesting, Reverdy Johnson cleverly broached the subject on his mind, and the President, indignant at the reports, denied them with much excitement, waxing eloquent as he talked. "They have no warrant, whatever," he said warmly, "in anything I have said or done, for believing that the President intends to do any act which is not in strict conformity with the Constitution and laws."

After an hour the party separated, all much gratified. The next day, Grimes imparted his own confidence to three other doubtful Senators. "You may rely implicitly upon this," he said. "I know Johnson's purposes in the event of acquittal. You need not fear his behavior will cause you to regret your vote, whichever way cast. He does not dread, personally, a verdict of guilty. He believes such a verdict would be disastrous to the Republic, and hence prays for acquittal. But he has no thought of wrong or rash doings."[8]

Thus, to their alarm, the Radicals found that several Moderates could be neither cajoled, bullied nor coerced. The terrorizing tactics of Tilton's caucus became so offensive to these men that on May 9 they began holding meetings of their own for self-defense.[9] The Senators who attended these meetings held the fate of Andrew Johnson in their hands.

There is Fessenden, spare, tall and his head crowned with a fine suit of iron-gray hair. A frown darkens his stern face. He is in earnest conversation with Lyman Trumbull, smooth-shaven, slight in frame, a scholar from the corn belt. The tall, lithe man with the commanding presence, standing next him, is John B. Henderson of Missouri, whose full beard gives him an air of dignity. One does not wonder that the young ladies of the day consider him a very handsome man. Listening to him intently is a clean-shaven, blue-eyed man of ordinary height and unimpressive mien, none other than Joseph O. Fowler of Tennessee. A former school teacher from Ohio, a poor talker, slow and halting in his words, and continually running his fingers through his wavy red hair, Fowler does not look the part of a statesman.

James W. Grimes is more impressive. White haired, almost six feet in height, with a well proportioned frame, he makes a striking appearance. Senate service has mellowed the rough manners of his youth, lending him dignity, suavity and grace. Grimes is plainly dressed, for he has long lived frugally and conducted himself without pretension. To strangers he seems at times cold and repellent, but to his intimates he is frank, hearty and "open as summer."[10] Grimes has no soaring imagination, but he perceives quickly and has a truly prodigious memory. Once he has made up his mind, he is tenacious of his convictions. His strong point is his fund of common sense. During the earlier crises of Reconstruction, Grimes has been carried along by the Radicals. But with impeachment, he has come to his senses with a start. While he believes that Johnson had been guilty "of many great follies and wickednesses," Grimes knows that the President is innocent of "those overt, flagrant, corrupt acts that constitute high crimes and misdemeanors."[11] His is a fine but not a happy face; who could be happy in Grimes' position, struggling with the pains of a fast breaking body and facing the spectre of political death?

The jolly, smiling chap, vainly seeking to cheer Grimes is Peter G. Van Winkle of West Virginia. But here in the corner is a little man, slight and unimpressive, who does not talk much, although he is listening intently to Henderson's excoriation of Grant. He is Edmund G. Ross of Kansas, Pomeroy's colleague, the man destined by circumstance to be the pivot of the impeachment vote. Ross is in a desperately bad position. Poor, ambitious and thoroughly convinced that his political future is staked upon his impeachment vote, his dilemma is pitiable. But the next few days are to prove him possessed of a rare virtue—of a courage such as few men have, the courage to do right although the Heavens fall.[12]

Both Sprague and Willey occasionally attend the meetings of the Moderates, and they have pledged that, if essential, they will vote not guilty.[13]

These were the men who were to determine the impeachment trial. They had come from every part of the country—from Maine to Iowa, from Illinois to Tennessee. As unlike in mind and temperament as in physique and physiognomy, they were temporarily joined in a determination—to use a phrase of

Fowler—so to conduct themselves that they would not become fugitives from themselves through time and eternity.

Ben Wade's shadow depressed the minds of several of this group. They feared that, upon becoming President, the repudiated Radical—Ohio had refused to reelect him to the Senate—would immediately intrigue for his own presidential nomination, thus upsetting the plans for Grant. On the other hand, if Wade were left off the ticket, it was anticipated that he would "make hay for himself while the sun shines upon his eminence," and that the resulting scandals would embarrass Grant's campaign.[14]

The Radicals had figured out a scheme to assure Fessenden's vote. In view of his chronic dyspepsia, they would make him Ambassador to Great Britain. There was another advantage to the plan—it was Pomeroy's concoction—it would get Hamlin back in the Senate without disturbing Morrill of Maine, a chief member of the cabal. But nothing came of the intrigue, for Fessenden had definitely made up his mind to vote for acquittal. Thereupon he advised a friend to be prepared "to hear me denounced as a traitor, and perhaps hanged in effigy. . . . I am utterly weary and disgusted with the great trial. . . . I should much like to see you all, to look at the garden, and feel that there are a few persons left in the world who love me none the less for not sacrificing my sense of right to outside clamor or party expectancy." "The public," he regretfully concluded, "when roused and excited by passion and prejudice, is little better than a wild beast, and, unfortunately, the men who now guide and control it are both dishonest and incapable. . . ."

His correspondence attested the correctness of this view. "Is it possible," a constituent wrote, "that you have turned traitor, and that your name will be handed down with that of Benedict Arnold?" Another begged him "not to crush the people of Maine with shame and misery." Rufus Dwinnell of Bangor, one of Fessenden's dearest friends, sent two urgent letters. He wrote: "You have no right to assume you know more than all others. If for nothing else, to satisfy those who elected you, you are bound to vote for conviction."

The Senator responded with indignation. "Do you know how atrocious such a sentiment is, addressed to a judge and juror acting under the solemnity of an oath?" he asked Dwinnell. "If I followed your advice, I could not look an honest man in the face. I should feel a degree of self-contempt which would hurry me to the grave. . . . You say you shall grieve over my downfall. Give yourself no anxiety on that account. The loss of office will be attended with no disgrace, . . . and will not do much credit to a people who reject a public servant because he had the courage to do his duty at the risk of forfeiting their good will."

Immediately before the vote, Fessenden's sorrows were increased by a letter from his intimate friend, Morrill of Vermont, urging "such a vote as you can defend without tearing your life out of you for the rest of your days. As an idol of a very large portion of our people, you would be knocked off your pedestal. You cannot afford to be buried with Andrew Johnson, nor can a poor devil like myself afford to have a cloud of suspicion thrown on the correctness of his vote by a wholly different vote given by yourself on a question of so grave consequence. . . . For your happiness, I trust you will be sure you are right."

Fessenden had made up his mind. None the less, he was grieved, he said, "at my time of life, after a long career, which I believe has been honorable, to find myself the target of pointed arrows from those whom I have faithfully served, for what I should know to be the one act of my life for which I am most entitled to the respect and confidence of all men."[15]

Henderson's experiences during the impeachment had been equally disturbing. Born in Virginia and orphaned in his 'teens, he had taken on his boyish shoulders the care of several helpless children, whom he endeavored to support by teaching school. A few years later he entered the law, and soon drifted into politics as a Union Democrat, following Stephen A. Douglas to the latter's death. Upon coming to the Senate, Henderson affiliated with the Radicals from 1864 to 1867.[16]

But he was a lawyer and a good one, with a knowledge of evidence, and a passion for justice and truth. During the impeachment proceedings, he became convinced that Johnson was not guilty of the offenses charged. Thereupon commenced a struggle between conscience and ambition. Henderson was troubled not only about his own prospects, but about the effect of a vote of acquittal upon a charming girl who had promised to be his bride, Miss Mary Foote, daughter of Johnson's Commissioner of Patents. Immense pressure began to be brought to bear on him. Insolent letters descended upon him. Radical newspapers hectored him. He was threatened with political annihilation. Greatly troubled, towards the end of April the Senator from Missouri laid the situation before his fiancée. "This impeachment trial, I am afraid, is going to be hard on you, Mary," he began. "If I vote for Johnson, it is sure to cost me reelection to the Senate, and I know you will not like that."

"You go ahead, John," the plucky girl responded. "Don't consider me. I don't care at all. Do what you think is right. That is the way I will be happy."[17]

A day or so later, Henderson was invited to a ten o'clock breakfast at Grant's house. After the other guests had left, the General asked him to remain, lighted the inevitable cigar and proposed a walk. What did the Senator think as to the result of the impeachment.[18] "You may rest assured that impeachment will fail," the latter answered. Grant expressed surprise; the Managers were very confident. "They have no substantial grounds for such confidence," Henderson shot back.

Then Grant revealed that the Managers were so sure of success that the members of Ben Wade's Cabinet had already been selected. Amazed, Henderson asked who they would be, and Grant told him that Butler had been picked for Secretary of State. "These men who are counting on the success of impeachment," he added, "offer me their influence as the nominee to succeed Wade, in case he becomes President by the removal of Johnson."

"What are the conditions?"

"That I shall agree to take over Wade's Cabinet."

"Good God, General," the Senator expostulated, "you didn't consent to that, did you?" Grant answered that he had not made any promise.

About a week later, Grant sat down by Henderson on a street car and again took up the impeachment matter. Had Henderson changed his mind? The answer was negative. Did the Senator think he could defeat it? "Well, I can't warrant that," Henderson answered. "We have friends enough against it to defeat it, but I cannot give a pledge that we shall actually defeat it."

"I hope you won't," Grant snapped back. Astonished, Henderson asked if he meant he would impeach. "Yes, I would," he answered brusquely, "I would impeach him, if for nothing else than because he is such an infernal liar."

By this time Henderson was boiling with rage at Grant's attempt to sway him. "I very much regret to hear you say it," he said rebukingly. "I regret it because on such terms it would be nearly impossible to find the right sort of man to serve as President." Nonplussed, Grant quickly left the car.

During these heartbreaking days, the President regarded the proceedings on Capitol Hill with grim amusement. One day toward the end of the trial, a Tennessee lad wonderingly observed the stream of people passing through Johnson's study and the affability with which the President, pleasant and smiling, received them. Noticing the boy, whose father was his good friend, Johnson beckoned him in and asked: "Have you been to the show?" When the boy said that he couldn't get in, the President gave him a ticket, and sent him up to the Capitol to enjoy the farce.[19]

With the President always awaiting the return of his counsel from the Senate or the conclusion of some important conference, there were many midnight vigils at the White House. Mrs. Patterson was ever at her father's side, seeking to soothe his troubled spirits. A brass chafing-dish played a part in the proceedings, and at many a midnight hour Johnson, Evarts, Stanbery, Curtis and Nelson were refreshed by a Welsh rarebit or some other trifle prepared by Martha Patterson's hands.[20]

Welles was struck by the President's lack of despondency. He attributed it to "an honest and sincere consciousness that he has been, to the best of his ability, faithful, that he has done his duty, and that a good Providence will not permit him to be sacrificed under these circumstances." At the beginning of the trial, according to the recollection of one of his secretaries, the President had "betrayed a great deal of anxiety as to its result, and a terribly bitter enmity to those he regarded as conspirators not only against him, but also the Constitution of the United States." But these natural passions soon subsided, and he became "quite philosophic," reading and re-reading Addison's "Cato," memorizing its dramatic passages and at times reciting them against the conspirators, "with great vehemence but without violence."

One Sunday, after church, Johnson came into the White House library with a Bible in his hand, which he exhibited to Moore, and then read him Chapter XII of the First Samuel, laying emphasis on the third verse: "Behold, here I am: witness against me before the Lord . . . whose ox I have taken? or whose ass I have taken? or whom I have defrauded? whom I have oppressed; or of whose hand I have received any bribe to blind mine eyes therewith? and I will restore it to you." The President had been "impressively struck" with the pertinence of the verse to his own case.[21]

The President was thoroughly familiar with the records, personalities and characters of most of the Senators now trying him, and would frequently discuss them with his family and friends. Firmly convinced that right would be rewarded and wrong punished, Johnson applied this doctrine of compensation and the law of retribution to his enemies. He liked to recall the fate of the men who had signed the death warrant of Charles the First. Some of his friends were shocked at the way in which the President, with inexorable logic, would trace the sequence "of dire events to the Nation and calamities to individuals that would follow the wrong, the evil, the crime of his expulsion."[22] But on May 10, when a Boston reporter interviewed him on the situation, Johnson declared that he had never allowed himself "to believe or feel that the American Senate would prostitute its great power of impeachment to base party purposes. I shall not believe it until I know the vote of conviction has been recorded."

"But whatever their opinion may be," he continued, "I shall cheerfully bow to the authority of the Constitution." When the reporter suggested that this declaration was not in line with Bingham's hint that it was doubtful if he would obey the Senate's judgment, the President indignantly brushed aside the "base" suggestion, asking: "Why should I not obey the mandate of the Senate, if all the forms and requirements of the Constitution are complied with? If Senators misuse or abuse the great power thus entrusted to them, it is not for the party impeached and convicted to attempt to set aside the judgment of the Senate. The people alone can settle with their agents. . . . . Mr. Bingham well knows that I have never failed to yield a cheerful compliance with all requirements of the Constitution. I have endeavored to the best of my ability to protect, defend, and preserve that great charter of our liberties, and I am more than willing to surrender my official responsibility whenever called upon to do so, according to the premises and requirements of that sacred instrument."[23]

Two days later Stillson laid before the President the efforts which the impeachers were making to convince the wavering Senators that, if acquittal came, he would "proceed to rule or ruin the country." The correspondent could not finish his recital before Johnson interrupted him: "and, in fine, set up anarchy in general, and preside over it with a sceptre, if I can." "I anticipated just such nonsense," he commented. "These men, I suppose, will stop at nothing. It will be strange though, if they make any unprejudiced Senators believe all the exaggerated statements afloat."[24]

Had Andrew Johnson been in the Senate Chamber on Monday, the eleventh, he would have realized that "unprejudiced Senators" were rarities. For that day had been set aside for Senatorial oratory. For fifteen minutes each "judge" could fulminate against the President to his heart's content.

Before the oratorical field day had got started, Buckalew made the motion "that the views of the Chief Justice be entered upon the journal." Chase, who had been debating whether or not to "charge the jury," had concluded it was not incumbent upon him to do so. Accordingly, his views as offered were merely upon the way in which the vote should be taken and not on the merits of the case.[25]

As the triers spoke, their opinions passed beyond the closed doors of the Senate chamber, to the elation or depression of the waiting Radicals. John Sherman let it be known that he considered himself bound by his Senate speech of the previous year as to the President's right to dismiss Stanton. He would not vote for the first article, but he would for the second.[26] "Poor Sherman!" Welles penned in his diary. "He thinks the people fools. They know him better than he does them."

The Ohio Senator, after carefully assuring his colleagues that his view was "binding upon no one but myself," asked how he "who made it and declared it to you, and still believe it to be the true and legal interpretation" could pronounce the President guilty, and vote to remove him "for doing what I declared and still believe he had a legal right to do. God forbid!" None the less, he was willing to vote for Johnson's conviction on several other articles.

After Sherman had thus stultified himself, Grimes, Trumbull and Fessenden came boldly forth and repudiated all of the eleven flimsy articles. Fessenden would consider himself un-

worthy of a place among honorable men if, from fear of public
reprobation, "I should disregard the convictions of my judgment and my conscience." Trumbull spoke with a great tremor
in his voice. The example of such a conviction, he pointed out,
would be a damning one: "No future president will be safe who
happens to differ with a majority of the House and two-thirds
of the Senate. . . . In view of the consequences likely to flow
from this day's proceedings, should they result in conviction, on
what my judgment tells me are insufficient charges and proofs,
I tremble for the future of my country. I cannot be an instrument to produce such a result." This announcement was a
"thunderbolt" to the Radicals, who excoriated the Senator for
his "deceit" in not informing the Illinois delegation in advance
of the stand he planned to take.[27] Grimes repudiated political
considerations, refusing to "agree to destroy the harmonious
working of the Constitution for the sake of getting rid of an
unacceptable president."

After carefully disposing of the first eight articles, Henderson declared that the eleventh was the only one as to which
he had ever entertained serious doubt. His quarter of an hour
ended before he reached any analysis of it. Doubtless he welcomed the respite Chase's gavel afforded. But the Radicals
were alarmed.[28]

On an impeachment trial, Fowler said, a Senator's position
was one of personal responsibility. "He can neither shun it
nor escape from it in any way, and is no more bound by the
wishes and purposes of those outside of the Court than is a
juror or a judge." He thus rebuked the Brownlow legislature
for its resolution demanding that he vote to convict. "Any
efforts to bias or influence his judgment by threats or appeals
to his personal prejudices or party affiliations or demands are
not less pernicious to the ends of justice than personal violence
or bribery to accomplish the same result. . . . I cannot shun
the ever watchful presence of God, and cannot afford to disregard His voice; nor can I dare to become a fugitive from
myself through time and eternity."

The opinions of the members of the Radical caucus were
chiefly interesting for their casuistry; several sought to give
the cloak of judicial merit to their votes by announcing unwillingness to vote for this or that article. But Sumner had
little patience with these devices. He flatly announced that he
intended to vote this "Pharaoh" guilty on all articles. "It is

very wrong," he said, "to try this impeachment merely on these articles. It is unpardonable to higgle over words and phrases." To him, any "act of evil example or influence committed by a President" constituted an impeachable offense. In the Impeachment Trial, if any doubt had existed on any point, "the benefit of those doubts must be given to the country"—that is, against the President. He sneered at "that swarm of technicalities, devices, quirks and quibbles which . . . have infested this great proceeding," brushed aside the defenses for the President, and scored Johnson's lawyers: "Nothing ever occurred so much calculated to bring the profession into disrepute. . . . Give me a lawyer to betray a great cause." His duty was "to vote guilty on all the articles. If consistent with the rules of the Senate, I should vote 'Guilty of all and infinitely more'!"[29]

The forecast of the vote based upon these committals gave the Radicals great alarm. It showed that there would be twenty votes against the first article—the twelve Democrats and Conservatives were against this, as they were against the other articles. Eight Republicans, including Sherman and Howe, had also indicated they could not vote to convict upon it. There would be twenty-one Senators against the fourth; although Sherman and Howe would vote to convict upon it, Edmunds, Ferry and Morrill of Vermont had announced that they would not. Edmunds and Ferry were against the fifth article; Ferry, Howe and Morrill against the sixth, Ferry opposed the seventh, Edmunds the eighth, thus insuring failure upon the four conspiracy articles. The ninth and the tenth seemed hopelessly lost. Sherman, Edmunds, Ferry, Morrill of Vermont, Howe and Howard ranged themselves against the former, and the first four of these similarly denied the tenth. If the President were to be convicted at all, it would have to be either on Thad Stevens' lovingly fashioned *omnium gatherum*, article eleven, or upon the second and third, ascribing a crime to the President's making Lorenzo Thomas Secretary *ad interim*.[30]

The probable votes had been immediately tabulated, and by the time of the dinner adjournment, the collapse of eight of the eleven articles stood revealed. The tenor of the opinions gave hope that the "infamous and dastardly conspiracy" would fail.[31] When Evarts heard that the first article had fallen, he remarked, "Then all the articles are lost, for no respectable Senator can acquit on the most important and then convict on those of trifling importance." Such a thing was "too monstrous for belief."[32]

As each Senator spoke, a note would be sent the President about the attitude he emphasized. Suddenly transported from the depths of despair to the heights of hope, McCulloch entered the President's study overjoyed. Soon Groesbeck appeared with a word of quiet confidence. "The work is accomplished," he cautioned, "but there must be no exulting outbreak." The optimistic Randall predicted twenty-two votes for the President, if not more. The gloomy Welles did not believe Randall was an accurate man.

Profoundly disturbed by the indications of the afternoon, the Radical caucus realized that if the vote were taken on Tuesday, as had been ordered, the President would be acquitted. But if a few days' delay could be gained, they believed that they could whip into line, at least on the eleventh article, enough doubtful Senators to convict. Therefore the caucus decided to force postponement.

When the Court took a recess for dinner, the Radicals noticed that Henderson had accompanied Reverdy Johnson, Sprague and Chief Justice Chase in Sprague's carriage to Chase's home, where they had dined together. Ben Butler rushed into the house. "We are sold out," he shouted. The apprehensions of the impeaching Members of the House became very great. Stevens immediately brought in from his Reconstruction Committee a bill to admit into Congress North Carolina, South Carolina, Louisiana, Georgia and Alabama, and the House made it a special order for Wednesday. Here was a threat that ten carpetbag Senators would be added to the Impeachment Court.[33] That evening the fears of the Radicals increased perceptibly. Van Winkle talked so "unreliably" that hope in him was abandoned. Ross maintained a dogged silence. "Monday night was one of the darkest ever witnessed in Washington," the *Independent's* correspondent reported, "I mean, among loyal men." A last-minute effort was made to relieve Wade of his embarrassment. Senator Henry Wilson and Speaker Schuyler Colfax both promised to withdraw as candidates for the Republican vice-presidential nomination, if only Wade would immediately resign as President *pro tempore* of the Senate, and cast the needed conviction vote.[34] There was no sleep that night for the friends of impeachment.

Before the Senate met on Tuesday, a drastic attempt was

made to force the hand of the backsliding Henderson. Five of Missouri's eight Republican Members of the House met and determined to demand that Henderson vote to convict, or resign. With them went a member of the Missouri legislature, who asserted that the Senator had told him that Johnson should be impeached, and that while he could not vote for any other article, he might vote for the eleventh.

This insistent group pounced upon Senator Henderson. They reminded him that he had been burned in effigy at Macon on the evening of the tenth[35] and that this was but a minor prelude to his political fate if he should persist. They told him in determined language that the Union party of Missouri almost unanimously demanded Johnson's expulsion from the White House. Henderson seems to have lost his self-possession, to judge from his answer to these insolent demands. He explained that, as a man of honor, he could not and would not vote for the first ten articles. He was in doubt only as to the eleventh. He was willing to telegraph his resignation to the governor, and the latter could appoint his successor, who could be sworn in and vote by Saturday, to which time Henderson knew the caucus had determined to adjourn. But the Congressmen were far from satisfied. It was not Henderson's resignation they wanted, but his vote to convict. The Senator then asked them to retire and to send him their advice in writing.

A little later, a singular document reached this Senatorial judge. "On a consultation of the Republican members of the House of Representatives from Missouri," it began, "in view of your position on the Impeachment Article, we ask you to withhold your vote on any article upon which you cannot vote affirmatively. This request is made because we believe the safety of the loyal people of the United States demands the immediate removal of Andrew Johnson from the office of President of the United States."

When the Senate convened at noon, the galleries were crowded with spectators eager to see the final scene. But Zach Chandler arose to announce that his Radical colleague, Senator Howard, had been taken very ill.[36] While his colleague was willing to come, "even if it imperilled his life," Chandler continued, there should be an adjournment until Saturday. Several Conservatives sought to substitute Thursday or Friday, but the Radicals held their lines and forced the four-day adjournment. "The President was more disturbed at the post-ponement than I have ever seen him," Welles noted, "but he soon rallied."[37]

The capital city, swarming with political harpies, reminded Fessenden almost of an Inauguration day. Gamblers thronged the saloons, making great wagers on the vote. The whole evil brood of place-seekers was on hand, lusting for the offices Ben Wade would parcel out. As their hopes rose and fell with the rumors of the hour, "so rose and fell the character and repu-tation of those Senators upon whose votes the result was supposed to depend; while the telegraph was at hand to carry over its wires to the homes and friends of those Senators every calumny which disappointed ambition or cupidity and malignity could invent, and while a portion of the press, claiming for itself a character for decency and even Christian virtue, stood ready to indorse and circulate the lie."[38]

The city was "a seething cauldron," alive with rumors of attempts, successful and unsuccessful, to bribe Senators to vote for Johnson. "The tongue of scandal was employed as a weapon of coercion." Intimidation and violence "were both threatened and intended." The excitement was "overmaster-ing." Truly, "passion ruled the hour."[39]

Pomeroy's caucus straightway fell to work. Impeachment had now become a "measure of desperation," and they were beginning to fear that failure would bring "political disgrace and personal obloquy" upon them.[40] In calmer days General Schenck, Ohio Congressman and Chairman of the Republican National Committee, had contemptuously termed the Presi-dent "an irresolute mule." Now he proclaimed him a "genius in depravity," a man bent upon the destruction of the country.[41] On the heels of the Senate's adjournment, the General dispatched this telegram to scores of party leaders in Maine, Rhode Island, Illinois, Kansas, Iowa, West Virginia and Tennessee:

Washington, D. C., May 12, 1868.

Great danger to the peace of the country and the Republican cause if impeachment fails. Send to your Senators public opinion by resolutions, letters, and delegations.

ROBERT C. SCHENCK, Chairman.

That evening the Missouri Representatives saw Henderson again.   Having now somewhat recovered his self-possession, he told them that he could not meet their written request without a degree of "humiliation and shame" to which he was certain they did not desire to subject him.   The Congressmen withdrew their letter, but continued to insist that his party demanded a vote for conviction upon one article, if that vote meant Johnson's removal.   The Senator expostulated.   Other members, he said, were likely to change their views at any moment before the final vote.   Then he showed his callers a list of thirty-six guilty votes, on the eleventh article, excluding Wade's and his own: the President might be deposed without assistance from him. The delegation answered that conviction was what they were after, Henderson need not resign unless it should appear that his vote was absolutely indispensable and he could not make up his mind to vote for the eleventh article.   The Senator then promised to try to find out how Anthony, Sprague, Willey and Van Winkle were going to vote.   With this, Loan and his fellow Radicals withdrew.

Schenck's "monstrous prostitution"—the phrase is Welles' —had already begun to bring results.   At a Republican campaign club meeting that evening in Chicago, one speaker publicly warned Lyman Trumbull that he had better stay off the streets of Chicago during the Republican National Convention. Otherwise, "the representatives of an indignant people will hang him to the most convenient lamp-post."   The club solemnly resolved "that any Senator, . . . elected by the votes of Union Republicans, who at this time flinches and betrays, is infamous, and should be dishonored and execrated while this free government endures."[42]

It was a typical exhibition of the response to Schenck's appeal.   Letters, telegrams, resolutions, delegations demanding the conviction of the President, poured into the Capital. Holden, Johnson's first provisional governor, telegraphed from Raleigh, "Strike the usurper from his seat."   The hesitating Senators were burned in effigy by indignant Radicals back home.   Papers thundered at them; ministers prayed for them at special prayer meetings.

Wednesday morning, while "Sunset" Cox was visiting Henderson, the Senator received a telegram from E. W. Cox, Radical St. Louis politician, inspired by Schenck's Macedonian appeal.

"There is intense excitement here," it read. "A meeting is called for tomorrow night. Can your friends hope that you will vote for the eleventh article? If so, all will be well."[43]

The two men read it with indignation, and Cox helped Henderson draft the answer, which read: "Say to my friends that I am sworn to do impartial justice . . . and I will try to do it like an honest man." At midnight Cox carried a copy of Henderson's telegram to the White House. He found the President very gloomy, believing that his fate depended on the Missourian's vote and that this was lost. When Cox showed him Henderson's staunch answer, a "festivity was improvised, and the morning dawned with roseate hues."[44]

The composition of this mild rebuke seemed to have restored Henderson's peace of mind. He immediately determined to go further and to inform the Missouri Congressmen that he intended to do his duty at any cost. "If I resign and a successor should come," he wrote them, "perhaps a proper sense of delicacy would prevent him from violating every precedent on this subject by casting a vote at all. . . . If he voted affirmatively . . . this manner of obtaining conviction would likely neutralize in the end every advantage to be derived from impeachment."[45]

The Radicals met with less success in arranging a similar demonstration of their House Members against Lyman Trumbull. At a caucus of the Illinois Republican congressmen it was proposed to address a joint letter to the Senator, urging that if he would not vote for conviction, at least he should refuse to vote at all. But five of the Representatives objected so strenuously that no letter was sent.

The Radical organs boiled with rage against "the four apostates"—Fessenden, Trumbull, Fowler and Grimes. They were particularly violent against the Senator from Iowa, Forney's *Chronicle* and Greeley's *Tribune* excoriating him as a traitor and a Judas. A man of quick feelings and tender sensibilities, Grimes suffered keenly under these assaults. For weeks he had been laboring under increasing mental excitement, brought about by the estrangement of old associates and the bitter attacks of political friends. On Wednesday afternoon he could sustain the strain no longer, and was stricken with paralysis.[46] The Radicals proclaimed this seizure a veritable judgment of Providence.

The great annual Conference of the Northern Methodists was then in session in Chicago. Its leading figure was Bishop Matthew Simpson, whose activities in the Radical cause have already been alluded to. On May 13 the Bishop inspired a motion before the assembled Methodists that an hour be set aside for prayer for the conviction of the President.

But an aged delegate did not approve the Bishop's partisan resolution. "My understanding is that impeachment is a judicial proceeding," he objected, "and that Senators are acting under an oath. Are we here to pray to the Almighty that they may violate their oaths?" Under these plain words, the motion failed.

The next day Bishop Simpson made another effort for the forces of the church formally to be put behind the impeachment. This time direct exhortation that Senators vote for conviction was omitted. But the resolution recited "painful rumors" in circulation "that, partly by unworthy jealousies and partly by corrupt influence, pecuniary and otherwise, most actively employed, efforts were being made to influence Senators improperly, and to prevent them from performing their high duty." Accordingly, an hour should be set apart the following day for invocation to the Almighty, "to save our Senators from error." When this cunning resolution was adopted without dissent, the *Nation* remarked that it had been "aimed at Senator Willey of West Virginia, rather than at the Throne of Grace."[47]

The African Methodists, then meeting in Washington, took their cue from the "white folks" to order an hour of prayer of their own. But here there was no subterfuge—the prayer was addressed not to God, but directly to the American Senate.[48]

From the shelter of his War Department barricade, Stanton worked frantically, overlooking no possible agent to influence doubtful Senators. The army list was carefully gone over. Every officer who, because of previous friendship with a Senator, was known to have influence with him, was brought to headquarters and given precise instructions as to what to do. The generals who had been removed by Johnson were directed against their senatorial friends. All of Grant's cronies were proclaiming that the General thought "Johnson ought to be removed," and his aides-de-camp rushed back and forth as upon a battlefield.[49]

Strangely enough, a roly-poly Kansas girl, Vinnie Ream, was to play a part in the acquittal of the President. Possessed of a talent for sculpture, in 1866 she had been commissioned by a generous Congress to carve the careworn form of Lincoln for the government. She worked faithfully on her figure of the martyred Emancipator, and at the Capitol crypt, which had been assigned to her for a studio, she received her many friends. Radicals and Conservatives alike smiled upon her and wished her well. Vinnie was a pet of the Ewings and of Senator Ross. General Sherman was very fond of her.[50]

During the Impeachment, Ross and other Conservative Senators bethought themselves of Vinnie's studio in the crypt —a quiet place for conference, unvexed by importuning Radicals. On occasions, General Thomas Ewing and his father met Ross in Vinnie's presence. Pomeroy's caucus heard rumors of these meetings, and that the charming sculptress herself was urging Ross to vote to acquit. Thereupon the cunning Julian was sent to warn her that this course would bring trouble on her head. It was later charged on the floor of the House that he had "threatened her that if she did not use her influence for conviction, it would be the worse for her."[51]

At the time of Julian's warning to the frightened girl, the suspense as to Ross' vote had grown too great for the Radicals to endure. They determined to find out at any cost. Pomeroy undertook the task, and on the 13th he began his attack. He noticed Ross entering the room of the Sergeant-at-Arms of the Senate in Trumbull's company, followed them, heard them discussing impeachment, waited until Trumbull left, and then beset his enigmatic colleague.

The Radical had in his hand a senatorial roll call, upon which he had indicated the Senators whom the caucus expected to vote for conviction, with the articles upon which that vote was expected. Exhibiting it, he bluntly told Ross that he was canvassing the Senate, had the names of thirty-five pledged in their own handwriting for conviction, and he wanted to know how Ross would vote. They must have his vote to make conviction sure.

When Ross glanced at the list, he found his own name indicated for conviction on the first, second, third, eighth and eleventh articles, and expressed amazement. Pomeroy explained that he had based these checks on Ross' previous talks with him. The badgered Senator then noticed that all the

marks on Pomeroy's slip were written in the same hand, concluded that his colleague was seeking to entrap him, and sharply
rebuked Pomeroy's presumption. Then he defined his position.
He would probably vote for the first article. In his judgment
it embraced all there was in the whole affair. He would not vote
for the eighth. As to all the others, he was undecided. If the
first carried, he might vote for the others; if it lost, in his
opinion all the others would go down with it.

This declaration was but cold comfort to Pomeroy and his
caucus. Sherman, Howe and others had already said they
could not vote for the first. A vote from Ross upon it would
not countervail the loss. Pomeroy must try again. Accordingly, the next evening Pomeroy trailed Ross to Van Winkle's
rooms, to find Henderson, Trumbull and Willey also there. But
the presence of these others did not abash the leader of the
Radical caucus. He boomed forth his belief that conviction
was sure, by a single vote, on article eleven. "Am I counted in
the affirmative?" Ross asked, and when Pomeroy answered yes,
he renewed his words of the day before, warning Pomeroy not
to count on him under any circumstances. The Radical quickly
left and reported the conversation, and instructions went forth
to extreme men throughout Kansas to bring more pressure to
bear on Ross.

By Friday, with the vote scheduled for the next day, Radical efforts reached their peak. That morning Ben Wade was
so sure of success that he called on General Grant at the
latter's office. "General," the near-President announced, "I
am here to consult with you about my Cabinet, in case Mr.
Johnson is found guilty." Badeau remained in the room and
took note of the interview. The Ohio Radical went over the
list of his Cabinet, starting with Ben Butler for Secretary of
State. Grant said he had no objection to any of those mentioned. After an half hour's earnest conversation, Wade departed.[52]

The Chief Justice had continued to be a target of the impeachers. Theodore Tilton had gone so far as to call at
Chase's home to hector him. Thinking that he was talking to
his quondam warm personal friend rather than to the fanatic
editor, Chase defended himself vigorously against Tilton's imputations. He was amazed and chagrined when the *Independent*
came out with a vicious editorial, captioned "A Folded Banner," which purported to describe Chase's conversation,

charged him with befriending the President so as to win the
Democratic presidential nomination, and termed him a traitor
to the cause. The Chief Justice wrote Tilton an indignant
letter, informing him not only that he had no right to make
such use of a private conversation, but also that the article was
a tissue of half truths and false inferences. He was "neither
candidate nor aspirant for any nomination. . . . I said I
would not take the Republican nomination if I could have it.
. . . I knew I could not have it . . . if I proclaimed my opinions on impeachment, military commissions, military government and the like; and I wanted no nomination with concealed
or unavowed opinions. . . . I am content to be read out of the
Republican party. I can afford to be, so long as I retain my
old principles and my old fidelity to the cause of the oppressed
and the needy."[53]

On the day before the vote, although Chase was "entirely
uncertain as to the result," he was righteously indignant over
the pressure being brought to force conviction. "Think of
legislatures, political conventions, even religious bodies, undertaking to instruct Senators how to vote, guilty or not guilty,"
he wrote Hiram Barney. "What would be thought of such
attempts to drive the decisions of any other courts? All the
appliances to force a measure through Congress are in use here
to force a conviction through the Court of Impeachment."[54]
But one thing he did know: "If the vote were deferred for six
weeks, until after the Chicago nominations, conviction would
be impossible."

Chase's conclusion seemed entirely sound. Already the
reaction to the Radical campaign had set in. The impeachers
had badly overdone it. Even the Chicago *Tribune* became
alarmed at the angry passions being evoked, and began to
fear that they might react against the Republican party. On
Thursday of conviction week it reprehended the assaults upon
the doubtful Senators as a party blunder.

"The man who demands that each Republican Senator
shall blindly vote for conviction upon each article," Medill declared editorially, "is a madman or a knave. . . . We do now
protest against the degradation and the prostitution of the
Republican party to an exercise of power so revolting that the
people will be justified in hurling it from place at the first opportunity. We protest against any warfare by a party or any
portion of it against any Senator who may, upon the final

vote, feel constrained to vote against conviction upon one, several, or even all of the articles. A conviction by the free and deliberate judgment of an honest court is the only conviction that should ever take place on impeachment. . . . To attempt to drive these Senators out of the party for refusing to commit perjury, as they regard it, would cause a reaction that might prove fatal, not only to the supremacy of the Republican party, but to its very existence."[55]

"Can any party afford to treat its leading men as a part of the Republican press has been treating leading Republicans during the last few weeks?" the *Nation* asked at about this time. "We have, during the last week, heard language applied to Mr. Fessenden and Mr. Trumbull, for instance, which was fit only for a compound of Benedict Arnold and John Morrissey." Godkin had become disgusted with the leading Radicals, "a class of roaring, corrupt, ignorant demagogues, who are always on 'the right side' with regard to all party measures," and predicted that they would destroy the Republican party.[56]

These expostulations had little effect upon Pomeroy, Schenck or the caucus. If anything, they increased their pressure on the few remaining doubtful votes. Friday afternoon, a telegram inspired by Schenck arrived from Leavenworth, addressed jointly to Ross and Pomeroy. "Kansas has heard the evidence," the telegram read, "and demands the conviction of the President." It was signed, "D. R. Anthony and 1,000 others." Pomeroy sent word to Ross to come by for a copy of the telegram. When he arrived, Pomeroy persuaded him to remain to dinner and pleaded again for him to vote for conviction. Ross finally answered that he was freer to vote for the eleventh article than for any other.

Soon after the badgered Ross had departed, the Radical caucus gathered in Pomeroy's large library. Tilton made a brilliant speech. The caucus was confident that tomorrow would mark Andrew Johnson's doom.[57] Pomeroy reported that Ross had said "he was freer to vote for the eleventh than for any other." Forthwith they determined that the initial vote must be upon the eleventh article. Serenely confident, Wade brought forth the final list of his Cabinet, and the caucus agreed upon it. Many of this "Cabinet" were among those present and congratulations were the order of the hour.

About midnight a triumph was reported. A group of the Radicals had kept after Willey, upon whom Simpson's Methodist maneuvers were having great effect. After being badgered until late in the night, the West Virginian finally capitulated, and agreed to vote guilty on the eleventh article.[58] Harlan and the Bishop were much rejoiced.

Nor was Fowler to escape these culminating assaults. Members of the caucus remembered that in January, at a meeting of the Union Congressional Committee, the Tennessee Senator had voiced some opinions on impeachment. His words had been too unimportant to be taken down at the time, but now "Pig-Iron" Kelley wrote out what he declared to be a report of Fowler's remarks, took affidavit that it was "their tenor and phraseology," and that Fowler often had "pressed the same views" upon him. Thereupon General Schenck and seven other Radicals signed a certificate that Kelley's report was accurate, and the document was put into type. On Friday evening a copy of it was sent to Fowler. Later that night, when three Radicals visited him to poll his vote, he was threatened with "exposure." But the Tennessee Senator was made of sterner stuff than Willey.

Toward midnight, Ross was seen at a downtown restaurant with Henderson and Van Winkle. It was suspicious company in the eyes of the Radicals, and the lobby was aghast. Stanton got hold of General Sickles and dispatched him to Ross' room to make a final assault. But the Conservatives were not altogether idle. They heard of Sickles' mission, and Vinnie Ream offered to keep the General from importuning poor Ross. Her plan proved successful. Sickles prided himself on being a great "ladies' man." Vinnie waylaid him on his way to Ross' room, and he did not make his plea to Ross.[59]

On Saturday morning Forney's *Chronicle* brought forth Kelley's great document against Fowler. As he was hurrying to his seat, Fowler ran into the committee that had called upon him the night before and now threatened him with investigation, exposure and expulsion from the Senate. But they secured little comfort from their threats. Fowler stood firm.[60]

Earlier that morning—and, incidentally, it was "one of the loveliest," a correspondent noted—Radical spies had tracked Ross and Henderson to a breakfast at the house of Perry Fuller. A little later Ross had answered Anthony's telegram: "I do not recognize your right to demand that I shall vote either for or against conviction. I have taken an oath to do impartial justice . . . and I trust I shall have the courage and honesty to vote according to the dictates of my judgment and for the highest good of my country."[61]

Ten minutes before Wade's gavel fell, Pomeroy made a last attempt on Ross, warning him that if he voted to acquit, his political death would follow, and threatening that such a vote would bring upon him an investigation on a charge of bribery! Thus the Radicals kept up their pressure to the very moment when Chief Justice Chase directed the Senate to be in order for the vote.

The Senate is slow in opening. Its hour as a legislative body has been set at 10:30 in the morning, and at five minutes before that time, not more than ten Senators are in their seats and the galleries make "a beggarly show of empty benches."[62]

Most of the Radical Senators are late; they had been holding a final caucus. But when Wade raps for order at the half hour, the Senate quickly fills, reporters sharpen their pencils, ladies enter the galleries, and special police take their stands in the Senate aisles and in all the galleries, including the Diplomatic. The legislative session is the sheerest routine, but the now crowded galleries watch it with breathless attention.

The House of Representatives is formally notified to attend the coming spectacle. Preceded by the Managers, its members advance two abreast, from the other end of the Capitol. Here they come, Bingham and Boutwell, Wilson and Butler, Logan and Williams, and now Thad Stevens, borne in a chair by two henchmen. Bingham seems impressed with "a comical solemnity"; Boutwell frowns grimly. Wilson's lips are tense and rigid. They stream past a plaster statue of Abraham Lincoln, illumined by a beam of sunlight. In an angle in the hall, a mournful looking old woman has apples and oranges for sale. Hucksters selling trinkets mingle with the milling throng in the corridor. The Managers file in and take their seats, nervously awaiting the dénouement of the drama. All of the President's counsel except Judge Curtis—he had been called back to Boston—are in their chairs.

At high noon, Wade announces in a "peculiar haggard voice" that he yields to the Chief Justice. Chase comes in from a side door, his robes rustling, takes his seat in a stately chair, and nervously twirls an eye glass. A crier intones the usual command, and the crisis of impeachment is at hand.

The scene is impressive. Despite the valorous efforts of

numberless gas jets, the Senate Chamber is encompassed in a soft and richly colored gloom. The galleries seem "glowing embankments, ascending from edge to summit under a burden of beauty." Hundreds of women flutter with fans and ribbons. The Diplomatic Gallery is now occupied, a scattered and strange group studying with curious brows this great farce produced by the government to which they are accredited.

On the Senate floor, the spectacle is much less vivid. General Sickles goes on the floor and holds a whispered conference with Senator Ross; Conservatives among the spectators look anxiously at the two. Fowler of Tennessee leaves his accustomed seat, advances into the midst of the Radicals and sits down there, apparently in happy communion with them. Conservative onlookers again are apprehensive. Van Winkle whispers in Hendricks' ear. Anti-impeachment stock goes up. The Radical Drake addresses low but earnest words to Trumbull. What is the meaning of this?

With the exception of the stricken Grimes, every one of the fifty-four senatorial judges is on hand. Quitting his stretcher, Howard of Michigan is brought in, supported by two friends, and slips into his seat, a great shawl wrapped about his shoulders. Before the Chief Justice can direct the Secretary to read the first article for the vote upon it, Williams of Oregon, who is acting as floor leader for the Pomeroy caucus, leaps to his feet to make the motion that the Senate rescind its rule to ballot on the articles in their numerical order. This is carried. He next moves that the eleventh article be voted on, and then the other ten successively. It is a patent trick, but by a vote of thirty-four to nineteen, the Radicals push it through.

Edmunds then moves that the Senate proceed to vote. Fessenden arises and asks a half hour's postponement to enable Grimes to be brought in from his sick-bed. Reverdy Johnson arises; in his lace shirt and frilled cuffs there is a suggestion of the fathers of the Republic. "He is here," he announced. "I have sent for him. He is down stairs. . . . He will be in the chamber in a moment." There is a bustle at the door, and Grimes is brought in, wan and feeble, and is slowly helped to his chair by his friends, amid the scowls of the Radicals.

After the Chief Justice has admonished the galleries to silence, he directs the secretary to read the eleventh article. There is a hush after the reading, and Chase orders: "Call the roll." The call is alphabetical, Anthony of Rhode Island being the first name pronounced by the clerk. Chase's friend arises in his place. "Mr. Senator Anthony, how say you?" the Chief Justice solemnly inquires. "Is the respondent, Andrew Johnson, President of the United States, guilty or not guilty of a high misdemeanor, as charged in this article?"

Anthony, although pale and a little tremulous, is assured. He gazes calmly into Chase's eyes, answers firmly, "Guilty," and wilts into his seat. There is an excited whisper. The next two names are of Democrats; both answer in the negative. Simon Cameron is so anxious to be on the proper side that before the question to him is half complete, he shouts "Guilty," breaking the tension and causing a titter that is quickly stilled. The next seven votes are guilty, followed by three for acquittal and three more for conviction.

"Mr. Fessenden,"—these two words electrify the Senate and the audience. It is the name of the first doubtful Republican. Fessenden rises, calm, self-contained. He stands erect as a pillar and looks the Chief Justice straight in the eye as the question is being put to him. A second elapses before he answers; during it the tinkle of an ear-ring could have been heard. Then comes the firm reply, "Not Guilty." The Chief Justice allows a little longer delay than usual to elapse after Fessenden's vote. There is a sigh of relief in the galleries.

The nervous strain has been too much for the Tennessean, Fowler, whose name is next. His answer is low, almost inaudible, and is taken to be "Guilty." Sumner jumps to his feet. "Did the Court hear his answer?" Chase repeats the question; now Fowler thunders "Not Guilty!" in tones to satisfy the hungriest ear.

The roll call reaches the stricken Grimes. The Chief Justice announces: "Mr. Grimes need not rise." The Senator from Iowa will not hear it, but struggles to his feet and votes for the President. Howard, likewise ill, is offered the same privilege, but arises to vote to convict.

Now Henderson's name is called. The spectators in the galleries crane their necks. The Senator from Missouri rises nervously. He looks "haggard, weary and over-worn." Conkling, Thayer, Patterson, Conness and Drake lean forward in anxiety. The Missourian's voice rings out "Not Guilty!" There is a sigh of relief. The President's friends breathe more freely.[63] The spectators settle back in their seats.

The next ten votes have been counted for conviction. They

are voted according to expectation. This makes twenty-four votes for guilty. Ten more are sure. They count upon Willey, now that the Methodist church has done its work. But how will Ross of Kansas go?

The undertone of banter and indifference in the galleries ceases when his name is called. There is a preternatural stillness. Chief Justice Chase's great voice booms forth and he leans forward, anxiety written on his brow. The Senators concentrate their gaze upon their Kansas colleague. The galleries rustle apprehensively. Ross has been occupying himself with his usual diversion of tearing sheets of paper into strips and littering his lap. He rises to his feet, a remnant of congressional foolscap clinging to his fingers, and announces, in a clear but conversational tone, "Not Guilty."

The tension is over. The contest is ended. The Radicals turn sour looks upon the "traitor from Bleeding Kansas." The Kansas Congressmen are purple with wrath that must be suppressed. "There is no remedy for this but the knife," one mutters. Ross resumes his seat and again tears paper into strips. The Conservatives are hard put to it to restrain their glee.

The roll call proceeds. The votes go as had been expected. Trumbull and Van Winkle say not guilty. Now that acquittal is assured, Willey goes with the Radicals. Wade's name is called. He thunders guilty, a useless and debased vote. Wade is not to occupy the White House; his Cabinet of the night before will remain on paper. The President is acquitted by a single vote.

The Chief Justice immediately announces: "The Secretary will now read the first article." Senator Williams moves for a fifteen minute recess. He is voted down. Chase again directs that the first article be read. Williams now moves for adjournment until May 26. Reverdy Johnson asks for the declaration of a vote on the eleventh article. The clerk repeats the senatorial roll call. Then the Chief Justice solemnly proclaims:

> Upon this article, thirty-five Senators vote guilty and nineteen Senators vote not guilty. Two-thirds not having pronounced guilty, the President is, therefore, acquitted upon this article."

Cameron renews Williams' motion for adjournment. The Chief Justice rules that it cannot be entertained, because the

MRS. ANDREW JOHNSON

A Portrait of Andy's Beloved Eliza McArdle, Taken During Her
White House Days.

Senate is in process of voting. An appeal is taken from his ruling, and the Radicals push their adjournment through. This adjournment, the *Nation* said, "not only deprived the process of all value, but converted it into a national scandal and disgrace."[64] But what cared the Radicals for such judgment on their procedure? They wanted ten days for further lobbying. They would not give up hope of conviction.

During the balloting, a stream of telegrams came to Johnson's White House study, telling every new detail of the vote. He opened them quietly and sent them on to his family. Even the dispatch indicating Ross' vote of not guilty did not alter his "placid spirit." He was disappointed at Willey's desertion, and remarked on how men crumbled under pressure. Then in came the message announcing acquittal on the eleventh article. The President's face flushed a little, and he made a quiet remark.

Young William Crook, Johnson's body-guard, had been sitting in the Senate gallery keeping tab on the vote. After the last Senator had voted, he did not wait to hear the verdict announced, but dashed down the stairs. The dense crowd which, unable to secure entrance into the Senate gallery, had packed the lobby and the corridors, was shouting impatiently: "What was the verdict?" Crook saw Thad Stevens held high above it, on the shoulders of two attendants being carried across to the House. His face black with rage, Old Thad was waving his arms and shouting in reply, "The country is going to the devil."

The Secret Service man did not pause to gloat over Stevens' discomfiture, but ran out of the Capitol and down the Avenue as fast as his legs would carry him. When he reached the White House, he saw a happy group about the President's study. He went on to Mrs. Johnson's room and entered. She greeted him with a gentle smile of welcome. The happy man could not restrain himself. "He is acquitted!" he cried. "The President is acquitted." The frail little lady rose from her chair, tears in her eyes, and grasped his right hand in hers. "Crook, I knew he'd be acquitted; I knew it."[65]

The moment that the verdict was announced, Nelson and Stanbery burst from the Senate chamber, leaped into a waiting carriage and drove like mad down the Avenue. When the White House was reached, they dashed from the vehicle and rushed upstairs. Despite his lame foot, Nelson made the better speed, and flung himself into the President's study "reeking with perspiration and hot with glee." In a moment, Stanbery panted in behind him, exuberant with joy. Presently Seward came over from the State Department, "very jolly," to invite Johnson to a party at his house that evening.

With the announcement of the acquittal, a great procession of callers thronged to the White House. There was "an avalanche of cards," and the White House was "as hilarious as a royal palace after a coronation." A watching newspaper correspondent noted the unfamiliar faces which appeared. Throughout the day the President demeaned himself with the greatest dignity and forbearance. He quietly expressed his gratification at the result, "confirming his lofty opinion of the character of the Senators who had voted against impeachment."[66]

"Never did a man behave himself," an observer testified, "more without arrogance, or an appearance of unseemly joy."

O<small>N</small> Saturday, after the Senate had adjourned, Fessenden walked through the Capitol's crowded lobbies. No hand of friendship was held out to him. There was no smile to cheer him on. With ashen face, but holding himself sternly erect, he threaded his way among the angry Radicals and went slowly to his lonely chamber. There, for the first time, his great heart faltered and, sobbing, he threw himself upon his couch.[1]

But Sunday morning broke more cheerfully for him and for the other recusant Republican Senators. They awoke to find an avalanche of congratulatory telegrams from the best men of the country awaiting them. Their party might have singled them out for punishment, but their country was filled with gratitude. Indeed, on Saturday night, delighted citizens at Catskill and Poughkeepsie, and at Westfield, Mass., fired one hundred guns in honor of the verdict. That night there was a torchlight procession at Bridgeport, Conn., and great mass meetings of celebration were held at Troy, Utica, Newark, Boston, Baltimore and New York.[2] Throughout the Union, the hearts of the Conservatives were glad.

Andrew Johnson was deluged with congratulations. From Lancaster, Thad Stevens' home came the message, "Ten thousand hearts are throbbing with exultations of joy. . . . Justice has triumphed over party." From Paris, John A. Dix sent word of his "unfeigned satisfaction." The assembly of the Harvard Law School formally congratulated the President. "I have not esteemed this proceeding of very great personal importance to you," Judge Curtis wrote his client. "But to the country, it was of such importance that it would be difficult to overstate it." In London, Lord Clarendon told John Van Buren, "I rejoice in his acquittal." In New York, Samuel J. Tilden wrote the President earnestly asking an office for one of his henchmen, and casually concluding with congratulations upon the result.

But the extreme Radicals were unrestrained in their abusiveness. Andrew Johnson had now ceased to be the great criminal of the age, being pushed into second rank by the magnitude of the crime of Fessenden, Trumbull, Fowler, Grimes, Henderson,

Van Winkle and Ross, in their treason to their party. As to Ross, the *Independent* stated bluntly that Washington "was filled with charges of his positive and downright corruption for money." Henderson was "to be confronted with affidavits alleging that he had positively agreed to vote for the eleventh article." As to Fowler, no other Senator had so "absolutely and irredeemably stultified himself as this wretched man."[3]

Horace Greeley's *Tribune* termed the seven Senators corrupt and shameless scoundrels, charging that they had taken bribes from the whiskey ring. Ross was "the greatest criminal of the age," and Greeley consigned him to "everlasting infamy," the only question being how much he received for his vote. Grimes had voted chiefly because he hated Ben Wade and also because Chase had seduced him! Going even further, Greeley took note of Joseph Medill's backsliding as to the dragooning of the Senators, and declared that Grimes owned stock in the Chicago *Tribune* and that Medill had influenced him to vote to acquit.[4]

On May 18 Greeley categorically charged the Chief Justice with the failure of impeachment. "He decided the vote of Mr. Van Winkle," the *Tribune* thundered. "He did his utmost, happily in vain, to carry off Messrs. Anthony and Sprague. We doubt that Mr. Henderson would have voted as he did but for the Chief Justice's exertions." Chase was indignant, and wrote Greeley in protest: "More lies seem to be afloat about me than I thought invention capable of. I have not interchanged a word with Mr. Van Winkle on the subject of impeachment, that I remember, and my acquaintance with him is very slight. I have not exerted myself to influence anybody, one way or the other. . . . The stories about dinner are mere bosh, and so are the stories about rides, except that there is a grain of fact sunk in gallons of falsehood."[5]

Yet the stories as to Chase's complicity would not down. It was said with particularity that he had said this to Anthony, and that to Van Winkle, and this again to Sprague; that he had started talk of a third party with himself as its nominee for President, and that he was after the Democratic nomination as well. All these matters provoked denials from the Chief Justice, for he seems not to have been able to understand that what the Radicals wanted was not truth or justice, but some culprit upon whom to hang the blame for their failure to thrust out the President.[6]

Regardless of who was responsible for the first acquittal, Greeley was determined not to be balked of his prey. Forney seconded him with malignant vigor, his Washington *Chronicle* and Philadelphia *Press* being, if anything, more vituperative than the *Tribune*. They began a campaign for new members to be added to the Impeachment Court. Referring learnedly to the trial of Warren Hastings and to the way in which the composition of the House of Lords had altered between its commencement and its final vote, these Radical editors therefore suggested that the bill which the House had already passed to readmit Arkansas into statehood and into Congressional representation be taken up by the Senate and immediately passed. This would add two votes for conviction to the Senate Court. If that would not suffice, there were four other Southern States which had selected sound Radicals for the Senate. These States could be rushed back into the Union and thus the South, from where Andrew Johnson had come, would furnish the necessary votes to eject him from the White House.

But the acquittal had awakened other feelings among the moderate Republicans, whose view was well typified by E. L. Godkin's candid comment in the *Nation*. The failure to convict, he wrote, might be regretted for several reasons, "but that it leaves Mr. Johnson in the Presidential chair we no longer include among the number." Nor was the acquittal likely to strengthen the country's confidence in the Radicals. The House had shown up badly in the trial. After announcing that it would have the case tried on high moral grounds, "it put in the forefront of its battle a lawyer whose opinion on high moral questions . . . nobody heeds . . . and whose want . . . of decency, throughout the case gave the President a constant advantage. . . . The managers were overmatched throughout in learning and ability," and they had sought to repair their deficiencies in law and logic "by warmth of language." It must be extremely mortifying to the Impeaching Members that they had failed "after having spent a week in holding the most honored of the party leaders, its wisest heads and purest characters, up to execration as perjured villains," an "amazing burst of folly."

Godkin analyzed the substance of Greeley's diatribes in the *Tribune*. "A Republican Senator might say on his oath," he satirized, "and yet be an honest man, that the removal of Mr. Stanton and the appointment of General Thomas did not constitute a high crime and misdemeanor; and he might say on his oath, and yet be an honest man, that the wild speeches of 1866 did not constitute a high crime and misdemeanor; but if he says on his oath that he believes the removal of Mr. Stanton in February, 1868, was not done in pursuance of a plan formed by Mr. Johnson in 1866, and of which the only evidence is a fragment of a stump speech made in that year, . . . although Mr. Johnson has ever since gone on acknowledging the validity of Congressional legislation day by day in the ordinary course of business, he must be a corrupt scoundrel—bribed to violate his oath by fraudulent distillers. His guilt is evident; he is not only to be driven out of the party, but to be held up to execration as a dishonorable man. . . . This is the charge against the dissentient Republican Senators, and the whole of it."

On the contrary, the *Nation* believed that "the thanks of the country are due to Messrs. Trumbull, Fessenden, Grimes, Henderson, Fowler, Van Winkle, and Ross, not for voting for Johnson's acquittal, but for vindicating, we presume nobody but themselves knows at what cost, the dignity and purity of the Court of which they formed a part, and the sacred rights of individual conscience. They have afforded American young men an example such as no politicians have ever afforded them in the whole course of American history, and at a time, too, when the tendency to put party claims above everything is rapidly increasing."[7]

It must not be assumed, however, that the impeachment-mad Radicals had given up their enterprise. The *Nation*, the Chicago *Tribune*, and the New York *Evening Post* might seek to immortalize the seven Senators. Extolling telegrams might pour in upon them from the four corners of the earth; guns might thunder in their honor; but the Republican party intended to have another try at the President. The sole purpose of the ten days' adjournment had been to afford further opportunity for pressure. The great criminal had been saved by but a single vote. During the recess, surely one of these traitor Senators might be made to realize the consequences of betrayal. Impeachment was far from being over.

The Pomeroy caucus continued with more intensity than before. During the week leading up to the vote on the 16th, a House committee had been at work ferreting out all the scandalous stories about pressure, bribery and influence on the

President's behalf. Newspaper correspondents related scandal, members of the Radical caucus told of their suspicions, and a nauseous mess of perjured villainy was kept boiling in the pot. No sooner had the vote on the eleventh article been taken than the Radicals in both Houses fell furiously to work.

Upon Chase's quitting the Senate, as soon as it had adjourned as a court, Wade immediately called it to order legislatively. Before it was a House resolution proposing a recess until the 25th, to enable Senators and Congressmen to attend the Republican National Convention in Chicago. Wilson of Massachusetts strenuously objected. The House had already passed bills to restore Arkansas and five other Southern States to statehood and to representation in Congress, he insisted. The Senate must stay in session to pass these bills.

Sumner did not mind adding these new judges to the Court, but he felt that it was unbecoming for the Senate legislatively to transact any business with the President; it was "as if the judge on the bench should continue to transact business with the criminal in the dock." Let the Senate put the Arkansas bill into a law "before the sun goes down," urged the more practical Nye. Senator Yates, Trumbull's Illinois colleague, wanted the two votes from Arkansas; but he also longed for a recess, "for members to go home and breathe the breath of popular opinion among their constituents, and understand how a great people feel outraged and indignant at the verdict which has been pronounced here today. . . ." The Senate first refused to adjourn; then it reconsidered and adopted the House resolution; but before it had done so, the House had also reconsidered. The formal adjournment was not had, but many Radical members sped to Chicago, nevertheless.

During the Senate's discussion of whether it would take up the bill for the admission of Arkansas, the question was raised as to whether Senators thus admitted could become members of the Impeachment Court. The Conservative Dixon referred to the campaign Greeley and Forney were making in their papers to gain these new votes for the Court, and warned that the Radicals intended the carpetbaggers, if made Senators, to become members of the Court. "Of course they can be," retorted Sumner. But Fessenden said he would not envy any Senator who might propose to administer the trial oath to Senators from Arkansas, and, "still less should I envy the condition of anyone who proposed to take the oath and to act as a member of the Court under such circumstances."

When it was pointed out that the ten days for consideration of a bill granted to the President by the Constitution would prevent admitting the Arkansans until after the trial had been concluded, it was countered that another adjournment of the Court would be quite as easy and fully as justifiable as the first. But the admission of Arkansas was too bold a play. The Radicals did not dare to bring it to a vote.

The activities of the House were even more unbecoming. On the Court's adjournment, the Managers snatched up their papers and rushed into secret session. After a few moments of excited consultation, they filed into the House, and Thad Stevens, sustained again by the burning fires of unquenched hate, recited that "Information has come to the Managers which seems to them to furnish probable cause to believe that improper and corrupt means have been used to influence the determination of the Senate upon the Articles of Impeachment." Therefore, he offered a resolution that, "for the further and more efficient prosecution of the impeachment of the President," the Managers be empowered to summon witnesses, seize persons and papers and look into the foul crime. Bingham hinted that the House was "clothed with full power" to demand the sequestration of the seats of Senators whose votes had been corruptly influenced. After a vain effort by the Democrats to secure membership on this new investigating body, the Radicals adopted the resolution and the Managers immediately set to work.

Ben Butler again took the lead. Newsboys were hawking on the streets a flaming extra, "Suicide of Ben Butler," but this hardy scoundrel, unabashed at the defeat, undertook the congenial task of befouling the Senators who had resisted the Radical attack.[8]

The necessary authority had hardly been conferred before the telegraph offices in Washington and Baltimore were impounded, and every message which had been sent or received for the last four or five days was scrutinized by Butler and his crew. The Washington banks were compelled to furnish the bank-accounts of the suspected Senators and of others as to whose activities the Managers wished information. A warrant was made out for one Charles Woolley, a Mid-Western gambler who had been betting heavily on Johnson's acquittal. This mysterious person gave Butler great concern by disappearing and then suddenly appearing. Put on the stand, he answered all questions readily to a certain point, when he became as silent as the grave. Almost frenzied by his refusal to answer questions, the Managers ordered him put into close confinement for contumacy. Unwilling to trust the jails of the city, they selected the Capitol crypt for his dungeon and ejected Vinnie Ream from her studio, despite her tearful protest that to move the model of her statue of Lincoln would mean its ruin.

On Monday Thad Stevens introduced a resolution asking the Senate for a certified copy of its proceedings on Tuesday, the 12th, and Saturday, the 16th. He explained to the House that he wanted it so as to have an official record of the senatorial votes. No one could doubt, he said, "that there has been great, manifold, deep damnation. . . . I charge nobody with anything. But to me it seems amazing that a body of that kind, having before it a body of men of the highest character, will give to themselves and to others the character which they have given. . . . We are therefore asking that . . . every opportunity shall be allowed for the purpose of ascertaining who have been willing to listen and who have refused to listen to the instruction of the accused."

When this insolent demand came before the Senate, the Conservatives were indignant at the implied insult, and inveighed against it as an encroachment on the prerogatives of the Senate. But Sumner could not understand this attitude. "We know from the evidence before us," he expostulated, "something of the character of the President. . . . We know how utterly unprincipled and wicked he is." The Senate ought to give the House every assistance in damning the recusant Senators. Only the lack of a quorum prevented Sumner's motion from prevailing.

Butler kept throwing out his dragnet, and finally seined in a bit of evidence to which the Radicals listened with great dismay. One of Pomeroy's Kansas henchmen,—it was the same Legate—had gone on the stand to purvey some vicious stuff about Ross. In his anxiety to smirch Ross, Legate overreached himself, and implicated Pomeroy in the solicitation of a bribe! According to his own henchman, Pomeroy had offered his own vote and those of three or four of his caucus, to the President's friends for $40,000! Pomeroy's brother-in-law had been his agent. Legate backed up his evidence by producing a copy of Pomeroy's letter of April 16, 1867, to Postmaster-General Randall pledging his vote for acquittal if the Administration would give Legate the Leavenworth Postmastership.[9]

Here was a pretty mess. The Managers had been hoist by their own petard. Pomeroy rushed on the stand to deny that he had written such a letter; the denial, however, was weak, for Randall produced a copy of the letter, attesting that he had seen the original, and the copy was a true one. "Senator Pomeroy either intended to dispose of three votes (his own, Nye's and Tipton's)," Thurlow Weed publicly proclaimed, "or he was willing that his friends should use his name to make money; or, as some believe, there was a conspiracy between Butler and Pomeroy to implicate the President, thus obtaining new material for impeachment."[10]

Henderson was also a target of the inquisitors, who sent him a formal demand to appear to give testimony. Terming their request an insult to the Senate, he refused. "If a member of the Court," he replied in rebuke, "can now, before the rendition of the judgment, be withdrawn from consultation and subjected to the inquisition of the prosecutors, that inquisition may reach all proceedings, and thus subvert the dignity and independence of the Senate."

The House Democrats had asked for a committee of their own to investigate the attempt of the Missouri Radical representatives to intimidate their Senator. Henderson appeared before it and freely answered all questions asked, relating the occurrences as they have been given. He also met "all questions propounded in reference to the conduct of Chief Justice Chase, the reported organization of a new party, the rumors of new Cabinet appointments, reported Presidential promises of protection to what is foolishly termed Conservative Senators, dinner-table talk with friends, and even my own private opinions."

On May 21 he submitted the impeachers' demand, his reply and the account of his testimony before the other committee to the Senate and asked its pleasure, telling his colleagues that he objected to submitting to an examination so insulting to the Senate and so contemptuous of the personal honor of its members. But the ingenuous Sumner could not see why any Senator should seek to impede justice by talk of the dignity of the Senate. "Let justice have a free course and take its way," exhorted this model of impartiality, "the way of justice cannot be stopped. Technicalities are out of place; they do not belong to a case like this." And he made use of a phrase which rankled with the Missourian: "It is the wounded bird that flutters."[11] The Senate refused to give Henderson any support in his stand.

The activities of Ben Butler and his committee formed but one phase of the Radical drive for the needed vote. While Butler and Stevens kept at their Washington scavenging, Bingham and Logan hastened to Chicago to make sure that the Republican convention took the needed steps.

A Convention of Soldiers and Sailors was held simultaneously with the Republican gathering—such devices to link the party of "high moral ideals" with the triumph of the Federal Army in the Civil War marked this period of Republicanism. It was resolved by the veterans' gathering that those Senators who had voted to acquit the President had been unfaithful to their duty, and were "unworthy of the confidence of a brave and loyal people."

The impeachers presented to the Resolutions Committee of the Republican Convention a formal declaration reading the seven recusant Senators out of the party; but wiser counsels prevailed there, and the platform as reported did not go quite so far. It lost little in vigor, however, from this omission. Andrew Johnson was a criminal of the deepest dye, it recited, a man who had been "justly impeached . . . and properly pronounced guilty . . . by the votes of thirty-five Senators."

Fessenden derived grim amusement from the convention's failure to read him out. "It now remains for us to decide whether we choose to stay in," he wrote. "If the party desires to swap me off for Ben Butler, I shall enter no protest."[12]

As the delegates rushed forward to the unanimous selection of Grant, Logan cheered them on by announcing that the General had "stood at the back of the Managers in Congress during the whole course of the trial." The selection of General Grant had been a foregone conclusion since he had deliberately given the lie to the President and his Cabinet. But Ben Wade was doomed to disappointment; his name was hardly mentioned for the vice presidential nomination. After a few ballots, "Smiler" Colfax got the place.

Several days before the "Court" was to reconvene, the Radicals realized that there was only one man of the nineteen who had voted in the negative on the fateful Saturday whom they could hope to secure. There was no use trying to tamper with Fessenden, Grimes and Trumbull. Their written views repudiating all the articles had already been filed for printing with the report of the trial. While Henderson was being badgered, he told the Senate that he expected to vote not guilty on all the articles. Van Winkle had had doubts only on the eleventh article, and on it, he had already voted no. In response to a congratulatory telegram on his vote on the 16th, Fowler had answered: "I acted for my country and posterity, in obedience to the voice of God."

Ross was the only man whom under any circumstances they could hope to win. With him there was still a possibility. Had he not told Pomeroy that he was inclined to the first, and was undecided as to the second and third articles? Perhaps they could bully him into line on one of these last. The spotlight of publicity was focussed on his mild and shrinking form. "Tell the damned scoundrel," came a message from Ben Butler, "that if he wants money, there is a bushel of it to be had."[13] Pomeroy kept up his pressure. The Managers' committee threshed over every hint and imputation against him. The Vinnie Ream story was thoroughly ventilated. Ross' connections with Perry Fuller, an Indian agent at whose Washington house Vinnie and her mother lived, was made much of. It was charged that the Ewings had seduced him, and tales of bribery floated through the air. Appeals, demands and threats from the Radicals back in Kansas continued. They would show this "skunk and perjurer" what it had cost him to sell out. There was even a desperate project to kidnap Ross and cause his resignation by force, so that a successor could be named in time to give the needed convicting vote.

One can imagine the feelings of this unhappy man. His reputation had been torn to tatters. He had dug his own political grave. His party had repudiated him. His former associates pretended to believe him guilty of accepting a bribe. And yet through it all, as DeWitt well puts it, "he bore the ordeal with the fortitude of a stoic and inscrutability of a sphinx."

Thus, on the morning of the 26th, when the Senate sitting as a Court of Impeachment once more assembled, there was universal uncertainty as to Ross. Although the general impression prevailed that the President would again be acquitted,

Welles by no means considered it certain. He was not sure about Ross: "It is claimed he is committed for the second and eighth. . . . Intrigue pervades the whole atmosphere."

Shortly before the Court was due to assemble, Pomeroy's caucus held a hasty meeting and determined to force adjournment for four more weeks. But none of the seven recreants had been invited—about half the impeachers themselves were absent—and this dictum of the caucus failed to be adopted when brought up in the Court.

The preliminary votes proved highly alarming to the President's friends. Williams, floor leader of the impeachers, offered a resolution to rescind the previously adopted order of voting on the articles. The Chief Justice ruled it out of order, but the Senate overrode him by twenty-nine to twenty-five. In that ballot Ross had voted with the Radicals! Next, Conkling offered a substitute that the voting proceed under the rule; the Radicals voted it down, Ross again being numbered with them. When Trumbull raised a point of order, Ross again joined Pomeroy's cabal to vote it down. Morrill of Maine sought to adjourn until June 23, and Ross moved to amend to fix the date as September 1; when this was lost, he voted for Morrill's motion.

All attempts at adjournment having failed, Williams' motion to rescind the order of balloting adopted ten days before, came up. This shabby effort to evade taking a vote upon the first article disgusted Fessenden, who told Wilson that it was "a nasty mean trick." John Sherman was annoyed that at least one of the articles voted on did not give the chance to vote no, so that he could justify his stand on opinion day.[14] But the caucus was adamant, insisted on the motion and carried it, Ross again voting with the Radicals. This succession of votes with the Radicals on the preliminary motions gave the impeachers the highest confidence in the outcome, while the Conservatives were almost convinced that the Kansas Senator had weakened under the pressure put upon him and had determined to save his political life.

Finally, at the Chief Justice's direction, the secretary read the second article, and began to call the roll. The Senators' responses showed that neither the ten day adjournment, nor Butler's villainous investigation, nor the Chicago platform, had shaken Fessenden, Fowler, Henderson or Grimes.

When Ross' name was called, stillness settled on the Senate.

On that day this obscure man from "Bleeding Kansas" was the most important member of their body, the pivot upon whose vote the fate of the President depended. As Ross arose from his chair, the click of a knife blade could have been heard throughout the Chamber. The Managers were motionless, their mouths agape. Senators ceased to whisper, spectators leaned forward, newspaper correspondents poised their pencils.

The Chief Justice spoke: "Mr. Senator Ross, how say you, is the respondent, Andrew Johnson, President of the United States, guilty or not guilty of a high crime and misdemeanor, as charged in this article?" Ross' answer came, clear as a bell. "Not guilty!" With it was heard a sigh of relief in the galleries. Johnson's friends grasped one another by the hand.

Hoping against hope, Williams immediately moved for the third article to be balloted upon. The result was identical with the other two. Ben Wade buried his chin in his shirt collar and seemed overcome with grief. Sumner's eyes were damp from unshed tears. Conness grew purple with indignation, while Howard seemed to be suffering a stroke of apoplexy. Others of the Pomeroy caucus were dazed and overcome. Now indeed impeachment was dead. "The great criminal" remained President of the United States.[15]

The Chief Justice thereupon directed that the vote proceed upon the first article. But this would never do. For then Sherman's vote and Howe's would be lost for conviction and, as article succeeded article, the votes against the President would become less and less. Williams jumped up to move that the Senate, sitting as a Court of Impeachment, adjourn without day. The Conservatives vainly sought to block this motion. The Chief Justice ruled the motion out of order. The Radicals overrode the opinion of the chair, and forced a vote upon adjournment.

The Chief Justice was determined on one point. Before announcing the result of the vote for adjournment, he informed the Senate that he was ordering an entry in the journal that the President had been acquitted. Thereupon the Court adjourned. The Impeachment farce was at an end.

The 26th was Tuesday, a Cabinet day, and so, while the final scenes of the Impeachment were being enacted on Capitol Hill, the President and his constitutional advisers were in session, contemplating the problems of government. Browning took note that Johnson was "calm and self-possessed as usual, and the Cabinet proceeded with business." The telegraph, *via* Willard's, kept them in touch with developments. When word as to Ross' vote on the preliminary motions was received, it put a damper on their spirits, a feeling intensified by the change in the order of articles to be voted on. Then came word that voting was in progress on the Second Article, quickly followed by a dispatch: "Ross stands firm and has voted right; the Article is beaten, 35 to 19." As the messages were brought in, the Secretary of the Interior carefully observed the mien of the President. "He was calm, dignified, placid and self-possessed," Browning noted, "with no outward sign of agitation, whatever passions may have glowed in his breast."

After the adjournment *sine die*, there was general jubilation among the Cabinet members. The President's face lighted up with "a pleasant and satisfied smile," but he retained his accustomed "calm, quiet composure."[16] Impeachment might be dead, but Andrew Johnson did not propose to dance on the fresh-turned grave. The victory was not his, but the country's and the Constitution's. "God's will be done," he told his callers that day.[17]

The reaction of the country was one of unfeigned satisfaction. Only the most extreme Radical organs continued to fulminate. The *Independent* might insist "that the President was not *honestly acquitted*," and might call his triumph "victorious shame";[18] Greeley might press forward for the punishment of the "corrupted Senators," but the country was regaining its common sense; the smallness of Johnson's offending and the enormity of the means used to convict him were beginning to be understood generally. "We shall hear no more of Impeachment," said the *Nation*, "and we are glad of it. After what happened, a verdict of guilty could have no moral weight." Editor Godkin went a step further and called attention to the fact that "the Butler investigation has thus far fastened suspicion on two of those who voted for conviction, a circumstance which we trust will not delay or impede inquiry. But no censure or punishment will be complete which does not reach the Missouri delegation, General Schenck, and the author of the Kansas telegram to Mr. Ross."[19] "Let a grateful people return thanks," rejoiced the Baltimore *Times*, "the nation is saved."

Butler's committee of investigation of the bribery of Senators came to an unlamented close. On May 20 the committee finally adjourned, "in disgust" at the lack of evidence.[20] But on May 25, the day before the second vote on the impeachment, the irrepressible Massachusetts demagogue had issued a "preliminary" report, made up of half truths, half suppressions and artful and malicious inferences. He was safe in his work of distortion, for none but rabid Radicals were members. Even so, while seeking to throw suspicion on the Senators who voted for acquittal, Butler was forced to admit that the only direct imputation had been against Pomeroy and his senatorial intimates, an imputation he brushed aside because they were "gentlemen of the highest honor!" In other words, only those who voted to acquit could be suspected. Henderson pointed out that such "logic" was "as vicious as the motives prompting the proceeding."

After the Court's final adjournment, Butler kept his probe going fitfully, more as an agency to wreak petty spite on his enemies than as a means of securing information. One by one, the members of his committee fell away from him. In July when he sought their signatures to the final "report," not a man would permit his name to be used. Butler alone signed this last outpouring of the scavengers, which was filed on July 4.

Fessenden wrote Grimes that it was "the most discreditable public paper ever issued in this country." Henderson said it was "a work of vengeance," designed to further the "selfish and malicious purposes" animating its "contemptible author." Fowler called Ben Butler "a being bloated by his own corrupt and discreditable passions," who had "sought to convert the Senate of the United States into a political guillotine." Even the mild-tempered Ross, stung by Butler's insults, referred to his "inefficiency and cowardice" in the war, and said that his "proneness to slime and uncleanliness" had caused the public "to insult the brute creation by dubbing him 'the beast.'"[21] From these characterizations of the report and its author, few modern students would dare dissent.

There were a few further echoes of the trial. On June 3 Sumner laid two resolutions before the Senate, seeking to declare the constitutional responsibility of Senators for their impeachment votes. The first asserted that, even assuming that the Senate was a Court, "Senators cannot claim that their votes are exempt from the judgment of the people." The second insisted that impeachment "is from beginning to end political, and that the vote of a Senator on impeachment, though different in form, is not different in responsibility from his vote on any other political question." To Grimes these resolutions were "the last straw," and he wrote Fessenden that they would be fatal to Sumner, if only someone would expose them.[22]

Ebullitions of wrath continued in the House. Thad Stevens kept proclaiming his intention of proposing further articles of impeachment. On July 7, on the eve of the Democratic convention, he made good his threat by offering five further articles. But their purpose was merely to offer opportunity for a characteristic tirade—almost his last. Never again, he thought, would a chief executive be "removed by peaceful means. If he retains the money and the patronage of the Government, it will be found, as has been found, stronger than the law, and impenetrable to the spear of justice." "If tyranny becomes intolerable," he prophesied, "the only resource will be found in the dagger of Brutus."[23]

It was Old Thad's valedictory, the last message to his followers of the Apostle of the Age of Hate. Within two months he was being consigned to self-selected ground in a negro cemetery in Lancaster.

There was little further talk of bribery. A committee had been named by the Senate to make its own investigations. On the last day of Johnson's term, its chairman announced that the committee had no formal report to make. "From no quarter," he said, "have we received any information which would even justify us in entering upon any regular investigation. . . . Nothing has appeared to justify any imputation upon any member of the Senate."[24]

The real epilogue to impeachment is not to be found in the shadow-boxing of the Radicals in the Halls of Congress, but in the way the avenging furies of party malice pursued the Senators who voted to acquit the President.

The number of Republicans who voted for the President was, strictly speaking, not seven but ten. In addition to the "seven traitors," Doolittle of Wisconsin, Dixon of Connecticut and Norton of Minnesota had been originally elected as Republicans. The difference between the situations of these three men and of the more famous seven was that as early as 1866,

Doolittle, Dixon and Norton had adopted the President's policies almost in their entirety and from that time on had been numbered as Johnson Republicans. Their votes for the acquittal of the President had been forecast from the beginning of the trial. Nevertheless, all three met short shrift with their legislatures. The Wisconsin legislature passed resolutions denouncing Doolittle's conduct and demanding that he resign. When he did not do so, he was emphatically rejected for reelection, and retired with Andrew Johnson, as did Dixon of Connecticut. Norton died in July, 1870, only a few months before he had completed his term; his successor had already been chosen by the Minnesota legislature.[25]

The verdict of history has been that "the glory of the trial was the action of the seven recusant Senators."[26] Their courage was of a rare order—almost beyond compare. And yet the malevolent predictions of Pomeroy's caucus as to their political fate proved all too true.

Fowler's term expired on the fourth of March, 1871. The Tennessee legislature relegated him to the discard. He did not return to the State, but remained in Washington until his death, a bookish man who spent much time browsing over musty volumes in Lowdermilk's. Nor did the West Virginia legislature dally with Van Winkle. His successor appeared in Washington at the beginning of Grant's first term. The Radicals were vexed at Trumbull's status. He still had five years of his Senate term to serve and nothing could be done with him until 1873. But the end of his term brought his inexorable retirement to private life.

Two days after the final vote, Grimes sent for Browning to express his wish that the Administration "be prudently and wisely conducted," a message promptly conveyed to the President, and cordially received by him.

Grimes never completely recovered from his paralytic stroke, but was not spared the Radical lash. Papers in Iowa sneered at his "recreancy" and said that he had voted "as none desired."[27] The stricken Senator remarked plaintively to a friend that perhaps he had done wrong "not to commit perjury by order of the party, but I cannot see it in that way."[28] And yet there were those who did not join in the clamor. The *Independent*, in the midst of scorching condemnation of the others, declared: "Grimes stands conspicuous as an honest exception among the conspirators. He was openly, frankly opposed to impeachment, and never deceived anybody."[29] Chase called upon him at his bedside to inform him, "I would rather be in your place, Mr. Grimes, than to receive any honor in the gift of our people."

"I shall always thank God that He gave me the courage to stand firm in the midst of the clamor," Grimes wrote a friend in January of the following year. "Neither the honors nor the wealth of the world could have induced me to act otherwise, and I have never for a moment regretted that I voted as I did."[30] A few months later, he resigned his seat and sought health and forgetfulness in a journey abroad.

Death spared Fessenden the humiliation of a defeat for re-election. Great honor came to him for his stern and rugged courage—but it did not come from the State of Maine. Eminent Bostonians might "all heartily recognize and admire" his "courage and conscientiousness under circumstances of peculiar difficulty" and invite him to a testimonial dinner. To the invitation might be signed such names as Francis Parkman, James Russell Lowell, Charles Eliot Norton and Charles Francis Adams, Jr., but the Radicals of Maine were after his political scalp. His term was due to expire in 1871. In the fall of 1869, Senator Fessenden discovered that the Radicals were organizing to oppose him. Newspapers in Bangor, Rockland, Calais and Biddeford opened a propaganda campaign against him, and the situation began to assume serious proportions. Always a fighter, this time Fessenden was not put to the test. On the last of August, he was stricken, and on the morning of September 9, 1869, died this man whom Grimes fondly termed "the ablest man of his day."[31]

Ross' trials were the most grievous of any of the seven, for he was to experience the full flavor of Kansas war-time passion. One of the justices of the Supreme Court of Kansas telegraphed him, shortly after his acquittal vote: "The rope with which Judas Iscariot hanged himself is lost; but Jim Lane's pistol is at your service."[32] He was burned in effigy throughout the State. At a mass meeting at Lawrence, presided over by Hugh Cameron, Ross was warned not to come back to his State. On the expiration of his term, he was remorselessly retired.[33]

The poverty-stricken ex-Senator went back to Kansas and opened up a printing shop in Coffeyville. He had barely got established when D. R. Anthony of Leavenworth, the same who had sent him the "perjurer and skunk" telegram, came to Coffeyville "to beat him up." A giant of a man and a bully of the worst sort, Anthony rushed into Ross' printing shop, knocked down his victim and beat him so unmercifully with his cane that Ross never completely recovered his health.

Ross' lot was hard in more ways than one. A cyclone struck the little town and scattered the contents of his printing shop over the prairie. When a local relief committee appealed for help for the impoverished ex-Senator, Trumbull gave $200 to the fund.[34] In 1875, Ross sent his congratulations to Andrew Johnson upon his election to the Senate. The note was written in pencil on paper of the cheapest kind, for Ross was living in the direst penury. His act of conscience had blasted his career.

There is, however, a single bright spot in his story. When he became President, Grover Cleveland appointed Ross Governor of the Territory of New Mexico. Ross was surprised one day by the arrival of an ancient patriarch with long gray beard and homespun garments. It was Hugh Cameron, the man who had presided at the Lawrence mass meeting. He had now walked all the way to New Mexico to apologize for his act.[35] In the late 'Nineties, an inquiring young man named Ashurst sought out Ross and tried to talk to him about his experiences in the Impeachment Trial. Although the old man seemed most reluctant to discuss the trial, his mind was as clear as a bell, and he impressed his questioner as having a well ordered intellect and as being a man "above the ordinary politician in force of character."[36]

A little before his death, Congress voted Ross a pension for his service as a soldier in the Civil War. In 1908, leading Kansas citizens undertook to have Ross' statue placed in the Hall of Fame at Washington.[37]

Although John B. Henderson did not escape immediate obloquy at home, the later phases of his career made it perhaps the least unpleasant of any of the seven. At the outset, the attacks on him were savage and relentless. Two days after the first vote, the St. Louis *Democrat* (despite its title the organ of the Missouri Radicals), declared that Henderson had made "a shameful record," having "insulted the moral sense and outraged the convictions" of his party, and that Missouri "will treat him as he deserves." Another paper charged that the Senator was "the meanest, the most white-livered, and the most

craven-hearted of them all." The St. Charles *Cosmos* thought
that he had received "a portion of that $10,000,000 which was
raised in Wall Street for the purpose of buying Radical Senators," and that, in any event, Henderson would find himself
"between Hell and the iron works."[38]   After his impeachment
votes, not only Henderson but his fiancée were burned in effigy
throughout the State.

In July the Senator carried on his campaign in Missouri,
defending his position and vigorously attacking his detractors.
At Macon, where he had twice been burned in effigy, he put his
case so staunchly that a Radical meeting tendered him an expression of "sincere thanks and improved confidence."[39]   But
such resolutions could not save his Senatorship any more than
could a curious declaration of Grant, then President-elect, that
Henderson's vote against impeachment ought not to hurt him,
since the Republican party would have lost the election if impeachment had succeeded.[40]   Missouri's Radical legislature
elected Carl Schurz, and Henderson returned to St. Louis to
resume the practice of law.

In Grant's first term, Henderson was government counsel
in the prosecution of General John MacDonald, General Orville
E. Babcock, one of President Grant's intimates and secretaries,
and others of the "whiskey ring."   The ex-Senator so flayed
Babcock's part in the liquor scandals that the President directed   the   lawyer's   dismissal   as   government   counsel.
Grant's famous phrase, "Let no guilty man escape," had
a hollow sound.   A little later Henderson took a leading part in
the organization of the Liberal Republican movement which
culminated in the ill-starred Greeley campaign of 1872.

In 1884 Henderson was selected for permanent chairman
of the Republican National Convention in Chicago.   When his
name was reported, the assembled delegates quickly caught its
significance, and cheer after cheer of applause followed.   He
was the only one of the seven "traitors" whom the party of the
Impeachers ever publicly forgave.[41]   He moved to Washington
in the 'Eighties, made some extremely sagacious realty invest-
ments, and lived until 1912, respected and honored by a great
host of friends.

Henderson told an interesting story of the aftermath of
the impeachment.   There had been a marked coolness between
Henderson and Charles Sumner ever since the latter's slur: "It

is the wounded bird that flutters." Several years after Henderson's forced retirement to law practice in St. Louis, he had occasion to go to Washington to argue a case before the Supreme Court. While there, he was much surprised to receive an invitation to dinner with Charles Sumner, but he accepted. After dinner, when the Missourian was about to leave, Sumner asked him to remain and when they were alone, he told Henderson that for several years he had wanted to have a private talk with him about the impeachment trial, adding impressively: "I want to say that in that matter you were right and I was wrong." When Henderson expressed his pleasure at this statement, Sumner continued: "I didn't want to die without making this confession, that in the matter of impeachment, you were right and I was wrong." After a moment's silence, he added: "But if it is just as convenient to you, I would rather you would say nothing about it until I am dead . . . and I won't live many years."[42]

A FEW hours after the Senate's adjournment *sine die* as a
Court of Impeachment, Edwin M. Stanton wrote this note
to the President:

> Sir: The resolution of the Senate of the United
> States, of the 21st of February last, declaring that the
> President "has no power to remove the Secretary of
> War and designate any other officer to perform the
> duties of that office *ad interim*," having this day failed
> to be supported by two-thirds of the Senators present
> and voting on the articles of impeachment preferred
> against you by the House of Representatives, I have
> relinquished charge of the War Department and have
> left the same and the books, archives, papers, and the
> property heretofore in my custody as Secretary of
> War in care of Brevet Major General Townsend, sub-
> ject to your direction.

Then he instructed Townsend to take charge of the Department, "subject to the disposal and directions of the President," dispatched that officer to the White House with his letter, gathered his personal belongings, and withdrew from his
battlements. No word of response came from the White House.
Johnson was of course happy to be rid of this thorn in his side,
but he was determined not to recognize the treacherous minister, even in his reluctant exit. Stanton went out, Welles
believed, "without respect, except on the part of ignorant and
knavish partisans."[1]

The next day the President had an order drawn under which
the Secretary of State was "authorized and empowered to perform the duties of Secretary of War temporarily, according to
law," but it was not issued. Lorenzo Thomas, who remained in
title the Secretary of War *ad interim*, was still fluttering about
the White House, but he received no fresh directions to take
over Stanton's abandoned citadel.

General Schofield's nomination had been sent to the Senate
a month before. But that body was loath to act upon it, because it read that Schofield had been nominated "in place of

Edwin M. Stanton, *removed*." Despite Johnson's acquittal, the Radical majority in the Senate would not admit Stanton's legal dismissal, while the President was equally determined not to yield. On the 29th, Seward determined to get in touch with the Radicals on the subject. "I will go to see Roscoe Conkling. . . . No mischief can go on without him." He did so, and Conkling suggested a new nomination of Schofield, without reference to his predecessor.[2] But the President would not listen. Finally the Senate took the bull by the horns, and adopted a resolution denying that Stanton had been removed and in the next breath confirming General Schofield in his place.[3]

With Schofield's entry, the President's troubles at the War office were over. When Welles asked if he considered Schofield reliable, the President answered that it would depend on the turn things might take. If the Conservatives seemed likely to win, the General would be with the President; if the Radicals succeeded, he would be with them. "In other words, Schofield is for Schofield." None the less, no Cabinet crisis arose in the remaining months of Johnson's term, and Schofield was later to pay tribute to the conduct and character of his chief.

There was another vacancy in the Cabinet—that of Attorney-General. Following the final acquittal, the President promptly nominated Stanbery for his old post. But the Senate, still smarting under the defeat of impeachment, pettily rejected him as a fitting rebuke for his having appeared as counsel for "the great criminal." Johnson next tendered the appointment to Judge Curtis, who declined. Seward then urged Evarts' name, the President consented, and he was nominated and confirmed. During his stay in Washington, Evarts livened up the Cabinet with his wit, and delighted Capital society by his dinners and levees.

The acquittal was followed by a train of rumors of wholesale Cabinet changes. The Democrats were eager to have at least Seward and McCulloch ejected, and the President gave a very careful consideration to a shift in the Treasury, but finally refrained.[4]

The Democratic presidential nomination was now occupying the attention of politicians. The Republicans, conscious of the many weak spots in Grant's political armor, were apprehensive; the Democrats believed that there was an opportunity to rehabilitate their party; while a host of Conservatives hoped against hope that the Democrats would so conduct themselves that the revolutionary Radicals would be overthrown.

There were a host of Democratic candidates, with George H. Pendleton of Ohio, McClellan's running mate four years before, Senator Hendricks of Indiana, General Hancock, and Horatio Seymour in the van. Chief Justice Chase had again been smitten with presidential fever, and the incomparable Kate Chase Sprague was in New York, managing his campaign. In the White House Andrew Johnson was nourishing great schemes about vindication at the polls.

Early in June public demonstrations for Chase began to be made, apparently under the direction of Horatio Seymour, who was felt to be "subtle, artful and not always sincere." On June 10 a secret meeting was held in Philadelphia, ostensibly to further the Chief Justice's candidacy; but the suspicious Welles believed that Seymour "means to be, and his friends mean that he shall be nominated, and their side moves are false and deceptive."[5]

Although early in the Impeachment Trial Chase had frowned on talk of presidential nomination, as its end approached he began to listen with eager ears to suggestions that he be made the Democratic nominee. The striking contrast between the Chief Justice's Radical views on the subjects of suffrage and political reconstruction and those held by the bulk of the Democrats was recognized as an almost insuperable obstacle by all except Chase and his most devoted advocates. But the Chief Justice bestirred himself to discover a Democratic platform, which would please the party members without his stultifying himself. He wrote to a friend in Cincinnati that the Democrats could assure a union of the anti-Radical elements by a platform assuring equal and exact justice for all men, the full restoration of the excluded States on the basis of universal suffrage and universal amnesty, and firm opposition to military government. On such a platform, he admitted, he "would not be at liberty" to refuse the nomination.

Late in May Chase receive a "private and confidential" letter from August Belmont, predicting that he would be named. The Chief Justice responded that he still remained a Democrat "upon questions of finance, commerce and administration generally." The slavery question was now settled, but national good faith required the vote for the freedman. Therefore he favored so much of the Radical program as based Southern

reorganization upon universal suffrage. He was unalterably
oppcsed to the exclusion of Southern citizens, the establishment of military despotism in the South and the use of military
commissions to try civilians in time of peace.

While Chase would welcome a Democratic nomination, he
made it plain that it must come upon such a platform as would
not make him stultify himself. Such a platform was drafted
and published a month before the Democrats gathered in Tammany Hall, and was praised in the press. James Gordon Bennett, that "strange old man, betrays a singular energy in your
behalf," an agent reported to Chase.[6] Seymour pretended to
be seeking to turn the New York delegation toward the Chief
Justice. The charming Kate Sprague sped to New York to
insure "this bright jewel" for her father's mundane crown. So
zealous was she in her electioneering that Chase sought to
moderate her zeal. "I am afraid that you are acting too much
the politician," he wrote. "Don't do or say anything which
may not be proclaimed from the housetops."[7]

Johnson's friends were equally determined. About the
middle of June, W. W. Warden, who had been so helpful in the
impeachment, proceeded to New York. A little later R. W.
Latham, Ralph Newton and Edmund Cooper joined him.
"Your friends have an awful load to carry in the Treasury,"
Latham soon reported. "Can't you confidentially give some of
us here either the news of a bold stroke at the Cabinet or something to say in explanation?" Newton pleaded.[8]

The Society of St. Tammany, then in the full flower of its
patriotic benevolence, under the leadership of Fernando Wood,
A. Oakey Hall and William Marcy Tweed, acted as hosts to
the convention, and Tammany Hall on Fourteenth Street had
been garishly decorated for the occasion. The long hair and
slouch hats of the Southern delegates, the friendly reception
accorded Vallandigham and other Copperheads, were seized on
by Radical papers as means to reincite the hatreds of the war.[9]
The Spiritualists, too, surrounded the Hall with their "batteries," to hurl their invisible missiles against the sweltering
delegates, hoping against hope to force Andrew Johnson's
nomination. Mrs. C. A. Coleman set up "within five rods of
Tammany Hall, and ceased not day or night her labors." Amy
Genner, a celebrated trance medium, was at work in Irving
Place, while Mrs. Stotts was nearer Tammany Hall. "Batteries are established wherever influential bodies are congre-

gated," a friend informed Johnson. "It may mean something and it may not."[10]

But the Democrats exhibited a tougher armor against the spirit world than had the judges of impeachment. Both the *World* and the *Herald* determined to ignore Johnson's claims for the nomination. As a counter-stroke, his agents urged a Cabinet shake-up and a new amnesty proclamation. "Your friends here are much disheartened," Latham reported. "They say it is impossible to elect you if nominated, with McCulloch and one or two other members of your Cabinet to carry."[11] But the President would not hearken to these hints.

"I am not ambitious of further service," he wrote on July 2. "I may add, indeed, of further endurance in that elevated and responsible position, unless by a call so general and unequivocal that it would serve as a plain indorsement by the people of my endeavor to defend the Constitution, and the reserved rights of the several commonwealths. . . . On such approval in the present temper of parties, I can perhaps have no reasonable expectation."

About this time he began work upon a new proclamation of general amnesty. "What I want," he told Colonel Moore, as they considered Seward's draft, "is to strike out all exceptions. . . . Take Jeff Davis' case, for instance. Suppose you except him? Do you not at once make him the martyr of the South? . . . I suppose there will be a howl made. But I don't care for that. The question is: Is such a step right? And if it is, I am going to take it." After preparing his draft, the President called in Reverdy Johnson, who remarked on the impolicy of the proposed amnesty, and then praised it. After he had left, the President told Moore, "if I issue a proclamation at all, I will make no exceptions. I will not mince matters." The proclamation was duly issued on the Fourth of July. It conferred free and unconditional pardon upon all persons under Civil War proscription, except those then actually under indictment. The Radicals received it with maledictions; some wrote the President that he deserved "curses and calamity." But a friend reported that it had been "beneficial in the extreme" in the New York convention, particularly with the Southerners.

On July 3, Colonel Moore cautiously sounded out the President as to the Democratic nomination. "Before God," the latter responded, "I would rather this moment pack up and leave this house and go to my old business than remain here subject to the insults and annoyances of the past." He told Moore that he was being asked: "Why don't I joint the Democratic party?" "Why don't they join me?" was his response.[12]

The amnesty, it proved, was insufficient to attract the nomination. And yet, by the morning of the 7th, Johnson was "anxious for the nomination," and told an intimate that, if nominated, he would resign his office, to make a vigorous campaign. In truth, the President was more anxious over the New York convention than he had been over impeachment. He was obviously "worried and nervous." On the 7th, however, Edmund Cooper sent word that "the indifference with which you are treated by the Northern Democrats, and the ingratitude of the Southern leaders, is well calculated to cause one to doubt the honesty and integrity of mere politicians."

Stung by Thad Stevens' speech to the House that "the only recourse from intolerable tyranny is Brutus' dagger," the President telegraphed Cooper in New York that his own nomination was demanded by the renewed Radical assaults. "How is it possible," the message read, "for me to maintain my position against a vindictive and powerful majority, if abandoned by those who profess to agree in principles with and to be supporters of the policies of the administration? Such an abandonment at this moment, when the heaviest assaults are being made, would seem an admission that the Administration was wrong in its opposition to the series of despotic measures which have been and are proposed to be forced upon the country." He felt sure that the will of the public, if truly reflected, would not be doubtful, but he had experienced ingratitude so often that no result would surprise him.[13]

In asking permission to publish the dispatch, Cooper commented upon the unpopularity of Seward and some other Cabinet members. Johnson immediately replied for his agent to exercise his own judgment as to publication, but as to the Cabinet, "are we not doing well in carrying seven Cabinet officers who were Republicans in favor of all the measures that the Democrats profess to support? Accessions of strength from some quarter [are] indispensable to the overthrow of the Radical order. Is it not also equally important to keep before the public the question of impeachment, in which Judge Chase and seven of their most respected, talented and influential Senators stood with us?"

The President insisted that it was no time for the Conservatives to change front. He pointed out that Grant had already been met twice and routed, and in the second encounter the General had been "met and convicted of deception and falsehood." In the impeachment, although Grant "was standing behind the seven Managers, . . . again he was repulsed, and driven back in shame and disgrace. And now, when the final issue is made, it is not time to change front, and while the enemy is in the field, to select some new leader to fight the last battle."

The convention quickly came to a deadlock. On the first ballot Pendleton had received the largest vote, with Johnson next. He was advised that if the New York and Pennsylvania delegations had united on him at any time on July 6, his nomination would have ensued. Johnson's managers were dazzled by Seymour's promises. The New Yorker, who was presiding over the convention, carefully outlined to Philo Durfree, one of Johnson's leaders, how the nomination could be secured for the President. It involved Seymour's own selection and his refusal in Johnson's behalf! Durfree trusted in Seymour and set out to carry out his scheme.[14] Chase's men were similarly beguiled. On July 9 Seymour was suddenly and unanimously selected. He did not decline. All that the convention had for Johnson was a weak platform indorsement, and for Chase, one even weaker. Welles was with the President when the telegram announcing Seymour's nomination came. He noted that while Johnson received the news calmly, "he was disturbed and disappointed."[15] When word came to Chase, his first remark was: "Does Mrs. Sprague know?" When told that she did, the Chief Justice asked, "And how does she bear it?" and seemed relieved when informed that she was calm in her disappointment.[16]

On July 11, Doolittle returned from New York to tell the inside story of the nomination; both he and the President expressed their distaste for it, the latter remarking that Seymour had not lifted a finger to sustain the Administration during its struggles, and that it was difficult for him to support such a ticket. Welles urged that Grant was even worse.[17]

Yet, although Johnson felt that Grant had treated him very badly, it does not seem to have warped his perspective as to the General's services during the war. In August the President wrote a long discursive letter to Ben Truman, in California. "Grant was untrue," he wrote. "He meant well for the first two years, and much that I did that was denounced was through his advice. . . . But Grant saw the Radical handwriting on the wall, and heeded it. I did not see it, or, if seeing it, did not heed it. Grant did the proper thing to save Grant, but it pretty nearly ruined me."

To this harsh judgment, he added, "I might have done the same thing under the same circumstances. At any rate, most men would. . . . Grant has treated me badly; but he was the right man in the right place during the war, and no matter what his faults were or are, the whole world can never write him down."[18]

Seymour's choice was an unhappy one. The Radical *Tribune* termed the Democratic nominee the deadly enemy to slavery's abolition, and lamented that if he were to be elected, "the patriot blood poured out like water . . . was shed in vain." The Conservative *Herald* saw "a clear field for General Grant."[19]

From Cincinnati, where he had resumed his practice, Henry Stanbery urged the President to keep his old Cabinet; "these gentlemen have stood by you faithfully on many trying occasions," he wrote. "I cannot see what possible advantage can be gained at this time by any change. . . . You will retire from office with a record of which any man might be proud, and which will grow brighter as the future develops the soundness of your views." But there was now no further question about Cabinet changes to assuage the Democrats. The question now perplexing Johnson was whether he should support Seymour and Blair. Dixon wrote him from Hartford that he felt that the nomination really had belonged to Johnson; but for the latter's courage and patriotism, what would the Democrats have to offer? Nevertheless, he felt the President should support the Democratic ticket.

The Democrats handled the hustings rather badly; among other errors, they indulged in flings at the War Democrats. "They are denouncing War Democrats as bitterly as Abolitionists," Edgar Cowan of Pennsylvania wrote Johnson. "These fellows think the President ought to give them all the offices in consideration of their forgiveness of him for the part he took in the great struggle, and I am getting tired of them."[20]

During the summer, many administrative problems pressed upon the President, and none more gravely than the condition of affairs in the Internal Revenue Bureau of the Treasury. E. A. Rollins, Commissioner of this bureau, was as violent a Radical as the executive service contained. Under him the whiskey ring had its origin, and evidence is not wanting that he was himself involved in the machinations of this far-flung cabal.

It has been the habit of several historians of Reconstruction to appraise Andrew Johnson on the basis of the faint praise bestowed on him by Secretaries Seward and McCulloch. But the truth seems that credit is due to Johnson for retaining these two Secretaries, rather than to them for remaining. The records show all too plainly that both Seward and McCulloch were devious and uncandid in their treatment of the President, and that both conducted their departments not in the interest of his Administration, but in their own, and often to his hurt.

McCulloch's case is an illustration. He was too close to Jay Cooke & Co., one of whose men visited him every morning, and often "made a good thing." His assistant secretary, William E. Chandler of New Hampshire, a Radical of high degree, almost flauntingly joined Stevens and Sumner in their war on his chief. The same was true of Rollins. Yet McCulloch would do nothing to eliminate these and other bitter enemies of Andrew Johnson from the department. The President smarted under this state of affairs. On June 8, he told his Secretary of the Treasury, in the presence of Colonel Moore: "We might take a loaded swivel and fire it into your department, without fear of injuring any of our adherents." When Chandler resigned, and the President nominated his Tennessee friend, Edmund Cooper, for the vacancy, McCulloch was charged with being responsible for the Senate's rejection of his name. The evidence as to Rollins' part in the whiskey scandals was damning, but McCulloch so feared to incur the anger of the Commissioner's Radical friends that he prevented effective prosecution.[21]

In the late summer of 1868, Rollins was brought to trial in a Federal court in New York, but the whiskey ring controlled the United States Attorney in whose district the trial was held, and he hampered the Government's special counsel at every stage of the proceedings.[22] The Washington lawyers who were pushing the case asked for a special fund to purchase a great mass of conclusive evidence offered to them. "For God's sake do something," read one appeal to the White House. But Johnson had no funds—the Radicals had seen to that—and McCulloch allotted a paltry $1,000 for the case!

The President was so concerned over the situation that he sent a confidential agent of his own to New York to ascertain the true situation. After investigation, the latter wrote that the only question was: "Shall the whiskey ring conquer the Government, or shall the Government conquer the whiskey ring?" After a visit to New York, Senator Doolittle reported that the District Attorney had sneeringly informed the Court that Fullerton, the special counsel employed for the case, had no status there to represent the Government, and had excluded him from any part in the trial, bringing the case to immediate disaster. In the three years in which the District Attorney had held his office, Doolittle continued, he had bought a brownstone house worth $40,000, and had otherwise grown very rich.

In the end, Rollins escaped conviction. The whiskey ring was fated to grow bolder and bolder under Grant, and the slimy trail of these public spoliators was to be found stretching into Grant's private circle, and leading to General Babcock, Grant's secretary and intimate friend.

Johnson's unsuccessful attempt to prosecute Rollins and his confederates aptly illustrates the practical effect of the Tenure-of-Office act upon public affairs. Because the Commissioner of Internal Revenue was a leading Radical, he must be protected in office, no matter what his official incompetence or dishonesty. Party attachment was deified while the public service was defiled and disgraced. The Tenure-of-Office Act tied the hands of the President; he was practically helpless either to promote efficiency in government service, or to prosecute and punish the betrayers of the public trust. Such was the extremity to which political partisanship, in its zeal to punish a President for daring to be merciful to a war-scarred people, had reduced the Chief Executive of the United States. As one indignant official wrote Johnson, Rollins' trial afforded "a most astounding disclosure of the rottenness of Congress."

To return to the political follies of 1868—the public did not warm up to Seymour, and even the Democrats remained rather lukewarm. Yet while Sanford Church, Dean Richmond, S. J. Tilden and other New York leaders maneuvered to secure the President's vigorous support, Seymour himself during most of the campaign did little to aid his managers, remaining at home and refusing to speak.

The Vermont and Maine elections in September, resulting in increased Radical majorities, confirmed the general belief that Seymour's nomination was disastrous.[23] The Democrats were so depressed that the Radicals whipped up considerable enthusiasm over Grant, as colorless a candidate as the nation ever saw. Although the General wisely refrained from making any campaign speeches, much political capital was made of his visit to Sherman in St. Louis. Then, when the two war heroes went together to call on Sheridan, the Radical presses shouted for joy.

Grant had been a tanner, and so "Tanneries" were organized throughout the country, the Republicans seeking to recreate the atmosphere of the "Tippecanoe and Tyler too" campaign. Grant's national committee levied heavily on the land-grant railroads and other large beneficiaries of Radical bounty. "The Boys in Blue" were carefully outfitted in new uniforms, and every effort was made to link patriotism and party in the public mind. "Let us have peace" was flaunted on transparencies, as was "William Penn was a carpetbagger."

As Radical efforts increased, so did Democratic apathy. Frank Blair, Seymour's running mate, stumped the West, and this had an unfavorable effect in the East. Seymour made a speech or two at county fairs, but that was all. Some of Chase's managers at the New York convention published embarrassing revelations as to Seymour's conduct there. He had approved Chase's platform of universal suffrage and sound money, they said. Now he was running on a platform quite the reverse. After his nomination, they continued, Seymour had gone to his room and had wept "for hours like a new-weaned baby."[24] "Prince John" Van Buren wrote the Chief Justice that Seymour had "never ceased a single day since the convention to reproach himself for 'yielding.' "[25] The Democrats had a candidate indeed.

The October elections but confirmed the omens in September of Vermont and Maine. The Radicals made great charges of Tammany directed frauds in Philadelphia and other large cities in Pennsylvania, Indiana and Ohio, which held October elections, but all three States went Republican. Hendricks lost the Indiana governorship; the Radicals carried Ohio by 17,000 and

Pennsylvania by 10,000. The Republicans had emerged, the *Nation* declared, "with a perfect certainty of success" in November.[26]

With this fresh disaster, came many suggestions for Seymour's withdrawal from the ticket and the substitution of Johnson or Chase. The New York *World* urged that now was the time to correct a mistake; let both Seymour and Blair retire.[27] The Democratic National Committee was agitated by the suggestion. It was reported that Seymour had forwarded his resignation and that it was in the Committee's hands.[28] This proved incorrect, for the nominee felt it would be "mean to shift his misfortunes upon some other's shoulders."[29]

Chase was strongly pressed as the man to save the situation for the Conservatives; his nomination even as a third candidate was urged. But the Chief Justice would have no hand in it. The *National Intelligencer* proposed Andrew Johnson as a refuge for the dispirited Democrats. The President received many letters urging him to force Seymour out. Senator Dixon confessed that every day it was more apparent that a grave error had been made in not selecting the man who had done "more than any living man" to give vitality to the Democratic cause. But Johnson was not beguiled by these urgings. He realized, as did the Democratic National Committee, that confusion would be worse confounded by a change at the last minute. He hoped that Seymour could be stung into effective activity, and telegraphed the nominee insisting that he take the stump against "the despotic power now ready to enter the very gates of the citadel. . . . I trust you may speak with an inspired tongue."

Seymour at last responded, and spoke at Cleveland, Buffalo, Detroit, Chicago, Indianapolis and other places. Democratic enthusiasm was engendered, but it was too late. The tide could not be stemmed. The results of the election on November 3 justified the apprehensions of the Conservatives. Seymour and Blair carried only eight States, and four of these were in the South. Tammany tactics accorded New York to the Democrats by 10,000, and New Jersey by 3,000. Delaware, Oregon, Georgia, Kentucky, Louisiana and Maryland completed the list. Seymour had been a great mistake.

One cannot help wondering what would have been the outcome had Andrew Johnson been the nominee in place of the inept New Yorker. To judge from the results in 1867, a

Thurlow Weed

Seward's *Alter Ego,* of Whom He Said "Weed's Seward, and Seward's Weed."

strong reaction in his favor had already set in. The Spring
elections of 1868 in New Hampshire and Connecticut during
impeachment gave further evidence of this same trend. It
seems certain that the Old Warrior had a greater hold on the
hearts of the common people than Seymour. Whatever else
might be said, Johnson would have carried his case to the
country. The election would not have been lost by default.

Although at first he seemed disheartened that "the country should have voted to continue Radical," the election outcome was no surprise to the President and his advisers. But
they did not regard it as a true referendum on the Administration; the issues had not been squarely presented to the people.
The election had been lost because of stupid nominations and
gross mismanagement of the campaign.

Johnson and his associates now bent their energies to clean-
ing up the unfinished business of the Administration, prepara-
tory to the induction of Grant and the Radicals. The most
vexing was the controversy with England over the *Alabama*
and other Civil War claims. When Reverdy Johnson had been
sent to England in the summer of 1868, he had carried instructions to come to an agreement for the arbitration of these
disputes. He found Lord Clarendon quite willing to negotiate,
and the result was the Johnson-Clarendon convention, which
was duly signed in London and dispatched to Washington in
November.

When Seward examined the treaty, he was disturbed. Ambassador Johnson had failed to secure many of the verbal
admissions of British guilt and responsibility which Radical
amour propre desired, and which were particularly sought by
Sumner, Chairman of the Senate's Foreign Affairs Committee,
who had been "twisting the lion's tail," to the amazement and
rage of his titled English friends.

Late in November Seward showed up at the Cabinet meeting with a puzzled look on his face. He told Welles that he
was sick over a "damned queer thing" from Reverdy Johnson—
the protocol! The whole thing was wrong and contrary to his
instructions. When the President examined the treaty, he
was not equally displeased, and told Welles that he wanted to
accept it. When Seward read to the Cabinet a proposed letter
of reprimand and new instructions to Reverdy Johnson, it
was generally disapproved. The President insisted on the

draft treaty's submission to the Senate. Thus the controversy would either be disposed of during his Administration, or the Senate would bear the responsibility for the failure. Soon thereafter, Seward changed his tune and became more optimistic over the negotiations.

When Congress assembled on December 8, it was in no cordial mood toward the acquitted President, and his message was not calculated to appease the Radicals. Johnson had drafted it without consultation with his Cabinet, and seemed desirous to embody in it, for the people and posterity, a final record of his views.

The reconstruction of the South was visited with his strong condemnation, the message pointing out further instances of its direful operation and praying for peace for a prostrate folk. In regard to national finances, after urging the strictest economy in appropriations, with a check to be put upon the Radical bounty to selfish private interests, he discussed the burden on the nation because of the outstanding United States bonds. These, he said, had been bought with the depreciated war-time currency; why should they be paid in gold? He thought it possible to pay interest on them for sixteen years and a fraction, which should serve in lieu of payment of the principal. The President's unorthodox ideas on finance were seized upon as repudiation by the Radicals. Johnson seemed not to have considered that his plan would have involved a national breach of faith. None of his Cabinet approved of it; indeed, none had known of it in advance.

In addition, the President urged several amendments to the United States Constitution—changes virtually the same as those he had urged many years before in his campaigns in Tennessee: direct election of United States Senators, direct election of the President, popular election of federal judges, etc. To the Conservatives of the day they seemed foolhardy, but the first of them has already been grafted on to the basic law.

After the Senate's reading clerk had read the first few paragraphs of the message, the Radicals rose in wrath, termed the communication an insult to Congress, and angrily forced adjournment with the bulk of the message unread. In the House, the message, after being listened to in silence, was denounced as infamous, and General Schenck insisted that it not be printed. The next day the Senate submitted to the completion of the reading, but a great attack was launched against the reference to the public debt. The President, who had expected the Radicals to be pleased with his plan, was surprised and disappointed at this reception.[30] He had not understood the high tariff and contracted currency support behind the Radicals. He did not understand the economic basis of the Sumner-Stevens assaults on him.

With the beginning of this Congress, there were premonitory symptoms of that carnival of corruption which was to mark Grant's administration. In their zeal of battle against the President, the Radicals had ceased to battle against the looting of the public treasury, and many of them became involved in the toils of the plunderers. The *Crédit Mobilier* scandals were already under way. Johnson struggled ineffectually to prevent the swindling of the government. He realized that evil things were being fostered. In December, Browning, Secretary of the Interior, brought the railroad scandals before the Cabinet, and there was general indignation. "The government and people have been terribly swindled and plundered by schemers," it was agreed, as one of the results of lavish subsidies and grants by Congress, "for party ends."[31]

The absorbing public question was Grant's Cabinet. Speculation went so far as to charge that Seward, Evarts and Mc-Culloch were seeking continuation in office. This aroused the indignation of the Secretary of the Treasury, who wrote the President that "if anyone in your Cabinet desires to retain his position under General Grant . . . *I am not the man.* With your Administration, my connection with public life ceases."

The Tennessee tailor's last months in the White House were not all toil and trouble, politics and petty war. Johnson had relaxed from the tension of the struggle with the Radicals, and now seemed eager to get what joy he could from entertaining his friends of all ages and degrees.[32] The White House had never been so brilliant and so popular. Never had it contained more bright and happy faces, heard more laughing voices and shouts of joy.

On December 29, the President's sixtieth birthday, there was a great children's party at the mansion. Households throughout the city were set agog when tiny tots received engraved cards saying that "The President of the United States" desired their presence. All of Marini's Dancing Academy was invited; in all his years at the White House, said Colonel Crook, "There never has been a children's party so wonderful."

The President, wearing a frock coat and striped trousers, stood at the entrance to the Blue Room and greeted his guests with open arms, as if to embrace them; his face beamed and his eyes smiled with the greatest affection as the children were presented to him, in groups. Mrs. Patterson and Mrs. Stover stood with him, equally happy. His wife, Eliza Johnson, departed from her usual custom and came down stairs to see the party. Dressed in black, with a lace cap falling to her shoulders, she received the children seated in a large arm chair, and smiled through tears at the happy throng.

The White House, brilliantly illuminated and profusely decorated with japonicas and azaleas, "looked like fairyland."[33] The dancing was in the East Room, where Marini's advanced pupils exhibited their fancy steps. Belle Patterson, the President's granddaughter, "a beautiful creature with fine golden hair to her waist, and a face like a beautiful flower," was running, jumping, playing and hanging on to Johnson's arm. Little Miss Garburri danced a Spanish dance; and there was a "Highland Fling" and then the "Sailor's Hornpipe." Finally the whole company lined up for the Virginia Reel. After that, the President led the way to the dining room for the refreshments, which little Mary DuHamel remembered for years and years—"gorgeous refreshments of ice cream and cakes and beautiful *glacé* fruit."

On New Year's Day there was another great reception at the White House. Three days before, the papers had announced that General and Mrs. Grant had left Washington to spend New Year's Day in Philadelphia; that they had done so in order that the General might avoid calling on the President on New Year's Day, as the custom of the service would have required had he been on hand. As if to mock this churlish attitude, Washington came to the President's reception in an unprecedented throng. By noon there was such a jam of Cabinet ministers, judges, diplomats and politicians that people could hardly move. Not only did official Washington call to pay its dutiful respects, but the people turned out by the thousands, as they had in Jackson's time. From eleven in the morning until late afternoon, they passed the President in a steady and congratulatory stream.

There was one unwonted figure in the procession: Ben But-

ler, with the leering eyes, bald head and strong, evil mouth.
Although startled to see him, and firmly convinced that Butler
was "the most daring and unscrupulous demagogue" he had
ever known, the President did not fail in formal courtesy to
this unexpected guest, but grasped the hand of the man who
had vilified and slandered him as badly as Old Thad had done.[34]

Grant's absence had been so disrespectfully conspicuous
that Johnson and his Cabinet began to discuss how the President should demean himself on Inauguration Day.   Welles
pointed out the precedent of 1829, when John Quincy Adams
and his Cabinet declined to attend the Jackson ceremonies.
Johnson, who had not known of this, was glad to be informed.

As January progressed, the Radicals on Capitol Hill began
to make ready for the new Executive.   On January 11, Butler
persuaded the House to repeal the Tenure-of-Office Act, thus
pointedly hinting to President Johnson that it had been passed
only for him.   The Senate did not immediately repeal the law—
such an admission would have been too bald—but it took great
pleasure in rejecting Johnson's nominations.   "Sunset" Cox
and H. A. Smythe were both rejected as ministers to Austria.
Two appointees to St. Petersburg and three to Ecuador were
thrust aside.   Five times, the President's nominations for a
successor to the shady Rollins failed of confirmation.   Similarly, Reverdy Johnson's treaty with England was violently
denounced by the Senate, Charles Sumner leading the attack.

On February 10, Congress counted the electoral votes, and
declared Grant duly chosen "with or without the vote of
Georgia."   Three days later a Radical committee formally
notified the General of his election, Oliver P. Morton of Indiana,
who headed it saying that "the friends of liberty throughout
the world" rejoiced at his election. Grant answered glumly, and
the ceremony was at an end.

During February, another amendment to the Federal Constitution was initiated by the Radicals.   It was declared briefly:
"The right of citizens of the United States to vote shall not be
denied or abridged in the United States, or by any State, on
account of race, color, or previous condition of servitude."
Once more Charles Sumner irritated his fellow extremists by
objecting to their plan.   He insisted that Congress already
had full power to enfranchise all negroes without any further
sanction of the Constitution.   There was a feeble suggestion of
votes for women; one or two Senators shamefacedly admitted

that perhaps an intelligent white woman had as much right as an ignorant negro plow-hand to determine the destinies of the nation. But there seemed little political advantage in women suffrage, and one by one the Radicals went back on their promises to Elizabeth Cady Stanton, Lucretia Mott and Susan B. Anthony. At the end of February, the Fifteenth Amendment was sent on its way to the legislatures of the Union, and women were left without the ballot for another fifty years.

Andrew Johnson contemplated these Radical preparations with disapproval, but there was nothing that he could do. In his usual, orderly way, he set about preparing for his departure. He called for all the bills he owed and paid them. He received and declined many offers of free transportation to Europe from the steamship companies. He carefully supervised the filing of all of his official papers. "I found nothing here when I came," he remarked, "and I am going to leave nothing here when I go." His voluminous correspondence was boxed up, his official records, pardon registers, appointment registers, and scrap books, were removed for shipment to his old home in Greeneville.[35]

As Inauguration Day neared, Welles' apprehension as to Grant became more pronounced. "Horse flesh has more charms for him than brains or intellect," he commented. "He loves money, admires wealth, is fond of power and ready to use it remorselessly." Father Gideon felt sure that Grant did not propose to study public affairs, but would let his Cabinet Members rule their departments like military commanders. "The appointment of his friends to office is the extent of his ideas of administrative duties."[36]

On February 21 Welles urged the President not to go to the Capitol on March 4 to sign bills, but to remain at the White House until noon. At a dinner at General Schofield's a day or so later, after discussion, it was generally agreed that all members should tender their resignations and should not induct their successors into the departments.

On Washington's Birthday the White House was the scene of another great reception, among those attending being a committee of seventy-five distinguished citizens of Baltimore with Mayor Banks at their head. They presented a resolution of their city council inviting the Old Warrior to visit Baltimore as the city's guest, before returning to Tennessee. The President was greatly touched by this tribute.[37]

On March 1 it became known that Grant had told the Committee on Inauguration Ceremonies that he would neither ride in the same carriage with Andrew Johnson nor speak to him. The Tennessean was no more willing to ride in the carriage with Grant than Grant was to ride with him. Crook overheard him bluntly refuse to sit beside the man who had lied to and betrayed him.[38] Dismayed at these developments, the Committee suggested a plan for the retiring and incoming Presidents to ride in separate carriages, and it was even suggested that there be two processions. But Andrew Johnson put an end to such tastelessness. He was determined to observe a certain decency and self-respect.

Evarts and Seward were still urging him to go to the Capitol to be present at the inauguration itself. Johnson hesitated, and finally evaded a decision by directing that the various members of the Cabinet meet at the White House at nine o'clock on Thursday morning, March 4, when they would decide what to do.[39]

On Tuesday, faithful Vinnie Ream asked the President to come to her Capitol crypt to look at her figure of Lincoln. "You are both good and great," she wrote, "and if you approve, the criticism of others would not so much dishearten me."

On the evening of March 3, the White House was jammed with a great reception; hundreds of friends and officials gathered to pay their respects, and hundreds of others were forced to drive away, unable to obtain entrance. Welles commented scornfully that many of those who were there "were the wild fanatical partisans who have busied themselves in slandering, defaming and misrepresenting the President." None the less, the occasion was generally interpreted as a great triumph for the President.

At nine o'clock the next morning, the members of the Cabinet began to assemble at the White House. The President remained sitting at his desk, examining and signing bills. "I think we will finish our work here," he informed Welles, the first arrival, "without going to the Capitol." Welles was glad. Other members entered, but still Johnson remained at his desk examining the last minute bills from Congress. Evarts came in, but did not take off his overcoat, so anxious was he to be off to the Capitol. A little later, McCulloch said that they were expected at the Capitol. Seward entered puffing a cigar. After a few minutes he interrupted to ask: "Ought we not to start immediately?" "I am inclined to think," the President answered, "that we will finish up our work here by ourselves." But he did not utter a word of complaint against anyone that day.[40]

A little after twelve, Johnson arose and announced that the time had come for them to part. He shook hands with each, uttered a few cordial words of farewell, and descended to the portico. All the White House attendants were gathered there for a final word. With a "God bless you," he entered his carriage and was driven off. The Cabinet Members followed quickly behind him.[41]

A few minutes later, President Grant drove up the Avenue, entered the White House and was greeted by the eager throng awaiting him. The Radicals at last had complete control of the Government.

Andrew Johnson's last public act as President was a message to the American people. It was speeding over the telegraph wires as General Grant was taking the oath in front of the Capitol. It was more than a defense of his administration. It breathed the tailor-statesman's three chief public attachments—the Union, the Constitution and the Common People. It was a plea for justice and for peace.

After calling attention to the outrages of the Radical majority in Congress, to the acts of conscription and confiscation, the denials of personal liberty, the imposition of bayonet rule, the humiliation of the whites and exaltation of the negroes "for party ends," he turned his attention to the scenes of corruption which had followed inevitably in the train of tyranny. "The servants of the people, in high places, have boldly betrayed their trusts," he declared. They had inflamed prejudices, retarded the restoration of peace, and "exposed to the poisonous breath of party passion the terrible wounds of a four years' war." They had engaged in class legislation, and had encouraged monopolies "that the few might be enriched at the expense of the many."

But Andrew Johnson's thoughts had been different. They had been "those of peace, . . . My effort has ever been to allay contention among my countrymen." "Forgetting the past," he concluded, "let us return to the first principles of the Government, and unfurling the banner of our country, inscribe upon it in ineffaceable characters: 'The Constitution and the Union, one and inseparable.'"

Of Johnson as President, a German historian has written an estimate which soundly states the case. "The evidence," this scholar found, "proves him firm in character, and a wise man. . . . History, an unprejudiced judge, will recognize the great merit of his work for the Union, and will consign to deserved oblivion all evil slander."   In Andrew Johnson, "integrity of character paired with practical wisdom and honorable intent."[42]

W HEN he left the White House, a private citizen for the first time in thirty years, Andrew Johnson was driven to the house of his devoted friend, John Coyle, one of the proprietors of the *National Intelligencer*. Mrs. Patterson and her family were visiting the Welles family. They were to stay in Washington two weeks longer to procure the necessary articles to make habitable the Greeneville home to which, despite proposals of European tours, Johnson had decided to return.

In accordance with his promise to the Baltimore committee, the former President left Washington on the morning of March 11, on his visit to that city. A committee of distinguished Marylanders had come to escort him. Upon his arrival, the square around the Camden station was found to be filled with a great applauding throng. When Johnson descended, a troop of cavalry and a battery of field artillery stood at attention and a great band played. The ex-President entered an open carriage drawn by four gray horses, and the parade began. The streets were lined with men and women and children, cheering, shouting and waving handkerchiefs and flags.

A little later a great levee was held, and thousands of people waited for hours to shake hands with the Defender of the Constitution. When a number of pretty young ladies stepped up, the President showed a new trait of his character by kissing them one by one resoundingly on the cheek, while the spectators "seemed to derive as much pleasure from the operation as the ex-President himself."[1]

That evening a great banquet was given, with covers laid for 275. The toast to "Our Guest" expressed Baltimore's admiration of "the patriot statesman . . . the bulwark of equal rights, and the defender and martyr of the Constitution." Johnson gratefully responded. "My deliverance," he concluded, "has been the greatest case of emancipation since the rebellion commenced." The next day he returned to Washington with Maryland's plaudits ringing in his ears.[2]

On March 18 the Johnson party began its homeward journey to Greeneville. In addition to the retiring President, there were Mrs. Johnson, now a frail old lady; Martha Patterson and her husband, whose Senatorial term had ended on the 4th of March; Robert Johnson, and the children. At Lynchburg enthusiastic citizens entertained the party in a manner quite different from that which had marked Johnson's stay there eight years before. At a great reception in his honor, the ex-President said that he was on his way to his home in Tennessee, where he planned to go into retirement, but that he was bearing "the advice of Cato to pray for Rome."[3]

There was also an impromptu reception at Bristol. The special train carrying the party from Bristol to Greeneville had to stop at almost every station along the way so that the people might see and hear the returning warrior. At Limestone, where the crowd shouted that Johnson would have to run for governor, he remarked to a newspaper correspondent: "Yes, there is a good deal of life in me yet."

Eager to receive its distinguished townsman with proper honors, the Greeneville town council had met on March 17 and passed a resolution that it would go to the station in a body to receive and welcome him, without specific indorsement or repudiation of the policies of his presidential career. But the Mayor of the town, a petty Radical, said that the reception was intended to indorse Johnson's policies, and vetoed the council's resolution![4]

None the less, there was a jollification as the train arrived. Four of Greeneville's prettiest girls—Lulu Evans, Maria Harmon, Bert and Kitty Crawford, all granddaughters of old friends of the statesman—presented him with great bouquets of flowers and led the procession that escorted the Johnson family to the house of a friend. There, from an open porch, addresses of welcome were made to him, and Johnson replied.

"I feel proud," he said, "in coming back among old friends to help them bear the burdens, if I can do nothing to relieve them." Then came a note of warning. "If the Constitution is not wrested from the hands of the usurper, in a few years the government will be gone," he prophesied. And at the last there was a phrase of disillusion: "An old man, weary with the cares of state, has come to lay his bones among you."[5]

Thus, after eight years, Andrew Johnson again took up his abode among the Greene County folk who loved him. With his return to Tennessee, there came much speculation as to what he planned to do. Would he really go into retirement, to live among the bitter memories of his presidential years, or would he reenter Tennessee politics?

By frugality and prudent investment, Johnson had accumulated what for those days was considered a substantial fortune. In the spring of 1869, he was worth probably $150,000. He began to improve his Greeneville property, and a little later bought a large brick business building. The rumor grew that he planned to use it either to organize a bank or to reopen a wholesale and retail tailoring establishment. People of the town noted him as he walked down the street, his hands clasped behind his back, a silk beaver hat resting on his head bent in meditation. Frequently he would take long walks through the woodlands.

Johnson enjoyed this interlude of relaxation, but he had made up his mind to get back into the fight. Even while beset with presidential cares, he had commented that, in his case, to live he must be busy. He dreaded the effect of retirement and rest, and he had welcomed the talk of entry into Tennessee politics which came to him two months before he left the White House.[6] A. A. Kyle of Rogersville wrote urging on him the public duty of running for governor, while Colonel Cooper reported that he found "the people—the masses—more than anxious" for Johnson to enter the race.

Late in March, he intimated to his friends that, while he was out of public life "for the time," he owed all that he was to the people of Tennessee, and if they commanded, he would try to help them lift their burdens. A week later he told a Knoxville audience of 5,000 that the measure of his ambition had been satisfied and he sought nothing more, "but in returning to your midst, is it anything unnatural that I should desire to set myself right before you, and not be misunderstood?"

Early in the summer, Johnson made a great tour throughout the State. He went to Knoxville, spent several days there with the richest man in town, and held a levee, making friends with his former secessionist foes.[7] He rode from city to city in a special train, and made many speeches. In these he took pains to set himself right with the negroes. His objection to negro suffrage, he declared, had not been that he did not want the negroes to vote, but that granting suffrage was a State, not a federal function. But his chief theme was that Congress had usurped the functions of the government and had pushed aside the Constitution; under the Radicals, it was becoming a vast and remorseless empire. How long would the people bow their necks to despotism?

In June, when he visited Washington to see his son in school there, the ex-President told a New York *Herald* correspondent that Grant did not "understand the philosophy of a single great question, and is completely lost in trying to understand his situation. He is mendacious, cunning, and treacherous. He lied to me flagrantly, by God, and I convicted him by my whole Cabinet."[8] While in the capital, a throng of several thousand called upon him, clamored for a speech and cheered him to the echo.

On his return to Tennessee, he continued his exhortations. At first, his Tennessee audiences had received him with deference; now they manifested increasing approval. The Tennessee Radicals took alarm and adopted counter-measures. On August 2, at Maryville, they organized a mob to break up a Johnson meeting, and made three charges on the speaker's stand. Unawed by the tumult, the Old Warrior abashed them and forced them back every time. The better element of the State was humiliated at this ruffianly conduct, and vigorously expressed its disapproval.[9]

The occasion for this statewide appearance of the former President was the pending election of a Governor of Tennessee and the members of the legislature. Late in February, when Brownlow had resigned as Governor to accept Patterson's seat in the Senate, D. W. C. Senter, speaker of the Senate, had succeeded to the gubernatorial chair. Already unpopular with Tennessee's Radical leaders, Senter wanted to be elected to succeed himself. For commissioners of registration he named Republicans who had favored a liberal interpretation of the Radical franchise laws. In May his policy was strengthened by a decision of the State Supreme Court that any person with an old election certificate could use it. Thus a great anti-Radical vote was created in Middle and West Tennessee. Senter had the support of the Conservative elements in his campaign. Johnson stumped the State, urging Senter's election and the choice of a Conservative legislature. In every speech, he carried the war into Africa by his assaults on the Radicals.

The results were the triumph of the Governor over his Radical opponent and the election of a Conservative legislature. After these unexpected events, the State began to buzz with the possibility that the former President might be elected to the Senate which so lately had tried his impeachment.

Upon this prospect, Radicals of the North and the South showed their apprehensions. President Grant told a Tennessee Radical that he would regard Johnson's coming to the Senate as "a personal insult" to himself.[10] Boutwell, now Secretary of the Treasury, cried in alarm that Johnson's election "will raise gold from 136 to 200 and thereby endanger the national debt." The Radicals tried to inflame the apprehensions of the bondholders, and the report was circulated that a large sum of money had been raised to use in the Tennessee legislature to encompass Johnson's defeat.

To this chorus of attack, the Conservative and Democratic papers responded vigorously. "No man in the State," the St. Louis *Republican* declared, "could represent Tennessee with greater ability or usefulness." The Nashville *Union and American* predicted that "he may be thrust into office against his will," and a great demand went up in the State from the common people that their spokesman throw his hat into the ring.

Democrats in Washington were watching the Tennessee situation with keen attention. On August 8 Samuel J. Randall wrote Johnson of "the great joy which has been expressed by your friends . . . over your triumph in Tennessee. I know of no political event of recent years which can compare with it. You have once again fastened your foot upon the necks of your enemies and traducers." But Randall warned him that the Radicals were raising money in Washington and through the North "to corrupt the legislature of Tennessee and thus defeat your election as Senator," and suggested that the Tennessean have Edmund Cooper report any evidence of the expenditure of any such fund, so that the Democrats in Congress would expose it.[11]

Tennessee was bitterly divided. It was urged against Johnson that East Tennessee already had one Senator. Others feared that his selection would tie the State to his personal grievance. One editor hinted that Johnson would give offense to Grant. But the Old Warrior went straight ahead, putting his devoted friend Edmund Cooper, now a state Senator, in charge of his campaign.[12]

The legislature met in October, and on the 19th, Cooper put Johnson in nomination. His "reputation as a statesman of broad and comprehensive views and of incomparable integrity and unflinching courage," he said, "is coextensive with the nation itself." On the first ballot, Johnson received eleven votes in the Senate and thirty-two in the House. The fourteen Senators and forty-nine representatives against him were divided among the number of candidates. On the second and third ballots, Johnson's manager complimented his brother, Henry Cooper, a Senator from Davidson County, by voting for him, but on the next four he returned to Andrew Johnson.

On the eighth ballot, Johnson had lacked but two votes of the necessary number for success. Some of his ambitious and determined friends determined to be "practical," and secure the needed men. They set to work and presently one of them, a former president of the Nashville and Chattanooga Railroad, said: "Mr. President, you will be elected tomorrow." Johnson expressed his doubt. The friend answered that he had secured the necessary two votes.

"How?" Johnson inquired.

"I have to pay $1,000 for each vote," the railroad man replied.

"You will do no such thing," Johnson answered indignantly. "Go and tell those rascals the deal is off."

Upon his friend's demurring that he could not do it, as he was in honor bound to complete the deal, Johnson thundered: "But it is my honor that is involved. If I am elected by those purchased votes, as sure as the Lord lets me live, I will go before the legislature and expose the fraud and refuse to accept the election."[13] And Johnson had his way.

On the evening of October 21, one of the roistering young blades of the town, very much in his cups, staggered into Johnson's room in the Maxwell House, cursed him wildly, and announced his intention of cutting the ex-President's throat. The young drunkard was quickly hustled out of the room, but the story was magnified a thousand times, and added to the excitement of the packed hotel lobbies.[14]

That same evening, a secret caucus was held at the City Hotel by the Radicals and the few Conservatives who, because of private bitternesses, were willing to join with anyone to block Johnson's election. Emerson Etheridge, old line Whig and Unionist though he had been, announced that he would support and vote for any man upon whom they could unite, "even if it were a negro."[15] Other Conservatives who personally hated Johnson expressed similar sentiments. One of the editors of the *Republican Banner*, the Nashville organ of the Radicals, suggested that they center upon Henry Cooper, in order to attract the vote of the brother of their candidate, Johnson's friend and manager! The group seized upon the plan. Edmund Cooper had not been in the caucus and was much embarrassed and disturbed at its decision, but finally agreed to the plan. On October 22, a Radical nominated Henry Cooper, and he received fifty-five votes to Johnson's fifty-one, and was thus duly elected to the Senate of the United States.[16]

Conservatives the country over were regretful over the outcome. The New York *Herald* suggested that Johnson had fallen between two fires; the bitter Radicals and the equally bitter ex-Confederates had combined against him, the former because of his policy of mercy to the South while President, the latter because of his support of the Union while the war itself was being waged. But it was not Johnson's presidential policies which had defeated him, the Nashville *Union and American* declared. "The members of the legislature that contributed mostly to his defeat were those who sustained his policies both during the war and during his presidential term. It was his Democracy that defeated him."[17]

Yet, bitter though he was against the Coopers, Johnson did not blame all the legislators, for he later gave a great supper to the assemblymen, and filed away in his papers the receipted bill from the Stacy House for $664.00.[18]

During this same session of the legislature, the Conservative majority decreed a new constitutional convention. Johnson followed the sessions with sympathetic attention. The new

Constitution was ratified at the polls, and in 1870 went into force. The legislature immediately repealed the Radical election and franchise laws, a step which the Radical North interpreted as the undoing of Reconstruction. Threats were made that Federal bayonets would be sent to Tennessee to insure negro rights. When Governor Senter's request for legislation to suppress the Ku Klux Klan was not met, he asked Congress to reconstruct the State, and the Reconstruction Committee held a prolonged investigation.

Stirred by these developments, the speakers of the two Tennessee Houses issued a joint statement claiming that the legislature had done everything in its power to remove all political distinction against the negroes. To the general surprise, Grant did not send troops into the state. General Forrest announced that the Tennessee Klan had disbanded, and federal interference was avoided.

Early in 1870, it was disclosed that the Radical who represented the First Tennessee District in Congress had sold a West Point cadetship. In March, the House passed a vote censuring him and took up the question of whether or not to expel him. But as the Radicals feared that Andrew Johnson would be sent to succeed this worthy, the motion for expulsion fell short by twelve of the necessary two-thirds vote.[19]

During this year, Johnson remained at Greeneville, and rumors revived that he planned to reenter business. He spent most of the time in his study, talking to old friends, reading newspapers, and writing letters and articles in defense of his policies. Whenever there was a court day, his house would be filled with friends from the country. His conversational style must have been somewhat difficult. He would state his views and then would demand that his listener "Answer that!"

The former President seemed ever keen to extend the circle of his friendship. Two young lawyers from the North established themselves in Greeneville, and he quickly cultivated them. Another young man, a former colonel in the Confederate Army, came to Greeneville to practice law. Two or three days after he had hung out his shingle, a distinguished gentleman entered his office, saying, "Mr. Reeves, I suppose; my name is Andrew Johnson." He paced up and down the office floor, telling the briefless lawyer that fees would come to him slowly at first. "I have traveled the road of poverty, and have felt its pinch," he continued. "If at any time you shall be in need of some financial help, just call on me, and it will be my pleasure to aid you." Then he said "Good day" and walked out. A little later Reeves was given a place on the *National Union*, Johnson's organ at Greeneville, and was formally appointed secretary to the tailor-statesman.[20] The addition of an ex-Confederate to his staff was a crafty political stroke. Johnson subdued his prejudices to accomplish his great ambition—his vindication by the people of Tennessee.[21]

He was urged to run for Congress from his old district, but refused; he did not think this a great enough vindication. Yet his mind could not keep away from politics and public problems. In the summer and fall of 1870 he made a few speeches, chiefly concerning the onerous nature of the public debt and the villainy of Congressional Reconstruction. He predicted that Grant would be reëlected because the majority sentiment against him in the nation could not be consolidated. Thus he kept his views before the people of the State.

In 1872, under a general redistricting bill, Tennessee was accorded an additional member of Congress, and there was some discussion about selecting him from the State-at-large, rather than from a newly created congressional district. In May the Nashville *Union and American* announced authoritatively that if such a course was followed, Johnson would be a candidate. His friends became active in his behalf, and Colonel Reeves was dispatched to Nashville.

According to instructions, the night before the Democratic State Convention at which the Congressman-at-large would be nominated, Reeves called on the Old Warrior in the latter's favorite room, No. 5, at the Maxwell House. After locking the door, Johnson told his aide of the pressure on him to become a candidate, but that he could not do so, because he had laid plans to run for the Senate to succeed Brownlow in 1875. "I would rather have the vindication of my State," he continued, "by electing me to my old seat in the Senate of the United States than to be monarch of the grandest empire on earth. For this I live, and will never die content without. . . . Go to the convention tomorrow, and if my name is put in nomination, promptly withdraw it on my authority."[22]

The ex-President's directions were carried out, and on June 21 General Cheatham, Reeves' old Division Commander, was nominated by acclamation. Horace Maynard was selected by the Radical Republicans.

On his way home, Reeves was amazed to read an announcement from Nashville that Johnson had announced an independent candidacy for Congressman-at-large. The ex-President never explained this sudden change to his Confederate secretary, nor gave him an opportunity to ask about it.[23]

The announcement aroused furious public discussion. The former Secessionists were vitriolic in their denunciation of this candidacy, which they rightly feared would result in Cheatham's defeat. A pamphlet was issued, in which the ex-President was raked fore and aft for all the sins of his career. F. C. Dunnington of Columbia, with Johnson's pardon in his pocket, assailed him as having "betrayed" his State, and quoted the harsh phrases of the first month of the Presidency about "traitors" needing to be "made odious and impoverished." With Johnson, he charged, ambition had become a passion; he had never "passed an eulogy on any living thing, except himself."[24]

But Johnson's friends were equally enthusiastic and combative in his behalf. There was a great demonstration in Nashville late in August. A band of workmen headed a monster procession to the public square, ending in a meeting at which the Old Warrior was formally put into nomination.

This campaign was one of the great political battles of Tennessee, ranking with the forensic combats of James K. Polk and "Lean Jimmy" Jones, Johnson's own tilts with Gustavus A. Henry and Meredith P. Gentry, the more recent War of the Roses between Bob and Alf Taylor, and the Patterson-Carmack joint debate. But the former President was greatly handicapped. Most of the Conservative papers had already committed themselves to Cheatham. The chief incident was a great three-cornered debate. The candidates opened at Bristol, and proceeded westward through the state. One meeting of the three aspirants took place in a cedar grove near Lebanon, a little Middle Tennessee college town. Cheatham was no orator. He haltingly read the speech the editor of the Nashville *Union and American* had prepared for him, but the crowd applauded him to the echo. His main theme was that, after twenty-seven years in office, Johnson ought to give him a chance.

Earnest, quiet, deliberate, Johnson spoke without a trace of bombast.[25] His appearance was dignified and courtly, but "while he never ranted, his eyes were ablaze." His words, readily understandable, revealed mastery of the English language and breadth and play of intellect. The impression he made was not of eloquence, but of impressive truth; his chaste, well chosen language, his homely, apt illustrations, and his remarkable magnetism compelled people to listen to him.

General Cheatham had denounced Johnson with bitterness. The ex-President, while assailing Toombs, Yancey and other Southern leaders who had precipitated Secession, was courteous toward Cheatham himself, but minced no words in defending his own support of the Union. He had stood for the Union and the Constitution in 1861 and recanted not a single word. He was still for the Union and the Constitution and therefore was determinedly opposed to the Radical Reconstruction scheme.

A crowd of rowdies kept crying out: "Tell us something about Mrs. Surratt." But having learned a costly lesson in the "Swing Around the Circle," Johnson ignored these shouts from the crowd, and kept to his closely reasoned speech. At the beginning, the great majority of the crowd was unfriendly to him, but upon his conclusion he received a great ovation.

The debate was closed by Horace Maynard, then in the height of his power as an orator; "he wielded the blade of an Aladdin," one who heard him there recounted. None the less, Johnson had the honors of the triangular argument. His sincerity had won the crowd.

Many stories yet linger concerning this famous campaign. A beginning lawyer at Jasper was amazed to see the former President toss off a tall tumbler of peach brandy with as much unconcern and with as little perceptible after-effect as if it had been water.[26] After a speaking engagement in the Sequatchie Valley, Johnson had himself driven to the Tennessee River, to cross it and catch a train to Chattanooga. When the yawl in which he was being ferried ran aground and he saw the train approaching, the campaigner jumped into the river and waded to the bank.[27] That afternoon he was on hand at old James Hall in Chattanooga to cross swords with his two competitors.

The meeting lasted all afternoon. Cheatham, as usual, was

brief in his discussion, and Maynard masterful in his attack on Johnson's Administration. But the former President carried off the honors. "His impressive earnestness," an auditor declared, "was penetrating. No competitor indulged in an anecdote but once. Mr. Johnson made the orator ashamed of himself for wasting the time of the people when the momentous issues of their country were under discussion." At the close of the debate, Maynard retired to his hotel "as exhausted as a race horse that had run four miles." But a crowd, with a band of music, appeared to serenade Andrew Johnson, who came out of his hotel, mounted a baggage truck at the Union Depot, and made a touching speech. As he approached, the crowd warmed up and one old Irishman jumped on the truck and took the speaker in his arms, shouting, "It's the same Andy of 1856!"[28]

"Maynard will be elected," Johnson told friends before the vote, "but I have succeeded in breaking up that military ring in Nashville."[29] His prediction was verified. Maynard received 80,000, Cheatham 63,000, and Johnson 37,000 votes. The tailor-statesman was not disappointed, for he had "reduced the rebel brigadiers to the ranks."[30]

In 1873 East Tennessee was visited with a fearful cholera epidemic. Johnson and his family had the means to flee the plague, but this did not seem an example to set and they remained in Greeneville. At length, the ex-President was seized with the cholera. For a while he was at the point of death; after several weeks he rallied, but he never fully recovered his strength.

On June 9, when his infirmities seemed about to overcome him, the stricken statesman gave a last message to his friends. "Approaching death to me is a mere shadow of God's protecting wing," he wrote. "Here I know can no evil come; here I will rest in quiet and peace beyond the reach of calumny's poisoned shaft; the influential, evil and jealous enemies; where treason and traitors in States, where backsliders and hypocrites in the church, can have no place, where the great fact will be realized that God is Truth, and gratitude the highest attribute of man."

Later that year, the famous Johnson-Holt controversy over the case of Mrs. Surratt arose. Holt began it by a long diatribe in the Washington *Chronicle* of August 25. The Judge-Advocate-General had been so harried by the reports that he had suppressed the recommendation of mercy that he sought to deny the charge. Surprised at this bold declaration, Johnson wrote some of his old associates, including Colonel Moore and Gideon Welles, for their recollections, and in October published a dignified but crushing reply.

The panic of 1873 was wreaking havoc in the country. Among the banks which failed was the First National Bank of Washington, which at the time had on deposit $73,000 of Johnson's savings. His loss was so generally discussed in the press that he issued a statement that even if the entire amount was lost, his resources would be sufficient to maintain him.[31]

Later that fall, someone asked if he planned to be a candidate for the Senate. "Of course I will," he answered jocularly. "The damned brigadiers having been destroyed, what hinders me from going to the Senate?"[32]

When Johnson started his campaign for the Senate in the fall of 1874, no one thought he had any chance. But he planned very shrewdly. First, he sent Reeves around to check up on the preferences of the new legislators. Then he himself opened a powerful campaign against Governor Neil Brown, one of the candidates for Brownlow's seat, with incidental denunciation of the Coopers. Most of the legislators were divided in their attachment between Governor Brown and General Bate, the latter having a slight advantage.[33]

Johnson was much pleased at Reeves' report. "Brown can't be elected, but he is desperate," he told his aide. "Brown will not let Bate, and Bate, being the stronger of the two, will not let Brown be elected, therefore the two will fight each other instead of fighting me; my plan is working just as I have contrived."[34]

The response to Johnson's Swing Around the Circle in the State was also gratifying. He covered Tennessee from Bristol to the Mississippi, and everywhere attacked Brown alone of the Senatorial competitors. In every speech he also denounced the Cooper brothers, this excoriation forming the climax and culmination of his speech. It was a blistering invective. He was scheduled to speak at Columbia, the home of Colonel D. B. Cooper, half brother of the "traitors." Before he reached the town, word came that if he repeated his denunciation there, he would be killed.

On his arrival, he learned that a bitter political enemy had secured the Court House and was talking against time to keep him out. Thereupon Johnson instructed two young men to find some goods boxes, and put them outside the Court House—he would speak from them. They placed them under D. B. Cooper's window.

"I have been told," the Old Warrior began his speech, "that if I repeated here today what I said on former occasions, perhaps I would be assassinated. But these two eyes have never yet beheld the man that this heart feared. I have said on former occasions, and I repeat it now, that Jesus Christ had his Judas, Cæsar had his Brutus, Charles I had his Cromwell, Washington had his Benedict Arnold, and I have had my Edmund and Henry Cooper." As he paused, pistols were cocked and trained on Cooper's window. But there was no sign of trouble. Johnson went on with his speech.[35]

The legislature, which met on January 4, 1875, was made up of ninety-two Democrats and eight Republicans. On January 19, it proceeded to the Senatorial election. In addition to Johnson, Brown and Bate, William H. Quarles, William H. Stephens, Edwin H. Ewing and John H. Savage were put into nomination. On the first ballot, Johnson had ten more votes than any other candidate. A deadlock between Brown and Bate quickly developed, and the feeling between their supporters grew more bitter day by day. As Johnson predicted, each was determined that the other not be named.

The former President stayed in his room at the Maxwell House, listening to reports and impressing all comers with his optimism. But he was not without wile. General Nathan Bedford Forrest had come to Nashville to work in behalf of General Bate. "When the gods arrive, the half-gods depart," Johnson told Forrest. "If the people really wanted to send a Confederate military hero to the Senate," he said, "they would elect Forrest himself, instead of a 'one-horse general.'" Struck by the force of this observation, the Wizard of the Saddle abandoned his efforts for Bate, and went back to Memphis.[36]

After four days of exciting and fruitless voting, Brown, Stephens, and Quarles withdrew, and their strength went to Andrew Johnson. On the 44th ballot, Bate had forty-eight, just one shy of the necessary number; the former President had forty-two. "I may not be elected, but Bate never will be,"

Johnson declared, on learning this news. "When a man gets that close, and does not get the final one vote necessary, he never will get it."[37] His prophecy proved correct.

Bate withdrew the next day and Brown reentered. On the fifty-fourth ballot, Johnson secured three new votes in the Senate. He maintained his strength in the House, and was thus chosen, by a majority of one, to succeed Parson Brownlow in the Senate of the United States.[38]

Upon the election, young Alf Taylor, Republican Representative from Carter County, ran from the Capitol to the Maxwell House, dashed up the steps to Room No. 5, shouted: "Mr. Johnson, you are elected!" and then fell in a faint. The new Senator was dashing water in his face when the less speedy Reeves arrived. In a moment N. B. Spears of Marion County, a huge giant of a man, lumbered in, seized the new Senator by his feet and trotted around the room with him, dancing and capering with joy. As the news spread over Nashville, a great crowd assembled at the Maxwell House to cheer the vindicated statesman.[39]

The night after Johnson's election, a great mass meeting was held in his honor. George W. Jones, the saddle-maker who had become the watchdog of the Treasury, and then had followed his State, presided. It was a great moment when he introduced his life-long friend, the tailor who had gone with his nation, to the throng in his hour of final triumph. The new Senator made a speech in which he paid tribute to the affectionate perseverance of his friends. "Look to the legislature," he said, "and see how many Confederate soldiers supported me. How many Republicans do you think supported me? . . . There they were all united around the altar of the country, and gave their decision in favor of me."[40]

Nor did he neglect to thank individual legislators, and to tender them sound advice. "What I have to say seems very simple and unimportant," he said to young Benton McMillin, then finishing his first term in the General Assembly. "But it is of the utmost importance to one who seeks favor of the public. If you should continue in public life, be sure of one thing . . . that you always strive to keep in touch with and on the side of the *common people*. With them for you, corporations and combinations may organize against you . . . but they will war in vain. . . . Keep the common people on your side and you will win."[41] It was advice from the depths of his heart.

This final triumph caught the attention and aroused the admiration of the country. No "common man," Thurlow Weed wrote the editor of the New York *Tribune*, "could have dug himself out of a pit so deep and so dark as that into which he had fallen."[42] Every mail brought the new Senator congratulations from the whole nation. General Custer wrote delightedly from Fort Lincoln. Groesbeck and Stanbery were almost transported with delight. "I have received so many personal congratulations," wrote the latter, "that I almost began to think I was myself the successful candidate—such a shaking of hands I have not gone through for many a day. . . . There is more real satisfaction in your success than I have known upon the election of any Senator."

In Buffalo, exultant New York Democrats fired one hundred guns in honor of the great triumph. Citizens of Atlanta held a great public meeting on January 30 to pass resolutions of delight. In transmitting them, W. M. Lowry added, "Who knows, my dear sir, but that in the whirl of events you may be the next Democratic candidate for President?" Ex-Governor Joe Brown, now President of the Western and Atlantic Railroad, sent him an annual pass and asked him to visit the Georgia capital. From Chattanooga, D. M. Key wrote of the genuine joy that Johnson's election had given "to all parties, not only in your own State, but throughout the nation."[43]

The newspapers of the country, Radical and Conservative alike, paid tribute to Johnson's indomitable pluck. The St. Louis *Republican* termed his election "the most magnificent personal triumph which the history of American politics can show." The Nashville *Union and American* said that he had never been greater than in the moment of his victory. The Cincinnati *Commercial* testified to the common people's abounding faith in him, and the New York *Times* predicted that he would have something to say well worth the Nation's hearing. Johnson's "personal integrity was beyond question," said the *Nation*, "and his respect for the law and the Constitution made his Administration a remarkable contrast to that which succeeded it."[44]

President Grant soon called the Senate into extra session to act on a treaty with the ruler of the Sandwich Islands. It was to begin on March 4, and Johnson proceeded to Washington. On March 4 the Senate galleries were packed, and as the new Senator from Tennessee walked down the aisle, thunderous applause burst from them.

The Senate was to organize the next day. Johnson's desk was covered with flowers sent by admirers. A little after noon, the ex-President entered the Senate, his sturdy form clad in old fashioned broadcloth, and a group quickly formed around him. Edmunds of Vermont, who had voted to impeach him, was addressing the chair. He looked at the group about Johnson, faltered in his speech, "kicked over a lot of old books on his desk, and abruptly sat down." Roscoe Conkling pretended to read a letter, but looked slyly at Johnson from the corner of his eye. Frelinghuysen sank to his knees after a book. Carl Schurz, now a liberal Democrat, stood up. John Sherman at first seemed not to know what to do; then he approached and shook hands. Oliver P. Morton was in a dilemma. First he had supported Johnson and then he had voted to convict him. But the Tennessean magnanimously stretched forth his hand. "He wore the same kindly smile as in times before," Morton later said. "That showed nobility of soul. There are not many men who could have done that!" Boutwell sat at his desk, perhaps meditating on "the hole in the sky" to which seven years before he had proposed that Johnson be consigned. Physically, the former President had changed less than almost any other Senator on the floor. His hair was somewhat thinned, but the *Herald's* correspondent noted that there were neither "hard lines, nor deep wrinkles in his face"; his expression, however, showed a mixture of earnestness and sadness.

The clerk began to call the roll for newly elected Senators to take the oath. "Hannibal Hamlin" he called, and Lincoln's first running mate responded. "Andrew Johnson" he continued, and Lincoln's second running mate answered, "Present." Then Johnson's Tennessee colleague—it was Henry Cooper!— came down the aisle, bowed stiffly, and with Senator McCreery of Kentucky escorted the new Senator to the Vice Presidential desk, where he stood beside Hamlin and Burnside of Rhode Island. Vice President Henry Wilson of Massachusetts, who, seven years before, as a Senator, had voted not only to convict Johnson of high crimes and misdemeanors, but likewise "for his disqualification from hereafter holding any office under the Constitution he has violated and the government he has dishonored," administered the oath. After he had sworn, the Tennessean turned and shook Hamlin's hand and then that of the Vice President, to a tumult of applause and cheers. As he went to his seat, a little page stepped up and handed him a bouquet.[45]

Throughout this scene, Johnson bore himself composedly, but to avoid its continuance he retired to the cloakroom, followed there by former enemies eager to shake his hands. "I miss my old friends," he told McCreery, with tears in his eyes, "Bayard, Buckalew, Reverdy Johnson, Fessenden, Fowler, Trumbull, Grimes, Henderson, Ross, all gone, all but yourself." Gone likewise were some of his enemies. Sumner's fine figure was no more to be seen. Ben Wade had been removed by the people of Ohio. Of the thirty-five Senators who voted to convict, only thirteen remained.

There was a good deal of speculation throughout the country as to how Johnson would conduct himself. "I have no wrongs to redress but my country's," he told a correspondent. "My election settled all personal injuries ever inflicted. I come now to deal only with present issues."[46] When the *Tribune's* correspondent commented that his two rooms on the second floor of the old Willard were not as commodious as his former home on the Avenue,[47] the Old Warrior answered, with a twinkle in his eye, "But they are more comfortable."

A day or so after he had taken the oath, Johnson sent for his old friend Crook to come to see him. He wanted to know where in his scrap books he would find the notices about Grant. "You remember where you pasted them in," he said to his old attaché; "I don't." Crook turned the pages, put in the proper markings and rose to go.

Then the ex-President unburdened himself, "Crook, I have come back to the Senate with two purposes," he said. "One is to do what I can to punish the Southern brigadiers. They led the South into Secession, and they never have had their deserts." Crook asked what was the other. "The other is to make a speech against Grant, and I am going to make it this session."[48]

Sure enough, his one speech during the special session of the Senate was on Grant. He made it on March 22, in connection with a resolution which Grant men had introduced into the Senate to approve that President's action in using Federal

troops to prop up the unspeakable Kellogg's villainous administration in Louisiana. Announcement had been made that the
Tennessean planned to speak, and the galleries were filled with
people eager to hear him turn the tables upon Grant. The
subject was fruitful, for it is doubtful if any of the Southern
carnivals of corruption which masqueraded as governments were
more shameless than that in Louisiana. The crowning outrage
—thus far—had come when Grant presumed to ignore the verdict of a State, and to place by force an expelled adventurer in
the Governor's chair.

"The President of the United States assumes to take command of the state and assign these people a governor," the
indignant Senator from Tennessee proclaimed. He read Grant's
weak excuse that the election at which Kellog had been displaced was "a gigantic fraud." If such were the case, Johnson
commented, both candidates were disqualified. But the truth
was that "the President finds a usurper in power, and he takes
it upon himself to make the Government of the United States
a party to his usurpation. . . . Is not this monstrous in a free
Government?"

The Constitution had been trampled under foot so often
that no one knew whither things were drifting. "Is Louisiana
a commonwealth as it now stands? Or is her government maintained by military power, and that through the President of
the United States? Is it his government?" He urged the
Senate to defeat the resolution for Grant's indorsement, and in
its place to make him the Catonian answer: "Bid him disband
his legions; return the commonwealth to liberty." These
alarums of Southern outrages, he hinted, were planned so that
"in the midst of the war cry," Grant could "triumphantly ride
into the Presidency for a third presidential term." "And when
this is done," he shouted, "farewell to the liberties of the country." The galleries broke forth into wild applause, which was
repeated when he asked, "How far off is empire? How far off
is military despotism?"

His conclusion had the ring of his speeches on the eve of
Sumter: "Give me the Constitution of my country unimpaired.
. . . In the language of Webster, let this Union be preserved
'now and forever, one and inseparable.' Let us stand equals in
the Union, all upon equality. Let peace and Union be restored
to the land. May God bless this people, and God save the
Constitution."

It was Johnson's last great public speech. Two days later the Senate adjourned, and he returned to his home in Tennessee. He stayed at Greeneville for several weeks, seeming particularly happy with Martha Patterson and her children. On July 28, he set out to visit his other daughter, Mary Stover, who was living in Carter County, about two miles from Elizabethton.

On the train from Greeneville to Carter Station, the ex-President talked with Alf Taylor, who found him "never more interesting." Captain W. E. McElwee of Harriman, another old friend who was on the train, elicited from Johnson this retrospecting: "More than a hundred times I said to myself: 'What course may I pursue so that the calm and great historian will say one hundred years from now, "He pursued the right course"?'" McElwee remembered that Johnson had termed Stanton the "Marat of American politics" and had explained that he was not assassinated by Charlotte Corday, "but had cut his damned throat from ear to ear." It was kept out of the public press, Johnson continued, but Stanton had cultivated his vindictive anger until "his reason was dethroned."[49]

When Johnson alighted at Carter's Station, his daughter's buggy had not arrived, and young Selden Nelson, son of his counsel in the impeachment, procured him a horse.[50] He had not ridden far when the Stover buggy met him, and he reached his daughter's farm about an hour before noon.

Johnson had often said that, when he died, he hoped and expected to go "all at once and nothing first."[51] His hope came true. After lunch that day, his granddaughter, Lillie Stover, walked to his room with him. As she was going out, she heard a heavy thud; Johnson had fallen on the carpet. It was a stroke of paralysis. As he lay in bed the next day, he talked of the days of long ago, of his tailor shop, political campaigns, the battles of ante-bellum Tennessee. Another stroke followed, and he became unconscious. He lingered on, until at 2:30 on the morning of July 31, Andrew Johnson died.

The Stover house was filled with mourners, plain people from the hills. Early Sunday morning, the family set out for Greeneville with the body. The town was draped in black. The old tailor shop was hung with mourning. With difficulty a suitable casket was secured for the body; the silver plate upon it was engraved: "Andrew Johnson, Seventeenth President of the United States." "When I die," he had said several years before, "I desire no better winding sheet than the Stars and

Stripes, and no softer pillow than the Constitution of my country." Remembering, his friends wrapped him in a fine new flag with thirty-seven stars, while they placed his worn and much thumbed copy of the Constitution beneath his head.

Knoxville, Nashville and Memphis each asked the privilege of affording burial to the departed statesman. But his family denied them all; in Greene County's soil he should be laid to rest. He had himself selected the spot for his burial, a cone-shaped hill about half a mile from his home. With his own hands he had planted there a willow from his yard, the offshoot of the tree brought from Napoleon's St. Helena tomb.[52]

All Tennessee and much of America was represented at the funeral. The procession, more than half a mile in length, included the great and the humble, the statesmen from the national capital, and the unkempt mourners from the hills. Blackstone McDannell walked at the head of the coffin, and the procession slowly made its way through the little town to the chosen hillock.

After the sonorous phrases of its burial, a Masonic choir chanted the requiem, a bugler sounded taps, and Andrew Johnson was at rest.[53]

Among those who attended the funeral was a boy of seventeen, a young printer on the Knoxville *Chronicle* named Adolph Ochs, on his first news story. He had telegraphed to several papers seeking the assignment to "cover" the obsequies, and Henry Watterson's Louisville *Courier-Journal* had ordered 250 words. About a year later, when young Ochs, now a reporter for the Knoxville *Tribune*, revisited Greeneville, he found that Johnson's grave had not been marked. After the publication of his story telling of this, his paper received a letter from Mrs. Patterson, explaining the reason for the delay. The Master Tailors' Association of the United States, she wrote, had asked the privilege of erecting the monument to the nation's only tailor-President, and the family had agreed. But the association had been slow in carrying out its plan.

Soon thereafter, the Pattersons themselves undertook the erection of an appropriate monument.[54] A few months later it was unveiled with fitting ceremony, and Andrew Johnson's life-long friend, George W. Jones, made the chief address.

There, in the friendly soil of his beloved Greene County, rests Andrew Johnson, his head cushioned on the worn copy of the Constitution, his body wrapped in the Stars and Stripes. Carved on the simple shaft above him are the words: "His faith in the people never wavered."

APPENDIX

AUTHORITIES CONSULTED AND CITED IN
THIS VOLUME

MANUSCRIPT:

Bates, Edward, Ms. Diary, Miss Helen Nicolay, Washington.
Black, Jeremiah Sullivan, Mss. Library of Congress, Washington.
Bradford, A. W., Mss., Maryland Historical Society, Baltimore.
Breckinridge, Family Papers, Library of Congress, Washington.
Chase, S. P., Mss., Library of Congress, Washington.
Comstock, Chas. B., Mss., Library of Congress, Washington.
Ewing, Hugh, Mss., Hon. George Ewing, Columbus, Ohio.
Ewing, Thomas, Mss., Library of Congress, Washington.
Fowler, Joseph O., Mss., Mrs. Fowler Shankland, Los Angeles, Calif.
Holden, W. W., Mss., North Carolina Historical Commission, Raleigh, N. C.
Holt, Joseph, Mss. Library of Congress, Washington.
Johnson, Andrew, Mss., Library of Congress, Washington.
Johnson, Andrew, Mss., Pennsylvania Historical Society, Philadelphia.
Johnson, Andrew, Mss., Col. A. J. Patterson, Greeneville, Tennessee.
Johnson, Robert, Mss., Col. A. J. Patterson, Greeneville, Tennesee.
Logan, John A., Mss., Library of Congress, Washington.
Moore, W. G., Diary Transcript, Library of Congress, Washington.
Nelson, Thomas A. R., Mss., Lawson-McGhee Library, Knoxville, Tennessee.
Stanton, Edwin M., Mss., Library of Congress, Washington.
Sumner, Charles, Mss., Harvard College Library, Cambridge, Mass.
Surratt, Mary E., Record of Military Commission, War Department Archives, Washington.
Welles, Gideon, Mss., Library of Congress, Washington.

CHIEF NEWSPAPER AND PERIODICAL SOURCES:

American Historical Review
Banner, Nashville, 1869-75

Century Magazine, New York, 1912-3
Chronicle, Washington, 1866-8
Congressional Globe.
Evening Post, New York, 1868
Herald, New York, 1865-8
Independent, New York, 1865-9
Nation, New York, 1865-9
Plain Dealer, Cleveland, Ohio, 1866
Press, Nashville, 1864-5
Star, Washington, 1865
Taylor-Trotwood Magazine, Nashville, 1908
Tribune, Chicago, 1868
Tribune, New York, 1865-8
Union and American, Nashville, 1869-75
Whig, Jonesboro, Tenn., 1845
World, New York, 1868-9

PUBLISHED VOLUMES:

American State Trials, St. Louis, 1917, Vol. VIII
Andrews, Eliza F., *War Time Journal of A Georgia Girl,* New
York, 1908.
Andrews, Sidney, *The South Since the War,* Boston, 1866.
Andrews, Marietta Minnegerode, *My Studio Window,* New
York, 1928.

Badeau, Adam, *Grant in Peace,* Hartford, 1887.
Baker, Lafayette C., *History of the United States Secret
Service,* Philadelphia, 1867.
Bates, David Homer, *Lincoln in the Telegraph Office,* New
York, 1907.
Bacon, G. W., *Life of Andrew Johnson,* London, n. d. (ap-
parently 1866).
Beale, Howard K., *The Critical Year,* New York, 1930.
Belmont, August, *Letters and Addresses,* New York, 1890.
Benjamin, Marcus, Ed., *Washington During War Time,* Wash-
ington, n. d.
Beveridge, A. J., *Abraham Lincoln,* Boston, 1928.
Blaine, James G., *Twenty Years of Congress,* Norwich, Conn.,
1884.
Bowers, Claude G., *The Tragic Era,* Boston, 1929.
Brabson, Fay W., *The Political Career of Andrew Johnson From
His Retirement From the Presidency to His Death,* unpub-
lished thesis, Vanderbilt University, 1912.
Bradford, Gamaliel, *Union Portraits,* Boston, 1916.
Brigham, Johnson, *James Harlan,* Iowa City, Iowa, 1913.

Browning, Orville K., *Diary*, J. G. Randall, Editor, Springfield, Ill., 1930.

Bryan, W. B., *History of the National Capital*, New York, 1914.

Burgess, John W., *Reconstruction and the Constitution*, New York, 1902.

Butler, Benjamin F., *Butler's Book*, Boston, 1892.

Butler, Benj. F., *Private and Official Correspondence*, Norwood, Mass., 1917.

Callender, E. B., *Thaddeus Stevens*, Boston, 1882.

Caskey, W. M., *First Administration of Gov. Andrew Johnson*, East Tennessee Historical Society *Publications*, Knoxville, Tenn., 1929. *Second Administration*, etc., Knoxville, 1930.

Carpenter, F. B., *Six Months in the White House*, New York, 1866.

Channing, Edward, *History of the United States*, New York, v.d.

Clarke, Allen C., *Abraham Lincoln in the National Capital*, Washington, 1925.

Clemenceau, Georges, *American Reconstruction, 1865-1870*, New York, 1928.

Colman, Edna M., *Seventy-Five Years of White House Gossip*, New York, 1925.

Correspondence with Provisional Governors, Washington, 1866.

Cowan, Frank, *Andrew Johnson Reminiscences*, Greensburg, Pa., 1894.

Cox, S. S., *Three Decades of Federal Legislation*, Providence, R. I., 1885.

Craven, John J., *Prison Life of Jefferson Davis*, New York, 1866.

Crook, William H., *Memories of the White House*, Henry Rood, Editor, Boston, 1911.

Crook, William H., *Through Five Administrations*, Margarita S. Gerry, Editor, New York, 1910.

Curtis, George Ticknor, *Memoirs of Benjamin Robbins Curtis*, Boston, 1879.

Depew, Chauncey M., *My Memoirs of Eighty Years*, New York, 1922.

DeWitt, David Miller, *The Impeachment and Trial of Andrew Johnson*, New York, 1903.

DeWitt, David Miller, *The Judicial Murder of Mary E. Surratt*, Baltimore, 1895.

Dicey, Edward, *Six Months in the Federal States*, London, 1863.

Dickinson, John R., *Daniel S. Dickinson*, New York, 1867.

Dunning, W. A., *Reconstruction, Political and Economic,* New York, 1907.

Eckinrode, H. J., *Rutherford B. Hayes,* New York, 1930.
Ellis, John B., *Sights and Secrets of the National Capital,* New York, 1869.

Fertig, James Walter, *The Secession and Reconstruction of Tennessee,* Chicago, 1898.
Fessenden, Francis, *Life of William Pitt Fessenden,* Boston, 1907.
Fleming, Walter L., *Documentary History of Reconstruction,* Cleveland, 1906.
Foulke, William Dudley, *Life of Oliver P. Morton,* Indianapolis, 1899.

Gorham, George C., *Edwin M. Stanton,* Boston, 1899.
Gouverneur, Marian, *As I Remember,* New York, 1911.
Greenhow, Rose, *My Imprisonment at Washington,* London, 1863.
Gurowski, Adam, *Diary,* 1861-2, Boston, 1862; 1862-3, New York, 1863; 1863-5, Washington, 1866.

Hall, Clifton R., *Andrew Johnson, Military Governor of Tennessee,* Princeton, 1916.
Hamlin, C. E., *Life and Times of Hannibal Hamlin,* Boston, 1898.
Hesseltine, W. B., *Civil War Prisons,* Columbus, Ohio, 1930.
Hitchcock, Henry, *Marching with Sherman,* New Haven, 1927.
Holden, W. W., *Memoirs,* Durham, N. C., 1911.
Hudson, Frederic, *Journalism in the United States,* New York, 1873.

Impeachment Investigation, Government Printing Office, Washington, 1867.
Impeachment Trial, Government Printing Office, Washington, 1868.
Irelan, John Robert, *Times of Johnson,* Chicago, 1888.

Jones, James S., *Andrew Johnson,* Greeneville, Tenn., 1901.
Julian, George W., *Political Recollections,* New York, 1883.

Keckley, Elizabeth, *Behind the Scenes,* New York, 1868.
Kendrick, Benjamin B., *Journal of Reconstruction Committee,* New York, 1903.
Kirkland, Edward Chase, *Peacemakers of 1864,* New York, 1927.

Lamon, Ward Hill, *Recollections of Abraham Lincoln,* New York, 1911.

McCarthy, Charles H., *Lincoln's Plan of Reconstruction,* New York, 1901.
McClure, A. K., *Old Time Notes of Pennsylvania,* Philadelphia, 1905.
McClure, A. K., *Lincoln and Men of War Times,* Philadelphia, 1892.
McCulloch, Hugh, *Men and Measures of Half a Century,* New York, 1888.
McPherson, Edward, *Political History of the United States During the Rebellion,* Washington, 1882.
McPherson, Edw., *Political History of U. S. during Reconstruction,* Washington, 1880.
Moore, Frank, *Speeches of Andrew Johnson,* Boston, 1865.
Morgan, James Morris, *Recollections of A Rebel Reefer,* Boston, 1917.
Morrow, Honore Willsie, *With Malice Toward None,* New York, 1928.
Morse, John T., *Abraham Lincoln,* Boston and New York, 1896.

Nicolay, J. G., and John Hay, *Abraham Lincoln, a History,* New York, 1890.
Nevins, Allan, *Fremont, The West's Greatest Adventurer,* New York, 1928.

Oberholtzer, Ellis P., *A History of the United States since the Civil War,* New York, 1917.
Official Records of the Union and Confederate Armies, Washington, v. d.

Pearson, Henry Greenleaf, *John A. Andrew,* Boston, 1904.
Perry, Benj. F., *Reminiscences of Public Men;* First Series, Philadelphia, 1881; Second Series, Greenville, S. C., 1889.
Piatt, Don, *Memories of the Men Who Saved the Union,* New York, 1887.
Pierce, Edward L., *Charles Sumner,* Boston, 1893.
Polk, James K., *Diary,* Chicago, 1910.
Pollard, Edward A., *The Lost Cause Regained,* New York, 1868.
Poore, Ben: Perley, *Perley's Reminiscences,* Philadelphia, 1886.

[Rayner, Kenneth], A National Man, *Andrew Johnson,* New York, 1866.
Republican Party, Proceedings of First Three National Conventions, Minneapolis, 1893.

Rhodes, James Ford, *History of the United States*, New York, 1914.

Richardson, Albert W., *A Personal History of U. S. Grant*, Hartford, Conn., 1868.

Richardson, James D., *Messages and Papers of the Presidents*, New York, 1901.

Riddle, A. G., *Benjamin F. Wade*, Cleveland, Ohio, 1886.

Ross, Edmund G., *The Johnson Impeachment*, Albuquerque, N. M., 1896.

Russell, W. H., *My Diary North and South*, Boston, 1863.

Salter, William, *Life of James W. Grimes*, New York, 1890.

Sandburg, Carl, *Abraham Lincoln*, New York, 1926.

Savage, John, *Life of Andrew Johnson*, New York, 1866.

Schofield, John M., *Forty-Six Years in the Army*, New York, 1897.

Schucht, J., *Andrew Johnson*, Leipzig, 1875.

Schuckers, J. W., *Life of S. P. Chase*, New York, 1874.

Schurz, Carl, *Reminiscences*, New York, 1907.

Schurz, Carl, *Speeches, Correspondence, etc.*, New York, 1913.

Sherman, John, *Recollections*, Chicago, 1896.

Sherman *Letters*, [Correspondence between General and Senator Sherman], New York, 1894.

Sherman, W. T., *Home Letters*, New York, 1901.

Sherman, W. T., *Personal Memoirs*, New York, 1890.

Smith, Edward Conrad, *The Borderland in the Civil War*, New York, 1927.

Smith, Matthew Hale, *Sunshine and Shadow in New York*, Hartford, Conn., 1868.

Stearns, F. P., *Life of George Luther Stearns*, Philadelphia, 1907.

Storey, Moorfield, *Charles Sumner*, New York, 1900.

Stryker, Lloyd P., *Andrew Johnson*, New York, 1929.

Sumner, Charles, *Works*, Boston, 1883.

Tarbell, Ida, *Abraham Lincoln*, New York, 1900.

Taylor, Richard, *Destruction and Reconstruction*, New York, 1877.

Temple, Oliver P., *Notable Men of Tennessee*, New York, 1912.

Tennessee General Assembly, *House Journals*.

Thayer, William Roscoe, *John Hay*, Boston, 1915.

Thompson, Samuel H., *Southern Hero Tales*, Morristown, Tenn., 1914.

Tuckerman, Charles K., *Personal Recollections of Notable People*, London, 1895.

Warden, W. W., *The Private Life and Public Services of Salmon P. Chase,* Cincinnati, 1874.

Warmoth, Henry Clay, *War, Politics and Reconstruction,* New York, 1930.

Warren, Charles, *The Supreme Court in United States History,* Boston, 1922.

Weed, Thurlow, *Autobiography,* Harriet A. Weed, Ed., Boston, 1883.

Welles, Gideon, *Diary,* Boston, 1911.

White, Horace, *Life of Lyman Trumbull,* New York, 1913.

Whitman, Walt, *Specimen Days,* Philadelphia, 1883.

Wilson, Francis, *John Wilkes Booth,* Boston, 1929.

Wilson, James H., *Life of John A. Rawlins,* New York, 1916.

Winston, Robert, *Andrew Johnson,* New York, 1928.

Woolley, Edwin C., *The Reconstruction of Georgia,* New York, 1901.

NOTES

CHAPTER I

1. Coming from the South, the war time traveler had to arrive by boat upon the Potomac.

2. Letter of James E. Murray, Assistant to President of Baltimore and Ohio Railway Co., to the author, Baltimore, November 12, 1928.

3. W. H. Russell, "My Diary North and South," Boston, 1863; 31.

4. John B. Ellis, "Sights and Secrets of the National Capital," New York, 1869; 21, *et seq.*

5. During the Civil War most of the Union troops to the Army of the Potomac came through this famous old station; Lincoln arrived in it en route to his first inauguration, and it was through this station that his body was carried on its way to burial at Springfield. It was used until 1905.

6. Ellis, 24.

7. It was latitude 38 degrees, 55 minutes, 48 seconds, north; longitude 77 degrees, 1 minute, 48 seconds west from Greenwich.

8. W. B. Bryan, "History of the National Capital," New York, 1914; II, 496.

9. Washington *Star*, March 6, 1865.

10. Edward Dicey, "Six Months in the Federal States," London, 1863; 94.

11. Benjamin F. Taylor, Chicago *Evening Journal*, June 16, 1864.

12. Edna M. Colman, "Seventy-Five Years of White House Gossip," New York, 1925; 279.

13. A. K. McClure, "Lincoln and Men of War Times," Philadelphia, 1892; 203, *et seq.*

14. Colman, 281. The present State War and Navy building now stands on this site. Cf. also McClure, Lincoln, 203.

15. Brainard H. Warner, in "Washington During War Time," Marcus Benjamin, ed., Washington, n. d., 191, *et seq.*, Cf. Bryan, II, 509; Colman, 279, and Washington *Star*, August 8, 1863. The canal was not arched and covered until 1870.

16. *Congressional Globe*, Second Session, 40th Congress, 687.

17. Washington *Chronicle*, April 14, 1861.

18. Colman, 279.

19. Bryan, II, 531.

20. Warner, 190.

21. Colman, 285.

22. Lafayette C. Baker, "History of the United States Secret Service," Philadelphia, 1867; 245.

23. Ellis, 452.

24. Ellis, 458.

25. Baker, 245.

26. Ellis, 400, *et seq.*

27. Baker, 241.

28. Russell, 33.
29. Russell, 51.
30. New York *Independent*, Jan. 23, 1868.   Editorial by Theodore Tilton.
31. Ellis, 228.
32. Ellis, 231.
33. Allen C. Clark, "Abraham Lincoln in the National Capital," Washington, 1925; 47.
34. He also made it a point to read carefully the papers from over the lines, and often found in the Richmond *Enquirer* news of moment and unexpected comfort.
35. Washington *Post*, August 3, 1924.
36. Walt Whitman, "Specimen Days," Philadelphia, 1882; entry for August 12, 1863. Cf. also Clark, 36-7.

CHAPTER II

1. It had come near doing so, however. Cf. Washington *Star*, March 9, 1861, for account of the first reception, the final scene of which had been tragi-comic. Perhaps not one in ten of that large assemblage departed with the same outer garments they wore on entering. Some thieves seemed to have taken advantage of the opportunities to make a grand sweep. By 1864 these affairs were handled better.
2. Ellis, 237, *et seq.*
3. Washington *Star*, March 9, 1861.
4. Colman, 289; See also Ellis, 242. The death of the first President Harrison is said to have been hastened by such reception bruises of the hand.
5. Ellis, 244.
6. Russell, 38.
7. Russell, 43.
8. Washington *Chronicle*, March 11, 1863.
9. Rose Greenhow, "My Imprisonment at Washington," London, 1863; 202-3.
10. Clark, 59, quoting "Dobbs Family in America."
11. Washington *Chronicle*, Feb. 20, 1864.
12. Russell, 34-43.
13. Ben: Perley Poore, "Perley's Reminiscences," Philadelphia, 1886; II, 148.
14. Edward Conrad Smith, "The Borderland in the Civil War," New York, 1927; 390.
15. Adam Gurowski, "Diary," '61-2, Boston, 1862; 242-7.
16. James G. Blaine, "Twenty Years of Congress," Norwich, Conn., 1884; I, 422, *et seq.*
17. Blaine, I, 444.
18. Benjamin F. Butler, "Private and Official Correspondence," Norwood, Mass., 1917; III, 99; 111-15; 150. III, 115-115. H. G., as Parton called him, "a naturally disinterested man," was interested in: 1—Senator

from New York. 2—Secretary of the Interior. 3—Governor of New York. Parton's book on Butler sold 100,000 in three months.

19. Adam Gurowski, "Diary," '63-5, Washington, 1866; 33.

20. Clark, 52, quoting Ward H. Lamon.

21. Gideon Welles, "Diary," Boston, 1911, II, 154-5, attributed this *mot* to Seward himself. This diary, while one of the most illuminating contemporary sources, needs to be used with some caution, inasmuch as Father Gideon edited it before his death, and his son re-edited it before publication. In essential references, comparisons have been made with manuscript of the diary.

22. Matthew Hale Smith, "Sunshine and Shadow in New York," Hartford, Conn., 1868; 317, *et seq.*

23. Cf. Welles, II, 549.

24. Russell, 42.

25. "Radical" as used in Civil War and Reconstruction had a connotation strange to twentieth century ears. It indicated those men who not only were determined to achieve the complete emancipation of the blacks, but also held the further test of political faith that the freed negroes must be enfranchised and established (in the South) on a plane of complete political, economic, and social equality with, if not superiority to, the whites.

26. Edward Bates, "Diary," (Mss.), Feb. 13, 1864; 39. For permission to inspect this diary, I am indebted to Miss Helen Nicolay, of Washington, who now owns it.

27. C. E. Hamlin, "Life and Times of Hannibal Hamlin," Boston, 1898; 452.

28. Russell, 406.

29. Honore Willsie Morrow, "With Malice Toward None," New York, 1928; 62; Cf. also Russell, 411.

30. Count Adam Gurowski's Diary reflects the plans, aims, passions, ambitions and hatreds of the Radicals better than almost any other printed source. Russian authorities had condemned him to death for revolutionary activities in Poland, but he escaped and reached America in 1849. In 1861 Sumner secured him a position as translator in the State Department. He was a singular old man, small in stature, stout of figure, ugly in feature and disfigured by a pair of green goggles. He was an intimate of Wadsworth, an ardent admirer of Ben Butler, and almost an idolator of Thad Stevens. Cf. Ben: Perley Poore, II, 140; Marian Gouverneur, "As I Remember," New York, 1911; 246-7. In Gurowski's "Diary," 1863-5; 164, he thus outlines his self-imposed task: "I attempt to dismantle the strongholds of shams, and disrobe false gods. . . . I offer no incense to idols. I point out those great criminals whose imbecility or cowardice cost the people the lives of scores of thousands of its best children. I dare to shake to the foundations the clay pillars of the sham temples. I am a bad man, but I cannot help it—and I shall continue to record doings, and to call things by their right names."

31. Butler, "Correspondence," III, 348-9.

32. *Ibid.*, 351.

33. "Official Records of the Union and Confederate Armies in the War of the Rebellion" Series i, XXXIII, 552, hereafter referred to as O. R.

34. Gurowski, January 28, 1864. Butler's further career as a soldier

was anything but glorious. Its finale came in the attempt to capture Fort Fisher, near Wilmington, N. C., in December, 1864, an attempt which ended in Butler's precipitate and unnecessary withdrawal of his troops. As a result, General Grant relieved him of command. This exploit gave Butler the further derisive title of "the Hero of Fort Fisher."

35. Butler "Correspondence," III, 442.

36. Welles, I, 345.

37. Welles, I, 501-2-3.

38. A. K. McClure, "Old Time Notes of Pennsylvania," Philadelphia, 1905; II, 133, et seq.

39. Gurowski, "Diary," '63-5; 60.

40. J. W. Schuckers, "Life of S. P. Chase," New York, 1874; 499-450.

41. W. W. Warden, "The Private Life and Public Services of Salmon P. Chase," Cincinnati, 1874; 573-74.

42. Butler, "Correspondence," III, 553-4; 574.

43. McClure, "Old Time Notes," II, 140.

44. B. F. Butler, *North American Review*, October, 1885.

45. In 1891 Butler reaffirmed this statement in a letter dated Boston, July 14, to Col. McClure in which he further said that he had understood "it had been determined on by Mr. Lincoln and his friends that somebody else, if it were possible, should be nominated instead of Mr. Hamlin."

46. Butler "Correspondence," IV, 29; According to *Ibid.*, 66, a rumor had reached the White House in April, that Butler, Fremont, Chase, and Banks planned to make common causes to defeat the President's renomination. If we are to believe one of Butler's Washington political lieutenants, great consternation ensued. Tom Ford of Ohio, a close friend of the General, was rushed to the White House; he denied to the President that Butler was participating in any such move. Lincoln was delighted—"Butler's stock had the greatest rise it ever had with Lincoln."

47. General Frank Blair, Montgomery's brother, Fremont's patron in 1861, had become the "Pathfinder's" bitter enemy, the feud between them tearing the Missouri Republican party in two. By 1864, the Fremont Radicals were thirsting for Montgomery Blair's blood, and were only a little less anxious to punish Lincoln himself.

48. Edward McPherson, "Political History of the United States During Rebellion," Washington, 1882, (4th ed.); 410-411.

49. *Ibid.*, 403.

50. J. G. Nicolay and John Hay, "Abraham Lincoln—A History," New York, 1890; IX, 40.

51. Ida Tarbell, "Abraham Lincoln," New York, 1900; II, 192-3.

52. In this, Sumner's attitude was quite unlike that of that other outstanding leader of the Radicals, Thad Stevens of Pennsylvania. There was no "Miss Smith" in Sumner's life.

53. A. J. Beveridge, "Abraham Lincoln," Boston, 1928; II, 339, et seq.

54. Charles K. Tuckerman, "Personal Recollections of Notable People," London, 1895; 85-87.

55. Hamlin, 464-5.

CHAPTER III

1. Portland, Me., *Express*, July 16, 1891; Hamlin, 466.
2. Statement of A. J. Waterman, Massachusetts delegate, quoted Hamlin, 467.
3. As late as the day before the convention, it was generally believed that either Dickinson or Dix would be nominated. New York Evening *Post* June 7, 1864. Cf. Welles, II, 45: "Should New York be united on Dix or Dickinson, the nomination would be conceded to the Empire State; but there can be no Union in that State."
4. John R. Dickinson, "Daniel S. Dickinson," New York, 1867; II, 650-1, "I have not been at any time . . . in the confidence of the Republican leaders," some of whom "have been jealous of my popular *éclat;* have been fearful of my advancement, and have at all times done all they dare . . . to disparage my efforts."
5. Dickinson, II, 656.
6. Blaine, I, 235-6.
7. Frederic Hudson, "Journalism in the United States," New York, 1873; 376.
8. Welles, II, 35-6.
9. Nicolay and Hay, IX, 72.
10. Gurowski, "Diary," '63-5; 246.
11. See also Nicolay's letter to Mrs. Hannibal Hamlin, July 7, 1891, in which he asserts that Lincoln replied that "he deemed it unbecoming in him to advocate the nomination of any one of them; that privately and personally he would be best pleased if the convention would renominate the old ticket . . ."
12. Letter from Pettis, Meadville, Pa., July 20, 1891, quoted McClure, "Lincoln and Men of War Time," 470-1.
13. Philadelphia *Times,* July 9, 1891. See also McClure, "Old Time Notes," II, 139.
14. McClure, "Old Time Notes," II, 143-144.
15. When McClure first made his revelation of this interview, in the Philadelphia *Times,* July 9, 1891, Nicolay challenged it with heat, and wrote to Mrs. Hamlin that McClure's declaration "is entirely erroneous," intimating that McClure had not even seen Lincoln on the day he declared the interview took place. McClure responded crushingly: "I saw Abraham Lincoln at all hours of the day and night during his presidential service, and he has himself abundantly testified to the trust that existed between us—I was one of those called to the inner councils of Abraham Lincoln—and there were scores of confidential conferences in the White House of which John Nicolay never heard." He then repeated his story with great detail. His testimony is entitled to weight, for he later became an enemy of Johnson; and at the time he wrote his recollections, no friendship existed for the impeached president to cause him to color his story to Johnson's advantage.
16. Chauncey M. Depew, "My Memories of Eighty Years," New York, 1922; 60.
17. Baltimore *Sun,* June 6, 1864.
18. Gurowski, June 10, 1864: "Find out how many bargains were made

in advance, how many promissory notes were delivered and similar facts, and the true character of that convention would be understood, and the people would see how it was cheated out of its trusts."

19. McClure, "Old Time Notes," 140-141.

20. Cooke's statement, Associated Press telegram, July 9, 1894. In another interview about the same time, Cooke said: "I know he would have been pleased with the nomination of Hannibal Hamlin." Nicolay and Hay, *loc. cit.* In the 90's Nicolay assembled a mass of testimony to prove that Lincoln wanted Hamlin as his running mate. According to it, many Lincoln delegates called at the White House in a vain attempt to get the President to name his choice. These included Dr. F. A. Powell, of Illinois; Dr. Isaac Jenkinson, an Indiana editor, and Robert Gardner, of California. According to the recollections of the first two, Lincoln refused to express a choice.

21. New York *Sun,* and Brooklyn *Eagle,* July 11, 1891; Chicago *Post,* July 12, 1891.

22. Gurowski, "Diary," '63-5; 247: "Many true patriots such as Potter of Wisconsin and Thaddeus Stevens of Pennsylvania . . . are sent by the people to the convention, but they are in the minority. Their communities instruct them to vote for Lincoln, and therefore the current cannot be stayed."

23. Indiana, which had instructed for Lincoln and Johnson, was an exception.

24. Nicolay and Hay, IX, 62.

25. John Savage, "Life of Johnson," New York, 1866; 288, *et seq.*

26. Savage says that all the Tremaine votes, and part of those cast for Johnson, were really Dickinson votes.

27. *National Republican,* Washington, June 7, 1864.

28. King's statement to John W. Babson, March 10, 1865, quoted Hamlin, 468.

29. Letter from Morrill to Hamlin June 9, 1864, quoted Hamlin, 481.

30. Baltimore *Sun,* June 8, 1864.

31. Nicolay and Hay, IX, 65.

32. Letter of Desha Breckinridge, Lexington, Ky., March 16, 1928, to author. Search of the Breckinridge papers in the Library of Congress reveals no written evidence to support this tradition.

33. Nicolay and Hay, IX, 65.

34. Although born in Massachusetts, in 1814, Maynard had moved to Knoxville, Tennessee in 1839; first a teacher, in the 'Forties he was admitted to the bar. He entered politics as a Whig. He was a member of the 35th, 36th, and 37th Congresses, being elected as an "American." When Tennessee was debating secession, he joined with Johnson, Brownlow, Nelson, and others in opposing it with all the vigor at his command. Maynard had "risked much to stand by *you* and had been hunted from place to place by Confederate troops."

35. Maynard's speech has passed into political history as a classic, as one of the few convention speeches which actually affected delegate votes. For its text, see "Proceedings of First Three Republican National Conventions," Minneapolis, 1893; 188-9.

36. Proceedings, etc., 198-9.

37. Gurowski "Diary," 1863-5; 250. "The efforts of patriots are to

carry the point that Mr. Lincoln be admonished by the convention to mend his ways, and change his constitutional advisers. The Wisconsin delegation, filled with Radicals, takes the lead in this."

38. Nicolay and Hay, IX, 69. This sixth resolution also deemed it "essential to the general welfare that harmony should prevail in our national councils . . ."

39. Proceedings, etc., 227, *et seq.*

40. They did, however, though rather ungraciously, vote to make Lincoln's nomination unanimous. See Proceedings, 233-4.

41. Nicolay and Hay, IX, 73. Lincoln "received the dispatch announcing the nomination of Andrew Johnson before he was informed of his own."

42. Proceedings, 235.

43. Welles "Diary," June 8, 1864. Mss. form: "The delegates and people of my state generally have disapproved of Hamlin's course toward me, and I have no doubt it contributed to their casting an united vote at the start. Hamlin and his friends will give me credit for influence which I do not possess and ascribe to me revenge or malevolence I have never felt."

44. The Iowa vote roused rare controversy. See Hamlin, 477, *et seq.*, which declares: "Mr. Hamlin was cheated out of the vice presidency, and the presidency also, by the unscrupulous action of William M. Stone, then Governor of Iowa. He falsified the vote of his state, and turned the tide to Johnson. When Iowa was called, Stone jumped to his feet . . . , usurped the functions of the chairman of his delegation, and cast the vote of Iowa for Andrew Johnson . . . The delegation divided . . . Johnson 8, Hamlin 4, Dickinson 4 . . . There is overwhelming evidence that Stone falsified Iowa's vote."

45. Proceedings, 239, *et seq.*

46. See Senator Morrill to Hamlin, Baltimore, June 9, 1864, quoted Hamlin, 481.

47. David Homer Bates, "Lincoln In The Telegraph Office," New York, 1907; 267-8. See also Ward Hill Lamon, "Recollections of Abraham Lincoln," New York, 1911; 112-3. Lincoln was reminded of an incident following the 1860 election. While reclining on a lounge at Springfield, he saw double image of himself in the looking-glass, one with his face reflecting the full glow of health and life, the other with the face showing a ghastly pallor. He took this illusion as a sign, the first betokening a safe passage through his first term, the other that death would overtake him during his second term. Johnson's enemies later claimed that Lincoln received the news with dissatisfaction. Major Albert E. Johnson, Stanton's secretary in 1864, in a statement made on January 15, 1897, declared that Charles A. Tinker, War Department telegraph operator at the time, slipped into Major Johnson's office and whispered to him that Lincoln, on reading the dispatch, had sighed deeply, and said: "Well, I thought possibly he might be the man. Perhaps he is the best man, but . . ." For such accounts, see Hamlin, 482-3, and appendix, 611-2-3. Despite the apparent corroboration, this testimony is of little value. Major Johnson and the others joined with Stanton in a bitter hatred of Andrew Johnson. Their statements were given long after their prejudices had colored their remembrance.

48. Robert Winston, "Andrew Johnson," New York, 1928; 257.

CHAPTER IV

1. Winston, 3, *et seq.*

2. Johnson Mss., Vol. 135, No. 20,329, letter from George Casely, Almwick, Northumberland, England, March 26, 1868. "My father has for a long time past requested me to write you, he being under the impression that you would like to have fuller information of your ancestors from your speech." The occasion referred to was Andrew Johnson's address at the unveiling of a monument to his father at Raleigh. Casely said that Jacob Johnson "had one brother, Thomas. There were also several sisters, one of whom, Isabella, was married to my paternal grandfather . . . My Aunt Isabella has in her possession the last letter received from your father." Cf. *Magazine of History*, Randolph County Historical Society, Elkins, W. Va., 1929; 19-21.

3. A National Man, [Kenneth Rayner], "Andrew Johnson," New York, 1866; 3, quoting Raleigh, N. C. *Star,* Jan. 12, 1812.

4. James S. Jones, "Andrew Johnson," Greeneville, Tenn., 1901; 14.

5. Jones, 13-14. Winston, 9, puts the date of the fishing party in December, 1811, and has Jacob Johnson dying "shortly afterward."

6. Johnson Mss., Vol. 116, No. 16,106, letter from Neal Brown of Raleigh, July 15, 1867. Brown, a boyhood chum of Andrew Johnson, wrote the President to recall to his mind "one who in our boysh days spent so many happy moments in our boysh plays," and gave the above cited description of them.

7. John Robert Irelan, "Times of Johnson," Chicago, 1888; 20-29, quoting Nashville *American,* Nov. 4, 1880, which had reprinted long interview of Louisville *Courier-Journal* correspondent with Lomsden, who wrote freely and with much detail about Johnson's life in Raleigh.

8. Johnson Mss., Vol. 153, No. 24,464. W. I. Anderson, Winona, Miss., April 8, 1869. "I was shown by Mr. Joe Selby of Holly Springs, Miss., a few months since a certificate of which the following is a true copy, and which he informs me was the original document by which you were apprenticed to his father, James J. Selby . . ." Anderson copied the cross mark by which Andy's mother had signed.

9. Winston, 8.

10. Jones, 14. Oliver P. Temple, "Notable Men of Tennessee," New York, 1912; 357, quotes the statement of W. W. Jordan, a neighbor and intimate friend of Johnson, in Greeneville, who said that Johnson told him that Selby had been a "hard and cruel master."

11. His name was Litchford, and he was alive in 1866, when the former apprentice had become President and admiring biographies were being rushed through the press about him. To John Savage, perhaps the best of these contemporary biographers, Litchford gave his reminiscences of "Andy" Johnson as an apprentice tailor. See John Savage, "Andrew Johnson," New York, 1866; 15.

12. Cf. Temple, "Notable Men," 357, quoting Jordan's statement that Johnson ran away "because of illtreatment, after giving Selby a good whipping."

13. The advertisement is dated Raleigh, June 24, 1824, and says the apprentices ran away on the night of the 15th.

14. Winston, 11, says Johnson stayed in Carthage "for several months."

15. Benjamin F. Perry, "Reminiscences of Public Men," [second series] Greenville, S. C., 1889; 250; quotes Judge Orr as saying that Johnson told him the incident when they were serving together in Congress. According to letter of Mrs. John F. Bolt, Sarah Word's granddaughter, to Col. A. J. Patterson, Laurens, S. C., March 28, 1930, the old quilt is still in existence.

16. Nashville *American*, Nov. 4, 1880; quoting long interview with Lomsden in Louisville *Courier-Journal*.

17. Account of Colonel Allan Brown, of Maury County, Tennessee, to A. M. Hughes, Nashville *Banner*, Dec. 18, 1927. Col. Brown was the son of the man in question.

18. There is a legend in Mooresville, Ala., that Johnson first stayed there a while.

19. Col. Sims Latta, Columbia, Tenn., May 22, 1929, to author, describing his own conversations with Ex-President Johnson on the subject, and "that while he [Johnson] worked for James Shelton, Mrs. Shelton helped him with his studies and was a mother to him. . . . That Johnson did live in Columbia was not questioned until after all the older people that knew the facts had passed away." See also A. M. Hughes, Nashville *Banner*, Dec. 18, 1927, quoting his own conversation with Shelton.

20. Savage, 17, quotes Litchford as saying Johnson told him he, Andy, wouldn't let Litchford go his security.

21. Johnson Mss., Vol. 146, No. 22,883. February wrote President Johnson from Jonesboro, Tenn., October 6, 1868, recalling to Johnson's memory "your old friend, A. D. February, who came across the mountains with you in 1826 with a wagon, with your stepfather and mother, as a journeyman tailor."

22. Temple, "Notable Men," 376.

23. Samuel H. Thompson, "Southern Hero Tales," Morristown, Tenn., 1914, 46.

24. Johnson Mss., Vol. 146, No. 22,883.

25. See Temple, "Notable Men," 357, for another and equally lyrical account of the arrival of the Johnsons at Greeneville.

26. Letter of J. L. Pemberton, Knoxville, Tenn., May 23, 1928. Mr. Pemberton is a collector of Johnson data to whose statements of fact I attach confidence.

27. Lieut. Col. Fay Brabson, U. S. Army, "The Political Career of Andrew Johnson From His Retirement From the Presidency to His Death," an unpublished thesis at Vanderbilt University in 1912. He based his statement on a conversation with Mrs. W. A. Harmon, of Greeneville, a local antiquarian.

28. J. L. Pemberton, Knoxville, Tenn., Sept. 11, 1929, to author.

29. For descriptions of Eliza McArdle, see Jones, 18, 391; Winston, 20.

30. Savage, 16.

31. Temple, 360, Savage, 23, calls it "The American Speaker," and gives Johnson himself as the source of his information. Winston, 10, prefers the title, "Enfield's Speaker."

32. Temple, 361. He secured his information from Joseph S. Fowler, a Reconstruction Senator from Tennessee, whom he terms, "at the time of Mr. Johnson's death, perhaps his most intimate friend." Fowler once saw this book in Johnson's library. It was burned, with the rest of Johnson's library, by the Confederates during the war. Savage, 22.

33. Perry, Second Series; 250. See also Temple, 361; Raynor, 4 and 5. Raynor's book was written in consultation with Johnson; Cf. also Moore, Introduction, vi, and Savage, 15, *et seq.*, Winston, (20) however, accepts the story that at the time of his marriage, Johnson could only "spell just a little," and "read simple words."

34. Letter of Dr. Charles Oliver Gray, President of Tusculum College, Greeneville, to author, Jan. 9, 1929. There is much incorrect information in other accounts of Johnson's early years in Greeneville concerning these colleges, which Dr. Gray's letter clears up.

35. In 1927, Tusculum College received $1,100 for two of these volumes, of which it had duplicates, much to the delight of its president.

36. Savage, 20.

37. The three colleges, Greeneville, Washington and Tusculum, remained in active competition until the Civil War. At the close of the war Greeneville and Tusculum were united under the name Greenville and Tusculum College, and in 1912 this title was shortened simply to Tusculum College.

38. Winston, 22.

39. Jones, 19.

40. Winston, 18-19.

41. Savage, 22.

42. Usually misspelled McDaniel; see letters to and from him in Johnson Mss., also the headstone on his grave at Greeneville bears the name "McDannel."

43. Jones, 29.

CHAPTER V

1. G. W. Bacon, "Life of Andrew Johnson," London, n. d. (apparently 1866), 6, 7, quoting statement to him of Alexander Hawthorne. Hawthorne's account does not comport with the traditional story that, in order to be elected, Johnson made a bitter campaign against the town aristocrats. Cf. Winston, 23-4; Jones, 20; Savage, 19.

2. This tally sheet, a facsimile of which is printed facing page 136, is in the possession of Mrs. S. A. LaRue, of Greeneville, Tenn., a greatgranddaughter of Blackstone McDannel. There were twenty-seven candidates voted upon. The successful ones were: J. W. Harold, 31 votes; 'Squire Mordecai Lincoln (the same who married Johnson and Eliza McArdle) 26; McDannel, 26; D. Alexander, 25; A. Brown and J. Lister, 19 each, and Johnson, 18 votes.

3. Winston, 29-30.

4. Jones, 21.

5. Temple, 363.

6. Temple, 363, never a friendly critic of Johnson, claims that in this first campaign Johnson exhibited a "disposition to pander to the prejudice of the people," that "he was almost brutal in his assaults," and that "all the kindly amenities of high debate between gentlemen were wanting."

7. Jones, 22-3.

8. Temple, 366, *et seq.*, contends that in 1835 Johnson was a Whig, that in 1836 he supported Hugh Lawson White for president, and that he did

not become a Democrat until after his defeat of Campbell in 1839. Inasmuch as Senator White was a Tennessean, the idol of East Tennessee, and inasmuch further as the dividing lines between Whig and Democrat had not yet been so clearly drawn as later, Johnson's 1836 position is not impossible to reconcile with that he later took.

9. Temple, 371, *et seq.*, has an unusually illuminating tribute to Johnson's popular leadership.

10. Edward Channing, "History of the United States," New York, 1926; VI, 124.

11. Temple, 372.

12. Temple, 373.

13. Temple, 216-217, claims that while Johnson was in the State Senate, he had passed a Redistricting Bill, adding to the hitherto strongly Whig First Congressional district enough Democratic counties to insure his own election to Congress next year.

14. Jones, 32.

15. Thurlow Weed in New York *Tribune,* Jan. 29, 1875.

16. Johnson Mss., Vol. 1, No. 94, true copy of page 121, ledger of Sergeant-at-Arms. In 1860, he counselled his son Robert, then a member of the Tennessee legislature, "I would in the receipt of my *per diem* be very careful not to take pay for any more time than I was employed as legislator . . . It will be worth more to you in the future than it is now."

17. Jones, 34. It is to be noted that the resolution passed, and Old Hickory was repaid.

18. Jonesboro *Whig,* July 4, 1845. On July 23, Brownlow charges that Johnson is, among other things, an Abolitionist! I am indebted to the late Selden Nelson, of Knoxville, Tenn., for these rare and racy issues.

19. The late John Trotwood Moore, *Saturday Evening Post,* April, 1929. Mrs. Moore has kindly furnished me with a copy of the full text of Mr. Moore's article, which was printed only in part by the *Post.* According to Moore, in his inquiries at Raleigh, Johnson "thoroughly disproved the slander," and secured numerous affidavits of good people still living to disprove the charge. No Raleigh paper of the day contained any reference to Johnson's visits. In a letter to Josephus Daniels, Moore claimed, in May, 1929, that Johnson had issued a pamphlet on the subject. This pamphlet is unknown to Johnson collectors. One fable about Johnson's recognition of illegitimacy is destroyed by Pulaski Cowper, late private secretary to Governor Bragg, of North Carolina. In 1867, Cowper heard Johnson's oration over the monument to his father, and says that Johnson referred to "the reputed grave of my father," rather than to "the grave of my reputed father." For this information I am indebted to Mr. Josephus Daniels of Raleigh, in a letter of May 11, 1929.

20. "Diary of James K. Polk," Chicago, 1910; II, 36-41.

21. Johnson Mss., Vol. I, No. 33.

22. Temple, 219.

23. Polk, "Diary," IV, 265.

24. Winston, 130, *et seq.*, has an excellent summary of the Homestead situation when Johnson started his fight.

25. Temple, 230.

26. Polk, IV, 265, says (Jan. 1, 1849); "If he had the manliness or independence to manifest his opposition openly, he knows he could not again be elected by his constituents."

27. Greeneville *Spy*, April 17, 1851.

28. Temple, 378; I. A. Graham to Franklin Pierce, Jonesboro, Tenn., June 24, 1852; Pierce Photostats, Library of Congress, Washington.

29. Letter to Sam Milligan, July 20, 1852; Mss. Pennsylvania Historical Society, Philadelphia.

30. Letter to Sam Milligan, Washington, Dec. 28, 1852; Mss. Pennsylvania Historical Society.

31. House Journal, Tennessee Legislature, 1851-2; 75.

32. Among these were Isham G. Harris, Joseph Conn Guild, J. G. Pickett, and Edwin Polk.

33. W. M. Caskey, "First Administration of Governor Andrew Johnson," East Tennessee Historical Society *Publications,* I, Knoxville, 1929; 45-6. Caskey found that of the 39 counties reported, 12 gave Johnson as first choice, to only six for Isham G. Harris, the next man.

34. According to George W. Jones, Memorial Address at Greeneville, June 5, 1878; 9, Johnson's letter had requested Ewing "to withdraw his (Johnson's) name from before the convention in the event he should think it necessary to do so in order to harmonize the convention."

35. Caskey, 48.

36. Henry did, however, have the satisfaction of a biting retort. At one debate, Johnson had ridiculed the "Eagle Orator," and said the eagle had not left any marks on him. "No," Henry replied, "the eagle is a noble bird, and will not feed on carrion."

37. Savage, 46.

38. House Journal, Tennessee Legislature, 1853-4; 297.

39. Caskey, 58.

40. Savage, 49.

41. Temple, 383. The growth of the Know-Nothings was so sudden and the affiliation of the secret order with the Whigs was so general that Democratic leaders of the North and the South had been much perplexed to know how to handle it. Stephen A. Douglas was among the first to denounce it, in a heated speech at Philadelphia on the Fourth of July, 1854. He called upon all Democrats to stand together against the "allied forces of Abolitionism, Whiggism, Nativism, and religious intolerance, under whatever name or on whatever field they may present themselves." See Beveridge, Lincoln, II, 227, Henry A. Wise, made a campaign in Virginia for governor, attacking the Know-Nothings, just about the time Johnson made his Tennessee onslaught.

42. W. M. Caskey, East Tennessee Historical Society Publications, II, 34 *et seq.*

43. Gentry, who had been similarly questioned, evaded a direct answer. Late in the campaign, however, the Temperance forces gave him their support.

44. Nashville *True Whig*, April 27, 1855.

45. Temple, 385-6; Rayner, 50-51; Savage, 46. The Kansas-Nebraska Bill was the next most important issue in the campaign, Johnson pressing

and Gentry evading taking a position upon it. Cf. also John Trotwood Moore Mss., 18.

46. Savage, 49.

47. It cost the state $48,000. Tennessee tendered the property to the Federal government for use as a site for a Southern branch of the military academy at West Point. The military affairs committee of the House reported favorably, but Congress adjourned without action. Johnson suggested that if Congress continued to ignore the proffer, the Hermitage should be used as a home for future governors of Tennessee. Jones, 58-9. In January, 1857, Governor Johnson went to Washington to urge President Pierce to accept the Tennessee offer. He was unsuccessful. On his way home, his train jumped the track near Chattanooga. Johnson's right arm was broken, and he was in poor health for months. As a result of this accident, his handwriting thenceforward was crabbed and awkward.

48. Caskey, East Tennessee Proceedings, II, 46-54.

49. Ms. letter to Sam Milligan, Dec. 10, 1856, in Pennsylvania Historical Society, Philadelphia.

50. Rayner, 53.

51. Possibly this unfortunate affair between Johnson and Bell kept the former from supporting the Bell-Everitt ticket in 1860. The fact that Johnson was so staunchly battling for the Union in the winter and spring of 1861, quite probably slaked Bell's Union fervor and caused him to support secession in April, 1861. Had Bell joined hands with Johnson, probably Tennessee would not have left the Union.

52. Savage, 60-71.

53. Rayner, 76-77.

54. Johnson Mss., Vol. 2, No. 250. Letter to Robert Johnson, April 8, 1860. But he added, "If you and Milligan will go [to Charleston], I will pay the expense of both."

55. Ms. letter to George W. Jones, Washington, Mar. 13, 1860; Pennsylvania Historical Society, Philadelphia.

56. A. Ten Eyck to Andrew Johnson, Detroit, Feb. 20, 1860; Johnson Greeneville Mss.

57. Sam Milligan to Andrew Johnson, Greeneville, May 10, 1860; W. C. Whitthorne to Johnson, Charleston, April 29, 1860, and Johnson's reply; W. H. Carroll, to Johnson, Charleston, May 2, 1860, and Johnson's reply; Johnson Greeneville Mss.

58. Ibid., Sam Milligan to Johnson, Baltimore, June 22, 1860; Jones, 64-5.

59. John J. Craven, "Prison Life of Jefferson Davis," New York, 1866; 261, et seq.

CHAPTER VI

1. Johnson Mss., Vol. 3, No. 517.

2. Among his reading at this time, according to Library of Congress records, were such volumes as Holmes' "American Loyalists," Wheeler's "History of North Carolina," and Haywood's "History of Tennessee."

3. Temple, "Notable Men," 396, et seq.

4. Cincinnati *Commercial*, Feb. 1, 1875, giving interview of Victor Redfield with Stephens.

5. Ms. letter to John Trimble, Washington, Jan. 13, 1861; Pennsylvania Historical Society, Philadelphia.

6. Ms. letter to John Trimble, Washington, Jan. 13, 1861; Pennsylvania Historical Society, Philadelphia.

7. Johnson Mss., Vol. 3, No. 517; Sam Milligan to Johnson, Greeneville, Tenn., Dec. 25, 1860.

8. Grinnell was afterwards a member of Congress and a leading Radical assailant of Johnson as President.

9. Gov. Harris telegraphed Lincoln: "Tennessee will not furnish a single man for purposes of coercion, but 50,000, if necessary, for the defense of our rights and those of our Southern brothers."

10. James Morris Morgan, "Recollections of a Rebel Reefer," Boston, 1917; 36, *et seq.*, Young Morgan thought it the greatest exhibition of courage he had ever witnessed.

11. Johnson Mss., Vol. 94, No. 10,912. Statement of Alexander G. Greenwood, April 26, 1866, about the incident. Greenwood stated that "the undersigned was warned by Jefferson Davis, the President of the Confederate States of America, to move the cars by Bristol so as to avoid the danger that threatened the life of Mr. Johnson. The undersigned, in obedience to the orders of President Davis, and to save Mr. Johnson's life or him from bodily harm, ordered the instant progress of the cars to Jonesborough, which order was obeyed. And thus Mr. Johnson was saved by interposition of Mr. Davis. How Mr. Davis *knew* of Mr. Johson's danger the undersigned does not know. He only obeyed a positive order and claims no credit therefor, and had no personal feeling at the time to avoid or thwart the mob."

12. Temple, "Notable Men," 399-400.

13. Statement of Judge T. A. R. Nelson, Knoxville, Tenn., December 10, 1927, to the author. Judge Nelson, a son of Johnson's associate in this campaign, accompanied his father on the month's trip. Fourteen years of age at the time, he remembered campaign incidents vividly.

14. Temple, 400-401. It indicates too, that the Southern vote for Breckinridge was by no means altogether a secession vote.

15. W. G. Brownlow to Blackstone McDannel, Knoxville, June 3, 1861; original in possession of Mrs. S. B. LaRue, Greeneville, Tenn.

16. The phrase is Horace Maynard's.

17. Diary of Samuel R. Glenn, correspondent of New York *Herald,* April 30, 1862, quoted Savage, 257.

18. Johnson Mss., Vol. 18, No. 4106.

19. Johnson Mss., Vol. 22, No. 4939.

20. Rev. Lucien Clark, Address, Columbus, O., September 12, 1915, 26-7-8; Jones, 82-3; F. B. Carpenter, "Six Months in the White House," New York, 1866; 102-3. Moody shortly thereafter told this story to Lincoln, who enjoyed it greatly.

21. Glenn "Diary," October 21, 1862.

22. Andrew Johnson to Captain James St. C. Morton, October 27, 1862. The original is in possession of Arthur V. Morton, Philadelphia. A photostat copy is now in my possession. One of the most interesting facts

about this letter is that it was not written for publication, was not given to the papers for Johnson's glorification, and is now finding its way into print for the first time.

23. See Clifton R. Hall, "Andrew Johnson, Military Governor of Tennessee," Princeton, 1916, for the best general account of the military governorship.

24. After one such incident, Lincoln telegraphed Johnson: "Do you not, my good friend, perceive that what you ask is simply to put you in command in the West? I do not suppose you desire this. You only wish to control in your own localities, but this you must know may derange all other parts."

25. O. R. Series iii, III, 77.

26. Original in J. Pierpont Morgan's Private Library, New York. Photostat in author's possession.

27. O. R. Series iii, II, 675.

28. O. R. Series iii, III, 789.

29. Johnson Mss., Vol. 38, No. 8929.

30. Hall, 118.

31. Johnson Mss., Vol. 39, No. 8655.

32. *Ibid.*, Vol. 40, No. 8893.

33. *Ibid.*, Vol. 40, No. 8847.

34. Hall, 123, estimates that had Lincoln's amnesty oath been the only one required, the vote would have been double that actually cast.

35. Benjamin C. Truman, "Anecdotes of Andrew Johnson," *Century Magazine*, January, 1913; 437.

36. A careful examination of his correspondence in the winter and spring of 1864 affords no evidence, not even a trace, of any campaign on his part for the vice presidential nomination. There is preserved no letter from Johnson to Lincoln, or from Lincoln to him on the subject.

CHAPTER VII

1. According to Johnson's application to Phoenix Mutual Life Insurance Co., No. 11,173, on April 14, 1865, H. A. Brewster, the company's agent at Washington, who forwarded the application, gave Johnson's weight as 178 pounds, his height as 5 ft. 8 in., his figure as "good" and his general appearance as "sound and healthy." His chest expansion was 39 inches, his pulse standing, 78, sitting, 71. I am indebted for a photostat of this application to Mr. C. T. Steven of the Phoenix Mutual's home office.

2. Truman, *op. cit.*, 436; Memorial Address, George W. Jones.

3. Temple, "Notable Men," 451.

4. William H. Crook, Mrs. M. S. Gerry, Editor; "Through Five Administrations," New York, 1910; 81.

5. Statements to author of James F. Duhamel, Washington, D. C., Dec. 4, 1928, and Mrs. Mary D. Clagett, Washington, Dec. 7, 1928.

6. Edward McPherson, "Political History of the United States During Reconstruction," Washington, 1880, 46-47.

7. David Rankin Barbee, of Washington, has quite a collection of such testimonials to Johnson. Letter to author, Sept. 3, 1929.

8. Bates "Diary," Ms., 87.

9. Gurowski, June 9, 1864.

10. Butler "Correspondence," IV, 337.

11. Johnson Mss., Vol. 46, No. 10,034.

12. Johnson Mss., Vol. 47, No. 261.

13. Letter to J. W. Wright, Nashville, Aug. 31, 1864; letter in possession of David Rankin Barbee, Washington.

14. Johnson Mss., Vol. 45, No. 9855.

15. Warden, 611-619, Welles, II, 62-65.

16. Charles H. McCarthy, "Lincoln's Plan of Reconstruction," New York, 1901; 194, *et seq.* The oath pledged support of the Constitution and the Union, and of the slavery legislation enacted during the war (unless such acts were repealed by Congress or modified or annulled by the Supreme Court), and adherence to all executive proclamations on the subject, subject to judicial constructions.

17. Nicolay, IX, 120-22.

18. Annual Cyclopædia, 1864; 307-10. Johnson had agreed thoroughly with Lincoln's pocket veto and proclamation. On July 13, he telegraphed the President "Your proclamation with regard to Winter Davis' bill. . . . is just as it should have been; and the *real* Union men are satisfied with it."

19. William Roscoe Thayer, "John Hay," Boston, 1915; I, 173-4.

20. Nicolay & Hay, IX, 189.

21. Nicolay & Hay, IX, 198.

22. Allan Nevins, "Fremont, The West's Greatest Adventurer," New York, 1928; II, 663. For Weed's intrigue, see letter of E. L. M. Barlow, Johnson Mss., Vol. 76, No. 6731. "He was with us and against the Republicans for about a month," Barlow wrote. "Then we lost him, and shall never find him again with our consent."

23. O. R. Series i, XLI, Part 2, 595.

24. Butler "Correspondence," IV, 464.

25. *Ibid.*, IV, 534.

26. Bates "Diary," Ms:, 111-112. Welles, II, 81. For Butler's side of the controversy, see Butler "Correspondence, IV, 576-593.

27. At the first Cabinet meeting following his re-election, Lincoln brought out the sealed paper, with the signatures of the members on the back, and read it. He had resolved, he told them, "in case of the election of Gen. McClellan, . . . that I would see him and talk matters over with him. I would say, 'General, the election has demonstrated that you are stronger, have more influence with the American people than I. Now let us together—you with your influence, and I with all the executive power of the government—try to save the country. You raise as many troops as you possibly can for this final trial, and I will devote all my energy to assisting and finishing the war.'"

Seward interjected, "and the General would answer you 'Yes, Yes'; and the next day when you saw him again and pressed those views upon him, he would say, 'Yes, Yes': and so on forever and would have done nothing at all." Lincoln responded, "At least I should have done my duty, and have stood clear before my conscience." Diary of John Hay, as quoted, Thayer, I, 134.

28. "Letters and Addresses of August Belmont," New York, 1890; 140-1.

29. E. C. Kirkland, "Peacemakers of 1864," New York, 1927; 131-2.

30. Proceedings of the 1864 Democratic National Convention, 25-28.

31. No sooner had the convention adjourned than the Democratic stupidity became apparent. On September 2, Sherman captured Atlanta. Five days later, McClellan himself recognized the error of the platform. "The re-establishment of the Union in all its integrity," he said, "is and must continue to be an indispensable condition of any settlement." Weed's keen nose "scented out the heresies" of the Democratic platform, and he began to support the Lincoln ticket.

32. Edward L. Pierce, "Charles Sumner," Boston, 1893; IV, 196, *et seq.*

33. Johnson Mss., Vol. 48, No. 532-C.

34. Annual Cyclopædia, 1865.

35. Bates "Diary," Ms., September 23, 1864; p. 133. Blair had added Stanton to their ranks by a characteristically injudicious remark. During Early's July raid, the Confederates had burned the Postmaster-General's country house. When a friend sought to express sympathy, Montgomery Blair burst out: "Nothing better could be expected while poltroons and cowards have the conduct of military affairs." Hallock heard of it and wrote an angry letter which Stanton thrust in Lincoln's hands. See Welles "Diary," II, 8.

36. McPherson, "Rebellion," 409.

37. Johnson Mss., Vol. 50, No. 962. Lincoln's Cabinet members were levied on for $250 each. See Bates "Diary," Ms., 128.

38. Johnson's state of mind at this time is reflected by his expression when he learned of the capture by the Federal forces of A. J. Watkins, a former member of the United States Congress, and George Heiskell, a member of the Confederate Congress. Applications were made for their release and the Military Governor opposed them. These two, he wrote, "are bad men . . . and deserve as many deaths as can be inflicted upon them . . ." See Johnson Mss., Vol. 47, for similar illuminating bits.

39. Hall, 146, *et seq.*, gives an extended review of the maneuvers of the Tennessee 1864 campaign.

40. Frank Moore, "Speeches of Andrew Johnson," Boston, 1865; xxxvi, quoting Cincinnati *Gazette* account.

41. Blaine I, 531.

42. John W. Forney, to Andrew Johnson, Johnson Mss., Vol. 55, No. 1825. At that time Forney had not yet made his trade with the Radicals. He wrote Johnson: "It will look very odd if the legislators from the free States endeavor to confer the right of suffrage upon the as yet illiterate negroes, just delivered from slavery, in the South, when in nearly all the free States the negroes are wholly disfranchised."

43. McCarthy, 351.

CHAPTER VIII

1. Johnson Mss., Vol. 51, No. 1229.

2. Johnson Mss., Vol. 52, No. 1271.

3. Johnson Mss., Vol. 53, No. 1394.

4. New York *Tribune*, March 1, 1865; dispatch from correspondent at Columbia, Tenn., February 20; "Governor Johnson has been ill in Nashville for the last two weeks. . ."

5. John Trotwood Moore, **Ms.**, states that Johnson's physicians "told him that to go to Washington for this inauguration would doubtless be fatal."

6. Johnson Mss., Vol. 55, No. 1947.

7. Johnson Mss., Vol. 55, No. 1981, and Vol. 56, Nos. 2016-17.

8. Johnson Mss., Vol. 57, No. 2344.

9. Nashville *Press*, Feb. 27, 1865; Nashville *Dispatch*, Feb. 25, 26, 1865.

10. Washington *National Republican*, March 2, 1864, adds "his health has much improved."

11. Johnson Mss., Vol. 57, Nos. 2422-7.

12. Truman, *op. cit.*, 437-8.

13. Washington *Star*, March 6, 1865.

14. Johnson Mss., Vol. 57, No. 2434; Cf. also Washington correspondence, Boston *Commonwealth*, March 11, 1865, for contemporary Hamlin account.

15. There are several accounts of this unfortunate incident. Hamlin left two,—the first is in a contemporary newspaper interview to be found in Johnson Mss., Vol. 45, No. 4021. The second was written some time later, after he had broken with Johnson politically. This last, which is to be found in his grandson's idolatrous biography, paints the incident much darker than does the first one. Doolittle told Senator John B. Henderson the full story, and Henderson incorporated Doolittle's account in an article in the *Century Magazine*, December, 1912. The Doolittle and the first Hamlin account seem more dependable.

16. The words are Hamlin's. In his later account he claimed that Johnson twice filled a full glass to the brim and drank it down without any water. Doolittle said it was brandy, Hamlin it was whiskey that Johnson drank.

17. This phrase is not found in any of the published speeches, but according to Parson Brownlow, who was informed of it and related it to his family with much gusto, Johnson used these very words, which were suppressed in published accounts. Interview with Walter G. Brownlow of Knoxville, Tenn., December 27, 1927.

18. Hamlin leaned forward, pulled Johnson's coat tail, and whispered, "Stop! Johnson, Stop!"—all to no avail.

19. Hamlin, 498. This same authority, 505, asserts that a few days later Sumner offered a resolution asking Johnson to resign!

20. New York *World*, March 7, 1865; "Ricardus" to C. D. Warner, March 5, 1865, Mss. Div. L. of C.

21. See Welles "Diary," Mss. form. March 4, 1865.

22. Johnson Mss., Vol. 65, No. 4021. This newspaper clipping of the Hamlin interview was sent anonymously to Johnson when the latter became President, in a letter urging that Hamlin "should be called to some position near you at Washington . . . None but a true friend could utter so kind and sublime a sentence" as the one we have just quoted. Interestingly enough, the handwriting of this anonymous letter bears some resemblance to that of Hannibal Hamlin. See also New York *Sun*, March 11, 1865, quoting Boston *Advertiser*. L. D. Campbell to Andrew Johnson, Hamilton, O., Mar. 16, 1865; Johnson Greeneville Mss.

23. Browning "Diary," March 4, 1865; this and later Browning "Diary"

references are to Vol. II of the Diary, to be printed in the fall of 1930 by the Illinois State Historical Library, Springfield, Ill. To Dr. J. G. Randall, of the University of Illinois, who has edited it, I am indebted for advance proof-sheets, to which my references are. Henderson, *loc. cit.*

24. *Independent*, March 16, 1865.

25. However, the New York *Tribune* account of the inauguration festivities has it that at the White House reception that evening, "Vice President Johnson was present for some little time and paid considerable attention to Mrs. Lincoln." See dispatch signed "J.R.S." N. Y. *Tribune*, March 5.

26. Washington *Times*, March 11, 1865.

27. Henry Greenleaf Pearson, "John A. Andrew," Boston, 1904; II, 262, quoting Albert Brown, Jr., to Andrew, Mar. 21, 1865.

28. Welles "Diary," Ms. form, March 7, 1865.

29. Hugh McCulloch, "Men and Measures of Half a Century," New York, 1888; 373-4. This was the view in Tennessee. Brownlow wrote Chase that he had never charged Johnson with being a drunkard; "in fact, nobody in Tennessee ever regarded him as being addicted to the excessive use of whiskey." A month later, on April 14, Johnson confided to the examiner of the Phoenix Mutual Life Insurance Co. that although he had "occasionally drank liquor," he was "temperate," and was not "addicted to habits of intemperance."

30. New York *World*, March 7, 1865.

31. *Independent*, March 9, 1865. In this it chided the *Tribune*, the *Times* and the *Evening Post*, for "pardoning with silence the great disgrace which Andrew Johnson inflicted that day upon his country," and insisted that if such an appearance was to pass without public rebuke, there no longer remained to the press any duty of impartial criticisms of officials.

32. Johnson Mss., Vol. 57, No. 2448. At that time the proceedings of Congress were not, as now, printed currently. Only a limited number of columns were printed in the *Globe* each day, and toward the end of a session ten days or two weeks would often elapse before the printing in the *Globe* was completed. It was the custom then as now for speeches to be revised and undoubtedly Johnson's remarks were revised and corrected, for as published in their official form they show no particularly horrible aspects. The correction was probably made by D. F. Murphy, official reporter of the Senate from 1848 to 1896, who revised and corrected all manuscripts before publication. His nephew, James W. Murphy, was official reporter of the Senate in 1928 and has many interesting recollections of stories told him by his uncle and his father, both of whom were present at Johnson's inauguration. Letter of James W. Murphy, Washington, February 28, 1928.

33. Johnson Mss., Vol. 58, No. 2503.

34. W. T. Sherman, "Personal Memoirs," New York, 1890, II, 324, *et seq.;* for Porter account, see Sherman II, 328-331.

35. Porter felt that the terms of the armistice which Sherman later made with General Johnston "were exactly in accordance with Mr. Lincoln's wishes. He could not have done anything which would have pleased the President better. Mr. Lincoln did in fact arrange the (so considered) liberal terms offered General Joseph Johnston, and whatever may have been General Sherman's private views, I feel sure that he yielded to

the wishes of the President in every respect. It was Mr. Lincoln's policy that was carried out . . . I was with Mr. Lincoln all the time he was at City Point, and until he left for Washington. He was more than delighted with the surrender of Lee, and with the terms Grant gave the Rebel general, and would have given Joseph Johnston twice as much had the latter asked for it . . ."

36. Mr. John Gray, in the congregation that day, communicated the account I have used to Miss Lucy Smith, of New Orleans, to whom I am indebted for it.

37. *Independent*, April 13, 1865.

38. Winston, 267.

39. Johnson Mss., Vol. 58, No. 2564. The Provost-Marshal General's permit for the trip is indorsed "Free Transportation." Some of the Radical writers attempt to quote Lincoln, on seeing Johnson in Richmond, as having exclaimed in disgust to keep the Vice President away from him. I can find no trustworthy authority for any such remark. For Warmoth story, see Henry C. Warmoth, "War, Politics and Reconstruction," New York, 1930; 25-27.

40. Campbell had been a member of the United States Supreme Court, reluctantly resigning upon the secession of his native State. He had become Confederate Assistant Secretary of War in the latter days of the Davis regime.

41. Walter L. Fleming, "Documentary History of Reconstruction," Cleveland, 1906; II, 113-4.

42. James Ford Rhodes, "History of the United States," New York, 1914; V, 133.

43. Ben: Perley Poore, II, 168.

44. McPherson, "Rebellion," 609-10.

45. Ben: Perley Poore, II, 168.

46. Pierce, IV, 236.

47. Johnson Mss., Vol. 154, No. 24,795. On July 21, 1869, Gideon Welles wrote Johnson a twenty page letter transmitting to him from his precious Diary the full particulars of this last Lincoln Cabinet meeting. Welles discovered in this early Stanton plan the origin of the 1867 Congressional scheme for military districts in the South, a project which when first presented by Stanton "was disallowed and otherwise ordered by President Lincoln himself. It was probably the last official act of his life."

48. Welles, II, 282-3. I have transferred from indirect to direct quotation all but the last paragraph of Lincoln's reference to his dream; in the last paragraph Welles quoted Lincoln directly, as above.

CHAPTER IX

1. In this account of Johnson's learning of the news of Lincoln's assassination, I have followed Farwell's detailed statement, as given in writing in March, 1866, to Senator J. R. Doolittle of Wisconsin and formally transmitted by the latter on March 12, 1866, to the Wisconsin State His-

torical Society. The original document is in the Manuscript Division of the Library of Congress.

2. See Washington *Star*, April 16, Pierce, Sumner, IV, 241; *National Intelligencer*, April 15; Washington *Chronicle*, August 26, 1865; *American Historical Review*, XXIX, 515. In his reminiscences, Senator W. M. Stewart, of Nevada, 194, charges that Johnson did not know of Lincoln's assassination until late the next morning, when the Nevada senator went to the Kirkwood House, awakened Johnson from a drunken sleep, took him to the White House, and through Stanton, secured a barber, a doctor and a tailor, to make him look presentable! A more outrageous lie has seldom been told in history. See also *Atlantic Monthly*, April, 1930; 463-5, containing diary entry of Moorfield Storey, Sumner's private secretary, to whom Stanton claimed to have sent for Johnson to come to the death bed; and Sumner to have had him sent away because of Mrs. Lincoln's "strong personal dislike" for the Vice President.

3. McCulloch, 375.

4. Pierce, IV, 241; Storey, to *Atlantic Monthly*, *loc. cit supra*. Welles, II, 287, *et seq.*

5. Moore "Diary" Transcript, March 18, 1868. Stanton related the incident to R. W. Latham, who told it to Moore, adding that "this shocked even so mean a man as Stanton, and he has never recovered from it."

6. Warden, 369, quoting Chase's Diary.

7. Schuckers, 519, quoting from Chase Diary, April 15.

8. McCulloch, 376.

9. According to a paper that Chase gave his biographer several years later, he had been requested by Johnson to write an address to the people of the United States, which the new President could make public and so went home to write it. Returning in about half an hour with the draft he had prepared, he was told that Johnson had already made a brief address to the group; Chase handed his draft to the President, who carefully filed it away. This is what Chase had prepared: "Fellow Citizens of the United States: The ways of God are inscrutable. In the midst of National rejoicings, because of the brightened prospects of restored, benign, and permanent peace, Abraham Lincoln, the revered and beloved President of the United States, has fallen by the hand of an assassin. The blow was stricken yesterday evening about half-past ten; and he died this morning at twenty-two minutes past seven. The agonizing grief which seizes all hearts fills my own. Oppressed by this sorrow and profoundly conscious how much I shall need the support and favor of my countrymen, I have taken the oath prescribed by the Constitution and have entered upon the duties of the great office so suddenly and so sadly made vacant. It will be my sincere endeavor to perform them faithfully and to justify the trust which has been reposed in me by the American people. In this endeavor I earnestly ask the co-operation of all patriots and the prayers of all Christians; and reverently invoke the gracious favor of Almighty God."

10. The new President was savagely criticised for this particular phrase; it seems to the author criticized unjustly, for it has a fine Roman ring. Its language is suspiciously similar to that employed by Sam Milligan five years earlier in connection with Buchanan's non-execution of federal law in seceded South Carolina. See *ante*, 103.

11. Warden, 640-1; Chase left a detailed account of Johnson's assumption of the presidency, with a careful notation in his diary, different portions of which are given by both of his immediate biographers.

12. McCulloch, 376. Apparently this verbal promise of the tender of formal resignations was never carried out. Had it been done, the unfortunate Stanton imbroglio could have been avoided and perhaps Johnson would not have been impeached!

13. Welles, II, 289.

14. McCulloch, 376.

15. Welles, II, 289-90. See also Col. W. G. Moore, "Diary" Transcript, Library of Congress, Washington, May 20, 1867. Moore, Johnson's executive secretary from 1866 to 1869, kept a diary in shorthand. A portion of the entries were transcribed by him in longhand, apparently early in April, 1868. These are published, *American Historical Review*, Vol. XIX, 98-132. The original shorthand notebooks are in the Johnson Mss. in the Library of Congress. During my examination of the papers, I compared the notebook dates with those printed, and saw that much was omitted. Consequently I urged the Library authorities to secure a competent shorthand expert to decipher and transcribe the notes in full. This has been done, and the result is of rare historic value. Whenever the transcript has essential changes from the printed notes, I have followed it. The printed diary references are: Moore, "Diary." In his own transcription, Moore constantly toned down his entries. He transcribed none after April 8, 1868. The new transcript, however, covers all of impeachment and the rest of Johnson's term.

16. McCulloch, 373-4.

17. Johnson Mss., Vol. 154, No. 24795, Welles letter of July 29, 1869, to which reference has been made ante, Chapter VIII, 181. See also Welles "Diary," II, 291.

18. George W. Julian, "Political Recollections," New York, 1883; 243-4.

19. Julian, 255-6.

20. Julian, 255.

21. Claude G. Bowers, "The Tragic Era," Boston, 1929; 6 *et seq.*, quoting Julian "Diary," Ms. Cf. also Moore "Diary" Transcript, April 26, 1868.

22. Julian Mss., Diary, April 16, 1865.

23. Johnson Mss., Vol. 60, No. 2977. Adam Badeau, "Grant in Peace," Hartford, Conn., 1877; 26. A. D. Richardson, "Personal History of U. S. Grant," Hartford, 1868; 503.

24. Johnson Mss., Vol. 58, Nos. 2597, *et seq.*

25. Welles, II, 293.

26. William T. Sherman, "Personal Memoirs," II, 242, *et seq.* But while at Savannah, the Secretary likewise called in a group of Savannah negroes and catechized them concerning their opinion of Sherman, surely a strange procedure in the case of a General who had accomplished the greatest military success of the war.

27. Sherman, II, 252.

28. Sherman, II, 346, *et seq.*; Browning "Diary," April 18, 1865.

29. Sherman, II, 253. The General insists that neither Breckinridge nor Johnston "wrote one word of that paper. I wrote it myself."

30. McPherson, "Reconstruction," 121-2.

31. Henry Hitchcock, "Marching With Sherman," New Haven, 1927; 304.

32. To Welles' pleasure, although Grant was opposed to Sherman's arrangements, he "was tender to sensitiveness of his brother officer, and abstained from censure."

33. Welles, III, 247.

34. This was Lincoln's telegram of March 3, to Grant: "The President directs me to say to you that he wishes you to have no conference with General Lee, unless it be for the capitulation of General Lee's army, or on some minor and purely military matter. He instructs me to say that you are not to decide, discuss, or confer upon any political question. Such questions the President holds in his own hands, and will submit them to no military conferences or conventions." Though Stanton signed it, Lincoln himself had written the words. Why Stanton had not transmitted this dispatch to Sherman six weeks earlier has never been explained.

35. George C. Gorham, "Edwin M. Stanton," Boston, 1899; II, Ch. LXXXV-VI, for a discussion of Stanton's side of this episode.

36. McPherson, "Reconstruction," 122. Compare this statement of Stanton with Lincoln's unsigned statement to Campbell in Richmond.

37. Gorham, II, 195.

38. *Ibid.*, 194. But Gorham insists that Sherman's motives were not questioned. He did not know his Stanton.

39. Welles, II, 294, *et seq.* Many years later, revising his diary under the light of the sober judgment of time, Welles placed a note at this point to the effect that he was satisfied that Sherman in his armistice "was substantially carrying out the benignant policies of President Lincoln to which Stanton was opposed . . . Strange stories were told us, and it was under these representations, to which we then gave credit," that Sherman's act had been so insultingly disapproved.

40. For such accounts see Rhodes, VI, 8, *et seq.*; Ellis P. Oberholtzer, "History of the United States since the Civil War," New York, 1917; I, Chapter I; Pierce IV, 241-7; Blaine II, 66, *et seq.* The last named blames it all on Seward.

41. Sumner to John Bright, May 1, 1865, quoted Pierce IV, 241. The business was in regard to the President receiving Sir Frederick Bruce, Lord Lyons' successor as British Minister to the United States.

42. Sumner to F. W. Bird, April 25, 1865, quoted Pierce IV, 241.

43. Sumner Mss., Harvard College Library, Letter from F. W. Bird, Boston, April 15, 1865.

44. Sumner Mss., Letters from F. W. Bird, Boston, April 15; George B. Loring, Salem, April 17; J. W. Phelps, Brattleboro, Vt., April 14; S. S. Southworth, Morrisiana, April 23; George L. Stearns, April 30, and May 8.

45. Pierce, IV, 245.

46. See Pierce, IV, 241-247.

47. Sumner Mss., Harvard College Library, Stevens to Sumner, May 19, 1865. At the same time that he was writing to Sumner, Stevens wrote President Johnson that "reconstruction is a very delicate subject. The late Congress, and I expect the present, looked upon it as a question for the legislative power exclusively." He suggested "the propriety of sustaining the reconstruction until the meeting of Congress. Better call an extra

session than to allow many to think that the executive was approaching usurpation." See Johnson Mss., Vol. 63, No. 3553.

48. Julian, 263.

49. A. G. Riddle, "Benjamin F. Wade," Cleveland, O., 1886; 268.

50. Chase Diary, Ms., April 29, 1865, quoted, Oberholtzer, I, 39-40; Chase to Johnson, Washington, April 18, 1865, Johnson Greeneville, Mss.

51. Welles, III, 194; see also *Ibid.*, II, 580.

52. State Historical Society of Wisconsin *Proceedings*, 291; Thurlow Weed in letter to New York *Tribune*, Jan. 29, 1875; Cf. Thurlow Weed, "Autobiography," New York, 1883; I, 474; II, 450. For Johnson on Lincoln, see Truman, *op. cit.*, 440. Johnson did not mean "to detract from the name of Washington, but Washington was an Englishman, after all."

53. Eliza F. Andrews, "War Time Journal of a Georgia Girl," New York, 1908; 172-3; 291.

54. David Miller DeWitt, "The Impeachment and Trial of Andrew Johnson," New York, 1903; 12, *et seq.* Three of the governors thus rebuffed were McGrath of South Carolina, Clark of Mississippi and Joseph E. Brown of Georgia.

55. Julian, 360, *et seq.*

56. The reference was to Morton's difficulties with Indiana Copperheads.

57. McPherson, "Reconstruction, " 44, *et seq.*

58. McPherson, "Reconstruction," 47-8.

59. Judge E. H. East of Nashville, who was in the party, communicated this recollection to the father of David Rankin Barbee. About that time, Col. John Overton, a rich Tennessee landowner called on the President to ask remission of his confiscated property. After Johnson said he had "no favor for any damned Southern aristocrat," Overton withdrew in despair. James A. Lyon, a noted Presbyterian preacher, who had known Johnson in East Tennessee, went to the President and sharply criticised his treatment of Overton. Johnson then gave the order. Incident communicated by A. Lyon Childress, of Nashville.

60. Welles, II, 300.

61. Welles, II, 329.

62. Welles, II, 301, *et seq.*; Pierce, IV, 244.

63. Welles, II, 302.

64. Welles, II, 303.

65. Welles, II, 303.

66. McPherson, "Reconstruction," 9.

67. See Sherman, II, 376, *et seq*; Ben: Perley Poore, II, 191; Sherman had come to Washington with deliberate intent to snub the Secretary. When passing through Richmond en route to the grand review, he embraced the opportunity to insult General Hallock. On May 10 he wrote his wife (Sherman's "Home Letters," New York, 1901; 352-3), "Unless Grant interposes from his yielding and good nature, I shall get some equally good opportunity to insult Stanton . . ." Grant did not interpose.

68. W. W. Holden, "Memoirs," Durham, N. C., 1911; 47.

69. Holden, 55.

70. This turned out to be worth about $150,000, and enabled Holden to carry on the administration, and to turn over a balance to Jonathan Worth in December, 1865, when the latter succeeded Holden as governor.

71. Holden, 75.

72. For full text of this proclamation, see Fleming, I, 168, *et seq.*

73. For a full text of this proclamation, see James D. Richardson, "Messages and Papers of the Presidents," New York, 1901.

CHAPTER X

1. New York *Herald*, June 27, 1901, quoted in Francis Wilson, "John Wilkes Booth," Boston, 1929; 15.

2. Wilson, 66.

3. These were Booth himself, Surratt, Louis Payne, whose true name was Powell, Samuel Arnold, Michael O'Laughlin, George A. Atzerodt, and David E. Herold.

4. "American State Trials," St. Louis, 1917. Trial of George A. Atzerodt, XIII, 164, *et seq.*

5. "American State Trials," VIII, 75. Testimony of William A. Browning, that "between four and five o'clock on the 14th of April, I left the Vice President's room in the Capitol and went to the Kirkwood House, where we both boarded. Noticed a card in my box which was adjoining that of Mr. Johnson, and Mr. Jones, the clerk, handed it to me. . . . I had known J. Wilkes Booth when he was playing in Nashville, Tenn." This card of Booth's addressed to Browning later was used by Radicals in their effort to implicate Andrew Johnson himself in the Lincoln assassination plot.

6. See argument of Atzerodt's counsel before Military Commission, American State Trials, VIII, 145, *et seq.*

7. On December 1, 1864, the *Dispatch* of Selma, Alabama, had published an advertisement signed "Box X, Cahawba, Alabama," stating that if the citizens of the South "will furnish me with the cash, or good securities for the sum of one million dollars, I will cause the lives of Abraham Lincoln, Wm. H. Seward, and Andrew Johnson to be taken by the first of March next. This will give us peace, and satisfy the world that cruel tyrants cannot live in a land of liberty . . ." Stanton depended on such "evidence" for his belief as to Confederate responsibility for the plot.

8. See David Miller DeWitt, "The Judicial Murder of Mary E. Surratt," Baltimore, 1895; 6-8.

9. *Ibid.*, 7; Dr. William B. Hesseltine, of the University of Chattanooga, in his "Civil War Prisons," Columbus, O., 1930, 245, recounts an apocryphal story of a visit to Capt. Wirz, under sentence of death for alleged crimes at Andersonville prison, of a secret emissary from a high Cabinet officer to offer to reprieve a criminal if he would make a confession which would convict President Davis of conspiring to murder prisoners. The condemned man indignantly denied any contacts with the Confederate President.

10. Welles, II, 303.

11. DeWitt, "Mary E. Surratt," 13.

12. DeWitt, "Mary E. Surratt," 16, 18, 19, particularly testimony of James J. Gifford, who had been in prison in 1865 with Weichman, had

evidence given in John H. Surratt trial, in 1867, testified that Weichman had told him that an officer of the government warned him "that unless he testified to more than he had already said, they would hang him too."
13. Johnson Mss., Vol. 62, No. 3260.
14. Welles, II, 299-300. Hunter was chief clerk of the Department of State, secretary *ad interim* during the convalescence of the Sewards. I have changed the tense of the Welles quotation from past to present.
15. Bates, "Diary," Ms., 222, entry for August 21, 1865.
16. Johnson Mss., Vol. 62, No. 3494. But in November Davis was writing the *Nation* denouncing the President for his Conservatism. "We remember his declaration that traitors should be punished, yet none are punished; that only loyal men should control the States, yet he has delivered them to the disloyal; that the aristocracy should be pulled down, yet he has put it in power again; that its possessions should be divided among . . . laborers of all classes, yet the negroes are still a landless homeless class." See *Nation*, Nov. 30, 1865.
17. Welles, II, 303. He adds that "the rash, impulsive, and arbitrary measures of Stanton are exceedingly repugnant to my notions, and I am pained to witness the acquiesence they receive. He carries others with him, sometimes against their conviction as expressed to me."
18. Johnson Mss., 62, No. 3499.
19. Welles, II, 305.
20. Johnson Mss., Vol. 62, No. 3303. Naturally enough their generals were chiefly former Democrats or Conservatives! Scott, Grant, Sherman, Meade, Rosecrans, Howard, Burnside, Hancock, Hooker, Schofield, Wright, Dix, Cadwallader, Emory, Blair, Pleasanton, Logan, Steel, Peck, Hatch, Franklin, Rodman, Alexander, Canby, Reynolds, Meagher.
21. General Cyrus B. Comstock, and Col. Horace Porter, were the two who refused the assignment. See DeWitt, "Mary E. Surratt," 23.
22. They were Major-General Lew Wallace; Brigadier-General James A. Ekin; Colonel Charles A. Tompkins; Major-General August V. Kautz; Brigadier-General Thomas M. Harris; Brigadier-General Albion P. Howe, and Lieut.-Col. David R. Clendenin. Hunter had written Johnson on April 16, begging for "a situation near your person, where I can secure, under Providence your valuable life to the nation." Johnson Greeneville Mss.
23. DeWitt, "Mary E. Surratt," 26.
24. In 1873 General Hartranft, who had been provost-marshal for the trial, entered the Johnson-Holt controversy to deny that Mrs. Surratt had been chained. The evidence is against him. Testimony of eye witnesses of the trial is unanimous that Mrs. Surratt was burdened with these iron anklets. The Northern press was full of details, and this was deemed appropriate treatment for a person already in the public mind convicted of guilt as charged. See DeWitt, "Mary E. Surratt," 28, 29, 30. Col. Burnett, in a paper delivered before the Ohio Society of New York, on April 18, 1892, denied the charge, as was natural.
25. Lafayette C. Baker has the audacity to claim that "during my visits to the prisoners before their execution, Mrs. Surratt confessed to me her implicity in the conspiracies so far as the intended abduction was concerned, but affirmed that she reluctantly yielded to the urging of Booth in aiding the plot of assassination!" See his "History of the United

States Secret Service," 563. Such testimony fortunately, has not the slightest weight.

26. "American State Trials," VIII, 40.

27. "American State Trials," VIII, 43-4.

28. Mrs. Surratt's active counsel were both young and inexperienced advocates, Frederick A. Aiken, aged 28, and John W. Clampitt, aged only 25. Doubtless it was no easy matter for persons accused of such heinous offenses to secure even beardless youths to defend them.

29. DeWitt, "Mary E. Surratt," 49.

30. "American State Trials," VIII, 63, testimony of Lewis F. Bates.

31. "American State Trials," VIII, 233, et seq. Testimony of George Cottingham, Mrs. Emma Offut, John Nothey, Joseph Nott, J. Z. Jenkins, Andrew Kallenbach, James Lusby, and others.

32. Ibid., VIII, 238, et seq. Testimony of Anna E. Surratt; Honoré Fitzpatrick; Mrs. Eliza Holahan, and Anna Ward.

33. DeWitt, "Mary E. Surratt," 101.

34. Spangler received a six year sentence, and the two others were sentenced to imprisonment for life.

35. DeWitt, "Mary E. Surratt," 98-110, has a singularly penetrating statement and analysis of the sentence sessions, debates and arguments of the commission. I have followed it, as the overwhelming weight of authority is on DeWitt's side.

36. DeWitt, "Mary E. Surratt," III.

37. Johnson Mss., Vol. 159, No. 25,817. Gideon Welles wrote Johnson a long letter on Nov. 5, 1873, based on his diary, for Johnson's use in the controversy with Holt over the Surratt case. Holt had stated that Johnson had submitted the commission's sentence of Mrs. Surratt to the Cabinet, and that it had "as a unit" concurred in denying the petition of the court for mercy.

38. Joseph Holt Mss., Library of Congress, Vol. 67, No. 9165, R. D. Mussey to J. H. Holt, Aug. 9, 1873. Mussey had then become a Radical of Radicals, and was eager to back up Holt.

39. Holt expressed his claim in these words.

40. In August, 1865, when Benn Pittman wanted to publish the proceedings of the trial, Holt turned over the file to him, cautioning him to print every word. Pittman's printed account contains no word of or reference to a recommendation of mercy. Johnson consistently claimed that "no recommendation for a commutation of her punishment was mentioned or submitted to me." The President said he knew nothing of the existence of such a document until 1867, when it was referred to in the trial of John H. Surratt. He immediately sent for the file, and examined it, remarking to Browning that the petition was "now attached in such way as to show it was subsequently done." Browning "Diary," Aug. 9, 1867.

41. DeWitt, "Mary E. Surratt," 121.

42. Holt Mss., Vol. 67, No. 6195. Mussey letter already cited.

43. DeWitt, "Mary E. Surratt," 120, et seq.

44. New York Herald, July 8, 1865; a graphic account by George Alfred Townsend, noted Washington correspondent of the day.

45. DeWitt, "Mary E. Surratt," 125.

CHAPTER XI

1. Carl Schurz, "Speeches, Correspondence," etc., New York, 1913; I, 258. Letter to Charles Sumner, dated Bethlehem, June 5, 1865.

2. *Ibid.*, I, 209.

3. For text see Carl Schurz, "Reminiscences," New York, 1907; II, 394. In writing his reminiscences, the General did not print Lincoln's letter. But the editors inserted it.

4. Walter P. Brownlow, "Defense and Vindication of Andrew Johnson," *Taylor-Trotwood* Magazine, Nashville, 1908.

5. *Ibid.*

6. Johnson Mss., Vol. 45, No. 9955; Vol. 46, No. 10,003.

7. During Andrew Johnson's presidency, Carl Schurz cuts a rather sorry figure, but his later career did much to re-establish his reputation. After the Radical excesses of Grant's first term, Schurz split with them, took a lead in the liberal protest, became a great Civil Service reformer, and a figure of some distinction in the politics of the country from 1872 until his death. Brownlow's phrase "as big a fraud as he was a reformer," seems not altogether just.

8. Johnson Mss., 66, No. 4243.

9. Sumner Mss., Letter from Benjamin F. Loan, St. Joseph, Mo., June 1, 1865.

10. Sumner Mss., Letters from T. Gilbert, Boston, June 3; M. D. Conway, London, June 14; J. W. Alden, New York, June 14.

11. New York *Tribune*, June 2, 1865.

12. Pierce, IV, 246, 247.

13. Oberholtzer, I, 37.

14. Sumner Mss., Letter from Thaddeus Stevens, Caledonia, Pa., June 14, 1865.

15. *Ibid.*, Sumner to Schurz, Boston, June 15, 19, 1865.

16. Schurz "Speeches," I, 264, Schurz to Sumner, Washington, June 16, 1865.

17. Johnson Mss., Vols. 66-70, for several such letters.

18. *Ibid.*, Vol. 66, No. 4381.

19. *Ibid.*, Vol. 67, No. 4716.

20. Unfortunately, a search of the letters received in the Sumner collection at Harvard does not reveal this letter. I have constructed this account of it from internal evidence to be found in Sumner's replies of June 22, 29, and July 11.

21. Sumner Mss., letter to Schurz, Boston, June 22, 1865.

22. Schurz, "Speeches," I, 265; Schurz to Sumner, Bethlehem, Pa., June 27, 1865.

23. Though they might dislike the President's policy about negro suffrage, the Radicals were anxious enough to get every government job they could. One finds General John A. Logan asking for appointment as federal marshal for the Southern district of Illinois; Hannibal Hamlin insisting that a pet of his named Brown be re-appointed navy agent at Boston, and John W. Forney, writing from Philadelphia, that one or two of his friends ought to have certain jobs. See Johnson Mss., Vol. 70, No. 5425; Vol. 71, Nos. 5478, and 5506. Gideon Welles was indignant at

Hamlin's attitude, and in his diary accused the ex-vice president of being a silent partner in the fat fees Brown received. See Welles, II, 332, *et seq.*

24. Sumner Mss., letters to Schurz, June 29, and July 11, 1865.

25. DeWitt, 18; Rhodes, VI, 12; Gorham, II, 416.

26. Rhodes, VI, 12-13.

27. "Correspondence Between General and Senator Sherman," New York, 1894; 251.

28. Adam Badeau, "Grant in Peace," Hartford, Conn., 1887; 31.

29. Sherman, "Home Letters," 353; O. R., Vol. XLVIII, part 3, 411, 462.

30. New York Evening *Post,* June 20, 1865.

31. Oberholtzer, I, 22, quoting *Press,* June 28; *Ledger,* June 13.

32. New York *Herald,* June 2, 1865.

33. Johnson Mss., Vol. 76, No. 6759.

34. Sept. 28, 1865, quoted Rhodes VI, 20-21.

35. Johnson Mss., Vol. 64, No. 3970.

36. But on May 23, the New York *Times* had called for a special exception to amnesty in the case of "every rebel officer who was concerned directly or indirectly in the torturing or murdering our prisoners." Dr. Hesseltine has collated many illustrations of the vigor of the North's insistence on vengeance on Southern prison officers.

37. Johnson Mss., Vol. 68, No. 4839.

38. *Ibid.,* Vol. 70, No. 5420; for recent Southern attitude on the black codes, see J. G. de R. Hamilton, in W. A. Dunning, "Studies in Southern History and Politics," New York, 1914.

39. Johnson Mss., Vol. 74, No. 6282.

40. Johnson Mss., Vol. 74, No. 6213.

41. Johnson Mss., Vol. 76, No. 6712. Doolittle to Johnson, Racine, Wis., Sept. 9, 1865.

42. *Ibid.,* Vol. 70, No. 5217.

43. Johnson Mss., Vol. 69, No. 5021.

44. Sumner Mss., Letters from James Harlan, Washington, August 21; Hugh McCulloch, Washington, August 22; Henry Wilson, Washington, Sept. 9.

45. Pierce, IV, 250-252.

46. Rhodes, VI, 17.

47. Francis P. Blair was outraged at these intimations from Massachusetts. He termed the projected exclusion of Southern representatives from Congress "simply an attempt at revolution, a breach of the Union by the vote of Congress." He urged Johnson to change his Cabinet, so that only loyal men would be about him, changes which must be made at once.

48. Welles, II, 393, *et seq.*

49. Oberholtzer, I, 45; see also New York *Tribune,* June 30, 1865. Horace Greeley particularly chafed at the situation. Oberholtzer says, "he must defend a Republican President, but this President was beginning to be viewed favorably by men whom he had taught himself. . . to hate as the minions of the Evil One."

50. Johnson Mss., Vol. 71, No. 5536.

51. Johnson Mss., Vol. 71, No. 5654.

52. *Ibid.,* Vol. 74, Nos. 6190-6191-6193.

53. *Ibid.,* Vol. 76, No. 6731.

54. Johnson Mss., Vol. 60, No. 2957.

55. *Ibid.*, Vol. 62, No. 3365.

56. New York *Herald*, June 27, 1865; "If this pressure of the last few weeks is kept up, it is doubtful if he will be able to stand it."

57. Digest of Washington Papers, Johnson Mss., Vol. 70, No. 5247.

58. Welles, II, 329-330.

59. Winston, 292, *et seq.*, gives an attractive picture of the Johnson family during this summer.

60. Knoxville *Whig,* Jan. 17, 1866, quoting an exchange's account of the reception. The little boy of the luncheon incident was James F. Duhamel, son of a Washington physician. My account of this incident is based on an interview with him on December 4, 1928.

61. Winston, 295. For a pleasant picture of the Johnsons' private lives, see Crook, "Through Five Administrations," 88, *et seq.*; for mouse story, see Moore "Diary" Transcript, July 31, Aug. 1, 1868.

62. McCulloch, 406.

63. Elizabeth Keckley, "Behind the Scenes," New York, 1868; 222, *et seq.*

64. Frank Cowan, "Andrew Johnson Reminiscences," Greensburg, Pa., 1894; 13.

65. Truman, *op. cit.*, 438; but William kept asking him for a United States marshal's job in Texas. Finally Johnson remarked to Truman: "That isn't *much*. Better give it to him, hadn't I?"

66. Oberholtzer, I, 21. When the equipage was sold at auction, it brought only about half the $6,000 which had been paid for it.

67. But there is a story of Johnson's accepting a gift. The Phoenix Mutual Insurance Company at that time made a practice of offering to each president, while in office, a policy for $2,000. According to the company tradition, Lincoln refused while Johnson accepted. Examination of the photostat of the Johnson application No. 11, 173, discloses that Johnson signed the application on April 14, 1865, while Lincoln was alive and Johnson still Vice President. His beloved Eliza was the designated beneficiary. It was received in Hartford on April 17, and indorsed in the home office as "Andrew Johnson, President." The blank bears the mark of $124.80 as the premium. To me it seems likely that Johnson paid for the policy.

68. For this information, I am indebted to the late Winslow Russell, Vice President of the Phoenix Mutual, who searched his company's records and furnished this information, as well as a photostat of the Johnson application and examination blank. Mr. Russell added that "it would appear that Mr. Johnson accepted the policy without premium payment for one year, but we have nothing to prove it either way."

69. Cowan, 5, 6, 7, *et seq.*; Howard K. Beale, "The Critical Year," New York, 1930; 21-22. Dr. Beale's picture of the true Johnson is one of the best ever written.

70. *Ibid.*, 10.

71. John Silva Meehan, librarian of Congress from 1829 to 1861, instituted a system of receipt books in which were kept the record of books borrowed and returned. Some of these books were lost in the fire of December 24, 1851, which destroyed more than half the books in the library. There remain, however, receipt books covering the 21st, 31st-9th Con-

gresses. I am indebted to Mr. Herbert Putnam, Librarian of Congress, and to Mr. R. F. Roberts, Superintendent of the Reading Room of the Library of Congress, for the painstaking work of searching these receipt books and preparing from them lists of the books Andrew Johnson borrowed, as indicated in the receipt books now remaining.
72. Moore "Diary" Transcript, Jan. 10, 1867; July 8, 1868.
73. Cowan, 13.

CHAPTER XII

1. Welles, II, 315-316.
2. McPherson, "Reconstruction," 12.
3. Sharkey was nearly 70 years old and had for the last 18 years been chief justice of the Mississippi Supreme Court. James Johnson, a conservative lawyer, opposed Secession, but "had gone with his State." He was timid, but of "strong sense and good principles." Parsons, a lineal descendant of Jonathan Edwards, was a New Yorker by birth, but had been a resident of Alabama since 1840. Although he had held a seat in the "rebel legislature," he was Unionist in feeling and sympathy. When the war commenced Hamilton was a Texas slaveholder, but supported the Union and removed to the North. Although appointed Brigadier General of volunteers by Lincoln, he saw no service in the war. Benjamin F. Perry was a native South Carolinian. As a young lawyer, Perry opposed Calhoun and Secession, but during the war reluctantly accepted office under the Confederate government. Marvin, a United States District Judge at Key West in 1861, remained at his post until 1863, when he removed to New York.
4. Johnson Mss., Vol. 63, No. 3379.
5. *Ibid.*, 62, No. 3490.
6. *Ibid.*, Vol. 63, No. 3585.
7. Johnson Mss., Vol. 56, No. 4843.
8. *Ibid.*, Vol. 66, No. 4320.
9. *Ibid.*, Vol. 67, No. 4718.
10. Johnson Mss., Vol. 66, No. 4268. "Jefferson Davis has fallen into disfavor, if not odium," he likewise reported.
11. Even such a rabid Radical as Governor Brownlow of Tennessee protested against the use of negro garrisons. "They are too ready to shoot and use the bayonet," he informed the President.
12. Johnson Mss., Vol. 67, No. 4685.
13. *Ibid.*, Vol. 69, No. 4987.
14. Johnson Mss., Vol. 70, No. 5263.
15. Schurz's report was published as Senate Executive Document No. 2, 39th Congress, first session. The reader will find sufficient excerpts of the Schurz report to indicate its character in Fleming; Vol. I.
16. Sumner Mss., Sumner to Schurz, Boston, Aug. 28, 1865.
17. Schurz "Speeches," I, 268-9.
18. New Orleans *Times*, Sept. 5, 1865; Johnson Mss., Vol. 75, No. 6601.
19. Schurz "Speeches, Letters, Etc.," I, 272-3.
20. Sumner Mss., Sumner to Schurz, Boston, Oct. 20, 1865. Johnson to

Bancroft, Washington, October 29, 1865, Bancroft Papers, Massachusetts Historical Society, Boston.

21. Schurz "Speeches, Letters, Etc.," I, 277.

22. Oberholtzer, I, 32, quoting Philadelphia *Press*, July 10, 1865.

23. Johnson Mss., Vol. 73, No. 6035-39.

24. Johnson Mss., Vol. 74, No. 6264. J. A. Stewart to the President, Rome, Ga., Aug. 12, 1865.

25. *Ibid.*, Vol. 67, No. 4511.

26. *Ibid.*, Vol. 69, No. 5128.

27. Johnson Mss., Vol. 81, No. 8002.

28. *Ibid.*, Vol. 80, No. 7610.

29. Welles, II, 337-8-9.

30. *Ibid.*, II, 366. At this point Welles characterizes the Chief Justice as "cowardly and aspiring, shirking and presumptuous, forward and evasive; . . . an ambitious politician; possessed of mental resources, yet afraid to use them, irresolute as well as ambitious." The diarist said that "the President detests the traits of the Judge," as exhibited in the Davis affair.

31. Johnson Mss., Vol. 78, No. 7210; Vol. 79, No. 7354.

32. Sumner Mss., Sumner to Schurz, Boston, August 28, 1865.

33. "Correspondence with Provisional Governors," Washington, 1866; 221-2. For a typical proclamation, see Fleming, I, 174.

34. "Provisional Governors," 221.

35. Perry, "Reminiscences," (Second Series) 229-241. Despite these remarks, anyone who reads the speech as a whole will agree with Perry that it castigates Confederate leadership much more vigorously than it does the Abolitionists of the North.

36. Johnson Mss., Vol. 74, No. 6314; 6340.

37. For telegraphic correspondence between Johnson and various provisional governors, see "Provisional Governors," 220-259.

38. Welles, II, 318, 358.

39. "Provisional Governors," 55, *et seq.*

40. "Provisional Governors," 229.

41. Johnson Mss., Vol. 77, No. 6929.

42. Oberholtzer, I, 146.

43. Johnson Mss., Vol. 76, Nos. 6817, 6813, 6809.

44. Letter of Bishop Thomas F. Gailor, Sewanee, Tenn., Sept. 5, 1929, to author.

45. Sidney Andrews, "The South Since the War," Boston, 1866; 33, 38. Andrews, the correspondent of the Boston *Advertiser*, and the Chicago *Tribune*, covered the constitutional conventions of South Carolina, North Carolina and Georgia in the fall of 1865. He was a Radical, but a shrewd and dependable observer.

46. Andrews, 67.

47. Johnson Mss., Vol. 80, No. 7670.

48. Andrews, 133.

49. Andrews, 243-244.

50. *Ibid.*, 251.

51. Johnson Mss., Vol. 80, No. 7772.

52. "Provisional Governors," 236-7.

53. Oberholtzer, I, 145.

54. Johnson ordered the Provisional Governors to maintain their posts until further instructions. On Dec. 4, 1865, Secretary Seward notified all but Hamilton of Texas to give way to their elected successors.

55. Popularly known as "the ironclad oath." By Act of Congress of July 2, 1862, it must be taken by every person elected or appointed to any office of honor or profit under the government of the United States, either in civil or military or naval departments of the public service, the President alone being excepted. Before he should enter upon his duties or receive any pay, the officer must "swear he had never voluntarily borne arms against the United States:" nor had voluntarily given aid, countenance, counsel, or encouragement to persons engaged in armed hostility to the national government, that he had "neither sought nor accepted nor attempted to exercise the function of any office whatever under authority or pretended authority in hostility to the United States;" and finally, that he had "never yielded a voluntary support of any pretended government within the United States, hostile or inimical thereto."

56. McPherson, "Reconstruction," 109; Oberholtzer, 1, 134.

57. Blaine, II, 113.

58. Johnson Mss., Vol. 78, No. 7243.

59. Johnson Mss., Vol. 76, No. 6819.

60. Ibid., Vol. 78, No. 7259; Vol. 79, No. 7423.

61. Ibid., Vol. 81, No. 7945.

62. Ibid., Vol. 77, No. 6945.

63. Johnson Mss., Vol. 78, No. 7291.

64. F. P. Stearns, "Life of George Luther Stearns," Philadelphia, 1907; 358, et seq.

65. New York World, October 19, 1865.

66. Stearns, 361.

67. Sherman Letters, 257.

68. Ibid., 259.

69. Johnson Mss., Vol. 82, No. 8061.

70. No use has hitherto been made of this account in the study of Johnson-Sumner relations. Campbell wrote Johnson in the spring of 1868, when the impeachment matter was at its height, to refresh the President's mind as to occurrences at the interview. See Johnson Mss., Vol. 134, No. 19,985.

71. Sumner, "Works," Boston, 1883; XI, 25, quoted Lloyd P. Stryker, "Andrew Johnson," New York, 1929; 259-260.

72. Pierce, IV, 268.

73. Welles, II, 395.

CHAPTER XIII

1. Johnson Mss., Vol. 82, No. 8054.

2. E. B. Callender, "Thaddeus Stevens," Boston, 1882; 9.

3. Stevens' first step was to introduce a resolution calling for a committee "to inquire into the expediency of providing by law for making Freemasonry a good cause of peremptory challenge to jurors in all cases when one of the parties is a Freemason and the other is not . . ." See Callender, 27.

4. Schurz, III, 212-7.
5. Stryker, 248.
6. Blaine, I, 325.
7. Blaine, I, 325.
8. Stevens reminds one somewhat of John Randolph of Roanoke of two generations before. The two men were equally brilliant, equally bitter, but Stevens was a better driver. Randolph was a soured idealist, however, and Stevens never forgot to be a practical man. It is doubtful if an American Congress ever saw a leader who approached Stevens in the ability to force unwilling men to support a policy which many bitterly despised.
9. Recollection of George Hensel, Jr., Quarryville, Penna., to author, September 29, 1927.
10. Benjamin B. Kendrick, "Journal of the Reconstruction Committee," New York, 1903; 139.
11. Welles, II, 387.
12. The Radical Independent, Dec. 7, 1865, said McPherson "deserves the thanks of the country."
13. We have already noticed Maynard's history. He had been "in the furnace of treason" along with Parson Brownlow and the President. Of his loyalty there could not be the slightest doubt, but Welles suspected that Maynard was in Stevens' game.
14. An Indiana Congressman offered a resolution to admit these applicants to the House privileges pending the determination of their cases. Stevens countered by a motion to adjourn, thus preventing a vote on the Indianian's motion.
15. Moore "Diary," Transcript, July 14, 1866; May 15, 1868. Blaine II, 112.
16. Welles, II, 392.
17. Blaine, II, 112.
18. Independent, Dec. 7, 1865.
19. Johnson Mss., Vol. 60, No. 2998.
20. Ibid., Vol. 80, No. 7785. Some recent historians, notably W. A. Dunning, have made much capital of Bancroft's connection with the message. While the style is that of this historian, there is no doubt that the thoughts are those of Andrew Johnson.
21. Richardson, "Messages and Papers of the Presidents," VI, 353, et seq.
22. Nation, December 14, 1865; McCulloch, 219-220; Johnson Mss., Vol. 110, No. 14, 634.
23. Rhodes, VI, 33.
24. Blaine, II, 126.
25. See ante Chapter XI, p. 260.
26. Welles, II, 399.
27. Ibid., II, 402-3.
28. Hugh Ewing Mss., Thomas to Hugh Ewing, Jan. 7, 1868.
29. Welles, II, 417.
30. Congressional Globe, 39th Congress, First Session, 74, et seq.
31. Stevens did not elaborate as to how he would give homesteads to the negroes, but in a speech at Lancaster, on Sept. 6, he disclosed the method.

"The real estate of 70,000 Rebels who own 200 acres each," was to be confiscated and split up for the negroes.

32. Blaine, II, 130; Stevens' reference was to Taney's Dred Scott decision.

33. Richardson, VI, 372. Covode had made him no report.

34. *Congressional Globe,* 39th Congress, First Session, 78.

35. Welles, II, 400.

36. *Ibid.,* 30.

37. Blaine, II, 149. A little later Sumner indirectly qualified his harshness by denying that he wished to reflect on the patriotism or the truth of the President. "Never in public or in private have I made such reflection, and I do not begin now. When I spoke, I spoke of the document that had been read at the desk."

38. Blaine, II, 92.

39. Act passed November 22, 1865. For a good compilation of such Southern laws governing freedmen, see Fleming, I, 273-312.

40. Blaine, II, 94.

41. Blaine, II, 100.

42. The *Galaxy,* May, 1872, 671.

43. Blaine, II, 106.

44. *Ibid.,* 90.

45. The votes were Senate, 27 to 10; House, 136 to 33. Senators Dixon, Doolittle and Norton, staunch Johnson defenders, went with the caucus, as did Henry J. Raymond in the House.

46. McPherson, "Reconstruction," 52, *et seq.*

47. James M. Embrey, who heard it, wrote Johnson (Johnson Mss., Vol. 86, No. 9001) that Stevens, Sumner *et al.,* had planned, originated and matured Douglass' speech as part and parcel of the Radical conspiracy.

48. New York *Tribune,* Aug. 29, 1875, letter from the Rev. A. Toomer Porter, Aiken, S. C.

49. Johnson Mss., Vol. 86, No. 9057.

50. Sherman "Letters," New York, 1894; 261-2.

51. Bates "Diary," Mss., 273.

52. Welles, II, 432.

53. Richardson, VI, 398, *et seq.* Johnson Mss., Vol. 87, Nos. 9208-66.

54. J. R. Hawley to C. D. Warner, Washington, Jan. 30, 1866; Hartford *Times,* Jan. 15, 1930.

55. Welles, II, 438.

56. Feb. 29, 1866. *The Independent.*

57. McCulloch, 393; Doolittle to Browning, Washington, Oct. 7, 1866, Browning Mss., Illinois State Historical Library.

58. I have followed the text of the speech as printed in the Washington *National Intelligencer,* for Johnson carefully corrected proofs of this account before its publication and preserved the proof sheets in his papers, where any inquiring student can find them today. The account in Forney's Washington *Chronicle* is badly garbled, as might have been expected in a turncoat sheet.

59. Statement of Col. A. M. Hughes, to author, Washington, Dec. 12, 1928. Hughes also said that Johnson was "cold sober" at the time.

60. Forney, whose attachment to Johnson had been so ardent in 1864 and the first half of 1865, had come to the conclusion that the Radicals were stronger than the President, and had therefore made a complete about face, becoming as villainous a critic as Johnson had. The columns of the *Chronicle* teemed with abuse of his former friend. The appellation "dead duck" clung to him the rest of his life.

CHAPTER XIV

1. *Nation*, Mar. 1, 1867.

2. E. K. Smart of Camden, Me., sent the President a copy of a letter which Paul Stevens, assistant librarian of the House of Representatives, had written to friends in Maine, on February 25, making the statement quoted above. Johnson Mss., Vol. 91, No. 10,141. Gurowski busied himself "repeating the dirty scandal." Forney's *Chronicle* was "scandalously abusive, and personally indecent, false and vindicative," Welles, II, 439.

3. A typical note was that from a man in Syracuse who "must hurrah for the blood of Old Hickory, or bust."

4. Johnson Mss., Vol. 87, No. 9374.

5. Johnson Mss., Vol. 88, No. 9604.

6. Sherman Letters, 263-265.

7. Johnson Mss., Vol. 88, No. 9550, letter dated Washington, Feb. 26, 1866.

8. No biographer of James Gordon Bennett should neglect a careful study of the letters from Phillips to Johnson, beginning with this one and ending with Johnson's presidency. I am at a loss to fathom the motive back of them. Whether Bancroft instructed Phillips to correspond with the President to deceive the latter or whether Phillips actually betrayed his secret analysis of his too commercial chief, I do not know. The present letter is to be found, Johnson Mss., Vol. 87, No. 9386.

9. John Sherman, "Recollections," (popular edition) Chicago, 1896; 312.

10. Welles, II, 447.

11. John Sherman, "Recollections," 314.

12. DeWitt, "Impeachment," 62.

13. Welles, II, 452.

14. *Congressional Globe*, 1st. term, 39th Congress, 1307-8.

15. Johnson Mss., Vol. 91, No. 10,151.

16. Johnson Mss., Vol. 90, No. 10,055.

17. *Ibid.*, Vol. 90, No. 10,100.

18. See Chapter XV.

19. DeWitt, "Impeachment," 65.

20. One can readily understand that such intransigeance irritated the more practical Radicals. Nye of Nevada arose to inform Sumner that he "mistook twinges of dyspepsia for constitutional scruples." There was vivid self-revelation in Sumner's answer: "I have never had dyspepsia in my life." Pierce, IV, 286.

21. For complete facts in the Stockton case, see *Congressional Globe*, First Session, 39th Congress, 1564, *et seq.* For a clear abstract, see DeWitt, "Impeachment," 65-83.

22. Blaine, II, 158.

23. Even so partisan a radical as Blaine, (II, 159) admits that the ejection "can hardly be justifiable," and that the Senate had acted without "magnanimity or generosity."

24. Blaine, II, 172, *et seq.*, Dixon voted for it, Cowan and Norton against it, and Doolittle did not vote.

25. McPherson, "Reconstruction," 78-80.

26. Johnson Mss., Vol. 79, No. 7572.

27. *Ibid.*, Vol. 91, No. 10,180.

28. William Dudley Foulke, "Life of Oliver P. Morton," Indianapolis, Ind., 1899; I, 466.

29. John Sherman, "Recollections," I, 369. After the veto, he accused Johnson of being insincere; "he has deceived and misled his best friends." See Sherman "Letters," 276. •

30. Welles, II, 459.

31. Welles, II, 463, *et seq.*

32. Rhodes, VI, 74, 75, 68.

33. McPherson, 74, 78. After this veto, the *Independent* called him "Nebuchadnezzar" and said that his position was that the Constitution should not be amended until Lee and Davis submitted amendments. See its issue of April 5, 1866.

34. DeWitt, "Impeachment," 80. However, the New Jersey ousting, although it resulted in a decrease of one in the Conservative strength, did not add a Radical vote, for a recalcitrant member of the New Jersey legislature, who held the balance of power there and had been won by Johnson with Federal patronage, prevented the Senate from going into joint meeting. Thus New Jersey went on from day to day without electing a senator. Thad Stevens sent repeated telegrams belaboring the recalcitrant, who was unmoved. Finally the New Jersey legislature adjourned in despair, and Stockton's stolen seat remained vacant for a year.

35. Moore "Diary" Transcript, undated, on page 15 of transcript.

36. Sherman "Letters," 278.

37. Blaine, II, 189.

38. *Ibid.*, II, 192.

39. Blaine, II, 199.

40. McPherson, 103-4.

41. Blaine, II, 205.

42. Benjamin B. Kendrick's introduction to his "Journal of the Reconstruction Committee," and his annotations to the text, afford valuable insight into the maneuvers and motives of the committee leading up to the amendment.

43. It is notable, however, that the disqualifying clause received a House majority of only 5.

44. This ban could not be removed by executive pardon, but only by a two-thirds vote of both Houses of Congress.

45. Warden, 647-8.

46. For Rhodes' discussion of this amendment, see Rhodes, VI, 80-95.

47. McPherson, "Reconstruction," 147-8.

48. See Chase Mss., Library of Congress, Vol. 97, No. 14,555 A. Brownlow had been in open war with the President for more than a year, and in

June wrote to Chase about the President: "I have long since given him up. He has conceived the idea of a second term."

49. "Some of the members . . . conducted themselves in a very refractory way to prevent a quorum," read Thomas' dispatch of July 14. "The Governor cannot manage them . . . and has appealed to me for military assistance."

50. Welles, II, 554-5.

51. These members secured writs of *habeas corpus* from Judge Thomas Frazier of the local state court. The Brownlow legislature promptly impeached, convicted and ousted the judge.

52. Richardson, VI, 395, *et seq.*

53. Patterson had been a state judge, his circuit being in a Unionist section. In 1862, a new election had been called and he had been re-elected by loyal neighbors over a Confederate candidate by 4,000 majority. The Confederates occupied the section at the time, and Patterson could not serve unless he took the Confederate oath. His neighbors were importunate that he do so in order to protect them from military oppression. He agreed, announcing at the same time that he owed no allegiance to the Davis government, and did not consider that part of the oath binding upon him. In September, 1863, he managed to escape from the Confederate territory and did not return home until the end of the war.

CHAPTER XV

1. Welles, II, 443.

2. The embarrassments imposed on the Federal service by the test oath is an example. The Secretary of the Treasury and the Postmaster-General found it next to impossible to secure good men for collectors, assessors, postmasters, and the like in the Southern states, because men who could take the oath were undesirable because of incompetence or bad character. Yet when the matter came before the Cabinet, and McCulloch proposed to address a strong and emphatic letter to Johnson which the latter could send to Congress, thus making a direct issue and informing the country of the Administration's practical difficulties, the Cabinet Radicals objected, Harlan fearing that such a confession "would operate injudiciously just at this time," while Stanton doubted the expediency of such a letter. They did not wish to see the President do anything to aid his case.

3. A son of Zachary Taylor; he had been a lieutenant general in the Confederate forces.

4. When Taylor revealed the incident, the President appeared confused, and Montgomery Blair, who had been privy to the negotiations, believed that Johnson himself had told Stanton of the matter. Nothing came of the Grant-Taylor plan. Blair revealed it to Welles on March 25, 1867. See Welles, III, 7203, and also Richard Taylor, "Destruction and Reconstruction," New York, 1877; 244, *et seq.*

5. The *Independent*, Feb. 29, 1866; Tilton termed Stanton "one of the truest, bravest and greatest men of the government."

6. This distrust of Speed seems to have been quite general. On the

night of March 14 Thomas Ewing had urged the President to select a new Attorney-General, and the next day had written Johnson to emphasize that "it is due to yourself, and also to the court" to have a stronger attorney-general. Speed "is not a competent legal adviser, especially in the present critical condition of affairs . . . You ought not to turn him adrift, but make him district judge somewhere, say in Mississippi." Ewing recommended for the place Henry Stanbery of Cincinnati, "who stands at the head of the western bar"; he also suggested Orville H. Browning, probably for the Interior Department, "a den of plunderers since 1861," badly needing a man like Browning to purify it.

7. For Doolittle's talk with Welles, and the latter's conversation with the President, see Welles, II, 480-484. In this sentence I have altered Welles' indirect discourse to direct quotation; for Johnson's estimate of Harlan and Speed, see Moore "Diary" Transcript, May 7, 1867.

8. McPherson, "Reconstruction," 15.

9. According to Badeau, Grant, 37, Johnson came "uninvited."

10. Welles, II, 478.

11. DeWitt, "Impeachment," 87, et seq.

12. Johnson Mss., Vol. 94, No. 10,974.

13. For one such instance, see Johnson Mss., Vol. 92, No. 10,528.

14. Johnson Mss., Vol. 95, No. 11,228. The lawyer was Henry Nicoll. The discussion grew so warm that the President had Dr. George E. Cooper, who had succeeded Dr. Craven as surgeon at Fortress Monroe, report to him on Davis' physical condition. It was bad. The prisoner was "considerably emaciated, . . . his skin much shriveled. His muscles are small, flaccid, and very soft, and he has but little muscular strength." His nervous system was greatly deranged, due to want of sleep, chiefly caused by the creaking boots of sentinels tramping about his cell. See Johnson Mss., Vol. 94, No. 11,016.

15. Schuckers, 534. The indictment was based on an Act of Congress of July 17, 1862. If convicted, Davis could have been fined up to $10,000, imprisoned up to ten years, or both.

16. On October 6 the President addressed a formal question to the Attorney-General in relation to Jefferson Davis. It appeared that there would be no session of the United States Circuit Court at Richmond that month. "There now existing in the view of the Executive, no reason why the Civil Courts of the United States are not competent to exercise their jurisdiction in Virginia, I wish to be advised what further may be proper or expedient to be done by the executive in the premises." Stanbery answered that "to avoid any misunderstanding on the subject, an order be issued to the commandant of Fortress Monroe to surrender the prisoner to civil custody whenever demanded by the United States Marshal, upon process from the Civil Court." This was the procedure eventually used to admit Davis to bail. Johnson Mss., Vol. 103, Nos. 12,994-6-9.

17. Welles, II, 454. Pomeroy also claimed that Johnson kept a mistress at the White House.

18. Ibid, 461-468-472-473.

19. Gamaliel Bradford, "Union Portraits," Boston, 1916; 193.

20. DeWitt, "Impeachment," 246-7.

21. Carl Sandburg, "Abraham Lincoln," New York, 1926; II, 42. See

also, Bradford, "Union Portraits," 177; and Beveridge, "Lincoln," II, 575-84. The case was the famous Reaper case of McCormick vs. Manny.

22. DeWitt, "Impeachment," 252-3.

23. Welles, I, "Introduction," xxxi.

24. Ida Tarbell, "Abraham Lincoln," New York, 1900, II, 279.

25. Welles, I, 129; 67; Donn Piatt, "Men Who Saved the Union," 79; Russell, 596-598-9; John T. Morse, Jr., "Abraham Lincoln," I, 328. And yet this man kept the ashes of his first-born child in an urn at his bedside; see Sandburg "Lincoln," II, 41.

26. Winston, 188.

27. Perley Poore, II, 27-8.

28. Browning "Diary," May 2, 1866; Browning called at the White House the morning after the Cabinet meeting, and asked if the *Intelligencer's* account that morning was correct. "All . . . and a great deal more," Johnson answered, and then outlined the meeting in detail to Browning.

29. Welles, II, 495-7 gives the best account of this meeting. The Washington *National Intelligencer* of May 2, 1866, has an extended account which, Welles says, over-stresses Stanton's statements. Doubtless Col. Moore, Johnson's shorthand secretary, took the notes and wrote out the abstract.

30. Welles, II, 498.

31. *Ibid.*, II, 501.

32. Johnson Mss., Vol. 95, Nos. 11,143; 11,274.

33. Winston, 353.

34. Welles, II, 512-13; Górham, II, 301.

35. See Gorham, II, 302-310, for the text of this speech.

36. Johnson Mss., Vol. 96, No. 11,405.

37. *Ibid.*, Vol. 96, No. 11,451.

38. Browning "Diary," May 2, 1866, Moore "Diary" Transcript, May 7, 1867; Welles, II, 523.

39. Welles, II, 524-5. On June 12 McCulloch and Welles told Seward there was need to come to an understanding; the latter "looked a little sharp," but had no objection. Welles could not read his mind, but believed that Seward was acting deviously.

40. McCulloch, 391.

41. On May 21 Sumner wrote John Bright that the Cabinet was "nearly equally divided," that he spoke according to his personal knowledge; "Seward encourages him; McCulloch is bitterly with him; Dennison sometimes with him, and sometimes against him; Welles is with him; Stanton, Harlan and Speed are against his policy. See Pierce, IV, 288.

42. Browning "Diary," June 11, 1866.

43. Welles, II, 529. John A. Andrew of Massachusetts took a similar attitude.

44. *Ibid.*, II, 535. His judgment was that the proposed convention "has no basis of principles. It will be denounced as a mere union with Rebels."

45. McPherson, "Reconstruction," 118.

46. With characteristic sagacity, Alexander H. Stevens wrote Montgomery Blair that while he cordially indorsed and approved the convention's purposes, he doubted the propriety of his own attendance. Cf. Oberholtzer, I, 387.

47. Stanton Mss., Library of Congress, Vol. 30, No. 56,000.

48. Johnson Mss., Vol. 100, No. 12,201 A, B.

49. Blaine, II, 219, discloses that Dennison had remained as long as he had because he wished "to restrain the President from using the patronage of the government in aid of his policy" and that Harlan, too, had been "extremely reluctant to surrender the large patronage of the Interior Department to the control of a successor who would undoubtedly use it to promote the reconstruction policy of the President."

50. On July 8 Senator Sherman wrote his brother, the General, "to avoid all expressions of political opinion," that the Radicals and the President were drifting into open warfare. Johnson was becoming "Tylerized." "Elected by the Union party, he now deserts and betrays it . . . I almost fear he contemplates Civil War." John Sherman. "Recollections," Popular Edition, 328-9.

51. Johnson Mss., Vol. 99, No. 12,035.

52. Johnson Mss., Vol. 98, No. 11,930.

53. Welles, II, 573-4. I have transformed indirect into direct discourse in some of the sentences.

CHAPTER XVI

1. For a thorough-going study of the economic background of the Johnson-Radical battle, Beale, "The Critical Year," and the same author's "The Tariff and Reconstruction," *American Historical Review*, XXXV, 276-295, are admirable.

2. Oberholtzer, I, 379; Welles, II, 570. In his first telegram to the President sent the day after the riots, Sheridan said white men, "political agitators and revolutionary men" had got up the scheme, and "that the convention plan was one certain "to produce breaches of the peace." See Johnson Mss., Vol. 99, No. 11,939.

3. Fleming, "Reconstruction," I, 231.

4. New Orleans *Times*, July 26-August 10, 1866, has a thorough contemporary account of the background and details of the troubles.

5. Richardson, VI, 590.

6. Moore, "Diary," 102.

7. See Johnson Mss., Vol. 98, Nos. 11,782, 11,801-2, and 11,810.

8. See New York *Tribune*, July 31, 1866: "The hands of the rebels are again red with loyal blood. Rebel armies have once more begun the work of massacre." For a more considered Radical estimate of the riots, see Blaine, II, 236-7.

9. Pierce, IV, 298, Sumner to Bright, Sept. 3, 1866.

10. *Independent*, August 9, 1866; *Nation*, Aug. 9, 16, 1866. Memories of the New Orleans riots lingered in the minds of the Northern people, and Johnson's friends pressed the President to take some action to counteract their effect. On August 27 Senator Dixon wrote him from Hartford that "the Radical press is exciting popular opinion most deeply, and I fear we are losing ground in consequence of it. What I would suggest is that some action be taken to show that the Administration is unjustly accused." Why not displace Mayor Monroe by orders to Sheridan? This "would

entirely counteract the Radical effort to make capital. Depend upon it, we are in danger of losing thousands of votes . . . by the falsehoods circulated on this subject." See Johnson Mss., Vol. 100, No. 12,344.

11. Report of the Committee of the House, Second Session, 39th Congress, Document No. 12,304, 27; 252.

12. *Independent*, August 9, 1866.

13. Johnson, Mss., Vol. 99, No. 12,106.

14. *Ibid.*, Vol. 99, Nos. 12,094, 12,097.

15. Stryker, 321.

16. DeWitt, "Impeachment," 112.

17. Blaine, II, 220-21.

18. When the President received a message telling of the Couch-Orr incident, tears of joy filled his eyes and he could not finish reading the telegram. Cf. Oberholtzer, I, 390.

19. Blaine, II, 223.

20. Rhodes, VI, 99-100, quoting *Scribner's Monthly*, June, 1880.

21. McPherson, "Reconstruction," 240-1.

22. Welles, II, 581-2.

23. Grant had been especially invited, and the General, according to the not quite trustworthy account of Adam Badeau (p. 38), went to the White House, "with the intention of excusing himself," but found the party already assembled. When the President sent him word to join them in the East Room, the General "thought that, without positive rudeness, he could not refuse. So he stood by Johnson's side during the entire demonstration, greatly to his own distress and chagrin, and returned to his headquarters afterward full of indignation."

24. McPherson, "Reconstruction," 127.

25. Welles, II, 582.

26. About this time, Sumner informed John Bright that the President "goes on from bad to worse . . . His apostasy is complete." The Senator likened Johnson to "another James II, with Seward for his Sunderland." It was a "gloomy prospect . . . Perhaps war again." See Sumner Mss., Sumner to Bright, August 17, 1866. The *Nation*, Aug. 30, 1866, belabored the convention's resolutions as "specious and clever . . . mainly devoted to proving what nobody denies and passing over the only questions on which the public wanted to be enlightened."

27. Oberholtzer, I, 392; Warmoth, 49-50.

28. Blaine, II, 226. After he had seen his words in print, Speed seems to have been frightened at his boldness, for he wrote a note to Johnson (Johnson Mss., Vol. 101, No. 12,526) stating that he had said "tenant," not "tyrant," of the White House.

29. Johnson Mss., Vol. 101, No. 12,626.

30. *Ibid.,* Vol. 101, No. 12,695.

31. *Ibid.*, Vol. 104, No. 13,348.

32. Blaine, II, 230-2.

33. The phrase is an old one in Tennessee, where, from the days of Andrew Jackson it had been the custom for candidates for Governor and Senator to "swing around the circle" in the State, from Sullivan county to Shelby, and Obion to Polk. As an aspirant in the Volunteer State, Johnson had done so many times. He now applied the phrase to the larger field.

34. Welles, II, 584-5.

35. Richardson, "Grant" 526, asserts that the President was so eager "to avail himself of the General's popularity" that he asked Grant again and again to go on the tour; and that finally, in order to put the General under such obligations that he could not refuse, Johnson turned over to the General the selection of officers from colonel to second lieutenant in twenty-six newly created regiments, whereupon Grant consented.

36. Johnson Mss., Vol. 100, No. 12,355; Browning "Diary," Aug. 27, 1866.

37. James H. Wilson, "Life of John A. Rawlins," New York, 1916, 334; quoting Rawlins.

38. Stryker, 343-4, has collated the authorities on this New York celebration *in extenso*, and gives a full, graphic account of it.

39. New York *Herald*, Aug. 30, 1866.

40. This banquet cost the City of New York $100 per plate, according to Albert D. Richardson, "Personal History of U. S. Grant," 527.

41. Richardson, "Grant," Hartford, Conn., 1868; 527.

42. Welles, II, 592-3.

43. Weed, to New York *Tribune*, Jan. 29, 1875.

44. Wilson, "Rawlins," 330. According to another of Grant's biographers, (Richardson, 528), after the party had passed Buffalo, the General, "thoroughly disgusted" at Johnson's assaults on Congress, remarked to a friend: "The President has no business to be talking in this way. I wouldn't have started if I had expected anything of the kind."

45. Wilson, 335, quotes Rawlins' judgment on September 1, to the effect that "the chances are favorable to the Conservatives and Democrats in New York state," and that the Johnson party would probably carry the Empire State by 40,000 majority. Phillips of the New York *Herald* wrote the President: "We are all rejoicing at the extraordinary good effect of your journey."

46. McPherson, "Reconstruction," 134; Cleveland *Plain-Dealer*, Sept. 4, 1866.

47. For text of the Cleveland speech, see McPherson, "Reconstruction," 135, *et seq.*, "Impeachment of the President," Washington, 1868; I, 326, *et seq.*, Cleveland *Plain-Dealer*, Sept. 6, 1866.

48. This charge was two years later to become a "high misdemeanor in office" in the impeachment trial of the President. See Trial, I, 328, *et seq.*

49. Welles, II, 593.

50. Johnson Mss., Vol. 101, No. 12,405. A. J. Goodman was his informant. See also Oberholtzer, I, 409.

51. Johnson Mss., Vol. 101, No. 12,554.

52. Cleveland *Leader*, Sept. 4, 1866.

53. Oberholtzer, I, 405.

54. Keckley, 226-7.

55. For text of this speech, see McPherson, "Reconstruction," 137.

56. Richardson, "Grant," 530, completely acquits the President of charges of intoxication at any time on this journey. The President "was not intoxicated by liquor, as many supposed, but only by his own passions," says this biographer of Grant, who went on the Swing as a newspaper correspondent. So does Benjamin Truman, who was with Johnson from beginning to end. See his article *Century* Magazine, Jan., 1913; 438. It was

Grant, not Johnson, who was drunk on the tour. Browning "Diary" Dec.
3, 1866, relates Postmaster General Randall's statement to him that "on
the presidential tour, when it was reported that Grant had left the party,
he was simply drunk, and put on board a steamer for Detroit to hide
him." For corroboration of this, see Welles "Diary," Mss. form, Sept. 17,
1866. Grant, drunk, had become stupidly communicative to Mrs. Farragut.
See also Beale, "The Critical Year," 13-14.

57. *Independent*, Sept. 6, 1866.
58. The *Nation*, Sept. 13, 1866.
59. Blaine, II, 239.
60. Wilson, "Rawlins," 330.
61. Welles, II, 594.
62. *Ibid.*, II, 595.
63. Richardson, "Grant," 530.
64. Welles, II, 591.
65. Author's interview with Col. A. M. Hughes, Washington, Dec. 8,
1928. The colonel was an eye-witness of the President's return home from
the Swing Around the Circle.

CHAPTER XVII

1. Johnson Mss., Vol. 107, No. 14,103.
2. Welles, II, 595-6.
3. Welles, II, 603. It should be remembered that Gideon Welles, the
author of these stinging words, was no Republican, no ex-Whig, but an
old-fashioned Democrat of the Van Buren stripe, a Free-Soiler and a
State Righter at the same time.
4. Hugh Ewing Mss., Letter to Hugh Ewing, Feb. 21, 1867.
5. Welles, II, 616-8.
6. Johnson Mss., Vol. 101, No. 12,586.
7. *Ibid.*, Vol. 102, No. 12,840.
8. *Ibid.*, Vol. 102, No. 12,933.
9. *Ibid.*, Vol. 100, No. 12,286.
10. Johnson Mss., Vol. 103, No. 13,009. Oulahan, "Head Centre" of the
Fenian Brotherhood for the District of Columbia, Maryland and Virginia,
had earlier besought Seward to seek reprieve from the English government for the "Manchester murderers." Seward had brusquely refused.
The delegation had then gone to Johnson, who was sympathetic, and representations were made to Downing Street. Letter of Richard Oulahan (II),
to author, Washington, July 15, 1929.
11. For text of these questions and for Child's attempt to explain, see
Johnson Mss., Vol. 103, Nos. 12,977-89.
12. Chase Mss., Library of Congress, Vol. 97, No. 14,624. Letter from
General B. R. Cowan, chairman of the Ohio State Union Central Executive
Committee, Columbus, October 12, 1866.
13. Browning "Diary," Oct. 25, 1866. Rawlins also told Browning that
Grant "was not a man of ability outside of the profession of arms, and
was a man of strong passions and intense prejudices!"
14. Johnson Mss., Vol. 102, No. 12,867. No answer of the President to

this request is preserved, but the appointment register shows that Major Hall was named Paymaster and Wharton White became Second Lieutenant. One cannot help feeling, however, that the necessity of resorting to such methods went against Andrew Johnson's grain.

15. Welles, II, 615.

16. Analyzing the Pennsylvania results, an Ohio friend told the President he should not be disheartened, that the Radicals had secured a majority of only two per cent in a total vote of 600,000. But this was cold comfort to the President.

17. Johnson Mss., Vol. 105, Nos. 13,560-13,469.

18. Welles, II, 620.

19. Johnson Mss., Vol. 105, No. 13,525.

20. A New York friend of the President wrote that he had been "most shamefully betrayed" by A. T. Stewart, who "after his most liberal subscription . . . to sustain the noble policy which you had proposed, also subscribed *far more* in aid of the Radical Republicans." See Johnson Mss., Vol. 106, No. 13,792.

21. George O. Glavis to Johnson, New York, Oct. 28, 1866; Johnson Greeneville Mss.

22. While the President was being overwhelmed in the North, the Johnson tickets were correspondingly successful in the Southern states. The Democratic majority in Texas was 40,000; in North Carolina, 25,000 and in Arkansas, 9,000, futile victories; these Congressmen were barred in advance. The Border States were divided, Delaware, Maryland and Kentucky giving strong Democratic majorities, while West Virginia and Missouri went Radical.

23. Rhodes, VI, 110.

24. Oberholtzer, I, 422.

25. Johnson Mss., Vol. 105, No. 13,499. See also my Chapter III.

26. Boutwell in *North American Review,* Dec., 1885, June, 1886.

27. Johnson Mss., Vol. 105, No. 13,637.

28. *Ibid.,* Vol. 105, No. 13,477.

29. For partial text of message, see McPherson, "Reconstruction," 143-7; Browning "Diary," Nov. 15, 1866.

30. Johnson Mss., Vol. 106, No. 13,868.

31. New York *Tribune*, December 4, 1866.

32. *Nation*, December 6, 1866.

33. DeWitt, "Impeachment," 149, declared that by December, 1866, a majority of the Republicans in the House already favored impeachment.

34. Welles, iii, 74.

35. For text of this act, see McPherson, "Reconstruction," 159.

36. Johnson Mss., Vol. 108, No. 13,193. Charles Sumner to "My dear General," a copy sent to the President for his perusal.

37. *Nation*, Jan. 10, 1867. It further objected that Johnson "talks of whiteness with as much reverence as Froissart talks of 'gentle blood.'"

38. See *Supra,* Chapter XVIII, for Impeachment Committee hearing details.

39. Welles, III, 10-13. I have changed Stanton's declaration from third to first person; Browning "Diary," Jan. 8, 1867.

40. For text of bills and votes thereon see McPherson, "Reconstruction," 163-6.

41. The veto was in Johnson's best style. For text see McPherson, "Reconstruction," 160. For Nebraska bill veto, see *Ibid.*, 164.

42. Moore, "Diary," 105.

43. Welles, III, 25-6.

44. *Independent*, January 17, 1867.

45. Moore, "Diary," 104-5.

46. Welles, III, 32, 34.

47. Sherman "Letters," 288.

48. *Ibid.*, 289.

49. Johnson Mss., Vol. 108, No. 14,333; Browning "Diary," Jan. 26, 1867.

50. *Ibid.*, Vol. 109, No. 14,487.

51. He told Blair he "would not have Greeley on any account." Out of his sanctum, the editor "seemed like a whale ashore, . . . all heart and no head; . . . a sublime old child." See Truman, *op. cit.*

52. Moore, "Diary," 105. I have changed some of this from third to first person. See also Truman, *op. cit.*, 439. Johnson believed that if he had made the changes Blair had urged, there would have been no impeachment. Andrew and Morton particularly would have strengthened him, and "no Senator would have dared to vote for my impeachment with those two men in my Cabinet." But he had become sincerely attached to several of his associates, notably Seward, Welles, Stanbery and Browning, and was unwilling to disturb them.

53. Johnson Mss., Vol. 109, No. 14,576

54. *Independent*, February 21, 1867.

55. *Ibid.*, February 28, 1867.

56. *Independent*, February 28, 1867.

57. Welles, III, 49; 58; 59.

58. The purpose of the Tenure-of-Office bill was frankly admitted by the Radical *Independent*, on March 7. It was to make it impossible for the President "to remove faithful and competent officers, and fill their places with his tools. Thus does a liberty-loving loyal nation protect itself from the treachery of a faithless executive. Impeachment is the step next in order."

59. *Congressional Globe*, 2nd Session, 39th Congress, 525.

60. *Congressional Globe*, 2nd Sesson, 39th Congress, 1039-46.

61. *Congressional Globe*, 2nd Session, 39th Congress, 1515-18.

62. Welles, III, 49.

63. Johnson Mss., Vol. 110, Nos. 14,596 and 14,616.

64. Moore "Diary" Transcript, Feb. 18, 1867.

65. Welles, III, 50-1; Johnson suggested that "both the War and the Navy help," inasmuch as Welles had already prepared a paper on the subject, but Stanton and Seward did not call on Welles. As to the virtual request for Stanton's resignation, see Browning, "Diary," Feb. 26, 1867, Mar. 31, 1868, Moore "Diary" Transcript, Aug. 12, 1867.

66. For text of this veto, see McPherson, "Reconstruction," 166-173; for text of the veto on the Tenure-of-Office bill, see *Ibid.*, 173-6.

67. Rhodes, VI, 134.

68. *Nation*, March 7, 1867.

69. Issue of March 14, 1867.

CHAPTER XVIII

1. Milligan, an Indiana Democrat, had been arrested by the military authorities and tried in October, 1864, by a Military Commission on the charge of conspiracy against the government, giving aid and comfort to the Rebels, initiating insurrection, etc. In this prosecution Colonel Burnett won the laurels which the next spring brought him to Washington to aid Stanton and Holt in the military trial of the Lincoln conspirators. The commission found Milligan guilty and sentenced him to be hanged on May 19, 1865. On May 10 he petitioned for a writ of *habeas corpus* and the matter came before the Supreme Court. The constitutionality of trial by military commission in a State where civil laws were operative was impressively challenged by David Dudley Field, James A. Garfield and Jeremiah Sullivan Black. The latter's argument has become a legal classic. On April 3, 1866, the decision of the court that the Milligan trial was unlawful was announced, but the opinions in which this decision was imbedded were not made public until December 17 of that year. See Charles Warren, "The Supreme Court in United States History," Boston, 1922; III, 145-176.

2. See Warren, 147-176.

3. In outlining the developments of the Radical mind, the files of the *Independent* have been extremely useful and illuminating. Theodore Tilton, the editor of the *Independent,* was the most vigorous and vindictive of the Radicals. He spent a great deal of time in Washington in close communion with Sumner, Stevens and other Radical leaders, and is thought by some modern historians really to have been the mainspring of the entire impeachment scheme. Tilton's editorials and the letters to the *Independent* of its various Washington correspondents reveal intimate and confidential knowledge of the Radical perplexities, plans and maneuvers.

4. *Independent,* January 3, 10, 17.

5. A second section of the Missourian's proposal declared it also the duty of the Congress "to provide for the faithful and efficient administration of the executive department."

6. *Congressional Globe,* 2nd Session, 39th Congress, 319-321.

7. *Congressional Globe,* 2nd Session, 39th Congress, 443-6.

8. Welles, III, 239.

9. Moore, "Diary," 107. The wife of a clerk of the House Judiciary Committee came to the White House to inform the President of this "understanding," the purpose of which was to insure an impeachment resolution in July, so as to aid a gold flurry.

10. Judiciary Committee Report, *Imp. Inv.,* 110.

11. *Imp. Inv.,* 2, 7.

12. *Imp. Inv.,* 384-394.

13. Judiciary Committee Report, *Imp. Inv.,* iii.

14. The present Nashville, Chattanooga and St. Louis.

15. "Impeachment Investigation," Government Printing Office, Washington, 1867, henceforth to be referred to as *Imp. Inv.* For this incident, see 183. None the less, Johnson did object, as an entry in Moore "Diary" Transcript, Mar. 25, 1867, reveals. After the bank cashier had called,

Johnson remarked to Moore: "I have had a son killed, a son-in-law die during the battle of Nashville, another son has thrown himself away. . . . I think I have had sorrow enough without having my bank account examined by a committee of Congress."

16. See Johnson Mss., Vol. 113, No. 15,406.

17. *Imp. Inv.*, 28, 32, 275, 280, 323, 324, 408, 450, 457, 483, 672.

18. Italics mine. *Imp. Inv.*, 285.

19. *Imp. Inv.*, 829.

20. So, at least, Pinkerton later told Henry S. Monroe, a Chicago Democratic attorney. Pinkerton said he had a pretty girl make up to the Committee's stenographer (they were male in those days) and she quickly began furnishing verbatim reports of the hearings. Communicated by Miss Harriet Monroe, Chicago, Oct. 23, 1928.

21. DeWitt, "Impeachment," 143, 147; Welles, III, 31.

22. Apparently, Matchett did not know that in addition to being physician for the Old Capitol Prison, Dr. Duhamel was President Johnson's personal physician. On the next day the Doctor wrote the President confidentially, laying before him Matchett's infamous proposal. Ashley's tool had further asked Duhamel to warn Surratt that "he need not look to Andrew Johnson, as he dared not interfere or pardon him." Johnson Mss., Vol. 110, No. 14,634.

23. Johnson Mss., Vol. III, No. 14,906.

24. *Ibid.*, Vol. 111, No. 14,914.

25. Johnson Mss., Vol. 112, No. 15,328. Dr. Duhamel to Colonel Moore, May 8, 1867.

26. *Ibid.*, Vol. 113, No. 11,369.

27. Johnson Mss., Vol. 117, No. 16,215.

28. *Imp. Inv.*, 1194–1208.

29. McPherson, "Reconstruction," 188-9.

30. *Congressional Globe*, 1st Session, 40th Congress, 1825.

31. Johnson Mss., Vol. 108, No. 14,342. Letter from Frank Smith, 48 Pine Street, New York, January 23, 1867.

32. *Ibid.*, Vol. 106, No. 13,774. From Halpine's next sentence, it would seem that Greeley's support was not without its price: "Mr. Greeley authorizes me to say that he would most heartily support and indorse the nomination of Mr. J. G. Savage for Postmaster."

33. Johnson Mss., Vol. 108, No. 14,369.

34. Welles, III, 60-1.

35. *Ibid.*, III, 62; Browning "Diary," Mar. 8, 1867.

36. Cowan, 12.

37. McPherson, "Reconstruction," 143.

38. *Independent*, May 9, 1867.

39. The *Nation*, Jan. 10, 17, 1867; *Independent*, Feb. 28, 1867.

40. Sherman, "Letters," 289.

41. *Independent*, March 14, 1867.

42. *Ibid.*, March 28; April 4, 1867.

43. Nor did the President change his views about it. "I shall go to my grave," he wrote Ben Truman (*op. cit.* 440) privately in August, 1868, "with the firm belief that Davis, Cobb, Toombs, and a few others of the arch-conspirators and traitors should have been tried, convicted and hanged for treason. There was too much precious blood spilled on both

sides not to have held the leading traitors responsible. If it was the last act of my life, I'd hang Jeff Davis as an example. I'd show coming generations that, while the rebellion was too popular a revolt to punish many who participated in it, treason should be made odious and arch-traitors should be punished. But I might lose my head," he added plaintively, "for Horace Greeley, who made haste to bail out Jeff Davis, declares daily that I am a traitor."

44. *Independent*, May 30, 1867.
45. *Ibid.*, July 11, 1867.
46. *Ibid.*, July 23, 1867.
47. *Nation*, Aug. 22, 1867.
48. *Independent*, August 15, 1867.
49. To Hugh Ewing, Lancaster, Sept. 16, 1867; Hugh Ewing Mss.
50. *Independent*, October 24, 1867.
51. Oberholtzer, I, 462. The President's friends charged that Churchill was a Judas, who has sold his honor for promises of Radical support later on. Welles believed that he had done so "to aid Wall Street speculators in the gold market." Welles, III, 239, said that aside from Boutwell and Williams, the signers of the pro-impeachment report were "smooth-borers, men of small calibre and intense partisanship."
52. *Imp. Inv.*, 110.
53. According to the *Independent*, Dec. 12, 1867, there were "not less than forty speeches ready for delivery," and the general desire of the House to dam this flood of oratory hastened the vote.
54. To Hugh Ewing, Washington, Dec. 18, 1867; Hugh Ewing Mss.

CHAPTER XIX

1. *Nation*, March 7, 1867.
2. *Independent*, March 14, 1867.
3. *Independent*, March 14, 1867.
4. *Nation*, Aug. 22, 1867.
5. Thad Stevens had actively sought the succession of Edgar Cowan, but Stevens could not rule the politicians of Pennsylvania as he did those in Washington. Although Old Thad left his seat in Congress and hastened to Harrisburg to watch the outcome, "Dead Duck" Forney accompanying him, Cameron received forty-six votes, Governor Curtin twenty-three votes and Stevens only seven. Caliban's defeat was cold comfort to the White House. No worse man than Stevens could have been elected, but Cameron was as staunch an impeacher as Wade or Sumner could have asked.
6. *Independent*, April 4, 1867.
7. Welles, II, 551-2.
8. *Congressional Globe*, Second Session, 39th Congress, 2003.
9. *Independent*, April 4, 1867.
10. *Independent*, March 21, 1867.
11. *Congressional Globe*, First Session, 40th Congress, 262-3; 364. Bingham's words were those which General Grant, according to rumor, had

contemptuously applied to Butler at the time of the failure to take Fort Fisher.

12. For text of measure see McPherson, "Reconstruction," 178-180.

13. *Congressional Globe,* First Session, 40th Congress, 315-17.

14. Welles, III, 60, 64.

15. The generals selected were, for the first district, General John M. Schofield; second, General Sickles; third, General George H. Thomas; fourth, General E. O. C. Ord, and fifth, General Phillip H. Sheridan. Thomas asked to be relieved and General Pope was named in his place.

16. Welles, III, 64-5. Justice Field of the Supreme Court went to see Welles to warn him that Sickles was a bad man, and to commiserate with the Secretary "as to the peculiar characteristics of the President, and the misfortune which he has brought on himself and the country by failing to act promptly on his own convictions, and listening to the advice of those who are not his friends."

17. *Independent,* March 21, 1867.

18. *Ibid.,* April 11, 18, 1867. See also Welles, III, 77-8.

19. Moore "Diary" Transcript, May 2, 1867.

20. Boston *Advertiser,* May 20, 1867, quoted Rhodes VI, 168.

21. *Independent,* May 23, 1867.

22. See *Imp. Inv.,* 544-578 for this testimony.

23. See Warren, III, 172.

24. Sharkey had taken this step without prearrangement or counsel with the President. See Springfield *Republican,* April 13, 1867.

25. Welles was amazed that O'Conor did not use the Milligan decision in his argument—III, 86. For a description of the courtroom scene, see Warren, III, 178-9.

26. Rhodes, VI, 184.

27. See Warren, III, 185-6. Justice Grier was believed to have been in favor of admitting the amended Mississippi plea. Probably his absence prevented the immediate test of the constitutionality of these oppressive Radical laws.

28. Warren, III, 179, 181, 186.

29. Welles, III, 90-1.

30. Johnson Mss., Vol. 112, No. 15,314.

31. *Ibid.,* Vol. 113, No. 15,506.

32. Johnson Mss., Vol. 114, No. 15,672; Moore, "Diary," Transcript, July 5, 1868.

33. Johnson Mss., Vol. 115, No. 15,854.

34. Welles, III, 109-110.

35. Memorandum of Stanton on Cabinet meeting, quoted Gorham, II, 361, *et seq.*

36. Rhodes, VI, 173. This historian, however, declares that "the tenor of the Attorney-General's opinion was excellent. The acts were harsh. Any mitigations of them. . . were very much to be desired."

37. *Independent,* July 4, 1867.

38. *Ibid.,* July 18, 1867.

39. Johnson Mss., Vol. 112, No. 15,169, indorsed "True Copy—O.S.R."

40. Italics Mine. For dispatch see Johnson Mss., Vol. 115, No. 15,903.

41. The report was correct, and Stanton's own biographer admits as much. See Gorham, II, 373.

42. Moore, "Diary," 107-8.

43. Welles, III, 149-152.

44. Johnson Mss., Vol. 117, No. 16,283. When this letter of General Grant's was finally made public in response to the call of Congress, the *Independent* said of it: "his letter, written in behalf of a bad cause, would be impertinent; but written in behalf of justice, it is an exceedingly courageous remonstrance."

45. Moore, "Diary," 108.

46. I have discussed the presentation of this record to the President on July 6, 1865, in my Chapter X, see *infra*, 207-9. DeWitt, "Impeachment," XX, 273-5 has a good account of the President's belated discovery of the document.

47. Moore, 108.

48. Welles, III, 160-165; Moore, 109.

49. Moore, 109.

50. Moore "Diary" Transcript, Aug. 11, 1867; Welles, III, 167.

51. Johnson was careful to suspend Stanton without reference to the Tenure-of-Office law, and sought to satisfy Welles that in suspending him, he was not giving adherence to this unconstitutional act. In addition, the President was anxious for the fact that Stanton together with Seward had prepared a veto of this bill, to be made public, along with Stanton's emphatic denunciation of its principles and its unconstitutionality. See Welles, III, 167-8.

52. Welles, III, 240.

53. For text of letter see McPherson, "Reconstruction," 261. Grant was greatly irritated at the phrase "submit to superior force."

54. Moore, "Diary" Transcript, Aug. 12, 1867.

CHAPTER XX

1. Thomas Ewing to Hugh Ewing, Lancaster, Ohio, Sept. 16, 1867, Hugh Ewing Mss.

2. *Nation*, Aug. 22, 1867.

3. Gorham, II, 399-404. This adulatory biographer searched Stanton's correspondence at this time, and excerpted practically every letter Stanton had received. In all there were only eighteen, and most of the writers were very minor figures! Senator Howard urged Stanton not to yield an inch. The Radical Governor of New Jersey held that immediate circumstances furnished Stanton an exception to the general rule compelling men of honor to resign when their services were no longer wanted. Senator Morrill of Maine wrote that Stanton must neither abandon nor be driven from his post.

4. Welles, III, 169; Browning "Diary," Aug. 16, 1867.

5. Moore, 110.

6. Johnson Mss., Vol. 118, No. 16,563.

7. *Ibid.*, Vol. 118, No. 16,573. This document is omitted from McPherson and from the other Radical texts of the time.

8. Moore, "Diary," 110-1.

9. *Ibid.*, 111.

10. Schuckers, 543-4.

11. Johnson Mss., Vol. 118, No. 16,551.

12. *Ibid.*, Vol. 118, No. 16,664.

13. Welles, III, 182-3.

14. Welles, III, 185.

15. *Ibid.*, III, 187. I have changed Grant's remarks from indirect to direct quotation.

16. Moore "Diary," 111-113. I have changed some of the President's remarks to Grant from third to first person.

17. The *Independent*, Aug. 29, Sept. 5, 1867. Grant had surrendered to the President. In the supplementary Reconstruction Bill, Congress had intended that district commanders be subject to the General, "since he was a man whom Congress could trust and not subject to the President, since he was a man whom the Congress could not trust." And yet Grant surrendered.

18. Welles, III, 207.

19. Johnson Mss., Vol. 120, No. 16,888.

20. Johnson Mss., Vol. 119, No. 16,664.

21. Some of Johnson's appointees were having a hard time. The Postmaster at Schenectady wrote Randall that the Radicals, "after having passed resolutions in favor of impeachment and denouncing the Cabinet, have the audacity to assess this office in support of their ticket this fall." This Postmaster refused to pay, and the Radicals threatened that they would have him removed. *Ibid.*, Vol. 123, No. 17,666.

22. Cf. New York *Herald*, Nov. 9, 1867, which printed a rumor of the reorganization of the Cabinet. Thereupon Bennett's secretary wrote Johnson that the report had aroused the Commodore's zeal "to the old fever heat, if such a program of men and measures should be carried out . . . The *Herald* will go to work at once in urging the change and supporting the men."

23. Moore "Diary" Transcript, Feb. 4, 1868. Johnson Mss., Vol. 119, No. 16,805.

24. *Ibid.*, Vol. 121, No. 17,078.

25. Johnson Mss., Vol. 122, No. 17,413. Apparently the President had tentatively offered a Cabinet position to Thomas Ewing, Jr., for the letter continued: "Do not tempt him with the offer. He can do more good to the country and to you where he is than if he had choice of the departments . . . And do not give McClernand of Illinois a department. He is a blatherskite and withal a false man."

26. Hugh Ewing Papers. The *Independent*, on Oct. 17, lamented that the Republican party "even yet quakes at meeting a negro by day as at seeing a ghost at night."

27. Johnson Mss., Vol. 122, No. 17,298. Letter from T. W. Egan, Washington, October 7, 1867. He also wrote that Chief Justice Chase was "actively making personal appeals to the Senators and Representatives against impeachment."

28. To Hugh Ewing, Nov. 6, 1867; Hugh Ewing Mss., "But even so I do not know where we shall land. We are in sight of breakers, but it is hoped the ship will come to feel the helm before it is too late."

29. Johnson Mss., Vol. 120, No. 16,908.

30. The *Independent*, Nov. 14, 1867, admitted that the election had had

this effect: "First, the impeachment movement is dead—unless the President, by fresh outrages, gives it a new impetus. The majority of Republicans will be against it . . . Second, all confiscation bills will fail. . . Third, Congress will not pass a national equal suffrage bill 'till after the presidential election."

31. Edward A. Pollard, "The Lost Cause Regained," New York, 1868; 163, *et seq.* Pollard derived his figures from a table of the election results in 1867, as compared with those of the year before. Senator Doolittle of Wisconsin had prepared it.

32. The *Independent*, Nov. 21, 1867; Browning "Diary," Oct. 10, 1867.

33. Johnson Mss., Vol. 123, No. 17,694.

34. *Ibid.*, Vol. 124, No. 17,782.

35. Johnson Mss., Vol. 123, No. 17,619. Sumner's interlocutor was M. H. Carpenter of Milwaukee.

36. A. W. Bradford to Johnson, Baltimore, Nov. 5, 1867; Bradford Mss., Maryland Historical Society.

37. Hugh Ewing Mss., Thomas Ewing, Jr., to Hugh Ewing: "If impeachment is conducted in the form of law, there will be no resistance by the President; otherwise, I guess he will fight." He also told his brother that Grant "has expressed himself strongly against impeachment to several friends," and the Radicals, "if they get badly scared," would nominate the General for the Presidency the next year.

38. Welles, III, 189. In the conversation Johnson informed the General that he was not a candidate for the Presidency the next year, and Grant answered that he was not a candidate himself. When the President related this to Welles, the latter bowed his acquiescence without expressing regret.

39. McPherson, "Reconstruction," 283-4; Browning, "Diary," Oct. 8, 1867.

40. Welles, III, 222; J. Schucht, "Andrew Johnson," Leipzig, 1875; 134-5.

41. Johnson Mss., Vol. 125, No. 17,983.

42. When published, the message greatly pleased the Conservatives. Typical comments were those of Harvey Watterson, who termed it "masterly, conclusive, unanswerable, crushing" and of Thomas Ewing, who called it "a magnificent paper."

43. Johnson Mss., Vol. 125, No. 18,076.

44. *Ibid.*, Vol. 126, No. 18,202.

45. Welles, III, 237-8. Col. Moore also noted that the Cabinet had "unanimously determined that the power of suspension was one that could not be constitutionally exercised"; Cf. also Browning "Diary," Nov. 30, 1867.

46. Moore, "Diary," 113. I have changed from third to first person in the President's declaration.

47. Hugh Ewing Papers.

48. Johnson Mss., Vol. 125, No. 18,005.

49. Welles, III, 240. On Dec. 16, the *Independent's* Washington correspondent predicted that Stanton would be restored to his old position, and "that he will then resign it, not desiring to remain in the Cabinet. The Senate cannot admit that there is force in the President's reasons, and therefore cannot assent to his removal."

50. McPherson, "Reconstruction," 324.

51. But all the Radicals were by no means enthusiastic about Grant. Early in January, Horace Greeley contributed an article to the *Independent* of Jan. 16, 1868, urging Chase as the "ablest, strongest man" for the Republican presidential nomination, and asking suspiciously why the "Copperheads" were talking so strongly of nominating Grant.

52. Welles, III, 244-5.

53. Edwin C. Woolley, "The Reconstruction of Georgia," New York, 1901; 43.

54. Such opposition he construed even to preclude giving the State advertising or printing to newspapers which opposed Reconstruction! See "General Orders," Third Military District, 1867; 49. It must be said however, in Pope's behalf, that he did emphatically uphold the freedom of public opinion, and that he reprimanded the post commander at Mobile for interfering with a newspaper there.

55. Johnson Mss., Vol. 127, Nos. 18,473-6. Running through the President's correspondence of this date is an interesting personal thread concerning his son, to whom George W. Childs of the Philadelphia *Ledger* wrote on Christmas Day, inviting him to a party a Mrs. Watts was giving on January 3 and adding: "She has a lovely and amiable daughter. . . If you can get her, she would make a splendid wife and is so rich. Now is your chance."

56. Welles, III, 248.

57. Johnson Mss., Vol. 127, No. 18,411.

58. Welles, III, 246.

59. Moore, "Diary," 115.

60. The Committee's report prepared by Howard was a labored attempt to defend Stanton's conduct and to reconcile his authorship of the veto of the Tenure-of-Office Act with his subsequent refusal to resign.

61. Badeau, 125.

62. McPherson, 283-5. In constructing the details of the Saturday conference, I have followed Grant's letter to Johnson of January 28, and Johnson's reply of January 31, wherever the details agree; where there was a discrepancy, I have given the weight of evidence to the statements of the five Cabinet Members who were present at the colloquy between Johnson and Grant at the Cabinet meeting on January 14, in which the President sharply quizzed the General about the Saturday conversation and the latter admitted the truth of what the President had to say about it. For these last, see Moore, "Diary," 115; Welles, III, 259, 262. See also Badeau, 110, *et seq.*, who asserts that after his return to Army Headquarters, Grant had said he had told the President "that on no account could he consent to hold the office after the Senate should act." But Grant made no such claim before the Cabinet on January 14.

63. Badeau, 111.

64. Johnson Mss., Vol. 167, No. 27,604.

65. McPherson, "Reconstruction," 263; all of the 35 were Republicans, all of the 6 were Democrats. Among those not voting were such Republicans as John Sherman, Sprague of Rhode Island, Chase's son-in-law, Grimes of Ohio, Henderson of Missouri, Ross of Kansas, Van Winkle of West Virginia, and Yates.

66. Badeau, 111, Browning "Diary," Jan. 14, 1868.

67. DeWitt, "Impeachment," 323.

68. Badeau, 125-6. Grant had then gone to Stanton's house to tell him in advance what he intended to do and had allowed himself to be persuaded to send a highly complimentary letter to the man whose place he then took. See *ante,* 455. See also Browning "Diary," Jan. 14, 1868.

69. McPherson, "Reconstruction," 262.

70. Both Johnson and Welles now suspected that Grant had broken his word by deliberate prearrangement with Stanton, but William S. Hillyer talked with the General and with Rawlins on January 14, and wrote the President he was "now fully satisfied that General Grant never had any conversation or collusion with Stanton in regard to his restoration of the war office," and that Grant never expected that Stanton would resume the duties of the war office without giving him notice.

71. Moore, "Diary," 115.

72. Badeau, 112; Browning "Diary," Jan. 14, 1868.

73. In his letter to Grant on January 31, 1868, the President carefully recited the three questions; when Grant questioned the accuracy of it, Johnson submitted his statement to Welles, McCulloch, Randall, Browning and Seward, all of whom had been present at the interview and all of whom indorsed the substantial accuracy of Johnson's statement of the case. For text see McPherson, "Reconstruction," 284, 291. At the end of the controversy Grant disputed that he had made the promise to see the President again. The crushing weight of the testimony is, however, that he broke his word. See also Welles, III, 259-262; Moore "Diary," 115, 116, both of whom have full and complete accounts of the Cabinet session.

74. Welles, III, 262; Browning, "Diary," Jan. 14, 1868, insists that Grant admitted that these conversations had occurred. At the last, it adds, "the General stammered out some sort of excuse, which was not intelligible to me, and then left."

CHAPTER XXI

1. W. T. Sherman, Memoirs, II, 423. This General wrote his wife, "I was only a listener."

2. See Johnson letter, January 31, 1868, to Grant; McPherson, 285. In his reply Grant admitted that at that conversation: "I stated to you that I thought Mr. Stanton would resign, but did not say I would advise him to do so. On the 18th I did agree with General Sherman to go and advise him to that course."

3. Moore, "Diary," 116. See also Welles, III, 262.

4. Home Letters, 365-7.

5. *Ibid.,* 366-7.

6. Moore, "Diary," 117.

7. *Independent,* January 9, 1868.

8. *Ibid.,* January 16, 1868.

9. Badeau, 126; Welles, III, 267, 273-4; McPherson, "Reconstruction," 286.

10. Moore, "Diary," 116.

11. John M. Schofield, "Forty-Six Years in the Army," New York, 1897; 412-3.

12. Moore, 117.

13. Sherman, "Home Letters," 368.

14. Johnson Mss., Vol. 130, No. 19,080.

15. Johnson Mss., Vol. 130, No. 19,097.

16. "Impeachment Trial," Washington, 1868, I, 521; Sherman's testimony as to the conversation.

17. Johnson Mss., Vol. 130, No. 19,134.

18. *Ibid.*, Vol. 130, No. 19,069; Moore "Diary" Transcript, Jan. 29, 1868.

19. Impeachment, I, 529; Sherman, "Home Letters," 369.

20. For this correspondence, see McPherson, "Reconstruction," 282-293.

21. C. B. Comstock Papers, Ms. Div., Library of Congress.

22. Badeau, 114, says that the language of Rawlins' draft was afterward somewhat modified, but that its tone remained unaltered. He terms it "a stroke of political genius" in that it made the rupture with the President personal, and impossible to be reconciled, and it also made any other candidate than Grant impossible for the Republicans.

23. Moore, "Diary," 118; Welles, III, 269-70; Browning "Diary," Feb. 4, 1868.

24. Welles, III, 270-1; Moore, "Diary," 118.

25. Welles, III, 272.

26. New York *World*, February 6, 1868, dispatch from Jerome B. Stillson, Washington correspondent of the *World* and a newspaper intimate of the President. The *World's* dispatches signed "J.B.S." from February through June, 1868, afford an important source of information as to the occurrences of this exciting period.

27. *Ibid.*, February 7, 1868. This dispatch also tells how, in the growing tension, many absurd rumors were eagerly repeated, none more absurd than the story that Johnson, the Democrats in Congress and certain of the executives in the army had plotted a *coup d'état* by which the President would make himself dictator.

28. *Independent*, January 30, 1868.

29. *Ibid.*, February 13, 1868.

30. *Independent*, February 20, 1868.

31. New York *World*, February 12, 1868; Welles, III, 275.

32. *Ibid.*, February 14, 1868.

33. *Independent,* February 13, 1868.

34. Welles, III, 279. Welles was not greatly impressed with Thomas. "He is right, but not strong," he noted, "and there are so many who wilt down in these days, or who will misunderstand, or who are weak and unreliable." Stanton seemed never to have liked Thomas. When he became Secretary of War in 1862, he quickly displaced Thomas from the duties, though not the title, of Adjutant General, dispatching him through the country on unimportant details. Thomas seems to have reciprocated the disesteem.

35. Moore, "Diary," 118-119.

36. Following the revocation, Sherman wrote the President (Johnson Mss., Vol. 132, No. 19,530) "to assure you of my obligation for your personal kindness on many occasions, indeed on all occasions since I first had

the honor to meet you as President on May, 1865. . . . I do believe that all the orders you may give for the army will be promptly and fairly executed by General Grant. The unhappy difficulty existing in relation to the office of Secretary of War ought to be settled by the Supreme Court."

37. Moore, "Diary" Transcript, Feb. 14, 15, 16, 17, 18, 1868; Browning "Diary," Feb. 23, 1868.

38. Moore, "Diary" Transcript, Feb. 19, 1868.

39. Moore, "Diary," 120-1; "Impeachment Trial," 1, 419-29.

40. Welles, III, 284.

41. New York *World*, Feb. 23, 1868.

42. Welles, III, 284.

43. McPherson, 74, 78. After this veto, the *Independent* called him "Nebuchadnezzar" and described him as holding that the Constitution should not be amended until Lee and Davis submitted amendments. See issue of April 5, 1866. J. Schucht, "Andrew Johnson," Leipzig, 1875; 222-3. This German student, in passing final estimate on Johnson's presidency, termed the veto of the Civil Rights bill "not only unwise but also morally reprehensible, the greatest mistake of his life. . . . With this, he gave himself the moral death-blow."

44. "Impeachment Trial," I, 210.

45. "Trial," I, 427-8.

46. Moore "Diary" Transcript, Feb. 22, 1868.

47. "Trial," I, 232-3.

48. *Ibid.*, I, 429; Moore, *Diary*, 121.

49. Welles, III, 286. According to Ewing's grandson, the Hon. Thomas Ewing of New York, the President's first intention had been to nominate General Thomas Ewing, son of the Old Roman, as Secretary. But the father had objected to the needless sacrifice of his son's career by involving him in the fight between Congress and the President, and had almost quarrelled with the son about the matter. At any event, it was Thomas Ewing, Sr., who was named. See letter of Thomas Ewing to author, New York, October 22, 1928.

50. That body, however, was not in session, and the nomination was not formally laid before the Senate until Monday, the 24th.

51. Moore, "Diary" Transcript, Feb. 22, 1868.

52. Welles, III, 289.

53. For this conversation, see President's answer, Article IX, of Impeachment Articles; "Trial," I, 233-8. Emory's lawyer consultants were Reverdy Johnson and Robert J. Walker.

54. New York *World*, February 24, 1868.

55. New York *World*, February 24, 1868.

56. *Independent*, February 27, 1868, editorial account of Henry C. Bowen, proprietor of the paper, who went to Washington to witness the scene.

57. *Ibid., loc. cit.*

58. So he seemed to the *World* correspondent, but Bowen in the *Independent* described him as "calm and serene as a summer's morn."

59. New York *World, loc. cit.*

60. Richardson, VI, 627. See also Moore, "Diary," 122, which also reveals that on the morning of the 24th, Doolittle in great haste, sent John-

son a note urging him to address his message to both Houses. The President replied that he would do nothing of the sort. He had prepared his message in answer to the Senate's resolution and the House had nothing to do with it.

61. New York *World*, Feb. 25, 1868; *Independent*, Feb. 27, 1868.
62. *Independent*, March 5, 1868.
63. New York *World*, Feb. 26, 1868.
64. Moore, "Diary" Transcript, Feb. 24, 1868.

CHAPTER XXII

1. *Independent*, Feb. 22, Mar. 5, 1868; Francis Fessenden, "Life of William Pitt Fessenden," Boston, 1907; II, 154.
2. Warden, 550-3.
3. Welles, III, 297.
4. DeWitt, "Impeachment," 378-385.
5. John A. Logan, Mss., Library of Congress, Medill to Logan, Mar. 6, 1868.
6. For data connected with Senator Vickers, I am indebted to his grandson, Hon. Harrison Vickers of Baltimore, for family traditions, letters, and a scrap-book, "Five Years in the United States Senate," containing the Senator's public record.
7. Bingham received 114 votes, leading the list. Stevens was at the bottom with only 105. The House Democrats refused to vote.
8. "Impeachment Trial," III, 228.
9. New York *World*, March 5, 1868.
10. Ben Wade's wife was happily informing her sewing circle friends back in Ohio that "there seems to be no doubt in the mind of any that Johnson's conviction is inevitable." See autograph letter of Mrs. Wade auctioned by Stan V. Henkels, Philadelphia, Apr. 24, 1928.
11. For this debate, see "Impeachment Trial," III, 360-401.
12. "Impeachment Trial," I, 12.
13. Moore "Diary" Transcript, March 7, 1868.
14. New York *World*, Feb. 27, 1868. Thomas immediately instituted a suit for $150,000 damages against Stanton, charging malicious arrest and false imprisonment, but nothing ever came of it.
15. *Ibid.*, Mar. 10, 1868.
16. *Independent*, Mar. 6, 1868.
17. Johnson Mss., Vols. 132, 133, contains hundreds of such letters and telegrams.
18. The *Nation*, Feb. 27, 1868. Johnson, it said, had played Moses for the Impeachers Members and not the negroes, "with truly wonderful fatuity," and Godkin thought he should be impeached for a dunce.
19. Sherman Letters, 313. The Senator replied, protesting that he meant to give "a fair and impartial trial."
20. Welles, III, 293-6.
21. George Ticknor Curtis, "Memoirs of Benjamin Robbins Curtis." Boston, 1879; I, 408, quoting from letter of Henry Stanbery; Browning "Dairy," Feb. 28, 1868.

22. Curtis, I, 408: "The President was unable to offer the smallest compensation." The late Selden Nelson, son of Judge T. A. R. Nelson, another of the President's counsel, informed me that his father had never received a penny from the President, but that he and other counsel were invited to live at the White House during the trial, so as to reduce their financial loss.

23. Curtis, I, 410, 416-7.

24. Moore, "Diary" Transcript, Feb. 29, 1868.

25. *Ibid.,* "Diary," 123.

26. Moore, "Diary," 132.

27. Moore, "Diary" Transcript, April 8, 1868, and printed "Diary" I, 123. In the latter, I have changed Johnson's remarks from third to first person.

28. *Ibid.,* 125.

29. Welles, III, 311. Johnson seems to have taken pride in such publications of his views, and once remarked that nobody seemed to read his messages, but everybody read his interviews. None the less, as Welles grimly remarked, "it is in his position hardly a pardonable weakness." Cf. also Moore "Diary" Transcript, April 8, 1868.

30. "Impeachment Trial," I, 19-20. The Chase who had been impeached by John Randolph of Roanoke during Jefferson's term had been a relative of Salmon P. Chase's family.

31. "Impeachment Trial," I, 36-7.

32. Moore, "Diary," 124. Stanbery was so earnest and eloquent that Colonel Moore seized a pencil and took a shorthand record of his words.

33. Moore, "Diary," 125-6.

34. Moore, "Diary" Transcript, March 18, 1868.

35. Johnson Mss., Vol. Nos. 20,027; 20,127.

36. *Ibid.,* Vol. 134, No. 20,127.

37. Moore "Diary" Transcript, April 12, May 6, 1868, recounting lengthy conversations with President on Alta Vela; Jeremiah Sullivan Black Mss., Library of Congress; Vol. 48; Nos. 59,122, 59,124, 59,125, 59,136, 59,142; Johnson Mss., Vol. 134, No. 19,953.

38. Johnson Mss., Vol. 134, No. 19,914. This is a careful brief by Moore of the chronology of this Alta Vela crisis. DeWitt, *Impeachment,* 399, states that the elder Black had no knowledge that Shaffer and Chauncey Black had secured the letter from the Managers until after it had been done, but does not give his authority for the statement.

39. *Ibid.,* Vol. 134, No. 20,089.

40. Welles, III, 316, 321-2; Moore "Diary" Transcript, Jan. 8, 1870, for Black note secured by Radicals; entry in the same for May 6, 1868, says Black prepared a denial of the Forney article, but after the rupture with Johnson, did not issue it.

41. The late E. C. Reeves of Johnson City, Tenn., acted as a sort of political assistant to Andrew Johnson in the latter's post-presidential political battles in Tennessee. He asserted that he remembered Johnson's having told him that, before writing the letter of March 19, Black called upon him, referred to the Butler-Bingham-Stevens-Alta Vela note, and said: "I have pointed your way to acquittal and advised you to pursue it. You decline to do so. You will be convicted and removed from office. I prefer not to have you convicted on my hands, therefore I resign as one of your

counsel." Col. Reeves declared that Johnson made this reply to Black: "I regard your demands as dishonorable and insulting. Resign and quit. Before I will sign an order contrary to law, as I believe, and against my conscience, I'll suffer my right arm to be torn from its socket. I denounce the course you advise me to pursue and will not adopt it, for I will not purchase my acquittal at the cost of my integrity. You have announced your resignation as one of my counsel. It is my pleasure to áccept your resignation." In the Spring of 1927, the author had a lengthy interview with Col. Reeves, in which he related this reminiscence. It is also to be found on pages 829-830 of a Memoir, "The Real Andrew Johnson," written by Col. Reeves and printed as an appendix to Stryker's Biography. The careful brief of the incidents in the Alta Vela matter which the President had made and which is now to be found in Johnson Mss., Vol. 134, No. 19,914, makes no reference to any such interview. Neither Col. Moore's Diary nor Black's many letters to Johnson refer to this talk. At the time when he related it to me, Col. Reeves was in his 80's, and while his memory may have been remarkable, I find it difficult to give full credit to this purported interview. Old men's recollections, as is well known to historians, are not as dependable factually as are contemporary diaries, letters and records.

42. Moore, "Diary," 128. I have changed the last sentence from third to first person. Cf. also Moore "Diary" Transcript, April 28, 1868.

43. One wonders what defense Judge Black ever made of his conduct in this matter. Further angry letters from him to the President appeared in the latter's correspondence for the next two weeks, but none afford a satisfactory explanation. The "Reminiscences of Jeremiah Sullivan Black," written by his daughter, Mary Black Clayton, and published at St. Louis, in 1887, fails to give any inkling as to Black's defense. Indeed, its pages fail to mention that Black was ever connected in any way with Johnson's impeachment trial.

44. New York *World*, March 24, 1868.

CHAPTER XXIII

1. Hugh Ewing Mss.; letter dated Washington, Jan. 15, 1868.

2. Thad Stevens introduced an even more extreme bill expressly forbidding the Supreme Court to take jurisdiction in any case arising from the Reconstruction acts, but even the House refused to follow him on this.

3. Warren, III, 187.

4. *Independent*, January 30, 1868.

5. *Independent*, March 5, 1868, predicted a 5 to 3 vote, and added that this prospect "renders the vote of the Senate for impeachment certain; for with acquittal, and congressonal reconstruction overthrown, the government would speedly pass into the hands of the Rebels."

6. Warren, III, 197.

7. This bill is properly characterized by John W. Burgess, "Reconstruction and the Constitution," New York, 1902; 196-7, as "an abominable subterfuge on the part of Congress, and a shameful abuse of its powers."

8. Benjamin F. Butler, "Butler's Book," Boston, 1892; 927-9.

9. New York *Herald*, March 31, 1868.
10. New York *World*, March 31, 1868.
11. "Impeachment Trial," I, 88.
12. "Impeachment Trial," I, 90.
13. "Impeachment Trial," I, 116-7.
14. For text of Butler's argument, see *Ibid.*, I, 87-123.
15. Butler, 929-30.
16. "Impeachment Trial," I, 431-2.
17. Moore, "Diary," 131. Johnson deemed this article only a further indication that the Radicals were anxious for a military despotism. But Comstock, one of Grant's staff, told General Sherman that the statement was untrue. See Moore "Diary" Transcript, April 7, 1868.
18. Badeau, 136. For White House scrap paper incident, see Moore "Diary" Transcript, Jan. 8, 1870.
19. Fessenden, II, 184-5.
20. *Ibid.*, 187-8.
21. Schuckers, 558.
22. Julian, 317.
23. Warden, 680-683.
24. The inconsequential nature of the case against Johnson can best be appreciated by a careful reading of the 741 page first volume of the three volume official report of the trial. Volume I contains the evidence, arguments as to its admissibility, and the opening presentations of both the prosecution and defense; Volume II the argument of counsel and the vote; and Volume III the printing of the opinions of the Senators. Issued by the Government Printing Office, Washington, 1868.
25. Butler, 930.
26. New York *World*, April 10, 1868.
27. For Curtis' address, see "Impeachment Trial," I, 377-414.
28. For Welles' testimony and debate on its admissibility, see "Impeachment Trial," I, 663-704.
29. Welles, III, 334.
30. Sumner Mss.
31. "Impeachment Trial," I, 693.
32. The previous summer, Chase had told James C. Kennedy that Johnson "had an unquestioned right under the Civil Tenure act to remove Mr. Stanton. . . The President can remove at his option. . ." See Johnson Mss., Vol. 123, No. 19,587.
33. Warden, 685, 687.

CHAPTER XXIV

1. "Impeachment Trial," I, 628-31; Moore "Diary" Transcript, April 17, 19, 1868.
2. Moorfield Storey, "Charles Sumner," New York, 1900; 345.
3. Schofield, 413-8. The account is based upon a memorandum which Schofield carefully made at the time. Moore "Diary" Transcript, April 23, 24, 25, 1868.
4. Before Boutwell began, Logan of Illinois obtained permission to

insert in the record his 51 page written argument. Logan termed the President "the great criminal of the age," a sentence which typifies a speech patently addressed to his constituents.

5. "Impeachment Trial," II, 77.

6. Moore, "Diary," 123.

7. Julian, 313.

8. New York *World*, April 30, 1868.

9. Matthew Hale Smith, 536.

10. New York *World*, April 30, 1868.

11. Letter, auctioned by Stan V. Henkels, Philadelphia, Apr. 24, 1928.

12. The *Independent*, May 21, 1868.

CHAPTER XXV

1. Hugh Ewing Mss., Letter from Thomas Ewing to Hugh Ewing, Washington, April 15, 1868.

2. New York *World*, May 3, 1868.

3. *Ibid.*, April 21, 1868.

4. Senator John B. Henderson, *Century* Magazine, Dec., 1912; Welles, III, 349.

5. Welles, III, 358.

6. Johnson Mss., Vol. 141, No. 21,542.

7. Why, this author has been unable to discover, unless they had been influenced by Henry Stanbery's words in opening his argument for the President, that "unseen hands seem to guide me . . . unseen voices urge me on."

8. S. S. Cox, "Three Decades of Federal Legislation," Providence, R. I.; 1885; 591-4.

9. Henderson, *Century* Magazine, Dec., 1912.

10. William Salter, "Life of James W. Grimes," New York, 1890; 390-391.

11. Salter, 323.

12. For much of this description of Ross, I am indebted to Mr. Thomas Ewing, III, who knew him well.

13. W. A. Dunning, "Reconstruction, Political and Economic," New York, 1907, 107; White, 321.

14. New York *World*, May 3, 1868.

15. Moore "Diary" Transcript, May 2, 1868. Fessenden, II, 205-10.

16. From sketch furnished me by Missouri Historical Society, Columbia, Mo. There is an interesting story furnished me by Hon. Breckinridge D. Long of Washington that Henderson made a fortune by buying up depreciated bonds which had been issued by Missouri counties to help the South and then forcing their repayment at face value. In Washington he invested heavily in real estate, which increased enormously in value.

17. Interview of author with Mrs. John B. Henderson, Washington, March 23, 1928. Cf. Welles, III, 349. "Henderson is relied upon, through influence of Miss Foote and her father."

18. John B. Henderson, *Century* Magazine, December, 1912; 202, *et seq.*

19. Interview with Col. A. M. Hughes, Washington, December 18, 1928.
20. The chafing-dish is now in the possession of Mrs. W. H. O'Keefe, of Greeneville, Tenn., to whom it was given by Mrs. Patterson, in these words: "I want you to have this chafing-dish because it is so intimately associated with the most tragic period of my life, my father's impeachment trial." Mrs. O'Keefe to author, August 29, 1929.
21. Welles, III, 344; Moore "Diary" Transcript, April 12, 1868.
22. Cowan, 11-12.
23. Boston *Post,* May 12, 1868.
24. New York *World,* May 15, 1868.
25. Warden, 693.
26. Henderson asked Sherman if he remembered the attitude he had voiced as to the President's right to remove his Cabinet members. "I remember it very well," Sherman answered. Then Henderson asked bluntly, "You are not going to stultify yourself by voting for the eleventh article?" Embarrassed, Sherman answered, "No."
27. *Independent,* May 21, 1868.
28. In his printed opinion filed after his vote on the 16th, Henderson took firm ground against all the articles. "A cool and deliberate future will not fail to look with amazement on this extraordinary proceeding . . .," he wrote. "We are told that the people clamor for the President's conviction. It may be so . . . I cannot, in justice to the laws of the land, in justice to the country or to my own sense of right, render any other response to the several articles than a verdict of not guilty." But in the speech on the 11th, he was silent as to Articles IX, X and XI.
29. "Impeachment Trial," III, 247-281. Sumner had dressed carefully for the occasion, in lavender silk trousers and a brown Alpaca coat.
30. Edmund G. Ross, "The Johnson Impeachment," Albuquerque, N. M., 1896, Chapter X. Only three Senators—Sumner, Pomeroy and Tipton—pronounced Johnson guilty on every article. Wilson, Patterson of New Hampshire, Frelinghuysen, Cattell and Williams declared him guilty, without particularization, and Morrill of Maine, Yates and Stewart declared him guilty of removing Stanton, without indicating any specific article.
31. Welles, III, 351.
32. *Independent,* May 21, 1868.
33. DeWitt, "Impeachment," 521.
34. *Independent,* May 21, 1868; Moore "Diary" Transcript, May 6, 1868.
35. Macon, Mo., *Times,* May 30, 1868.
36. Welles, III, 352, says it was either brain fever or delirium tremens.
37. *Ibid.,* III, 353. At the news, Lorenzo Thomas, whom Browning thought was drunk, asked Johnson if he should demand possession of the War Office, and the President told him to let it alone. Browning "Diary," May 12, 1868.
38. Fessenden, II, 212.
39. *Ibid.,* II, 214, quoting Ross; Julian, 313-7.
40. New York *World,* May 10, 1868.
41. Julian, 313-17.
42. Horace White, "Life of Lyman Trumbull," New York, 1913, 314-315.

43. Missouri *Statesman*, May 29, 1868.

44. Cox, 594.

45. Cox, *Congressional Globe*, Second Session, 40th Congress, 2471.

46. Welles, III, 353.

47. White, 316-17.

48. DeWitt, "Impeachment," 531.

49. *Ibid.*, 531-2.

50. Letter from Thomas Ewing, III, to author, October 31, 1928. Vinnie was the daughter of a Kansas hotel keeper. Mr. Ewing remembers her consulting General Sherman about her proposed marriage, and the latter smilingly replying, "Well, Vinnie, if you are going to marry at all, it is about time, isn't it?"

51. *Congressional Globe*, Second Session, 40th Congress, 2674-5. Julian denied it, but admitted a conversation on the subject.

52. Badeau, 136-7.

53. Warden, 687-9.

54. *Ibid.*, 693-4.

55. Chicago *Tribune*, May 14, 1868.

56. *Nation*, May 14, 1868.

57. Schuckers, 559.

58. Welles, III, 358; Moore, "Diary" Transcript, May 10, 1868, has it that Grant set Simpson on Willey's trail.

59. Marietta Minnegerode Andrews, "My Studio Window," New York, 1928; 159; DeWitt, "Impeachment," 540-5; New York *Sun*, Oct. 25, 1896; Letter to author from Mrs. Richard L. Hoxie, Miami, Fla., Jan. 8, 1929, states that Sickles later wrote Vinnie that he was afterwards convinced she had not influenced Ross' vote.

60. *Congressional Globe*, Second Session, 40th Congress, 4507-10. It was an arrant forgery. "I did not utter one single sentence that Kelley has coined," the Tennessean later told the Senate. "He neither gives the spirit nor the connection nor the object of my remarks."

61. DeWitt, "Impeachment," 544. This manly message brought instant and discourteous retort from Anthony. "Your telegram received," he fulminated. "Your vote is dictated by Tom Ewing, not by your oath. Your motives are Indian contracts and greenbacks. Kansas repudiates you as she does all perjurers and skunks."

62. New York *World*, May 17, 1868.

63. For a general account of the balloting, I have followed the New York *World*, May 17, 1868, and DeWitt, "Impeachment," 549-54. For Henderson, see Jefferson City, Mo., *Weekly People's Tribune*, May 20, 27, 1868.

64. The *Nation*, May 28, 1868.

65. W. H. Crook, "Reminiscences," Margarita S. Gerry, Editor, New York, 1910; 133. W. H. Crook, "Memories of the White House," Henry Rood, Editor, Boston, 1911; 66-7.

66. New York *World*, May 17, 1868. See also Cowan, 13. This close observer thought that the President had become so convinced that he would be found guilty that he was really "disappointed and chagrined" at the acquittal.

CHAPTER XXVI

1. Fessenden, II, 219.

2. But Edward Brownell, of Troy, who arranged the firing of the guns there, wrote the President complaining that the Federal Revenue officers at Troy had refused to contribute to the cost of the celebration.

3. *Independent,* May 21, 1868.

4. Salter, 359. On May 26 Grimes wrote a card to the Chicago *Tribune* denying all these things. He had never had hostility to Wade; as to Chase, "I never had a word of conversation with the Chief Justice on that subject"; and as to the *Tribune,* he had never been interested directly or indirectly in that paper.

5. Warden, 696-9.

6. Thomas Ewing wrote Fessenden on May 12: "Chief Justice Chase has done himself much credit in this investigation. He has held the scale of justice even and with a firm and manly hand." Letter in possession Thomas Ewing, III, who furnished me a copy.

7. The *Nation,* May 21, 1868. The file now in Mr. Oswald Garrison Villard's possession carries a pencil notation that Godkin was the author of the editorial, an indication rarely given.

8. New York *World,* May 17, 1868.

9. For this letter see Butler's report, *Congressional Globe,* Second Session, 40th Congress, 3731.

10. DeWitt, "Impeachment," 570. Pomeroy's subsequent career showed clearly that he was not above any such attempt. It was only a few years until the Kansas legislature, on the eve of electing him to succeed himself in the Senate, was startled by a member rising, with a great mass of greenbacks in his hand, and announcing that Pomeroy had given them to him the night before, to secure his vote in the senatorial selection. This ended "Subsidy Pom's" political career.

11. *Congressional Globe,* Second Session, 40th Congress, 25,489; *Century* Magazine, Dec., 1912.

12. Fessenden, II, 223.

13. Ross, *loc. cit.*

14. Johnson Mss., Vol. 138, No. 20,964.

15. New York *World,* May 27, 1868.

16. Welles, III, 368; Browning "Diary," May 26, 1868.

17. *National Intelligencer,* May 27, 1868.

18. *Independent,* June 6, 1868.

19. The *Nation,* May 28, 1868.

20. New York *World,* May 20, 1868.

21. Salter, 361, quoting Fessenden to Grimes, July 7, 1868; *Congressional Globe,* 2nd Session, 40th Congress, 4463, 5, 4513, 4516-7.

22. Salter, 360.

23. *Congressional Globe,* Second Session, 40th Congress, 3790-1.

24. *Ibid.,* Third Session, 40th Congress, 1865.

25. Oberholtzer, II, 211.

26. Rhodes, VI, 267.

27. Browning "Diary," May 28, 1868; Johnson Brigham, "James Harlan," Iowa City, Iowa, 1913; 233-4, quoting Iowa *State Register.*

28. Salter, 357.

29. *Independent,* May 21, 1868.

30. Salter, 361-2.

31. Fessenden, II, 329, 350.

32. Letter from Thomas Ewing, 3rd, New York, Oct. 31, 1928. The allusion was to the weapon with which Lane, to whose seat Ross had succeeded by appointment, had committed suicide in 1866.

33. Letter from R. W. McGrath, Fredonia, Kan., Sept. 13, 1929.

34. White, 322.

35. McGrath Letter.

36. Interview of author with Senator Henry F. Ashurst of Arizona, Washington, Nov. 19, 1929. But Ross did tell Ashurst that each one of the seven who had voted not guilty had done so "knowing that each and every one was looking directly into his open political grave." Ross wrote an account of the impeachment trial and published it in his Albuquerque printing shop. It was, however, mainly an analysis of the constitutional basis of the trial and carried entirely too scant a story of the personal sufferings which Ross himself had been forced to endure.

37. White, 322: McGrath Letter.

38. Mexico, Mo., *Messenger,* May 23, 1868; St. Charles, Mo., *Cosmos,* May 21, 1868; St. Louis *Democrat,* May 18, 1868.

39. Jefferson City, Mo., *Weekly People's Tribune,* Sept. 16, 1868.

40. C. E. Moss in a letter to *Anti-Slavery Standard,* dated St. Louis, Jan. 3, 1869, reprinted Memphis *Avalanche,* Jan. 23, 1869. Moss declared again and again that Grant desired impeachment's defeat on political grounds, and that the General was "much interested" in Henderson's re-election at the time of the vote.

41. White, 326.

42. Henderson, *Century* Magazine, Dec., 1912.

CHAPTER XXVII

1. Johnson Mss., Vol. 138, No. 20,927; Gorham, II, 456; Welles, III, 370.

2. Johnson Mss., Vol. 139, No. 21,022. When former President Buchanan died at Lancaster on June 1, the House refused to adjourn for his funeral, and the Senate refused to appoint a committee to attend services. But it did pass a resolution tendering Stanton the "thanks of the country." For Seward incident, see Moore "Diary" Transcript, May 29, 1868.

3. "In the opinion of the Senate the said Stanton has not been legally removed from his office," this ingenuous document asserted, "but inasmuch as the said Stanton has relinquished," etc., the Senate did "advise and consent!"

4. Welles, III, 371; Moore "Diary" Transcript, June 24, 1868; McCulloch, Johnson told his secretary, was "considerably anxious."

5. Welles, III, 383.

6. For Chase's renewed presidential ambitions and endeavors, see Schuckers, 560-593; Warden, 699-716; Schuckers to Chase, Chase Mss., Vol. 100, No. 15,114.

7. Chase Mss., Historical Society of Pennsylvania, quoted Oberholtzer, III, 173.

8. Johnson Mss., Vol. 140, No. 21,445; Vol. 141, No. 21,495.

9. Oberholtzer, III, 171.

10. Johnson Mss., Vol. 141, No. 21,542.

11. *Ibid.*, Vol. 141, No. 21,551, 63, 78.

12. *Ibid.*, Vol. 141, No. 21,613; Moore "Diary" Transcript, July 1, 1868; *Ibid.*, July 3, 1868.

13. Johnson Mss., Vol. 142, No. 21,747.

14. Johnson Mss., Vol. 142, No. 21,753. Cf. Welles, III, 398; "His nomination has been effected by duplicity, deceit, cunning management and sharp scheming." See also Johnson Mss., Vol. 142, No. 21,775, from J. D. Perryman: "You were swindled in the very moment of victory,"—"Seymour has *deceived* from the beginning."

15. Welles, III, 398; Browning, however, ("Diary," July 9, 1868) "could form no opinion, from his manner or speech, whether he desired a nomination or not." The next day, Colonel Moore ("Diary" Transcripts, July 9, 10, 1868) noted that Johnson "felt the disappointment keenly." The next day, however, he was in brighter spirits, the suspense being over.

16. Warden, 706.

17. Welles, III, 402-3.

18. Johnson to Truman, Washington, Aug. 18, 1868; quoted Truman, *op. cit.*, 438-40. In this letter, Johnson termed Sherman "our greatest military genius," "erratic and stubborn, but he doesn't know how to lie," and said that Thomas was in many respects "the greatest general the war produced."

19. New York *Tribune*, July 10, 1868; New York *Herald*, July 11, 1868.

20. Johnson Mss., Vol. 144, No. 22,245.

21. Moore "Diary" Transcript, July 23, and Oct. 4, 1868; similarly, Johnson Mss., throughout several volumes, *e.g.*, a Revenue inspector at Bordentown, N. J., wrote that he had determined to give battle to the Radicals because of their open encouragement of frauds on the Government. "The immense frauds committed and glossed over, the attempts to conceal the extent of the whiskey frauds from the people by means of false official reports, the duplicity and dishonesty of the present Committee of Ways and Means on the liquor question"—all these things had disgusted him. Certain Radical Congressmen, he charged, had bought 70,000 gallons of whiskey, to be held until the assembling of the new Congress, when they would restore the old tax of $2.00 per gallon, and thus would profit privately from their public act.

22. For the truth as to Rollins, see the voluminous papers interspersed in Johnson Mss., Vols. 142-3-4-5. See also Welles, III, 434-5.

23. Welles, III, 439.

24. The *Nation*, Sept. 10, 1868.

25. Oberholtzer, III, 189.

26. The *Nation*, Oct. 15, 1868.

27. New York *World*, Oct. 15, 1868.

28. Welles, III, 457-8.

29. So he told John Van Buren. See Oberholtzer, III, 193.

30. Welles, III, 477-82.

31. Welles, III, 485.

32. On Christmas Day there came from the White House Johnson's final proclamation amnesty, giving without condition to everyone who might have been under penalty because of the Civil War a full restoration of all rights, privileges, and immunities granted by the Constitution. This proclamation embraced Jefferson Davis, and put an end to any further talk of prosecuting the President of the late Confederate States.

33. Recollections of Mrs. Mary DuHamel Clagett, who attended the party; given to author in interview, Washington, Dec. 7, 1928. See also Crook, "Through Five Administrations," 144-5.

34. Butler's effrontery in presenting himself was the subject of numerous newspaper dispatches. According to most accounts, Johnson's manner was frigid, but the *Herald* said it was quite the reverse. See also Truman, *op. cit.,* 440.

35. Crook, "Through Five Administrations," 145.

36. Welles, III, 483-4.

37. But it provoked wrath among the Maryland Radicals, the Baltimore *American* going so far as to caption its editorial protest, "Baltimore Disgraced."

38. Crook, "Through Five Administrations," 147.

39. Welles, III, 538.

40. Benjamin C. Truman, *Century* Magazine, Dec., 1912; 440.

41. Welles, III, 540-2; Crook, "Through Five Administrations," 148.

42. Schucht, 212.

CHAPTER XXVIII

1. Baltimore *Sun,* March 12, 1869.

2. David Rankin Barbee, Nashville *Banner,* Sept. 1, 1929.

3. Nashville *Union and American,* March 19, 1869. For the Tennessee newspaper references in this chapter and much of the other material on Johnson's Tennessee epilogue, I am indebted to the Brabson thesis.

4. Nashville *Union and American,* March 21, 1869.

5. Letter of H. H. Ingersoll, who was Johnson's host that night, to Col. Brabson. See also Nashville *Union and American,* March 28, 1869.

6. New York *World,* March 29, 1869.

7. David R. Barbee to author, Washington, Aug. 10, 1929; this despite Johnson's alleged aversion to rich men. When a principle was not at stake and a vote was, Johnson was not averse to flattery.

8. New York *Herald,* June 27, 1869.

9. Nashville *Union and American,* Aug. 5, 1869.

10. There is another version, given by J. B. Brownlow, the Parson's son, as to Grant's attitude. Brownlow was quoted in the Nashville *Union and American* of Sept. 4, 1869, as saying that Grant had said Johnson would suit him as well as any other Democrat, and had ridiculed the idea that the ex-President would be any special annoyance to his administration. For citation, see Johnson Mss., Vol. 155, No. 25,003.

11. Johnson Mss., Vol. 155, No. 24,834.

12. At one time Cooper had been one of Johnson's private secretaries.

Then he had been a Member of the House from Tennessee. Later the President had nominated him Assistant Secretary of the Treasury. In June, 1868, Cooper went to New York to manage Johnson's interests in the Democratic National Convention, and had written Johnson from the New York convention that the "ingratitude" which Southern leaders had displayed toward the President "is well calculated to cause one to doubt the honesty and integrity of mere politicians."

13. Reeves' statement, quoted Stryker Appendix, 831. Possibly the ex-President of the railroad referred to was Michael Burns.

14. Knoxville, *Whig*, Oct. 22, 1869, quoted in Knoxville *Journal*, Nov. 24, 1928.

15. Nashville *Union and American*, Nov. 1, 1874.

16. Conversation of Duncan B. Cooper with Col. Brabson, in Brabson's Thesis; Nashville *Union and American*, Oct. 23, 1869. Johnson never forgave either of the Coopers; for the new Senator-elect was also under obligation to him, inasmuch as in 1862, while Military Governor, Johnson had appointed him to a judgeship which he had held for five years.

17. Issue of Dec. 8, 1869.

18. Johnson Mss., Vol. 155, No. 25,012.

19. Nashville *Union and American*, Mar. 19, 1870.

20. Reeves, *op. cit.*, 826-7.

21. Reeves' help proved invaluable in defeating the "Confederate Brigadiers." Some shrewd students say that without it Johnson could not have won in 1875.

22. Reeves, *op. cit.* 832.

23. Col. Reeves told the author that the explanation he had arrived at in his own mind was that Johnson had acted under the influence of liquor. He also said that Johnson was not a man easily questioned about his conduct, that he preserved an air of great dignity even with his intimates, and, in all the six years of Reeves' association with him, never addressed his quasi-secretary except formally as "Mr. Reeves."

24. "Mr. Dunnington to Ex-President Johnson," Columbia, Tenn., Sept. 30, 1872; an extremely rare pamphlet, for photostat of which I am indebted to Mr. David Rankin Barbee of Washington.

25. Foster V. Brown of Chattanooga and Gen. Lillard Thompson of Lebanon, both of whom were in the audience that day, have kindly furnished me memorandums of their recollections and impressions of the speech.

26. Recollections of Foster V. Brown of Chattanooga, to author in conversation.

27. Reeves, *op. cit.*, 833.

28. Recollections of Col. W. M. Nixon, of Chattanooga, who was in the crowd; communicated to author, May 17, 1929.

29. Jones, 347-9.

30. Temple, "Notable Men," 142.

31. On November 10 the bank paid a dividend of thirty percent; on April 8, 1874, twenty percent; on April 4, 1875, ten percent, and Johnson's estate later was paid in full.

32. Winston, 498.

33. The Shelby County voters had likewise held an informal referendum on the Senatorship and Johnson had received a large majority. The

Memphis members announced that they considered themselves bound by this expression of the voters' will.

34. Reeves, *op. cit.*, 833.

35. A. M. Hughes, Nashville *Banner*, Dec. 18, 1927.

36. Temple, "Notable Men," 439-42.

37. Brabson Thesis, quoting conversation with Chancellor John Allison of Nashville.

38. Two of the men who changed explained that they did so because their constituents were overwhelmingly for Johnson. Of those who elected him, 44 were Democrats, 8 Republicans. Thirty ex-Confederates and 22 ex-Federals voted for him. Nashville *Union and American*, Jan. 29, 1875. The story of this election would not be complete without reference to the loyalty with which the Shelby county legislators had kept their pledge to abide by that county's referendum on the senatorship. Many of them were bitterly hostile to Johnson personally, and one, J. Harvey Mathes, had lost a leg at Chickamauga while serving on Bate's staff.

39. Reeves, *op. cit.*, 834.

40. Nashville *Union and American*, Jan. 27, 1875.

41. Statement of former Governor McMillin to author, Nashville, March 29, 1928.

42. New York *Tribune*, Jan. 25, 1875.

43. Johnson Mss., Vols. 163-4 are filled with these and similar expressions of delight over the ex-President's success.

44. *Nation*, Aug. 5, 1875.

45. Brabson Thesis; DeWitt, "Impeachment," 623-4; New York *Herald*, March 8, 1875; New York *World*, March 6, 1875; Crook, "Through Five Administrations," 150; Stryker, 809-10; Winston, 503-5.

46. Nashville *Union and American*, March 11, 1875.

47. New York *Tribune*, March 8, 1875.

48. Crook, "Through Five Administrations," 151-2.

49. McElwee statement in Tennessee State Library, quoted Chattanooga *News*, May 21, 1923.

50. Statement of the late Seldon Nelson to author. Nelson remembered how well Johnson looked that morning and derided the possibility of there being any truth to the canard that he had been intoxicated the night before.

51. New York *World*, Mar. 29, 1869.

52. Brabson Thesis.

53. Winston, 507-9; Brabson Thesis; Stryker, 822-3-4. Johnson's first Masonic degrees had been conferred by Greeneville Lodge, No. 119. He later was passed and raised, and became a Royal Arch Mason and a Knight-Templar. See Greeneville, Tenn., *Democrat-Sun*, Dec. 23, 1929.

54. Statement of Adolph S. Ochs, to author, Chattanooga, May 16, 1929.

INDEX

217; prevents Pennsylvania from indorsing Johnson, 224; seeks to persuade Johnson to give up policy, 224, 225; fears Dawes, 227; sketch of his life and personal traits, 262; plan of campaign against Johnson's policies, 265, 266; joint resolution for committee on reconstruction, 267; to exclude Southern representation in Congress, 277, 278; ridicules Johnson, 298; prepares Radical program for Congress, 378; speaks on Reconstruction Bill, 387; zealous for impeachment, 471; urges Reconstruction Committee to consider charges, 499; reads report of committee on impeachment, 511; impeachment resolution, 512; on committee to notify Senate, 513; disgust at mildness of articles, 517; author of 11th Article, 519; physically feeble, 520; concurs with Butler on Alta Vela, 536; carried to his seat, 576; Butler reads his final speech, 576; bill to admit Congressmen from Southern States, 596; demands investigation of Senate's impeachment vote, 618; insists it is open to question, 619; death and burial in negro cemetery, 627

Stewart, A. T., on committee that greets Johnson in New York, 360

Stewart, William M., accused of using Federal patronage against Johnson, 323, 324; tells how new Cabinet will kill impeachment, 533; defends limiting *habeas corpus*, 545

Stillson, Jerome B., tells of efforts to sway Senators, 593

Stockton, John P., elected Senator from New Jersey, his seat protested, 301-305; votes for himself to break tie, 304; ousted by single vote, 305; delegate to National Union Convention, 351

Stokes, William B., helps plan Tennessee's restoration, 110

Stoll, J. B., tells Johnson people despise Cabinet, 464; exhorts him to eject Stanton, 524

Stotts, Mrs., Spiritualist, 636

Street car system in Washington, separate cars for white and colored, 8; Sumner threatens charter, 8

Streets of Washington during war, 5

Sumner, Charles, protests against separate cars for white and colored, 8; threatens charter of railroad, 8; tender to Hamlin of Vice Presidency, 24; prefers Chase to Lincoln as candidate, 26; secret circular, 28; intrigues against Hamlin, 33; characteristics and antagonisms, 33 *et seq.*; "Bully" Brooks' attack, 34; Stevens' view of him, 34; Grant's retort on him, 34; Wade disapproves of him, 34; Bates' story of Julia Ward Howe's call on Senator, 34, 35; plot to force Fessenden out, 36; to use Dix or Dickinson as Vice Presidential candidate, 36; scheme to retire Seward, 36; view of status of Southern States, 53; reference to Lincoln in letter to Richard Cobden, 131; bars Louisiana representatives from Congress, 139, 140; comments on Lincoln's last speech, 157; secret paper read by Stanton, 167; sought to prevent Lincoln's renomination, 168; cultivates Johnson, 176; letter to John Bright, 177; letters to friends on Johnson, 177, 178; tells Radical caucus Johnson favors negro suffrage, 178; presses views on Johnson, 178; explains Chase's tour of South, 179; eulogy of Lincoln, 216; insists on Schurz making tour of South, 218, 219; agrees to assume expenses, 219; Boston *Advertiser* to publish his correspondence, 219; prevents Massachusetts from indorsing Johnson, 224; petition of 300 negroes on right

of suffrage, 225; writes to John Bright and Francis Lieber, 225; denounces Johnson to Cabinet members, 225; chairman of Massachusetts Republican Convention, 226; in close touch with Schurz on tour, 240; consoles him, 242; believes civil trial for Davis folly, 246; talk with George Bancroft on negro suffrage, 259; calls on President, 260; complaint against him based on negro suffrage, 260; denounces Southern policy, 275; President's message "whitewashing," 280; objects to admission of Colorado, 300; insists on negro suffrage, 311; bill for suffrage in District of Columbia, 381; exults in Johnson's impotence, 381, 382; three-day speech on Tenure, 392, 393; assists in finding evidence to impeach Johnson, 405; still proclaims necessity to impeach, 471; advises Stanton to stick, 504; "dignified and calm" on day of impeachment, 511; denies right of Chief Justice to preside, 551; Johnson guilty regardless of evidence, 564; moves to discipline Judge Nelson, 574; will vote guilty on all articles, 594; ready to further Stevens' demand, 619

Sumter, Fort, 7

Supplementary Reconstruction Bill vetoed, 431

Supreme Court, opinion in Milligan case, 401; injunction on Reconstruction acts asked, 438; denies appeal for lack of jurisdiction, 438

Surratt, Anna, attempts to make personal appeal to Johnson, 210

Surratt, John H., hears Booth's kidnapping plan, 191; arrested in Egypt, 412; approached to implicate Johnson, 412; his trial, 451

Surratt, Mrs. Mary E., her inn and boarding house, 203; defense discredits witnesses, 204; commission unwilling to impose death sentence, 205; scheme devised for having her hanged, 205; sentenced, 206; Johnson gets brief abstract of case, 207; death sentence read to her, 209; all appeals for mercy useless, 210; widow of Stephen A. Douglas seeks mercy in vain, 210; daughter Anna attempts to see Johnson, 210; writ of *habeas corpus* signed, 211; commission's recommendation for mercy turns up in trial of her son, 451; President never saw it, 452

Surrender of all Southern armies, terms of, 172, 173

Sutton, chief reporter of Senate, 150

Swain, D. L., confers with Johnson on North Carolina, 186

Swett, Leonard, law partner of Lincoln, 43; advises Joseph Holt on ticket with Lincoln, 45

"Swing Around Circle" occasioned by Douglas Memorial, 358; begins with large party, 358; itinerary of tour, 359; Grant and Farragut wildly cheered, 360; reception in New York, 360, 361; dinner at Delmonico's, 361; West Point review, 361; Seward ignored in Albany, 362; Radicals alarmed at ovations, 362; plan break-up of meeting in Cleveland, 363; Johnson heckled, 363, 364; unveiling of Douglas Memorial in Chicago, 365; Johnson heckled in St. Louis, 365, 366; newspapers call tour drunken orgy, 367; man killed in riot in Indianapolis, 368; Governors avoid meeting Johnson, 368; party in Louisville, 368; tour cut short by Seward's illness, 369

Talbot, Charles J., gets into secret caucus in Boston, 37

Tammany Hall, *see* Society of St. Tammany

"Tanneries" for Grant's campaign, 643

ADDENDA